ARLINGTON COUNTY VIRGINIA
A Modern History

by
SHERMAN PRATT

Books and literary efforts by this author -

Autobahn to Berchtesgaden:
    An Infantry Sergeant's view of WWII in Europe

Decisive Battles of the Korean War:
    An Infantry Rifle Company Commander's Assessment

Editor:
    "The Graybeards", Newsletter of the Korean War Veterans
        Association

    "The Mustang", Newsletter of the National Order of Battlefield
        Commissions

Contributor:
    Travel Section, the Washington Post
    The Magazine of The Retired Officers Association
    Miscellaneous historical and civic articles to
        Northern Virginia media

ARLINGTON COUNTY VIRGINIA
A Modern History
by
Sherman Pratt

*In consultation with and extensive
use of documents and other materials from the*

**ARLINGTON HISTORICAL SOCIETY
and
THE VIRGINIA ROOM OF THE
ARLINGTON PUBLIC LIBRARY**

1997

Copyright: @ 1997 Sherman W. Pratt, All rights reserved. Permission to reproduce in any form must be secured in writing from the author.

Library of Congress Catalog Card Number: 97-077077

ISBN: 0-9661795-0-1 $24.95

Editorial and proof reading assistants:
　　Sara Collins　　　　　　Seymour Stiss
　　Roye Lowry　　　　　　Sophie Vogel
　　Agnes M. Downey　　　Juanita Sayre Smoot
　　Robert & Laura Watson　Ingrid Kauffman

　　Publication of this book is facilitated by especially generous donations from:
　　Herman J. Obermayer　　J. Newman Carter
　　Seymour B. Stiss　　　　William & Virginia Knull
　　Evelyn Truitt　　　　　　Mr & Mrs William Graham
　　Christine Pratt　　　　　Herschel and Ruth Kanter
　　Paul Pratt　　　　　　　Sandy Bushue
　　Paul Ferguson　　　　　Jerry Gideon
　　Elizabeth Campbell　　　Walter & Carol Frankland
　　Hon. Allen H. Harrison　George Dodge, Esq.
　　Hon. M. Patton Echols, Jr.　Hon. Karen Darner
　　Benjamin Winslow　　　Hon. James Almand

Use of maps, charts, or significant quotations from media articles as identified herein, are with express permission of the source publication.

Profits from sales of this book will be donated to the Endowment Trust of the Arlington Historical Society.

* * *

Printed by
BookCrafters, PO Box 370, Chelsea, MI 48118

TO:

I proudly dedicate this chronicle to all those numerous citizens, known and unknown, some of whom have risen to important elected or appointed positions in local or other government, who have unselfishly volunteered their time, efforts and talents in many ways in civic activities to making my community, Arlington County Virginia, a better place for me, and my family and neighbors to live, work, and enjoy life.

I also dedicate it to my wife Anastasia, my son Paul Alexander, and my daughter Christine April.

* * *

Photographs, drawings or charts herein, unless otherwise indicated, are by the author or courtesy the Arlington Historical Society, or from other sources as indicated in the text.

A CAVEAT OR EXPLANATION

The literary purists may well take umbrage, or even develop heartburn over my generous use of photos, graphics, varied fonts, or other means of breaking up the solid pages of type. If so, then so be it. I am one who believes that masses of type are boring to the reader, unnecessarily difficult to cope with, and that it encourages careless reading or no reading at all. If this is displeasing to some, then it is a price I am willing to pay to make my narrative as easily read and enjoyable as possible for those who feel as I do.

AUTHOR

"Arlington County is one of best places to live".
"Oh? Who said so?"
"Our elected officials."
"Isn't that self serving?"
"Perhaps. But doesn't make it not so."
"Nor does it make it necessarily true."

FOREWORD

There is a wealth of historical information and data about Virginia and Arlington in particular in the Historical Society archives, in the Virginia Room of the County Central Library on North Quincy Street, and in the Library and community archives in the old Woodmont School building off Lorcom Lane and above the Potomac Palisades.

This impressive collection of priceless documents and other materials in the public library system has been mostly under the management and watchful eye of that walking and talking encyclopedia, widely known and highly respected and admired, Sara Collins and her helpers. In the Historical Society the materials in recent times have been safe guarded and catalogued by archivist James Palmer.

Sara Collins has now retired after many years of faithful and devoted service, but continues to serve her community in additional ways. At the Virginia Room she has been replaced by a gracious and knowledgeable lady, Judy Knudsen, who daily shows promise of becoming in time yet another Sara in her devotion and professional approach in overseeing the Virginia Room.

Most of the vast expanse of historical materials in the County library system, however, are not available for checkouts to the average snuffy or intellectual from the streets, nor is it, for the most part, assembled in any kind of single manuscript for easy and quick accessibility and reference. For extensive and detailed information on any particular event over the years in Arlington's past, one must usually nose into many shelves, files or cabinets at considerable laborious and time consuming effort.

In recent years, it has dawned on me that some effort should be made to assemble into a single volume some of the history, particularly of recent years, of our County. There has been only one such publication that approaches this need, and a good one, namely the work of the late C. B. Rose, with the help of Arlingtonian Ruth Ward and some others, <u>Arlington County - A History,</u> published in 1976 by the Arlington Historical Society and printed by the Port City Press in Baltimore, Maryland.

In my judgement, however, Rose's book is now deficient in a couple of important respects. First, through no fault of hers, since she passed away in the 1970's and closed out most of her writing around the mid 1960's, her book is dated. There is also a need for supplementation in some areas.

In the thirty years since Rose laid down her pen, or ceased her typing, enormous, important far reaching, and even "explosive" events have taken place in our County. We have seen mind boggling changes in the landscape. Undeveloped, or underdeveloped mostly open and semi-rural areas have been transformed into massive high rises and ultra-urban centers in Rosslyn and the Ballston and Jeff-Davis corridors. Less spectacular, but nevertheless historical and dramatic changes have also been made in other parts of the county since Rose's demise. This history needs to be catalogued and better addressed together with the circumstances, sometimes quite controversial, surrounding such changes, and herein I have made an effort to do so as the reader will note.

Secondly, with respect to a need to supplement, not substitute or replace, Rose's work I have noted that she mostly avoided, for reasons best known to her, any detailed coverage of the political, especially partisan, growth of the county and I have attempted to fill in that void with a chapter on Government and Political Growth and with a history of office holders in the Appendix. I hope readers and scholars will find this additional material informative and helpful. For sure there will be some variation in the description of some events that are covered by both Rose and me. That is to be expected especially when an author, such as myself, has been so heavily and personally involved in so many of these events. No two observers are likely to ever see matters in precisely the same light. If such differences are detected herein, I must leave it to the reader to determine what weight to give each version.

Like any devoted chronicler of history, I have tried to be modest and stay grammatically with the editorial "we" or the third person and away from the first person singular herein. In places it has been awkwardly difficult to do so since I have been so personally involved in my civic activism with many of the events herein depicted. Still, I have made every effort to minimize my personal involvement and not inject myself into the text herein. It is my hope that the reader will understand my predicament and indulge me where it is felt I have strayed from the accepted and expected practices of the historical writer.

* * * *

On the eve of publication time for this work an esteemed colleague and well established Arlington historian, editorial helper herein, and Society past president, who preferred to remain anonymous, noted correctly that I had failed generally and extensively to identify newspapers and other printed sources throughout the text by italics. To attempt to correct this oversight so late in the effort would be laborious and, more important in the remaining days of this aging author, very time consuming. So in the interest of expeditious publication while there is still time on my agenda I will not undertake to do so. I ask readers who may border on purism and perfection in print for their indulgence and forgiveness.

CONTENTS & CHAPTERS

Foreword		vii
ONE -	A Brief Glimpse at Early Residents	1
TWO -	Post Civil War Growth	33
THREE -	Government and Political Growth	83
FOUR -	Sources of Influence	107
	County Civic Federation	109
	Committee of 100	116
	Committee for School Improvement	121
	County Taxpayers Association (ACTA)	124
	Pentagon City Coordinating Committee)	131
	Political Parties and Movements	144
	Arlington Education Association (AEA)	169
	Chamber of Commerce	170
	Coalition on Transportation (ACT)	172
FIVE -	Major Community "Battles" and Controversies	173
	Retrocession to Virginia	174
	The Mackey Reform Movement	177
	The Battle for "Good" Schools	182
	The Battle for Metrorail	208
	The Prospect Hill Rezoning	221
	The Sickles Tract Rezoning	229
	The I-66 Controversy	238
	The Fight for Single Member Districts	255
	The Aurora Hills Branch Library	271
	The Pentagon City Rezoning	277
	The Struggle for I-395 Sound Walls	287
	The I-595 Upgrading Controversy	296
	The Sewage Treatment Plant Expansion	305
	The Football and Baseball Stadiums	317
	The Effort to Save The Abingdon Ruins	336
	The Acquisition of Ft Smith	364
	Saving Arlington House Woodlands	393
	Arlington-Falls Church Park Lands	407
	The Home Depot Proposal	413
	The Rosslyn Boathouse	419
	Less Than Major Controversies	421
SIX -	Post World War II Development	422
SEVEN -	Funding and Financing the County	445
EPILOGUE -		466
APPENDIX -		468
INDEX -		501

ARLINGTON HISTORICAL SOCIETY
PAST PRESIDENTS

Rear row standing L-R: Allen Kitchens (1985-85), Ruth Preston Rose (1978-79), Martha Orth (1977-78), Jack Foster (1962-63), Donald J. Orth (1974-75), Dow H. Nida (1961-62), and Sherman Pratt (1995-96).
Front row seated L-R: June Brumback Verzi (1975-76), Doris C. Bangs (1980-81), Sara J. Collins (1984-85, Catharine T. Saulmon (1986-88), and Elizabeth G. Clements (1990-91).

OTHER PAST PRESIDENTS ABSENT FROM ABOVE PHOTO DUE TO DEATH OR OTHER REASONS

1957-58 Harrison Mann
1958-59 Frank L. Ball
1959-60 Robert Nelson Anderson
1960-61 Walter E. Bell, Jr.
1963-64 Percy C. Smith
1964-65 Elizabeth R. Goebel
1965-66 John F. Burns
1966-67 Edward F. Sayle
1967-68 Chester M. Brasse
1968-69 J. Elwood Clements
1969-70 Donald A. Wise
1970-71 John L. Overholt
1971-72 Margaret H. Gibson

1972-73 John R. Herbert
1973-74 Dean C. Allard, Jr.
1976-77 Hyman J. Cohen
1979-80 Herbert R. Collins
1981-82 James E. Huddleston
1982-83 Libby S. Ross
1983-84 Warren D. Clardy
1988-89 Evelyn Reid Syphax
1989-90 June Robinson
1991-92, '94-95 Karl VanNewkirk
1992-93 Bruce Gregory McCoy
1993-94 Seymour B. Stiss
1996-98 Robert J. Watson

A Glimpse at Early Residents

CHAPTER ONE

A BRIEF GLIMPSE AT ARLINGTON'S EARLIEST RESIDENTS

THE INDIANS

Relatively little is known about the original aborigines who populated the area that is now known as Arlington County Virginia. They, like most or all other such peoples, or "Indians" as they were incorrectly called by Christopher Columbus and other early explorers, were illiterate. They had no alphabet for writings and thus left behind no voluminous tomes or libraries from which later civilizations might learn about their daily lives and activities.[1]

The Indians who settled in Virginia, and the other lands of the North American continent North of modern day Mexico, did not build enduring pyramids, great temples, or burial tombs with hieroglyphics, or sacred carvings and writings as did their contemporaries in Egypt, Persia, Greece, Central America, or elsewhere in the Oriental or Far Eastern worlds. Thus we have no meaningful record of their history.

Absent helpful writings by the early Indians of Arlington and the surrounding areas, most of our present knowledge of them stems from studies by scholars who depended mostly on extant accounts by early explorers or from recent archeological excavations.

---

[1] *For a more comprehensive, detailed, and well annotated account of this period the reader should consult Chapter One of C. B. Rose, Jr.'s book, Arlington County Virginia - A History., Port City Press, Inc., Baltimore, Md., 1976, available from the Arlington Historical Society, Box 402, Arlington, Va., 22210.*

ARLINGTON COUNTY VIRGINIA - A Modern History

The excavated Indian finds have, for the most part, been scanty and consist only of bones and occasionally stone and pottery fragments. Even these, in some instances, were accidently and clumsily uncovered by massive earth moving equipment during construction of the George Washington Parkway along the Virginia palisades of the Potomac River in the late 1960's, or other development in the area.

From the little that is available it seems to be established that native human habitation existed in the area from as early as 10,000 B.C. until shortly after the arrival of the first Europeans in the 17th Century. In the part of Fairfax County that is now Arlington, it has been determined that there were several Indian villages, mostly along the banks of the Potomac river from the modern Crystal City area to the county line above the Chain Bridge.

One Indian village was located just about where the National Center office buildings of the Navy are located in modern Crystal City and another three around the Virginia ends of the several bridges just east of the Pentagon building. There was a village near the Memorial Bridge site, another on Roosevelt, once Analostan, Island, and others farther up the river near Marcey Creek, Donaldson Run and Gulf Branch.

In a talk before the Arlington Historical Society (AHS) on January 8, 1971, reported in the Society's magazine of that year, Herman Friis from the National Archives described the Indians of the upper Potomac estuary. He said they had a "relatively highly developed and specialized culture" and had developed trade routes with other tribes from the lower Chesapeake and from as far away as what later became Canada. Friis said those aborigines were of Algonquian stock and that their chief town was called "Petomek", which, no doubt, is the origin of our present name of Potomac for the River.

Friis also recited in his Society talk an interesting account of the Indians' efforts to establish a mutually advantageous and friendly relationship with the arriving settlers. He said that as early as 1619, when the Europeans had been here barely a decade, the Potomac Indians sent a delegation to Jamestown with an offer to trade furs, oils, shell currency, dyes and other items for whatever the Europeans might have to offer.

The Funk and Wagnalls Encyclopedia (Vol 2, 1986) reminds the reader that, by and large, the Indians were rebuffed and became disenchanted with the new arrivals. Relations steadily soured. The Indians considered the Europeans to be despicable, stingy and intolerant of their religious beliefs and in their sexual and marital arrangements.

The Indians also ridiculed the Europeans for excessive reliance on a book - the Bible - and for not doing more of their own thinking. The Encyclopedia records that the Indians felt too that the new settlers were out of tune with nature, too mechanical, soulless and "wielded diabolical and ingenious tools and weapons to accomplish mad ends."

In any event, for a variety of reasons, to include the above, the incursion of hostile Indians from the north, and perhaps in the constant search for happier hunting grounds, the local Indians soon moved away from the Potomac basin to more interior habitats.

Official documents of 1679, roughly a century before the Revolutionary War, report that there were no longer any Indians on the Virginia side of the Potomac, which would include what is now Arlington County.

A Glimpse at Early Residents

YEARS OF HARDSHIPS AND TURBULENCE

The years leading to the departure of the Indians from Arlington and the surrounding areas were times of great hardships, upheavals, dislocation, dangers and anguish. There was an innovative system designated as "headrights" that provided immigrants who paid their own way to Virginia with 50 acres of land for each person imported. In spite of this, movement to the wild, unknown, unpopulated frontier wilderness remained slow. Settlement stopped altogether for several years because of the continuing Indian uprisings and an incident in 1676 known as Bacon's Rebellion.

Events that discouraged northern settlement and even flight by the few settlers who were there included the Indian massacre of over 300 settlers in March 1622 by the Powhatan Confederacy led by Chief Opechancanough. More slaughter later that year occurred following the English burning of the Nacochtanke village where the present day Anacostia Naval Air Station and Bolling Air Force Base are located in southwest Washington.

The Nacochtanke Indians in reprisal went on a rampage and massacred any Englishmen they could find. The following Spring, to reestablish trade with the Indians, the ship Tiger returned and Indians from the village were allowed to board the ship. They quickly fled when a sailor, perhaps accidently, fired a shot. The ship's Captain Henry Spelman went ashore believing the natives liked him and that he could reestablish a friendly relationship. He had in earlier days lived among them. He received an unexpected welcome, however, and sailors on board his ship watched as he was tortured and brutally killed on shore. The crew promptly weighed anchor and sailed away to safer waters of the Chesapeake Bay nearer Jamestown.

Settlement was further delayed by the Indian massacre of over 500 settlers in 1644, again led by the aged and ailing Chief Opechancanough. Settlers wreaked terrible vengeance on the Indians and captured and murdered the Chief. Conflicts with the Indians in the following years continued to discourage settlement on the Northern Virginia frontier and the confrontations helped to trigger an incident in 1676 recorded in history as Bacon's Rebellion

When Bacon's Rebellion is mentioned it usually draws mostly a blank reaction from the average American. Most people may have heard of it, but few, indeed, can explain in any detail just what it was or where or when it took place. The event gets its name from one Nathaniel Bacon who was an early settler in Henrico County on lands about 40 miles from James City near the mouth of the Chesapeake Bay. Bacon was young at 29, defiant, aggressive and fearless. He became increasingly dissatisfied with Governor Sir William Berkeley whom he considered corrupt, biased in filling government positions, and insufficiently active in putting down Indian aggressions that were making life critical and unbearable for settlers and were a constant threat on his lands. Bacon has been looked upon by some historians as a George Washington of the 17th Century, whereas to them Berkeley represented oppressive and aristocratic royal authority.

In September 1676, Bacon, with support from some landless colonists rose in revolt and drove Berkeley from James City, or Jamestown. Berkeley escaped across the Bay to the Eastern Shore and took refuge in "Arlington" the just finished home of John "Uncle Jack" Custis II. Arlington became the temporary capital of Virginia and Berkeley summoned all "loyal" men to join him under pain of being otherwise denounced as rebels.

The Eastern Shore, that had not faced Indian perils, did not rally to the aid of Bacon and the rebellion ended in less than a month when a flotilla of small craft under the command of Bacon's colleague William Carver became "wind bound" while anchored at Old Plantation Creek near Arlington. The crews were over powered by Berkeley men who boarded the craft pretending to be Bacon sympathizers. Carver and other Bacon leaders were promptly hanged. Bacon escaped that fate, however, when he succumbed a few days later to a brief but mortal illness back in James City.

The Indian massacres and the Bacon Rebellion had helped to forestall settlement in the far north as settlers fled south to safer places below the Occoquan River, that now forms the southern boundary of Fairfax County, or even farther. But with the ending of these events, movement and settlement northward resumed. Several events over the following years were to take place that would accelerate movement into the area by ever increasing numbers of new arrivals, or the return of the former settlers.

ARLINGTON'S FIRST RESIDENT LANDOWNER

In 1669, one John Alexander bought from shipmaster Robert Howson 6,000 acres of land along the Virginia banks of the Potomac River from the vicinity of the mouth of Four Mile Run, near the present National Airport, to almost what is now Rosslyn.

Alexander's land passed to his progeny and in 1740 or '41, his great-great grandson, Gerrard inherited the property. He then moved onto the plantation and into the house there known as Abingdon located near where the airport main terminal building is situated today. Gerrard Alexander thus became what is believed today to be Arlington County's first land owning resident. We will discuss Abingdon and its builder Gerrard in more detail herein in Chapter V. Here we will say only the following by way of brief introduction.

In the earlier years, land owners in what would someday be Arlington County, did not live on their lands in the county. This included George Washington at Mt Vernon and George Mason at Gunston Hall who owned large wooded areas along Arlington's present day Four Mile Run water shed, and elsewhere. In buying the tract and moving onto it, the Alexanders set a precedent and stimulated additional settlement thereafter.

The Alexander family was also to contribute to growth and development of the area in other ways. The town of Alexandria, chartered in 1749, was named after the family. The land was sold in 1778 to George Parke Custis and became the childhood home of two of the county's most distinguished historical figures. Nelly Custis, who would one day marry George Washington's nephew, was born at Abingdon in 1779; and George Washington Parke Custis, who was to build majestic Arlington House standing today in Arlington Cemetery and overlooking the National Capital area, was born across the Potomac at Mt Airy in Prince George's County Maryland when his mother was temporarily away from their home at Abingdon.

A Glimpse at Early Residents

Abingdon was burned to the ground in 1930. The crumbling ruins, mostly overlooked or ignored since, have remained in place on the ground purchased in 1940 by the Federal government for the National Airport. They commanded renewed interest and media and other attention in 1992 when it was revealed that the ruins were about to be plowed under or otherwise done away with to make way for a new garage as part of the airport expansion and modernization.

Ruins to Save?

Numerous letters to the editors appeared, a major campaign was launched, and the Virginia legislature enacted measures aimed at compelling the Washington National Airports Authority to save what was left of Abingdon. The story of that battle to save the Abingdon ruins and the site in place, is told in detail in Chapter V.

At this writing it appears the way has been found to make the necessary airport improvements and yet not lose an irreplaceable historical treasure. Such preservation has been done in numerous ways in this and other countries around the world and historical preservationists argue that there was no reason why it could not also be done for Abingdon if there was a strong enough will to do so.

18TH CENTURY SETTLEMENT

Settlement of Arlington proceeded steadily during the 18th Century, albeit quite slowly. Even the Revolutionary War came and went without any significant impact on the area.

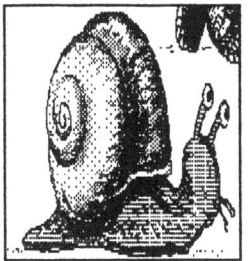

The years following, however, were quite another matter. Events of enormous magnitude, even if moving at a snail's pace, were just around the corner and about to engulf the region. The Northern Virginia area, to become in the 20th Century Arlington County, was simply the northernmost tip of the "Northern Neck" in the earliest days. That "neck" consisted of all the lands in Virginia between the Rappahannock and the Potomac Rivers.

As settlement progressed in the 1700's, especially in the areas stretching up from the Rappahannock, if not in the northern extremes, new divisions and counties were created. For most of this period, today's Arlington County was made up mostly of a number of large plantations and dairy and truck farms that provided food for Georgetown and Alexandria, and, after the Revolutionary period, for the District of Columbia. Food was usually ferried across the Potomac by ferry boats until the construction of the first bridge in 1797 that was replaced in 1808 by the first Chain Bridge.

In 1730 Prince William County was created in roughly the northern half of the neck, and 12 years later in 1742, the land north of the Occoquan River was designated as Fairfax County.

Thus when the Revolutionary War was in full swing, today's Arlington County and the city of Alexandria were simply the northernmost tip of Fairfax County .

Then, in 1789, with the adoption of the Constitution and the establishment of a new national government, there was the need for a United States capital. As any high school history student who is well read well knows, the founding fathers, after much bickering, compromising, give and take, settled on the Potomac River estuary as a location for the capital.

The capital area was to be a one hundred square mile zone ceded from the States of Maryland and Virginia. Presidential appointed commissioners were to make a survey to set off the limits and exact location of the square. The results of their deliberations had a long lasting and profound impact on what would become in later years Arlington County. It was from those deliberations the exact location and size of the County would be determined, with some adjustment to be discussed briefly hereinafter. The square, ten miles by ten miles, would straddle the Potomac River roughly at the upper limits of its navigable tidal waters with about two thirds coming from the State of Maryland and one third from the Commonwealth of Virginia.

One Virginia corner of the land thus ceded to the new National government was located at Jones Point near where the Great Hunting Creek empties into the Potomac, and now in the shadows of the Virginia end of the Woodrow Wilson Bridge on the I-495/I-95 beltway. The corner marking stone is in place partly under a later erected Coast Guard light house. The other Virginia corner of the square was located ten miles to the Northwest. The stone for that corner is also still in place and can be seen in the East Falls Church neighborhood just off Meridian Street and within sight and sound of the recently built I-66 Interstate highway.

Additional marker stones for the capital boundaries were placed at one mile intervals along the boundaries of the square and many of these are also still in place and being preserved with iron grills or otherwise. Others have been eliminated because of vandalism, road construction, or other urban development. The story of the 1791 survey for the National Capital boundaries by Major Andrew Ellicott and his assistants, to include the self educated Black astronomer Benjamin Banneker, is a fascinating one but is a bit beyond the scope of this narrative. There is no shortage of scholarly works on the project in most first class libraries and especially the Virginia Room of the Arlington County Main Library. Additionally, AHS members have contributed writings on the subject to the Society's Magazine. [2]

After the transfer of the Virginia land to the National government it was known as the Alexandria County portion of the District of Columbia and included the then city of Alexandria that today would be identified generally as "Old Town" Alexandria.

In the following years, as we shall see, this Virginia land would be returned to the State, and some parts would be annexed by the City of Alexandria. Eventually, in 1920 by Legislative action, that part outside the boundaries of the City of Alexandria formerly identified as the "country part" of Alexandria County would be officially

---

[2] *E.g., see Vol. 1, No. 1, (1957), The Boundaries of Arlington, Rose, Jr. C. B.*

A Glimpse at Early Residents

In the years leading to and through the establishment of Independence and a new National government, the lands that would someday become Arlington County continued to be mostly wooded and undeveloped and sparsely populated. One of the most reliable sources for populations and demographics in those years well before the taking of the national census each ten years, were church, county or parish records. The lands that would become Arlington County was within and a small part of the Truro Parish.

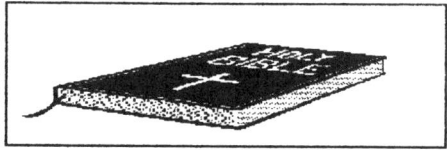

The Truro records of 1743, relied upon by many modern historical writers, indicate there were only 1,372 "tithables" (tithe-ables) in all the Parish and that category did not include all human beings. Thus the residents of the forthcoming Arlington County, which did not include all the Parish, could not have then numbered more than a few hundred.

In the first national census, as required each ten years by the new Constitution, the population of Arlington County, the "country part" of the Alexandria County of the District, was shown to be 978, of which about a third were slaves. There were no recorded concentrations of settlers in the area but a primitive map [3] of the day reveals several widely scattered homesteads or farms in existence.

The subject map contains designations for the Abingdon plantation at the present National Airport, and for the Wheeler, Griffin and Awbrey "Places" up the Potomac from about the Marine "Iwo Jima" Memorial to the southern edge of Rosslyn. The map does not show, and thus apparently predates, Arlington's Glebe House[4] currently standing on North 17th Street.

The John Ball house and mill are shown and there are Whitford and King houses, or farms, shown in the area about where Glebe Road intersects with I-395 in the present Nauck neighborhood. None of the early structures, or others, except for the John Ball house and the ruins of Abingdon are now known to exist. The John Ball house is in the Glencarlyn neighborhood of Arlington and will be discussed in greater detail herein in Chapter II concerning Post-Civil War Development in the County.

---

[3] *"An interpretive historical map of Fairfax County Virginia in 1760", by Beth Mitchell, on file in most Northern Virginia libraries, and the Virginia Room of the Arlington County Central Library.*

[4] *A "glebe" in early American days was a tract of farmable land allotted to a minister for use as a source for food. A glebe was not a house, but a small plot of farm land. The term "glebe house" referred to the structure, if any, on the glebe. Thus, the current practice of referring to Arlington's "Glebe", without including the word "house", on North 17th Street may not be exactly correct literally.*

ARLINGTON COUNTY VIRGINIA - A Modern History

PRE - CIVIL WAR DEVELOPMENT

In the early years of the 1800's leading to the Civil War, development and population growth in the future Arlington County, then part of the National Capital land, continued to be slow. The earlier cession arrangement provided that there be no erection of public buildings on the Virginia side of the Potomac. Some historians have written that the new President so requested since he owned lands on the Virginia side and did not want to be confronted with what might have appeared to be a conflict of interest in the nature of real estate speculation and enrichment.

Two developments of the period, however, merit mention in this sketchy overview of early Arlington history. The first of major importance is the building of the Arlington House, or the Custis-Lee Mansion, our current majestic landmark in Arlington Cemetery, the other is the return to Virginia of that portion of the National Capital lands that had been accepted from the Commonwealth at the time of the creation of the new National government.

ARLINGTON HOUSE - THE CUSTIS-LEE MANSION

The construction of Arlington House, initially called Mount Washington, was begun in 1802 by the grandson of Martha Washington, George Washington Parke Custis. who, as stated, had been born when his parents occupied the Abingdon house and plantation near where Donald Trump's shuttles, as well as planes from some other airlines, landed years later at National Airport.

Custis, with his sister Nelly Custis, had lived with his Grandmother and step Grandfather George Washington at Mt Vernon after his father died of fever in 1881 near the end of the Revolutionary War.

Upon reaching maturity Custis became heir to lands along the Potomac across from the Capital in addition to Abingdon that his father had obtained from the Alexanders. He also inherited adjacent lands from George Washington stretching to the Four Mile Run water shed several miles to the west. He thereby became the largest land holder in what is today Arlington County but, as stated, what was then known as the country part of Alexandria County of the District of Columbia.

Leaving Mt Vernon and needing a home, Custis chose for his new home the high and commanding ground within view of the Capitol building, the White House and other sights beyond the Potomac River. He ultimately decided to name it "Arlington" after the family ancestral estate down south on the Eastern Shore of Virginia.[5] Arlington House was designed by a young English architect, George Hadfield, who also was in charge of early construction. The wings were constructed in the period from 1802 to 1804, and the center section to include the portico was finished by 1817.

---

[5] *For a fascinating account of the source of the name, i.e. whether from Lord Arlington or a town in England by that name, one could refer to the article <u>The Arlington Connection</u> by Warren Clardy in the October, 1989 issue of the Arlington Historical Society Magazine.*

A Glimpse at Early Residents

In 1804 Custis's roving eyes came to rest on one Mary Lee Fitzhugh from Alexandria City. They soon married and moved into the part of Arlington house that was then completed. The couple had one daughter, Mary Anne Randolph Custis.

In 1831 young Mary Custis married a dashing young Lee from the Stratford Hall plantation in Westmoreland County on the southern banks of the Potomac River some 30 or so miles east of Fredericksburg.[6] That Lee was none other than Robert Edward Lee, who would become one of the most renowned, respected and established figures in American history.

Because of the union of a Custis and a Lee, Arlington House, pursuant to an Act of Congress, would also become known in later years, until today, as the Custis-Lee Mansion. The years ahead for Robert E. Lee and Arlington House were productive and historical, but also painful and turbulent. That record is well documented by numerous works in almost any first class library and available to readers who are interested in a deeper and more detailed account. Such an incisive examination is not within the scope of our brief glimpse of Arlington's early history and inhabitants, but it might be helpful to summarize some of the more important developments as background on more comprehensive treatment of later events herein.

* * *

We need not lean here on the almost endless and detailed accounts of Robert E. Lee's life before and during the Civil War. For our purpose and for brevity, it is sufficient to rely largely on the somewhat more abridged highlights provided by the late gifted and prolific Eleanor Lee Reading Templeman in her book Arlington Heritage.[7] Ms Templeman herself, as the Lee in her name indicates, was in the Lee family progeny. She was the great-great granddaughter of Richard Bland Lee, the brother of "Light-Horse Harry" Lee, and she lived most of her life, after 1935, in Arlington.

Templeman wrote many articles and books on the Lee family and Northern Virginia history and was widely known and admired. She related that Lieutenant Lee, from Stratford Hall on the Potomac and just out of West Point, proposed to Mary Custis, the only daughter at Arlington House in 1830. The couple were married on June 30th the following year at Arlington House in a festive and elaborate wedding attended by many distinguished guests.

In their years of marriage leading to the Civil War three decades later, Robert and Mary Lee made Arlington House their home for the most part, although they often were not there. The years were not without their share of hardships involving much travel or long periods of separation. In spite of stressful years, they managed to have seven children, three boys and four girls.

---

[6] *Other prestigious mansions and estates near Stratford Hall and around Warsaw, Virginia on the Northern Neck between the Potomac and Rappahannock Rivers existing today and dating from as early as the 18th Century, include Sabine Hall, Bladenfield, Grove Mount and Accakeek Farm.*

[7] *New York, Avenel Books, A Division of Crown Publishers, Inc., 1969.*

ARLINGTON COUNTY VIRGINIA - A Modern History

On some of Lee's military assignments, such as when he was Superintendent at West Point, or heading engineer operations to save the harbor at St Louis, his wife and children would accompany him. At other times when he was away in the Mexican War, or with the cavalry out west, or in command of troops at Harper's Ferry to recapture the Federal Arsenal occupied by the abolitionist John Brown, his family remained at Arlington House.

In 1853, Lee's mother-in-law died, and four years later his father-in-law also died at the age of 76, both at Arlington House. Upon the death of Mr Custis, Lee obtained extended leave, and an assignment nearby so he could manage and try to save the Arlington House and the estate. The property had been badly neglected by its owner in his advanced years and when he was all alone and deeply depressed at the loss of his beloved wife. Saving the estate proved to be no small financial challenge to Lee. He could have raised badly needed cash by selling off a number of the slaves, which he was urged to do, but he declined to do so. It is well recorded that the Lees objected to slavery, were compassionately attached to many of their slaves and preferred to grant them their freedom as rapidly as they could afford to do so.

Finally, in 1861, while living at Arlington House, and assigned duties at nearby Ft Washington, Lee, as is well known, was offered command of the Union Armies. While briefly pondering the offer, word arrived that Virginia had seceded and Lee declined. He and his family promptly left Arlington House, and never returned.

One contemporary writer put it this way in 1993.[8]

> *"When the news reached him that Virginia had adopted an ordinance of Secession on April 17, 1861, Lee was distressed. As an army career officer, and an opponent of slavery, he had supported the preservation of the Union his father and uncles had helped to create.*
>
> *"Nevertheless, Lee thought he owed his loyalty to his native state, and on April 20 resigned his commissioned in the Army. Two days later he left Arlington for Richmond to accept command of Virginia's military forces with the General Assembly's approval.*
>
> *"About a month later, as Union troops prepared to occupy the hills around Arlington to set up fortifications to defend Washington, Mrs Lee left her home after sending her children and some of the family valuables to safety..."*

Mrs Lee died in 1873 and rests with her husband in the lower part of the Chapel at Washington and Lee University in Lexington, Virginia.

Upon the departure of the Lees, Arlington House was occupied and claimed by the Union Army as a headquarters. It was badly damaged and abused during the war. Eventually, the property, after the war, was returned to the Lee family as a result of a long and bitter court suit. Lee died in 1870 and seven years later his son Custis filed suit to reclaim the Arlington House estate. In 1878 the Supreme Court by a 5 to 4 decision

---

[8] *Joe Farruggia, <u>Insider's Guide to Arlington</u>, The Arlington Courier, October 21, 1993.*

A Glimpse at Early Residents

ruled in favor of Lee and granted his request for ejection of all "trespassers". Much was at stake since the Federal government over the years had established a National Cemetery with thousands of war dead buried on the grounds. It was also using a part of the property for Freedman's Village to house hundreds of former slaves.

Historian James Edward Peters writes[9] that reasonable minds prevailed and Lee reissued his offer to accept compensation for the property. Peters wrote, in part,

> "...on March 3, 1883, the Forty-Seventh Congress appropriated the agreed sum of $150,000 to be paid to Major General Custis Lee. Upon receipt of this payment, Custis Lee executed the deed and following the approval of Secretary of War Robert Todd Lincoln, it was recorded at the Alexandria County Court House on May 14, 1883. At last, nearly twenty-two years after Union troops had first occupied the estate, Arlington became an official National Cemetery of the United States of America."

Thus ended an extraordinary and fascinating period of Arlington history concerning its most important and lasting structure built during the early years of the 19th Century and leading to the Civil War. Arlington House and its surrounding areas that include the graves of John F. and Robert Kennedy, is now a National historical treasure visited regularly by millions of people from all over the world.

THE RETURN OF CAPITAL LAND TO VIRGINIA

The other major event of the first half of the 19th Century to have a lasting impact on Arlington County thereafter can probably be said to be the return, or "retrocession", to Virginia of lands that had been ceded to the National Government for a capital at the time of the founding of the country.

The land involved was about 30 of the 100 square miles of the capitol area, or District of Columbia, that lay on the Virginia side of the Potomac River. The land was and is triangular in shape with the irregular Potomac River banks forming the Northeast, hypotenuse, boundary side and the straight line Southwestern boundary running ten miles between a stone corner marker at Jones Point at the Southern end of modern day "Old Town" Alexandria and another corner marker in East Falls Church.

By 1846, agitation for return of the former Virginia lands of the District reached a boiling point. Merchants in Alexandria, Historian Rose writes, especially were displeased with river constructions by the District government that made travel and trade difficult between Alexandria and Georgetown up the river.

In September 1846, following numerous conferences, public and legislative discussions, and Congressional authorization, a referendum on the matter for residents of the Alexandria county part of the District of Columbia was held.

---

[9] *Arlington National Cemetery. - Shrine to American Heros,* Woodbine House, Washington, D. C., 1986, p. 36.

The attitude of the Federal government, at the time, on the question of retrocession seemed to be one of general disinterest. Rose shed light on this with the following quote from the Congressional Act authorizing the referendum:[10]

"...no more territory should be held for the seat of government than is absolutely necessary and proper...and ... experience hath shewn that the portion of the District of Columbia ceded to the United States by the state of Virginia has not been, nor is ever likely to be, necessary for that purpose."

Rose follows the above quote with her own wry and quite pertinent and understated observation:

"In the light of the present day, it may be remarked that the crystal ball of the Congress was distinctly clouded!"

The result of the referendum on retrocession, was 763 for and 222 against. Most of the votes against were from the "country part" of Alexandria, or what would now be generally Arlington County. Rose suggested that a reason for the heavy vote against retrocession in the now Arlington County part of Alexandria County may have been related to the slavery question. The area, north of Alexandria and along the banks of the Potomac nearest the District, was said to have been a place of sanctuary for escaped slaves. On the Virginia side of the river they could seek help from abolitionists across the river, as was once reported by an Arlington official and historian Crandal Mackey at the turn of the century.[11]. But then Rose seems to have pondered further with the comment, "Nothing has come to light to suggest just why the country people were actively opposed to retrocession."[12]

In any event, following the referendum vote by the residents affected, President Polk issued a proclamation declaring the retrocession in full force and effect, provided Virginia formally extended its jurisdiction into the area.

This Virginia did, effective March 20, 1847, after some argument in the legislature on the question of representation for the new county. The governing body was known as the County Court, as with other Virginia Counties, and consisted of 13 Justices of the Peace, appointed by the Governor with no provision as to where the Justices must reside within the county. The delegate to the General Assembly was elected.

---

[10] *Rose, Ibid, p. 81*

[11] *A Brief History of Alexandria County, Falls Church, The Newell Printing Co., 1907.*

[12] *Rose, Ibid, p. 82.*

A Glimpse at Early Residents

Four years later in 1851, a new Constitution provided that the Justices would be elected and there would be 20 Justices of which 16 would be from wards in the City of Alexandria. The remaining 4 were to be elected "at large" in the country part of the County, i.e. present day Arlington.

ARLINGTON COUNTY IN THE CIVIL WAR

At the outbreak of the Civil War in 1861 the Northern Virginia areas across from the District of Columbia, and especially what is now Arlington County, still remained relatively unchanged from the times in 1791 when a part of Virginia was ceded for the new Federal Government for its capital.

As stated above, it had been only 15 years since the Virginia part of the ten miles square of the capital zone had been retroceded to Virginia and designated as the county of Alexandria.

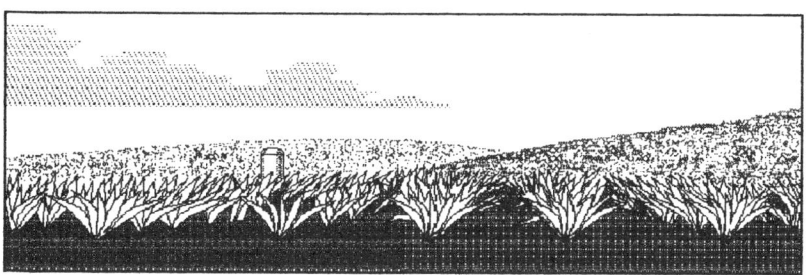

Much of the area to become Arlington County was then still in woodlands and the scattered farms or grazing fields that did exist were mostly owned by Virginians such as the heirs or successors of Lord Fairfax and others who did not reside in the area. There were no settlements that could be described as villages or towns and the only residence of significance was Arlington House overlooking the Potomac, built by George Washington Parke Custis, the grandson of Martha Washington as we have discussed above.

In 1861 there were only about 10,000 people in Alexandria County but over three quarters of those were in Alexandria City now, roughly, Alexandria "Ole Town". Only about 1,500 people were located in the "country part" of Alexandria County, that is what is today Arlington County. Of that number outside the City, almost half were slaves or "free colored".

Thus the "Arlington County" of 1861 stood in sharp contrast to the fully developed and completely urbanized community of the late 1900s with its Rosslyn, Crystal City and Ballston high rises, the Pentagon building, Fort Myer, Henderson Hall, Arlington Cemetery, and extensive high rise developments, shopping malls, and packed residential neighborhoods interlaced with massive interstates and road nets and a population of almost 200,000.

At the onset of the Civil War, Ft Sumter in the Charleston harbor, where the opening shot of the War was fired, fell to Union forces on April 14, 1861. A few days later Virginia withdrew from the Union and the soon to be famous Arlingtonian Robert E. Lee from his home in Arlington House, declined the offer to command the Federal Army.

Since the White House and other key Federal facilities were almost within range of cannon fire from the high ground on the Virginia side of the Potomac, it immediately became essential for the protection of Washington that the ground be occupied by Union forces as alluded to above. Arlington thus became a critical part of the defenses of Washington for the duration of the war.

Union army troops began occupying the "country part" of Alexandria County soon after on May 24th. As we know, the part of Alexandria County outside of Alexandria City was not to be known officially as Arlington County until years later in 1920 when it was so designated by the Virginia General Assembly to end the confusion over a county and a city of the same name.

The Federal, or Union, troops promptly occupied Mason Island earlier known as Analostan Island and today known as Roosevelt Island. The Island had been purchased by John Mason, son of George Mason, whose stately home was intact at the time of Federal take over. The home and island had been the scene of many gala affairs and receptions for national figures in the years leading to the antebellum period.

The John Mason home on Mason (Analostan/Roosevelt) Island before it was burned after the Civil War from undetermined causes.

The troops then crossed into Virginia (1) over the Long Bridge, roughly where the George Mason and Rochambeau Bridges are now located; (2) by water down the river to Alexandria City; and (3) on the mule trail along side the canal on the Aqueduct

A Glimpse at Early Residents

Bridge along side where the Key Bridge now stands.[13] The Alexandria force was under the command of Col Ellsworth who became the first casualty of the war.

Arlington House became the command post of the Union forces and action was quickly taken to secure the bridge and river crossing sites. Within the first week, construction was started on the first of a string of forts along the Virginia high ground. Priority was given to Ft Corcoran, overlooking the Aqueduct Bridge; Fort Albany about where the Navy Annex and new Arlington County detoxification Center is now on Columbia Pike; and Fort Runyan roughly where the north end of the Crystal City development is located.

Federal troops on Mason (Roosevelt) Island during the Civil War. The troops commuted from Georgetown (background) by Ferry.

In due course, the forts would stretch almost from Alexandria City up the Potomac to near the Chain Bridge. They would include Ft Smith on the palisades above the Aqueduct Bridge, Ft Corcoran, Ft Scott in South Arlington (now a small County Park), Ft Whipple (now Ft Myer), Ft Richardson on the Army Navy Club golf course, Forts McPherson, Tillinghast, Cass, Woodbury, Strong (or DeKalb), and Ft Marcy across the county line in Fairfax County. Some of the forts were to serve as intermediate or backup forts within cannon or small arms range of the main forts. Later in the war the Union forces constructed forts on or near present day Arlington land at greater distances from the Potomac such as Forts Ramsay and Buffalo along the Leesburg turnpike where Seven Corners is now located.

At the beginning, the Arlington forts were loosely organized and not very adequate to withstand a determined attack by the Southern forces. As time passed,

---

[13]*On the North side of the present bridge, near the Virginia shore, some remains of the piers of the old bridge can still be seen protruding above the water.*

however, they were constantly strengthened and expanded and occupied in strength by the Army of the Potomac. Although there were skirmishes and aggressive scouting from time to time in the area the fort areas never became actual battlegrounds.

Still, the forts had a tremendous impact on the Arlington County of the time. Normal commercial or social intercourse between the residents of the county that had not fled and Washingtonians across the river was interrupted. The Aqueduct Bridge was drained and converted into a planked bridge but was largely preempted for heavy columns of military traffic.

As the Union troops occupying the Virginia Forts swelled to probably over 10,000, friction grew with the relatively few locals, many of whom were known or suspected of having Confederate sympathies.

Rose relates that there were depredations by troops, requisitioning of houses and farm animals, stabling for horses, chopping of timber and numerous other hardships imposed on the local population by overwhelming numbers of Federal troops.[14]

Federal troops on Mason's (Roosevelt) Island during the Civil War. Note Aqueduct Bridge (now location of Key Bridge) in background.

Even the still existing but rebuilt Mt Olivet and Hunter's Chapel Churches were requisitioned to serve as hospitals and were later razed or damaged for their timbers. Most of the few private homes in the County were also taken over for hospitals or sleeping quarters for officers or troops.

---

[14] *Rose, Ibid, p 105-7.*

A Glimpse at Early Residents

Union troops at Arlington House during the Civil War. The Robert E. Lee family had fled the area in the opening days of the War.

Rose wrote "The times were unhappy ones for the residents of Arlington County and not much better for the occupying troops." She also quotes a northern artilleryman who wrote home "I wish you could come out here and see us and see what a country this is in mud about three inches deep and the damest(sic) weather you ever saw - the fog is so thick you can cut it with a knife."

During the Union occupation the Arlington plantation suffered badly. Furniture and other belongings left behind by the quickly departing Lees was damaged or missing. The grounds and gardens were disrupted by the large number of troops camping there, and after the battles of Bull Run the grounds became burial sites for Confederate as well as Union dead.

Eventually the Arlington estate was taken over by the Federal government because of bazaar circumstances that prevented the owner from paying delinquent taxes. As stated several pages back, it was recovered after the war in a suit brought by General Lee's son and then, in a settlement, purchased outright by the Federal government for its present use as a national cemetery, museum, and other purposes.

One of the major forts built on the Custis grounds, and the only one to survive to this day but renamed, was Fort Whipple. Construction was undertaken almost immediately upon occupation of the area in May, 1861. As its completion was nearing in the Spring 1863, there was a need to find a name to identify the fort. A Northern General, Amiel W. Whipple, had been wounded at the Battle of Chancellorsville (May

2-4, 1863)[15] and died in a hospital in the District on May 7th. It was decided to name the newly completed fortification Fort Whipple in honor of that fallen officer.

Union troops at Fort Whipple located about where the modern day Battleship Maine mast is located in Arlington Cemetery.

At the height of the Civil War a young Army officer, Albert James Myer, arrived in Washington and Fort Whipple. He was to become a most remarkable young officer and would make a lasting mark for himself and his new fort that would eventually bear his name. Myer would become known as the founder of the Army Signal Corps and plant the seed that would grow into the meteorology service as a part of the Signal Corps. He felt that better knowledge by military commanders of coming weather would be of great value for planning military operations and would also give the army a much needed peace time role. His meteorology organization, with mixed degrees of success, would later be transferred to the Department of Agriculture and become the U. S. Weather Bureau.

Myer was born in Newburgh, N. Y., on September 20, 1828. As related by Paul J. Scheips of the U.S.Army Center of Military History in a talk before the Arlington Historical Society on September 4, 1973, [16] Myer grew up in Buffalo and earned a Doctorate from the University there. In his dissertation he developed a sign language for the deaf and dumb based on the Bain telegraph alphabet. This experience apparently

---

[15] *Chancellorsville was one of the major and bloodiest Battles of the War. Lee sent Hooker reeling and started a Confederate drive north that did not end until July, the following year at Gettysburg.*

[16] *AHS Magazine Vol. 5, No. 2, (October 1974), p.29-43.*

A Glimpse at Early Residents

whetted his appetite for communications. In 1959 he obtained a qualified approval for his military signalling system from a board presided over by Lt Col Robert E. Lee. He was commissioned a major in 1860 on the eve of the Civil War, became the Army's first signal officer and was sent west to put his system to test in the Navaho Expedition. In the west he developed a kerosene lamps by night and flags by day expansion of his communication techniques.

When the war brokeout, Myer was returned east and served as an aide to General McDowell at the first Battle of Bull Run and then became McClellan's signal officer. He also organized a signal corps with officers and enlisted men from various Union departments. Here he apparently ran into trouble by encroaching on someone's turf and got himself removed from active service. Scheips described that Myer's efforts to get men from the established telegraph service was resented by those with connections to Secretary of War Stanton. Myer was exiled out west again and a year later placed on inactive duty where he remained until after the war. He won vindication in 1866 and resumed Signal Corps activities with renewed intensity, mostly at Fort Whipple, for the rest of his life.

The full extent and variety of Myer's post Civil War activities, and those who served with him, is a fascinating and dramatic tale but is beyond the scope of this narrative. Myer died in 1880. The following year the Fort was renamed Fort Myer in his honor and remains as such to this day.

While Myer may have died in 1880 the imprint of his efforts in the field of military communications did not. In the early 1900s the Wright brothers had made aviation history at Kitty Hawk with their first, but short, manned flight of an aircraft. It is fitting and proper in this narrative to stress that Arlington County and Fort Myer were to play key roles in the next steps in the development of the Wright airplane. Orville Wright arrived in Washington and Fort Myer in 1908 to test his airplane and try to interest the Army in providing money for, and using, the new Wright invention. He argued that it would be of great value to observation, as a means of communication and intelligence, on the battlefield.

Wright made several brief flights from the grounds of Fort Myer one of which, on September 17th ended in a crash that killed his passenger Lt Thomas Selfridge, and maimed Wright for life. Two years later Orville Wright returned to Myer to again demonstrate his aircraft for the Army, and the world. He successfully circled the field repeatedly as required and then made a cross country test which called for a flight of ten miles. That flight was from the Fort Myer grounds near the present flag pole eastward to Shooter's Hill in Alexander where the George Washington Masonic Memorial now stands and back. It was witnessed by AHS founder and past president, the late Frank L. Ball as a small boy, from a spot about where the present Fort Myer Post Exchange is located. [17]

Thus, Fort Myer became the location of the first cross country flight, and regrettably the first aircraft death in American and Arlington history. Today at Fort Myer there are markers commemorating and describing these events at the main gate, the

---

[17] Ball, Frank L., *The First Cross-Country Flight by Airplane*, AHS Magazine, Vol. 1, No. 3, (October 1959), p. 37-40.

ARLINGTON COUNTY VIRGINIA - A Modern History

Lt Thomas Selfridge and Orville Wright in plane at Fort Myer that crashed and killed Selfridge and maimed Wright.

clearing by the flag pole in front of Quarters One, next to the reviewing stand on the parade ground, and on the brick wall of the reviewing stand. But we have gotten ahead of our story. We must return briefly to the Civil War period and the Federal occupation of the Custis house and grounds.

General Albert James Myer, father of the Army Signal Corps, founder of the weather service, and the Army Officer after whom the Civil War Fort Whipple was renamed in 1881.

A Glimpse at Early Residents

Considerable damage to the Custis house occurred during the period of Federal Army use as has been well documented by numerous writers. Troops came and went in muddy boots, cooking and eating in the rooms, and often banging their heavy arms and equipment against walls, doors, and whatever furniture remained in the house. There was of course vandalism, and malicious or indifferent attention, and even theft for many of the items that remained behind when the Lees departed just prior to the arrival.

One development that aided in restoration after the war were the photographs that were taken by Mathew Brady and his staff and an Army photographer, at the instigation of Army Quartermaster Montgomery C. Meigs. The way in which the photographs, or pictographs, were used to compare post war conditions with those that existed before the war was the subject of an imaginative approach in an article by Agnes M. Downey for the AHS Magazine. Ms Downey (now Mullins) has been curator at the Arlington House and a Board member of the Society for many years.

In her article [18] Downey pretends to write a letter to the long deceased Brady and the anonymous Army photographer thanking them for taking the photographs of Arlington house and its grounds. She sets forth in repeated detail the manner in which the photos were helpful to show how certain parts of the building were designed and made, and from what materials, and other details, before damage or deterioration. In her letter dated January 19, 1960, Downey wrote in part;

> *Dear Sirs:*
> *It may be a shock to receive a letter at this late date, but your gifts and their value are increasingly appreciated with each passing year. It was thought that you might be interested in the part being played by your early photographs of Arlington in the restoration of that house..."*

Downey then referred to the Doric-columned portico and other portions of the house that were restored based on the photographs made during the war. She closed with the hope that "should either you or the Lees return to Arlington, you would find it looking much as you did that spring in 1861."

In addition to the impact on Arlington House resulting from its occupation and use by the Federal forces was to be the changes to the estate grounds around the mansion. Early in the War the decision was made to begin burying battle casualties on the estate and almost next to the house. The areas nearest the house were to be converted into a national cemetery. It is well recorded that the action was deliberate and pursuant to the orders of Quartermaster General Meigs to prevent the Lees from ever returning to their antebellum mansion.

---

[18] Downey, Agnes M., <u>Thanks For the Memory</u>, AHS Magazine, Vol. 1, No. 3 (October, 1959), p. 28-36.

ARLINGTON COUNTY VIRGINIA - A Modern History

In a series of articles in the AHS Magazines [19] Arlington practicing attorney, dedicated history buff, and Historical Society member George W. Dodge details the stages in which the Arlington grounds were converted into a military cemetery in the War years. Dodge wrote that the first battle casualty to be buried in Arlington Cemetery was a private William B. Blatt from the 49th Pennsylvania Infantry who had been killed in the battle of Spotsylvania on May 10, 1864, and buried on May 14th. Dodge wrote that Blatt was not the first soldier to be buried in Arlington but the third since two others who died of disease were buried one day earlier on the 13th. The grave of one of those soldiers, and that of Blatt are in Section 27 only a few paces from the mansion.

The graves of William Christman and William Blatt, first burials in Arlington Cemetery on May 13 and 14, 1864. Christman died of disease, Blatt in battle.

The graves closest to the mansion in Arlington Cemetery are those located in the Rose Garden almost at the front door steps of Arlington House. It was almost as though General Meigs, known as a very vindictive individual, wanted to rub salt into the aching wounds of the South and the Lees, by placing graves as near to the mansion as possible. Dodge wrote, "The proximity (of the graves) to the mansion was part of U. S. Quartermaster Meig's plan to make the property uninhabitable as he detested Confederate General Robert E. Lee."

The burial of the dead in the Rose garden took place throughout the summer of 1864 in the weeks following the first burials described above. The area was designated as a National Cemetery and burials have continued ever since. The first burials in Arlington were of troops killed in various battles of the times to include Cold Harbor, Petersburg, the Wilderness, Spotsylvania and at Fort Stevens on the outskirts of

---

[19] Dodge, George W., *Arlington National Cemetery's First Confederate Burials*, Vol. 9, No. 1 (1989), *The Rose Garden Burials*, Vol. 9, No. 2, (1990), *The First Battle Casualty*, Vol.9, No.4,(1992), *...Confederate Burials*, Vol.10, No.1,(1993).

A Glimpse at Early Residents

Washington in 1864. Before the war ended the grave number would swell to more than 16,000 Union dead from these and the many other costly battles in the area.

The Summer 1864 Union soldier Rose Garden burial sites in Arlington Cemetery. The sites were deliberately placed as close as possible to the mansion.

In modern times the graves in Arlington Cemetery have grown to more than 240,000 in its 612 acres. Adjacent lands in the Arlington County community have all been extensively developed making further expansion of the cemetery highly unlikely. Arlington is one of the two largest military cemeteries in the country and is almost full. The newer Columbarium for cremated remains opened in 1980 and will probably have burial space long after the rest of the cemetery is filled. Eligibility for burial in Arlington is rigidly limited to mostly active duty, retired, disabled, or decorated military personnel, and certain other nationally recognized distinguished figures. In June 1997, the TV Channel 7 newscast aired the information that waivers of the requirements for burial in the Cemetery had significantly increased in the President Clinton years to more than 50. The program reported that the waivers were opposed by some veterans and certain historical preservationists who were resisting the transfer to woodlands next to Arlington House for use as burial grounds as reported elsewhere herein in Chapter V.

There are two presidents buried in Arlington, John F. Kennedy and William H. Taft. The Tomb of the Unknowns from World Wars I and II, and the Korean War is located behind the Memorial Amphitheater with a continuous elite guard from the famed 3rd "Old Guard" Infantry Regiment stationed at Fort Myer. The remains of 2,111 Civil War reinterred unknowns rest under a granite sarcophagus in the Rose Garden only a few paces from the grave of those buried first.

There is also a monument and mass grave for the unknowns of the War of 1815 in Section 1, near the mansion. Their remains were moved to Arlington in 1905 after being discovered during excavation work in what is now the Washington Navy Yard.

All of the 409 Confederate soldiers buried in Arlington were reinterred around the base of the Confederate Memorial at Jackson circle in Section 16. Congress authorized the construction of the memorial in 1906 and it was dedicated in 1914. The gravestones of the Southerners are slightly different from those for Union soldiers. They have a pointed instead of a rounded top. Historian Philip Bigler in his "In Honored Glory", an account of the Cemetery, [20] wrote that legend had it that the pointed stones were originally designed to keep Yankees from sitting on the graves of their former opponents.

The mast of the Battleship Main with graves of its 260 crewman.

About 50 yards in front of the Amphitheater is the mast of the battleship Maine that was recovered from the ship salvaged from Havana harbor. Around the mast are the bodies of 260 men who lost their lives in Havana harbor when their ship exploded and sank in 1898. 164 of the number were reinterred from a Cuban cemetery. The balance were recovered from the ship after it was salvaged over a decade later in 1910.

Also in front of the Amphitheater and slightly to the right are the more recent

The Confederate Monument at Jackson Circle with 409 southern graves.

---

[20] *Vandamere Press, Arlington Va., 1987, available at the Cemetery Tourist reception center and in the Virginia Room, Arlington County Main Library.*

A Glimpse at Early Residents

graves of astronauts who died in accidents during launchings at Cape Kennedy, and just to the left is the grave of America's most decorated veteran of World War II, Audie Murphy.

Also interred in Arlington Cemetery is one of the saddest grave sites of any because it contains the remains of servicemen who died without just cause and in circumstances that can best be described as treacherous by a people that pretend to be friendly to America. There, in a remote and almost hidden corner of the cemetery are the bodies of 14 crewmen of the 25 that were killed when Israeli planes attacked the intelligence ship U. S. Liberty in the Middle East in June 1967. According to writer Bigler above, three of the bodies not identifiable, and some stray limbs and other body parts, are buried under a head stone listing the names of the three plus three other crew members whose intact bodies were never recovered from the sea. Bigler writes further that Israel later apologized for the attack, claiming it was a case of mistaken identity and that Israel had paid $3.5 million in reparations to the families of the 34 American sailors who were killed and a similar sum to the 171 wounded. Bigler, almost like an epitaph, had this to say about the incident;

> *"Inexplicably, the United States seemed content to dismiss the attack and accept the Israeli version of the incident while virtually ignoring the testimony of the Liberty officers and men which proved conclusively that the attack on the ship was both deliberate and premeditated..."*

The graves of George Washington Parke Custis, who built Arlington House and died in 1857, and his wife Mary Fitzhugh Custis, who died in 1853 as stated, are located within an iron grill enclosure in Section 13 of the present day Cemetery, about 50 yards from the corner of McPherson and Meigs Drives just inside the Fort Myer Chapel Gate.

The gravesite of George Washington Parke Custis and his wife Mary Fitzhugh Custis in Arlington Cemetery about 100 yards from Arlington House.

ARLINGTON COUNTY VIRGINIA - A Modern History

The list of important and distinguished national heros and personalities that are buried in Arlington Cemetery is seemingly without end. A few of the more important would have to include the following, other than those mentioned above, (not necessarily in order of importance): Generals Arthur MacArthur, Anthony McAuliffe (Bastogne "Nuts" of WWII), Montgomery Meigs (who ordered the first burials on the Custis estate), John J. "Black Jack" Pershing, Clair Chennault, Phil Sheridan, Creighton Abrams, Jr., George C. Marshall, Daniel Sickles, Phil Kearny, Hoyt Vandenberg, Walter Bedell Smith, Jonathan Wainwright, Omar Bradley, Henry "Hap" Arnold; Col Leonard Wood; Admirals William Halsey, William Leahy, Hyman Rickover, Robert Peary, Lt Thomas Selfridge (first aviation fatality in history at Ft Myer in 1908), Cpl Ira Hayes (one of statues of marines on Iwo Jima Memorial); Justices Hugo Black, Oliver Wendell Holmes, Earl Warren and William O. Douglas; James Forrestal (lst Sec/Def), Inventor George Westinghouse, newsman Frank Reynolds, Abner Doubleday, Bacteriologist Walter Reed, Mary Randolph (first burial at Arlington) Pierre L'Enfant, Boxer Joe Louis, Francis Gary Powell (shot down in spy plane over USSR); Actress Constance Bennett; composer Ignance Paderewski (to be returned when "Poland is Free"); Robert Todd Lincoln, William Jennings Bryan, Robert F. Kennedy, Medgar Evers (Civil rights Activist); explorer Richard Byrd, Jr., and British Field Marshall Sir John Dill (died in Washington in World War II - one of only two equestrian statues in the cemetery).

Throughout Arlington cemetery are also numerous trees with identifying or descriptive plaques planted by war veterans to commemorate their military organizations. There are monuments or memorials to honor various services or activities to include the Service Nurses, Navy Seabees, San Juan Hill Rough Riders, servicemen killed in 1983 Beirut car bombing, and arches, gates and roads named for famous national leaders and heros.

Arlington Cemetery, within the boundaries of Arlington County is a unique national and local asset. Local residents can well be immensely proud that it is located in their County. No local piece of real estate has played a more decisive, lasting and complimentary role in shaping the destiny and future of Arlingtonians.

* * *

Our brief halt in the Arlington County Civil War era would not be complete without touching on another event that was to profoundly affect the community both at the time and for decades thereafter. It had to do with the freeing of slaves at the height of the war and their arrival in the county and location in rapidly constructed temporary quarters that became known as "Freedman's Village", a place mostly unknown to Arlingtonians today, other than well read scholars or dedicated history buffs.

In 1863, following the Emancipation Proclamation, freed slaves, mostly from the closest areas surrounding the National capital, began drifting into the District of Columbia in ever increasing numbers. Prior to that time, the District had already become a haven for fugitive slaves from Virginia and Maryland, especially following President Lincoln's emancipation in April 1862 of slaves in the District.

The care and handling of the freed slaves rapidly became a problem of embarrassing and staggering proportions. Most arrived with tattered rags on their backs

A Glimpse at Early Residents

and little or no other possessions. They were without the skills or other wherewithal to provide for themselves and there was no gainful employment for them.

Writer Bobbbi Schildt, an esteemed historical writer and one of the most prolific and knowledgeable authorities on this subject, described the situation in a February 1985 issue of Northern Virginia Heritage. A number of other writers, to include Felix Janes and Donald Sweig, have also written about the matter. [21]

Workers at the wharf in Alexandria, Virginia 1862

Schildt wrote that the freed slaves were mostly located in crowded, unclean living quarters including McClellan's Barracks that was converted from horse stables. There was only one well for water in the camp and there was a foul swampy excavation adjacent to the camp which was thought to have contributed to an 1863 smallpox epidemic.

Schildt wrote further that a black surgeon, Alexander T. Augusta, tried to improve conditions in the camp and suggested that water be brought from the city's water supply. He also suggested that the stinking and polluted swamp be filled to lessen the problems of disease. After these suggestions were lodged, he was transferred to Baltimore.

It was increasingly apparent that measures had to be taken to cope with the deteriorating conditions in the freed slave camps and quarters. In due course, the Army

---

[21] *The works of these and other authors are filed in the Freedmen's Village records of the Virginia Room archives of the Arlington County Main Library.*

Quartermaster suggested that the inmates be relocated into a farming environment south of the Potomac River where there was "pure country air". Whereupon the freed slaves were moved from their location in the District on 12th Street and East Capitol Streets (now Folger Library) to the newly constructed and established community on the Arlington Estate of the Custis-Lee family that would become known as Freedman's Village.

The cluster of two story wooden buildings, and some accessory buildings of the village, were located where now is the eastern edge of Arlington Cemetery. The grounds of the village, however, took in considerably more land than would probably be considered farming acres. The map used by Rose in

Evelyn Syphax at the dedication of the Freedman's Village marker October 22, 1995.

her book (Ibid, page 123) shows the boundary of Freedman's Village stretching from modern day South Glebe Road to the Potomac River, from South Gate Road (extended to the River) on the south to almost Rosslyn on the north, excluding, generally, what is now the Fort Myer boundaries.

James in his 1967 Howard University Master's Dissertation wrote that the Village: [22]

> *"consisted of approximately 100 frame houses, each a story and a half high, with a bedroom on the second floor. The houses were neatly white-washed and divided in the center so that two families could be accommodated...each tenement was numbered and a rent of $3.00 a month was charged...there were workshops where the women and children could be trained in mechanical occupations which would aid them in becoming useful citizens instead of burdens on the community...the freedmen earned $10.00 a month in wages in addition to being supplied by the government with clothes, food and lodging...they were not to remain as permanent residents, but yield to others as soon as they could find employment."*

In later years following the war, the Federal government acquired much of the Arlington estate for burial, military and other purposes. The continued presence of the residents, and especially large numbers of unauthorized trespassers and squatters in the Village was increasingly undesired. The land of the village was needed, and the conduct and activities of the residents themselves were causing complaints. On November 12, 1887, J. A. Commerford, the Superintendent of the National Cemetery (Arlington

---

[22] *The Virginia Collection, Virginia Room, Arlington County Central Library. (VR/ACCL)*

A Glimpse at Early Residents

1887, J. A. Commerford, the Superintendent of the National Cemetery (Arlington Cemetery) wrote to G. B. Dandy, the Army Quartermaster as follows: [23]

> *"I would respectfully report that for years past some of the colored people who live on the reservation (Freedman's Village) have been in the habit of entering the cemetery during the late hours of the night for the purpose of getting wood for fuel. Upon my arrival here I was informed that several hundred young trees from 2 to 6 inches in diameter were cut down and carried away.*
>
> *"It has been the custom of these thieves to use a cross cut saw to cut down the trees.. it is said that few of the squatters buy fuel and depend mostly on what they can pick up within the enclosure.. It has been suggested, that the most effective way of preventing such thefts, is to cause the removal of these people from the reservation."*

Shortly after the dispatch of the above letter, the news appeared in the Virginia Star newspaper on December 7, 1887 that Freedman's Village, never intended as a permanent facility, was indeed to be closed. The item read, in part:

> *FREEDMAN'S VILLAGE MUST GO - The Secretary of War has issued an order requiring all the inhabitants of Freedman's Village, located on the Fort Myer military reservation in this county as well as anyone else who is living within the reservation limits to remove within thirty days... the immediate cause of the order was a complaint of the Superintendent that some of the inhabitants were cutting down trees...The Secretary decided to (also) rid the reservation of all outsiders who have lived on it by sufferance...there are a number of shanties scattered on the eastern side between the main road and the river...the inhabitants have no title of any kind but own the houses...which they will be permitted to move...the Village was an outgrowth of the war...the Secretary may extend the time for their removal, as otherwise they might be turned out houseless before the end of the cold weather..."*

By the end of the Century the Village had been terminated and its residents relocated into surrounding areas that in time became known as the Arlington neighborhoods of Green Valley, Nauck, Johnson's Hill, East Arlington and Queen City. Queen City was bull dozed in World War II to become the South Pentagon parking lot, but the other settlements remain today mostly as the Arlington View and Nauck neighborhoods. Two Baptist churches of the day, Mt Zion and Mt. Olive still survive and serve their members. Many of Arlington's most productive civic leaders have come from these neighborhoods over the years and many alive at this writing claim proudly to

---

[23] *The Virginiana Collection, Ibid.*

be direct descendants of the residents of Freedman's Village who relocated in the areas outside its boundaries in the late 1800s.

One such prominent citizen was George Vollin who was born in Arlington County almost a hundred years ago and is mentioned elsewhere herein in Chapter V as the lead plaintiff of a civil rights suit to change the manner of electing governing body menbers for the county. Vollin had lived in a segregated neighborhood known as Queen City located roughly where the South Parking lot of the Pentagon and the southern edge of Arlington Cemetery now exist. Vollin recalls that Queen City was razed during World War II to make room for the Pentagon. Vollin was for years a voluntary fireman and was a candidate for election to the office of sheriff at the time the county adopted the county manager form of government, and again in 1976. Vollin died on June 14, 1997 at the age of 93.

The author with Arlington View senior citizen George Vollin in the Spring of 1995.

Another such citizen, esteemed community leader, past school board member, and currently leading a drive for the establishment of a museum to honor Arlington's African-American past is Evelyn Syphax. Syphax on October 21, 1995 was featured in a community unveiling and dedication of a historical marker for Freeedman's Village at Arlington streets South Gate Road and South Oak on the southern edge of Arlington Cemetery. The ceremony was attended by County Board, Historical Society, and Historical Landmark Review Board members and other community figures. The Syphax family members were not residents of the Village but, rather, lived on the Custis-Lee plantation.

But again, at this point we have gotten a bit ahead of ourselves chronologically. We must return to the end of the Civil War. It was in the times following the war in the last half of the 19th Century that woods, farm fields and open spaces began to steadily disappear. They were replaced with clusters of houses that would form neighborhoods with names such as Cherrydale, Ballston, Glencarlyn, Clarendon, Ft Myer Heights, Walker Chapel, Nauck and others. Those seedlings were to provide the beginnings for the explosive growth of later years. In time, they would expand to convert the county into a truly urban and densely developed community. In our next chapter we will focus on that post Civil War growth and development in Arlington County to date.

A Glimpse at Early Residents

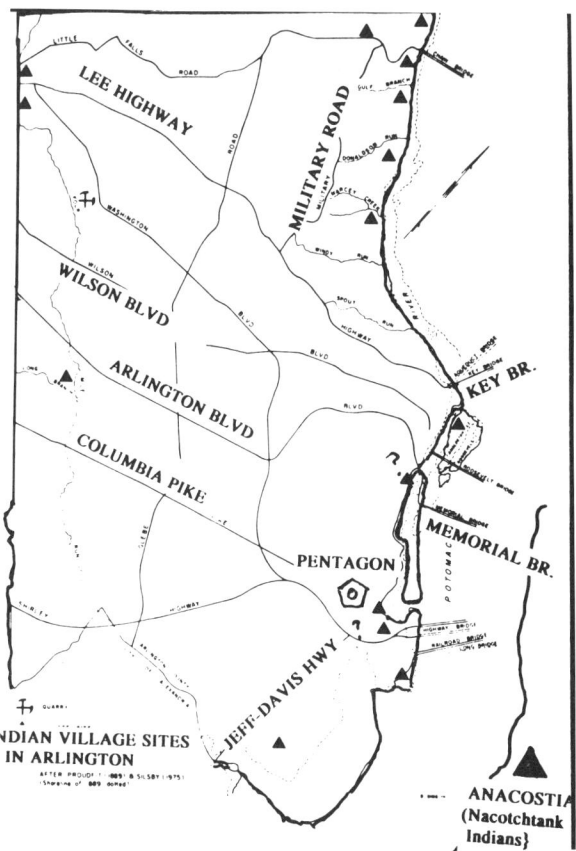

Indian villages (black triangles) of Arlington County before the departures of the last Indians around 1669. Most of the village sites are no longer extant due to massive earth movement incidental to the construction of the National Airport, the Pentagon building, the George Washington Memorial Parkway along the Potomac palisades, or other developments.

The Nacotchtankes Indian village at about where is the modern day Anacostia Naval Station is believed to have been one of the largest area villages of early Colonial days and was the locale of some particularly turbulent exchanges with the Indians. Early English visitors, or "traders", from the James Town settlement burned the village at the time of the infamous massacre of 1622. When the ship "Tiger" returned a year later its Captain Henry Spelman went ashore to negotiate with the Indians. He was brutally killed as the ship's crew watched offshore. Whereupon, the crew fled and the English stayed away for another decade.

LAND OWNERSHIP MAP 1669-1796
by Don Wise

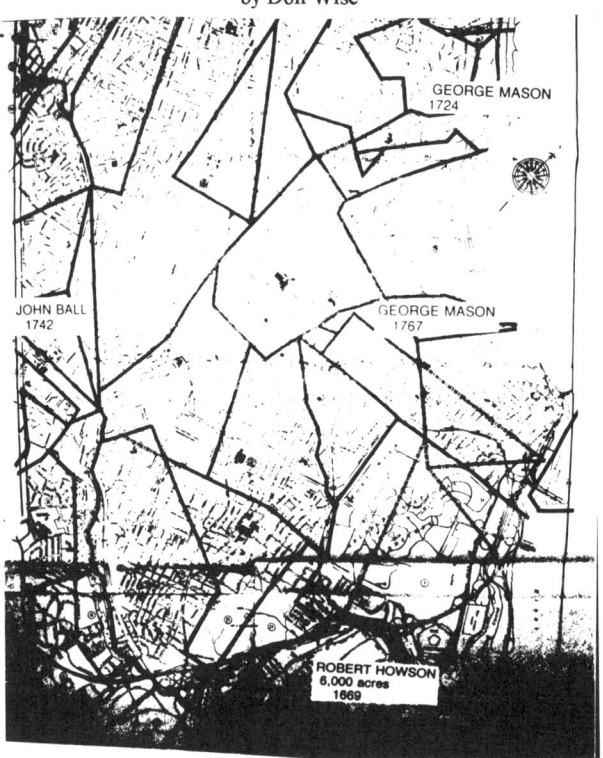

The above map, based on research by Arlington Historical Society member Donald A. Wise, was published by the Northern Virginia Sun in connection with the 1976 bicentennial observations.

A part of the lands of Robert Howson was purchased by the John Alexander family who built their "mansion" Abingdon. The structure burned in 1930, but the ruins are preserved and are now located near the entrance to the main terminal of the National Airport.

George Mason's son John eventually owned most of the lands including Analostan (Roosevelt/Mason) Island, the location of present day Fort Smith, and an extension reaching to the modern day Clarenden circle area.

John Ball built his log cabin on a part of his lands in the modern day Glencarlyn neighborhood. The cabin, with latter day exterior additions, is located on South 3rd Street.

ARLINGTON COUNTY VIRGINIA - A Modern History

AN INTERMISSION FROM THE TEXT
An Historical Vignette

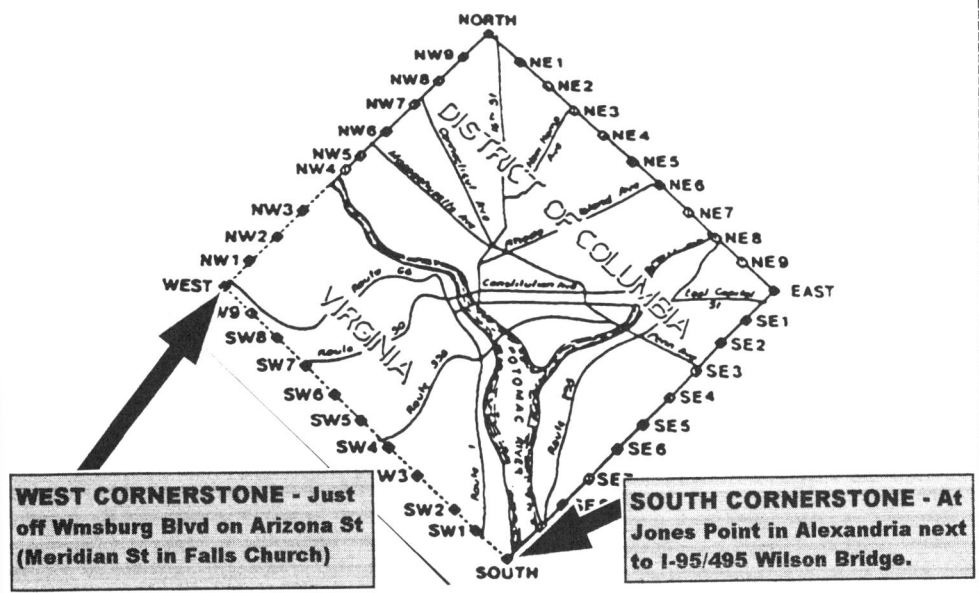

WEST CORNERSTONE - Just off Wmsburg Blvd on Arizona St (Meridian St in Falls Church)

SOUTH CORNERSTONE - At Jones Point in Alexandria next to I-95/495 Wilson Bridge.

The boundaries for the ten mile square (shown above) for the Capital City that included present day Arlington County were surveyed and laid out in 1791 by Major Andrew Ellicott with celestial sightings by a remarkable self-educated free Black man, Benjamin Banneker discussed on page 408 herein.

The starting point for the survey is marked by the South Corner stone now located under the abandoned Coast Guard light house (below) at Jones Point in Alexandria, in the shadows of the I-495 Wilson Bridge on the "beltway".

AN INTERMISSION FROM THE TEXT
An Historical Vignette

The West Cornerstone (above) of the original Capital City boundary stones as laid out in 1791. The stone is located on Arizona Street just off Williamsburg Blvd. It once marked the boundary between Fairfax County (the town of Falls Church was not chartered until 1875) and the District of Columbia but now delineates at that point the City of Falls Church, and the Counties of Fairfax and Arlington.

Boundary stone #9 (below) marks the boundary of the City of Falls Church and the County of Arlington at Van Buren and North 18th Streets. The stone is located in a County Park along Four Mile Run that was renamed the Benjamin Banneker Park in 1997.

CHAPTER TWO

POST CIVIL WAR GROWTH

RECONSTRUCTION AND AFTERMATH

After the Civil War, Arlington, along with the rest of Virginia, entered its period of "reconstruction" as part of a specially designated military district under the command of General John Schofield.[1]

Virginia's reconstruction was the briefest of any Southern State and by 1870 the State had ratified the new 14th and 15th Amendments to the U. S. Constitution

---

[1] *Gen. Schofield had fought with Gen. Sherman on his march through Georgia to the sea, and later served in Hawaii where his recommendations resulted in the establishment of Pearl Harbor as a naval base. Schofield Barracks on the island of Oahu, later day home of the 25th Infantry Division, is named after the General.*

concerning the rights and treatment of Black people and thereby was entitled to readmission into the Union and to welcome the end of military occupation.

Under a new Virginia Constitution that became effective on May 1, 1870, Alexandria County, later Arlington, as with other counties under the Constitution, was to be governed by a Board of Supervisors. Arlington's Board was to be elected from three single member geographically designated districts outside the incorporated City of Alexandria. This will be discussed further in a later chapter dealing with the growth of county politics and government.

In the post war period, Virginia, as with the other Southern States, undertook to try to heal the wounds and damage caused by the war and the fighting. Many of the major campaigns of the war such as Fredericksburg, the Wilderness, Petersburg, Bull Run, Cold Harbor, and Spotsylvania took place on Virginia soil leading to the surrender of Gen Lee to Gen Grant at the Appomattox Court House on April 9, 1865.

Since what is now Arlington was mostly unsettled during the Civil War, and no major fighting took place in the area, there was no widespread or massive damage to, or in, the county such as ordinarily might be expected in any urban area in the wake of a major war. Nevertheless, there were numerous claims filed following the fighting.

Union troops at Arlington House during the Civil War.

The county had no factories or industrial facilities of note, or congested neighborhoods or other urban type of developments that were victims of the war and that would have to be rebuilt or restored. There were, of course, constant scouting parties and skirmishes from time to time in the county as a "no man's land" and those military operations resulted in the destruction or devastation of most of the farm houses and barns

Post Civil War Growth

from whence the occupants had usually fled. In any event, there was only a handful of such structures. For the most part, Federal troops were concentrated in the aforementioned line of forts built near the Virginia banks of the Potomac River.

THE FIRST RESIDENTIAL CONCENTRATION
- FREEDMEN'S VILLAGE -

Probably the most pressing local project demanding attention in the years during and just after the end of the Civil War was the disposition and care of the large number of freed slaves on the grounds of the Arlington estate. Better housing and homes, sweet or not, had to be found for the hundreds there who were living under wretched conditions and dying from fevers, malnutrition and other causes. Although already mentioned in Chapter One, Freedman's Village merits some additional coverage in this Chapter covering post civil war developments for at least two reasons.

A sketch of a portion of Freedman's Village on the Arlington House grounds built during the Civil War for freed slaves.

First, is the probability that very few Arlingtonians today have ever heard of Freedman's Village in spite of the dramatic role it played in its day in the growth of the County. The Village existed a long time ago, it has long since been, in one way or another, done away with, and Arlington today is filled with recent arrivals from many lands who know little or nothing of the county's past. The role of Freedman's Village justifies periodic repetition.

ARLINGTON COUNTY VIRGINIA - A Modern History

Secondly, in our glimpse of Arlington's earlier neighborhood development years, we need to understand that Freedman's Village was perhaps the single most significant lunge ahead, immediately after the Civil War, in the growth of the country. Further, the Village, although to be gone before the last decade of the 1800's, would provide the seed for the establishment of other nearby neighborhoods, mentioned earlier, that exist to this day and form a viable and key part of the county and its affairs.

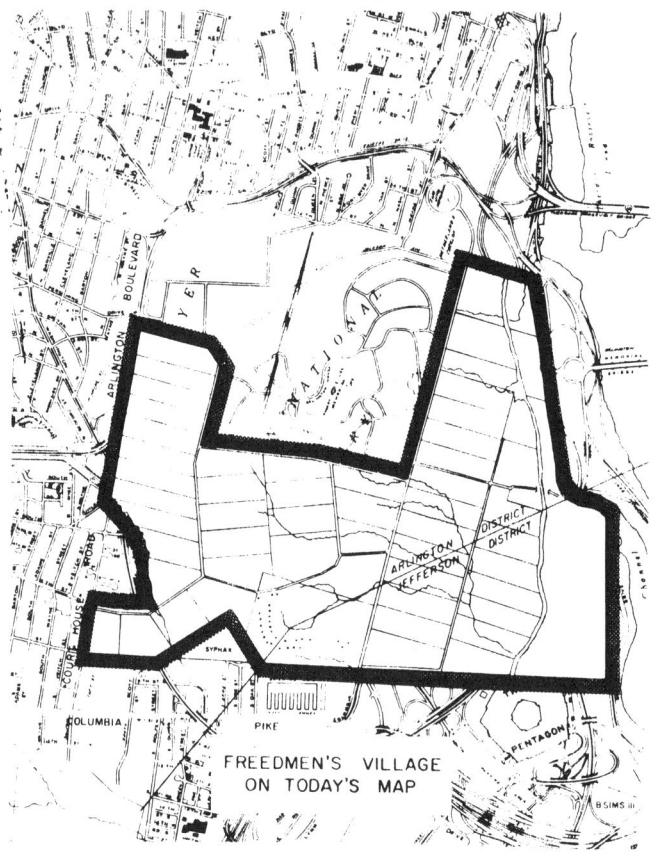

The above map from page 123 of Arlington County Virginia *(ibid) with some elaborations by this author, shows the outer limits of Freedmen's Village grounds which was much larger than the actual Village shown at the lower center straddling the Arlington and Jefferson District boundaries. As can be noted, the Village was next to today's Arlington View and other Green Valley neighborhoods. Within its borders are now the Henderson Hall Marine Barracks, the southern end of Arlington Cemetery, and a part of the Pentagon building and grounds.*

Post Civil War Growth

There are a number of excellent articles on the history of Freedman's Village in the Virginia Room of the Arlington County Central Public Library. Two of the better in this writer's opinion are by Bobbi Schildt [2] and Felix James[3]. Additional relative background on the status of Black people before and after the Civil War is available in an article also in the Virginia Room archives by Donald Sweig [4], a Research Historian for Fairfax County, Virginia. The reader interested in more detailed information on the subject may wish to refer to these writings or any number of others available in the Virginia Room of the Library.

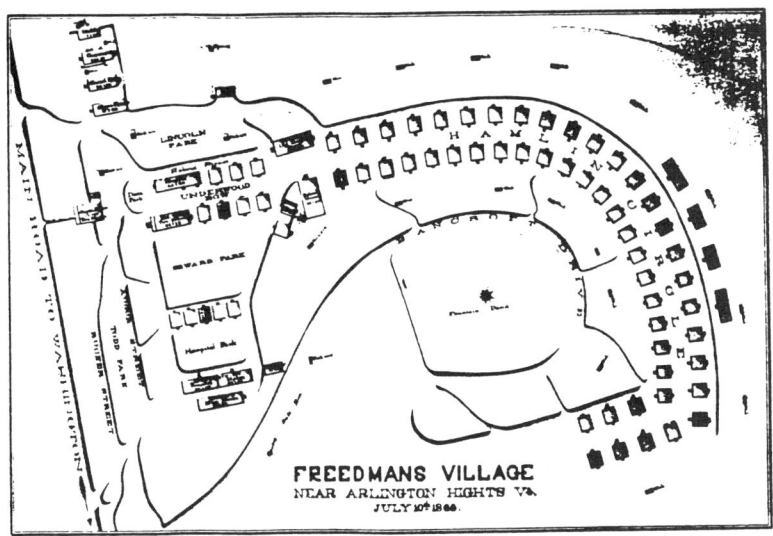

For our purposes we can review the background of Freedman's Village more briefly. The settlement was started even while the war was still in process and expanded or "improved" during the several years afterwards. It consisted of several dozen two story wooden duplex houses in an arched or semi-circle layout with a hospital, a park, a pond with fountain, and certain administrative structures. There were facilities for work and for limited schooling.

The Village was located at the Southern end of the Arlington estate and the National Cemetery and its boundaries ran to the Potomac River on the east. Located today within its boundaries then, is the Henderson Hall Marine Barracks, the southern

---

[2] *Freedman's Village,* Northern Virginia Heritage, February 1985, and AHM, 1974, p. 29-43.

[3] *The Establishment of Freedman's Village in Arlington Virginia,* The Association for the Study of Negro Life and History Incorporated, Vol 33, No. 4, April 1970.

[4] *Free and Black in Northern Virginia Before the Civil War,* Northern Virginia Heritage, February, 1983.

half of Ft Myer, the southern end of Arlington Cemetery, and the Northern tip of the Pentagon building and its adjacent grounds and parking lots.

Initially, Freedman's Village occupants were provided with food and clothing and certain other necessities, but were expected, when and if they worked, to pay nominally for these items.

The Village was chronically over crowded and disease and sickness abounded with deaths averaging two per day for much of the time.

Over the years, problems with the village increased. To the dismay of the residents, uninvited and unauthorized homeless people congregated and imposed on the villagers. They overflowed into surrounding areas to include the National Cemetery. They cut trees for firewood, littered, and otherwise constituted a nuisance. The aforementioned author James wrote, in part:

> "...inhabitants of the Village would not admit newcomers into their homes until they were clothed and placed in proper condition...the newly arrived freedmen -- were dirty, discontented, and uncomfortable while the residents of the Arlington camp were relatively neat, tidy, and very comfortable."

As more years passed, the appearance and condition of Freedman's Village steadily deteriorated, problems compounded and pressures mounted to abolish the settlement and relocate its inhabitants elsewhere. By the early 1880's many of the inhabitants of the Village had in fact left. Some had managed to find work of various kinds and establish themselves, modestly, in newly built neighborhoods nearby that, as stated, have comprised Arlington's Black communities that are now becoming increasingly integrated.

Finally, by 1887 the continued existence of the Village seemed intolerable. On November 12th, the National Cemetery Superintendent wrote to the Army Quartermaster and complained again about tree cutting and thievery by the "squatters" in the Village. He wrote, "...the most effective way of preventing such thefts is to cause the removal of these people from the reservation."[5]

---

[5]*Misc. papers, Freedman's Village files, Archives, Virginia Room, Arlington County Main Public Library.*

Post Civil War Growth

Three weeks later, on December 7, the Washington Star reported that the Secretary of War had ordered that "...all the inhabitants of Freedman's Village, located on the Fort Myer military reservation...be removed within thirty days." [6] The order was later extended to ninety days, but in due course Freedman's Village became a thing of the past and only history. It had, nevertheless, played a dramatic, critical and substantial role in developments in Arlington County in the days following the Civil War and laid the ground work for future long range developments.

A hymn sing by Freedman's Village residence of unknown date but probably soon after the end of the Civil War.

As an epitaph of sorts to the demise of the Village, the Alexandria Gazette afterwards wrote, in part:

> ...*The presence of negroes on the reservation has had a curious effect on the politics of Alexandria County. Numbering between 300 to 400 they have virtually controlled the county, electing, until very recently, their County Clerk, Commonwealth's Attorney, Overseer of the Poor and Board of Supervisors...It has been frequently argued that those people, being squatters on a government reservation, had no right to vote as citizens of Virginia, but this question has never been brought to a direct issue."*

---

[6] *Misc. papers, Freedmans Village files, Ibid.*

The irony of the Gazette story, and the political clout of the Village Black people, is underscored by the fact that it would be the last significant role to be played by Black people in the political activities of the County for almost exactly a hundred years later until the election of a Black man to the County Board in 1987.

* * *

In the quarter century following the Civil War, except for activities at Freedman's Village, development and growth in Arlington's country part of Alexandria County, sped forward at a near standstill, or at least at an extremely slow pace.

The Arlington area continued to be largely rural, uninhabited and undeveloped. At least there were no clustered settlements that could be classified as villages or "neighborhoods". One of the better, if not the best, records of the status of the area in those years is a map labeled Alexandria County, available for examination or purchase in the Arlington Historical Museum[7]. A notation on the map indicates that it is from G.M.Hopkins' Atlas of Fifteen Miles Around Washington D.C., 1878, and entered that year in the Library of Congress.[8]

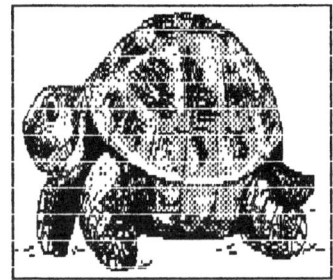

Pace of Development?

The subject map shows a network of about a half dozen unidentified roads that appear to be located about where are modern day Jeff-Davis highway, Glebe Road, Lee Highway, Columbia Pike, Military Road, Wilson Blvd., and some lesser roads that today may have disappeared as a result of later year developments. The map shows some several dozen scattered houses throughout the County, most of which are separated from the nearest structure by at least several hundred yards. Some of the houses are along the shown roads, but many are some distance from roads and were reachable, presumably, only by wagon or horse trails.

The Hopkins map shows the Long Bridge, about where the recent 14th Street bridge was located, the Aqueduct Bridge at Rosslyn, and the Chain Bridge near the Fairfax County Line. The map also shows the Washington and Alexandria Railroad lines in the county running alongside the Alexandria and Washington Pike from Long Bridge south into Alexandria. At the Alexandria Junction, a mile or two south of modern day Crystal City, a line of the Washington, Ohio and Western Railroad twists abruptly northwest and aligns with Four Mile Run and runs to the East Falls Church Station. Today the county bike trail runs along the route of those old WO&W tracks.

---

[7]*The Museum is located in its headquarters in the old Hume School Building at 1805 South Arlington Ridge Road.*

[8]*A considerably more detailed discussion of Hopkins' map and what it does and does not reveal, and its times, is contained in the article The Map of Arlington - 1878, by Rose, C.B.,Jr., in the October 1962 issue of the AHS Magazine.*

Post Civil War Growth

The rails of the railroad line to Falls Church have long since been removed but the abutments of the railroad viaduct over the road at the Alexandria Junction have not and can still be seen alongside Jeff-Davis Highway just short of the present U. S. Route 1 rail yard overpass.

The early 1900's Luna Park entertainment center at U.S. Route 1 and Glebe Road where the sewage treatment plant now operates.

The Hopkins map shows the Carlin Springs Pavilion, a spa and entertainment attraction served by the WO&W RR,[9] and "Balls X Road", where the Ballston shopping center is now located at Wilson Blvd and Glebe Road. Most of the scattered houses on the map include the names of the residents. Some of the names such as Donaldson, Marcey, Veitch, Carlin, Walker, Titus and King are familiar today since there are streets, streams or runs, parks, or other public facilities named after those early residents.

During the 25 years from the end of the war until 1890, the population of Arlington's portion of Alexandria County, to exclude the City of Alexandria, roughly doubled from 3,200 in the 1870 census to 6,500 in the 1890 census. Not a particularly dramatic increase for that period of time. In the 1890's and through the turn of the century, however, Arlington was to experience its explosive beginnings of a period that would see the area transferred from mainly a rural countryside to a full grown suburban and finally an urban community with several dense and congested high rise, "downtown" centers.

* * *

---

[9]*The site of the spa and pavilion is preserved today off South 3rd and Jefferson Streets as Four Mile Run Park. A historical marker explains that the spa once attracted Washingtonians who arrived by the railroad.*

In the first decades of the 20th Century, open space and farm lands were rapidly replaced with new subdivisions of single family homes grouped together in village type arrangements. Steadily the undeveloped spaces between such clusters disappeared until by the beginning of World War II, the county was for all practical purposes one continuous expanse of residential communities from border to border, except for vacant "pockets" here and there and for the Federal government occupied lands. Some developed, but non residential areas included zones along Jeff-Davis highway and the Four Mile Run.

The clusters of housing that grew into county neighborhoods over the years became known by various names such as Virginia Highlands, Nauck, Johnson's Hill, Barcroft, Glencarlyn, Cherrydale, Clarendon, Ballston, Fort Myer Heights, Rosslyn, and some others. In the years between the two World Wars, numerous "garden type" low rise apartment complexes emerged, many of which remain to this day.

THE BIRTH AND GROWTH OF ARLINGTON's NEIGHBORHOODS

The following are some brief overviews of Arlington neighborhoods that constitute the community's earliest known settlements. Additional information on these communities can be found in the Nan and Ross Netherton *Arlington County Virginia: A Pictorial History*, in Eleanor Templeman's *Arlington Heritage* and in the Historical Society's magazine issues cited below and elsewhere herein. These publications are available for reference in the Virginia Room of the Central Library and, in some instances for sale in the Historical Society headquarters in the Hume School on Arlington Ridge Road.

None of the named neighborhoods are official or legally established political subdivisions of the county. The dates shown for each neighborhood are those provided by Netherton. Obviously no neighborhood can be said to have been established precisely in any one year so the dates indicated are probably the years that Netherton considered to be about the times that aggressive development got underway. She also indicated she had relied on a list of Alexandria County postal villages for her information. She wrote on pages 81 and 82, in part; "many (of the named neighborhoods) grew up as stops along the railroads that began to traverse the county" and "As they did, real estate operators promoted the new subdivisions for residents who commuted to work in Washington and began to form genuine suburban communities".[10]

One antebellum neighborhood mentioned by Netherton and not today locateable with reliability was "Glebe Cottage", with a date of 1856. That neighborhood was not described with any particulars by Netherton but it may be an area now unofficially referred to as "The Glebe" northwest of Glebe Road and North of Chesterbrook Road in the area of Saint Peters Episcopal Church.

---

[10] *For more on Arlington County railroads see* History of Arlington County's Electric Railways, *by E. L. Tennyson, AHS Magazine, October 1984, P 39-48.*

Post Civil War Growth

The Potomac pontoon bridge during or shortly after the Civil War at about the location of the present Memorial Bridge.

1874 - BALLSTON

The Arlington neighborhood that can probably claim to be the first established, around 1874, is the Ballston section of the County in the area around the intersection of Wilson Boulevard and Glebe Road. The late Eleanor Lee Templeman, mentioned above and cited elsewhere herein, described the area as "the site of the County's earliest hamlet", [11] and related that it was first called Birch's Crossroads and later Ball's Crossroads after the Civil War. Ballston has also been called a "village" and a "hamlet". The 1927-28 edition of Polk's Washington Suburban Directory described the Ballston of that era as a "town" of 2,700. Templeman relates that there is extensive Birch family history in Arlington and that the Crossroads was first named after Joseph Birch whose forefathers settled in Virginian's Northern Neck and Westmoreland County as early as 1690. She writes that in 1798 Birch and John Ball acquired vast acreage in the area and that on July 15, 1799, Birch was appointed to "the important position of tobacco inspector for the Town of Alexandria which carried a bond of $4,000".

Templeman adds, "In the early 1800's one of the Ball family, probably a grandson of either John or Moses Ball, erected a two story log inn, "Ball's Tavern" at the southwest corner of Birch's Crossroads, which soon became known as Ball's Crossroads." This would be the corner across Wilson Boulevard from Bob Peck's Chevrolet dealership. In the following years, the tavern became an important gathering place, a voting precinct, general store, and even a Post Office. In time, the settlement and immediate surrounding area became known as Ballston. The earlier John Ball,

---

[11] *Ballston's Beginning*, AHS Magazine, October, 1959, p. 52 et seq.

mentioned above, had built a sturdy log cabin about 1740. The cabin, within a later built wooden clap board house, still stands, in part, on South Third Street in the Glencarlyn neighborhood. It is known as the Ball-Sellers House after its first and last owners. It was donated in 1975 to the Society by Marian Sellers and is one of two properties owned by the Historical Society, the other being the Hume School building on Arlington Ridge Road. Both are open on certain days to visitors.

The 1920 Ballston elementary school built on the same plan as the Hume school on Arlington Ridge Road.

The late Arlingtonian, Commonwealth Attorney, State Senator, civic leader and Historical Society member Frank Ball, was a direct descendant of the early Ball family. He was also a founder of the Society and a repeated contributor to its magazine. In the 1958 issue [12] Ball described the events surrounding the dedication of the County's new, and first Court House on November 10, 1898, which he witnessed. In the 1959 issue,[13] he wrote of the first cross county flight by an airplane from Fort Myer on a day in July 1909 that he also witnessed. Concerning the airplane flight, Ball wrote, in part:

> *"I went to the Fort Myer grounds with my older brother Wade...and younger brother Dallas...seeing the immense crowd and with full knowledge that we country men did not have a chance among the big boys, we decided to go to the south end of the field along the area where the old railroad track was. (this would be about where the*

---

[12] *Vol. 1, No. 2 P. 5-14*

[13] *Vol. 1, No.3 P. 37-40*

Post Civil War Growth

modern day Radar Clinic is located. AUTHOR) Wright rose and circled the field making his turn right over our heads. He then headed for Shooter's Hill (the site in Alexander where the Washington Masonic Memorial is located. AUTHOR) We watched him as he left Fort Myer until he flew over the Four Mile Run area where there was a depression ...and he went out of sight...you cannot imagine a more tense crowd...as we stood and stared and hoped he would come back safely. We had only a few minutes to wait before the buzz of the engine was again heard and the returning plane came in sight... There went up a terrific hurrah...and constant cheering from that moment until he landed...Thus ended the first cross country flight...perhaps the most famous event in the history of Arlington County"

Orville Wright with Lt Thomas Selfridge (who was killed in a crash and became history's first air casualty) at Ft Myer on September 17, 1908.

Frank Ball died in 1966. The Ball family burial grounds are located at 3427 Washington Boulevard, just behind the American Legion headquarters near Clarendon Circle. John Ball, son of Moses Ball brother of John Ball, Sr., and other Ball family members are also believed to be buried in the Carlin Cemetery next to the Glyncarlyn Branch Library at South Kensington and Third Streets where markers are missing.

Another early pioneer of note was Samuel Shreve who settled in Virginia in 1780. Shreve was a Revolutionary War officer from New Jersey and is buried near his homesite in the family graveyard between 829 and 839 North Abingdon Street. Templeman wrote that the pre-Civil War Shreve family house was once located on the northwest corner of Columbia Pike and Court House Road and that when it burned down in 1902, it was replaced with a handsome residence which was also demolished in 1958 for commercial developments. The Shreve family burial grounds are on the north side of Fairfax Drive between Frederick and Harrison Streets. An interesting grave stone is the one for Richard and Francis Shreve that indicates they were both killed by lightening on June 25, 1871.

Yet another early resident of the Ballston neighborhood was Ruth C. DeBevoise who told of her reminiscences in the October 1974 Historical Society magazine.[14] DeBevoise painted a picture of the primitive conditions that existed in the community around the turn of the century. She wrote that her parents bought lots on Ballston Avenue (now North Stuart Street) in 1898 that had been farmland until subdivided for the new trolley line. She wrote, in part;

> *"It was really pioneer days...drinking and other water was a block away....the three bedroom, two story clapboard house they built had no heat, or bath...my mother awoke one cold morning and found snow on her hair as there was no paneling around the window frames...the water in the pitcher froze and broke the pitcher...*
>
> *"My mother was asked to christen the first County Court house...she used a bottle of wine and in breaking it got wine on her hat...she was one of the founders of St. George Episcopal Church in Ballston..."*

The Ballston neighborhood is generally considered to be the area around the Wilson and Glebe intersection for a distance of about a half mile in all directions to include, roughly, the later day communities of Buckingham, Cathart Springs, Brandon Village, Waycroft, and perhaps a part of Westover Hills and Virginia Square.

A County blighted area on North Cameron Street between 17th and 18th streets on the edge of the Ballston area about 1935.

---

[14] *Vol. 5, No. 2 P 47.*

Post Civil War Growth

"Broadview", the Lacey house at 5151 No. 14th St., a prestigious residence from the early Ballston era. The house was featured in the book "The Secret of Old House", by Margaret Leighton.

During the Civil War, Ballston was a site for hot-air balloon intelligence gathering for the Union Army. One of the first high rise buildings to be erected in today's Ballston in 1986 is the Holiday Inn on the southwest corner of Fairfax Drive and Glebe Road. The hotel sits near the site of the old Lacey Station, a stop on the Arlington-Fairfax Electric Railway. It took its name from a Civil War officer who remained in the area after the war and purchased a large tract of land. [15] In the Hotel's "Lacey Station" restaurant there were for several years in the late 1980s and early 1900s photographs of various trolley scenes from the past and Historical Society charter members.

About a hundred yards south-southwest of the Wilson/Glebe intersection, or Ball's Crossroads, at 4516 North 7th Street is the home of Rudolph Wendelin, the Forest Service artist who created the famous Smokey Bear. The Robert Ball graveyard is on the northwest corner of Stafford and Fairfax Drive.

Templeman considered that many Arlingtonians felt it was unfortunate that the once prestigious shopping center built in 1951 at Ball's Crossroads was named "Parkington" instead of the historical name honoring one of the earliest pioneer families in the area. The earlier shopping center has now been greatly upgraded into the Ballston shopping mall and all around are the tall office and high rise apartment buildings that make up the western end of the "Ballston Corridor". Civic associations that lie within, or adjacent to the Ballston area include the Ballston-Virginia Square, Cherrydale,

---

[15] *Trolley Tour of Ballston,* Historic Arlington Day, 1994, AHS, P 8.

ARLINGTON COUNTY VIRGINIA - A Modern History

Ashton Heights (sometimes dormant)Lyon Village, Stonewall Jackson, Glebe Wood (sometimes dormant), and Waycroft-Woodlawn.

1886 - WALKER CHAPEL

The area of Arlington commonly known as Walker Chapel is located at the north end of Glebe Road, near the Fairfax County line and the Chain Bridge. One of the best extant accounts of the beginnings and development of the area is the article Reminiscences of the Walker Chapel Area by Harry E. A. Gutshall in the October 1974 issue of the Historical Society Magazine [16]. A footnote in the article reveals that Gutshall, a mail carrier, married the granddaughter of David Walker who settled in the area along Glebe Road at the head of the Chain Bridge in the mid-1880's.

David Walker arrived in the area apparently some years before his death in 1848 and built his home. An 1864 Civil War map shows the Walker house to be where is now the Cornwell house at 4446 North Glebe Road. It has an old stone foundation and was constructed of logs now covered with clapboards. Templeman wrote that his son Robert was employed by Henry Lockwood to oversee his Easter Spring Farm and that in 1871 he purchased land and built a log house. That house at Templeman's writing was stuccoed and is located at 4211 North Glebe Road. The Easter Spring Farm house built in 1856 stands still at 3722 North Glebe Road according to Templeman.

As related elsewhere herein, and as related by Gutshall, Walker Chapel was near the location of the Walker school in Ballston, one of the first three schools established in Arlington immediately after the Civil War. Although not precisely within the Walker Chapel neighborhood, the school could have served the area. On its southern edge are the meticulously maintained and carefully manicured open spaces of the Washington Golf and Country Club and the garden like grounds of Marymount University. To the east, Walker Chapel is bordered by the George Washington Parkway along the Potomac River and the Potomac Overlook Regional Park with its nature trails and Marcey Recreation center. The Center, as well as other Arlington landmarks are named after the early Marcey pioneer family.[17] One member of the family, John Henry Marcey was the head gardner at Arlington House and Arlington Cemetery, He lived with his daughter at 2554 North Military Road and died in 1957 near 102 years of age. Also within the Walker Chapel neighborhood are the Glebe Recreation area and the Gulf Branch Nature Center.

At the apex junction of old and new Glebe Roads is located the Walker Chapel United Methodist Church organized in 1871, and the Walker family burial grounds. The earlier Walker church, dedicated on July 18, 1876, was named in honor of the Walker family who donated a part of the Walker graveyard as a site for the church.

---

[16] *Vol. 5, No. 2 P 16-28.*

[17] *The Arlington Marcey family (with an "e") is not to be confused with the Army General Randolph Barnes Marcy, McClelland's Chief of Staff, in whose honor the civil war Fort Marcy was named.*

Post Civil War Growth

Glebe Road looking westward from the Lockwood farm toward Walker Chapel about 1900.

In the Society Magazine account, Gutshall described church, school and social conditions that existed in the area in its early years around the 1890's. He mentions the Cabin John car line that ran through the area on its route from Georgetown to Cabin John, and he tells of a restaurant "where you could get all you wanted to eat for lunch for 9 to 12 cents." He also mentions the C & O canal operations and fishing on the Potomac at the mouth of Pimmit Run. Gutshall included in his account some of the events during and following the Civil War. He said all the trees were cut down between the Forts of Ethen Allen and Marcy to clear the view for fields of fire and that the place where Henry Clay and John Randolph fought their duel was just to the north of Fort Marcy, about 50 or 75 feet.[18] There seems to be some doubt as to the exact location of the duel, but some remains of Fort Marcy are still preserved in the area as a historical treasure.

One of the earliest residences in Walker Chapel known as Birchwood at 4572 26th Street was renovated in 1940 and today is a modern home that has been designated as an historic site by the Arlington Historical Commission.

Today the Walker Chapel neighborhood is without doubt one of the loveliest and most treasured areas of Arlington County. It is probably the most residentially affluent part of the County with little or no high rise buildings or commercial activity. It is comprised mostly of upper middle income homes on gently rolling, picturesque landscape. The civic associations believed to be operative that lie within, or adjacent to, Walker Chapel are: Walker Chapel later Old Glebe (both now dormant), Donaldson Run, Rock Springs, Gulf Branch, River Crest, Arlingwood and Bellevue Forest.

---

[18] *For a detailed account of this duel the reader could refer to the article A Duel in Arlington, by Ruth M. Ward in the October 1981 AHS Magazine, P 18-21.*

ARLINGTON COUNTY VIRGINIA - A Modern History

1888 - HALL'S HILL (HIGH VIEW PARK)

Just south and west of the present George Mason Drive and Lee Highway intersection is the community long identified as Hall's Hill. The community was one of Arlington first black neighborhoods following the removal of freed slaves from Freedman's Village described above. Some of the families from the Village might have been resettled in the Hall's Hill area. If so, they were apparently far fewer than in the neighborhoods immediately adjacent to Freedman's Village. At least modern day census and demographic county records so indicate. In past days Hall's Hill was adjacent to a separate area a couple hundred yards to the south known as Highview Park. In modern times both names are often applied interchangeably to either or both sections. Templeman wrote that both sections are now known as High View Park but modern street maps do not exactly so indicate.

The Hall's Hill or High View Park section of the county enjoys a distinction not shared in any meaningful way by any other of Arlington's identifiable neighborhoods. It was the scene of an exchange of fire or "mini-battle" in the Civil War.

Sketch of Union troop camp believed to be between Hall's Hill and Munson Hill and south of present day Seven Corners.

In the early months of 1861 the Confederate forces began establishing a cavalry outpost line that extended across the western end of Arlington County and beyond. The Southerners wanted to keep an eye on the activities of the Federal forces. The "Feds" were busy building their own line of forts on the highlands overlooking the Potomac River and were undertaking increased cavalry patrols in the "no-mans" land to their south and front.

Post Civil War Growth

One of the strongest Confederate forts then in operation was at Munson Hill located approximately where Glen Carlin Road today intersects with Leesburg Pike (Route 7) about mid-way between Seven Corners and Baileys Crossroads. Munson hill had one of the highest elevations in the immediate area and from it the Capitol building, much of the Capital area, and the Federal positions could easily be seen, although at a distance. There is now a residential "Munson Place" street in the shadows of Munson Hill.

From their observation balloons at Fort Whipple (now Ft Myer) and Ball's Crossroads the Federals noted on a morning late in August that the Confederates were laboring diligently to build entrenchments at numerous places to include Upton's Hill (on Wilson Boulevard just short of Seven Corners near the present water tower).[19] They also noted that an estimated thousand men were constructing especially strong works at Munson Hill.

The Federals decided to sally forth to better examine the Confederate positions and if possible break them up. In the process, as they approached Munson Hill, there developed some confusing cavalry skirmishes and artillery exchanges along present day Lee highway to include the Hall's Hill areas. The Federals withdrew after concluding that "the works on Munson Hill were too formidable to be attacked", as Templeman worded it, but the events of that day bestowed on Hall's Hill a reputation as one of the few places in Arlington where any significant military confrontation took place in the Civil War.

Today Lee Highway (Route 29) along the north side of Hall's Hill is one of Arlington's busiest thoroughfares with heavy traffic especially during commuter hours. The mostly single family residential neighborhoods through which it passes, however, are among some of Arlington's most peaceful and enjoyable. They are in sharp contrast to the busy and congested high rise development in the Ballston Corridor and at Balls Crossroads just a stone throw away and in some ways within sight and sound.

In her Pictorial History of Arlington, Templeman included a photo taken by John Best of the present day Calloway United Methodist Church at 5000 Lee Highway in High View Park. The church is historically significant to the area because of its early beginnings in 1866 in Halls' Hill at 4840 Lee Highway. It is but one of several churches that serve the area. Other neighborhoods around Hall's Hill include Becket Glen, Merry Mews, Tara, Lee Lexington Village and Livingston Heights. Civic associations in the area of Hall's Hill are; Leeway, John M. Langston, Highland Park-Overlee Knolls, Tara-Leeway and Northwest Arlington.

1885-90 (?) ROSSLYN

The Rosslyn area of Arlington is not comparable to the other neighborhoods discussed above and below from the standpoint of being a lasting early residential or commercial area that merits consideration as a viable part of the county during its

---

[19] *In depth information on these balloon operations is contained in the article* <u>The United States Balloon Corps in Action in Northern Virginia During the Civil War</u> *by June Robinson, AHS Magazine, October 1986, P 5-17.*

developmental periods. We will mention it briefly in passing, however, since it has now become such a highly developed and widely known part of the County in modern days both locally and even nationally. The area began to be seriously transformed from farm and pasture lands in the years following the Civil War and by the end of the Century had become mostly a collection not of family residences but of infamous saloons, bordellos, gambling houses and other houses of ill repute until cleaned up during the Crandal Mackey era.

Rosslyn about 1956 at the Virginia end of the Key Bridge before high rise and Washington Parkway construction.

The name "Rosslyn" began showing up on area maps on the Arlington side of the Aqueduct Bridge site soon after the Civil War. It is not shown on the 1865 War Department Engineer Bureau Map of Northern Virginia Forts and Roads [20] although the name "Ross" does so appear at the Bridge end. The name was given to the area by William Henry Ross, an early settler, who, in 1860 received a large farm on the Virginia waterfront from his wife's father Joseph Lamden. According to some anonymous Historical Society chroniclers, based on articles in the Northern Virginia Sun, the name Rosslyn is a combination of the owners family name and "Lyn" or "lynn" that are obsolete spellings of "linn" that means, variously, a torrent of water running over rocks, a pool of water, or a ravine with precipitous sides. The chronologers wrote, "It is probably the first of these meanings which the Rosses had in mind since the property is traversed by a rocky stream."

---

[20] *Division of Maps, Library of Congress, Sep 31, 1951, distributed by Kate Waller Barrett Chapter NSDAR.*

Post Civil War Growth

It seems possible also that Ross may have named his farm Rosslyn by borrowing the "lyn" from the last letters in his wife's name of Caroline that is sometimes spelled "Carolyn". The Society chronologers also wrote that the occupation of Arlington by Federal troops during the Civil War drove the Rosses from their home, and they lived in France in 1869. From there, they sold the farm to a group of people who formed the Rosslyn Development Company and sold the acreage off for home sites in "The Town of Rosslyn".

The Ray Walls Sunday Bar, No. 2 Sunday Bar and Birch Bar in Rosslyn around the turn of the Century and before the Mackey "clean-up" drive.

After its transformation into a more "respectable" and acceptable neighborhood following the campaigns of Mackey, Rosslyn still did not experience any clear growth as a residential community. Until rather recent years, and a change in zoning ordinances that result in explosive growth following World War II, Rosslyn consisted essentially or a lumber yard, a winery, a lithograph print shop, a brick factory and several other commercial activities. Two of the most prominent features on the Rosslyn landscape in those years was a soda plant, the Cherry Smash Bottling Company, and the Consumer Brewing Company with its towering smoke stack and huge red brick building. When the 125-foot smoke stack was demolished in 1958 to make way for the Hot Shop Drive-In restaurant and later the Marriott Motel, there was much excitement. Templeman wrote in her "Arlington Heritage" [21];

> *"When the brewery building was being demolished I climbed through the rubble and asked ... the superintendent if he would save for*

---

[21] *Ibid, P 78.*

the Historical Society any of the horse shoes or brick in the debris...he phoned me the next day and said he would...the Arlington Fire Division cooperated by lending its ladder truck ...There was great excitement with fire trucks, police cars, reporters and photographers...We find no record of fanfare regarding the erection of the brewery, but its destruction caused more excitement than Rosslyn had experienced since the raids which broke up the gambling in 1904."

Wilson Blvd at Fort Myer Drive in Rosslyn looking west on March 24, 1937 long before high rise developments.

For many years Rosslyn was of particular importance as a transportation center. It was not only a turn around point for the Georgetown trolley but also the terminal for three trolley lines and two railroad lines. Rose (supra) wrote that Rosslyn was one of the first Arlington sectors to be provided a post office in 1888. Rosslyn today is a high concentration of recently built high rise office and apartment buildings. That development will be discussed later when we cover the explosive growth in Rosslyn, Crystal City, the Ballston corridor and elsewhere in the county following zoning ordinance changes in the early 1960's

1889 - NAUCK / GREEN VALLEY

The Nauck neighborhood is located in South Arlington generally east of Glebe Road and west of the Army-Navy Country Club and between Walter Reed Drive and Interstate highway I-395 (Shirley highway). This area together with a small "enclave" between Columbia Pike and I-395 east of the Country Club known as Arlington View

Post Civil War Growth

Sketch of the Rucker Lumber yard - familiar sight in Rosslyn until recent years and high rise developments.

(and Green Valley), were the areas where most of the residents of Freeman's Village were relocated when the Village was demolished around 1888. These neighborhoods have been Arlington's major historically segregated residential areas until recent years when some integration has taken place caused by shifting public attitudes, new townhouse projects, the civil rights movements, and legislation and court decisions that outlawed discriminatory practices in housing, and for other reasons.

The Arlington View sector is still designated on most land deeds of it and the surrounding areas as Green Valley. The designation derives from the fact that it, as well as the Nauck and Army-Navy Club lands and also the lands on the east side of I-395, were once a part of the Green Valley Manor estate of the Fraser/Sickles families. The Fraser graveyard is extant and located near hole 26 on the golf course of the Club on what was once the Fraser manor lands. The Fraser and Sickle families and lands are discussed in greater detail in Chapter Five herein.

The "Why Do We Call it...?" publication of the Historical Society [22] reveals that the "Map of the Town of Nauck" is recorded in the Arlington County Deed Book B4, on page 440, and that a survey of 1876 states that the area was "formerly known as Naucksville and Convalescent Camp" and covers land (46 acres) bought by John D. Nauck, Jr in 1874. The land was originally part of the Abingdon estate, (discussed in detail in Chapter Five). The Society publication states that Nauck's origins are obscure but that he is listed among the white voters of Arlington Magisterial District in a poll book for which the year has not been established. The publication also shows that Nauck

---

[22] *Special Publication No. 2, page 8, available for sale at the Society Museum, and for research at the Virginia Room, Arlington Main Library.*

Typical street in Queen City, next to Nauck and Green Valley neighborhoods, about 1912, and now a part of the Pentagon South Parking Lot.

The Pearson Brothers store at NW corner of Columbia Pike and Walter Reed Drive near Nauck area, now location of Arlington theatre.

was a resident of the County and State for one year, that his occupation was that of upholsterer and also that he served as a special policeman in 1878 and 1879 and was Justice of the Peace in 1890 and 1891. Just how much of the Nauck lands in fact came from the Abingdon estate, and whether some might have come from or relate to the

Post Civil War Growth

Fraser-Sickle lands mentioned above could be a source for fruitful inquiry by a future researcher.

1949 blight in the Green Valley area as seen from the Kemper School. Citizen pressure on officials caused clean up of this and other county "slums".

The Nauck and and other Green Valley neighborhood residents have been a vibrant part of Arlington's community life and have participated extensively in numerous social, political, education and other matters. The Nauck civic association is one of the most active in the county. The Hoffman-Boston school, one of the oldest in the county and discussed in Chapter Five describing county schools, is located in Arlington View.

One of the county's eldest citizens, George Vollin discussed in Chapter Five in the pages covering the battle for single member electoral districts, lived in Arlington View, as does Evelyn Reid Syphax, a renown and highly respected community leader and the wife of a direct descendent of Syphax families of the Civil War and slave period. She is also a past president of the Historical Society. The energetic and committed citizens of Nauck, Arlington View, and other surrounding neighborhoods are clearly destined to continue to play a vital role in the affairs of the County.

1893 - CHERRYDALE

Cherrydale is a part of Arlington that was not only one of the earliest definable settlements, along with the other communities listed herein, but is an area where some exceptionally historic events have unfolded. It has many "firsts" to its credit. Cherrydale, as reflected by its civic association boundaries, encompasses the neighborhoods north of present day I-66 between Utah and Taylor Streets on the west to a part of Old Dominion Drive to the north and east to Pollard Street, and then jumps Old Dominion to include several streets around Vacation Lane.

ARLINGTON COUNTY VIRGINIA - A Modern History

A typical street scene in the area around Cherrydale in the late 1930's believed to be North Stafford Street reflecting urban changes in later years.

In the area now designated Cherrydale there are no houses shown on the Civil War maps. It seems the area got its name from Robert Shreve, the son-in-law of the first settler, Dorsey Donaldson. Shreve had planted a small orchard of cherry trees along present day Quincy Street that was originally named Cherry Valley Road, presumably because of the Shreve cherry orchard. Shreve operated a store in which Donaldson requested that a post office be established. When he was asked to suggest a name, legend has it that he replied "Cherrydale". Templeman wrote that few if any of the original cherry trees remain, but that the local Women's Club had undertaken a drive in the 1950's to replant cherry trees in yards, schools and elsewhere. The cherry trees today along Spout Run Drive between Lorcum Lane and Lee Highway are the result of the Virginia Highway Department's contribution to that effort.

Cherrydale became firmly fixed on area maps in the early 1900's when it was designated as a stop, one of the first in the county, on the Great Falls and Old Dominion Railway. Cherrydale also can lay claim to having the first Arlington County fire engine, a hand propelled creation garaged in a shed behind the school. The Cherrydale elementary school built in 1917 was one of the oldest schools still in use when Templeman wrote her book Arlington Heritage in the 1950's. It was sold and razed, however, in later years to make way for a nursing home. The Donaldson home still stands today just behind the firehouse at 3900 Lee Highway. The Shreve house built in 1889 also still stands on Pollard Street a block north of Lee Highway. Civic Associations abutting Cherrydale are Waverly Hills to the west, Ballston-Virginia Square to the south, and Maywood to the north.

Post Civil War Growth

The railroad station at East Falls Church that served also Cherrydale until a station was established there also.

1895 - FORT MYER HEIGHTS

Fort Myer Heights is the area between Wilson and Arlington (Route 50) Boulevards east of Clarendon and South of Rosslyn. As the name implies, it is on high ground, that overlooks and affords a panoramic view of the nearby Fort Myer military reservation, to the extent that modern day high rise buildings do not block the view.

This neighborhood, still with a dominance of single family residences, and some medium rise or garden apartments, sits squarely on the Ballston corridor near and between stations at Rosslyn and Court House Square of the Metro rapid rail system. In view of this location, that is highly vulnerable to higher density development, it remains to be seen just how long the neighborhood will remain "low density" and not become an extension of the high rise construction in Rosslyn or the clusters around Court House and County offices just to the west.

Just across Arlington Boulevard and adjacent to the Marine Iwo Jima Monument and in view of Roosevelt Island where John Mason once built his manor is the community known as Radnor Heights.

But for the existence of the Arlington Boulevard freeway that splits the two neighborhoods, Radnor Heights, for all practical purposes, would probably be looked upon by local residents as an extension and a part of Fort Myer Heights. There is no civic association by the name of Fort Myer Heights shown on the County Board Clerks list of civic associations, although there has been in past years as reflected on a County map of Civic Associations dated 1989. It is possible that some residents of the neighborhood may be members of the adjacent Courtland or Highland Park Associations just to the west and north respectively.

The John Mason house on Analostan (Mason/Roosevelt) Island long since destroyed by fire and flood waters.

1896 - GLENCARLYN

The modern day Glencarlyn community is located just inside the County line between Arlington Boulevard, Four Mile Run and Long Branch. Although given the date 1896 by Templeman as its beginning, it is considered the first planned community in the County. It was established by the Carlyn Springs Company in 1887 that acquired part of the land owned by William Carlin who bought it in 1772 from the estate of the original settler John Ball. Ball, in turn, had derived title from Lord Fairfax in 1742. [23] A part of the log cabin home of John Ball is extant, as added to in later years with a clap board dwelling, at 5620 South 3rd Street. The house, owned and open to visitors by the Historical Society, as described in a Society brochure, "..is a landmark of pioneer Arlington and a rare example of homes where the working class people of the time lived."

Glencarlyn, like Cherrydale, is a part of Arlington County where perhaps more history has unfolded than most other parts of the county. The area was first known as Carlin Springs after William Carlin and his nearby spring along side Four Mile Run in the County Glencarlyn Park below Jefferson Street. The name Carlin was changed to

---

[23] Lane, Munson H., *a life long resident of Glyncarlyn, in a presentation before the Arlington Historical Society on November 14, 1969, as reported in the October 1970 issue of the AHS Magazine, P 49-55*

Post Civil War Growth

The John Ball house as it looked before being enclosed in its later day clap board structure on South Third Street.

Carlyn in 1896 at the insistence of the Post Office to avoid confusion with another town in Virginia of the same name. Glencarlyn can boast of the oldest community center in the county, Carlin Hall, built in 1892 and once used as a school. On the grounds of the Hall is the Ball-Carlin cemetery and beyond the Glencarlyn Branch Library. In the library on display with a descriptive plaque is a slice of the large tree that once served as a reference point in the land deeds that conveyed the land to and from its original owner John Ball.

There are several large, prestigious and historical houses in Glyncarlyn to include the Backus residences on 5th Street at 5432 and 5500 and several others of Victorian styles.[24] Additionally, there are numerous houses in Glyncarlyn that existed prior to its founding, but not all are extant. These would include the Burdett and Carlin houses located near the present library; (2) the Mary Carlin home on Carlyn Springs Road; (3) the Carlin house on Carlyn Springs Road (now the site of Kenmore School); Carlin Hall at 5711 Fourth Street[25], and the Reynolds house at a corner now marked by a traffic light on Carlin Springs Road and identified by a large holly tree. [26]

---

[24] *For a most informative account of early life in Glyncarlyn, the establishment of schools, holidays, and youthful antics see* Recollections of a Non-Native-Born Glencarlynite *by Florence C. Backus, AHS Magazine, October, 1988, P 35-39.*

[25] *For detailed history and background on Carlin Hall see* Carlin Hall, *by Gail Baker in the October 1993, AHS Magazine, P 27-33.*

[26] *Lane, Munson H., Ibid, P 51.*

Rear view of John Ball house. Entrance to steps leading down to the to log cabin interior is on the right beyond the two men.

Perhaps the most intriguing and today little known event in Glyncarlyn history was the establishment of the pavilions and recreation centers at the Carlin Springs Station as shown on the Baxler & MacGowan map of 1908-1910. It was there that rides for children, picnic areas, refreshment stands, and other facilities were created that attracted crowds from as far away as Washington that arrived on the convenient trolleys and trains of the day.

Author Rose wrote that the Carlin Springs picnic spot and resort was developed in 1872 by the Carlin family with a swimming hole, a bar, and a place for dancing. She related that a "certain amount of glamour was attached to the Carlin Springs area when a report was circulated in the mid-1870's that there was gold deposits there...apparently no mining operations were ever conducted. Perhaps the 'gold mine' was the rich rewards reaped from the operation of the resort". [27]

1898 - BARCROFT

The part of modern day Arlington known as Barcroft is located between Arlington Boulevard on the north and Columbia Pike to the south. To its east is George Mason Drive and Arlington Hall, the pre-World War II school for girls, commandeered in the war by the Army and more recently taken over by the State Department for its Foreign Service Institute. To the west is Four Mile Run, and the Glencarlyn community just beyond.

---

[27] *Rose, ibid, P 140.*

Post Civil War Growth

View of Columbia Pike at Four Mile Run in Barcroft area about 1931 where small shops and the county trash collecting point now exist.

Barcroft is excitingly rich in early county history. Although the Barcroft area was formally established by subdivision into homesites in 1903, some years after most of the earlier communities discussed above, Barcroft nevertheless has many of its roots extending back to the Civil War years.

Two particularly prolific writers and former residents of Barcroft who have provided especially detailed accounts of the birth and development of the area are M. Louise Payne and Mildred Handy Ritchie. The Payne account, "Reminiscences of Barcroft's History" appeared in the October 1959 issue of the AHS Magazine on pages 55-60. The Ritchie article "Barcroft, Arlington County, Virginia - A Village Metamorphosis" was published in the October 1980 issue of the AHS Magazine on pages 24-39.

Payne wrote that the Barcroft community was named in honor of Dr. John W. Barcroft, a native of New Jersey and a graduate of the Philadelphia Medical Society. She related that Barcroft arrived in 1849 and built a home and mill which were destroyed or badly damaged by Union troops during the Second Battle of Bull Run. She related that after the war Dr Barcroft returned and rebuilt his home and mill near the top of Barcroft Hill. She wrote in 1959 that the house was still standing.

Payne's account includes mainly details on the steady growth of the community early in the 20th Century, the building of houses, and of the establishment and operation of railroads and trolley lines. Especially touching is her account of the start of Barcroft's first school. She wrote that Sidney T. Marye and his wife had two school age children and that there were seven others old enough to start to school. Payne wrote, in part:

> *"The county would not pay for a teacher for less than ten children, and so Mr Marye persuaded the parents of the seven children to agree to send them, and he persuaded Mrs Edith Fairfax, who lived*

in the house adjoining the present Community House on the south to teach the children and to include her four year old child in the class to get the required ten. The children attended the first school in Barcroft in Mrs Fairfax's front room...the house was torn down in 1954."

Ritchie wrote that Barcroft was "long separated from the rest of the county by surrounding forests and (the) only means of access was by railroad or the east-west Columbia Pike." She related that in 1903 Barcroft had a water grist mill, a grocery-dry goods store, a 12 foot square yellow station on a single-track railroad line, a large cattle pen nearby and perhaps six houses scattered about within a half mile of the station on Columbia Pike. The Pike, she added, "became known as a major thoroughfare, a narrow two lane dirt road - rocky, rough and dusty, and in rainy weather, a quagmire of mud with deep ruts. It was travelled by draymen, drovers, buggies and walkers."

Ritchie added that the Mill, rebuilt after the Civil War as related by Payne, was on foundation of an earlier one erect by George Washington Parke Custis and that an even earlier mill had been built by George Washington. Ritchie also tells of several houses in the area built after the Civil War including the one of John Newlon who operated the mill for Dr Barcroft. Ritchie wrote that "fires were the most dreaded scourge of the rural area", which she said were often caused by sparks from the railroad engines operating through the heavily wooded area. She described fires that destroyed homes, the church, the mill, and other structures while the alarmed citizens could do little other than stand by frantically and watch them burn. Ritchie wrote an especially poignant account of the arrival of electricity in Barcroft;

"Electricity was still about a mile and a half away in 1912, and oil lamps furnished the evening light. The wish began to grow to try the new-fangled convenience. Mr Handy obtained an agreement with the Virginia Electric Company to extend poles and a line to Barcroft - if he could obtain 12 customers. He got fourteen and, as an electrician, wired the homes himself in his spare time. He added the school house...in 1914."

Perhaps the most significant contribution to Arlington history made by Ritchie is her account of the events leading to the change on the county name from Alexandria to Arlington in 1920. She wrote that local citizens had made arrangements with Bolling Air Base officials for a Court House fly-over in 1919 as part of a joyful demonstration for returning World War I veterans. She said it was stressed to the Base officials that the Court House in question was in Arlington and not the one in the city of Alexandria. In spite of that caveat, it seems the time arrived for the fly-over and no planes appeared. They had flown over Alexandria.

Ritchie wrote, "That did it! For years the confusion in name had increased since the building of the Court House (on present day Court House Road) in 1898." Ritchie wrote that Walter Handy of Barcroft and others urged a change of name for the County, that a committee was selected and meetings were held. At one, after much bickering and indecision, Handy suggested something for which the County itself was well known - "like

Post Civil War Growth

Arlington, for instance, the Custis home." A motion was made to that effect as Handy left for an appointment. When he returned he was "amazed and delighted" that a vote was taken and the new County name would henceforth be "Arlington". State legislature action was, of course, required to effectuate the change in name for the County, but the pride of writer Ritchie that Barcroft played a key role in generating the change is understandable.

Today Barcroft is by no means "separated from the rest of the county" by forests or otherwise. The forests have disappeared, except to the extent that trees still abound in the narrow Four Mile Run waterway. Nor is there open spaces in any quantity, if at all, on the community's edges that might provide a means of separating Barcroft from the rest of the County. Its neighboring communities have, in fact, grown along with Barcroft and today present such a merging of neighborhoods that a visitor would not likely know when he or she has left one and arrived in another. Such has been the development of Barcroft and its surroundings.

Barcroft today has its own civic association and is amidst the Alcova Heights, Glencarlyn, Columbia Heights, and Arlington Forest Civic Associations. The community has provided many energetic community leaders.

1900 - CLARENDON

For years Clarendon has been considered by many to be the "downtown" of the County. Most of the other neighborhoods described above were largely residential in nature that did not contain many or any stores, shops and other commercial enterprises to the extent that did the point where the main arterials of Wilson, Key and Washington Boulevards and Fairfax drive either crossed or converged. Clarendon prided itself on several large department stores such as Sears, Kahns and the JC Penney Company, and dozens of smaller merchants lined its streets. Over the years, many of the bus and trolley lines passed through or near the hub of Clarendon Circle where Wilson and Washington Boulevards met and crossed. While many of Arlington's remote or secluded neighborhoods may seldom be visited by citizens at opposite ends of the County, few residents can avoid passing through Clarendon at some time or the other, and probably often because of its location centrally and on key arterial roads.

Clarendon has also been distinctive in that it is one of the earliest, if not the first, neighborhood that grew from deliberate planning that included laid out streets. Historical writer Templeman wrote that most of the County just "grew like Topsey, without much plan or design" with "scattered farm houses and planation homes conveniently built near the river and along existing roads which led to settlements in Fairfax or Loudoun county". Around the turn of the century, however, subdivisions began to be laid out, usually by real estate firms or developers with land to sell. The locations were usually related to trolley or railroad stops with growth therefrom somewhat like modern day developments around Metro rail stations in the Ballston corridor or elsewhere. Clarendon is claimed by some to be the first of these planned layouts with streets.

ARLINGTON COUNTY VIRGINIA - A Modern History

Clarendon circle in 1945. Note absence of high rise office building that now exists where are the clump of trees on the right.

The first court house of 1898 on the eastern edge of Clarendon long since razed for a tower structure which is also schedule for demolition.

Historical Society writer Dorthea E. Abbott, in her AHS Magazine article "The Roots of Clarendon,[28] provided a sketch by Gene Stewart "Plan of Clarendon,

---

[28] *October 1986, P 46-54.*

Post Civil War Growth

Alexandria Co, Va.," dated March 31, 1900. The plan showed laid out streets of several blocks north of the Washington and Wilson Boulevard intersection and included about two blocks of N. Jackson Street, and "Irving, Hudson and Herndon Streets". She also included a reprint of an advertisement by "Wood, Harmon & Co., Largest Suburban Real Estate Operators in the World" headed "Clarendon! What it Means" in which they announced the sale of lots in Clarendon at prices of $90-140. [29]

In her "Roots" article, writer Abbott pointed out, with a map for clarification, that the 25 acre Clarendon area was the northwest tip of an early Colonial period 500 acre land grant about a quarter mile wide and extending westward from the Potomac River to present day Jackson Street. The tract was known as the William Struttfield and Daniel Jennings land grant and had been obtained from its proprietors, Margaret Lady Culpepper and the 5th Lord Fairfax and his wife Katherine as recorded in 1709. Abbott traces the passage of the land over the following years in precise detail but for our purposes here it suffices to report that, in due course, the portion that concerns us here was obtained by George Mason and devised to his son John in 1792.

John Mason also came into possession of much land and numerous properties in scattered other places to include Mason's (Analostan/Roosevelt) Island in the Potomac at the eastern foot of the Struttfield-Jennings tract where he built a summer residence of some elegance in the early 1800's. Mason later had substantial business reverses and borrowed large sums of money from the Bank of the United States in Washington. When he was unable to repay the loans the bank took over most of his property and 1,822 acres in Virginia that included the Struttfield-Jennings tract with the portion that someday would become Clarendon. In the years after the Civil War there were further changes in ownership, and extensive subdivision that led to the 1900 "Plan of Clarendon" and its designated streets and blocks. There was a further subdivision in 1911 of an adjacent "Section 2" that consisted of a block of Hartford Street, and a portion of Highland, Garfield and Filmore Streets that intersected with Wilson Boulevard. John Mason's residence on his island was destroyed by fire and floods, or otherwise, after the War.

The origins of the name "Clarendon" is apparently the source of some disagreement between the two writers upon whom we lean the most for information about Clarendon and its beginnings. Abbott writes, "It has been inferred that Clarendon was named in honor of the Earl of Clarendon. However, there is no proof that this is the case." [30]. Templeman, however, alludes to the March 31, 1900 "Plan of Clarendon" and wrote without equivocation, except to say the reason was obscure, that "this real estate venture took the name from an English historian and statesman, the Earl of Clarendon (1609-1674). [31] Even without proof, however, Abbott seemed to concede that Clarendon might be named after the Earl and wrote, "On the off chance that

---

[29] *Additional and exceptionally scholarly and detailed information on Clarendon history is contained in the article* Clarendon *by the then 16 year old Woodlawn High School student Margaret Young in the AHS Magazine of October 1978, P 48-61.*

[30] *The Roots of Clarendon, Ibid, P 52.*

[31] *Vignettes of a Virginia County, Ibid, P 98.*

Clarendon was named in honor of the Earl of Clarendon, I did a little more research..." She related that her research revealed that the ruins of the Clarendon Palace are near Salisbury England and she described some of the events and family members of the Earl's days. She also noted as a sidelight that an early Virginia Secretary of State had written to Lord Clarendon on various matters concerning government organization.

Abbott ended by writing; "Perhaps some day material will come to light that will conclusively establish a stronger connection". Although Abbott wrote in 1986, 27 years after Templeman's "Vignettes" of 1959, she apparently had not yet been able to throw light on any material that would establish that connection. Absent such material, it would seem the safest bet would be to conclude that the source for the name of Arlington's Clarendon is the English Earl of the 1600's.

Clarendon can boast of yet another historical experience that is peculiar only to it, as compared to any other neighborhood in the County. In 1922, it applied for a charter to become a separate town and lost. Alexandria had, in 1915 and 1925, taken by annexation parts of the County near the Potomac and south of Four Mile Run (the Del Ray and St Elmo communities and adjacent areas to the west). The Virginia Supreme Court turned thumbs down on the Clarendon effort holding that Arlington County was a "continuous, contiguous, and homogeneous community" that could not be subdivided for the purposes of incorporating a portion of it. The Court permitted, however, the later 1929 annexation by Alexandria referred to above, but the General Assembly thereafter adopted legislation prohibiting any more annexations of Arlington County.

Clarendon can also claim a first, or near first, with respect to early activity in the field of civic associations. The area contained in both sections of the original "Plan of Clarendon" is now included within the boundaries of the Lyon Village Civic Association as shown in the County Board's Civic Federation membership list and the County maintained map of civic association boundaries. It is known, however, that the "Clarendon <u>Citizens'</u> Association" (emphasis provided) existed for several years prior to the organization of the Civic Federation in 1916. Templeman in her "Vignettes" quotes from a 1920 booklet published by the Association that sheds considerable light on the early years of Clarendon development, although the language may be somewhat excessively self congratulatory in spots. The booklet read, in pertinent part;

> *"(Clarendon) now covers an area of one square mile, contains nearly six hundred homes and boasts of a population of approximately 2,500...Clarendon is indeed a healthy place to live, the birth rate exceeding the death rate by more than double...During the past two years the Citizens' Association has become the most aggressively progressive civic organization in the State, with a membership of 350 men who are working together with the one idea of making Clarendon what it should and shall be - one of the most attractive spots within easy reach...*
>
> *"Under the forceful, stimulating influence of the Citizens' Association, the community has succeeded in purchasing the largest motor-driven chemical fire apparatus now operating in Arlington*

Post Civil War Growth

County...in securing house-to-house delivery of mail...and installing water and sewer systems."

Clarendon today is probably on the threshold of intensive urban high rise and other development. Except for several structures of historical value that have been or may be designated by the Historical Affairs and Landmark Review Board (HALRB) for preservation (the Masonic Temple Building and 1907 telephone building at Clarendon circle, the 1910 Maury School and the First Baptist Church) most of Clarendon consists of old single story or low density buildings (there are a couple of high rise office buildings in existence or under construction). Clarendon is the center of the County, if not the Northern Virginia, Vietnamese community. A three block section of Wilson Boulevard is lined with Vietnamese restaurants, clothing stores, oriental shops, even small department stores and other outlets with traditional and ethnic food and other items. The street is locally referred to as "Little Saigon".

The intensive high rise development that has rapidly taken place around the other County Board designated "bulls eye" Metro stops in the Corridor from Rosslyn to Ballston has not yet occurred around the Clarendon station. It is doubtful that Clarendon will much longer remain as the only Metro stop in the corridor not subjected to massive high rise development.

LYON VILLAGE

Another of Arlington's neighborhoods that must be included in this brief overview, even though it cannot claim to have been established as early as most of the above communities, is Lyon Village. That portion of the county has been an extraordinary source for Arlington leadership over the years, and its citizens have contributed generously and indespensibly to the advancement of the County.

Lyon Village is located between and a little west of the Potomac Palisades and Fort Myer. It is bounded on the north by I-66 and Lee Highway, on the South by Wilson Boulevard, on the west by Kirkwood Road and on the east by North Veitch Street. Its southern third or so would come within the Struttfield-Jennings (John Mason) lands referred to above in the Clarendon segment herein. The area gets its name from Frank Lyon, a lawyer, newspaper publisher, builder and land entrepreneur, who developed the area in the years immediately following the first World War as chronicled by Society member Carolyn V. Boaz.[32] His home at 4651 25th Street, North, still stands and is called Missionhurst.[33]

Among other things, Lyon Village is known as having more Sears homes than any other neighborhood in Arlington County according to Society member Darline

---

[32] Boaz, Carolyn V., *Lyon Village*, AHS Magazine, October 1993, P 17-26.

[33] For a scholarly and comprehensive background on Frank Ball see *The Role of Frank Ball...."* by Ruth P. Rose, AHS Magazine, October 1976, P 46-58.

Hannabass.³⁴ These were low cost prefabricated and disassembled houses that were widely marketed in the years between the two World Wars and many were sold to Arlingtonians of the day. The houses have proven to be quite durable and lasting and most still stand throughout the County. In her Society Magazine article cited in foot note 34, Hannabass lists the various styles of Sears houses in Arlington, their costs at time of erection, locations, and some other features.

The Lyon Village citizens (civic) association dates from 1926 when it held its first meeting in the offices of the Village developer, Lyon and Fitch. The Association quickly became a leader in the County and participated in many county projects to include raising money for zoning the county in 1929, generating interest in the 1930 referendum to adopt the county manager form of government, the street renaming efforts of 1932-35, and the establishment of the first central post office in Clarendon on Washington Boulevard and the Lyon Park Community House on Pershing Street.

Perhaps the greatest accomplishment of the citizens of Lyon Village, and one for which they "sweated blood" and can justifiably be quite proud, was the establishment of their Community House at 1920 North Highland Street. Writer Boaz points out that soon after the time of the start of the community the need for a community meeting house for the civic association and other purposes became apparent. Fund raising efforts to include carnivals, beauty contests, and even a rolling pin throwing competition, and some other approaches with the sponsorship of the American Legion post were not very successful. Whereupon, community leaders turned to the developers who had represented at the time of sales that 10% of the purchase price of each lot would be set aside in trust to provide a community house, a park and other amenities.

Boaz writes that when the developers failed to favorably respond and in so many words told the citizens to get lost ("let them sue") suit was filed in a case that went to the Supreme Court after being dismissed by the Circuit Court. The high court supported the home owners and sent the case back for settlement. Trustees were appointed, agreements were reached in 1944, and a trust fund of $20,000 was established. The War delayed the beginning of construction until 1949 by which time with inflation the trust proved insufficient and an additional $12,000 was raised by contributions and a loan. By 1964 the loan was paid off and a mortgage burning party was held at the Community House with much area publicity.

Boaz wrote, "The Community house not only serves Lyon Village residents but has become a community resource. It is a polling place, a church and a place for political parties, artists and clubs to hold their meetings".

Lyon Village has provided many County leaders over the years, one of the most notable being William Watt from Highland Street. Watt served as a trustee for the Community House fund, and also was President of his Civic Association and the countywide Civic Federation in 1945-46. He has also been a recipient of the Washington Star Trophy in 1946 for outstanding community service.

---

³⁴ Hannabass, Darline, <u>Sears Roebuck Houses in Arlington</u>, *AHS Magazine, October 1993, P 7-16.*

Post Civil War Growth

Boaz wrote further that "it is expected that Lyon Village will continue to be what the Washingtonian (magazine) described as one of the area's great neighborhoods".

ADDISON HEIGHTS (VIRGINIA HIGHLANDS)

The railroad station at 23rd street in the Addison area where a later fire station stood for many years and is now filled with ethnic restaurants

One other neighborhood that must not escape at least passing mention in our survey of principle Arlington early settlements is the community on the flat lands east of the Arlington Ridge and extending to about the modern day Jeff-Davis (Route 1/I-595) corridor and northward from present day South 23rd Street to about the new Pentagon City shopping complex. The area today is unofficially but widely known as Virginia Highlands but is shown on maps of the early 20th Century at the Historical Society Museum and on a 1900 subdivision as Addison Heights.

At one time the Addison property before subdivision apparently extended to the top of the Ridge and along present day Arlington Ridge Road where the Addison house is shown on the 1964 DAR Barrett Chapter map of Civil War Forts and Roads. The house seems to be located about where now is Ridge Road. Templeman in her "Vignettes" on page 166 writes more precisely that the Addison home "appears on both the 1864 and 1878 maps on the southeast corner of what is now Ridge Road and 20th Street South."

Until recent years there was in fact a vintage white wooden home on the subject corner owned and occupied by Lou Pappas, a South Arlington business man with numerous realty holdings in the commercial section of South 23rd Street near Jeff-Davis highway and elsewhere. The house was featured in the action adventure film "No Way Out" staring Kevin Cosner, a fictional account of a "mole" in the American Intelligence and Defense community. In the film shots, the house was used secretly by the Russian spy ring as an operational base and there were aerial sequences of the mole driving along Ridge Road and entering and leaving the driveway of the house. In the 1980's the house was razed and replaced with a larger and more prestigious brick structure.

There has been extensive remodeling of older homes in the Virginia Highlands community, and construction of new homes on every remaining empty residential lot. The proximity of the neighborhood to places of employment in the massive new high rise office buildings in Crystal City and Pentagon City, and the nearest of two Metro rail stations in the area for those who may work elsewhere has made Virginia Highlands a highly desired residential location. Many residents over recent years, however, have felt threatened by the dense developments they perceive to be closing in on them and have been highly active as citizens and in civic associations striving to cope with the situations and defend their neighborhood from commercial and high rise encroachment. Citizens of Virginia Highlands have been particularly involved in major community struggles to monitor and contain developments such as the Pentagon City project as discussed in more detail on Chapter Five herein.

A 1939 aerial view of the Agricultural Experimentation Farm (now at Beltsville, Md) and the Hoover Airport that ceased operation when National Airport was established in 1940-41. Note absence of the Pentagon. Queen City is on upper left and Jackson City on Lower right.

Post Civil War Growth

View of cars in 1935 enroute to the 14th Street Bridge (former Long Bridge) from Arlington on road across Hoover Airport. Road had to be closed and traffic halted when planes landed or took off.

The Virginia Highlands has its own civic association, the Aurora Highlands Association, and its leaders have worked often in joint efforts with the adjacent Arlington Ridge Association to oppose or consult with County officials on rezoning matters or projects perceived to adversely impact the residents such as expansion of the past trash collection and compacting points and the expansion of the Water Pollution (Sewage) Control Plant on Eades Street at South Glebe Road. Efforts to establish football and baseball stadiums have also been matters of intense citizen concerns in the Virginia Highlands and Arlington Ridge communities in the mid 1990's.

The Pentagon building under construction about 1941.

1935 aerial view of Roosevelt (Analostan/Mason) Island. Note absence of the Pentagon, National Airport, Teddy Roosevelt Bridge and Whitehurst Freeway. The Agricultural Farm and Hoover Airport are shown in upper middle background beyond Roosevelt Island. Note piers of the former Acquaduct Bridge along side the Key Bridge, lower right

A proposal to place a football stadium in the nearby former Potomac railroad yards was withdrawn in 1994 in the face of vigorous citizen opposition, but the prospect that a Northern Virginia baseball stadium may be located in South Arlington at the bridge ends between the Pentagon and the National airport, is pending at this writing and may be similarly opposed. Local residents have expressed strong concerns about the adverse impacts such a stadium would have on them such as oppressive traffic, parking, misconduct, noise, rowdyism and other consequences of large and boisterous crowds.

* * *

Post Civil War Growth

Sketch of one of the proposed, but rejected, designs for the Pentagon building. It seems likely that such a height was unacceptable in view of the expected flight paths of nearby National Airport about to open on the eve of World War II.

There are numerous other sections or developments in Arlington that are not included in this overview of the County's principal neighborhoods. Some may derive their identification from historical sources, others from the name of housing or apartment complexes. These areas would include Colonial Village, Buckingham, Shirlington, Alcova Heights, Columbia Forest, Arna Valley, Dominion Heights, Arlington Forest, Claremont, Lyon Park, and Shirley Park to name but a few. There may be a risk in offending some citizens by omitting these areas from our detailed treatment herein, but most have newer and more shallow roots or have been absorbed into or overshadowed by the more established neighborhoods covered herein.

* * *

The county's first high rise buildings, the Arlington Towers apartments between Route 50 and the Key Bridge were built in the late 1950's, followed by the 17 story River House apartment on South Joyce Street near the Pentagon building.

In the early 1960's the County Board relaxed its off street parking, height, and some other requirements for high rise developments. As a consequence, development in the Rosslyn, Ballston Corridor, Crystal City, and Pentagon City areas literally exploded and moved forward at an astounding pace. That construction has transformed the county dramatically from a semi-rural composition to a clearly urban business, commercial and residential component of the Washington metropolitan area. This will later be discussed in greater detail in Chapter Six.

DESIGNATED HISTORIC DISTRICTS IN ARLINGTON

The following Arlington locations or areas dating from the dates shown have been officially designated by the County Board as Historic Districts as shown on the web as of February, 1996.

1760 - THE BALL SELLERS HOUSE, 5620 3rd Street, South
1785 - BALL CARLIN CEMETERY, 300 South Kennsington Street.
1814 - BALL FAMILY BURIAL GROUNDS, 3427 Washington Boulevard.
1820 - THE GLEBE HOUSE, 4527 17th Street North.
1830 - TRAVERS' FAMILY GRAVEYARD, 1309 South Monroe.
1860 - ALCOVA, 3435 8th Street South.
1861 - FORT ETHAN ALLEN, 3829 North Stafford Street.
1863 - FORT C. F. SMITH, 2411 24th Street North.
1871 - WALKER CHAPEL AND CEMETERY, 4102 North Glebe Road.
1876 - EASTMAN-FENWICK HOUSE, 6733 Lee Highway.
1881 - HARRY GRAY HOUSE, 1005 South Quinn Street.
1891 - HUME SCHOOL, 1805 South Arlington Ridge Road.
1892 - HARRY CROSSMAN HOUSE, 2501 North Underwood Street.
1892 - CARLIN COMMUNITY HALL, 5711 4th Street South.
1909 - BARCROFT COMMUNITY HOUSE, 800 South Buchanan Street.
1909 - MAYWOOD NEIGHBORHOOD, Vicinity Glebe Road & Pershing Drive.
1910 - MATTHEW F. MAURY SCHOOL, 3550 Wilson Boulevard.
1921 - CLARENDON CITIZEN HALL, 3211 Wilson Boulevard.
1922 - LOMAX AME ZION CHURCH, 2704 24th Road South.
1934 - COLONIAL VILLAGE, Queens Lane and North South.
1937 - ARLINGTON POST OFFICE, 3118 Washington Boulevard.
1945 - DAN KAIN BUILDING, 3100 Washington Boulevard.
---- - BRANDYMORE CASTLE, North Roosevelt Street at Four Mile Run.

The Shreve family home on North Pollard Street that narrowly missed demolition for a bike trail in 1974.

Post Civil War Growth

Unpaved, muddy or dusty, Moore Street in Rosslyn in 1915. The Arlington Trust Company, reached by foot or horse wagon or train on left.

A worker plowing corn on the Agricultural Farm in 1908 where now is the east edge of Arlington Cemetery. Arlington House can be seen in background.

ARLINGTON COUNTY VIRGINIA - A Modern History

Listed below is a chronological table for some of the major events that shaped the developments of Arlington County in the years following the Civil War until near the end of the century. Some of these events were of considerable importance in the growth of the County but they are only briefly listed here since they are mentioned elsewhere herein or because a detailed treatment is well beyond the scope of this narrative. Further, the events should be well documented elsewhere by capable writers whose works are readily available in Arlington libraries.

1875 - A part of Arlington County, generally known as East Falls Church, lost when the Town of Falls Church was chartered by the General Assembly. The area was returned to the county in 1936 when the Falls Church lines were redrawn.

1881 - The Civil War Fort Whipple is renamed Ft Myer after Brig. Gen. Albert J. Myer, the post commander who had established a Signal Corps school and experimented with electric telegraph lines.

1878 to 1906 - The establishment of the County's first post offices at Rosslyn, Glencarlyn, East Falls Church, Ballston, Cherrydale and Clarendon.

1891 - Construction of Hume School on South Arlington Ridge Road, on land donated by early Arlington civic leader, and delegate to the General Assembly, Frank Hume. The school is the oldest existing school building in the County but ceased to be used as such in 1959. It was deeded in 1966 to the Arlington Historical Society for its use.

1898 - Dedication of the new County Court House after removal of the courts from the City of Alexandria. Although the court house was demolished in later years to make way for the court and administrative structures now standing at 14th Street and North Court House Road, the copper tip of the tower was retained and is now on display in the Historical Society facilities in the Hume School.

1900 - The Arlington Agricultural Experimental farm is established in the areas adjacent to, or a part of Jackson City, near the present 14th Street bridge system. The farm activities were relocated to Beltsville, Maryland in 1932. At the outbreak of World War II The Congress transferred the land used by the farm from the Department of Agriculture to the War Department and the construction of the Pentagon and its environs took place.

1900 - Period of intensive residential construction begins that quickly transformed county from an essentially rural to a suburban and then urban community.

Post Civil War Growth

1902 - Era of "Good Government" began with crusades to clean up gambling, prostitution, alcohol, and other illegal operations in the county, particularly near the Key and Long Bridges.

1903 to 1908 - First volunteer fire departments, or stations, organized in Cherrydale and Ballston, and followed in 1918 by a Black citizens company in Halls' Hill.

1906 - Opening of Luna Park recreational center by Pittsburgh entrepreneur at South Glebe Road and Route 1 where the County sewage treatment plant now is located. Luna Park had all the usual carnival type rides and merry-go-rounds, with slides and exhibition houses of Moorish, Japanese, Italian, Gothic and other nationality or artistic designs. It was located at the Four Mile Run station of the railroad line running from the District bridge to Alexandria. Operations lagged in time and profits apparently sagged. It was dismantled during World War I, or just before.

1906 - First steam railroad in Arlington began operating from the Key Bridge northward to the Great Falls area and provided service where electric railroads did not exist.

1907 and 1909 - World's first sustained air flights take place at Ft Myer by Orville Wright around the post and to Alexandria where the Masonic Memorial now stands. In one of the flights Wright's passenger Lt Thomas Selfridge is killed in a crash when Wright banked the plane too sharply. A plaque marks the place where the flights began on a grassy clearing with a spectacular overlook of the Capital and monuments. It is a short distance from, and on the same street as is, Quarters #1 where the Chairman of the Joint Chiefs of Staff usually resides.

1908 - Town of Potomac privately incorporated in the area south of Four Mile Run and east of present I-395 highway. The town and corporation ceased to exist when the area, mainly Arlandria, Del Ray, St Elmo, and Potomac Yards were annexed by Alexandria in 1915 and 1929.

1912 - County Board of Supervisors moves to establish a police force to supplement the offices of Sheriff and Constables.

1912 - Construction completed of Navy Department's Arlington Radio Station with three huge towers on land near Columbia Pike and present Washington Blvd. Messages from the station and towers to Veracruz, Mexico via a relay station on the U. S. S. Birmingham, and to Pearl Harbor and the Eiffel Tower in Paris were the first long distant communications overseas and of the human voice in history. When the new National Airport was built just before World War II, the towers were dismantled as a peril to air navigation.

1915 and 1929 - Annexation by the City of Alexandria of that part of South Arlington east of Quaker Lane and South of Four Mile Run, now, roughly, the Arlandria, Potomac Yards and Del Ray areas. The action followed intense and acrimonious confrontations to include extensive litigation. The annexations were resisted by Arlington that lost its two high schools, Mt Vernon and George Mason, and a major source of tax revenue from the railroad yards.

1916 to 1918 - The initiation of meaningful telephone service by the Chesapeake and Ohio Telephone Company that absorbed the limited facilities of the Falls Church Company.

1921 - Dedication of the Tomb of the Unknown Soldier in Arlington Cemetery.

1922 - Unsuccessful attempt by Clarendon to incorporate as a town. Virginia Supreme Court ruled that Arlington County was a "continuous, contiguous and homogeneous community", and that for purposes of incorporating a part of it, the county could not be subdivided.

1925 - Washington-Lee High School opened to replace the two high schools lost to Alexandria due to annexation, and to provide schooling for students in the central and northern portions of the county that had been attending schools in the District of Columbia.

1926 - Hoover airport opened on the site of old Jackson City. The airport closed just before World War II when the new National Airport, and the Pentagon were started.

1926 to 1932 - Construction of the Memorial Bridge.

1927 - Establishment of a county wide water system with water from the District of Columbia plant by way of main lines across the chain bridge and along Glebe Road. In later years the system was expanded to cover all of the county.

1930 - First steps taken to establish a county wide sewer system and a sewage treatment plant. Early plans called for two disposal plants, one in Rosslyn and the other at Four Mile Run. Implementation was delayed until 1933 because of community uncertainty over paying for the system, and other concerns needing resolution.

Post Civil War Growth

1930-31 - Legislation, referrendum and adoption of County Manager form of government.

1932 - First County Manager government assumes office with governing body members elected at large.

1945 - Hunting banned in all of Arlington County by the County Board.

1956 - Elected School board for the County, and throughout the State abolished during the "massive resistance" era following the Supreme Court ruling in 1954 in Brown v. School Board over turning the separate but equal doctrine of many years.

1959 - School integration begins without incident as four black students are enrolled at Stratford Junior High School.

1960's - Massive high rise development is launched in Rosslyn, Crystal City, Ballston and the Ballston corredor areas.

1960's and '70's - Construction and beginning of operation of the Metro Rapid Rail transportation system.

1970's and early 80's - Construction and opening of Interstate Highway I-66 following almost a decade of controversy and litigation.

1993-94 - Completion and dedication of new jail and court house across Court House Road from old facilities.

* * *

ARLINGTON COUNTY VIRGINIA - A Modern History

The Court House entrance in 1996 with the "tower" structure in background.

The partially dismantled court house tower in December, 1996. Demolition was completed by implosion charges in February, 1997.

CHAPTER THREE

GOVERNMENT AND POLITICAL GROWTH

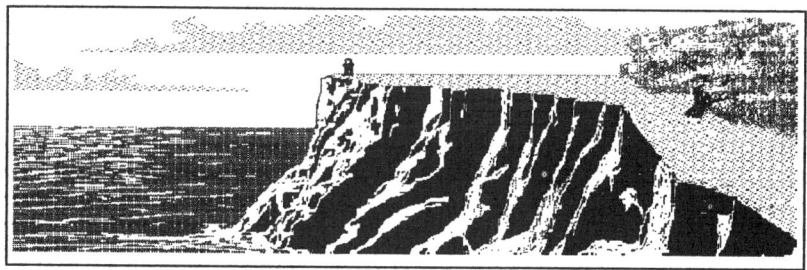

PRECIPITOUS TIMES FOR ARLINGTON COUNTY

THE BEGINNING - 1870

For all practical purposes, local government, politics, and political parties or movements in what is now Arlington County, can be said to have begun with the adoption of the Constitution of 1870 at the time of the readmission of the State into the Union.

Before retrocession in 1846, the area was a part of the District of Columbia. In the primitive period leading to the outbreak of the Civil War, Arlington as part of Alexandria County was governed by appointed magistrates. The Arlington area, with so few inhabitants, did not even have its own delegate to the legislature in Richmond, but shared a delegate with Fairfax County.[1]

During and after the war until readmission, the area was under martial law as a part of the Virginia Military District.

The new constitution, among many other things, provided that counties would be governed by an elected board of supervisors from no less than three districts. It excluded cities with more than 5,000 population from being a part of a district. Thus, the City of Alexandria with more than that much population, ceased to be a part of Alexandria County, leaving only, essentially, what is now Arlington County. The constitution

---

[1] *For a list of Arlington representatives in the General Assembly from retrocession to 1960 see AHS Magazine, October, 1969, p. 34.*

provided for numerous other elected offices but later amendments abolished some and provided for appointment of others.

A Governor appointed commission divided the new Alexandria County, (Arlington) into three districts, each about equal in area, with arbitrary straight lines across the county. The commission thus created Washington District in the northern portion, Jefferson to the south and Arlington in the middle. Freedman's Village was included in the Jefferson district.

Supervisors elected from each of the districts formed the County Board of Supervisors. Terms of office were for one year until 1885 and two thereafter until 1904 when the terms became four years. The first election, to include supervisors, was held on May 28, 1870 and it is interesting to note that one of the members, appointed because of the ineligibility of one of the elected members to serve, was James C. Roach. Roach was a land owner and apparently a citizen of considerable influence. He had built his prestigious home Prospect Hill overlooking the Abington plantation and the confluence of the Anacostia and Potomac Rivers on high ground that is now known as the Arlington Ridge in South Arlington. The mansion stood until the late 1960s when it was demolished to make way for the Representative high rise condominium. We will return later herein to Roach and his mansion and the rezoning controversy that resulted in its destruction.

In the mid 1960s a Research and Records Committee of the Arlington Historical Society (AHS), at considerable and diligent effort, compiled a list of all Alexandria County (Arlington County after 1920) governing body members from the first election in 1970 to and through 1960.[2] A scan of the list, included here in the Appendix, will show that the Board of Supervisors for the period until the end of 1931, at which time the County Manager form of government was adopted, consisted of three members with one from each of the magisterial districts.

The Research Committee list reflects considerable fluidity in the composition of the board in those early years of existence, and does not always show the terms of office as being for full calendar years. It may be that the dates shown reflect the periods of actual meetings, and not the overall terms of office.

The Society Committee reported that the supervisors could draw $3.00 a day (later $4.00) when meeting, but only for a maximum of ten days (later 18). They were thus "apt to accomplish their business as expeditiously as possible", as indicated in one document used by the Committee.

Many members are shown to have not completed their terms of office either because of resignations, perhaps death, or other causes. The list, and the report accompanying it, does not indicate the political parties, if any, of the members of the Board. The committee indicates it had to rely largely on Board of Supervisor "Minute Books" and wrote, in part, that there were "...some gaps in the record, and some mysterious appearances and disappearances of individuals."

---

[2]*The Committee's report was published in the AHS Magazine for October, 1967, p.36.*

Government and Political Growth

Nevertheless, the report and list compiled by the Research Committee of the Historical Society stands as probably the most authoritative and complete available and constitutes a most worthwhile contribution to our knowledge of the early political composition of Arlington County government.

The designation in 1920 by the State Legislature of "Arlington" as the official name for the country part of Alexandria County, did not alter the manner of election of county governing body members.

CHANGE OF GOVERNMENT 1930-32

In the period from 1930-32 an event was to take place that would profoundly affect Arlington and its future and government for most of the rest of the Century, for the better or worse, depending upon one's point of view.

As a result of constitutional amendments adopted in 1928, and new laws enacted pursuant thereto,[3] Arlington voters in the November 1930 election chose to change to the new County Manager form of government previously mentioned. They also voted, by a rather close vote,[4] to elect their five County Board members "at-large" in a single county wide electoral district, rather than individually from single member districts as had previously been the case.

A very detailed and learned account of the background and circumstances leading to the adoption of the Manager form of government, and at-large voting, can be found in the October, 1958 Magazine of the Historical Society in an article entitled "Arlington Adopts the County Manager Form of Government", by Robert Nelson Anderson. A later analysis of the at-large system in operation can be found in the article "Arlington's At-Large Electoral System A Study in its History, Strengths and Weaknesses" by this author [Pratt] in the October, 1995 issue of the Society Magazine.

Anderson was obviously a strong advocate of the changes and a leader in the very energetic community drive to bring them about. He states that he was President of the Better Government League that apparently was the catalyst more than any other group that worked toward the goal of adopting the changes. He describes the actions by his group to obtain legislative authority for a referendum on the question and then the campaign locally to ensure that the measure, once on the ballot, would be approved by the voters.

---

[3] Chapter 14, Title 15, Code of Virginia.

[4] *The Alexandria Gazette on Nov 5, 1930 reported the election results as 1,650 for at-large and 1179 for single member districts. The vote in the Virginia Highlands and Arlington areas where most Black people lived was heavily for single member districts; i.e. 368 vs 216.*

Anderson wrote, in part, as follows:

> "..the Better Government Committee labored unceasingly to the end that every voter ...should have complete information on the subject as a basis for an <u>intelligent</u> vote...every question raised in the public discussion has been fully answered, and every objection to the change raised by the opposition <u>had been shown to be without foundation</u>" (emphasis supplied).

Presumably Anderson concluded that only votes for his recommended changes were "intelligent" and that votes against were unintelligent. It seems doubtful that the substantial percentage, but minority, of citizens that voted against the changes would agree with that assessment. Additionally, it is interesting to note the finality with which Anderson disposed of the arguments, with which he did not agree, of his opponents. They too, might not agree that their positions were without foundation.

Anderson summed up his discourse with a rather glowing and self serving, but not necessarily incorrect, tribute to himself and his co-workers:

> "Suffice it to say that as a result of this adoption and the dedicated effort and ceaseless interest on the part of the officials and employees of the County and scores of its civic minded citizens we constitute today, one of the most progressive, happy and prosperous communities in the United States."

In its flyers in support of the proposed changes in government, the Better Government League had written, in pertinent part:

> "...under our system of government anyone may become a candidate...merely by announcing his or her intentions of doing so...the result is there are so many candidates ...the vote is split up and no candidate has a majority of the total votes cast and in many instances the affairs of the County are conducted by individuals who have received considerably less than a majority of the votes cast and who consequently do not represent a majority of the people of Arlington County".

There is evidence that some citizens at the time were not as delighted and euphoric as Anderson and those who felt as he did. It seems some citizens felt the change, or at least the adoption of an at-large voting arrangement was racially motivated, to discourage Black citizens from filing and running for public offices. Of course this would be most difficult if not entirely impossible to document at this late date, or perhaps even at the time of the voting on at-large districts. Persons with an objective of improperly discriminating seldom ever commit their motives, actions or views to writing.

Government and Political Growth

Additionally, in the years since, questions have arisen as to whether the "at-large" or the "single member district" electoral system best serves the overall public interests of the county. There are those who feel that in practice the at-large arrangement has operated to the distinct disadvantage of certain sections or neighborhoods of the County. This will be discussed in more detail in Chapter Five, "Major Controversies".

In any event, in the election of 1931, members to the new five member County Board were elected from 51 on the ballot, including three Black candidates. This was the year of the Franklin D. Roosevelt Democratic landslide in the national elections.

All five of the successful candidates of the new Board were among the top six recommended by Anderson and the Better Government League. None, however, received more than a small portion, about 7%, of the total votes cast. If Anderson and his group were concerned over the fact that their candidates received "considerably less than a majority of the votes" and therefore "did not represent a majority of the people of Arlington" as set out in their flyers, this writer could find no record of such concern. Perhaps they would have been more displeased if the election turned out other than as they wished.

Be that as it may, the winners in Arlington, were elected for four years terms and they took office on January 1, 1932. The five were, Fred A. Goznell, Harry A. Fellows, Elizabeth B. Magruder, John C. Gall and Lyman M. Kelley. The votes for the five ranged from a high of 2088 for Gosnell who came in first to 1465 for Kelley who was fifth, out of a total vote of just over 27,000 for all 51 candidates. Thus, as stated, none of the winners could claim more support than about 7% of the electorate.[5]

The Alexandria Gazette reported on November 4, 1931, that Ms Magruder was believed to be the first woman to become a member of any county governing body in the State. The list of 51 candidates on the ballot included three with "(col)" after their names. They were Mrs Mary B. Harris, Dr. E. T. Morton, and C. H. Moseley.

TERM LENGTHS - SOME CHANGES

Inasmuch as the first County Board members under the Manager form of government were elected for four years, the second election did not take place until four years later in 1935. Two of the early Board members, Magruder and Chew, would set longevity records by serving on 16 Boards, or the equivalent of four 4 year terms. Those records would not be broken until the reelection in 1993 of Board member Ellen Bozman for a sixth term who at this writing has served on 23 boards that will expand to 24 by the end of her current four year term in 1997.

A few County Board members have resigned over the years, and in 1952 three, Robert W. Cox, Alan L. Dean and Daniel A. Dugan, were removed by Court order because they were found, as Federal employees, to be ineligible to serve in local offices. Two Board members, Leo C. Lloyd in 1947, and David L. Krupshaw in 1960, died in office.

---

[5] *The County Board members from 1932 to date are shown in the Appendix.*

ARLINGTON COUNTY VIRGINIA - A Modern History

For a record of elections and board members in the earliest years of the manager form of government we must rely, to a major extent, upon the research conducted by a library volunteer, "R. Singleton"[6], and by Historical Society and Board Member Norman Novach as published in the October 1994 Magazine on pages 61-66 and reproduced in the Appendix herein. Researcher Singleton reported that in the second election only Mrs Magruder and William A. E. McShea, who had apparently been appointed to replace Gall who had resigned in office, were elected to the new board, along with three new members to include W. R. Ames and F. Freeland Chew who would serve on the board for extended periods. The Chairman of the second board was George M. Yeatman.

In 1938 the voters approved changes in order to stagger the terms of the board members. Thus, in the third election, in 1939, members were elected for varying years with the results as follows:

Magruder	4 years
Chew	4 years
Edmund D. Campbell	3 years
Basil DeLashmut	2 years
Leo Lloyd	1 year

All of the board members were Democrats. Ames, ran for reelection but lost. McShea and Yeatman, both Democrats, ran in the primary and lost. Two other candidates, one a Republican and one apparently an independent, ran and lost.

In the election of 1940, only Lloyd, the one year member, ran. He was reelected for four years. Likewise, in the election of 1941, the two year candidate DeLashmut ran for reelection. He too was reelected for four years.

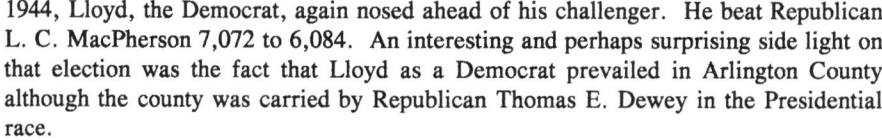

In 1942, Campbell, the three year member, ran unopposed and was reelected.

In 1943, the terms of four year members Chew and Magruder expired and they ran successfully for reelection. In 1944, Lloyd, the Democrat, again nosed ahead of his challenger. He beat Republican L. C. MacPherson 7,072 to 6,084. An interesting and perhaps surprising side light on that election was the fact that Lloyd as a Democrat prevailed in Arlington County although the county was carried by Republican Thomas E. Dewey in the Presidential race.

In 1945, Board member DeLashmutt ran for reelection and won, leaving the membership of the board unchanged.

Thereafter, the pattern to date has continued to be annual elections for one county board member, with an election for two members each fourth year, i.e. 1947, 1951, 1955, et seq.

* * *

---

[6] *On file in the Virginia Room of the Arlington main (Central) Library, and also in the office of the Voting Registrar, Arlington County government.*

PHILOSOPHICAL COMPOSITION OF THE BOARD

Over the years from 1932 to date, it seems the Arlington County Board has shifted from a rather conservative beginning lasting almost three decades, to a two decade period of fluctuating philosophical composition, to the past two decades of mostly, and at times exclusively, liberal membership.

The categorization of political people as "liberals" or "conservatives" is not, of course, without certain hazards. Some people object to being labeled either way. This writer had found no shortage of individuals who will assert that they are neither liberal nor conservative, but are moderates that swing slightly to the right or left depending upon a particular issue, or the personality of a candidate running for office. It is further this writer's belief that most Arlingtonians, at least in modern days, fall into this category.

Many others, however, will eagerly and proudly claim that they are from one side or the other of the political spectrum, but even they will usually add that they are only "moderately" so. Such people are usually the dedicated party workers for Arlington's two major political organizations.

Few if any local people will admit, in our days, to being extremists on either the right or left. Odds are heavy today that one could beat the brush in vain to find a trace of a far left wing radical or quasi-communist, or a right wing near-Fascist in or around Arlington. Books can, of course, be written on this subject without resolving much, but for our purposes here, we can make certain assumptions to get on with a reasonable treatment of the matter insofar as it applies to our narrative and Arlington County.

ARLINGTON COUNTY - LIBERAL OR CONSERVATIVE ?

Generally speaking, in modern American politics, locally or nationally, it seems safe to say that Republicans are looked upon as conservatives, and Democrats as liberals, allowing for the fact that some Republicans will be viewed as more liberal than their colleagues, and some Democrats may also be viewed as more conservative than other Democrats.

A major historical exception to this somewhat simplistic classification has been the Southern Democrats who were considered to be clearly in the conservative camp. More often than not, they voted in the National legislature with the Republicans rather than with their fellow Democrats to the great disenchantment of Democratic leaders to include Presidents Roosevelt in the New Deal era and Johnson in the 1960 period when major civil rights legislation was enacted.

With respect to the philosophy of the Arlington Board members from 1932 to 1946, all of whom were Democrats, it seems safe to conclude that they were conservatives. There is a dearth of information in available records on this point, but given the fact that prior to World War II, Arlington was still very much a part of the "old South" and the Southern State of Virginia, it would seem that the philosophical leanings of Arlington's Democrats would be no different from that of other Southern Democrats, i.e. clearly conservative.

Although it is true that the early Board members were also mostly, or all, the same leaders who crusaded for a change to a manager form of government, that issue could be correctly considered by many as neither liberal nor conservative but more as a "progressive" move toward more efficient government that could easily be embraced by both ends of the political spectrum.

The records reveal that those early Democrats also pushed hard for the at-large electoral system as described above. That fact may be far more revealing concerning the political philosophy of those early Arlington Democrats. The at-large voting system, especially if adopted to deny Arlington Blacks equal access to the democratic process, would hardly be considered by most modern day liberals as a liberal arrangement.

With the emergence of civil rights movements in the last several decades, the at-large electoral system has been vigorous opposed by liberals everywhere. It has also been struck down throughout the United States by the Supreme Court as regressive and constitutionally impermissible on the grounds that it is unlawfully discriminatory, dilutes minority voting strengths, and denies them equal access to the democratic process.

Thus, absent more persuasive evidence to the contrary, it must be concluded that Arlington's earlier, board members (i.e., those from 1932 to about five or so years after WWII) were all conservative Democrats.

THE ADVENT OF ARLINGTON LIBERALISM

In the years immediately following WWII, politics in Arlington County took a definite swing to the left, or toward more liberalism.

During the war, and afterwards, large numbers of "outsiders" arrived in the Nation's Capital area, and in Arlington. Many of the newcomers were government appointees or workers in the Roosevelt and Truman Democrat administrations and thus could be considered more liberal in their thinking and positions that the prevailing local residents.

The newcomers to Arlington, together with many long time residents, expressed a displeasure with conditions in Arlington and especially educational facilities. They began to hold "town meetings" and in 1946 formed an organization named the Citizens Committee for School Improvements. We will treat this movement in more detail later herein.

The Citizens Committee, with the acronym CCSI, claimed to be "county-wide and non-partisan in character, with members of both major political parties from all parts of the County". [7]

The CCSI stated that it believed that Arlington schools should be the best; that there were insufficient schools rooms with too many students per teacher; that working conditions of teachers, salary and school plants should be improved; that school board members must have "broader vision and ability to plan for long range needs and courage to make responsible decisions..."; and that the school board should be elected by more direct methods.

---

[7] *CCSI flyers and newsletters, Virginia Room archives, Arlington Central (which is the main or principal County) Library.*

Government and Political Growth

CCSI launched a public bond effort to achieve these objectives and they began to field candidates for the County and School Boards who would work toward the accomplishment of their programs. In the election of 1946 they made their first breakthrough by nominating Daniel A. Dugan who ran as a Nonpartisan and won in a big upset by defeating longtime regular Democrat Ed Campbell.

Dugan took office on the 1947 Board. In that same year, Board member Lloyd died, as stated, and a conservative, or "Official" Democrat Alfred E. Frisbie was appointed as his replacement. On May 17th, another conservative, Harry W. Cuppett was appointed to replace Magruder who had resigned from the Board. The Board now consisted of four old line conservative Democrats and one liberal "Independent".

In the election of 1947, "Town Meeting" and CCSI, now also identified as the Better Government League[8] candidate Mrs Florence Cannon ran as a Nonpartisan and won. She took office on the 1948 board. Thus the board then had two liberal members and was closing the gap. Board member Chew also ran for reelection as a Greater Arlington Association candidate and won in a race with a total of nine candidates running as Independents, Nonpartisans and Greater Arlington Association affiliations. Cuppett, the Magruder appointee earlier in the year, ran but was defeated. The race was close with all four leading candidates, Chew, Cannon, T. Oscar Smith and Cuppett in that order, receiving from 4,920 to 4,474 votes.

In the election of 1948, Board member Frisbie won reelection over his CCSI liberal candidate L. Lee Potter, in a photo finish of 9,181 to 9,052 votes. This left the 1949 philosophical membership of the Board unchanged.

1950 - LIBERALS GAIN CONTROL OF BOARD

In the 1949 election, however, a land mark and historical event in Arlington history took place. The liberals gained control of the 1950 Board with the election of Nonpartisan Robert W. Cox who had attended the first "Town Meeting" that launched the CCSI in 1946. Cox's election, upon taking office in January 1950, ended 17 years of conservative control. Cox by a vote of 7,308 to 6,306 had defeated conservative Basil DeLashmutt, who ran as an Official Democrat and had served on ten Boards for the longest period to that date, after Magruder and Chew as mentioned above.

The defeat of DeLashmutt, and the clout of the new liberal movement, was apparently somewhat of a shock to the county. Most of the political leaders of the day had something to say about the outcome of the race [9] but the victorious candidate, and his liberal compatriots on the Board seemed to demonstrate no vindictiveness. Cox was quoted as saying:

---

[8] *The Sun, Arlington Virginia, July 25, 1947, page 1, column 5.*

[9] *The Sun, Arlington Virginia, November 10, 1949, page 1, columns 6-7.*

ARLINGTON COUNTY VIRGINIA - A Modern History

The 1951 County Board, L-R: Ruby Simpson, Clerk, Daniel Dugan, Robert Cox, Florence Cannon, Freeland Chew, Alfred Frisbie, and Albert Lunsberg, Manager.

"...the election results show that the people of Arlington County want real non-partisan elections for the County Board...I deeply appreciate the confidence shown in me..."

Dugan, on the Board, added:
"I am extremely glad that Mr Cox won and wish to reiterate the statements I made during the campaign concerning the personal integrity of Mr DeLashmutt. Mr DeLashmutt is a thorough gentleman and I expect to remain, as I have been, one of his friends."

There was no change of the Board's membership in 1951 with liberal Dugan's successful run for reelection in the 1950 elections. During the campaign Dugan, with CCSI support and indorsement, continued to push for approval of school bonds and argued that school facilities remained inadequate. It was probably the major issue in the campaign and bitter acrimonious disagreement developed between the County Treasurer, John Loche Greene, and the school administration that charged, in effect, that Dugan and the CCSI were misrepresenting class room construction and other costs.[10]

An interesting sidelight of the 1950 election was a statement in the Dugan campaign flyer, Dugan Speaks which read in part: "Federal Workers need not hesitate to actively campaign for Dan Dugan, who is himself a Federal employee."[11] In the second year of Dugan's term, he would himself be removed from office by Court order,

---

[10] *Letter, To The Citizens of Arlington, W. A. Early, Office of the Superintendent, Arlington County Public Schools, October 30, 1950, VA room Archives, Central Library.*

[11] RE-ELECT DANIEL A. DUGAN TO ARLINGTON COUNTY BOARD, *Campaign Bulletin #2, October 22, 1950. Campaign flyers referred to throughout herein are on file in the Virginia Room, Arlington Central Library.*

Government and Political Growth

as we shall see, because he was a Federal employee. This in itself, however, did not prove his statement untrue in substance. The Court stopped short of ruling that Federal workers could not work in his campaign, which was supposedly non-partisan. The ruling might have been otherwise, in view of the Federal Hatch Act, had Dugan been running as a partisan Democrat or Republican.

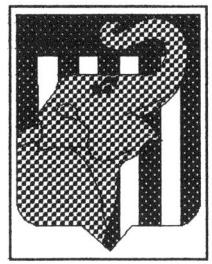

1952 BOARD - THE FIRST REPUBLICAN MEMBER

Beginning with the election of 1951, changes would occur that would see the swing of the County Board composition back to the conservatives for the next several years, but under Republican, not conservative Democrat, control.

In the 1951 election Board member Cannon did not run for reelection but long term member Chew did in a race with nine candidates. The election for the two opening seats was won by Nonpartisan Alan L. Dean and new comer Robert A. Peck who ran as an "Official" Republican.

Peck was widely known in the County because of his automobile business and as an active member of several community organizations to include the Optimist Club, the Chamber of Commerce and Cancer and Red Cross Committees. Chew, who shared the record of the longest service on the Board with Magruder, finished a distant seventh with only 2,718 votes as against Peck's 5,299 and Dean's 4,777. Peck's running partner, George M. Rowzee, Jr., a local banker, came in fifth in the race with 3778 votes.

Surviving participants in the 1951 election advise me that it was an exceptionally bitter and strenuous campaign year. In their literature the Nonpartisan, or "Town Meeting", candidates pointed proudly to their record in the two years they had controlled the Board. They claimed they had, among other things: provided a six year improvement and development plan; adopted a zoning ordinance; established a Department of Real Estate Assessment; established a merit system for County employees; met the needs of the school system for operating revenue; improved training of police; and fought the system of milk price fixing. The Nonpartisan also advocated voter approval of bonds on the ballot for sewers, roads and parks.

REPUBLICAN ISSUES RING OUT

The Republican candidates challenged Nonpartisan claims and contended that Arlington's greatest immediate need was for a more businesslike management approach to government problems. They also endorsed the proposed bonds for roads and sewers, but their flyers did not mention the park bonds. The Republicans condemned wasteful and extravagant policies of the Nonpartisan County Board, and criticized Nonpartisan interference in the performance of the County Manager, an apparent reference to some past incidents.

When asked to what he contributed his victory and Chew's defeat, Peck did not allude to philosophical or operational issues but replied only, "I simply ran a high profile and energetic campaign. I was rather widely known around the county, and I was able to spread my posters just about everywhere. I drove around the county in my car with

ARLINGTON COUNTY VIRGINIA - A Modern History

eye catching signs. Chew lost mainly because of his fondness for the bottle. He was seen publicly in some compromising situations under the influence and I think it ruined him. The Nonpartisan lost because they were discredited with the voters."[12]

With the election of one liberal, Nonpartisan Cox, and one conservative, Republican Peck, it might be said the 1951 election ended in a draw.

* * *

The 1952 Board year began on a cheery note for the Liberals. Members Dugan and Cox with newly elected Dean formed a majority of 3 liberals to 2 conservatives, Republican Peck and Democrat Frisbie.

The early 1952 County Board, L-R: Ruby Simpson, Clerk, Alan Dean, Daniel Dugan, Robert Cox, Robert Peck, Alfred Frisbie, and Albert Lundberg, Mngr.

As the months passed, however, their fortunes waned and faded. A suit was filed to have all three liberals, or Nonpartisans, removed from the Board on the grounds that as Federal employees they were ineligible to serve on a local governing body. Circuit Judge McCarthy ruled in favor of the plaintiffs and ordered all three liberals removed, and he appointed three replacements to serve until the end of the year. He also ordered elections to fill the three vacant positions in the regular election in November.

1953 - A SOLID CONSERVATIVE BOARD

In the regular election of 1952, three conservative candidates, Leone B. Buchholz, Robert H. Detwiler and Alvin F. Kimmel, were elected to serve for the remainder of 1952, or about seven weeks.

Additionally, George M. Rowzee, Jr, an Official Republican, Kimmel, a Republican running as an Arlington Independent Movement (AIM) candidate, Buchholtz,

---

[12] *Interview with the author, in the Peck Chevrolet offices, November 27, 1992.*

Government and Political Growth

an AIM candidate, and Detwiler, an AIM candidate were respectively elected to 4, 3, 2 and 1 year terms.

Thus, 1953 witnessed the return of County Board control to a solid conservative membership. The same held true in 1954 with the election in November 1953 of conservative Wesley W. Cooper who ran as a Regular Democrat. He replaced Detwiler who was elected, as stated, to a one year term in 1952 and did not run for reelection in 1953.

Although the Nonpartisans had lost all their seats on the County Board, they occupied all five of the seats on the School Board. Thus, in those critical Korean War days of turmoil abroad all the ingredients existed on the home front for acrimonious confrontation in Arlington with its County and School boards completely comprised of philosophically opposed memberships. But it would not be for long. The liberals were to soon rise again as we shall see.

1955 was a relatively uneventful year insofar as philosophical composition of the County Board was concerned. Buchholtz ran for reelection at the end of her two year term and she was elected in a close race by defeating Nonpartisan Ivan Booker. Former Board member Dugan ran as an Independent and came in a distant fourth. Thus the Board remained all conservative.

LIBERAL CLOUT EMERGES

1956 was to be a notable year, however, with a renewed showing of liberal clout. The remnants of the Town Meeting and Nonpartisan organizations and the CCSI had been merged or reformed into a new group that adopted the name Arlingtonians for A Better County, or ABC. We will hear more about the ABC organization later herein and especially in Chapter Four, "Sources of Influence".

The new ABC group stated "Our ranks include Democrats, Republicans, and independents in national and state affairs". They claimed they were seeking to "Secure for Arlington a government responsive to all the people", but the Washington Post on March 30, 1955, in its report on the new Arlington political organization indicated its purposes or aims might be otherwise. The Post headline on the article read: "New Group to Fight AIM in Arlington".

In the 1955 election the ABC group fielded two candidates for the County Board, Ralph Kaul, and David L. Krupsaw who ran as ABC candidates against two AIM candidates. The issues in the campaign were essentially the same as they had been in the earlier years. School operation continued to be a hot issue and each group contended they could do a better job of running the schools. The Republicans attempted to capitalize on the fact that Arlington's U. S. Representative and the President were both Republicans. Their campaign flyer urged, "Let's Join the Eisenhower-Broyhill Team!!".

The two ABC candidates won the election and the 1956 Board, thus, then had three conservatives and two liberals. The new ABC organization was off to a flying start in its announced intention of regaining control of the County Board, as well as the School Board.

But it was not quite yet to be. In the 1956 election, AIM candidate Lucas H. Blevins nosed ahead of ABC candidate Curtis E. Tuthill by a hairs breadth of only 118 votes in a final tally of 17,963 to 17,845. In the campaign, ABC lashed out at AIM and

95

charged it had conducted a "vicious attack on the Arlington public school system by appeals to bigotry and fear.[13]

During the year the local right to elect school boards had been abolished by the General Assembly following Arlington's response to the U. S. Supreme Court decision of 1954 in Brown v. School Board striking down segregation in public schools. Undoubtedly, as a consequence, school desegregation in Arlington had become a local political issue as reflected in another flyer for Tuthill in which the ABC organization promised to work to restore the right to elect School Board members.[14] The flyer proclaimed, in part;

> *"AIM, through its control of the County Board, has hacked away at our rights as voters and citizens, voted to slash school budgets and fought school improvement, undermined the master zoning plan, road blocked the Planning Commission, wasted tax money by unbusinesslike policies and given special favors to its supporters".*

Blevins campaign flyers stressed his record of extensive participation and involvement in church, Masonic, civic, Committee of 100, charitable and other community activities. It also accused his opponent of condemning his own Democratic members of the County Board and the "legislative action" of Democrats Charles Fenwick, Harrison Mann, Kathryn Stone and William Winston for having sponsored the Moncure Bill that did away with elected school boards in Virginia.[15]

In an apparent appeal to Arlington voters concerned about the prospects of school racial integration the Blevins flyer proclaimed, in part:

> *"A.I.M.'s opponent has many N.A.A.C.P. backers who are suing our School Board to force integration on our children. People who previously had not seen the real purpose of the A.B.C. Agitators in now revealed, are joining the large group of BLEVINS SUPPORTERS. They are now actually working in our campaign to see that his policy of moderation is victorious on Tuesday, November 6th."*

THE 1958 BOARD - THE DEMISE OF THE CONSERVATIVES

The AIM/Republican conservative apparatus had managed to retain control of the County Board for another year with the election of Blevins in 1957, but it would be their last Board. In the next election they would lose, the Board control would pass to the

---

[13] *Flyer, Tuthill Campaign Committee, 3037 No. Stafford St., Arlington 7, Va.*

[14] *ABC campaign committee flyer for Curtis E. Tuthill on November 6th, 3037 No. Stafford St., Arlington 7, Va.*

[15] *Blevins A.I.M. flyer, Committee for Your County Board, undated, Virginia Room archives, Arlington Main Library.*

Government and Political Growth

liberal ABC organization and it would so remain for over a decade with no conservative membership at all in some years.

In the election of 1957, ABC candidate Herbert L. Brown, Jr., would defeat his AIM opponent by a comfortable margin, and the following year Leo Urbanske, Jr., would edge out Buckholtz, creating a 1959 Board of four ABC members to one AIM member, Blevins. Buchholtz had ran as an independent when the AIM organization was dissolved.

The membership of the 1960 Board remained unchanged, except that member Krupshaw, as stated earlier, died in an airplane crash in Jamaica in January and was replaced by Ernest Wilt, an ABC indorsed appointee. Wilt was a local banker, businessman and a member of the Board of Zoning Appeals. His appointment by Circuit Court Judge Walter McCarthy and the other two Judges was warmly embraced by ABC Council Chairman Lawrence J. Latto, and ABC Board members Brown and Urbanske.

In the 1960 election, ABC new comer Thomas Richards defeated Blevins in a close race, 19,939 to 19,442, and Wilt ran unopposed for a term of three years, the remainder of Krupshaw's term.

Thus the Board in 1961 was comprised of only ABC members and it was to remain so through 1962 and 1963. The Board membership, however, would change just once in 1962 when ABC candidate Roye L. Lowry replaced Brown who did not run for reelection in 1961.

An interesting sidelight of the 1961 election was the candidacy of a local bakery operator, Julius Brenner who ran as an independent. Brenner's business had caught fire and was badly damaged. He felt the fire engines had been slow in arriving in response to his alarm and he ran mostly on the single issue of improving the efficiency of the Fire Department.

1964 - A CRACK IN ABC DOMINANCE

At the end of 1963, the terms of Board members Wilt and Kaul expired and neither ran for reelection. In their wake, Republican Harold J. Casto, a local stock broker and World War II combat paratrooper, and ABCer Joesph L. Fisher, an economist and educator, were elected.

Thus the 1964 Board again had a conservative member. In the campaign, the ABC candidates promised to continue to work toward past goals concerning parks, schools, taxes, regional cooperation, and orderly development to preserve residential areas and the Potomac Palisades.

RALPH KAUL
The only ever truly independent Board Member?

ARLINGTON COUNTY VIRGINIA - A Modern History

The 1964 County Board, L-R: Bert Johnson, Mngr, Harold Casto, Thomas Richards, Joseph Fisher, Roye Lowry, Leo Urbanske, Phyllis Ferari, Clerk.

The Republicans joined the ABC in advocating the protection of "the residential complex of our community" and promised to "protect the American two party system of government at the local grass-roots level." [16] No doubt as a response to community concerns over the methods of complying with demands for school integration, the flyer contained the following concerning one of the major county schools in South Arlington that had been historically all Black:

> "KEEP HOFFMAN-BOSTON SCHOOL OPEN - Stop the tax-wasting ABC scheme to bus colored children out of a modern high school (which is under capacity) in their own residential area to already overcrowded schools in other areas of the community."

The membership and political composition of the Board did not change in 1965, but the Republicans picked up an extra member for the 1966 Board when Arlington Dentist Kenneth M. Haggerty defeated ABCer Lowry in the 1965 election. The Board thus stood at three ABC members and two Republicans. The ABC campaign issues remained essentially unchanged. They pledged to continue the programs they had long advocated and had been implementing. Lowry stressed his proven experience and responsibility and he was strongly endorsed by the Washington Daily News, the Evening Star and the Northern Virginia Sun.

The Republicans, on the other hand, injected some new issues. Their campaign flyer [17] announced that they believed in...

---

[16] *Flyer, Casto & Matthews for County Board, 2825 Wilson Blvd, Arlington, Virginia.*

[17] *Flyer, Haggerty for County Board Committee, 4620 Lee Highway, Arlington, Va., Virginia Room archives, ibid.*

Government and Political Growth

> *"Stopping the continuous Arlington tax and spend spiral; Reduce Arlington's 66% increase in major crimes under ABC rule; invest Arlington's recreational dollar in Arlington. The ridiculous misappropriation of taxpayers' money to purchase park-land in Prince William County is indefensible; and protect the residential complexion of our community. The present ABC Board issued a record 93 high density zonings in less than 2 years of their control."*

Haggerty contended that a vote for him would be a vote for strong leadership and a voice for recreation, and for parents, property owners, taxpayers, commuters and apartment dwellers. Lowry, in his flyers, also claimed, essentially, that he would be a better voice for these, and other, citizens. Lowry also campaigned in support of integration of the Hoffman-Boston and Thomas Jefferson schools, and in opposition to the building of the Three Sisters Bridge across the Potomac River below Spout Run. The casual observer and voter was left to sort out which candidate was voicing mere political rhetoric or solid substance.

1967 - RETURN OF CONSERVATIVE CONTROL
BEGINNING OF VACILLATING PERIOD

The Arlington Board of 1967 returned to conservative, or Republican, control with the election of Columbia Cemetery manager Ned R. Thomas who defeated ABC member Urbanske in the 1966 election. The year also marked the beginning of almost a decade of annual swings in the Board control as the liberal ABC-Democrats vied in close races with the conservative, and sometimes moderate, Republicans for a Board majority.

The 1968 Board returned again to ABC control with the election of Jay E. Ricks who defeated Casto in the 1967 race. In that election the voters also approved the sale of liquor by the drink locally and almost two hundred million dollars in bonds for transit, schools and recreational, and state projects, by a margin of about two to one. The local bonds had been proposed by the ABC controlled Board, but Phillips had not campaigned against them in substance. Reflecting a disenchantment with past Board budget hearing policies, Phillips pledged:

> *"the public will be assured of an opportunity to be heard on budget matters. Never again would over 75% of the budget be approved without public hearings."*[18]

In 1969 the Republicans regained a 3-2 majority with the election of A. Leslie Phillips who defeated Wholey in a close race with only a difference of 895 votes out of over 50,000 cast in the 1968 election.

The 1970 Board composition remained unchanged, thus the Republicans retained their 3-2 control when Haggerty ran for reelection in 1969 and won. The voters also

---

[18] *Flyer, Haggerty for County Board, undated.*

approved in that election, the sale of bonds for roads, a jail, a branch library swimming pools storm drainage, parks, and neighborhood conservation. The Republicans charged that too many projects were being funded by bonds that should more properly be allotted to annual operating expenses.

In the November General election of 1970, however, newcomer ABC candidate Joseph S. Wholey, a budget planner and self-proclaimed "think tanker", trounced Casto 33,747 to 18,724 and the Board returned again to ABC control in the new term beginning January, 1971. Baker Brenner also ran in the 1970 election, but received only 2,640 votes.

The Board would remain under ABC control from 1971 until 1979, and in the years 1974 and 1975 it would be comprised of only ABC members.

* * *

In the 1973 election year, this writer entered a three way race with ABC candidate Ellen Bozman, a local civic activist, and Republican Henry Lampe, a local stock broker and former member of the Legislature.

Bozman won the election with a comfortable lead over Lampe of 17,908 to 14,026 votes. Running as a true independent without any major political party backing, I trailed far behind with 3,158. Still, my supporters and I had some satisfaction. We had not expected to win against such formidable opponents. Rather, in the race every effort was made to focus public attention, for the first time, on the perceived Board neglect of the southern half of the County. On issue there was a feeling we had succeeded.

In the campaign, we made the issue of South Arlington neglect the center plank of the platform. Of course that matter would appeal to South Arlingtonians, to the extent it could be conveyed in a brief time, but not necessarily to voters in the North half of the County, as reflected in the precinct voter tabulations.

In the 15 or so years that followed, during which the Southern half of the County continued to be unrepresented on the Board, as described elsewhere herein, there was clearly some increased attention and sensitivity to the concerns of South Arlington, but not completely so as will be pointed out. The Post said that Pratt conducted a "raucous" campaign, but had done better than any other genuine independent candidate in recent memory.

Another event of the period worth noting in passing was the temporary return to the Board of ABC former member Richards in 1975. He was appointed to fill the unexpired term of Fisher who had been elected to the Congress.

The year 1976 was another milestone in the Board's composition in that two Republicans were elected in the November 1975 General election. Dorothy Grotos, a civic activist with specialties in environment, recreation, and youth programs, and Walter Frankland, a West Pointer and combat veteran of the Korean

Government and Political Growth

War, with extensive business and professional involvements, comfortably nosed out two ABC candidates and independents Julius Breener and George B. Gary.

Both Republican and ABC candidates had extensive and impressive records of heavy involvement in county civic affairs and community activities. All came well armed with knowledge of the county and its problems. It may have been, however, with a protracted period of only ABC membership on the Board, that there was a public feeling of a need for change, or more balance on the governing body. If so, that sentiment did not carry over into the next campaign.

In the 1976 election, ABC Board member John W. Purdy, a local lawyer, came up for reelection and was challenged unsuccessfully by Republican and retired and now deceased Air Force Lt. Gen. Daniel Graham. Graham has national prominence as an advocate of military missile defense weapons that later became known as SDI, or Star Wars during the Reagan Presidential years.

During the Purdy-Graham campaign an acrimonious dispute arose concerning the distribution of Purdy campaign literature in the publicly owned teacher message and mail boxes in the school system. Graham filed suit in the Federal District Court for an injunction to halt the practice, naming as defendants Purdy the candidate, the other County Board Members, the School Board members, the School Superintendent Larry Cuban, the Arlington Education Association President Karen Darner, and Patricia Pope, the Arlington Political Action Committee President. [19]

The Plaintiffs' suit came on for hearing before Judge Albert Bryan, Jr, but was dismissed as moot when counsels for the Defendants assured the Court that the practice had been discontinued.

In the General election Purdy received a little over 30,000 votes to Graham's 26,000. The Board composition in 1977 thus remained three ABC and two Republican.

In the 1977 campaign, this writer again ran, this time with Republican backing, against Bozman who was up for reelection. Bozman won easily but not greatly, roughly 17,000 to 13,000 votes. A third candidate, Arthur Vogel, also now deceased, received just under 2,000 votes. The party, or philosophical, tally of the Board in 1978, therefore, remained at three ABC and two Republican members.

REPUBLICANS REGAIN CONTROL

The following year was to see a change. The control shifted again to Republican with the election of Stephen Detwiler, to fill the seat vacated by Wholey who did not chose to run for reelection. Detwiler eased ahead of challenger ABC candidate Joseph N. Pelton by a vote of 21 to 19 thousand. Detwiler, a local banker, may have been helped by running on the same ticket with successful Congressional Republican candidates John Warner and Frank Wolfe.

Pelton, with a background in satellite communications and degrees in political science, had been extensively involved also in community affairs with the Civic

---

[19] *U. S. District Court for the Eastern District of Virginia, Civil Action No 76-800-A.*

Federation, the Committee of 100, and other local groups. Although Pelton was backed strongly by the ABC organization, his campaign literature seemed to downplay his ABC connections in favor of his Democratic Party activities. He had been campaign manager for an Arlington Delegate to the General Assembly, Warren Stambough, also deceased.

Republican control of the Board was to last for four years with the Frankland-Grotos-Detwiler majority through the year 1982. In the election of that year, Mary Margaret Whipple, former Chairman (person) of the School Board, defeated Detwiler in his bid for reelection.

Like Pelton before her, Whipple in her campaign literature seemed to soft peddle her ABC connections.[20] It was no great secret around the country, however, that she was strongly supported, morally, financially, with precinct and other workers, and otherwise, by the ABC-Democrat organization.

Thus the Board of 1983 returned to ABC, or ABC-Democrat, control with the Bozman, Whipple and John G. Milliken who was elected in 1980 to replace Purdy who did not chose to run for reelection. The Board has remained under ABC-Democrat control ever since and to this date.

Significant changes in Board membership in the recent years of ABC-Democrat control have included Michael E Brunner, a Republican in 1984; and ABC-Democrats Albert C. Eisenberg in 1984; William T. Newman, a local lawyer, and the first Black to be elected to the Board since the days of Reconstruction following the Civil War, in 1989; and James B. Hunter, III, elected in a special election in 1990 to replace Milliken who resigned to accept an appointment as the Virginia Secretary of Transportation.

In 1993, a Republican, Benjamin Winslow, was elected resulting in a board comprised of one Republican and four ABC/Democrat members. Winslow had been opposed by an admitted homosexual, Jay Fisette, in a special election to fill the seat vacated by board member William T. Newman, who had been appointed a Circuit Court Judge. There was much private, but little or no public, discussion as to whether Democrat Fisette's sexual orientation played any part in his defeat. His losing race was one of many by Democrats, but most others in Arlington that were being consistently won. Observers were left to draw their own conclusions but it appeared strongly that Arlington voters were not yet ready to accept a member of the Gay-Lesbian community to serve on the governing body.

Winslow's term on the board, however, was short lived. With two seats on the board to be filled in the election of 1995 he and his Republican colleague, Hennriette Warfield, lost to Democrat new comer Paul Ferguson and board member Al Eisenberg who ran for re-election. The following year, Democrat Christopher Zimmerman was elected to a board seat, and the board remained all Democrat in membership.

In 1997 the Arlington County Board membership consisted of Ellen Bozman as Chair, and members Albert Eisenberg, James Hunter, Paul Ferguson and Christopher Zimmerman.

---

[20] *Flyer, undated, Rinker and Whipple for Arlington County Board, 3260 Wilson Blvd, Arlington Va, 22201, By authority of James B. Hunter III, Treasurer.*

Government and Political Growth

* * *

In summary, it can be noted that the Arlington County Board over the 60 years since the community adopted the County Manger form of government in 1931, has been for most of those years comprised of and controlled by Democrats, either conservative or liberal.   Only in the following years has the Board been under the control of Republican or AIM/Republican members:

1953	1967	1980
1954	1969	1981
1955	1970	1982
	1979	

Few observers, if any, would disagree that Arlington County as a Metropolitan Washington urban community has been most fortunate in being spared from unqualified or inept, unethical, dishonest, or corrupt candidates for public office. There has been no incidence of graft or mismanagement of a type that would reflect on the character or integrity of any elected official in the County or any candidate for election.

The success or failure of a candidate seems clearly, although successful candidates may disagree, to have turned not so much on the personal qualifications of candidates, but more on either the issues surfacing at the time of a particular election, or upon the effectiveness of the political organization involved.

In that respect, objective and impartial citizens will contend that the success of the ABC-Democrat organization is largely attributable to an over powering, better financed and highly orchestrated and expertly managed political apparatus.

An examination of campaign expenditure reports will show that in almost every election in the past 30 years, the ABC-Democrats have far out spent their opponents. Additionally, they ordinarily, to their credit, have far more campaign workers involved in elections and their voter records and control is by far superior to their opponents.

Arlington voters, until just recently when a large influx of lower income foreign immigrants have altered the demographic composition of the Country, are mainly middle income, moderately disposed urban voters. Arlington with its heavy percentage of government, or government oriented, population is neither heavily Republican or Democrat in its political commitments or activities. For this reason, to a large extent, the voters tend to sway from party to party since no political group in the country seems to stray very far from the middle of the road in its political philosophy.

Whether this will continue, or for how long, remains to be seen. Changing demographics may well alter significantly the political outlook of Arlington voters. Only time will tell. There clearly is a need at this writing for more diversity on the governing body that is still comprised of only one political faction.

Impatient citizens waiting to speak?

At a meeting of the County Civic Federation on January 7, 1997, Board member Eisenberg, in response to a question from a delegate, expressed warm approval of the extensive demographic diversity in the County resulting from recent widespread immigration. He indicated that such diversity was "healthy and advantageous" for the County. He did not indicate why he did not feel that more political diversity in County Board membership might also be in order.

As 1997 neared an end, the picture concerning board composition became quite intriguing and complex with an unexpected development. In August, Board member Hunter announced his retirement because of advanced cancer thus generating an election for two board members, instead of one, in the November general election. Announced candidates for the seats being created by the retirement of long time member Ellen Bozman are Independent Amy Jones-Baskaran endorsed by the Republicans, and Democrat G. N. "Jay" Fisette, Jr. For the Hunter seat the candidates are Republican Benjamin Winslow and Democrat Barbara Favola who nosed out Diane Smith in a hastily called Democratic primary. An additional Independent candidate is African-American Joszet Hudson a former Democrat reported at "miffed at the Party" by writer Mike Allen in the September 25, 1997 Washington Post.

* * *

The late 1997 County Board, L-R: James Hunter (died January, 1998), Christopher Zimmerman, Ellen Bozman, Albert Eisenberg and Paul Ferguson.

AN INTERMISSION FROM THE TEXT
An Historical Vignette

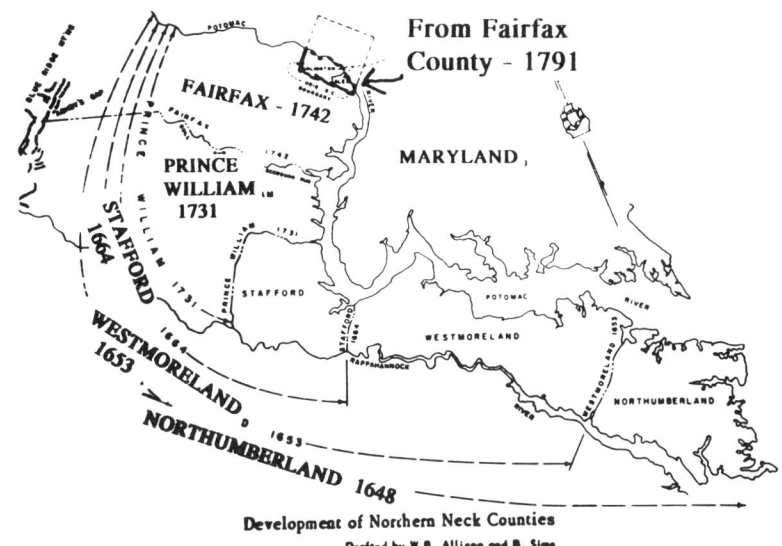

Development of Northern Neck Counties
Drafted by W.B. Allison and B. Sims

The area of Northern Virginia that became known as Arlington County in 1920, has been under more political jurisdictions that most, or any, other American community since the early days of Colonial settlement. The identity of those jurisdictions and the years the County was a part of them are:

Northumberland County	1648(?)-1653
Westmoreland County	1653-1664
Stafford County	1664-1731
Prince William County	1731-1742
Fairfax County	1742-1791
The District of Columbia	1791-1846
Alexandria County (less City of Alexandria)	1846-1920
Arlington County (less southern areas annexed by the City of Alexandria)	1920-

A TEXT INTERMISSION
An Historical Vignette

FEATURING
Night Bathing

100 Clean Amusements

ARLINGTON AMUSEMENT BEACH
SOUTH END HIGHWAY BRIDGE

Wonderful Shade Trees Clean Sand Beach
Clean, Clear, Fresh Water Always a Cool Breeze

Over the years, Arlington County residents have enjoyed numerous recreational facilities that are no longer extant. These included a beach and marina in the "twin bridges" area (above post card); a miniature "Disney World" or Coney Island type Luna Park where later was located the sewage treatment plant on South Glebe Road; and a picnic grounds, swimming hole, bar, dance hall, restaurant and "pavilion" at the Carlin Springs stop on the Washington and Ohio railroad line.

LUNA PARK

Government and Political Growth

AN INTERMISSION FROM THE TEXT
An Historical Vignette

Historical Society 1996 annual banquet speaker Roger Mudd presents an award certificate to member Darline Hannabass as Society President Sherman Pratt looks on.

Arlington County Board Chairman Albert Eisenberg (2nd from Rt.) presents 1996 "Historical Day" Proclamation to the Historical Society at the Hume School Museum. Society members, (L. to R.) Laura Watson, Virginia Knull, Norman Novak, Robert Watson (President), Mr Eisenberg, and Agnes Mullins.

AN INTERMISSION FROM THE TEXT
An Historical Vignette

The Thomas Selfridge grave and monument in Arlington Cemetery at about the location of the former Civil War Freedmen's Village. Selfridge, an Army Lieutenant, was killed in 1908 in the Fort Myer crash of a plane flown by Orville Wright. Selfridge, thus, became history's first airplane casualty as mentioned herein on pages 45 and 79.

CHAPTER FOUR

SOURCES OF INFLUENCE

Influence Source	Page
COUNTY CIVIC FEDERATION	109
COMMITTEE OF 100	116
COMMITTEE FOR SCHOOL IMPROVEMENT (CCSI)	121
COUNTY TAXPAYERS ASSOCIATION (ACTA)	124
PENTAGON CITY COORDINATION COMMITTEE	131
POLITICAL PARTIES AND MOVEMENTS	144
ARLINGTON EDUCATION ASSOCIATION	170
CHAMBER OF COMMERCE	171
COALITION ON TRANSPORTATION (ACT)	171

Arlington County, as with most American communities of any significant size, has its share of non-governmental, or "private" organizations, associations, or other such groups that meet and carry on their business and activities in and around the County. The Clerk of the County Board maintains a list of such groups and their leaders that, at this writing, is almost 26 pages in length.

The groups well nigh cover the spectrum for political, business, social, ethnic, religious, educational, professional, recreational, veterans, civic, and other activities. There are over forty neighborhood civic associations of homeowners, tenants and others.

Additionally, there are the usual "knife and fork" luncheon groups such as the Lions (4 clubs), Kiwanis (3 clubs), Rotary, JAYCEEs (2 clubs), Optimists and Soroptimists.

There are also organizations that operate essentially as a service, or to further the cause of, their own members such as the Police Beneficiary Association, the County Bar Association, the Professional Firefighters Association, the Business and Professional Women's Clubs (2), Girl and Boy Scouts Councils, certain Vietnamese, Chinese, Korean, Middle Eastern or other ethnic groups, the YMCAs, the Freemasons, service clubs, womens groups, and even the Gay and Lesbian Alliance.

Aside from the foregoing, there are also charitable, religious, educational, or other self supporting organizations that provide a public interest related service such as the Red Cross, the Historical Society, the Medical Society, the Food Assistance Center, the Arlington Extension Homemakers Council, the Children's Theater, Friends of Arlington Parks, League of Women Voters, or the Meals on Wheels of Northern Virginia, and of course churches of nearly all denominations. Lawyers and doctors may well feel that the Bar and Medical Associations more properly belong also in these categories. And well they might.

Arlington groups deliberate

Few, if any, of these organizations or activities, however, exert any significant influence on the County or its government officials with respect to the adoption of legislation, policies or practices or operational direction insofar as the institutions are concerned, although their members may do so individually, or by cross membership in other activities or groups as will be hereinafter discussed.

Indeed, most of the above groups were not organized and do not exist or function for such purposes as their names, LOGOs or descriptive titles will reflect. The Lions Clubs, organized in Chicago in 1917 claims its purposes to be "...to promote civic improvements, education, health, and international amity."

The Kiwanis charters provide that the purpose of the organization of men's fraternal clubs is "to cooperate in creating and maintaining that sound public opinion and high idealism which make possible the increase of righteousness, justice, patriotism and good will." The Optimist Clubs in their goals place heavy emphasis on youth recreational, patriotic, educational and other efforts to promote good citizenship and patriotism. The activities of these groups are closely related to the interests of the groups members, and few in their constitutions or bylaws provide for local political or civic activity to mould or control governmental policy or practice.

In contrast to the more passive Arlington county groups mentioned above, there are a number of activities, civic and political or otherwise, that have been active and heavily involved in trying to influence or persuade government bodies to their points of view. The subject groups appear before Boards, Commissions, Staff offices, or whatever other responsive ears available that are perceived to have power or authority. The groups lobby, provide forums, generate and carry on publicity promotional efforts, adopt civic or political positions, or otherwise try in various ways to educate or orient the public and local government to their points of view.

It is to these more "influential" groups and activities we will now turn our attention. In describing a particular group or the nature and history of their operations

Sources of Influence

they are taken in no particular order, nor is there an attempt to assess their relative effectiveness. That role will be left to the reader or the observer of past or contemporary county events.

* * *

THE COUNTY CIVIC FEDERATION

The Arlington County nongovernmental organization that has probably had the greatest influence on county affairs, in widely varying degrees from time to time, over the longest period, has been the Arlington County Civic Federation. The Federation membership in recent years has consisted mainly of some 40-50 neighborhood civic associations.

The Federation's membership, however, has also included over the years many additional community organizations and activities. These include, at this writing the following:

The League of Women Voters;
The American Association of University Women;
The Arlington Education Association;
The Arlington Heritage Alliance;
The Arlington Historical Society;
The Arlington Taxpayers Association;
Delta Kappa Gamma;
The Arlington Jay Cees;
Friends of Arlington Parks; and
The Pro-Bolivian Committee.

From time to time, when a controversial, or exceptionally important issue arose, certain ad hocs groups have also been members of the Federation for short or temporary periods.[1]

The origins of the Federation, based on its records and available sketchy information in the Virginia Room of the Arlington County Central Library, in whose Community Archives the Federation records are filed, seem to date from the year 1916. At that time, six local civic associations in Arlington, then still known as the "county part of Alexandria County" joined forces in what was to become known today as the Arlington County Civic Federation.[2] The concern of the groups then was primarily roads and schools, both of which the groups wanted improved.

---

[1] *A list of all Federation members is included in the Appendix.*

[2] *Arlington Historian Bruce Gregory McCoy records that the County's first neighborhood citizens association of record was the Cherrydale Citizens Association, dating from 1900; followed by the Ft Myer Heights, Ballston, Clarendon and Parkway Associations in 1912, 1913 and 1914, respectively. McCoy's list probably should have included the Glencarlyn Association also organized about 1900.*

ARLINGTON COUNTY - A Modern History

One of the first actions of the new Federation was to attempt to prod the Alexandria County Supervisors into action on a number of matters of concern. Records in the Arlington Library's Virginia Room indicate that the following letter was sent to the Supervisors on March 14, 1916.

> *"At the last meeting of the Civic Federation an extensive discussion was had of the various improvements which are urgently needed in the County viz; good roads, a larger school building, a water supply system and a sewage disposal system.*
> *"We hope for improvements; or any future solution, except by bond issue.*
> *"We come to urge you to determine the cost.*
> *"We suggest the State Highway Commission send an engineer to estimate the cost of road and State building necessary.....*
> *"We believe a splendid future lies before this county. You have an opportunity to do great constructive work.*
> *G. S. Luckett, Sec."*

A brief description of the Federation history and functioning appears in the 1967 issue of its Constitution and By-Laws, and includes the following:

> *"One of the Federation's greatest contributions to the county has been to serve as a sounding board for all citizens on matters of civic interest. Its delegates represent the grass roots" opinions of the ordinary citizens, regardless of political or partisan affiliation, on civic matters, and thus it may be truly said that the Federation is the Voice of Arlington".*

As stated, the influence of the Federation seems to have varied considerably over the years. At certain times the prestige of the Federation reached high levels and a cursory review of the newspapers in some years reveal that seldom was there an issue without a lead page one story reflecting the influence and energy of Federation actions. For example the Alexandria Gazette on November 6, 1929, carried the following story on page one.

> "Arlington County Civic Federation
> Passes resolution at last Night's Meeting.
> MANY AT MEETING

Sources of Influence

The following letter addressed to Mr Edward Duncan, chairman of the Arlington County Board of Supervisors, was adopted last evening unanimously at the regular monthly meeting of the Arlington County Civic Federation with a goodly number in attendance and was signed by the various delegates there...."

Other prominent page one lead story press coverage of the Federation's actions selected at random and considered typical of the period, include the following:

CIVIC FEDERATION FAVORS ELECTION OF SCHOOL BOARD MEMBERS
Arlington Chronicle, June 9, 1944.
FEDERATION TOLD COUNTY MUST HAVE INCINERATOR NOW
The Arlington Sun, Jan 5, 1945.
FEDERATION SEEKS TO COORDINATE WAR MEMORIAL PLANS
The Sun, Feb 9, 1945.
FEDERATION FAILS TO ACT ON PROPOSAL TO BOOST REVENUE
The Sun, March 9, 1945.
CIVIC FEDERATION VOTES 29 to 10 AGAINST (TAX) INCREASE
The Sun, April 6, 1945.
FEDERATION OFFERS 3 FOR SCHOOL BOARD
The Sun, May 4, 1945.
FEDERATION URGES CONTRACT SYSTEM FOR DOG POUND
The Sun, June 8, 1945.
FEDERATION ASKS BOARD MEMBERS BE ELECTED AT ONE TIME
The Sun, October 5, 1945.
FEDERATION ASKS SPEEDIER PURCHASE OF PLAYGROUNDS
The Sun, Nov 16, 1945.
FEDERATION ASKS GAS RATE PROBE
The Sun. Sept 13, 1946.

A study of the records of the press for extended periods before and after the above cited articles reveal that the omission of mention of the Federations actions and positions following Federation monthly meetings, was the exception rather than the rule. The Federation seems to have almost always gotten prompt attention and on page one in one of the lead stories of an issue.

In more recent years the contrary seems to have been the practice. When this writer was active in the Federation in the 1960's and early 1970's as Chairman of the Legislative and Local Government and Executive Committees, and as President, and in the years thereafter to date, publicity for the Federation was almost non-existent. Further, the minutes of the County Board meetings are not lacking in instances where the Board took actions and made decisions, contrary to the positions and recommendations of Federation representatives appearing before the Board.

ARLINGTON COUNTY - A Modern History

FEDERATION FUNCTIONING

Pursuant to its Constitution the Federation meets monthly, except during July and August, unless the President calls a special meeting. For many years it met in the Dawson Terrace Recreation Center on North Taft Street, and at the Lyon Park Community Center near Pershing Drive and South Filmore Street, but more recently at the Arlington Hospital Social Hall on George Mason Drive.[3]

Each member Association or Group is authorized to designate four delegates, and four alternates any four of which may attend Federation meetings, each with one vote. Ordinarily only one or two delegates from each member association or group attends Federation meetings. Membership dues were $20 per annum until 1985, at which time they were increased to $30.

Once a year the Federation holds its annual banquet, at various locations around the county but most recently at the Sheraton National Hotel on Columbia Pike, and, in 1997, at the Fort Myer Officers Club. At the banquet, the delegate, or committee, who has made "the greatest contribution to civic endeavor in Arlington during the year" is presented with a Trophy known as the Evening Star Award until the late 1970's when that newspaper ceased publishing. Afterwards the Journal Newspapers have presented the award. Additionally, from 1936 to 1960, eight individuals have been designated as "Members of the Order of Distinguished and Meritorious Service."[4]

* * *

The bulk of the Federation's activities center around the work of its various standing committees, and their reports to the assembled Federation for its consideration and action, if any. Delegates are appointed to the committees based on their interests or backgrounds and committee chairmen are appointed by the Federation President, usually with help from the Executive Committee, following the annual election of officers.

For many years there were 14 standing committees in the Federation but in 1985 they were reduced to 11, to wit; Membership, Constitution and By-Laws, Public Services, Legislation, Transportation, Planning and Zoning, Conservation and Beautification, Schools, Revenue and Expenditures, Parks Recreation and Cultural Affairs, and Housing.

The busiest committees on a continuing bases have probably been the Zoning and Schools committees since they consider matters, proposals or problems that are regularly considered by the appropriate county authorities throughout the year. The Revenues and

---

[3] *At this writing the Hospital consolidated with another health facility and became known as the Columbia Arlington Hospital.*

[4] *The names of the persons thus designated, and recipients of the Star and Journal Trophy Awards are shown in the Appendix hereto.*

Sources of Influence

Expenditures Committee is most busy during County or School Board budget consideration times each year. The work of other committees is concentrated at times when a matter arises that is within their area of interest or concern.

In early 1993 the Federation published an Index of the subjects that had been considered and acted upon for the period 1986 to 1993. In addition to the usual and routine matters such as the County budgets, schools, legislation, parks, land use, or public safety, the index reflected that the Federation had also considered many diverse matters to include the following:

Preservation of the Abingdon Plantation ruins at National Airport.
Proposals for County actions to cope with the AIDS problems.
Actions with respect to creating Affordable Housing.
Operation of the Airport Authority (National and Dulles).
County actions concerning the Chesapeake Bay preservation.
Establishment of detoxification centers.
Elderly care centers.
Proposals concerning the establishment of Family Life Programs.
Shelters for the homeless.
A proposed urban forestry program.

Positions of the Federation on a particular issue or matter are usually reported by the Committee Chairman, or other Federation leadership, to the decision making bodies of the County at the next regular meeting. These include the County Board, the School Board, the Planning Commission, and sometimes, the Board of Zoning Appeals. Contacts are also often made with the County Manager staff.

The Federation Constitution provides that there shall be a President, Vice President, and Treasurer, elected at the annual June meeting and a Secretary chosen by the Executive Committee. Although the Constitution does not specify how many terms an officer may serve, the well established custom has been for Presidents to serve no more than two terms.

CIVIC ASSOCIATION MEMBERSHIP

The names of the neighborhood associations that comprise the membership of the Federation usually indicate the geographical part of Arlington County that is represented by a particular association, such as Claremont, Donaldson Run, Lyon Village, Nauck, Arlington Ridge, East Falls Church, Columbia Pike, Central Arlington, Glencarlyn or Washington-Lee.[5]

Since each association determines its own boundaries not every part of the County is necessarily represented by a civic association, although most citizens of the County will reside within the boundaries of one or more associations.

---

[5] *A list of member neighborhood Civic Associations in included in the Appendix.*

The resolution of disputes by associations as to their boundaries are attempted by the Membership committee, but not always successfully. There have been instances when two adjoining associations claimed the same street or block in which case a resident could claim membership in either or both of the associations. Most associations endeavor to build their membership to the maximum and are loath to deny membership to anyone residing within their claimed boundaries even if they overlap with another association.

Citizen interest in civic associations has often been determined by events that are perceived to affect the population, and particularly themselves, for better or worse. There is no legal requirement in law that there be a civic association, or that citizens join and pay dues to an association. Most associations can claim only a fraction of the residents within their boundaries as dues paying members, and usually no more than a dozen or two members or guests attend monthly, or periodic, meetings of most associations except when there is an issue of extraordinary interest or concern.

For these reasons, among others, spokespersons for associations are often looked upon by County officials with some cynicism or doubt. This writer remembers on more than one occasion appearing before the County Board to report on a position taken by the Arlington Ridge Civic Association on a matter in controversy only to have a  Board member peer inquisitorially and ask, "How many of your members were present when that position was taken, and how many voted for or against the position?"

Neighborhood associations have been known to spring into existence, or fade away into inactive status from time to time, depending on the emergence, or resolution, of some particular problem or controversy over which the citizenry becomes concerned. These matters could include the proposed construction or enlargement of a road or highway such as Interstate I-395 or I-66, or a major development such as Pentagon City, or the location of a County operated facility such a detoxification center, a fire station, a sewage treatment plant, or any other proposal that is believed to impact, adversely or not, on the locality in particular, or the County generally.

For many years the Federation sponsored an annual "Federation Recognition Day" during which the goal was to more widely promote the purposes and activities of the organization so that wider participation could be generated. To achieve better press coverage the Executive Committee of the Federation at that time asked this writer to prepare letters to the Editors describing the Federation and its work. Whereupon this author wrote such an item for the Federation that was published in the Northern Virginia Sun on March 4, 1975, and in other local newspapers at about the same time. The item highlighted the history, operations, functions and purposes of the Federation and is in the Appendix herein.

SOME AUTHOR OBSERVATIONS

But for all the weakness of the voluntary and unofficial neighborhood civic associations as a barometer of public sentiment, there seems to be no more reliable gauge of the collective local public will in the neighborhoods of Arlington County than the Civic Federation's member Associations - other than, perhaps, the official ballot box in

Sources of Influence

the duly conducted official elections. This seems especially true since the governing County Board members are elected at-large by county wide voting without any requirement that they reside in any particular, or "local" part of the County.

Thus there is no one member of the governing body that can be said to be the exclusive representative for any particular local part of the county, no matter how strongly defenders of the at-large voting system may feel otherwise. So long as Board members are elected at-large, the neighborhood civic associations provide the only real and most correctly attuned, or the most effective, local voices before county decision making bodies, or the Manager's staff for any parts of the county in which a board member does not reside.

* * * *

Arlingtonians waiting for local County Board Member?

115

THE COMMITTEE OF 100

Through the years, there has been no shortage of media attention for Arlington County's Committee of 100.

On January 13, 1979, Arlington Journal writer Jim Wolfe, with a headline "Arlington's 'Think Tank' is 25", reported that the County's Committee of 100 was meeting to celebrate its 25th birthday. He described the Committee as a place "where people of diametrically opposing viewpoints can gather to talk calmly and rationally about their (civic) differences.

Washington Post writer Evelyn Hsu, on June 13, 1987, in an article headlined "Arlington's Committee of 100 wields a lot of Quiet Influence" described how the Committee "has played a pivotal role in Arlington's civic life"..."as a forum where current and often controversial issues are discussed". She pointed out that almost everyone from State Senators and Delegates, to County and School Board and Planning Commission members, and other elected officials, to business community leaders, civic activists, and countless other community groups, were Committee of 100 members and faithful and regular participants.

15 years after Journal reporter Wolfe's account, on June 1, 1994, Arlington Courier staff writer Joe Farruggia, reported that the Committee was meeting on June 8th in the dining room of Marymount University to celebrate its 40th anniversary with a special program "Challenges in Arlington's Future" Farruggia wrote that the committee was a "select group of Arlington civic and business leaders, politicians, educators and other shakers and movers ... meeting monthly to tackle the most pressing issues facing the County and its citizenry".

Writer Wolfe explained that the seeds for the Committee were planted when "eleven moderate Arlingtonians joined together after a liberal County Board had just been dismantled by businessmen who used an obscure state law to remove three members of the old 'Non-Partisan' party".[6] Wolfe wrote that the liberals had infuriated the business interests by seizing control of the county planning commission and by voting large increases in business taxes. Wolfe quoted an early founder, Lyle Bryant, (see below) as saying, "We (the moderates) decided something had to be done, so we decided to form a committee to become a forum...the community divisions had grown so sharp the country government was virtually paralyzed".

With respect to the reasons and circumstances that brought about the 1956 formation of the Committee of 100, the group has this to say, in part, in a brochure dated

---

[6] *The three board members were removed by court order because they were Federal employees and found ineligible to serve. This is discussed in more detail in Chapter III herein.*

Sources of Influence

December 1989 entitled, "The Arlington Committee of 100, A forum of Civic Leaders Seeking solutions to Community Problems.":

> *"The aim from the beginning was to counteract the polarization of thinking about community problems which had developed in Arlington's civic and political life after World War II. People without economic stakes in the County beyond home ownership - and particularly new arrivals - tended in their social civic and political as well as their economic activities, to be walled off from the County's business and professional people...invective had all but replaced thoughtful discussion of public issues...there was a stalemate because in both camps political activity was aimed mainly at frustrating initiatives from the other camp without regard to merit...The founders of the Committee sought a way out of the impasse...they sought to turn conflict into constructive channels by building and maintaining bridges over...the chasm...Accordingly, they undertook to being together, in roughly equal proportions and in an atmosphere favorable for their getting to know each other as persons, the more moderate of the "local" and the "commuter" leaders for thoughtful discussions of community concerns. The dinner-forum session preceded by a social hour was hit upon as a means for creating the right atmosphere."*

FOUNDING

The Committee of 100 was founded in 1954 at a meeting in Hogates Restaurant on Wilson boulevard by a group of eleven individuals headed, mainly, by Lyle C. Bryant, a resident of Arlington since 1941.[7] Bryant was to remain active, and a driving force in the organization until his death in 1983. He was a native of Wisconsin and held degrees from Beloit College and the University of Chicago. He held a number of professional positions with the federal government and on the faculties of colleges and universities. Bryant focused on community urban planning and development and was a member of a long list of Arlington and metropolitan committees, commissions and other civic groups. Bryant stressed the importance of providing programs of deep substance and initiated the practice of preliminary "dry runs" or warm-up practice sessions before each meeting to insure the programs would be well organized and effectively implemented.

In a statement adopted at a later meeting on November 10th, the Committee announced that its purposes were:

> *"To study the essential interest, problems and goals of the people of the County for the purpose of furthering a general and common understanding of older and newer problems and the efforts*

---

[7] *The group included prominent Arlingtonians Lucas H. Blevens, Kingsley Higgins, Barnard Joy, B. Alden Lillywhite, Leon Logan, Clyde Merriam, John Newdorp, Charles Rideout, Thomas Sebrell III, and Dorothy Terborgh.*

necessary to their reasonable solution. As a group not to influence directly action for or against local issues or urge approval or disapproval of specific projects or propositions."

Journal writer Farruggia echoed these sentiments years later in his 1994 report. He wrote, "the Committee...does try to solve problems as much as offer a forum through which all sides can express their views and raise questions".

MEMBERSHIP

The November statement provided that membership in the Committee of 100 was to be classified as:

"Commuters" who were Arlingtonians who worked outside the County, or Federal workers who were employed in Arlington;
"Local businessmen" who represented different types of business or professions who earned their living from operation of a business or were employed in a business located in Arlington, and;
"Unclassified", that included retired persons, employees of County or State government, and those holding local public office.

The November statement further provided that membership in the Committee was to include "ample representation from the different service clubs, apartment dwellers as well as home owners, and women and young adults as well as older persons". Married women were to be classified on the basis of the occupation of their husbands. Persons could become members upon invitation of 2/3 of the Membership Committee, but their membership could be forfeited at the end of any quarter in which their attendance fell below 60%.

ORGANIZATION

The November 1954 statement provided that the officers of the Committee of 100 "shall be an Executive Committee of 9 members, and a co-chairmen, with such other officers, committees or officials as the Executive Committee deem to be necessary to carry on the work of the organization" and that the officers "shall be elected each year to serve for one year terms". The statement also specified that there would be an Executive and Nominating Committee, and other committees such as membership, arrangements and publicity and such other committees as the Executive Committee determined to be needed. The head of the Committee is known as the Chairman.

MEETINGS

The first regular meeting of the Committee of 100 took place on September 15, 1954. The subject was "Transportation - problems and implications". There was another meeting in September, two in October, none in November and one in December. In 1955 there were two meetings in January and two in February, and one each month

Sources of Influence

thereafter to date except for Summer months of July and August. In recent years the Committee has met on the second Wednesday of each month in the dining room of Gerard Phelan Hall of Marymount University on North Glebe Road. Attendance is by reservation only and is limited the capacity of the dining room, usually about 175.

The subject scope of the Committee's meetings include just about any and all matters of major importance or concern to the community from taxes, education, crime, development and recreation to energy, environmental, consumer, housing, and other affairs. Most of the subjects programmed have been repeated many times as conditions change over the years. A tabulation of the program subjects, and the times they have been presented, is listed below: (as of 1989 and as listed by Committee documents)

Subject Classification	Number of Programs
Citizen involvement	10
Collective bargaining	4
Committee of 100 - internal affairs	5
Communications media	7
Community goals and leadership	20
Community role of the church	2
Consumer Problems	2
Crime and Justice	17
Cultural Development	9
Economic Development	29
Energy and Environmental Issues	13
Fiscal Affairs	17
Higher Education	17
Housing	9
Human Resources Conservation and Development	27
Land Planning and Development	31
Minority Participation	10
Organization of County Government	16
Parks and Recreation	4
Perspective on the Urban Crisis	3
Political Process	5
Population growth and Demography	12
Regionalism - Metropolitanism	9
School Problems	25
State Issues - Commonwealth Relations	16
Transportation	22

Through its years the Committee of 100 has remained vibrant and influential. Although the group calls itself a committee of 100, the membership has usually varied from 200-300. The attendance at monthly meetings is not ordinarily more than 175 since that is the capacity of the dining room at Marymount University. Occasionally some additional persons will be accommodated when they attend without eating.

ARLINGTON COUNTY - A Modern History

The success of the Committee in achieving its goals and maintaining interest and participation can probably be attributed to a large extent on the policy of free and open discussion without rancor on subjects of keen local interest, and by avoiding taking positions on the matters discussed. In an article titled "An Integrative Force: Arlington's Committee of 100, in the May 1976 issue of National Civic Review, Mary E. Stowe, a staff member of the Northern Virginia Community Education Program, lists her reasons for the Committee of 100's success. First, she lists the rule of the group that all subjects be present on a nonpartisan basis, fairly and thoroughly with speakers and other discussants that are knowledgeable on the subject. She thinks that, knowing this, the majority of the members come to meetings open minded, waiting to hear the facts and then reasoning behind the proposals presented.

Secondly, Stowe believes a reason for harmony in the rules against ever taking positions on the subjects it explored. She writes that this is known thoroughly by even those few who come to meetings already committed to a point of view. She notes that even though arguments can be presented, there can be no attempt to introduce motions or to seek or expect actions by the Committee as a whole. In such circumstances, there can be no "victories" or losses, and thus no ill feelings or resentments.

Next, Stowe notes, as a benefit to the Committee, that the program committee deliberately chooses subject matter not yet explored by the community to any great extent, neglected subject matter, or angles so new that community leaders have not yet taken sides. She asserts that this practice not only helps bring neglected issues to public attention but also provides full exploration before too many people in decision making positions have split into opposing camps.

Lastly, Stowe points out that the Committee of 100 provides a diversity of participation found in no other county organization. Membership is conferred by the executive board, on the basis of nomination by present members, to those reflecting a wide range of local interests and are experienced in community leadership and thoughtfulness. She points out that from its beginning the organization has sought representatives of all significant elements; Republicans, Democrats, Independents, liberals and conservatives, local officials, national officials who live in Arlington even if they work elsewhere, and business, professional and industrial leaders, educators, church and civic leaders and various races and ethnic groups.

The Chairpersons of the Committee of 100 are listed in the Appendix herein.

* * *

Sources of Influence

CITIZENS COMMITTEE ON SCHOOL IMPROVEMENT (CCSI))

At the end of World War II, thousands of newcomers to Arlington who had arrived during the war to work for, or with, the Federal government, or the war effort, settled in the County as permanent residents. Many of these people and families, with an ending of the war effort, refocused their attention on peacetime problems and their own local community affairs. In particular they, as well as many longer time residents, were displeased with the Arlington school system and what they perceived to be a lack of priority on education.

On April 15, 1946, the Arlington County Board and the School Board that then was appointed, and not elected, met in a joint session to consider the school budget for the coming year. The lengthy meeting was well attended by citizens and speakers for organizations who strongly urged that more money be raised for school purposes. The need for an expanded school plant and program was stressed and that more money was needed to accomplish these goals.

To the disenchantment and intense displeasure of most of the speakers, the Boards adopted a resolution calling for only a five cent increase in the school tax. This was characterized as "niggardly" by the advocates of more school money, who claimed it would cover only additional operating expenses and would not permit the implementation of any new programs or buildings.

Three weeks later in May, a group of the disgruntled proponents for more educational money met and organized a new movement they called The Citizens Committee for School Improvement, or CCSI. They described their group as a "voluntary organization of citizens who are interested in improving Arlington's schools ...county-wide and non-partisan in character, with members of both major political parties from all parts of the county." [8]

No doubt there were citizens around at the time who wondered about the accuracy of that description of the new movement, but there can be no question that the group quickly became a dominant factor in County policies and politics for a period of over ten years until finally superseded, as a practical matter, by a later organized political group known as "Arlingtonians for a Better County" that exists to this day as elsewhere herein explained.[9]

The CCSI promptly announced their goals, generally. They wanted a change in the system of selecting school board members; i.e., by popular election rather than

---

[8] *CCSI file, Virginia Room, Main Arlington County Library.*

[9] *An examination of the CCSI and ABC files in the Virginia Room of the County Main Library will reveal that the leadership in the two organizations was substantially identical.*

appointment by either the courts or the County Board and the establishment of "democratic methods through which a nominating convention selects representative candidates for the school board". [10] They also initiated drives for bond issues for school construction in 1947, 1948, 1951 and 1952.

In more specificity, the CSSI stated their goals as follows.[11]

> "A change in the system of selecting the County School Board, to provide for election by the voters.
>
> Establishment of democratic methods through which a nominating convention selects representative candidates for the School Board.
>
> Election of School Board members having the background, interest and convictions required to raise standards of education throughout the system."

Over the decade or so of its most active existence, the CCSI worked energetically and effectively to achieve its goals in many diverse ways. One of its earliest successes occurred in 1947 concerning its announced objective of changing the method of selecting School Board members. The group had expressed particular dissatisfaction with the practice of Circuit Court appointment of board members based on recommendations of a School Trustee Electoral Board appointed by the Circuit Court. Many felt this procedure excessively removed the board from an adequate responsiveness to the public. CCSI members asserted that the procedure had not resulted in the appointment of individuals who were sufficiently experienced in educational matters or very highly motivated toward improving the school system. They believed that popular election would be more democratic and result in a correction of board shortcomings.

CCSI achieved the passage of special legislation to allow a referendum on the question of changing the method of selecting school board members and whether the selection should be by County Board appointment, or by popular vote.

Pursuant to the new legislation, in the Spring of 1947 CCSI filed a petition of 5,200 signatures with the Arlington County Circuit Court asking for an order for a referendum on the question of changing the method of selecting members of the School Board. Circuit Judge Walter T. McCarthy granted the petition and designating Tuesday, May 27 as the day for the referendum.[12]

The voters opted for an elected school board and in a heated election that followed, CCSI supported candidates won control of the school board.[13] Although the

---

[10] *CCSI file, Ibid.*

[11] *CCSI flyer, The Citizens Committee for School Improvement, WHAT - HOW - WHY - WHO, The Virginia Room, Ibid.*

[12] *The Arlington Sun, April 11, 1947, page 1, microfilm, the Virginia Room, Ibid.*

[13] *The successful candidates were; Elizabeth Campbell, Barnard Joy, Colin C. McPherson, C.E. Tuthill, and E. R. Draheim.*

Sources of Influence

new elected board member arrangement survived a subsequent court challenge, the victory for CCSI was somewhat short lived. In 1956, following the U. S. Supreme Court decision in Brown v. School Board that ordered desegregation of public schools, and the "massive resistance" policy of Virginia, the General Assembly terminated the authority of Arlington to elect its school board. Since that date until the return of the elected board in the 1990s the board has been appointed by the County Board. (see Chap V, p. 182)

New legislation in 1992, after many years of effort by proponents, provided authority for another referendum on the question of electing school boards. The issue was on the ballot in the November 1993 election and approved by the voters. Some dissatisfaction existed, however, since the ballot proposal called for the election of school board members at-large, without any requirement that they live in any particular part of the county. County sources who favored a return to single member electoral districts for governing body members, also strongly objected to the at-large election of school board members. They felt that a single member, multi-district system should also apply for school board members so that all county localities will be assured of a board member from their own neighborhoods. But such was not to be. At least for the time being.

The first chairman, and the founder of the CCSI is identified in CCSI literature as being one Oscar R. LeBeau, followed in 1948 by Co-Chairmen Mr and Mrs Joseph Wheeler of South 18th Street. The group was organized into 15 standing committees and met at regular meetings as determined by the leadership. Between the meetings, work was carried on by an Executive Committee consisting of the officers and the chairmen of the committees. There was an annual dues of $2 per family.

Almost immediately after organization the group became politically active. In the 1946 election CCSI threw its weight behind Independent "Town Meeting" independent candidate Daniel A. Dugan, and he was elected to the County Board on a platform containing most of the CCSI positions. Although the CCSI backed candidate Lee Potter failed to win a Board seat in the 1947 election, the influence and strength of the CCSI in the following years, and especially early 1950s continued to grow and school construction bonds endorsed by the group were steadily approved by the voters.

Although the CCSI has long ago faded into history as an active and vibrant part of Arlington affairs, its influence and after effects have not. As stated, many CCSI members became leaders in the ABC political movement of the 1950s and that organization quickly gained control of the county government and has held that control, often exclusively, for most of the past four decades. This development has not met, of course, with universal acceptance throughout the county.

Political opponents, usually Republicans, and some moderates and conservatives have complained that they have been all but completely excluded from participating in the governing process. Additionally, advocates of a more structured or traditional approach to education assert that the surviving, more liberal, education philosophies and practices of the progeny of CCSI are not best for Arlington's youth, as is discussed in more detail elsewhere herein.

* * *

THE ARLINGTON COUNTY TAXPAYERS ASSOCIATION

The ACTA Bulldog

Probably no organization in Arlington County credited with having influence on county affairs, is more controversial, contentious and adversarial to the governing apparatus, and the partisan political group that dominates the government, than is the Arlington County Taxpayers Association, or ACTA.

Representatives of ACTA appear regularly before the County Board, especially during annual consideration of the County budget, and testify concerning on-going or proposed County projects and expenditures, taxes and tax rates, and other fiscal and financial matters. Leaders and committees of the group meet periodically to study, analyze, and evaluate County programs and expenditures as to need and necessity or affordability, and then report their findings and positions, and often oppositions, to their members, the public, and the County Board at regular appropriate sessions.

It is also probably quite safe to write, that no other non-government activity or group in the county carries out a continuing study of government fiscal affairs that is more sophisticated, scholarly, in depth, detailed, comprehensive and evaluative than that performed by ACTA. The results of ACTA's deliberations are more often than not, critical and, therefore, not very popular with the county managers staff and especially the elected governing body political members. Nor, for that matter it seems, are ACTA's recommendations very often adopted by the County government. There are no shortages of instances, however, when county actions have been modified, altered, or even dropped, in the face of ACTA voiced opposition.

More, perhaps, than any other activity in the County, and, as stated, often the only voice in the county, ACTA will urge spending restraints, less waste, and more efficient and economical operation of the County government even if such moves might jeopardize pet social programs of what ACTA considers to be the strongly liberal governing body.

Sources of Influence

The Association was formed in 1974, initially as an ad hoc group, by a group of citizens who voiced concern over the size of government and what they perceived to be the constant increases in taxes and the budget. According to Ralph Baylor, one of the founders, ACTA was formed out of frustration by citizen who felt they were not heard by their elected officials.

"Why doesn't someone do something?", related Baylor. "They said I was always complaining, why didn't I do something? So I decided I would," he said. Whereupon the Association came into being. Early organizers of ACTA included such widely known individuals as Roy Newbold, Harrison Mann, George Mason Green, Ruth Graham, Scott McGeary, Philip King, James Olmsted. Norman Miller and Allen Harrison.

"Let's do something!!!"

The presiding officer of ACTA through the years has included some of the above early organizers, plus other prominent Arlingtonians to include John Torbet, Halvor Ekern, Robert Harrington, Dorothy Grotos and, in the late 1980's and early '90s, Benjamin J. Gault, John Rosso, Donald MacQueen, and Tim McCune. Directors and other leaders have also included many of the above, plus Leslie Haynes, Col Bruce Jones, Frederick Tutt, Paul Martin, Norman McChesney, George Gilmore, Angelo Iandolo, Donald MacQueen, Allen Schirmer, Former U. S. Department of Transportation Secretary Frank Turner, Francis Hewitt, a U. S. House of Representatives Appropriations Committee Staff director, who served as secretary and historian for many years until his death in the late 1980s, Timothy Wise, long time editor of the Association's newsletter "The Watchdog", and Aldyth Peterson the more recent secretary of the Association.

ACTA MEMBERSHIP

It can be pointed out that many, perhaps most, of the participants in ACTA over the years have also been active in County Republican affairs or served as Republicans in the State Legislature or on the County Board, or ran for public office as Republicans. Some, however, could more properly be identified as independents, or apolitical, such as Cindy Reed, Josephine Barber and Francis Hewitt. Although Taxpayer Association membership has included individuals from the dominant ABC-Democrat political establishment from time to time, to include the present, such involvement has usually been the exception rather than the rule.

INCORPORATION

The organization was incorporated on October 2, 1974 under the laws of Virginia with Articles signed by Ralph Baylor, Elizabeth Edmiston, Thelma Fruitman and Gideon Leslie Haynes.

1. To provide information on the principles of efficient government, public finance and taxation, and to engage in educational endeavors to carry out corporate purposes...

2. To promote honest, economical and responsible government and defend the rightful interests of Association members in the administration of governmental affairs affecting Arlington County...

3. To examine the assessment, collection, and expenditure of tax funds affecting Arlington County...

4. To make recommendations to appropriate elected and appointed officials in matters in which the Association has a rightful interest...

5. To inform members and citizens of government plans and policies that are of concern to them...

6. To analyze the County annual budget, and the budget formulation process, the School Budget, and joint enterprises with other jurisdiction to which the County may commit resources (i.e. Metro, parks, etc)...

7. To establish contacts with local, state, and/or federal officials and with others as appropriate to achieve the purposes and objectives of the Association..., and

8. To prepare, initiate, and/or support legislation and legislative changes necessary to serve the policies of the Association.

* * *

One of the first acts of ACTA, which earned it wide publicity, was to file suit against the County in Circuit Court in September, 1974. The suit claimed the County had violated its own regulations with respect to tax collections for 17 years since 1957. ACTA claimed the County had not printed and adopted formally an assessment manual so that citizens would know what procedures were used, and had been used, to determine their real estate values for taxing purposes.

The assessment suit, along with several others subsequently filed by ACTA against the County Board, resulted in changes, or county government actions, desired by ACTA. The suits also served to familiarize many citizens, and especially the County Board, with the existence of ACTA and that henceforth ACTA was a force to be reckoned with.

* * *

In an Arlington Journal May 8, 1975 article headlined "Taxpayer Unit: Watchdog or Pest?", staff writer Chris Jensen asked whether ACTA was;

Sources of Influence

    (1) A vigilant watchdog over the county's fiscal affairs, asking some very valid questions about how the county's coffers are filled and where the money goes; or

    (2) A bothersome group led largely by Republicans but using their professed "independent" status to launch attacks on the county's all Arlingtonians for a Better County (ABC) Democrat County Board.

Writer Jensen reported that ACTA's early, and perhaps first, Chairman Roy Newbold favored the first description, whereas ACTA critics, usually preferred the second. Jensen wrote that critics, "usually Democrats or members of ABC scoff at the ACTA claims of being non-political and say the group is just a front for the Republican Party. However, one top Democrat concedes 'some of the things they criticize deserve to be criticized'".

Not all journalists have been as critical of ACTA, openly or inferentially, as writer Jensen. Arlington Journal editorial page columnist Don Lynch in a 1994 article credited ACTA with "an exhaustive analysis of the county government's taxing and spending", and [ACTA] "has found that Arlingtonians keep getting less for more... One would think that with new technology, equipment and facilities, the government would be more efficient and productive. One would be wrong". Lynch then itemized items in the school budget, an increase in the number of county employees per family, the "luxurious jail", and several other items to support his position. He added, "..the County Board is able to confiscate and waste the earnings of its tax slaves as skillfully as its counterparts in Fairfax County and Alexandria".

* * *

Generally, over the years, ACTA has objected to tax increases, or the rate of increases with respect to real estate, and has repeatedly urged tighter rein on governmental growth, routine operations, and many spending projects that the association considered to be marginally necessary or not needed at all.

Some of the specific County expenditures that ACTA considers to be unnecessary, inappropriate or excessive and a violation of fiscal restraint, has included the following:

    a. County involvement in public housing, repeatedly rejected by the public in referendums, under the slogan "affordable housing" at a cost of ever increasing tax revenues; e.g. establishing the first so called "Special Affordable Housing Protection District" (SAHPD) by approving the site plan for the Pollard Gardens development, obligating taxpayer subsidies of at least $4,500.000.

    b. Overstaffing of County government which runs at 19 employees per thousand population, the highest in the State, as compared to an average of 6.34 for the other 94 Counties in the State and 16.25 for cities with comparable responsibilities.

c. The Arlington practice of granting housing subsidies to illegal immigrants which ACTA claims to be to the detriment of, and cost to, legal residents, and in violation of Federal law and regulations.

d. Laxity in administering medical and social services and improper screening to insure that aid is denied to ineligible illegal aliens.

e. County designation of parts of the Buckingham apartments on Glebe Road as a historical district that resulted in a law suit against the County alleging the County Board's purpose was to attempt to preserve residential portions as "affordable" housing by decreasing their value, inhibiting redevelopment and facilitating the ability of non-profit organizations which own and operate "affordable" housing to acquire the property.

f. County authorization of the sale in 1984 of $23.5 million of bonds to finance public parking in the Ballston Commons shopping center that has not resulted in an economically viable operation, with a $6 million shortfall in covering operating expenses.

g. Overpayment of county employees, such as a swimming pool managers with "exorbitant and outrageous" annual salaries of $65,000.

h. The use of the county's Industrial Development Authority to float bonds to enable the Arlington Housing Corporation to purchase 500 units of the Buckingham apartments for low-cost housing, that ACTA argued was prohibited by State law and could result in court challenges.

METRO RAPID RAIL SYSTEM

Probably no County fiscal expenditure, or commitment, has more annoyed ACTA over the years than the manner of local participation in the construction, maintenance and operation of the Metro rapid rail system and its implication to Arlington taxpayers.

In the early 1950-60 years of the rapid rail system planning it was represented that the system would cost about $2 billion, some of which would be supplied by participating metropolitan jurisdictions through bond sales as an indication of the sincerity of their commitment - the rest by direct Federal appropriations. It was further represented that the bonds would be retired in future years, with no ultimate cost to local taxpayers, by profits from the fare boxes.

In later years as the system construction neared completion, it became common knowledge that not only were operating profits insufficient to retire any bonds, but also they were woefully inadequate to even routinely operate the system, requiring continuing extensive annual subsidies from participating metropolitan jurisdictions.

Sources of Influence

ACTA historian Francis Hewitt labeled the system "The Monster in our Midst: Metro Financing" [14] and wrote "From the start, ACTA questioned (the candor) of the minimal cost of the system, first set at $2 billion, then $4 billion, then graduating upward in $2 billion leaps to $10 billion, with the ultimate cost somewhere in the stratosphere of imponderables."

Hewitt recorded further that ACTA leaders had pointed out that less than one third of Arlington residents would be users of the system, either bus or rail, ... that only 9% of the riders during peak periods would originate in Arlington, ... that fare proposals would provide totally inadequate financing in the long run... that there must be a less costly way to provide public transportation... that both the principal and interest of retiring revenue bonds will fall back on local governments, and that "future costs of operating the system will be so great as to be beyond the financial ability of our community" (to handle).

Hewitt cited an Arlington News article of March 27, 1975, reporting that Metro was already the largest single item in the Arlington budget other than schools, and that it was twice the combined cost of the Police and Fire Departments.

Hewitt summarized by quoting the Mayor of Alexandria who warned: "The capital commitment (for completing Metro) is but a pittance compared with the operating deficits we are committed to cover. All the local jurisdictions are in over our heads on the (future) operating subsidies." Hewitt then wrote, "As prophetic as his (the mayor's) voice was, he was but reiterating what ACTA had been warning of all along."

Citer Francis Hewitt?

* * *

In a July 8, 1993 Washington Post article headlined "Merits of Taxpayers Association Questioned", staff writer Charles W. Hall, described ACTA as an organization that has "vigorously challenged the county government's cherished self-image as one of the best-run, and most lightly taxed, in the Washington area.

Writer Hall quoted ACTA President John Rosso as saying, "We are trying to obtain cost-effective, efficient and responsive government...Our biggest contribution is in creating public awareness. After that, it is up to the public to decide what they want to do with that information."

Hall further pointed out that when County officials brag about their AAA bond rating and Arlington's national standing with bond-rating agencies, Rosso argues that the indicators have little meaning; that New York City also had a Triple A Rating but even so, its financial affairs were in disarray and in due course the State of New York became involved in the management or supervision of the City's fiscal affairs. Rosso was

---

[14] Hewitt, Francis, *A History of the Arlington County (Va.) Taxpayers Association,* unpublished, extensively annotated, with Appendices, 400 pages plus, on file with the Secretary of the Association.

credited with pointing out that, like New York, that Arlington's real estate tax bill goes up steadily over the decades.

Hall wrote also that on the County Board, ACTA "inspires both praise and anger". He quoted newly elected Board member Benjamin Winslow, Jr, the first Republican backed Board member in almost a decade, as saying, "I think they keep everybody alert to wasteful spending, and they force people to justify what they're doing. That's always valuable". And with a contrary viewpoint as though in rebuttal, Hall quoted Board member Albert C. Eisenberg as responding, "Right now ACTA is a plague on the process."

"ACTA says that?"

Four times a year ACTA publishes its periodic bulletin, "The ACTA Watchdog", edited at this writing by Timothy Wise. The organization holds annual Membership meetings, usually in April, at the Lyon Park Community Center on North Filmore Street. The annual membership dues is $15.00. *ACTA claims to have about 1,500 dues paying members.*

When asked about the future of ACTA, former President John Rosso replied, "The membership and leadership may change, but I am confident that ACTA will be around for many years to come. There is no other activity or organization in the County that is more energetic and able to pinpoint and challenge unwise and wasteful operations by the present liberal, free spending politicians in control than our organization."

The grave of Mary Randolph (1762-1828), the oldest grave in Arlington Cemetery. The brick enclosed grave is located alongside Custis Walk leading from the front of Arlington House to burial sites below including those of John F. and Robert Kennedy. The first Civil War burials of Privates William Christman and William Blatt did not occur until May, 1864. Mary Randolph was a direct descendent of Pocahontas and a cousin of Mary Lee Fitzhugh Custis, wife of the builder of Arlington House.

Sources of Influence

PENTAGON CITY COORDINATION COMMITTEE {PCCC)
&
CENTER FOR URBAN EDUCATION (CUE)

WORKAHOLICS ANONY MOOSE ?

This author feels safe in writing that in the modern period of Arlington County history, some three to four decades, no group of citizens has worked more diligently and energetically, over a longer period of time, at greater self sacrifice, on a civic cause, than those who consulted with private developers and county officials, and others, on the development of a tract of land now known as Pentagon City.

By the early 1970s the just under 120 acres tract was by far the largest piece of undeveloped land in the county, other than parks, golf courses or government lands. It was, and is, located in the southernmost part of the County between the Department of Defense Pentagon Building and the area along Jeff-Davis Highway (U.S. Route l), then rapidly being developed. The site is bounded by South Joyce and Eads Streets on the North and South; and 18th Street and Army Navy Drive on the East and West; less the Western Electric Company block in the center between Hayes, Fern, 12th and 15th Streets. As stated, most of the area was zoned for commercial or high density uses but was open and undeveloped.

DEVELOPMENTAL PLANS

When it became increasingly known about 1971 that the owners of the lands, the Cafritz-Tompkins interests, were negotiating for the sale and development of the subject tract, certain residents in the adjacent or nearby surrounding neighborhoods became

ARLINGTON COUNTY - A Modern History

intensely concerned. Mainly, they were members of the Arlington Ridge Civic Association and, in due course, organized themselves as a committee of the Association.

It was generally recognized by these individuals that the land was already zoned for dense or high rise uses, but the citizens were interested in just how high or high dense the development would become and what more desirable features could be included.

The citizens around the proposed Pentagon City development were especially worried over the possible adverse impacts the development could have to include congestion, parking, pollution, traffic, or other matters that would lessen the enjoyability of living conditions in their residential neighborhoods.

The worried citizens were mostly from the nearby single family Virginia or Aurora Highlands and Arlington Ridge Civic Associations areas located in the Arlington neighborhoods North of Glebe Road and East of the I-395 roadway. The leadership in the group consisted mostly of citizen activists who had long been heavily involved in civic association and other community causes.[15]

1975 - RUMBLES OF PERILS

By 1975, the citizens group had requested and were granted permission to meet with representatives of the developers, and the members of the county planning and zoning staffs. As the months passed, repeated, lengthy and complex negotiations occurred at which many citizens requested modifications or alterations in design and proposed uses were made. In addition to developer-staff-citizens meetings during these periods, the concerned citizens also met continuously in homes, at civic association meetings, and other occasions for planning, briefing, study, and other reasons. The number of man hours, evenings, weekends and other contributions by the citizen activists for this cause can never be known with certainty, but would for sure be enormous and mind boggling.

Over the months of citizen-developer-staff meetings the developers adopted many recommendations made by the citizens or the staff. As the time grew closer, however, for consideration of the matter by the County Board, it became apparent that there were many remaining gaps in the positions of the citizens and the owner-developers and the County staff that seemed more often than not to side with the developers. It became increasingly clear that full agreement was not

"No parks or jogging trails?"

---

[15] *Included in the early activists were well known South Arlington civic leaders John & Joan Quinn, John & Willa Marr, Derk & Nancy Swain, Anita Treadway, Walter & Pat Bauman, Richard & Deborah Herbst, Francis & Mary Hewitt, Robert Harrington, Bud & Maryanne Annon, Robert and Sunny Cook, Henry and Polly Franklin, and several others from North Arlington to include widely known activist Louise Chesnut.*

Sources of Influence

possible and a confrontation before the County Planning Commission and Board at the required rezoning hearing would be inevitable.[16] Battle lines were steadily forming.

By the end of 1975 events were unfolding in rapid fire order. The citizen activists had designated themselves as the Pentagon City Coordinating Committee, or "PCCC". On November 13 the Planning Commission considered the plan for Pentagon City development and in December there were numerous meetings with the County Manager Staff and a "work session" by the County Board. At all of these formal and informal meetings, spokespersons for PCCC attended and conveyed their opposition to, or positions on, the development as proposed.

1976 - YEAR OF SETBACKS

On January 28th, the County Board met and by a close vote (3-2) did not disapprove the Pentagon City plan, but instead decided to give "further consideration to upzoning" and scheduled the matter for hearing on its regular zoning meeting on February 25th. On that date, the Board, after hours of testimony by witnesses for and against the proposed plan, voted 4-1 to rezone the Cafritz-Tompkins tract as requested.

Members of PCCC were keenly disappointed, if not infuriated by the County Board's action in disregarding citizen opposition and granting the requested rezoning. The PCCC members met promptly in further planning sessions and decided to continue their opposition to the development of Pentagon City as planned and now approved. The group, recognizing that the struggle would be long and difficult, decided to incorporate, retain legal counsel to initiate suit against the County Board, and to launch a vigorous fund raising effort.

INCORPORATION

On June 2, 1976, PCCC was incorporated in the State of Virginia as a nonprofit membership corporation. Its stated purpose was to be, in general,

> "to promote and protect the health, welfare and quality of life of the community which it serves, and, in particular, to promote sensible and temperate development of the Pentagon City tract and surrounding area, and to coordinate community efforts to that end, consistent with the general purpose of the Association."

---

[16] *The nature and detailed development of the long drawn out confrontation between the principles in the Pentagon City rezoning dispute are dealt with in more detail in Chapter Five, Major Community "Battles" and Controversies, herein.*

The articles of incorporation provided that membership was open automatically "...to all members in good standing of the Arlington Ridge Civic Association, the Aurora Highlands Civic Association, the Crystal City Civic Association and the River House Tenants Association". It was also provided that the membership could be extended to others "...sympathetic to the purposes of the Association.

The articles and by-laws also stipulated, in part, that the Association "...shall not... devote a substantial part of its assets or activities to influencing legislation" or "..participate in any political campaign or support any candidate for public office."

On July 3rd, the day following incorporation, PCCC, Inc., through its attorneys, filed suit in the Arlington County Circuit Court aiming to overturn the County Board's action in rezoning the Pentagon City tract to permit development as proposed. The suit claimed the Board action to be "arbitrary and capricious" and therefore "unlawful", and asked the court to invalidate the rezoning.[17]

The PCCC suit also charged that the Board failed to consider and pay proper heed to the "adverse impact which the rezoning will or is likely to have upon the public health, safety, convenience and welfare of the citizens of Arlington County as a result of increased traffic and environmental pollution...".

In the following months, PCCC members were intensively involved in numerous meetings with counsels, the law firms of Covington and Burling and Siciliano, Ellis, Sheridan and Dyer, for planning sessions and to take testimony and prepare pleadings, depositions, and filings in the pending court suit. Additionally, time demanding meetings were held to devise methods of fund raising to defray mounting and significant legal expenses for the suit underway.

PCCC budget records dated July 1976 indicate that the group expenses at that time, mostly for fact finding and legal fees, exceeded $58,000. The proposed, but not yet realized, income to meet these expenses were to be raised by coffees and picnics, neighborhood canvases, walk-a-thons, and by foundation, personal and business donations.

In the first of a number of "Update" bulletins of the PCCC, it was announced also in July that the group would meet every other Thursday evening at the Quinn home on South Knoll Street. The bulletin also announced that the PCCC had expanded its

---

[17] *Marilyn Chase, Staff writer, Arlington Journal, June 10, 1976, p. C10*

Sources of Influence

involvement to additional areas of development, other than Pentagon City, to include the construction of I-595 roadway in Crystal City and the Shirlington Redevelopment plan, a shopping center west of I-395 and generally, between Glebe Road and Route 7 (King Street), an area once part of George Washington's lands along Four Mile Run.

Much of the time of PCCC members in the months following the filing of their suit to reverse the County Board "higher density" zoning action for Pentagon City was spent in fund raising to finance the suit, marshalling of community support for their efforts, and consultations with their lawyers that would pursue the suit in the Arlington County Circuit Court.

PCCC distributed fund donation cards throughout the community in public places and door to door drops, under its name, and reading "We're all in this together". The cards asked for donations by pledge or otherwise in the amounts of $50 to $1000, or "other", and that donations be payable to the Association treasurers Mr and Mrs Walter Bauman at 2757 South Ives Street. Additionally, in this period, PCCC began in earnest a series of neighborhood spaghetti dinners, picnics, "coffees" and similar events for fund raising purposes. The group also operated a speakers bureau for county wide seminars and civic association meetings.

In its September, 1976 "Update" bulletin, PCCC announced that a court date had been set for November 15, on the pending suit, and also a preliminary hearing date of September 23 on the defendants' motion to remove the PCCC and certain others from the list of plaintiffs.

The September bulletin also announced to the membership that PCCC had joined the Arlington Ridge and Aurora Hills Civic Associations, the Hospitality House and Stouffer's Motor Inn in Crystal City, in a suit against the U. S. Department of Transportation and the Virginia Department of transportation to stop the construction of Interstate Highway I-595 through Crystal City.[18]

Additionally, concerning the Shirlington shopping area, the bulletin reported that the County Board had approved a new zoning classification to be used "...in the redevelopment of the deteriorating neighborhood shopping area". The bulletin did not indicate any PCCC position with respect to the new classification.

After almost three weeks of testimony in the PCCC Arlington Circuit court suit, including night sessions, Judge Paul D. Brown on December 22, issued his ruling that upheld the County Board's February rezoning decision. PCCC members were far from pleased with that "Christmas present" from the judiciary. Shortly thereafter, on January 6, 1977, PCCC met and decided to appeal the decision to the Virginia Supreme Court. The appeal was filed in the first week of February.

---

[18] *The issues, developments, and details of the I-595 project and court suit are covered elsewhere herein in Chapter 5, "Major Controversies and Confrontations in Arlington County".*

1977 - A VICTORY - A LOSS

In its January, 1977 "Update" PCCC announced with obvious pleasure and delight that The Alexandria Federal Court had, in November, issued a permanent injunction against the construction of the "expensive, useless, and environmentally dangerous I-595, a proposed elevated connector roadway between I-95 (I-395) and the National Airport." Thus, said PCCC, the Association "ended 1976 with one tremendous success and one 'temporary' setback".

In the bulletin, PCCC reported a new member, the River House Tenant's Association, and it continued its appeal for funds to carry on its work. It said, in part,

> *"With your help we can set another precedent which will help make land developers accountable to the local citizens. We can preserve the integrity of our region and prevent its over-development into a suburban wasteland. Our opponents have millions of dollars -- WE DO NOT. We need your support... fill in the form below and mail it in with your contribution."*

In its annual report of February 24, 1977, PCCC announced through its Chairman John Quinn that during 1976 it had revenues of just over $9,000 and expenditures of just under $8,000. It reported that it owed: $18,500 thus far for legal fees on the Pentagon City litigation, but had not received a bill from one of the two law firms; and $16,500 legal fees for the I-595 litigation. The report indicated that fund raising efforts were to continue with a goal of raising $200,000 over the next couple of years.

PCCC FUNDS? OR DEBTS?

Soon after the annual report, on March 31st and in May, Quinn outlined a fund raising plan to the Board of Directors. He estimated that known or expected indebtedness of PCCC was approximately $124,000 but that pursuit of the Pentagon City appeal, and further proceedings with respect to the highway through the Jefferson Davis corridor (I-595), might alter those figures. To liquidate that indebtedness $50,000 was immediately needed, with an additional $150,000 to be raised over a three year period, by December 31, 1979. Quinn listed numerous methods by which the money could be raised, to include kick-off dinners, contacts with business men or groups, recruitment and training of workers, preparation of "white papers", personal contacts with 2-5,000 people, the organization of implementation teams, and various other means.

* * * *

On September 13th, Chairman Quinn advised the PCCC leadership that the law firm of Covington and Burling had informed him that the Supreme Court of Virginia had rejected the petition for reconsideration in the law suit against the County Board. He wrote that the question of a further appeal to the U. S. Supreme Court would be discussed at the next board meeting. He also reported that "no progress in raising the substantial funds required to pay the bills totaling approximately $48,250 ... or for the unbilled charges... Our current bank balance is $1,306.89."

On December 3rd, Chairman Quinn submitted his final report to the PCCC leadership advising them that he would not be available for reelection when his term expired at the end of the year. He informed the group that Covington and Burling had filed a petition for certiorari in the U. S. Supreme Court, that the Court had denied the petition, and that there had been no changes of any consequence in the PCCC's financial situation.

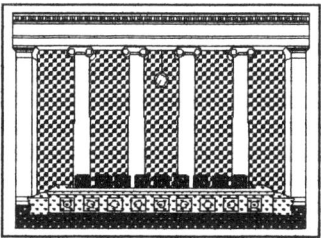

"We affirm Judge Brown"
VA Supreme Court

1978
CHANGES IN LEADERSHIP

On January 24, 1978, outgoing PCCC Chairman Quinn submitted his final and "Second Annual" report, and also a Memorandum for the leadership. He indicated that the candidates for election at the membership meeting at the Calvary Methodist Church on South 23rd Street on that date would be:

Chairman	Derk Swain
Vice Chairman-Finance	John Quinn
Vice Chairman-Comm. Rels.	Barbara Naquin
Secretary	Margaret Gaffen
Treasurers	Walter and Pat Baumann

In his final and somewhat comprehensive report, Quinn described the PCCC activities during the past years that centered around further developments in the Pentagon City and I-595 projects. He stated that the Pentagon City construction was beginning but that the developers continued to file applications for modification of their building permits and site plans that required constant monitoring by PCCC to insure that adverse pollution, parking or other environmental impacts did not occur. His reported indicated again that no significant success had been realized in fund raising to meet outstanding obligations, mainly legal costs, but that $8,000 had been borrowed from the National Bank of Washington ($2,000 of which was repaid) which had been used to retire a part of the bills owed for legal services.

With his final reports, Quinn included and introduced a Memorandum for future and continuing fund raising under his direction as the new Vice Chairman for Finance. In the Memorandum, he said, in part:

> "...no significant progress has been made in curtailing (our) indebtedness...our credibility is impaired with the very experts we need to consult in order to carry on ... these debts were incurred after full discussion... to our undertaking Pentagon City (and) I-595 litigation... as a Board and as a community of respectable citizens we must renew and strengthen our efforts to raise the money to pay the debts..."

ARLINGTON COUNTY - A Modern History

1979 TO 1985
A CHANGE OF NAMES AND?

In the following year or so, PCCC filed an application with the State Corporation Commission to change its name from the Pentagon City Coordinating Committee, Inc., to the Center for Urban Education., Inc.

The change in name, no doubt, reflected the feeling of many in the group that with the controversy over the nature of the Pentagon City development rapidly passing into history, and its construction all but a "fait accompli", it was no longer realistic, nor was there a continuing need for the PCCC group to be identified by a name linking it to only that project. Additionally, the other two issues that had preoccupied PCCC, the I-595 construction, and the Shirlington Shopping area redevelopment, were also completed and in being. It appeared clear that the group should either fold up its tents and wind up its affairs or to branch out into new and other concerns.

In a flyer dated April 4, 1981, the new Center for Urban Education, Incorporated, or "CUE" described itself in much the same way as the old PCCC, to wit:

"The Center for Urban Education is a non profit corporation, organized in 1976 to promote the development of an environmentally sound community and thus to help avoid community deterioration. It collects and analyzes information concerning air pollution, noise pollution, transportation problems and related matters, particularly as such problems relate to land use decisions..."

The description made no reference to past Pentagon City, I-595 or Shirlington issues, nor did it limit its henceforth interest to only those areas or to any other limited or particular part of Arlington County.

The flyer listed John Quinn as the President, John Marr as Vice President, William Massa, Jr., as Secretary and Clyde Heasly, Jr., as Treasurer. The 27 Directors included especially well known civic activists Doris Bangs, Louise Chestnut, Richard Herbst, Kathryn Hughes, Herman Jensen, Joan Quinn, John and Willa Marr, Derk and Nancy Swain, and William Wallace.[19]

In 1984, in a follow-up flyer, CUE urged citizens to join the organization at an annual membership dues of $3.00. It listed its current areas of activity as (1) transportation in Arlington, (2) the National Airport-reduced use, (3) Compatibility of high density development and residential neighborhoods; (4) air pollution, (5) Neighborhood conservation, and (6) Education in Arlington.

The flyer asserted that CUE's focus was to:

---

[19] *Also included in the Directors were the Officers, and citizens Betty Constantz, Robert Gazzola, Jean Harrett, Charles Henck, Lloyd Herman, Leonard Kojm, Carol Noggle, Susan Schruth, Marie Schum-Brady, Robert Shefner, Robert Steadman, Susan Wilder and Fred Wood.*

Sources of Influence

        (1) promote citizen involvement,
        (2) Develop and evaluate all issues in terms of people (services, age, economics, housing, children, public education, healthy environment),
        (3) Promote sound planning to review impacts on neighborhoods,
        4) Provide planning leadership, and
        5) Support regional approach to planning.

The flyer listed the leadership to be:
    President - Mary Kathryn Hughes
    Vice President - (Planning) Nancy Swain
    Vice President - (Fund Raising) John Marr
    Treasurer - Clyde Heasly
    Executive Secretary - Sally Boss

Overworked CUE volunteer?

In its early years of activity, CUE met regularly and with its talented and artistic president, published highly professional periodic news bulletins generously sprinkled with eye catching and communicative art work.

The bulletins were mailed with regularity to the membership and distributed elsewhere throughout the county to libraries, county government agencies and to other regional sources that were felt to have an interest in conservation and environmental threats to the better quality of living in Northern Virginia.

1981-86 - YEARS OF FINANCIAL CHALLENGE AND VICTORY

    Soon after the creation of CUE, a remarkable and dramatic development took place with respect to the wherewithal of the organization to retire its indebtedness, mainly created by its Pentagon City and I-595 litigation. With the demise of those controversies, PCCC\CUE found itself saddled with almost a quarter of a million dollars of debt, a staggering amount for a group of private citizen activists without outside support or assistance.

    With its fund raising efforts to that time, consisting of neighborhood coffees, dinners, and miscellaneous solicitations, the leadership had raised but mere pocket change. For example, in 1977, perhaps a typical year, the Treasurer reported that an I-595 workshop had netted only $66. The same year, an EPA water quality workshop realized only $400, a Stauffer's hotel fund raising dinner $560, and a Herbst fund raising effort $408. The total of all other donations amounted to only $2,980 for an overall total of only about $6,000. At that rate, it seemed a $250,000 debt could not be finally and completely paid off until another 40 years or until about the year AD2022.

    Faced with this discouraging dilemma, several of the stalwart leaders in the PCCC\CUE movement met one evening in early January of 1980 in the home of Dick

ARLINGTON COUNTY - A Modern History

Herbst on South Knoll Street for a collective effort to find ways or means to solve the group's crushing financial predicament and pay off its staggering debts. The assembled CUE members included loyal supporters and workers John Marr, Dick Herbst, John Quinn, Derk Swain, and several others. After a period of relative silence, head scratching, hand wringing and soul searching, slowly, and almost inaudibly one of the assembled members spoke hesitatingly.

"Why don't we run a bingo game?" asked CUE member and leader John Marr.

"A bingo game?" some one responded in surprise as each and all of the group looked from one to another searchingly.

"Where on earth did you get that idea?" someone asked Marr.

"Well," explained Marr, "I ran into an ole buddy the other day in the grocery store and he mentioned his recent experience with bingo games in the school where his children attend. Seems there was some hanky-panky and misdirection of funds and the games had to be closed down. But he said they had been most profitable."

"Could bingo by our group also be sufficiently profitable?",

"Would it be permissible?"

"Who would operate the games?"

"Where would they be held?"

"Would anyone come?"

The questions came thick and fast.

"Wouldn't we be required to get a permit? Would we be qualified for a permit?" Quinn asked.

"Yes," Marr answered. "I understand permits are required, and few activities can get them. I believe we would qualify as a non-profit organization operating for community or educational purposes. Our local tax assessor Gerry Whiting would be the source for the permit. There is a nominal annual license fee. I think it is $25." [20]

---

[20] *Section 18.2-340 of the Code of Virginia provides, in part, that an "organization operated exclusively for religious, charitable, community or educational" purposes may be granted a bingo license. Additional sections requires that a license be obtained from the local governing body with an application fee of $25, that profits be used only for the purpose for which the organization is formed and that auditing and specified operating requirements be followed.*

Sources of Influence

Before the meeting adjourned the group had decided to pursue the suggestion to raise money by conducting bingo games. In the following weeks an application for a permit was filed on which, among other things, CUE leaders had to establish that their organization had been in existence for at least two years as required by the Virginia Code and they had to familiarize themselves with other statutory requirements for conducting bingo games. In due course a permit was obtained, game crews were organized and on July 11, 1980, the first of the weekly scheduled bingo games was held in the cafeteria of the Gunston community center on South Lang Street.

The idea to undertake bingo games operation proved to be little less than a stroke of genius. Gradually, with energetic promotion within the community, and considerable efforts by dedicated CUE organizers and operators who donated endless hours of their time to organizing and operating the enterprise, attendance increased and profits quickly reached an average of about $1,000 a week.

By 1985 almost a quarter of a million dollars in profits had been realized, enough to pay all the organizations legal and other indebtedness. In 1985 the games were suspended for several months to give operating individuals a breather, and to recruit replacements. After the 1985 break the games were resumed for another 2-3 years to finance additional projects undertaken by the organization. They were then permanently discontinued.

* * *

The past major developmental and urban growth controversies with which the group centered its activities and concerns have long since been completed or otherwise resolved. In recent months the group had focused its attention on the proposal by Redskins football team owner Cooke to build a stadium for the football team on the railroad property just south of Crystal City. That issue disappeared, at least for the time being, however, when the proposal withered and became dormant after intense local citizen opposition both in the City of Alexandria and in Arlington County as discussed herein in Chapter V.

In 1993 CUE representatives attended, and in certain instances spoke or furnished written testimony, or both, at various hearings including those related to retaining the U. S. Navy at Crystal City in Arlington; the National Commission to ensure a Strong Competitive Airline Industry; the FAA "Meeting" on the aircraft noise at National Airport; the aspects of the Vice President's task force relating to the FAA; on National Performance Review commonly referred to as "Reinventing the Government"; and a recommendation concerning examination of air pollution from aircraft made to the chairperson of the Air Quality Committee of the Council of Governments.

* * * *

At this writing, CUE continues to exist and function, although, it seems, with considerably less steam and fire. No doubt some members will feel it has passed its peak performance. Denis O'Sullivan, a South 22nd Street resident, serves as the group's

President, John Marr as Vice President, Bette Keiger as Secretary, and Larry Straus as Treasurer. The Board of Directors has nine vacancies [21]

On January 7, 1994, CUE President Denis O'Sullivan distributed his notice of the Annual meeting of the organization on January 26th at the Oakridge Elementary School in South Arlington. The specified agenda was to consist of several administrative items including the approval of minutes of the 1993 Annual meeting, financial reports, and the nomination and election of officers. Although some members had expected that the question of taking a position on the easing up or continuing the restrictions on commercial aircraft sizes and hours of operation at the National Airport might be discussed, there was no mention of the item on the notice of annual meeting. The group held its 1997 annual meeting on January 22, in the Oakridge Elementary School. A principle item of business was to decide whether the organization would disband or go to a standby status.

The "Peaking" of PCCC and CUE?

The future of CUE is shrouded somewhat with uncertainty. Member Louise Chestnut suggested at the 1992 annual meeting that perhaps the organization should be disbanded since the purposes for which it was initially activated have been accomplished, or no longer exist. Other members felt that such action might be premature and that the group should remain functional or on a standby status and ready to cope with any future challenges to "an environmentally sound community".

No matter what the future of CUE may be, its record of past performance in terms of time and effort contributed unselfishly by dedicated citizens volunteers to preserve the quality of their community as a desirable place to live and work, seems unmatched to date. Nor does it seem that the efforts and accomplishments of CUE will be exceeded anytime soon hereafter since there are no longer any large areas of undeveloped land in the County around which controversy is likely to swirl and that would need a CUE to cope with. Many CUE members without doubt will enthusiastically agree.

---

[21] *In January 1994, the Board was comprised of the following individuals, other than the officers, only three of which reside in the Arlington Ridge Civic Association area where the group was originated in 1976: Suzanne Bolton, Don Brady, Louise Chestnut, Betty Constantz, Sylvia Courembis, Bob Dreher, Phyllis Furnari, Bob Gazzola, Jim Landrum, John Quinn, Ted Saks, John Wettroth and Susan Wilder.*

Sources of Influence

The Pentagon City complex in South Arlington between I-395 and Crystal City as seen from the heights of Arlington Ridge Road above and to the west. In the foreground, but beynd the multi-level parking structure, are (L to R) the buildings of the Macy Department Store, the MCI Office Building (and main entrance to the Fashion Center Shopping Mall), the Ritz Carlton Hotel, the Nordstrom Department Store and the Park Vista Apartments. The Pentagon City development was completed in the early 1980s on open space and has become one of the most popular shopping centers in the Washington Metropolitan area with its own Metro rail station underground.

Beyond the buildings of Pentagon City are the highrises of Crystal City in the Jeff-Davis corridor and beyond farther the Potomac River and National Airport.

POLITICAL PARTIES OR MOVEMENTS

"Only our party can save Arlington from chaos...!!"

As with most any American community, partisan political movements, parties, groups or associations cannot be omitted as a major source that influences, directs, or controls the direction in which the community moves or impacts on its citizens. Learned observers may well differ as to whether it is the efforts and activities of these groups, i.e. "politics", that control events, opinions and positions of people, or whether the groups merely reflect the issues, problems, controversies or other circumstances that prevail in a given area. In other words, which is the cart and which the horse, or the chicken and the egg, and which comes first. Probably it is a little of either, or a combination of both.

In Arlington County, since the days of "reconstruction" following the Civil War, these groups have consisted first of the Democratic and later the Republican Parties, and assertively independent groups to include the Arlingtonian Independent Movement (AIM) and Arlingtonians for a Better County (ABC) of the 1950s and the Volunteers for an Independent Arlington Coalition (VIA) of the 1990s. [22]

---

[22] *Additional information on the formation and composition of Arlington government after adoption of the Constitution of 1870 can be found in the AHS Magazine for 1962 on page 36, in the article* <u>County Officials in Arlington 1870-1960</u> *by the Research and Records Committee.*

Sources of Influence

Additionally, in the early years after World War II, increasingly, individuals have run for the governing body or other positions and identified themselves in campaign literature or otherwise, as "independents", as "Non-partisans", as "Town Meeting" candidates, and as "liberal" or "regular" Democrats. Also in the period there were candidates who called themselves "official" democrats, "official" republicans, or "endorsed" democrats and republicans. One example, and perhaps the only one, of a true and legitimate independent not beholden to any specific political group or party could have been Ernest Wilt who unofficially ran successfully in 1960 for the board unopposed and was appointed on January 29. He was supported by the ABC, Democrat and Republican organizations.

In some instances, as anywhere, political titles other than Democrat or Republican may have reflected a clear non-affiliation with, and a true independence from the established major political parties alluded to above. The use of qualifying titles may have simply reflected a position different from that held by the majority of the established political party. For example, in 1950 Robert Cox, a Town Meeting participant, ran as an "independent" Democrat for a board on which also sat Freeland Chew and Alfred Frisbie who were recognized as "regular", or conservative democrats.

The use of qualifying designations or non-democrat or republican identifications may also have resulted from a perceived or real need by a candidate, or his or her supporters, especially after the court removal of three Federal employees from the County Board in 1952, to not identify with a partisan political party to avoid conflict with the proscriptions in the Federal Hatch Act.

In the November 1952 election, Leone Buckholz, Robert Detwiler and Alvin Kimel, all recognized in the community as dedicated Republicans, ran as AIM candidates for a board that included Robert Peck, another known Republican who had ran as a Republican. Thus, there were, in essence, Republicans on the board simultaneously that were identified as Republicans and others as AIM members. It may also have been possible, in the rapid growth of population in the county following the war and uncertainty as to political affiliations of the voters, that individuals in both parties felt that party ties could have been counter productive in wooing voters who were believed to be largely non-affiliated with either party, that is, bona fide independents.

Complicating this confusion further, and doubtlessly contributing to it, for better or worse, was and is the Virginia electoral arrangement that does not list candidates on the ballots by party affiliation. Nor is there any such party designation requirement for the voter in order to vote. Consequently, no one can ever say with any degree of certainty how many Arlington voters are Republicans or are Democrats. Neither do the political parties know this information and therefore they must direct their campaign efforts not so much at their own relatively few members whose votes they can depend on, but rather at the public at large most of which are clearly independent from any partisan political group.

The parties themselves, by membership and participation, as we shall see below, are comprised of only a small number of the overall county citizenry. Neither major party can claim to have any particular number of "members". They do not require dues or applications to join the parties, nor do they issue membership cards that would identify any particular voter as a party member. Both parties, undoubtedly maintain lists of workers and of voters that they consider to be their core supporters based on known activity and participation and perhaps financial contributions. Election law requires, in fact, that periodic reports be made during and at the conclusion of campaigns of all significant contributions. Even this indication of "membership" may be flawed, however, since many voters or business or other organizations or activities are known to contribute to both parties just to insure that they are covered no matter who wins the election, a cautious and crafty technique widely practiced at all levels of campaigning nationally as well as locally.

Probably the nearest membership composition that can be determined for any political group would be the ABC and especially the VIA groups. They both maintain membership lists that consists only of individuals who have in some formally or overt manner "joined" the organization and who pay an annual dues or in the case of the ABC, a "registration" fee. No formal or express dues are required for "membership" in either the Republican or Democrat parties.

THE DEMOCRATIC PARTY

By far, the partisan political group with the most seniority in the geographical area now comprising Arlington County is the Democrat Party. It clearly dates from the adoption in 1869 of the Constitution of 1870, although candidates in elections and holders of offices initially were not specifically identified by the Democrat label. Following the adoption of the County Manager form of government in the election of 1930, and the election of other officials in the election of 1931 to take office in 1932, party designations began to appear in the records of the County Registrar or were self proclaimed in the campaign literature of the candidates. [23]

In the period 1932 to 1946 only Democrats are shown to have been elected to the County Board and other elective offices. The first indication of a split in the ranks appeared in the 1947 election creating a board of 4 democrats and one "independent" (Daniel Dugan), and in the next five years until 1952 "regular" or conservative democrats (e.g., Basil DeLashmutt or Freeland Chew), shared the board in minority numbers with NP (non-partisan) and GAA (Greater Arlington Association) members. [24]

---

[23] *Based on studies compiled by library volunteer R. Singleton on file in the Virginia Room, Arlington County Main Library.*

[24] *In recent years, widely known and esteemed Elizabeth Campbell and her late husband Edmund have been recognized as "founders" of the Arlington Democratic Party, presumably meaning the current party as distinguished from the pre-World War II Southern conservative Democratic Party.*

Sources of Influence

In 1953 Democrats disappeared entirely from a board comprised of 2 Republican and 3 AIM members, but Democrat membership was restored in 1954 through 1957 with the election of "regular" Democrat Wesley W. Cooper. In 1956 for the first time ABC members appeared on the board with AIM members until 1960 and thereafter only with Republican members beginning in 1964, except for the 1961 independent Ernest Wilt referred to above. From 1962 to date the board has consisted of only ABC members, or a combination of ABC and Republican members, although beginning in the 1980s the ABC members began running as Democrats as explained in greater detail below.

A CHANGE IN PHILOSOPHY

In the last half of this century the Democrat group has undergone considerable transformation concerning its philosophical makeup, outlook and active workers. For some 75 years from the period immediately following the Civil War until the end of World War the party, like the party elsewhere generally in the South, could best be described as ultra-conservative and much unlike its increasingly liberal counterparts in the Northern and some other parts of the United States.

Virginia Democrats were firmly "Dixiecrats" within the popular and widely understood meaning of the term. In philosophy concerning governmental authority, economic outlook, racial relations, states rights, and many social issues, the Harry Byrd Democrats of Virginia were little different from the Talmadges of Georgia, the Rankins of Mississippi, the Longs of Louisiana, or those of any number of "Old South" political dynasties. All held firmly to the perpetuation of the status quo and the Jeffersonian conservative approach that the government that governs best is the one that governs least and that human and society needs could best be met by private sector financing and efforts and not by relying on extensive governmental involvement. Most such conservatives contended that their goals were the same as liberals but that they should be reached by emphasis on the private sector, rather than the less efficient and more wasteful and bureaucratic government. They agreed that government assistance could be justified to help those who could not help themselves, but that the line between inability and unwillingness for self help should be tightly drawn. Many conservatives held that the line was often too generously and unrealistically applied by liberals.

During and following World War II, however, large numbers of Federal government workers arrived in the area and drastically altered the Arlington County demographic makeup and philosophical outlooks of its people with respect to needed local governmental involvement in community affairs. These self proclaimed liberals soon dominated the political landscape. When they surveyed the schools in particular they were greatly dissatisfied with what they saw and set about to generate change by electing school and county board members that would implement their goals as described in more detail herein in Chapter Five.

The early liberal activists, first operating under "Town Meeting" and "Non-Partisan" labels, soon evolved, as stated elsewhere, into the operating political apparatus and organization titled Arlingtonians for a Better County or ABC. With the emergence of the ABC the Democratic party ceased to run Democrat candidates for the County Board although the Democrats generally supported and worked for the ABC candidates for County Board. ABC continued through the years to run, or at least actively support,

Democrat candidates for other local offices and for the State legislature. These included local positions such as the constitutional offices of Commonwealth Attorney, Commissioner of Revenue, Treasurer, and the State offices of Senator and Delegates to the House of Representatives.

It is near impossible in a climate absent any requirement for voters to officially designate their party preferences or membership to track with certainty the individual philosophical or partisan movement of voters. Nevertheless, it is probably quite safe to say that in the emerging period of ABC growth and the influx of persons with liberal views, that most conservative Democrats moved from the Democratic to the Republican parties in their loyalties, activities and financial support, and that the Democratic party became increasingly if not wholly moderate to liberal in its composition and outlook.

One clear and probably typical example of the definite swing toward liberalism of the Arlington Democratic establishment exists in the outcome of the special election of March 11, 1969. The purpose of that election was to select a replacement for the 9th Senatorial District to replace the recently deceased Arlingtonian Charles R. Fenwick. Long time Arlington Delegate Democrat C. Harrison Mann promptly filed as a candidate feeling that his "experience and years of service in the House of Delegates" clearly established him as the individual "most qualified and entitled to the advancement to Senator".[25] Mann, however, was not sufficiently liberal for the party leadership. He was perceived by some as being too much from the "old line Southern Democrats" and thus "too conservative",[26] although he insisted that he was not. Whereupon, a known liberal, Wallace G. Dickson, was caused to also file as a candidate to run for the office opposite Mann and the Republican candidate M Patton Echols, Jr. As a consequence, the Democratic vote was split and Republican Echols won by a plurality. The vote was Echols 6111, Mann 5800 and Dickson 4916. Thereafter to date, no admitted conservative is known to have run for election in Arlington County on the Democratic ticket or as an ABC candidate.

In the ensuing years any distinctions between the Democrat and ABC political organizations have all but completely disappeared. Although some candidates for offices other than county board will be identified in campaign literature and posters as Democrats, the candidates for both groups have appeared generally on the same campaign literature and their workers at voting places and elsewhere conduct joint efforts on behalf of both ABC and Democratic candidates. In recent years, however, the trend has been for candidates to run as Democratic Party candidates as explained in more detail below. Both groups will routinely and formally at meetings, or otherwise, endorse the candidates of each other.

MID CENTURY ARLINGTON
Which party or candidate is liberal? Or conservative?

---

[25] *As stated to author in an interview in the Mann residence on Arlington Ridge Road in December 1972.*

[26] *Ibid.*

Sources of Influence

The Party and its candidates positions, which usually cannot be distinguished from those of the ABC as reflected in its campaign literature, has included the following.[26]

1950s

- Increase spending for schools and teacher salaries.
- Establish of a Department of Real Estate Assessment with full time professionals operating without favoritism.
- Establish a merit system for County employees rooting out the spoils system.
- Meet school operating revenue needs.
- Improve police training and public utility services and establish citizen advisory committees to implement same.
- Full citizenship rights for Federal employees with eligibility to serve in local offices.
- Vigorous continuation of Arlington's Capital Improvements Program for sewers, streets, parks, swimming pools and public services.
- Full distribution of tax load by (a) increase business taxes, (b) full assessments of property tax, (c) re-establish Department of Real Estate Assessments, and (d) prompt collection of delinquent taxes.
- Proper zoning with adequate protection of residential areas.
- Improvement of cross-county bus service and elimination of low flying by aircraft over residential areas.
- Cooperation with State and Federal authorities for more Potomac bridges.
- Adoption and use of code of ethics for County officials and employees.
- Strengthening laws to protect game, fish and water resources, enforce anti-pollution laws and create a State park for Northern Virginia.
- Opposition to a County sales tax and finding ways to attract new businesses.
- Establish a master plan for the development of the County.
- Establish (and re-establish after elimination in the mid 1950s) an elected school board.
- To keep the public schools open (when it appeared they might be closed by the State during the Court ordered integration period).
- Achieve the lowest possible taxation through more efficient operations.

1960s

- A continuation of the goals of the 1950s.
- Resist real estate speculators who want to pack the community with high density apartments.
- Resist those who want to recklessly slash school budgets.
- Dynamic planning for the future.

---

[26] *From campaign literature on file in the archives of the Main Library Virginia Room.*

♥ Cooperation with neighbors to clean up the Potomac River.

♥ Continuation of non-partisan (ABC) elections for Arlington County.

♥ Support the County Manager and Police in maintaining order and moving forward with school integration; if public schools are threatened, support legal action to preserve them (in the early 1960s).

♥ Expansion of land acquisition efforts for parks.

♥ Develop needed transportation facilities with emphasis on and support for bonds for a mass transit system.

♥ Full cooperation with neighboring jurisdictions to solve regional transportation, water resources, recreation and sewage problems.

♥ Protect, conserve and revitalize neighborhoods.

♥ Expand kindergarten, summer school, and mental retarded school children programs.

1970s

♦ Continue protection of County's residential neighborhoods by opposing construction of sewers for a greatly expanded population, and 30-story office buildings.

♦ Improved operation of the Consumer Protection and Tenant-Landlord Commissions.

♦ Oppose and prevent the construction of Interstate Route I-66 inside the I-495 "beltway".

♦ Fight to retain the at-large electoral system for County Board members.

♦ Expansion of tax and rent relief to meet higher costs of living.

♦ Construction of an 80 mile bicycle trail system.

♦ Neighborhood pre-school day care programs financed by sliding scale fees.

♦ Renovation of neighborhood shopping areas.

♦ Encourage construction of nursing and retirement homes.

♦ Develop programs to reduce crime, improve lighting on streets, increase police patrols and beef up robbery and burglary prevention programs.

♦ Support drug and alcohol treatment programs; provide for the special needs of Spanish and Asian-Americans and the Black community.

1980s

♣ To continue the previous efforts concerning rental housing, crime prevention, schools, parks and libraries.

♣ To meet the needs of senior citizens, maintain excellence in schools, provide quality community services and be fiscally responsible.

1990s

In the 1990s, the Arlington Democratic political goals and campaign issues seemed to undergo a degree of transition from "things to be accomplished" to "accomplishments to be retained". The party seemed to be saying that much had been done in the past through the election of its candidates, but that the time had come to hold on to, or expand, what had been achieved. The party proclaimed that its candidates had

Sources of Influence

caused the establishment of "a top quality school system", "affordable housing for all income levels", "a safe and protected environment", "a strong, comprehensive public safety program" and "efficient, responsive public services...with the lowest tax burden".[28]

The party seemed to concede, however, that there was still some work to be done but it hastens to insist that it can best done by its candidates. In its campaign literature it also asserted that "youth organizations and drug abuse programs" should be expanded, that more "affordable housing" should be created, "the supply of quality child and elderly day care services" should be developed and expanded, that "Arlington's play fields and recreational facilities" should be improved, that the "development of the Rosslyn-Ballston Corridor as an attractive, livable community" should be ensured, "air quality "should be improved, "library services and community cultural programs" should be expanded, and that commercial land owners "should pay their fair share of real estate taxes". [29]

When asked about the relationship of the Democratic Party and the ABC organization in Arlington, Democratic leaders indicate their belief that there would continue to be a need for the ABC for the foreseeable future although there is considerable overlapping of memberships and activities between the two groups. [30] The leaders indicated that the bulk of the party's efforts were directed at local, state and national elections other than membership on the Arlington School and County Boards, whereas the ABC group focused primarily on the board races. That information, however, seemed to conflict with that contained in the party's campaign literature. All of the flyers referred to above, and others in the early years of 1990 decade, urge voters to vote "Democratic" for the national, state and local candidates listed that invariably included the Arlington County Board candidate without no, or inconspicuous, mention that the Board candidate is also endorsed by ABC.

Most recently, the Democratic Party headquarters has been located in the Long and Foster Realty Building at 4620 Lee Highway. The Party has an Executive Committee with a mailing address of P. O. Box 1443, Arlington, VA, 22210. In addition to periodic campaign literature during election times, the party distributes a newsletter *Democratic News,* edited and managed by Tony Taylor, editor, Robert Platt, Layout, and Susan Prokop, Photography.

The Arlington Democrats, as stated, do not charge any membership fee or issue membership cards but they do not discourage contributions to help in administrative and mailing costs. There is a $10 registration fee for Executive Committee members, and $25 for persons attending nominating meetings, or caucuses, but there is a liberal policy of forgiveness for anyone who claims an inability to pay the fees.

---

[28] *Eisenberg-Newman campaign flyer* The Messenger, *1991, and Hunter campaign flyer, 1996, both prepared and released by Arlington County Democratic Committee.*

[29] *Eisenberg-Newman flyer, 1991, Ibid, Hunter flyer, 1992, Ibid, Bozman campaign flyer* Bozman Banner, *1993.*

[30] *Interview with Charlene Bickford, Party Chair on October 17, 1996, and with former party chair Kevin Appel on October 23, 1996.*

The Party Chair at this writing is Charlene Bickford, a historian and accomplished author with the First Federal Congress Project at the George Washington University. In an interview with the author at her home on North 5th Street, Bickford listed as party goals the continued success in elections, and upgrading committees.

Bickford's predecessor from 1991-95 was Kevin Appel, a native Arlingtonian with Master Degrees in Law and Psychology who at this writing is employed in the County Treasurer Office.

The Democratic Party has normally met for candidate selection or other purposes in the auditoriums or cafeterias of either the Washington and Lee High School, or the Thomas Jefferson Intermediate school. The party leadership estimates its core of year round workers to be about 125 with an additional 2,000 or more precinct workers and financial contributors during election campaigns.

When asked in an interview with this author, what were his objectives in assuming the leadership of the Party in 1991, Appel replied, "To continue the successes of the Party with emphasis on expanding its outreach to the rapidly growing immigrant community." Appel pointed with pride to the Party's accomplishments during his term in office when he said it carried every precinct in the County from 1992 to 1995.

Appel attributes the success of the Democratic Party primarily to its ability to field superior candidates that have more extended community involvement and service on committees and civic organizations as compared to Republican Party or other opponents. This in turn, he said, attracted workers and supporters in sufficient numbers to insure victory at the polls. Appel did not feel that party organization or structure were particularly critical in the Party's successes. He also felt that the Democratic Party was more attuned to community expectations and not as extreme in its positions as was and is its opposition. When asked what were the party objectives in the 1996 elections, Appel said, "winning every precinct". This last goal was achieved with some irony in the November, 1996, at least insofar as the County Board race was concerned. Incumbent James Hunter running with no opposition carried every precinct.

THE ARLINGTONIANS FOR A BETTER COUNTY (ABC)

As stated or alluded to repeatedly herein, the most dominant, influential and effective partisan political group in Arlington in the second half of the 20th Century, if not the oldest, clearly has been the Arlingtonians for a Better County, or "ABC". The group was formed in the early 1950s from the remnants of the "Town Meeting", and "Non-Partisans" groups and some other activists who were dissatisfied with school and other conditions and concluded that no remedies existed within the existing and controlling political establishment. Whereupon, they organized to create their own political apparatus and ABC came into being.

On March 30, 1955, the Washington Post and Times Herald carried a news story by reporter C. K. McClatchy headlined, "New Group to Fight AIM in Arlington". (We will elaborate more on AIM, the Arlington Independent Movement, hereinafter). McClatchy wrote, in part, as follows:

> *"Formation of a new political group - the ABC - was announced yesterday in Arlington...The letters stand for Arlingtonians for a Better county...the alliance will select two county board candidates to oppose those of AIM...*
>
> *"Formation of ABC [by 55 well known Arlington residents] marks the end of the Non-Partisan group [that] controlled the County Board [until] three members were removed from the board on September 17, 1952 [because] of their status as Federal employees...The Republican and Democratic organizations have said they will not support candidates in the November Board election.*
>
> *"ABC co-chairmen are Edward Hincks, vice president of the Civic Federation, and Edmund Campbell, former board member and defeated 1952 Democratic Congressional candidate, and Korkley Coulter, former chairman of the Republican County Executive Committee."* [30]

Post writer McClatchy listed the leadership of ABC as also including: Leo Urbanske, Jr., Chairman of the Democratic Party Executive Committee, Mrs Robert L. Groom, wife of the former chairman of the Republican County Executive Committee, Mrs Kathryn Stone, Democratic member of the House of Delegates, Brian Bell, defeated candidate for the County Board in 1954, and Ivan Booker, defeated Non-Partisan candidate for the County Board also in 1954.

The Washington Evening Star on the same day, editorialized "The stage is set for a lively County Board race this fall...with a brand new group calling itself ABC...with the remnants of the once-powerful Nonpartisan movement. Its liberal aspect is attested by the fact that it intends to compete with the conservative AIM for dominance of the county board election...". The Star editor alluded to an earlier election in which the conservative candidate had won with only a margin of 162 votes because of divided opposition and wrote that the new ABC leaders "are seasoned campaigners who know the value of united action" which will give the AIM candidates "no clear field this year".

---

[30] *Other well known organizers of ABC included Herbert Brown, Emory Hackman, Leo Urbanske, Ralph Kaul, Davis Krupshaw, Barnard Joy, James Stockard, Warren and Ruth Cox, Alan Dean, Alden Lillywhite, Robert Groom, Curtis Tuthill, Eloise Newdrop and Julian Serles.*

Shortly after its formation, the ABC issued a paper entitled "Statement of Principles" It set them forth as follows:

"ABC is a citizens' organization which seeks to secure for Arlington a government responsive to all the people. Our members and supporters expect for themselves only those benefits which flow generally to the community as the dividends of efficient and responsible government.

"We in ABC are not cast in one mold, and we differ on some of the crucial problems which confront us. Our ranks include Democrats, Republicans, and independents in national and state affairs. Our common bond is our desire for good government in Arlington.

The ABC Statement also included its definition of good government as (a) according equal political weight to all citizens and denying political rights to none; (b) encouraging the broadest possible participation in public discussion, voting and office holding; (c) responding to the needs and interests of all sections of the community with no special favors; (d) practicing economy and recognizing that true economy is rational management and not penny-pinching or wastefulness; and (d) operation in a way that acts are openly arrived at and subject to public scrutiny and evaluation.

The ABC Statement also included a list of the rights of citizens. Among these were: (a) opposition to any limitation with a purpose of disfranchisement of all qualified voters; (b) objection to the exclusion of Federal employees from service on the County Board; (c) a belief that Board members should be elected on their individual qualifications, stands on local issues, and; (d) accomplishments in community affairs. The statement also urged repeal of the poll tax.

POLITICAL IDENTIFICATION

Through the years of ABC existence and operations, the political labeling of its candidates has undergone a period of gradual transition. At the out set, candidates selected, endorsed or supported by ABC were clearly identified as such in campaign flyers and elsewhere; e.i., Ralph Kaul and David Krupshaw in 1955, Curtis Tuthill in 1956, Herbert Brown in 1957, Leo Urbanske in 1958, Kaul and Krupsaw again in 1959 (i.e., "Vote ABC! Reelect Kaul and Krupsaw"), and Roye Lowry in 1961. A minor deviation in this approach appeared in the 1960 campaign of Tom Richards and Ernest Wilt. While some of the literature urged voters to "Vote ABC! Elect Richards and Wilt", other flyers presented the two as "Candidates for the County Board endorsed (emphasis supplied) by Arlingtonians for a Better County, a coalition of Republicans, Democrats and independents". During this period, ABC mainly directed its critical rhetoric at the AIM organization and candidates. Board candidates Joseph Fisher and Irene Rock in 1963, Tom Richards in 1964, and Roye Lowry in 1965 were clearly identified in campaign flyers as ABC candidates, but to identify Joseph Wholey in 1968 as an ABC candidate required examination of the smaller and inconspicuous print on campaign flyers.

Sources of Influence

The 1970 election seemed to signal a shift in ABC strategy with respect to labeling of candidates for the County Board. It seemed that the ABC label, at least in the view of some ABC leaders and tacticians, was perceived as a possible liability insofar as attracting voters was concerned and that a candidates connections with ABC should be down played. The flyer for the next campaign of Wholey in 1970 proclaimed him an "<u>Independent</u> candidate for Arlington County Board...<u>endorsed</u> first by the Arlington Democratic Party and secondly by Arlingtonians for a Better County (emphasis supplied). Not only had the candidates ceased to be primarily ABC candidates, but they now were also designated, at least inferentially, as Democratic Party Candidates that were endorsed by ABC and some Democrats even served on the ABC Executive Committee. The same held true in 1971 for the campaign of Joseph Fisher and Everard Munsey. In a flyer dated October 27, and signed by the candidates, they asserted "We are the Independent candidates for the Arlington County Board". In several places there is reference to the "Independent County Board majority", not the ABC majority although some of the board members had clearly been elected as ABC candidates. At no place in the Fisher-Munsey flyer, or the sample ballot on its reverse side, was there any mention of ABC.

The practice of not labeling candidates as primarily ABC but rather Independent candidates endorsed by first the Democratic Party, and secondly by ABC continued through the 1970s and specifically in the campaigns of Wholey in 1974, Richard Barton and Steve Krum in 1975, John Purdy in 1976, Ellen Bozman in 1977, Joe Pelton in 1978 and Charles Rinker and Mary Margaret Whipple in 1979. Some of the literature of Barton and Krum does not even mention ABC endorsement but only that of the Democratic Party.

By the 1980, the identification of liberal ABC/Democratic candidates seemed to have made a full swing. It appeared that the old days of undesired association with a Democratic party known to be conservative had ended. Candidates would begin to be unabashedly identified in campaign literature as Democrats a label generally identified with the "new" Democratic Party established by Edmund and Elizabeth Campbell in the late 1940s. The flyer of John Milliken in 1980 read, "Democrat for the Arlington County Board, endorsed by Arlingtonians for a Better County". Although the literature for Bozman in 1981 and 1985 continued to proclaim that she was "Endorsed by the  Arlington Democratic Party" and ABC, the flyers for Whipple in 1982, for Al Eisenberg in 1983, Milliken again in 1984, and Eisenberg and William Newman in 1987, all expressly identified the individuals as candidates of the Democratic Party.

By the mid 1980s, the news media also had all but completely ceased referring to these candidates as being from the ABC. Following the election of Eisenberg and Newman on November 3, 1987, the Arlington Journal the following day carried a banner page one headline "Democrats sweep (Arlington County) Board" and the Washington Post on December 31 published an article by writer Evelyn Hsu with the headline "Arlington Board is All-Democrat", not mentioning ABC at all.

ARLINGTON COUNTY - A Modern History

The practice of ABC supported and/or Democratic Party candidates running expressly and openly as Democratic candidates has continued into the 1990s. On November 7, 1990, the Arlington Journal, following the re-election of Whipple wrote, in part, "Arlington voters reaffirmed the Democratic Party's grip on the county government...". Successful candidates Eisenberg in 1992, Chris Zimmerman in 1994 and Paul Ferguson in 1995, all ran expressly on the Democratic ticket as did the unsuccessful self admitted Gay candidate Jay Fisette in a special election in the Spring of 1993. The Arlington Journal on March 22 in a page one article by writers Amy Resnick and Jay Sherman announced "<u>Democrats</u> Nominate Fisette" (emphasis supplied).

Just what this shift from open and deliberate running of ABC candidates to "independent" candidates endorsed by ABC and finally to candidates labeled primarily or only as Democratic Party candidates with no, or almost no, mention of endorsement by ABC means is by no means clear. Nor is it possible to conclude whether this means the demise of the ABC group as an operating and influential player in county politics.

There can be no doubt that the organization claiming to be independent was greatly assisted in its original launching by the then crippling restrictions of the Hatch Act in a community with a heavy percentage of residents who were Federal employees. But the Act has been all but detoothed by the Congress and the courts and there is no longer any pressing need, as discussed elsewhere, for politically active individuals to masquerade that they are individuals working in a "non-partisan" election to avoid conflicts with the restrictions in the Act. Thus, from this stand point, there may not be any longer a continuing role for a non-partisan organization such as the ABC. But there are views to the contrary.

When asked about the future of ABC, the current chair Bonnie Franklin insisted, like Mark Twain in years gone by, that reports of ABC's obituary are clearly premature. She said, "Oh you can bet we are going to be around for a good many years to come. We have a role to play in County affairs." Past Democratic Party President and 1995 president elect of the County Bar Association Kevin Appel agreed. In an interview with the author he said he felt ABC would continue to be a meaningful factor in the local races for School Board seats and County Board appointed positions, areas to which the Democratic Party could not, or would not, devote its undivided attention.

Northern Virginia Sun staff writer Carolyn L. Bennett also seemed to agree. In a May 9, 1996 article headed "ABC Maintains Dominant Role After 4 Decades of Controversy", Bennett quoted ABC vice chair John McCracken who said, "There were many non-partisan organizations for better government and schools in the '40s and '50s, but ABC survived.

While ABC as a political and civic organization may well survive for some years to come, its days of running candidates, as stated above, seems to have drawn to a close. Courier writer Joe Farruggia on June 2, 1993, reinforced that conclusion in an article headed, "An Arlington tradition ending: the 'Independent' candidate". Farruggia wrote that the era of independent candidates in Arlington elections may be over and he attributed it, in part to a federal case arising out of an Alexandria City Council election. In that case the court placed further restrictions on the Hatch Act and seemed to open the

Sources of Influence

gates wider to federal employees running as party candidates. Following the decision, Farruggia wrote, Ellen Bozman, who had run as an independent with Democratic Party endorsement since 1973, announced she would run in 1993 as a Democrat.

The ABC organization at this writing maintains a dues paying membership of about 250-300. Its mailing address is PO Box 1203, Arlington Virginia 22210. The group ordinarily has met for nominations or other business at the Lyon Village Community Center on North Highland Street at Lee Highway. The group periodically, and usually monthly, publishes a newsletter, "The Arlington Way" edited by long time ABC activist Maury Flagg, with staff assistance from Virginia Klarquist, Jim Clayton, George Day, Tom Whipple, and others.

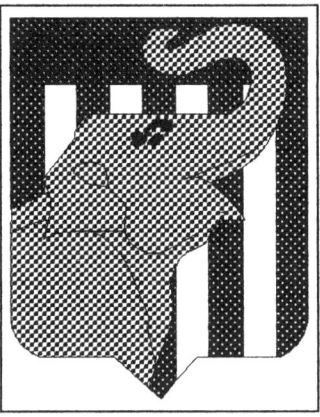

THE REPUBLICAN PARTY

The birth of the Republican Party as a meaningful and viable partisan political force in Arlington County can reasonably be said to have taken place in 1952 and 1953 with the election of Republican candidates Robert A. Peck and George M. Rowzee, Jr., to the County Board, and Joel T. Broyhill to the U. S. House of Representatives in 1952. There were for sure Republicans around, but they had not made much impact, if any, on local affairs, at least insofar as achieving the election of officials to local government. I. Lee Potter had ran for the Board earlier in 1948 as a Republican-Nonpartisan but he had lost, albeit by a narrow margin, (9,181 to 9,052) to Alfred Frisbie.

Although no candidates specifically labeled as Republicans were to successfully run for the County Board in the next few years, several individuals with known sympathies for, or activity in, Republican causes were to run successfully but under the banner of the Arlingtonian Independent Movement, or AIM. These were; Alvin Kimmel for a part term in 1952 and a three year term beginning in 1953; Leone Buchholz for a part term in 1952, a two year term beginning in 1953 and a regular term beginning in 1955; Robert T. Detwiler for a part term in 1952 and a one year term in 1953, and Lucas H. Blevins in 1956.[32] Buchholz ran again in 1958 as an Independent when the AIM group was dissolved but she lost to ABC candidate Leo Urbanske in a rather close race (13581 to 11892).

The success of the Republican or conservative oriented AIM candidates in this period resulted in County Boards not controlled by liberal Democrats or the ABC for a period beginning in November 1952 and lasting through 1957. During these years

---

[32] *This complicated length and staggering of terms situation resulted from the removal and replacement of board members following the court decision in September, 1952 that Federal employees were not eligible to serve in elected positions.*

candidates ran as Republicans for other offices, e.g., in 1952 C. Wynne Tolbert for County Attorney, Dr. John A. Tillema for County Judge, Charles O. Pratt for Commonwealth Attorney, Neil Foss for Sheriff, Theodore Nickson for Commissioner of Revenue, Col. C. Fuller Groom for the Virginia House of Delegates, and Richard L. Parli for County Board in 1953. In these cases, and most or all others, where and when Republicans ran for local offices, they were not successful.[33]

In most of the years of Republican campaigning to date, the issues have normally been directed at asserted incompetence or unwise and too liberal policies of the ABC. Republicans claimed their goals were much the same as their opponents but that those goals and objectives could better be achieved by the Republicans. A campaign flyer for Blevins in his unsuccessful 1960 race for re-election asked, "What are the Big Issues in the County Board Election...?" The flyer then identified them as harmful ABC domination of the Board, inequitable, discriminatory spot assessment with ever increasing taxes, and failure after three years of repeated promises to provide a Master plan for zoning to protect residential areas. The flyer added that the ABC had spent $700,000 for the office of planning "with nothing to show for it except a higher tax bill".

In the 1961 election, the Republican Party fielded candidates for the House of Delegates and Kenneth B. Ludwig for the County Board. A "Vote Republican" campaign flyer proclaimed the difference between the Republican and Democrats to be:

1. Government is best when smallest;
2. Respect liberty for the individual;
3. Hold taxes lower - and at home - to strengthen local government;
4. No tax increases ...and attract industry providing jobs;
5. A free public school system preserved and improved;
6. Remove the appointive powers of Judges so that they may devote their full time to judicial duties;
7. Equitable re-apportionment of legislative seats by population;
8. Assistance to urban localities perplexed by urban development.

In its other County Board campaigns in the 1960s to include that of Casto in 1963, Haggerty in 1965 and 1969, Ned Thomas in 1966, and A. Leslie Phillips in 1968, the Republicans raised issues concerning the closing of Hoffman Boston High School, the barring of YMCA clubs, forbidding prayers in schools, the violation of private property rights and the concealment of tax raises.[34] The closing of the Hoffman Boston School became a controversial matter in the wake of court ordered school integration. The closing of the school, in the segregated Arlington View neighborhood in South Arlington, by a school board appointed by a county board comprised only of members from white

---

[33] *Republican flyer 1952 Outstanding Local Candidates offered by GOP, Arlington Republican Executive Committee flyer, 1951, signed by I. Lee Potter, Chairman, Arlington Republican Executive Committee, and "Vote Republican" sample ballot for November 3, 1953 election.*

[34] *Harold Casto & James Matthews flyer in campaign for board in 1963.*

Sources of Influence

North Arlington neighborhoods was viewed by some as unnecessary and a means to avoid bussing white students from those areas into a black neighborhood. Ironically, in later years the move would also be questioned by the black leadership near the school as is pointed out elsewhere herein in Chapter Five in the discussion of school developments in the county.

The Republicans also charged that major crime had increased 66% under the ABC leadership, that continuous tax spiraling should be stopped, that money for parks should be invested in Arlington rather than regionally, and that the ABC Board had issued a "record 93 high density zonings in less than 2 years.." and "...if the practices of control by pressure groups and speculators is allowed to continue, Arlington will lose its residential identity." [34] The justification for Republicans to complain on some of these issues might be questionable since they had members on the board at the time and, in fact, in 1967 had a controlling majority.

Twilight for Republicans?

In the campaigns of Phillips in 1968 and Haggerty in 1969, the matter of repealing the ABC imposed 14% utility tax was picked up as an issue. Phillips maintained in his flyer that school improvements and maintenance of neighborhood school concepts, and protection of citizens rights to fair and impartial zoning hearings were areas that had declined under ABC domination and that improvements would be realized if he were elected to the Board.

In the 1970s, the Republicans continued to concentrate on many of the same issues they campaigned on in the previous decade. They charged in the Sid Dewberry and Frank Harding literature of 1971 that their opponents were failing to cope with the needs of balanced transportation, the alarming rise in the crime rate, and the spreading drug addiction problems. The extent to which the public accepted these criticisms, valid or not, is not documented, but it can be noted that both candidates lost the election.

In 1972, candidate Leslie Phillips, running for re-election, accused his opponent and the opposition in his flyer of making "all sorts of promises to bag the apartment tenant vote...with the usual political slanders thrown in...". Phillips listed, as the "key issues", inadequate funding for schools, the conflict of interest of his opponent (John Purdy) as an employee of the National Education Association when dealing with school related matters, and fiscal mismanagement with respect to money for road maintenance. He also listed excessive rezoning for high rise use at the expense of single family residential neighborhoods, a position more often claimed by his liberal opponents.

Republican candidate for County Board Henry Lampe campaigned heavily on the need for maintaining a Republican voice on the board. The lone Republican member, Haggerty was not running for re-election and Lampe stressed that if his opponent Ellen Bozman was elected, the board would consist only of members from one political group. Lampe failed to nose out his opponents, as did Dorothy Grotos on much the same theme the following year.

---

[34] *Kenneth Haggerty campaign flyer for 1965.*

ARLINGTON COUNTY - A Modern History

In 1975, however, Grotos, together with Walter Frankland, emerged comfortably ahead of their opponents Steve Krum and Richard Barton arguing that the board should have a balanced political and philosophical makeup. They contended, as issues, that there should be more open government, improved tax assessment, new initiatives to attract business, that government operations should be simplified and the school board should be more responsive to community needs.

In the 1976 race between incumbent John Purdy and Republican Daniel Graham, in addition to the extant issues, a new and different issue arose. During the campaign political flyers headed "APAC Arlington Political Action Committee", and the address 915 North Stafford Street, and with John Purdy's name and telephone number, together with a flyer reading "Come and Meet Jimmy & Rosalyn Carter at a Northern Virginia Rally" at a time and place designated, were found to be distributed throughout the county school system in teachers message boxes.

Upon learning of the distribution of the flyers, Republican candidate Graham filed suit in the U. S. District Court in Alexandria asking that he be granted a restraining order enjoining any further distribution of the flyers. He named as defendants the County and School Board members, the School superintendent and officials of the Arlington Education Association. At a hearing on January 7, 1977 before Judge Albert V. Bryan, Jr., the defendants' attorney advised the court that the practice had been discontinued, whereupon Judge Bryan dismissed the matter as moot.

"It is now Moot."

"Flyers in Schools?"

In the 1977 campaign, the Republican endorsed candidate Sherman Pratt, this author, a resident of the southernmost part of the county, made as the principle issue in the campaign the geographical imbalance on a board comprised only of members who lived in the extreme northern corner of the county. It seems that either his message did not reach the voters sufficiently, or they were indifferent to the matter since he did not succeed in defeating the incumbent Bozman although the vote was close.

Ironically, on November 11, 1977, the Washington Post published an article by staff writer Jay Matthews headed "Many South Arlington Residents Unhappy at Dominance of North". As explained in more detail in Chapter Four, the article was accompanied by a map of the County that plotted the residences of the County and School Board members, the legislative delegates, and the elected constitutional officers of the county. The map showed them all to live in the extreme north portion of the county, except one black school board member who lived in the county's black Nauck neighborhood in the South end of the county. It is interesting to speculate on what effect this publicity would have had on the election had it appeared before instead of after the election day.

After the Pratt-Bozman election there were news items questioning whether Bozman had been eligible to run for the board at a time when she had accepted an appointment to, and was sworn in as a member of, the Arlington Hospital and Health Center Commission, a body established pursuant to the Virginia Code.

Pratt filed a complaint with the Circuit Court asking for a ruling on whether Bozman had been eligible to run, or whether she was barred from doing so by Sec 15.1-50 of the Code. That section provided, in pertinent part, that elected officials shall not hold more than one office at a time and that if a person is elected or holds more than one

160

Sources of Influence

office his [or her] qualifications in one shall be a bar to his right to qualify for the other. Pratt questioned whether Bozman qualified as a candidate, and that if not, her name should not have been on the ballot, and that the printing of her name on the ballot was unlawful, null and void. The matter was heard by a panel of three judges who held for Bozman and dismissed the complaint.

1980 ISSUES

The campaign themes for the Republican county board candidates in the decade of 1980s remained much as it had for preceding decade. Their announced goals were much the same as those of their opponents except that they claimed they could better and more effectively reach them.

In the 1980 campaign self designated Independent Sim Pace was included on the Republican election literature and claimed credit "in the last two years under the Independent-Republican [board] majority for cuts in the real estate and personal property taxes. He stated as his "position on issues" that county growth policy should be balanced and well-planned, that METRO operating costs should be kept under control and that "...we can make our neighborhoods safe for all of us..." In 1981, candidate Bob Harrington, a South Arlington resident, echoed mainly the same issues used by Pace but added the charge that "current real estate assessment laws are responsible for diminishing the availability of affordable rental housing" in the county.

In the 1982 race, incumbent Steve Detwiler, a businessman and son of 1950s board member Dr Robert H. Detwiler, faced off successfully against challenger Whipple. Detwiler stressed his extensive community involvement in many civic activities and listed the reduction in crime and taxes, improvement in educational quality, significant expansion in citizen participation and openness in government, and a growth in community pride as accomplishments by the Republican controlled board during his term of service. In an editorial on October 23, 1982, the Washington Post backed Detwiler and asserted "...Detwiler has a record of independent thinking and moderation that stands him in good stead as the pivotal vote. We think he deserves reelection."

Surprising developments that seemed to defy dispositive explanation by any political analysts in the county occurred in the 1983 campaign. Newcomer, youthful and heavily community involved Mike Brunner emerged as top vote getter in a four way race with Al Eisenberg, Richard Buffum and incumbent Walter Frankland. Both political factions used the same political issues, essentially, of revitalizing business, protecting neighborhoods, strengthening schools and affordable housing, except that both continued to claim that they could do the job better. Brunner and Eisenberg won the two seats being contested with votes totaled 17,100 and 16,500 respectively with Buffum and Frankland trailing with 16,200 and 16,000.

In 1984, candidate Peter Espada, an economist and financial analyst also claimed that spiraling METRO costs should be controlled, that tax rates should be kept low and public housing should be opposed. His flyer read in part, "The County Board's liberal majority would like to impose a public housing authority on Arlington. They tried in

1982 but the voters overwhelmingly said no. Now they want to allow the Alexandria Public Housing Authority to broaden its influence in the County! This shows insensitivity and disregard for the views of Arlingtonians." Espada proclaimed that his Republican backed colleague and board member Mike Brunner needed help to achieve these goals.

The following year, another South Arlingtonian, Richard Herbst, active in PTA, Civic Association and other community efforts, and additional candidates in the remaining years of the 1980s campaigned on much the same issues as their predecessors. Herbst, as had Harrington in 1981, argued that his election would give South Arlington a much needed and deserved position on the governing body. In the race of 1987 in which Democratic candidate William Newman was elected as the first black board member since the days of reconstruction following the Civil War, race was not raised by the Republicans, as least openly, as an issue.

1990 REPUBLICAN ISSUES

The first political event of perhaps major significance on the Arlington landscape occurred in 1993 with a special April election to fill the empty board seat created by the appointment of Democrat member Bill Newman as a judge on the Arlington General Court. Independent, but Republican supported, Benjamin Winslow, who had ran the previous year unsuccessfully was pitted against the Democrat Jay Fisette, a self proclaimed homosexual. To the surprise of many and in spite of the well established strength of the Democratic Party as evidenced in many previous contests, Winslow squeaked ahead with 50.49 percent of the vote, i.e., 9,348 to 9,143.

The Arlington Journal on April 21 in a page one banner headline put it "Winslow wins in a squeaker". Writers Will Schermerhorn and Scott Schraff attributed Fisette's loss to a low voter turnout and quoted Arlington voter registrar Charlotte Cleary as saying, "There are so few voters today that everyone coming into the polls gets a really bright reception." Winslow's election provided the board with its only Republican, or opposition, voice.

Fisette's gay sexual orientation openly had not been made an issue and was not publicly commented on by Winslow or his supporters in the campaign but in the view of many observers there could be no disagreement that it must have contributed to Fisette's defeat. [36] Just to what extent, if any, Fisette's sexual orientation caused his defeat can never be known with certainty, but it can be noted that no known "Gay" has ever been elected to any office in the County before or since. Winslow contended that other issues, and public discontent with the controlling Democratic "machine" had been the cause of his success. In this connection, it can also be noted here that Winslow was not successful when he ran for reelection against a straight" candidate at the end of his shortened term.

---

[36] *One exception reported by the Journal on April 22 was a supporter with children in school who wrote to 12 friends asking that they not vote for Fisette because he was Gay, but that when Winslow heard of it he asked her to stop sending the letter.*

Sources of Influence

Winslow had publicly proclaimed that he wanted to change the direction of the county government and that it was out of touch with many basic county problems. [37] Winslow stated that he was especially unhappy with the county's health insurance program and that a study could save the county money.

The Arlington Courier on April 7, editorialized that the election of Winslow "would provide a needed voice". The editor wrote that Winslow had done his homework, demonstrated that he had fresh ideas, and exhibited a long-standing interest in Arlington political and governmental affairs..." These specified qualifications were at variance with the views of some Democrats and ABCers who had long contended that Republicans lost elections because they never ran qualified and community committed candidates.

The need for single member electoral districts was injected energetically into the regular 1993 election by Republican candidate John Barr, as well as the lower crime, maintenance of neighborhood schools, and lower taxes issues of earlier candidates. Barr made the change in the method of electing county board members by abandoning the at-large system a major plank in his campaign. The single member district issue generated considerable response in area letters to the editor columns. On September 14, Kevin Appel, chairman of the Democratic Party, wrote the Journal criticizing the Republican party's support for single member districts.

On September 23 and 29 the Journal and Northern Virginia Sun, respectively, published responses from Charles Cervantes and George L. Vollin. [38] Cervantes and Vollin wrote, in part, "...the arguments against single member districts emanating from the Democratic majority are self-serving, disingenuous and specious. Why do we want single-member districts in Arlington? Because it will broaden representation on the board, and offer a level of accountability not currently enjoyed by Arlington's various minority populations...John Barr and the Republican Party he represents seek the same end in pushing hard for single-member districts...we hope they succeed."

In 1994 the Republican Party chose a new chair person, Deborah Phillips who had managed Barr's unsuccessful 1993 campaign. Barr again became the Republican candidate for a second attempt for a board seat, this time running against incumbent Whipple. He again lost and the Washington Post reported, "GOP Juggernaut Stalls in Arlington - Democrats Remain Dominant in the County". Barr had again campaigned heavily on the single-member district issue but apparently had again been unsuccessful in getting his message across to enough voters to propel him into a board seat.

In 1995 Republican county board member Winslow ran for re-election with Party regular and activist Henriette Warfield unsuccessfully against Board incumbent Eisenberg and new comer Paul Ferguson. Both Republican candidates stressed the need for a

---

[37] *Washington Post, April 29, 1993, Virginia Section, p. 4.*

[38] *Vollin, as an African American in the historically black Arlington View neighborhood, mentioned herein, had long favored single member districts and was the lead plaintiff in a court suit also mentioned herein to break up the at-large system.*

ARLINGTON COUNTY - A Modern History

Republican voice on the board. The party and the candidates also continued as a campaign issue their long simmering struggle to eliminate the Business and Professionals Occupational Licensing Tax ("BPOL") In their party newsletter, Pachyderm Press, signaling an intra-party conflict that would come to a head in the following year, several articles appeared over the months stressing the need for Party Unity. Journal staff writer Michelle Meyers in an article on August 15, 1995, quoted House of Delegates candidate J.P. Jerry Gideon, as saying, "There is a strong feeling of discontent with the [Republican] leadership in Arlington County." Jonathan Moseley, a committee member from the Arlington Forest neighborhood wrote in the March issue, in part, "We must close ranks behind the party winner...choosing and supporting a candidate is the essence of political parties."

One can only speculate on the future of the Republican Party at the local level in Arlington County. The Democratic candidate for country board, James Hunter ran unopposed in November 1996 and won, no doubt to the chagrin and disappointment of Republican or non-Democratic voters in the county. In a special election earlier on January 25 to fill a board vacancy created by the election of board member Whipple to the State Senate in November, Republican candidate Scott Stone lost to Democrat Chris Zimmerman. Stone no doubt was not helped by his service as campaign manager for party rightist Oliver North in a U. S. Senate race in 1994 with an Arlington County electorate that has not been, and is not now, known for right wing extremism, at least to the extent that North has been perceived to be. Zimmerman was an economist with the National Conference of State Legislatures, extensively involved in county political and civic affairs, and perceived as a party insider.

In the Spring a somewhat bitter and rancorous contest developed for party chairmanship between the incumbent Phillips and the just defeated county board candidate Warfield. Marketing executive Warfield won by a margin of 63 percent. The contest was described in the media as philosophical in nature  between conservative Phillips and more moderate Warfield. Journal writer Gigi Whitley wrote on April 5 that in the party election for chair and committee members, long time conservatives had been unseated, including Sen. Robert Dole's deputy chief of staff. Whitley wrote, in part, "...Years of backbiting and a string of humiliating losses have pushed Arlington Republicans to the margins, while Democrats have maintained control of nearly every elected seat in the county" (emphasis supplied). Whitley, of course, understated the situation since there were at the time no elected positions at all occupied by Republicans.

Near year end, as November election day neared, a controversy arose concerning numerous bonds on the ballot. Bond issuing authority being submitted for voter approval included $12.9 million for land acquisition and parks. The Republican committee held a press conference on September 21 at Arlington's Bluemont Park and announced its opposition to park bonds. The Journal's Robert Gehl quoted party chair Warfield as saying, in part, "We're taking a stand on this issue. We want the community to note 'no' on the bonds. The county does not need millions of dollars for more parks." Gehl wrote that former board member Winslow as also at the conference and who had joined in

Sources of Influence

opposing the park bond issue. Gehl credited Winslow as saying that the parks department had become "unmanageable" and "the department cannot maintain or manage the facilities they now control". These same views were repeated and elaborated on in an op-ed article in the October 27, 1996, issue of the Washington Post headed "A Bridge to Nowhere and Other Follies" and sub-headed "The proposal to buy more park land strikes many Arlingtonians as a bad case of confused priorities". Notwithstanding the opposition of the Republican Party and some others, the park bonds easily won approval by the voters in the November, 1996 election.

At this writing, the future of the Republican Party in Arlington, and its chances of prevailing in any election can only be described and gloomy if not, indeed, dismal. Time will tell whether future events will result in a turn around.

In an interview with Republican party chair Henriette Warfield at the party's headquarters on South Glebe road on August 20, 1996, Warfield was asked by this author how she felt in her role as chair person. She answered, "Wonderful!...a most exciting challenge against a formidable machine that has been in power for 40 years." When asked about the future goals of the party, Warfield said it would be a "strong policy force...we will concentrate on schools, jobs, business retention, crime, and safety..." and would build strength through intensified door to door precinct work. She said the Democrats were "out of touch and arrogant" and the movement dominated by people "interested primarily in personal power"

ARLINGTON INDEPENDENT MOVEMENT (AIM)

Voter cultivation?

The campaign efforts, successes and failures of the Arlington Independent Movement or AIM are discussed to some extent above. Some additional comment on the Movement's issues and activities might be warranted.

In an AIM "Dear Neighbor" letter dated October 23, 1952, political or community activists Ruth Price, Thomas Broyhill and W. L. Bragg, Sr., urged support for board candidates Alvin Kimel, Leone Buchholz and Robert H. Detwiler. The letter indicated that the candidates were also endorsed by the following citizens, who are reported herein as being affiliated, in various degrees and times, with the early ABC, Democrat or Republican organizations: Mrs Harry Green, Oren R. Lewis, Harrison Mann, I. Lee Potter, Dr L. H. Blevens, Kingsley Higgins, Basil M. DeLashmutt, and Robert A. Peck.

In the letter its writers set forth their positions as follows, in part:

> "We have watched the conduct of our county government with growing alarm. It has been appalling to see the waste that has resulted from inexperienced and impractical leadership...property taxes have more than doubled since 1948...personal property taxes have increased tremendously...county operating expenses...are now 287% of the 1948 level...this can be accounted for only in part by increased school population and inflation...there has been waste...[by] Non-Partisans and...former Non-Partisan board members.
>
> "Its time we changed to experienced, responsible and practical people...".

In a 1953 flyer plugging for the election of AIM candidates James R. Miles and Dolph Hays to the school board, AIM criticized what it considered the prevailing educational philosophy of its political opponents. In a column headed "This We Believe - What A.I.M. Stands For" it asserted, in part:

> "It is not our desire to criticize the school system as a whole...but only to work for what we believe to be desirable and necessary improvements in teaching methods, curriculum, administration and school construction programs in the interest of all the children in our schools...we are alarmed over the educational philosophy that is being developed in Arlington...we do not believe that the philosophy upon which our educational system was founded can be surpassed by any socialistic philosophy...Our philosophy has made America the greatest nation in the world...we believe steps should be taken to develop a program of teaching and learning that will produce children who are better prepared to function adequately in all that they do...this can best be done by teaching basic subjects such as English, Reading, Spelling, Mathematics, Pensmanship [sic], Geography, Civics, historical background of America, and the Sciences...we believe that grades and competition should be maintained...we believe the best way to improve our way of life is to give every student a thorough understanding of our American heritage which was founded upon Christian principles and a deep appreciation of his rights and duties as an American citizen. This requires teaching self-control, courteous behavior, discipline, self-sufficiency and good work habits..."

In her campaign flyer in 1954, Buchholz described herself a "a gracious lady...extremely honest, sincere and conscientious in all her decisions as a board member...considers the feelings of each individual citizen, regardless of race, creed or color". She listed her goals as promoting capital improvement for needed streets, sidewalks drainage and recreation, to improve education with full day sessions and adequate classrooms, to minimize and equalize taxpayer burdens, and to work with area governments in joint sessions to expedite traffic flow to and from Washington to aid Arlington residents who use the traffic arteries.

Sources of Influence

As stated, AIM for its brief period became a force to be reckoned with in Arlington politics by controlling the governing body for four years until it was compelled to yield to the power of the new ABC movement. With their Republican and Official Democrat Cooper colleagues of like philosophy they occupied a majority on the board from late 1952 through 1956. Their leader Buckholz disappeared from board membership at the end of 1958 and AIM as an organized and functioning political activity in Arlington County passed from the stage and into history.

* * * *

VOLUNTEERS FOR AN INDEPENDENT ARLINGTON (VIA)

"The Republicans and Democrats are unresponsive and inept.
We are the Volunteers for an Independent Arlington and we can better speak for the people"

In 1992 as the height of the presidential primaries, conventions and campaign, and as the to be nationally known Ross Perot was appearing on the scene, a group of Arlington citizens met in the Lyon Village Community Center. One by one they took the podium and expressed their dissatisfaction with the Arlington County political situation and the direction in which the local government had been moving. Like Perot, they were disenchanted with both major political parties. Also like Perot, they decided to form their own independent movement. They embraced many of the concepts and arguments advanced by Perot on the national scene, and formed what functioned, for a while, as a local source of support for the Perot movement. In time, after the erratic performance of Perot in withdrawing and then returning to the presidential race, the local group would drift away from the Perot camp.

The group decided to call themselves the Volunteers for an Independent Arlington, or VIA. Initially it was headed by Arlington civic activists Jim Charleton, John Antonelli, Ben Winslow, Lincoln Cummings, Amy Jones, Timothy Wise and Ernie Ragland. [39]

---

[39] *Early participants as of March 13, 1993 also included Herbert Aburn, Reade Bush, Jane Coates, Thomas Dennison, James Kovach, Pete Kurzenhauser, Arnaldo*

ARLINGTON COUNTY - A Modern History

VIA prepared and made available a membership application asking for a $15 donation to be sent to VIA Coalition, 222 No. Evergreen Street, Arlington, VA, 22203. The application asserted that "Since the 1970s Arlington County government has become non-democratic...Elected leaders are doing what they want. We the people are being left out...We the people own Arlington...an imprudent government has led this fine county of ours to the edge of financial bondage with bloated staffs and long-term borrowing that we will have to pay in the future... We can and must reform our government and elect fiscally responsible people to office."

The application listed VIA's specific purposes as:

* Promote accountability, integrity, stewardship, honesty, ethics and values in local government;
* Work for election of all VIA Coalition-endorsed candidates;
* Promote an informed public through political education and activity;
* Provide an open forum for public debate of issues affecting good, fiscally-sound government;
* Communicate community positions on issues.

The steering committee of VIA met on December 28, 1991 and January 2, 1992 and adopted organizational plans. The group began to meet about bi-monthly and on January 8, it adopted a planning schedule for steering committee and membership meetings extending through June. The schedule contemplated the appearance of speakers to include Congressmen Moran and Wolfe and County Manager Anton Gardner. VIA began publishing its own newsletter, The Arlington Volunteers and threw its support behind the election of Independent Ben Winslow for the county board in the special election in April 1993, discussed elsewhere herein.

In due course, the continuing president and nerve center of VIA became Amy M. Jones-Baskaran, an attorney with a civil litigation and immigration practice in her own law firm, American International Legal Group, in Washington. Jones is a graduate of Georgetown University Law Center, graduated with honors, and lives in Arlington's Cherrydale neighborhood.

Jones, together with Ernie and Leslie Ragland are the driving forces behind VIAs energetic activities. The Raglands also write, edit and publish the Ballston Virginia Square Newsletter of the Ballston Virginia Square Civic Association, a civic association newsletter unequalled elsewhere in the county in comprehensive and in-depth content concerning civic and community affairs in the county.

Under its more recent leadership VIA has turned its attention from just local political races and greatly expanded its concerns into broader fields. It has prepared and proposed comprehensive state legislation on the following matters:

a. repeal of the Virginia Jurisdictions' authority to impose local income taxes;

Lerma, Ruth Lunn, John Marshall, Ann Meager, Donald Mozingo, Alfred Olsen, Cameron Quinn, Sherman Pratt, Alice Sayre, Evelyn Staples and Enid and Paul Weitz.

b. strengthening and expanding public access to government and the legislative process through the use of the internet and otherwise;

c. amending the constitution to allow a return of the Initiative and Referendum procedures;

d. achieving legislation to strengthen Virginia's conflict of interest laws especially as it relates to the Limited Partnership Act;

e. reforming Virginia's Judicial Nomination Process; and

f. improving and tightening the Virginia procedures for handling ethics violations by public officials.

At this writing VIA continues to meet regularly at its office of record at 3130 North 10th Street. It is represented in the meetings of the Civic Federation and county boards and commissions. It appears that VIA will continue to play a part in formulating public opinion and governmental actions affecting Arlington citizens but with less, or no, direct participation in local political campaigns. It has no ties with the 1996 Perot presidential campaign. As an indication of the perceived continued need for an organization such as VIA, a principle VIA player, Timothy Wise, who is also the President of the Arlington County Taxpayers Association wrote a letter to the Washington Post published on October 3, 1996. Wise outlined what he considered County Board mismanagement in past months concerning financial losses in real estate disposals and wasteful incompletion of a road bridge in Rosslyn's loop road system. He wrote "While Arlington's government misfeasance is presumably preferable to the malfeasance of some government leaders, an arrogant lack of fiscal responsibility has become so institutionalized that is has locally engendered a popular name--Arlogance.".

* * *

THE ARLINGTON EDUCATION ASSOCIATION

In any enumeration of Arlington County groups or organizations that exercise influence on the direction in which the county moves, the Arlington Education Association cannot be entirely omitted even if its areas of interest are somewhat limited to only a part of the county governmental overall operations. The school system, with which AEA is primarily and so heavily involved, absorbs almost half of the County budget, (excluding the costs of debt service). But far more important, its members have in their hands, more than any others outside the home, the fate and educational welfare of the community's most precious and treasured asset - the youth of Arlington County.

The organization cannot officially characterize itself as a union of teachers since State law does not allow public employees to engage in collective bargaining. The group does, however, in many respects function as a union with respect to recruiting teachers and others as members, and by lobbying and representing their interests before governing officials.

The AEA headquarters operates from offices on Columbia Pike in Falls Church, just west of the Arlington County boundary line. Representatives from the Association regularly attend school board meetings and especially annual budget conferences of the School and County Boards. AEA also takes an energetic part in work sessions on behalf of its members. In its operations and functions AEA is subject to and guided by the by-laws and policies of the National and the State Education Associations.

At this writing AEA has just under 1,400 members consisting mostly of teachers but also administrators and others who have an interest in the goals and objectives of the Association. About 75-80% of Arlington teachers are members of AEA. To be eligible for membership a person must first, or similtaneously, be a member of the National and State Associations. The dues for the local Association are a little over $100 per year and about $450 for all three Associations. There is no requirement that Arlington teachers be a member of AEA, but they are encouraged to join at their initial orientations at the time of employment, and at periodic membership drives by the Association or its supporters.

In appearing before governing bodies, or otherwise advancing the causes of its membership, AEA representatives make recommendations on behalf of teachers and school system employees, relating to working conditions, hours of employment, compensation, retirement and other entitlements, and other matters of interest to its members.

AEA has a president, a board of directors, and an executive secretary with a small office staff. The Presidents of AEA have usually been teachers, or individuals of established recognition and involvement in County affairs. Such leaders have often advanced to elective or other offices of importance and influence in the county. The President of the AEA at this writing is James Schroeder, a teacher in the County educational system. A current Arlington delegate to the Virginia legislature, Karen Darner, is a past president of the AEA. The executive secretary is Marjorie McCreery, a civic activist who has occupied positions of leadership over the years in the Committee of 100, the Civic Federation, and other community groups.

Hard working teacher?

THE ARLINGTON CHAMBER OF COMMERCE

The Arlington Chamber of Commerce merits at least passing mention in this chapter of activities in the county that are a source of influence on county affairs. Although its concerns are directed mainly toward attracting business and commercial activities into the county, and creating and maintaining a friendly and healthy environment for existing businesses, the Chamber, nevertheless, makes a contribution to county governmental operations through liaison with elected and appointed officials and appearances before bodies that are considering matters that could affect business.

The Chamber office is located at 2009 14th Street, North, Suite 111 and acts as a clearing house for business information, publications, and programs. Its President at

Sources of Influence

this writing is Richard V. Doud, Jr., and its Chairman is Carolyn Settles. The Chamber has a Board of Directors comprised of members from the more than 900 Arlington businesses, and other community activities. The Chamber's members include the Arlington Symphony, Marymount University, The Arlington Historical Society, the Arlington Hospital, Northern Virginia Community College and the Arlington County Public Schools.

The Chamber Speaks!

The Chamber publishes a periodic newsletter "The Arlingtonian". It does not hold monthly luncheons as do many other Chambers of Commerce elsewhere in the State or Nation. Instead, according to President Doud, the Chamber holds an annual banquet at which it presents awards to citizens who have made outstanding contributions to the community, especially in the areas of public safety such as police and firemen.

In an "Introduction to the Chamber for New Board Members", the Chamber explains that the Chamber movement is an international activity having originated in France in 1599. The first U. S. Chamber was formed in New York and today there are approximately 4,000 local chapters in the United States. Virginia has over 130 chapters.

The Arlington Chapter is one of the three largest in Northern Virginia (the other two being in Fairfax County and Alexandria). In addition to the some 900 Arlington business, professional and other organizations, President Doud pointed out to this author that the chamber also has over 1,550 individual members.

The mission of the Chamber, as stipulated in its publication, "The Arlingtonian", is:

"to serve the interests of our membership and the business community by identifying and implementing activities which enhance the ability of business to prosper; to foster economic opportunity and growth by promoting a favorable business climate; to provide information and advocacy that sustains and enhances the economic environment; and to take a leadership role in promoting community pride and recognition".

"What's good for business is good for Arlington!"

When asked what he considered to be future challenges or goals for the Chamber, Doud said the possible loss of major tenants or business interests such as the Gannet Corporation in Rosslyn and the U. S. Navy in several office buildings in the Crystal City area. "The loss of these major activities could spell real trouble for Arlington County. They will be difficulty to replace", Doud said to this author.

* * * *

THE ARLINGTON COALITION ON TRANSPORTATION (ACT)

Among the more energetic and effective activities in Arlington County in past years, has been the group that was formed in the 1960s to oppose the construction of that part of interstate highway I-66 that was to pass through Arlington and inside the "beltway" (I-495).

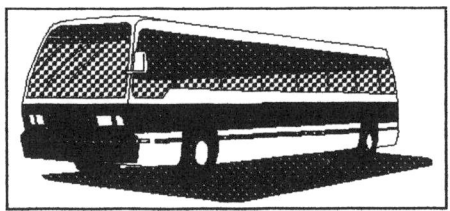

The group, known as the Arlington Coalition on Transportation or ACT, assembled a large number of members who were opposed to the highway and appeared before any and all local and higher bodies who had any decisional making role in the project. Eventually ACT filed a Federal court suit that held up construction for almost a decade until finally resolved. Few groups in Arlington, if any, have been more dedicated and committed to a project than the members and supporters of ACT. We will not, however, treat the movement further in this chapter since their campaign is described in much detail in Chapter Five "Major County Battles and Controversies".

CHAPTER FIVE

Major Community "Battles" and Controversies

Round I - Retrocession to Virginia	174
Round II - The Mackey Reform Movement	177
Round III - The Battle for Good Schools	182
Round IV - The Campaign for METRORAIL	208
Round V - The Prospect Hill Rezoning	221
Round VI - The Sickels Tract Rezoning	229
Round VII - The I-66 Controversy	238
Round VIII - Struggle for Single Member Districts	255
Round IX - The Aurora Hills Branch Library	271
Round X - The Pentagon City Rezoning	277
Round XI - The Struggle for I-395 Sound Walls	287
Round XII - The I-595 Upgrading Controversy	296
Round XIII - The Sewage Plant Expansion	305
Round XIV - The Football & Baseball Stadiums	317
Round XV - The Effort to Save Abingdon Ruins	336
Round XVI - The Acquisition of Fort C. F. Smith	364
Round XVII - Saving Arlington House Woodlands	393

Round XVIII - Falls Church Boundary Parks Lands   407
Round XIX - The Home Depot Proposal   413
Round XX - The Rosslyn Boathouse Proposal   419
Round XXI - Less than Major Battles   421

* * * *

Arlington County and its people, like most other American communities nationwide, have had their share of controversies, confrontations, arguments, disputes and disagreements down through the years. They have centered around issues ranging from land uses, public facilities, schools, zonings, taxes, transportation, and any number of other subjects that citizens perceive as effecting them and the enjoyment or value of their way of life, and even the County's very Virginia existence. We will here discuss some of the major disputes in the County in the days since the area has been a part of the United States of America in this Chapter, that is, post-revolutionary times.

Round I
RETROCESSION TO VIRGINIA

Probably Arlington's first "battle" of significance began when the area was still in its infancy only months after the adoption of the U.S. Constitution and the birth of the new Republic. It revolved around the question of whether the Virginia land ceded to the National government to form the Federal capital, should be returned to Virginia.[1] The land, some 26 square miles in size, ran along the Potomac river from the Jones Point corner stone in Alexandria, at the Virginia side of the modern day Wilson Bridge of I-495/95, to the northwest corner stone ten miles away along Meridian Street adjacent to Falls Church.

The signature ink on ratification documents was barely dry when in early years of the 1800s, demands were made by merchants in Alexandria, a minority view, that the Virginia lands be returned to the State. Georgetown interests had caused to be erected in the Potomac main channel a mole, or causeway, from the Virginia shore to Mason's Island (once Analostan and now Roosevelt Island). The mole interfered or blocked river commerce to the claimed detriment of the merchants in Alexandria. An 1804 Resolution introduced in Congress to effect retrocession was dropped, however, when opposed by the Mayor, citizens, and officials of Alexandria, but the issue did not disappear.

In 1824 another attempt at retrocession was made, but dropped, on grounds that citizens of Alexandria were deprived of their constitutional rights. Some claimed they could not exercise political power and were taxed without representation.

---

[1] *For more detailed treatment of this subject, see articles by Harrison Mann on pages 15 and 43, of the 1957 and 1958 issues of the AHS Magazine; and pages 80-82 of the C.B. Rose book, ibid., available at the Society Museum and the Virginia Room of the Arlington Central Library.*

Major Community "Battles" and Controversies

Finally, in 1846, prompted by financial problems stemming from the construction of the Alexandria Canal, the Virginia Assembly adopted a resolution agreeing to take back the Virginia part of the National Capital if the Congress agreed. The Congress did so agree on July 9, 1846 in an Act calling for a referendum under the direction of five commissioners to be appointed by the President. As an interesting sidelight, two of the commissioners duly appointed were George Washington Park Custis, builder of Mount Washington, now Arlington House in Arlington Cemetery, and James Roach builder of Prospect Hill manor on the high ground at the east end of Arlington Ridge Road over looking the Pentagon and Crystal City and now the site of the Representative condominium apartments.

The rationale for retrocession, as stated in the preamble of the Act, was that the national government should not hold territory more than that "necessary and proper" and that Virginia lands of the Federal government were not, or ever likely to be, necessary for that purpose.

In the Alexandria County referendum on retrocession on September 1 and 2, 1846 the vote was 763 for retrocession, and 222 against with most of the opposition centered in the residents of the "country" part of the county, i.e., those not in the Town of Alexandria. The days leading to the vote were filled with intense confrontations, meetings, and efforts by both sides to swing the outcome their way. The reasons on both sides are not well documented other, perhaps, than simply a matter of preference. C.B. Rose, however, in her Arlington history book, cited elsewhere herein, suggests at least a major reason for the opposition to retrocession by the people of the country part of the County, or present day Arlington, may be rooted in the slavery question of the day. Rose quotes a writing by Crandal Mackey, described below, that implies a racial, or discriminatory reason for opposing retrocession and the relinquishing of Federal control. Crandal wrote, in part:

> *"(Arlington County) ... by reason of accessibility, soon became an asylum for fugitive slaves, where they could seek the protection of the United States courts and the sympathy and aid of the early abolitionists residing in the District of Columbia. The slavery question becoming each year more acute the question of ceding back the county of Alexandria to Virginia became a political issue of the day..."*

Retrocession was not finally consummated with the referendum on the subject. There was yet to be contentious confrontation and continuation of the struggle by those opposing the return of the territory to the State. The Congressional Act authorizing retrocession provided that before the President could issue a proclamation declaring retrocession to be in full force and effect, Virginia had to extend its jurisdiction to the retroceded area. On January 7, 1847, a Bill was introduced in the General assembly to do so, and there it met extended and, for a while, uncertain treatment and outcome. Disagreements arose that by modern day standards could best be described as efforts to establish or defend political turfs both at the local levels and in the State legislature. Opponents of retrocession refused to "lie down and die", as former Arlington Delegate

Harrison Mann once put it. Various constitutional and other arguments continued to be made in support of the opponents positions. Numerous questions concerning the powers of the new territory, and its form of government and organization of courts and other instrumentalities had to be provided for in the jurisdiction measure.

The question that emerged and presented probably the most bitterness and controversy, however, was whether the County of Alexandria (to include the Town of Alexandria) would have its own delegate, or whether it would be represented by the delegate for Fairfax County. Rose wrote that the issue had all the overtones of "country boys" versus the "city boys". In any event it resulted in acrimonious parliamentary maneuvering, heated and closed deliberations, additional polls, and finally not an entirely clear resolution.

At one point the legislative committee of conferees presented a report denying Alexandria County a delegate and providing that Alexandria and Fairfax Counties should elect one delegate until a later reapportionment. The matter was much debated and there were efforts to lay the matter on the table or otherwise inconclusively dispose of it. At the time it appeared that Alexandria had lost the fight for its own delegate and the records of subsequent events do not shed much light on the matter. Delegate Mann observed: [2]

> *"It would be interesting to know if there were a gentlemen's agreement that at a later date, when the act authorizing retrocession could not be placed in jeopardy ... Alexandria would be given a delegate all its own. But the books are closed and lips are sealed on what occurred behind the scenes between the conferees and the leaders of the two houses fighting for a separate delegate".*

In any event, the Assembly on March 19, 1847, passed "An Act to extend the jurisdiction of the Commonwealth of Virginia over the County of Alexandria". The Act did not appear to clearly dispose of uncertainties concerning Alexandria County's entitlement to a delegate of its own. Retrocession, nevertheless, was consummated and Arlington's first major battle was over. The following December, two delegates, one from Alexandria County and one from Fairfax County showed up at the General Assembly, demanding to be seated, and both were. Mann wrote that this event lent "credence to the belief that a side agreement was made over the provision that caused the most difficulty".

Arlington's first significant battle, so critical to future relations with the State of Virginia and the National Government, was to quickly move to the background and pass into history. Just ahead on the horizon loomed the calamitous events leading to and through the Civil War, or the War Between the States, as some would label it. Clearly, there were to be more battles to command the attention of Arlingtonians.

---

[2] *AHS Magazine, October 1958, p. 50.*

Major Community "Battles" and Controversies

Round II
THE MACKEY REFORM MOVEMENT

Bars and saloons in Rosslyn

The next "battle" of major importance in Arlington history occurred around the turn of the present century and involved what could be considered the forces of "good" and "evil" in the most classical legendary and traditional uses of the terms. It took place just as Arlington County, then known still as Alexandria County, was in its early embryonic stages of transition into an urban community. There were growing numbers of scattered residential neighborhoods, as described elsewhere herein, but mostly the county was still undeveloped, with rolling woods and fields, and as yet with a relatively meager population of only about 6,000.

It seems, in this environment, at least in the view of some citizens, the county was going down the sinful drain with too many liquor stores, saloons, brothels, gambling houses and other houses of ill repute. There was also race track betting in the County to the intense disenchantment of church and other groups that usually consider themselves as the most virtuous elements in society. Most of these activities were located in Jackson City at the Virginia end of the Long Bridge, now the 14th Street Bridge and Lady Bird Johnson park complex, Rosslyn, and the lower reaches of Columbia Pike.

In the face of growing public impatience over these activities, there emerged in the early years of this century a promising and dedicated citizen to lead a charge for a return to law and order. In 1903 a civic activist, Crandal Mackey, ran for the office of Commonwealth Attorney, the position considered most critical in any effort to clean up the county.[3] The election was very close with Mackey receiving only 323 out of 763 votes cast, which, as a plurality, was sufficient to win. There were numerous heated charges of irregularities in the election and even court suits, but in the end Mackey was declared the winner.

Crandal Mackey stands as one of the more colorful figures in Arlington history.[4] Mackey was born in 1865 in Shreveport, Louisiana where his father, Thomas Jefferson Mackey, a Civil War engineer, had moved after the fighting. Later the family settled in South Carolina where his father served as Judge of the Circuit Court. When Crandal was 18, Historical Society member and past president Jack Foster writes, the family moved to Washington, D. C. where his father practiced law. Crandal attended Randolph Macon College and Georgetown University and there earned his law degree. In the Spanish American War he was appointed a Captain of Infantry Volunteers and after the war practiced law in Washington.

Upon taking office in 1904, Mackey swung into action to stamp out the "illegal activities" considered to be threats to law and order and a wholesome environment. In addition to prosecutorial measures in the courts, he organized posses that descended on the "houses of inequity". In her Arlington History book writer C. B. Rose described Mackey's tactical assaults, in part, as follows:

Crandal Mackey in Spanish – American War

"The area around Jackson City was dealt with in a different manner. A posse headed by Crandal Mackey armed itself with axes, sledge hammers, and at least one sawed-off shotgun, and boarded a train in Washington after arranging with the engineer to slow down long enough to let them off after it had crossed the Railroad Bridge. Here they entered the establishments where illegal activities were conducted, broke up the furniture, and generally wreaked havoc. ...there was a tale that a juke box knocked over in the melee played a popular tune of the times, "There'll Be a Hot Time in the Old Town Tonight."

Foster expands on Rose's account and writes that upon taking office, Mackey did not have the full support of law enforcement officers. He requested the sheriff to take the necessary action to shut down gambling but the sheriff stalled and requested more time. But after a delay of four months, Mackey decided more direct action was needed. He obtained warrants and made plans and organized his helpers.

---

[3] *Mackey and his campaign are also briefly discussed in Chapter Four herein.*

[4] *See article* Crandal Mackey, Crusading Commonwealth Attorney, *by Jack Hamilton Foster, page 22, AHS Magazine, October, 1984.*

Major Community "Battles" and Controversies

*Crandal Mackey and children at his home   (Now townhouses)
1711 No. 22nd St on Mackey Hill*

When Mackey descended on the Jackson City with the raid Rose describes, he found the place hidden behind a high board fence, but the gate had been left open because no raid had been expected. Foster notes that the Alexandria Gazette devoted little space to the Mackey raids, but that the Washington Star on May 31, on the contrary, gave the matter conspicuous attention, as follows, in part:

> *"Commonwealth Attorney Crandal Mackey and a number of law-abiding citizens of Alexandria County, Va. late yesterday afternoon visited several places in the county where gambling is alleged to have flourished and made a demonstration which is intended to give the lawbreakers an idea of what they may expect if they persist in operating* [5]
> *...Mr Mackey is being backed by the better people of the county, it is said, and yesterday when he called for volunteers the responses were numerous...the 'raiders' were anxious to put the pool room at St. Asaph's out of business first and then visit the smaller establishments. None of the proprietors was in place at Jackson City but a number of gamblers were engaged in various games. They suddenly recalled that they had engagements elsewhere and were in a hurry to keep them. It did not bother them whether they left through the open doors or the closed windows. They all wanted to get out in a hurry...when the posse*

---

[5] *Note the change in journalistic practices over the years. It is doubtful that modern day media writers would conclude that Mackey's posse were "law abiding", or that their targets were "lawbreakers" without a court determination to that effect.*

> *had driven the crowd from the place, the work of destruction was commenced and in a few minutes several hundreds of dollars of property had been destroyed...glassware was smashed and contents of the bottles, demijohns and decanters were allowed to flow, giving the room the appearance of having passed through a Potomac flood. Rosslyn was visited next...each place the party took paraphernalia enough to use as evidence...some of those in the party were anxious to apply the torch to the gambling places, but Mackey would not countenance such conduct..."*

In an editorial on May 1, 1905, the Star applauded the new county administration that had forced gamblers to leave the southern side of the river. The editors said that no longer were there degrading conditions on the high road from the city to the national cemetery or at the very gates of Ft Myer, both of which were of instructive interests to all visitors to the city. The paper said now it would be possible for tourists to inspect both these points without being subject to disgusting sights or unpleasant experiences.

In this early Arlington battle between the forces of good and evil, getting rid of the saloons proved to be especially difficult. In a referendum on the question the drys lost. Another community pillar of the day, Frank Lyon, joined the fray. The law required that liquor license applications must be accompanied by signatures of citizens supporting the license, and by a determination that adequate police protection existed before a liquor license could be issued. As editor of the local newspaper, The Monitor, Lyon threatened to publish the names of those supporting a liquor license, and in court suits he pointed out that in a county with only one sheriff and constable for each Magisterial District, there was not adequate police protection. The Judge agreed and denied applications for licenses, ending the sale of liquor by the drink in Arlington County.

After the raids on illegal activities in the County Crandal Mackey served two more terms as Commonwealth's Attorney. He also became interested in writing and publishing and wrote *A History of Alexandria County* as a member of a committee appointed by the Board of Supervisors. Foster writes that Mackey edited and published the Chronicle newspaper for many years and unsuccessfully ran for Congress in 1930. He also served as a director in the Arlington National Bank in Rosslyn and helped organized the Arlington Trust Company that had headquarters for many years in the building by that name on Court House Road opposite the County courts and administration. He resided most of his years in a home at 1711 North 22nd Street, now a vacant lot, in an area known as Mackey Hill just north of Rosslyn.

In her book, Rose summarized the early Mackey clean-up battle in this way:

> *"The struggle to clean up the County had been difficult and prolonged but with determined leadership and the support of a public-spirited citizenry the campaign was successful. Thereafter Arlington was able to develop rapidly, free from the stigma of being a refuge for lawless elements."*

Major Community "Battles" and Controversies

The County was also free to launch into its next community battle. And it was not long in coming.

The Crandal Mackey Grave in Arlington Cemetery

ARLINGTON COUNTY VIRGINIA - A Modern History

Round III
THE BATTLE FOR "GOOD" SCHOOLS

BACKGROUND

No narrative of the "battles" that Arlington and its residents have experienced down through past developing years would be complete without some reasonable mention of those surrounding the building and improvement of the county public education system.

In some respects it may be a misnomer to label this struggle as a battle. Battles, in war, or even a non-military environment, are usually of a limited time length or defined in terms of a set number of days, or even hours. The Arlington school struggle has taken on more the characteristics of a open ended campaign, or series of never ending "battles", in various directions and over differing causes, that began in the earliest days of the county and continues to this date.

To correctly assess the matter, consideration must early on be given to as clear an understanding as possible as to what is meant by "good" or "improved" schools and to recognize that what might be good or better so some, may not be to others. In this context the adjectives "good" and "improved" are both relative and subjective. In a primitive atmosphere, a good school might well be any school at all, especially if there has been none. To others, and probably most people today, a good school would at least require a proper and adequate meeting place, or school building, well qualified, motivated, capable and fairly compensated teaching and staffing personnel, and a sensible curriculum of subject matter with as many of the needed teaching aids and equipment as

Major Community "Battles" and Controversies

possible. People can also differ greatly in their views of "adequate schools" depending on what they perceive to be the objective of secondary public education, and what they want the finished product to be.

Still others may consider, especially it seems in recent years of widespread criticism and dissatisfaction with the products of public education, that good schools require more than just the above ingredients. They may feel that no matter how polished and ample may be the physical, technical and material aspects of public education, more yet is required to produce a properly educated student ready to take his or her expected place in society. As the 20th Century draws to a close, there has been ever increasing publicity concerning school disruption, disobedience, violence, guns, drugs, defiance, absenteeism, lowering of standards for "politically correct" or other reasons, and numerous symptoms of a deteriorating educational system both in Arlington as well as, generally, nationwide. Many taxpayers, parents, and other concerned citizens will question whether any system can be labelled correctly as "good", no matter how well financed and equipped, if disorderliness, disruption, and lack of control in the class rooms exist. Opinions in Arlington County vary greatly as to whether its school system has been, or is, "good" when all these factors are reasonably taken into careful and balanced account.

SOURCES OF INFORMATION ON SCHOOL HISTORY

For a record of the Arlington County effort to establish and develop its public educational facilities, one must look mainly to a small number of historians, or historical writers, who have labored diligently to document what information has been, or is, available from rather skimpy public or private records. It is mainly to these writers, and the references they annotate in their writings, that we will lean  on to cover the highlights of the building of Arlington's system, and obstacles encountered, as covered below.

Foremost among these writers, who have contributed articles to the Historical Society's annual magazine, are Seymour Stiss, Cecelia Michelotti, C. B. (Cornelia) Rose, Jr., and an anonymous "Research Committee" of the Historical Society. Rose (deceased) was, and Stiss is, long time members of the Society. Both are also past presidents. Rose was a founder of the Society and also author of the only comprehensive history book of Arlington to date, Arlington County Virginia, A HISTORY, cited elsewhere and identified in footnotes herein. Michelotti taught mathematics at Arlington's Wakefield High School and wrote her Master's Program paper at the University of Virginia on the subject of Arlington's schools. Rose's article on Arlington Schools in the 1870-1905 era begins on page 17 of the Society's 1965 magazine; the Research Committee article on community efforts to improve schools begins on page 41 of the 1966 issue; Stiss's article on school buildings appeared on page 3 of the 1979 issue; and Michelotti's article on school desegregation begins on page 3 of the 1988 issue. Limited additional information on this subject is available from the Virginia Room of the Arlington Main Library, from Historical Society archives, and probably from the State Historical Society in Richmond. Rose stated that the "Minute Book" of the Arlington School District from 1870 to 1905 formed the basis for her writing, but she alluded to "gaps" in the minutes and pointed out that they were "in many respects not complete" and "some results (of meetings) were not recorded". [6]

One additional source for information on schools used herein is Principal's aide Catherine Sue Kleinsfeldt, cited in footnotes, who prepared a paper on the history of Arlington Schools, and Abingdon Elementary School, for the Centennial Celebration of Arlington Schools in 1971.

Perhaps the most thorough, in depth, and well researched and documented account of Arlington School history, however, is contained in the December 1991 Historical Resources Survey 18 Early-Mid Twentieth Century School Buildings, prepared for the Arlington County Department of Community Planning, Housing and Development by Lois Snyderman and the Couture Denig Partnership.[7] The Survey, that is almost 500 pages in length, limits itself to Twentieth Century school buildings, presumably, because there are no 19th Century school buildings extant, except for the 1890s Hume School building on South Arlington Ridge Road. That building has not been used as a school since the 1950s and the ownership was transferred to the Arlington Historical Society. It now serves as the headquarters and museum for the Society.

As indicated in the title, the Survey authors examined 18 county schools with a goal "to identify those schools which have potential for historical district designation under Section 31A of the Arlington County Zoning Ordinance and landmark designation under the criteria established by the National Register of Historic Places". The Survey footnotes show that the authors heavily relied on the School Board minutes for their information, as did C. B. Rose cited herein, and also on County Neighborhood Conservation Plans, some newspaper articles, and on some Arlington School history and architectural writers to include Fletcher Kemp, Andrew Gulliford, Susan Gilpin, Jewel Griffin, Andy Johnson, F. Wallace Dixon, and public school teacher Judy Rundle.

The Snyderman survey lists, of the 18 schools, the Woodrow Wilson (1910), Hoffman-Boston (1915 and 1932), Barcroft and Washington-Lee (1924) as the oldest school buildings in the county and the Abingdon, Stratford (now H-B Woodlawn) and Oakridge schools (1950) as the newest. All of the others are shown to have been built in the years from 1925 to 1947 (Barrett, Drew, Fairlington, Stonewall Jackson, Langston, Robert E. Lee, James Madison, Randolph, Walter Reed, Swanson and Woodlawn. Schools built after 1950 such as Gunston, Kenmore, Thomas Jefferson, Wakefield, Yorktown and some others, would presumably be too new to have any particular historical significance.

---

[6] *Copies of the Board Minutes, as well as the issues of the AHS Magazine cited herein are available for examination by interested persons in the Virginia Room of the Arlington Main Library and the Society Museum archives in the Hume School on South Arlington Ridge Road.*

[7] *Copies of the Survey are available in County Manager and School system libraries and specifically in the Virginia Room of the Main Arlington County Library.*

Major Community "Battles" and Controversies

In assessing the community historical importance of a school building, the survey mostly relates a school to the development of the particular early or historical neighborhood served by the school such a Fairlington/Shirlington, Barcroft, Buckingham, Waycroft-Woodlawn, James Madison (Walker Chapel area near Chain Bridge), and Highland Park-Overlee Knolls ((Walter Reed). Exceptions to that criteria were applied to the Drew and Hoffman-Boston and Langston schools for their roles in the development of early black communities in North and South Arlington, and to Stratford as the first school to be desegregated as discussed in more detail elsewhere below.

Over and above these historical considerations, the Survey authors considered the Stonewall Jackson and Wilson schools to have special historical significance. The Wilson school (now an adult center) is noted to have been in continuous education use since 1910, longer than any other school in the county. It was first called the Ft Myer Heights school and served the neighborhood known also by that name in east Arlington at the "gateway" to Washington. The school building is located on what was once the farm of William Ross called "Rosslyn" that was subdivided and sold to developers after the Civil War. Part of the school site was once the Civil War Fort Corcoran. After the war the school area became a center for lawless elements that dominated the waterfront of Arlington until the Mackey cleanup campaign of 1904 as discussed in Chapter Four herein. In the early 1900s the Washington Golf and Country Club was located on the school grounds and in 1925 its name was changed to Woodrow Wilson in honor of the 28th president, a Virginian born in Staunton.

The Survey authors apparently felt the Stonewall Jackson school (now a special education center) was historically unique because of its location near renown Ballston, one of Arlington's first concentrations of residences and because the school served the early 1920 railroad subdivisions of Veitch and Bon Air. The school was first called the Bon Air school until changed in 1926 to honor the famous Confederate General. The Ballston intersection at Wilson Boulevard and Glebe Road was earlier known as Birch's and later Ball's Crossroads. It was a key stop on the electric railroad and the Washington Arlington and Falls Church Railway until 1930.

THE BEGINNING OF ARLINGTON SCHOOLS

Prior to the Civil War, or War Between the States as Southerners were wont to term the fighting, there seems to have been no public schools in the country part of Alexandria County (Arlington). Settlement then was still sparse and such school age children as there were, if they resided in the northern or eastern parts of the county, went to school in the District of Columbia, if they went at all. If they lived in the southern portions, they most likely attended schools in the City of Alexandria.

Just how many children attended school is not well recorded. Rose wrote that Statewide the more affluent residents sent their children to private schools or tutored them at home and that free public schools existed only for the "poor". She added that many people who could not afford private education hesitated to send their children to free public schools "to avoid the stigma of poor". As survey writer Snyderman put it, "Education opportunities were very limited, particularly for the blacks and middle class whites, and illiteracy was widespread". She pointed out that support for a public school system was slow to develop in Virginia, in contrast to other parts of the country, and;

> *"Public education, administered by the state, was looked upon by the aristocracy as being intended for paupers, and the poorer class resented the attempt to pauperize themselves by accepting aid from the state for the training of their children. Thus public education found no real place in the social fabric of the state until the middle class developed a truer conception of democracy than that which existed during the early days"*

Snyderman also contrasted the Virginia attitude on public education with that of New England where "nonsectarian public education had been an important issue since 1647 in the colonial period when the Massachusetts Bay Colony governing body enacted the first statute in the nation providing for the establishment of a system of public grammar schools and requiring selectmen in each township to provide school buildings. She mentioned too the Federal Ordinance of 1784 for the Northwest Territory that required states to establish permanent funds to endow public schools, using receipts from the sale of public lands. She wrote that the New England and Northwest Territory models did not flourish much in Virginia and the South, if at all, perhaps because of the lack of public lands to sell and finance any public school programs.

Upon the ending of the war, however, the adoption of the Constitution of 1869 and the reestablishment of operative State government, new legislation provided for the establishment of free public schools for other than just the poor. The schools were to be managed in each district by boards appointed by the State Board of Education (later they would be appointed by the Circuit Court). Arlington had three such districts, Jefferson, Arlington and Washington that also served as magisterial districts. The district members, collectively, formed the County School Board with the superintendent as *ex officio* Chairman. Uncertain financial support came from various taxes, but local supplementation was permitted.

School board officials in those early days were responsible for taking a census of the school population, hiring teachers, and determining the number and location of schools. Writer Snyderman quoted Kemp (supra) as saying the responsibility of the officials "...was to build up a public sentiment in favor of free schools. The people of Virginia were slow to realize the appropriateness of the state's undertaking an important part in the function of educating children both white and Negro."

The first Arlington School Board, with county population still under 5,000, held its organizational meeting on October 28, 1870. In the coming months, the Board established Arlington's first three schools. They were at the "Columbia House" on Columbia Pike at the corner of now South Wayne Street, at a building known as "Union League Hall"; at Freedmen's Village that became known as the Arlington School House, taking its name from the Custis-Lee Arlington estate where Freedmen's Village was located; and in Good Templars Hall (the Walker School) at Balls Cross Roads. They

Major Community "Battles" and Controversies

were designated Arlington Schools Number 1, 2, and 3 respectively.[8] Snyderman wrote that by 1871 there were five schools in the Jefferson and Arlington Districts (three white and two colored) with 333 students (126 white and 207 colored) and that by 1881 there were nine, all frame and with outhouses.

The 1891 former Hume School on Ridge Road, Arlington's oldest school building.

Writer Susan Gilpin (supra) wrote [9] that the first school for Arlington Blacks was established by the American Tract Society, a religious organization, in 1863 in the black settlement Freedmen's Village and that the school at its height had 150 children with a principal and four teachers and an evening school for adults. She related further that the school was acquired by the Arlington County system in 1870 and functioned until 1889 by which time most of the Freedmen's village residents had resettled elsewhere in the communities of Nauck in South Arlington, Johnson's Hill (now Arlington View), Butler-Holmes west of Fort Myer, or in new communities (razed at the beginning of World War II for the Pentagon building construction) such as East Arlington, Queen City, and South Washington.

In 1875, with the coming demise of Freedmen's Village and the Arlington School #2, two other colored schools were opened, one in Rosslyn and Kemper School in the Green Valley, or Nauck, neighborhood. The Kemper school was initially located in the A.M.E. Zion Church until 1893 when a two story brick school building was erected.

---

[8] *Kleinsfeldt, Catherine Sue, manuscript, The History of Arlington County Schools, on file in Virginia Room, Arlington Main Library.*

[9] *Arlington Black History, July, 1984, Vertical files, Virginia Room, Arlington Public Library.*

ARLINGTON COUNTY VIRGINIA - A Modern History

The Kemper school building was eventually replaced. With the Drew Elementary school, among others, it was included in the Snyderman survey.

Snyderman related that the educational goals of Arlington's early school was simple, clear and uncomplicated to teach reading, writing, spelling, arithmetic and good moral behavior.

Rose does not indicate specifically in her writings that the Arlington School (# 2) was integrated, but from available records, and a knowledge of racial relations and attitudes at those times, it can be safely assumed that it was not. She and her contemporary writers do mention the Kemper school was established for "colored" and they do not write, understandably, that the school was only for those children. Even if it were planned to operate the school as an integrated facility, it presumably soon would have become segregated under the prevailing conditions that existed in Southern States following the Civil War.[10] In any event the matter would have become moot within a decade as the Village population was resettled in the nearby communities, and the school was no longer needed and closed. Kleinsfeldt wrote that there was a difference in the number of days the schools operated each year. She wrote that the Arlington "colored" school was open for 180 days, almost twice the number for the other schools.[11]

ARLINGTON'S FIRST SCHOOL BATTLES

Two of the first "battles", or at best "confrontations" concerning school operations in the County arose and centered around School Number 1, on Columbia Pike and Number 3 at Balls Crossroads.

The Templar Hall, by available accounts, had served well as a home for Arlington School Number 3 (Ballston, or Walker) for a number of years but by 1877, with a steady increase in enrollment, it had become unacceptably crowded and the School Board considered obtaining an additional building near Balls Crossroads.

Herein lay the beginnings of trouble and problems. As Rose put it, "A foretaste of the difficulties to be encountered many years later in selecting a site for the Columbia School was experienced in the disagreements which immediately arose when a particular location was mentioned."

---

[10] *For details on personalities, costs, salaries, and other arrangements in the establishment of these early schools and School Board meetings, interested persons could refer to Rose's cited article in the 1966 AHS Magazine in the locations mentioned. That information is beyond the scope of this narrative, but one of the first Board members, Lewis Bailey, might bear mentioning. He was from the family for which modern day Bailey's Crossroads is named.*

[11] *Kleinsfeldt, ibid.*

Major Community "Battles" and Controversies

The Board received offers for sale and donation of the necessary land within 400 yards and the Crossroads and accepted a plan for the building to accommodate not less than forty "scholars". Days later, the Board received an offer at a very attractive price from another land owner presenting the board with a dilemma as to which offer to accept. Disagreement amongst the citizens developed and pressure mounted against the Board. Each of the sites were considered to be more convenient to certain citizens. The claim was made that most of the pupils attending the school lived "north of the Georgetown Road (Wilson Blvd) and the small tots would be unable to attend the school because of the increased distance if the first site was chosen. In the process, at least five other sites were taken into consideration, as the pot of contention heated. Eventually the matter was resolved with the selection of a site at the corner of what is now Wilson Blvd and North Randolph Street. Thus ended the first of Arlington's educational battles. But there were to be others as we shall see.

TRAUMA IN RELOCATING A SCHOOL

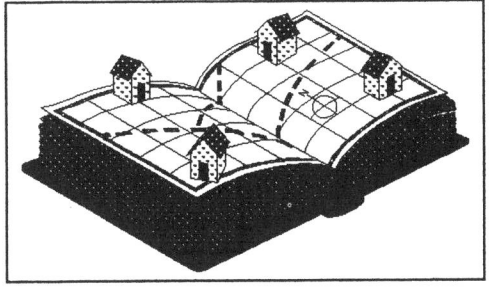

By 1900, the school population at the Columbia school, like Walker before it, had grown so much that the School Board looked around for a site to relocate and enlarge the school in the vicinity of Grey's corner, at about the present intersection of Glebe Road and Columbia Pike. It focused on a site known as the "Brown" lot on Columbia Pike just west of the present Walter Reed Drive. An election was held to get citizen approval. By a majority of 16 the citizenry opted for the Brown site. The dissatisfied losers, however, called for the creation of an appeal board under State law to hear the matter. The board was duly created, heard the matter, and ruled against the losers, whereupon they sought further review in the Circuit Court that, in turn, ruled that the losers challenge had no standing. The losers thus lost again.

Following the Court decision, the Board proceeded with plans to acquire the Brown lot and construct the school there. At least one Trustee continued his opposition. He filed a motion objecting to the site alleging that the water drainage was bad, the cost excessive, and the location next to the trolley line dangerous for children. The record is silent as to other reasons for opposing the school at the Brown site, but one could assume, as in modern times, that at least some parents might have desired the school to be nearer their homes, especially in the days before wide uses of school buses, and autos in every drive way. Others may have wanted it farther from their homes so as not to be disturbed by noisy children at recess or arriving and departing from the school.

In the meantime, the population at the Columbia school was continuing to grow and construction of a replacement had to begin. Despite uncertainties, arguments, hard feelings and disagreements over ceilings, privies, grading of grounds, concreting of basements, assembly halls, and other details, the school was finished and the School

Board met in its Hall in August 1904. But the friction was not yet over. The news media reported that there were complaints over the cost and size of the building that had increased from an original $5,000 to over double that amount to $10,515. Rose wrote, however, that the Arlington District School Board did, "have a building of which it was proud and which was acknowledged to be one of the finest school building in the State". Rose did not identify the source for that conclusion, nor does there seem to be any way of reliably determining the extent, if any, that her opinion was shared, or opposed, by others at the time.

ADDITIONAL SCHOOLS

In the closing years of the 19th Century, after the establishment of the first three Arlington Schools described above, and until 1905, the School Board established several additional schools. The Kemper school in the area now known as Green Valley or Nauck was opened to replace the phasing out Arlington school, and schools were established in Rosslyn, Glencarlyn, Fort Myer Heights and Clarendon (later the Woodrow Wilson School). [12] There were no particular controversies of record surrounding the birth of these schools although some difficulties requiring touchy resolution were experienced with contractors for the Glencarlyn and Clarendon schools concerning quality and building materials, designs and locations.

All of Arlington's first schools must have operated financially on shoe string budgets, even at those early day standards. Most had only one teacher, the pay ranged from about $25-40 a month, and the teacher was generally required to provide any supplies from her wages. Rose reported that an exception was made by the School Board for the Glencarlyn school. In that case they allowed the teacher $5 a month for rent, and paid for three tons of coal to heat the rented room. Kleinsfeldt wrote with somewhat more specificity, that teacher James Doharty was paid $35 per months, and teachers James Oresh and Miss C. C. Anderson received salaries of $40 per month. [13]

The establishment of schools in Arlington continued apace through the early years of the 20th Century and by 1922 there were a total of 16 schools. The County's first enduring high school, Washington-Lee was under construction and would be opened in 1924 for students who had been required to attend high schools in the District of Columbia or Alexandria. There were two earlier Arlington high schools, one located in the Delray section before annexation by the City of Alexandria around 1922, and another in a building purchased from the School Board by the St. Agnes private school on North Randolph Street in Arlington. Also in 1922, an event of some historical significance took

---

[12] *There appears to be an inconsistency in school numbers in Rose's book and in her AHS Magazine article. She lists six schools by 1905, less the Arlington closed school, for a total of 5. In her book on page 136 she writes "In 1881, there were nine school in the County...", and on page 138, she writes, "By 1900 there were 11 schools in the County...". Since Rose is deceased, and reliable records are scarce, there seems to be no way to reconcile these differences.*

[13] *Kleinsfeldt, ibid, p. 2.*

place when the three school boards, one from each District, were formed into a single board, pursuant to newly enacted State legislation.

Historical Society writer Seymour Stiss reports that as of 1922, the Arlington District had 8 schools and 34 teachers, the Jefferson District 4 schools and 24 teachers, and the Washington District 4 schools and 18 teachers. [14] Stiss stresses, however, that many of the schools would be later changed, renamed, or their buildings added to or replaced. Some would be closed. At the time that Stiss wrote in 1979, he lists 55 new schools as having been built in the County and 77 schools as having been renovated, or added to. Since 1979 there may have been some additional changes. The County's three high schools, Washington-Lee, Wakefield and Yorktown, were built in the years 1924, 1953, and 1950-60, respectively.

THE COUNTY COUNCIL OF THE 1930s

The efforts in early years to establish schools and an educational system in Arlington, as we are describing, certainly contained their moments and instances of discord, obstacles, road blocks, discouraging pain, and challenging frustration. The available records, however, do not seem to reveal much evidence of any really knock-down, drag out, bitter and costly engagements or any major blood letting that could be labeled as "battles", or at least not large and cantankerous battles.

County Council of 1930s

The first such engagement, to require a marshalling of forces for combat and an all out assault on a designated objective with a determination to emerge victorious, seems to have occurred in the early years of the Great Depression. February 9, 1931 marks the birth of the County Council of PTA's from Civic Leagues, Mothers' Clubs, Parents' Club, PTA's and others.

The purpose of the movement, and the new Council was to work for a bond issue to improve schools. By 1934 the Council launched its legislative program urging full 9 month school year sessions, a minimum teachers salary of $720 per annum, and free text books for children. In addition to these goals, the Council was armed with a report from the U. S. Bureau of Education recommending a construction program of $355,000, and a bond issue of $580,000 to cover that program and certain other outstanding loans. The report indicated that Arlington ranked 24th out of 28 cities of comparable size and situation in pupil expenditures.

In due course, the Council sent its troops to Richmond and launched an assault on the Legislature and State Government to achieve these objectives. In the following years they were successful in reaching most of these goals, as well as others. By 1935 the Council and its supporters were able to get a ruling that a child could enter school in his 6th year with the result that many 5 year olds were in school, and that children

---

[14] *Stiss, Seymour B., School Buildings in Arlington: 1922-1979, AHS Magazine, October 1979, p. 3.*

must attend school in their district instead of shopping around for their preferred school or teacher.

By 1937 the Council was bringing pressure on the County Board for more funds for school buildings and operations, especially for junior high schools. The Council aided the Page school PTA in its project to initiate training for handicapped children. In 1938, the Council, as reported by the Historical Society Research Committee, "undertook a program designed to create wide interest in, and better understanding of, the school program in Arlington, and to interpret to the public the Virginia new curriculum...". [15] The Council also wrote letters to State legislators opposing a Bill under which the County Board, instead of the Circuit Court, would be given authority to appoint school board members. The Council's position was that it wished to keep the selection of School Board members out of politics. Later school activists were to take an opposite position on this matter. The Council also aided in organizing safety patrols and increasing supervision of playgrounds. The record does not indicate that any of these projects or programs were especially contentious or very stiffly opposed by any particular group of citizens.

As the County and country approached World War II, the Council formed special committees that worked closely with the school board on matters of air-raid shelters, gasoline rationing, and increasing teachers salaries. Thus, Arlington's first significant battle over school operations and issues was being waged by untiring and unrelenting participants who were claiming repeated victories. Battles were being won with little or no opposition. That too was to change in future years as we shall see below.

THE POST WORLD WAR II PERIOD

As Arlington, like countless other communities nationwide, emerged from the trauma of World War II, it found itself confronted with the need to recover from many disruptions caused by burdens and sacrifices in the war years. The impact of large influxes of Federal wartime workers with families and children had over taxed many community services and facilities. In the view of some residents, school facilities especially were strained, over crowded, and in many ways woefully inadequate. There was a wide spread feeling that county officials were not responding to community

---

[15] *Community Efforts to Improve Schools in Arlington County, Virginia,* Research Committee, Arlington Historical Society, The Arlington Historical Society Magazine, October 1966, p.41.

Major Community "Battles" and Controversies

demands for greater attention and effort to public education and school needs. Arlington's second major "battle" over schools was about to get under way.

THE BIRTH OF THE CITIZENS COMMITTEE FOR SCHOOL IMPROVEMENT

It was with this backdrop that a group of Arlington citizens, headed by one Oscar R. LeBeau, met in May, 1946 and formed an organization they identified as The Citizen's Committee for School Improvement, or CCSI.[16] Its constitution stated that the objectives of the group were, in substance, (1) to obtain and publicize facts concerning the problems of public education, (2) to encourage citizens to participate in the guidance of their school administration through attendance at meetings and hearings and through support of well qualified candidates for the school board, (3) to cooperate with other civic organizations and mobilize public support for an improved education system for Arlington, and (4) to foster appropriate legislation for improvement of education and for revisions of governmental structure and procedure that will strengthen the school board.

County Council of PTAs

Certain members of the new group had appeared before the County School Board's budget hearings on April 15th, three weeks earlier, and urged that school appropriations be significantly increased to provide for an extensive building program, kindergartens, full day sessions for the first and second grades, and a more adequate and better paid teaching force. The action of the Board fell far short of meeting the recommendations of the citizens that had appeared before it at that meeting. The Board decided to "niggardly" recommend, as CCSI representatives put it (but in later years generally considered politically unacceptable language), that there be a five cent increase in the school tax rate to cover only additional operating expenses. It also recommended a budget to cover some of the costs of the improvements urged by LeBeau and his team, but did not include any recommendations for implementing any such program.[17]

Following its rebuff at the budget meeting, and perhaps as a consequence of it, CCSI announced as its objectives:

    a. a change in the system of selecting School Board members (appointed by the District Trustees) to election by the voters;

---

[16] *Others citizens involved in the early CCSI movement, as indicated on its literature, include, Harold Stone, Mr & Mrs Joseph Wheeler, Mrs Malcolm Miller, Mrs Sue Arcardo, Mrs. Herbert Thatcher, Ivan Booker, Edmund Struther, Mrs Irene Flack, W. H. Gammon, Mrs Charles Planck, Lem Banks, Joseph Ingram, Mr & Mrs James Pettee, Ralph Clark, Harold Lewis, Mrs Alice Mintz, Mrs Edward Hanwaring, Mrs Edward Hincks, Mrs Theodore Pryor, George Parker, and Mrs Florence Backus. In its early years CCSI was also chaired by Shelby A. Robert, Jr., B. Alden Lillywhite, Reed K. Pond, Dr John Newdorp, and James C. Pettee; VA Room archives, Ibid.*

[17] *Flyer, CCSI, Box 1661, Arlington Va., Dec 31, 1946, VA Room archives, Ibid..*

b. a nominating convention selection of candidates for the school board;

c. election of school board members with backgrounds, interests and convictions required to raise educational standards; and

d. passage of bond issues for school construction in years ahead.

With respect to the selection of school board members, it is considered pertinent to point out that this group of school improvement advocates, were somewhat at odds with the recommendations of the pre-war group who had favored no changes in the procedure whereby board members were selected by the District Trustees, as described above. The earlier group had opposed the suggestion that the County Board appoint school board members. Whether the earlier group would have supported a proposal for direct election by voters as LeBeau and his supporters urged, is not revealed.

CCSI promptly swung into action to implement their program and one of their first maneuvers was to appear before a meeting of the School Trustee Electoral Board in late May, 1946. The Board, that was appointed by the Circuit Court, had authority to appoint school board members and was meeting to fill an upcoming vacancy. CCSI in a flyer alluded to above, reported that the acrimonious and raucous meeting was packed with numerous  individuals and organizations urging the appointment of one Rev. Paul Hunter, a CCSI backed candidate, but that the Board selected one Harry W. Porter instead. The CCSI paper reported that the Arlington Daily newspaper on May 28th reported that "A near riot climaxed the public hearing...chagrinned by the selection of Porter, tempers reached a feverish pitch and citizens stubbornly refused to leave...Angry citizens demanded to know how the Board eliminated the Rev Hunter who had been heartily endorsed by the majority of civic organizations present...".

CCSI had clearly lost this first engagement in its battle for school improvement, but the campaign was just warming up. The war was by no means over. CCSI quickly fell back and effectively regrouped to continue its struggle. Failing before the Trustee Electoral Board to get its board candidate selected, the group turned for relief to the Circuit Court Judge who appointed the Trustee Board. It concluded that the membership of the Trustee Board had to be changed to one that would be more receptive to CCSI desires with respect to the appointment of school board members.

CCSI submitted the names of eight persons to Judge McCarthy for consideration for appointment to the School Board, along with names submitted by others for a total of 30 names. Included in the names submitted by CCSI were well known Arlingtonians to include Mrs Edmund Campbell, C. Harrison Mann, Harold Stone and William Watt. CCSI had also submitted to Judge McCarthy an "open letter" listing its view of desirable qualifications for school board members. The Judge repudiated the letter, in the view of CCSI, and made appointments that resulted in the Board remaining, as CCSI put it "under the domination of the same clique by which it had been controlled for years.".

CCSI was not to be deterred by its failure to get a candidate of its choice appointed to the school board by the Circuit Court in 1946 as related above. In the aftermath of that set back it stepped up its efforts. Since it could not get the Trustee

Major Community "Battles" and Controversies

Board to appoint its candidate to the School Board, and could not get the Courts to change the Trustee Board, CCSI set about to change the manner of selecting school board members by withdrawing that authority from the Courts and the Trustee Board. It proclaimed in flyers of the day that "we must have an elected school board that will be democratic and responsive to the citizens". Arlington school activists had thus swung full about and reversed course on this issue since the days before the war.

THE FIRST ELECTED SCHOOL BOARD

??? The School Board ???

Armed with petitions with over 5,000 signatures, CCSI members traveled to Richmond in the Spring of 1947 and persuaded the legislature in a special session to grant Arlington County the right to elect school board members. Strangely, the new Virginia law applied to only Arlington County, an exceptional arrangement that constituted no small feat for the CCSI representatives. The Arlington Sun reported on page 1 on April 11, 1947 that Circuit Court Judge Walter T. McCarthy had issued an order designating Tuesday May 27th for a referendum on the method of selecting members. Voters were asked to answer two questions on the ballot, whether they desired to change the method of selecting school board members and if so did they prefer a direct popular election or selection of members by the County Board. In that election voters opted to chose their school board members by popular election. In the elections that followed, to the obvious delight of CCSI and its supporters, a new school board was elected that favored massive school improvements as desired by CCSI. In later years, following the Supreme Court decision outlawing racial school segregation, and on the heels of acrimonious public exchanges between local activists and some legislators, the General Assembly cancelled Arlington's authority to elect its school board until restored in the 1990s (see below).

Having achieved a school board to its liking, CCSI next focused its attention on the County Board "that controlled the purse strings", as phrased in a CCSI flyer. Its objective was to elect a County Board that also would be sympathetic to its goals and that would appropriate the money needed to carry out the programs advocated by CCSI. In this project, CCSI had some wins and some losses.

It was about this time that yet another activist civic collateral group emerged known as the "Town Meeting" organization with the objective of fending candidates for the County Board. There was considerable cross membership in the two groups as reflected in their literature. The eventual goals of the two groups, with respect to school operations, appeared to be essentially the same. An observer could reasonably conclude that CCSI was the educational arm of the activists and the Town Meeting group served as their political arm. At any rate, in the election of 1946, as related elsewhere herein in Chapter Four, with the support of both groups, a candidate, Daniel Dugan, was elected to the County Board, to begin serving in January 1947. It marked the school activists first political victory in their campaign.

CCSI and the Town Meeting group won again in the 1947 board election with their candidate Florence Cannon, but lost the following year when the CCSI supported candidate Lee Potter was defeated by incumbent Alfred Frisbie. Thus, the County Board in 1949 remained in conservative control to the disenchantment of CCSI. The election later that year, however, was to see the day of fulfillment with the election of Robert W. Cox which gave the 1950 board a liberal, CCSI majority - Dugan, Cannon and Cox. But their victory would be short lived. In September, all three of the CCSI supported board members were removed by court order because of their Federal employment, as also is described in more detail in Chapter Four herein. The County Board then reverted to conservative control, but only for a couple of years.

ENTER THE
ARLINGTONIANS FOR A BETTER COUNTY

While the above election and other events were taking place, activists in the CCSI and Town Meeting groups were forming their own political organization. It would become known as the Arlingtonians for a Better County, or ABC. Many of the county's liberals Democrats eagerly joined the ABC movement either as members or workers. ABC claimed that it also had independents and some Republicans among its membership. With the advent of ABC, CCSI would gradually fade away.

ABC successfully ran two candidates for the county board in the 1955 election and another in the 1957 election and thus regained control of the 1958 Board for the liberals. The ABC-liberal Democrat coalition would maintain dominance on and control of the Board for almost all of the next 35 years and thereby were able to continue the implementation of the 1946-1955 CCSI school objectives. The CCSI group could justifiably claim little less than astounding success for their efforts beginning after the unsuccessful 1946 efforts to persuade the Trustee Election Board to name their candidate to the school board.

RACIAL DESEGREGATION ARRIVES

As the school improvement advocates were waging their struggles during the 1950s, other events were also transpiring at the time to attract their attention. In 1954, the U. S. Supreme Court handed down its landmark Brown v. School Board decision on public school desegregation and Virginia entered its "massive resistance" days. A special commission (the Gray Commission) was appointed to find ways to avoid compliance with the Court's decision and it recommended that desegregation be left to local option. The

Major Community "Battles" and Controversies

Commission also recommended a constitutional amendment to make public education a voluntary matter with a system of tuition grants for attendance in private schools.

Whereupon, Arlington, being far more liberal than the rest of the State and less opposed to the Court's decision, forthwith undertook as a local option to desegregate over a three year period. Society Historical writer Michelotti wrote that the news of desegregation action by Arlington "Fell like a thunderbolt on the State..." and that the legislature met in January, 1956 "...to consider additional action to meet the new threat to continued segregation..." One of the outcomes was a repeal of the legislation authorizing Arlington to elect its school board and instead have the board members appointed by the County Board. Thus, Arlington lost its right to elect school board members almost as quickly as it was extended.

When an NAACP suit to desegregate was filed in Federal Court in May, 1956, the prospect appeared to be that if Arlington complied with a Court order to desegregate, the Governor would close Arlington Schools. Faced with that prospect, and with the approaching demise of CCSI, Arlington school activists organized yet another group, or arm of CCSI, known as the Arlington Committee to Preserve Public Schools (ACPPS), and launched a "Save our Schools" (SOS) campaign.[18] In its literature the SOS group made frequent reference to CCSI and its officers. The two groups appeared in substance to be one and the same.

SOS reported in it literature [19] that it was "organizing person-to-person telephone talks, newspaper publicity, and a series of coffee conferences", and that "when speakers are needed, SOS can and does supply them on request." M. Singer, in an SOS Bulletin wrote, "One of the heartening developments in this campaign is the way people have stepped up to be counted...spokesmen for various religious denominations are participating...civic groups, educators and politicians are pitching in." Particularly influential and heavily involved in the SOS committee were, among many other Arlingtonians, Theda Henle, who would later help organize ABC, James Stockard, a School Board member, Attorney Edmund Campbell, and William Lightsey, a long time activist in Arlington and Virginia politics.

In the following months, SOS, or ACPPS, members made repeated trips to Richmond and had lengthy conferences with the Governor and other state officials with the objective of preventing the closure of Arlington schools.

In due course, with pressure from the Federal Courts mounting, Governor Lindsey Almond changed his position on school closings, Arlington school integration occurred, and the controversy was resolved. SOS was quick to take major credit, or blame, depending on one's point of view, for this development. Mr.Lightsey of ACPPS and SOS recalled:

---

[18] *There were many citizens involved in the SOS efforts, but two of the most active were lawyer Edmund Campbell, and Elizabeth Weihe who made repeated trips to Richmond to argue the matter before the Governor and other State officials.*

[19] *SOS Bulletin "School Improvement", Vol. II, No. 2, January, 1956.*

ARLINGTON COUNTY VIRGINIA - A Modern History

> *"The thing I remember most is the changed position of Governor Almond who had been originally an active leader in support of massive resistance...(he) told me it was not until after the statewide PTA conference in which an overwhelming vote called on the government...to keep the schools open, that he realized there was widespread support of that position throughout the state and that the work done by the Committee for Public Schools (SOS) had resulted in his changed position."* [20]

While there can be no doubt that the contribution of the Committee for Public Schools in influencing the governor to reverse his position on closing Virginia schools is significant, the version of Mr Lightsey may be somewhat over stated and excessively self congratulatory. B. Alden Lillywhite and Others, in their report "Citizens Fight for Better Schools in Arlington" prepared for the National Citizens Commission for Public Schools wrote: [21] *"It should be pointed out clearly that these accomplishments in Arlington County are by no means the results solely of the Citizens Committee for School Improvement. Other organizations in the County played major roles, as did a number of persons who never joined the Committee...the accomplishments are the result of cooperative effort on the part of many groups and interested citizens".*

INTEGRATION AT STRATFORD

Integration began in Arlington on February 2, 1959 when four seventh grade black students entered Stratford Junior High School in what the Washington Post headlined as "The Day Nothing Happened." Although there had been constant and near inflammatory media treatment of this event, and elaborate security measures had been taken by the School Board, the police, and others, the enrollment of the black students proceeded with little or no disruption either near or in the school building.

Stratford Junior High

Years later, Peggy Deskins, mother of Ronald Deskins, one of the four children involved in the Stratford integration, described the events, "...there was lots of publicity, our homes were filled with reporters and the streets with police, but Arlingtonians were very supportive and all seemed determined that there would be no violence. It was difficult times. I had some hate mail and there was a cross burned in the church yard. I had to have my telephone unlisted. But overall, there was more positive signs than negative, and the children were not subjected in public to any intimidation or dangers."[22]

With the Stratford integration, Michelotti wrote, "ninety years of dual education

---

[20] *Michelotti, ibid, p. 9.*

[21] *AHS Research Committee, Ibid, p 46.*

[22] *Remarks made at "Arlington Reunion" meeting, Auditorium of Arlington Main Library, January 18, 1996.*

came to a sudden halt". But there would still be another 12 years pass by before Arlington would have what activists called a "unitary, non-racial" school system. Writer Michelotti said she had spent much time pursuing the question of why it took so long to more fully integrate Arlington schools and said she had talked with many individuals in and out of the black community. She wrote that much of the delay centered on the black community where many students and parents were satisfied with their schools the way they were, and did not want their children bused out of their neighborhoods or their teachers transferred. Also many did not want the only black High School, Hoffman-Boston (also a junior or "intermediate" school), closed as would be necessary if its students were transferred to other high schools where there were white students.

On September 2, 1995, the Washington Post devoted much of its Virginia Section to the subject of school integration in Arlington. The article indicated that many Black families were now, almost 40 years later, having second thoughts about the desirability or need for racial integration, or at least the widespread busing and school closings to achieve it.

The Post article explained that in the 1970s the black Nauck neighborhood had lost its elementary school - Drew - as a result of court ordered desegregation. Drew was converted to a countywide alternative school. Black kindergarten students from Nauck continued to attend Drew, but other higher grade students were bused to one of three other elementary schools some distance away in white neighborhoods.

The Post reported that when black citizen Henry Briggs and his wife Maria moved from Hampton to Arlington's Nauck neighborhood in 1990 they were dismayed to learn that their two daughters could not go to Drew, which is only a few walking blocks from their home. "I had to go across town to talk to people who went to the school my daughter attended. Why should she have to be bused 35 minutes to school?", Briggs was quoted as saying. The Post article indicated that Brigg's feelings are shared by many other Black citizens. Ironically, these were the same sentiments that were expressed by white people in the early days of court ordered integration many of whom claimed they were not opposed to desegregation, but objected to extended busing of their children to schools far away from their residences.

In Arlington, a comparable school closing to accommodate integration, mentioned above, existed concerning the former black Hoffman-Boston high school in the Arlington View neighborhood in the southernmost section of the County. The school was also closed to nearby black high school students when they were bused out to Arlington's other three and larger high schools to achieve integration. When Briggs' daughter Cicelia goes to high school she will be assigned to Yorktown in the far northern tip of the County, the Post article read. "Why should she be bused so far to school, when there are kids who can just walk out their door and get to school?" Briggs asked.

CHANGING PUBLIC ATTITUDES

As the years have passed, at this writing, the sentiment for forced bussing of public school students has diminished as reflected in the Post and numerous other media articles. There is now increased talk in both the white, black, and new Asiatic neighborhoods for a discontinuation of busing when it is simply for racial balances.

ARLINGTON COUNTY VIRGINIA - A Modern History

Answers as to what to do about integration, busing, and racial balance problems and not just black and white are still being sought.

In a Washington Post article on July 1, 1993, staff writer Stephanie Griffith described the "late-night and often bitter" debates by an Arlington panel trying to advise school officials on how to cope "with a soaring number of immigrant students." She said the prospect of specialized high schools, changing boundaries and other proposals could dramatically change the way the county educates its children and has divided parents across the county. She said, further, that some parents, particularly those in mostly white areas of North Arlington "will fight changes every step of the way", whereas others in South Arlington who have seen classes over crowded with Hispanic and Asian immigrants "are more willing to make changes".

"Time for a change?"

Writer Griffith wrote that the immigrant issue had turned some Arlingtonians against the Democratic establishment in the last elections and provided what "some political observers believe was the margin of victory for Republican Benjamin Winslow, an underdog candidate." Winslow commented that his support for neighborhood schools was a key to his victory. He said, "Some people moved to this community for their neighborhood schools. Now they are being told 'Well, tough'. Certain things are sacrosanct." [23]

Further evidence of modern day disenchantment with integration was contained in an Washinmgton Post article on February 4, 1996, by Dusty Horwitt, a free lance Arlington writer. His article was headlined "When Arlington was Little Rock - Remembering a Forgotten School Integration Struggle". Horwitt quoted several of the four students who were integrated at Stratford 37 years earlier in 1959. He quoted Lance Newman, now an engineer in Torrence, California as saying,

> *"Desegregation isn't the panacea it was thought to be...schools are segregated again...you have a class thing...a lot of people send their kids to private school. Maybe I am part of the problem because of my grand daughter...my wife and I send her to a private school."*

Horwitt quoted Ronald Deskins, another of the four 1959 integrated students, and now with the Fairfax Virginia Fire Department;

> *I think there has been a lessening of academic excellence in the public schools...my wife and I have thought about sending our kids to private school".*

---

[23] *Winslow may have been correct, but he was defeated when he ran for reelection in November 1995.*

Major Community "Battles" and Controversies

THE RETURN OF THE ELECTED SCHOOL BOARD

"We're back!"
(Education Board)

As the end of the Century approaches in the 1990s, there is rarely any talk of the school improvement objectives once fought for with such vigor and determination by the CCSI and their forerunners and progeny. Most of those objectives have come about. An exception was the question of an elected school board that was lost to Arlingtonians, as stated, in the massive resistance days. Most Arlington civic leaders on both ends of the political spectrum had never ceased to favor an elected school board after the option was abolished in 1957. Legislation to achieve this had been introduced periodically by Arlington and other Northern Virginia legislators, but until recently, with no success. In the mid 1970s the interest in elected school boards reached a peak.

Arlington Journal writers Mark Crawford and Frank Davies reported that Arlington Delegate John Melnick introduced a bill in the 1975 legislative session calling for elected school boards for Arlington but that it was defeated by a vote of 48 to 41. He quoted Melnick as saying, "I started supporting the concept of an elected school board in 1973 and I guess I will again next year".

Journal writer Crawford reported again on January 29, 1976 in an article headlined "Elected School Board Concept Gains Support" that there was considerable support to bring back an elected board and that Melnick had again introduced his bill to achieve that goal. Mark Crawford wrote that Melnick said, "Attitudes about elected school boards are changing. Last year not a single citizen asked me about it. This year its the hottest thing I have going...I think it is time to let people decide...". Crawford pointed out, however, that public opinion on the issue was widely split and that many groups, including some usually liberal sources opposed elected boards. He wrote that they contended that school boards should not become politicized by having to run for election...that candidates for a school board without taxing powers can make wild promises about improving school to which they could not be held".

Earlier on March 13, 1975, the Journal had editorialized, in part, "We believe that the public has a right to directly select the people who are going to make vital decision affecting the education of their children...the old saw which is advanced by those who would perpetuate a bad system, (election causes politicizing) flies in the face of democratic practice..It assumes that people cannot really be trusted with selecting good school board members."

Finally, in the early 1990s the legislature enacted laws permitting a referendum on elected school boards. In Arlington a referendum was held and the voters opted for an elected board. The law left it to the County Board, however, to determine whether the elections should be at large or by single member districts and the County Board, itself elected at large, ordered that elections for school board members also to be at-large. This greatly displeased some citizens who felt that an at large school board member election in a community where one political faction, the ABC-Democrats, prevailed so strongly would simply mean that all school board members also would be from the same partisan political apparatus. Thus far, this fear has proven to be well grounded. In the two school board elections held to date, only ABC-Democrat supported candidates have prevailed.

Even with the return of the elected school board arrangement, however, controversy and contention continued. It was all but certain that to be elected to the school board a candidate must have the backing of the ABC organization. To obtain the backing of the ABC group a candidate had to be endorsed in an ABC "convention" and complaints arose concerning the manner in which the convention was conducted. To run in that convention, however, the ABC required candidates to agree to drop out of the race if they lost in the convention, a condition many considered to be undemocratic and unfair.

In an editorial headed "Wrong ingredients" the Arlington Journal on May 23, 1994 criticized the conditions placed on candidates for ABC backing and charged that the appetizing enhancement served up for the first Board election in 40 years "has become a heavy-handed, politically correct gumbo". The paper said further, in part;

> *"The ABC made two mistakes in concocting this stew. One, it required any candidate seeking endorsement to drop out if they don't win (at the convention) and Two, ABC allowed anyone who lives in Arlington -- even 'nonresidents' which means legal or illegal immigrants - to participates in the endorsement process...Because of the drop out requirement, people who are not citizens of this country will participate in dictating how honest-to-goodness Americans can vote in the November general election. We urge ABC .. to reevaluate this policy..(it) is a relic from the days of fighting the Byrd machine."*

Citizen and civic activist James Charleton wrote for the Journal letters column on May 20, 1994, "ABC has been transformed into the tool of entrenched and highly disciplined political machine, imposing loyalty oaths and suppressing rather than encouraging candidates for office...If citizens of Arlington understood how they were being manipulated by ABC, they would, like the 'robots' in Karel Capek's 'R.U.R.' revolt against their masters and insist on a truly nonpartisan School Board election".

In a special election on January 4, 1996 Diane Smith was elected to the school board. She had been endorsed and supported by the ABC-Democrat political group.

It seemed clear from these and similar reactions and developments that the return of the elected school board in Arlington was not quite what many advocates of the approach had expected.

LATTER DAY SCHOOL PROBLEMS

In the most recent years, the emphasis on school matters has shifted to questions concerning the efficiency, or lack thereof, in running the school system and, specifically,

Major Community "Battles" and Controversies

whether bond and other monies are being properly and effectively expended. Many of the CCSI's goals may have been accomplished, but there has been ample evidence of worrisome problems in other areas of school management and operations.

An example, and only an example since there are others, is alluded to in an article in the Washington Post on June 17, 1995 by staff writer Ellen Nakashima headlined "Arlington School Renovations come up $25 Million Short". She relates that parents who campaigned for bonds to finance school renovations were "outraged" over admissions by Superintendent Arthur Gosling, that there is a $25 million shortfall and that school officials did not closely monitor how the money was being spent." Nakashima wrote that school board member Charles Cervantes had resigned to protest the school administration's mismanagement.

As further evidence of mismanagement, Nakashima wrote in an article on November 11, 1995, that "Renovations in Arlington School Test Patience of Staff, Students". She told of sewage seeping into classrooms at H-B Woodlawn school, of "mess ups" in the heating system of one school where students wore coats, and where faucets in rest rooms were installed backwards. The Post reporter quoted Marty Swaim, president of the Arlington Education Association as saying, "There is reasonable evidence of mismanagement. This is a system and a county that is not used to that (and) where people expect that for their tax dollar they're going to get good services". She wrote further that school board member Mary H. Hynes was "furious that these problems keep arising" and quoted her as saying, "I'm upset that we have a building program that is making it hard for kids to learn right now. I see us bumbling".

Especially enlightening in what constitutes "good" or "improved" schools, or at least the direction in which education should be headed, a half century after CCSI is the "Futures Planning Steering Team" report of the Superintendent released in June, 1993. The report indicated that the prime concern of the school administration was not precisely those things that bothered CCSI and its supporters long ago but, rather, the need to face current and new challenges to the school system.

The three main challenges in the Superintendent's report were: QUALITY, CROWDING, and DIVERSITY. With respect to Quality, the report stated that standards and expectations must be high, curriculum constantly reviewed, instructional methods varied, and schools must provide a secure and positive learning environment. (emphasis supplied). One must infer that the latter provision must allude to problems of disruption, violence, crime, misconduct, and other conditions that detract from a learning environment. Such conditions are known to exist, although opinions may vary greatly as to just how serious and widespread they are in the Arlington school system.

With respect to Crowding, the report calls attention to the increased enrollment and a resultant over crowding of schools. It reports that the capacity of the elementary schools is approximately 8,500 but enrollment is expected to reach 9,500 by 1997-98; the middle schools capacity is 3,200 with a projected enrollment of 4,200 by 1997-98. The report indicated the situation with high schools was better with a capacity of 5,300 and an expected enrollment of 5,200 by those years. It could be noted that over crowding

ARLINGTON COUNTY VIRGINIA - A Modern History

was also a condition in the post World War II period that greatly displeased early CCSI activists.

The most dramatic element of education contained in the report is probably that of Diversity of students occasioned by the awesome change in demographics caused by the recent flood of immigrants. The report lists changes in white students in Arlington schools from 85% about 20 years earlier to 45% in 1992/93. It reports that minority students have increased from 15% to 55% with about 10% Asians, 18% Black and 27% Hispanic, and that percentages of students who have limited English proficiency is as high as 45-50% in some of the elementary schools.

The problems the county faces with language as well as racial diversity was also highlighted in a feature article in the Virginia supplement to the Washington Post on page 9 of the September 2, 1993 edition. The article pointed out that in the two largest high schools and in two of the five middle schools an average of three quarters of the students were Hispanic, Asian, or other minorities, and that in each of those schools an average of 20% of those students were limited in their English proficiency.

In some of the elementary schools, the situation was even worse, as also reported by the Superintendent in his above referred to report. In Glencarlyn 88% of the students were minorities with 45% of those not proficient in English. The Post too reported that in almost a dozen other elementary schools the language situation was only slightly less severe.

The Superintendent's report include a list of option available to cope with the above challenges but this aspect of the matter is beyond the scope of this narrative since no action

"So little English!"

at this writing has yet been undertaken in the matter, and thus no "battles" have emerged that can be included in this narrative. If battles do develop they must be left to later writers to relate.

The Arlington "battles" over the years in school matters have been contentious at times, and fought with vigor, determination and dedication with sometimes gains and other times losses. Whether they are more so than in most other American communities must be left to the observer or the educational specialists to determine. Opinions, as with most civic and community matters, will vary depending on many factors including the observers philosophy, political leanings, background and other related considerations.

LIBERAL OR CONSERVATIVE MANAGEMENT?
(Some author observations)

This then, is a narrative of the efforts of Arlington civic activists over the years to achieve what they term as public school "improvements" in the County's school system. Their success, for better or worse, for the most part has been profoundly impressive. Whether their accomplishments constitute improvements to the extent they claim is debatable. For sure, conservatives and other critics may have other views.

It is undeniable that this struggle has been, largely, if not almost totally, an effort, at least in the last half century, by the liberal element of the community. The

Major Community "Battles" and Controversies

early CCSI, SOS, and liberal wing of the Democratic party, and their supporters, formed the nucleus for the organization of the Arlingtonians for A Better County. The individuals involved in those movements have been almost the same. More moderate Democrats, such as Harrison Mann and Leo Urbanske, Jr., left the Democrat party, after some years, or otherwise fell into disfavor as related elsewhere herein in Chapter III. The self proclaimed liberal ABC group has dominated county politics and government and school management for almost all of the past several decades. They have therefore, been in position to implement their liberal or "progressive" concepts of educational content and techniques. They, therefore, are entitled to credit for advances in this area, but by the same token must accept blame for any failures in their approach.

On January 22, 1996, Washington Post writer Kevin Merida described in an article headlined, "Public Shows Rising Concern Over Quality of Education", teacher dissatisfactions and other related problems. He quoted Bedford, N.H. teacher Bonnie Venn at a presidential candidate Lamar Alexander political gathering as saying, "I am retiring from teaching because I got angry at what is going on...they tie teachers hands. A child could hit you, but how dare you put anything on their little bottoms." Merida wrote that in the question and answer period of the meeting, one after another of those present vented their feelings. He said they complained that schools were on the decline, there was no discipline in the class rooms, that teachers are given no incentives to innovate and that students were graduating from high school.

While parents and other may disagree over the extent to which these conditions apply to Arlington schools, there is evidence of dissatisfaction with the way the system is operating under Arlington's educational administration that some consider too "liberal". Journal Staff writer Whitney Wyckoff wrote in March 1993 headlined "Meeting leaves parents unhappy" of parent discontent with both management techniques and student achievements. Wyckoff described a school planning meeting intended to give parents a chance to discuss the school system's future but that "many who attended said their ideas weren't valued and the information they received was too vague. He quoted parent Jim Rock as saying "a lot of us feel that our input is either not wanted or ignored.. Its a closed process meant to avoid opposition from citizen groups." He wrote that parent Carol Sergeant was worried that students might be bused to other schools to achieve goals of racial and ethnic diversity without addressing other educational issues.

Nevertheless, the ABC group is more than satisfied with their school programs and accomplishments as reflected in their public statements and the contents of their political literature during election campaigns. They point to their past perceived accomplishments and urge voters to allow them to continue in their past direction concerning school management and other county affairs. Whether they are justified in claiming credit, or blame as some would see it, is open to question. Considerable money and effort has gone into the County school system over the years.

Arlington's schools, overall, are probably a model for the nation insofar as the "hardware" is concerned. Despite some current problems with over-crowding, maintenance and capital improvements, most schools are modern, roomy, and equipped with fully adequate libraries, media centers, swimming pools in high schools, cafeterias, arts and crafts facilities and other needs. Teachers are at or near the very top state-wise and perhaps nationally in pay and qualifications and on a par with other Washington Metropolitan jurisdictions. There is a curriculum that is extensive and also as diversified as almost any in other public school systems nationwide.

Nor can it be claimed, as did the early CCSI people, that the Arlington educational system is now, or recently has been, under-funded. Since the CCSI days of peak activity, the country has sold over $250-million school bonds (which will be roughly doubled when paid off with interest) and appropriated over $1.5 billion for school operations. In the 1995 fiscal year, $290-million is allotted for schools, or just under $10,000 per pupil, near or at the top nationally.

But are all these superior ingredients sufficient to guarantee a good and sufficiently "improved" educational system that turns out an acceptable finished product; i.e., a youngster that is second to none in public school education and reasonably well equipped to go forward to meet and overcome modern day society's challenges in the business, social and employment world? Some critics think not. They are maintaining that no matter how much money is spent and how superior the material things - personnel, buildings, equipment, libraries and a raft of other facilities - an education system will be no better than the direction, management and control exercised in its operation. In recent years, moderates and conservatives and even liberal educators have questioned whether unstructured, open class rooms, student freedoms, restrictions on teachers, lax or easy curriculums and lowering of standards and demands for social reasons, are the correct road to a good education, or whether they constitute "improved" schools. More and more voices are heard demanding "a return to the basics" - reading, writing and arithmetic - a disciplined and highly structured environment where the teachers, and not the students, are clearly in control. Some Arlington parents and taxpayers are asking why Arlington schools are not operated in that manner and whether it is time to look for a changed approach.

Defenders of the Arlington school system may well respond that simply yelling for a return to "the basics" is an unrealistic and overly simplistic approach to deep and complex contemporary problems confronting teachers and administrators. Great numbers of non-English speaking immigrants have been absorbed in the 1990s into the schools and it could well be reasonably argued that to hold the system in the 1990s to the same standards of acheivement possible in the 1960s, may be little less than an excercise in fantasy and wishful thinking. Those same defenders would probably also reject too much reliance, under the circumstances of large numbers of non-English speaking students, on test scores as a primary means of determining acheivement.

Arlington Taxpayer:
"More money for schools?"

Although Arlington's expenditures on its public education have stayed at or near the top in amount when compared to other communities nationwide, its students have consistently ranked only average nationally in SSAT and other testing scores. Many

Major Community "Battles" and Controversies

parents and others may well ask, if good education is a matter of spending lots of money, why doesn't Arlington stand at or near the top in student achievements nationally? With this in mind, it could also be asked by voters, parents, taxpayers and others whether or not the changes brought about over the years by the CCSI and its predecessors and successors have been in fact improvements as great as claimed by those who made them. The answers to these questions must come from others. They are beyond the scope of this narrative.

There does not, however, appear to be any great ground swell at this writing to cut back on public school expenditures in Arlington County (but see below). The contrary appears to be the prevailing citizen sentiment. At the County Civic Federation meeting on March 5, 1996 at the Arlington Hospital auditorium the Schools Committee endorsed the County Manager's proposed school budget of $148 million for the new fiscal year and recommended that the Federation go on record as favoring an increase of an additional $.3 million. Repeated efforts by some Federation delegates to delete that increase were defeated by comfortable margins.

* * *

Evidence that public attitudes with respect to the effectiveness and efficiency of school operations may be changing came to light just as this narrative was nearing publication. This author learned of the embryonic formation of an Arlington group that called themselves, at least as an interim identification, Arlingtonians for Better Schools or ABS.

The ABS group, comprised of school system activists, claimed they had long been intensively discontent with perceived inept management by the school board and its appointed superintendent, relatively poor achievement of students, wasteful monetary expenditures, and other matters under the control of top school officials.

Leadership in ABS included John DePauw, a retired army colonel, author and political science professor at the University of Maryland, his wife Barbara, an administrator in the Montgomery County, Maryland school system, Roger Morton, a communications engineer, and Sophie Vogel, a retired Arlington County public school teacher and librarian, mentioned elsewhere herein.

Speakers for ABS appeared at the County Board meeting on March 22, 1997 and indicated they would appear and speak again at the school budget meeting on April 12. On March 25 an "exploratory" organizational meeting was held at the home of Col. DePauw to select a permanent name for the group and to determine a course of action to get their message before the appropriate county officials. Complaints voiced by individuals at the meeting included; (1) test scores of Arlington public school students were only average nationally despite the fact that expenditures per student were at or near the top nationally, (2) school employees were weighted too heavily toward administrators, caretakers and others at the expense of teachers and teacher aids, (3) the school budget contained contradictory and misleading information concerning school costs, and (4) there were numerous items of waste in the upcoming budget of nearly $200-million.

The future course or impact of this group can only be speculated upon at this writing and thus must be left to future chronologists. (For more on school spending and county fiscal matters see comments of Ms. Vogel and Chic Hoagland on pages 464-5).

Round IV
THE BATTLE FOR METRORAIL

It was 3 a.m. on a frosty morning on Tuesday, November 5, 1968 in Arlington County, Virginia.

It was also election day in Arlington and elsewhere.

A handful of specially briefed shock "troops" of "General" Elizabeth Weihe's special task force were preparing to cross the line of departure (LD) to launch an all out assault on their assigned objectives. The troops were dedicated and highly motivated. Their tactical targets were the county's 39 voting precincts. Their weapons were stakes, hammers, staple guns and posters. Their mission was to mount their posters in quantity and as conspicuous as possible at all precinct entrances before daylight and the opening of the polls at 6 a.m.

The posters urged citizens to vote "yes" on the ballot item "Transit Facilities - Shall the County Board contract a debt in an amount not exceeding $54,000,000 for the purpose of providing funds for the construction of transit facilities in the Washington metropolitan area"; (translation, "METRORAIL").

Elizabeth Weihe trained and briefed her forces carefully. She was well qualified for her mission. She had long been active in civic affairs and had thirteen years of experience as a member of the County Planning Commission where she served much of that time as Chair of the group. She was well versed in community problems and development projects. She had been named to head the effort to obtain voter and citizen acceptance and approval of funding for the County's share of the costs of constructing the rapid rail transit system for the Washington Metropolitan area.

For weeks before election day, Weihe dashed around the county contacting movers and doers to solicit their assistance and support. She visited Milton Drewer,

President of the Clarendon Trust Bank and others and obtained "seed" money to buy bumper stickers and flyers to hand out at any kind of gathering. She obtain the loan of a Metro rail car and had it moved to the parking lot of the George Mason University on Wilson Boulevard near Clarendon Circle for public display. When visitors moved through the car she handed them a flyer urging them to vote for Metro bonds in the coming election.

Weihe also recruited helpers from among the civic activists in the County and organized them into a team to mount posters at the county polls. She assembled that team in her home on North 33rd Street for final instructions on the eve of election day. D-Day had arrived and her operation was launched.

METRORAIL BACKGROUND

Soon after the ending of World War II, there was talk in the Nation's capital of the need for a rapid rail transportation system. In the 1950s and early 1960s this talk accelerated and the matter became ever more pressing as the area grew in population and traffic increased to the point of strangulation, with endless gridlocks as commuters, visitors and others fought for parking spaces or places on clogged roads leading into and through the central Washington area. The need for a rapid rail transportation system to reduced vehicular travel became ever more apparent with each passing year.

It was recognized that any such system would be costly, and probably well beyond the means of area jurisdictions to finance. Community leaders were resigned to the fact that only by significant assistance from the Federal government could a rail system ever be achieved. It was also known that the sense of Congressional leaders was that the Federal government would not likely ever completely pay for a rail system for the Capital area. It was further recognized, that not even would the Congress provide any assistance at all unless the local jurisdictions would first indicate their willingness to share in the cost of constructing such a rail transit system. It was eventually decided that financing would be on a federal-local 2/3-1/3 matching funds partnership arrangement. Later there would be an unsuccessful drive to change the cost sharing to an 80% to 20% ratio.

There was considerable uncertainty, however, as to whether local citizens were willing to shoulder the considerable expense of their participation in financing the system. If even one of the numerous metropolitan jurisdictions declined to help finance the system, then there was much doubt that any of the others would do so. There could be no piecemeal approach to the project. As a practical matter, it had to be all or nothing.

IMPORTANCE OF VOTER BOND APPROVAL

Community leaders in Arlington County well recognized the criticality of the November 1968 referendum item on the election day ballot. For months speakers throughout the County had appeared before civic groups to include the Committee of 100, the Civic Federation, League of Women Voter, Chamber of Commerce, and numerous other organizations and groups to insure that the public was well informed on the matter and that there was wide understanding of how pivotal would be the upcoming election with the transit bond question on the ballot. The eyes of all jurisdictions in the area were on the voters in Arlington as well as its sister jurisdiction on this election day. If the voters in any of the jurisdictions rejected the transit bonds items, it would be a major setback, perhaps even fatal for years to come, for achieving a rail transit system for the area. General Weihe and her troops, and supporters throughout the County, were determined that would not happen in Arlington. They pitched in with vigor to do all they could to insure the passage of the transit bond item on the ballot.

As it developed, the fears and apprehensions of the rail system enthusiasts were not well grounded. Arlington voters approved the bonds for Metrorail by a near landslide. The vote was 42,718 for and only 11,658 against - a ratio roughly of 4 to 1 or 80% in favor. The bonds would be sold in the period from 1970 to 1974 and would constituted Arlington's first funding contribution to the construction of the system. There would be additional bond items on future ballots in the years from 1983 to 1996 in the amounts of 13, 13, 17.8, 4, and 8 million dollars. All of those bond issues passed but not always with such a comfortable ratio of pro and cons as in the first bond election of 1968. One issue of $25 million on the 1975 ballot that was defeated. The total bonds to be sold would amount to $109 million dollars, with $83 million dollars for interest, for a total of $193 million as Arlington's share in construction costs for the system. [24]

THE BIRTH OF WMATA

Although voting for Arlington funding for local contributions to the Metrorail system did not take place until 1972, work on organizing and planning the system had been under way for a number of years. As early as October 1966, Congressional action on the compact had been completed and the legislation was signed by President Johnson on November 6th. It was ordered executed by the Governors of Maryland and Virginia on November 17th and by the District of Columbia on November 22nd.

In October 1967, the Washington Metropolitan Area Transit Authority (WMATA) was created to build, and later manage and operate, a rapid rail system for the Washington Region. It replaced its predecessor, a federal agency, the National Capital Transportation Agency (NCTA). Shortly thereafter, WMATA began staffing for its mission to include absorption of many of the workers of NCTA. In 1973, WMATA acquired the region's four private bus companies. WMATA was to serve the District of Columbia, the Maryland Counties of Montgomery and Prince George's, the Virginia counties of Arlington and Fairfax, and the cities of Fairfax, Alexandria and Falls Church.

WMATA was to have, and has, a governing board consisting of 12 members with authority over all policy matters relating to the construction, operation and administration of the system. Each of the participating signatories, Maryland, Virginia and the District of Columbia, has two voting members and two alternates on the Board. To carry a policy issue, there must be four "ayes" including one from each of the three signatories, plus a fourth. That provision makes it impossible for one signatory to be overruled by

---

[24] *Memorandum, Arlington County Manager, Sept 8, 1994, Subject: "Information Provided to Citizens Regarding Arlington's investment in Metrorail...".*

Major Community "Battles" and Controversies

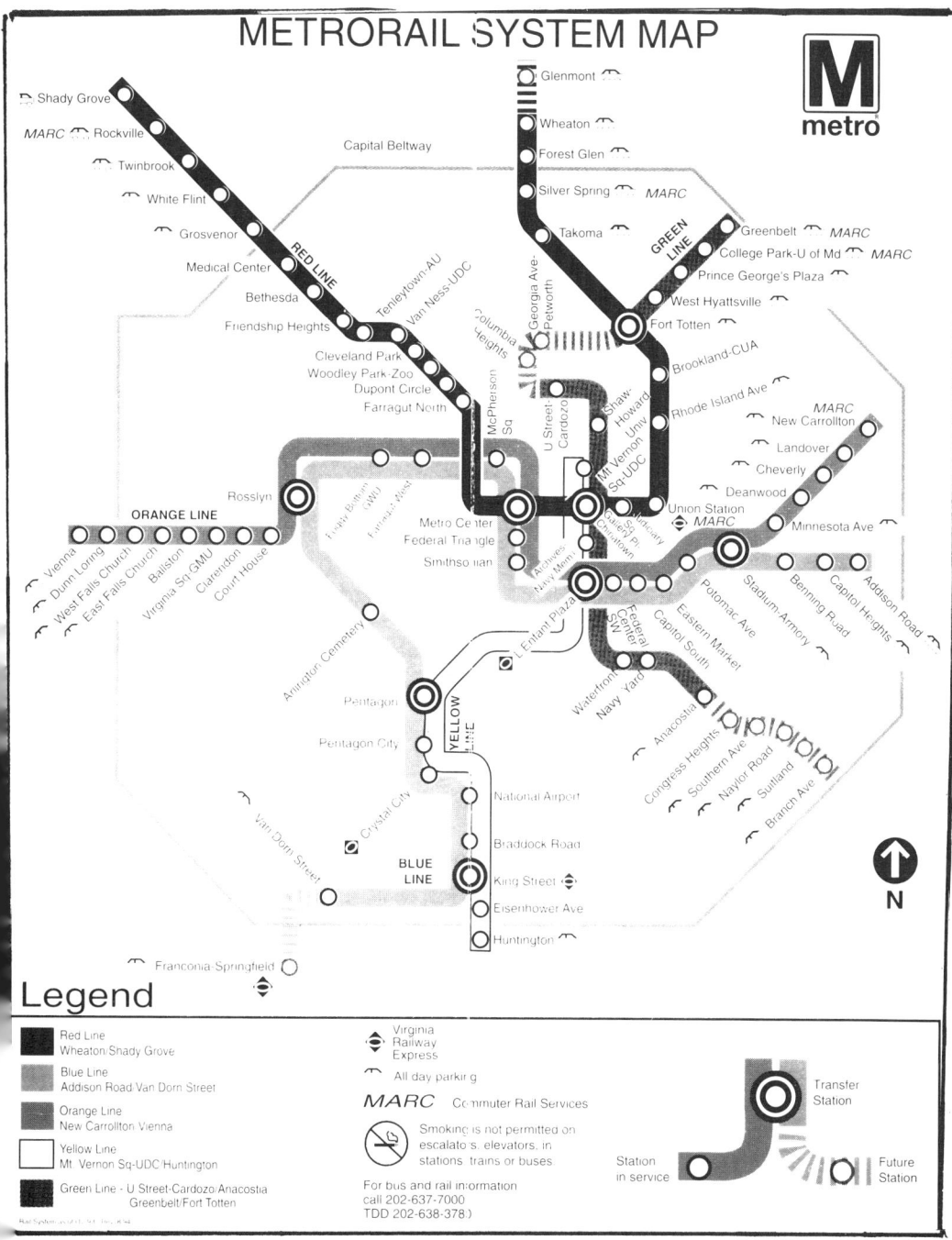

The Metrorail System as of January 1995

the other two.[25]

---
[25] *The Magazine of Metro*, Spring, 1992, p. 3.

ARLINGTON COUNTY VIRGINIA - A Modern History

THE METRORAIL SYSTEM

Metrorail was planned to be a 103 mile system with five lines running from downtown Washington, D. C. to the suburbs like spokes on a wheel, but somewhat zig-zagging and winding on some routes. The lines would extend to stations at Vienna, Franconia-Springfield and Huntington in Fairfax County in Virginia; and to Shady Grove and Glenmont in Montgomery County; and to Greenbelt, New Carrollton, Addison Road, Branch Avenue in Prince George County in Maryland.

The rail system would be entirely underground at the "downtown" stations, but surface at points near the Union Station, National Airport, the Arlington-Fairfax County line, and certain other outlying areas near the District and Maryland county lines. It was planned to have about 70 stations. A station at Arlington Cemetery was, after some uncertainty, later added to the plans. Concerning that station, the Washington Post editorialized on July 4, 1972 as follows, in part:

"*because Arlington Cemetery is one of the all-time popular stops along the tourist circuit here...a sensible effort has been under way to build a Metro station there...you would think this project would be a natural for congressional approval ...but subcommittees have rejected a $250,000 planning request...stations added to the original Metro lines...must be paid for by the government seeking to include them...in this case the Federal government...The station at Arlington Cemetery is too important to be lost because of a squabble over which agency pays for it..."*

In due course, the money for the station was provided and it has long been in operation as the Metro line reach and passed that point. A station at Ballston in Arlington was in danger of being eliminated in that same year when the County Transportation Commission, by a vote of 7-2, recommended its deletion unless the county decided to authorize intensive, high rise development for the area around the station. On May 25th, the Washington Post reported that board member Joseph Fisher, as one of a three member majority on the board, had called for limits on future high-rise development, but that Republican member Leslie Phillips said he thought the station "would serve nearby residents and should be kept". Later the county did designate the

Major Community "Battles" and Controversies

area for high-rise development, the station was retained in Metro plans, and the matter was thus resolved.

Metro suburban bus routes to downtown would, generally, be discontinued. The routes would terminate at and connect with outlying Metrorail stations such as those at the National Guard Armory on East Capitol Street in Washington, or Rosslyn and the Pentagon in Virginia. Large crowds of citizens and dignitaries gathered at Judiciary Square in the District of Columbia for the December 9, 1969 ceremony marking the start of construction of Metrorail. When the first leg of the system was completed citizens were offered a free introductory ride at the Rhode Island Avenue Station on March 27, 1976.

FUNDING AND OTHER METRORAIL PROBLEMS

Some early very critical assistance for Metro rail funding was provided by Congressional action in July 1992 when legislation was passed, and signed by President Nixon on July 14th, guaranteeing $1.2 billion in bonds to complete the rapid rail transit system. Washington Post writer Jack Eisen on June 27th reported that the measure passed the house by a vote of 280 to 75 although opponents argued that it would saddle the federal government with the full $1.2 billion. The purpose of the measure, mainly, was to make it easier for local jurisdiction to sell their now federally backed bonds, at better interest rates, in the bond markets.

At this writing, the system is about 95% completed with entire completion scheduled for the year 2001. There is already discussion of extending the system's lines to Dulles Airport in Virginia and deeper into the Maryland suburbs. The Senate, in fact, once went on record as favoring such an extension. Stephen Green wrote in the Washington Post on October 5, 1972 that the Senate had passed a bill authorizing extension of Metro rail system 16.7 miles from Falls Church to Dulles International Airport. He also quoted Rep. Joel Broyhill as saying "it is unlikely that the House will vote on this measure this year...", so the proposal to go beyond the existing station at Vienna apparently died in Congress.

The first and exceptionally critical battles in the campaign to establish the metropolitan rapid rail system was won with the passage of enabling legislation by the Congress and its signing by the President, and the acceptance of bond issues by the voters in the participating jurisdictions. But the war was far from over at those points. There were to be skirmishes and struggles on the rocky and treacherously pock marked battlefield ahead. Most of these were to swirl around the matter of how to continue financing the project. Additionally, there would be the threatening and harmful impact from other projects, such as the building of Interstate highway I-66 in Virginia and across the Potomac River.

There would, also, at one point even be a major cave in accident on Connecticutt Avenue in the District that would add to the woes of those trying to complete the project. On October 3, 1972, in midday with work in full progress, 85 feet of Connecticut Avenue at M Street dropped into the subway open excavation because of a collapse of shoring along the walls of the excavation. The Washington Post reported, "A construction superintendent on the site detected a shifting sidewalk and then instigated an evacuation of workers and passersby only a half-hour before 200 tons of wooden decking and steel under-pinnings caved in". Fortunately, the prompt action by the superintendent prevented any deaths or injuries.

In the period following the cave-in there was considerable publicity and finger pointing by Metro officials and the independent contractor Intercounty Associates as to who was responsible for the accident and whether required safety procedures had been followed. Construction at that location was only temporarily delayed and in due course the incident became mostly forgotten history, but the matter did not help Metro and its need for a good reputation with the public who would repeatedly be called on to approve more bonds for continued construction.

Another event that proved to be troublesome for the Metrorail construction program centered around the forthcoming building of interstate highway I-66 in Northern Virginia, described elsewhere herein. In April 1972, the Federal Courts enjoined highway officials from any further planning or construction of the highway inside the beltway I-495 until certain environmental and other studies were completed. Plaintiffs in the case also contended that the highway inside the beltway and through Arlington County was no longer needed and therefore should not be built at all.

Plans for much of Metrorail inside the beltway, however, called for rail-bed use of the median strip of the highway right of way that had been acquired by the Virginia Highway Department with road funds and no expense to Metrorail. It appeared that if the highway was not built, the cost of acquiring the right of way for the rail system would have to be borne by the Metrorail system, thus adding many millions of dollars to the costs of the rail construction program. Here again, the matter, in 1975, was eventually resolved to the benefit of Metrorail when the Federal Court requirements were met and an order was released permitting highway officials to proceed with I-66 construction. For a while though, it appeared that the Metrorail project had yet another major obstacle to overcome which the system and its officials by no means needed.

THE GROWTH OF FUNDING PROBLEMS

By far the most serious and troublesome challenge throughout the construction years for Metrorail was the need for adequate funds to carry on the extraordinarily costly project. This proved to be especially difficult as time wore on. At the outset of the project, it was represented by advocates, both Metro officials and local supporters, that the cost of the system would be around $2.5-billion, a third of which would be paid by local jurisdictions through bonds that would be paid off over the years by profits from the fare boxes. The local contributions thus, it was argued, would impose no actual

Major Community "Battles" and Controversies

financial burden on area taxpayers other than those who rode the system, and there was, therefore, no justifiable reason for voters to reject bonds issues at election times. The experience as of this writing, contrary to predictions, has been that there have been no operational profits to pay off construction bonds. Even more disappointing the local jurisdictions have been called on to heavily subsidize Metro operational costs to avoid drastic fare increases that would surely have decreased the number of riders and greatly worsened Metro's operational viability.

Step by step, however, voters and taxpayers began to realize that the cost of the system would not stop at the $2.5 Billion initially claimed. By 1995, with the system not yet completed, $7.8 Billion in federal and local funds had been spent on Metrorail construction and it was estimated that another $1.8 Billion would be needed to complete the remainder of the 103 mile system, for a total cost of $10.6 Billion.[26] When interest of about $8 Billion is added to this amount, it seems reasonable to conclude that the total cost of the system will be in the neighborhood of a around $20 Billion, or even more, if Arlington County's experience on interest costs can be used as a model. The total of Arlington bond issues to date and projected amount to $109 Million, with interest calculated at $83 Million, or about 80% of the bond values.[27] 80% of $10.6 billion would bring the total to near $20 billion.

In light of these staggering and ever increasing construction costs, and oppressive operational deficits and subsidies, Metro transit supporters have been hard pressed to retain public support for the system. Over the years, various efforts have been made to obtain relief from the steady increase in subsidies. For Arlington County the subsidies have varied annually from $130,000 in 1977 to $3,650.000 in 1995, and in two years amounted to $8 million for a total of $87.150 million.[28] As early as 1972, legislation was introduced in Congress to provide a Federal subsidy for the financially strapped D.C. Transit system. On February 1st, Jack Eisen in the Washington Post reported that the leaders of the nation's transit industry were pleading with a Senate subcommittee to support a government subsidy to keep city bus and subway fares from rising beyond what passengers could afford.

In March, Post writer Eisen reported that the House District Committee had agreed to a one-year subsidy up to $3 Million for the system intended to keep fares from rising above 40 cents. Eisen wrote that the bill would be the first general transit operating subsidy and could become a model for a national program along similar lines. The Post reported on May 9th, however, that the House had overwhelmingly rejected the proposal by a vote of 270 to 50, thus effectively ending for the time any hope for subsidies from the Federal government to relieve Arlington and other localities in their contribution to transit system losses.

[26] *Northern Virginia Transportation Handbook, P. 31.*

[27] *Memorandum, Arlington County Manager, Sept. 8, 1994, Ibid, P. 8.*

[28] *Memorandum, Ibid, P. 10.*

As mentioned above, the problem of transit operational losses did not go away through the years. Much later, in 1980, Arlington and Fairfax County members Dorothy Grotos and Marie Travesky of WMATA pushed for an increase in Metrorail fares as a means of coping with the heavy operational losses. Post writer Joseph Whitaker on November 27th, wrote that Arlington member Dorothy Grotos, however, opposed an increase in bus fares saying "We felt the 22 percent increase in bus fares earlier this year was enough". Member Travesky agreed, but said that river crossings and zone charges could be increased by 35 cents.

FUNDING PROBLEMS CONTINUE

As construction, and eventually operations, got underway Metro was to be continuously plagued, as stated, by funding problems. Most would be overcome but sometimes not without considerable anxiety and large dozes of ingenuity and perseverance. In a Washington Post article headlined, "Broyhill Warns President on Possible Metro Freeze", writer Stephen Green highlighted the possible threat to Metrorail resulting from Appeal Court rulings stopping planning and work on the proposed Three Sisters Bridge as a part of the interstate highway construction in the area.

On April 26, 1973, Arlington Journal writer Beth Price in an article headlined "Metro Still Seeks Funds, but Faces Hill Roadblock", wrote that Northern Virginia "is still left with virtually empty pockets and with enormous mass transit bills". She told of the efforts of the Northern Virginia Transportation Commission (NVTC) to tap into the "sacred highway trust fund" for use to finance Metrorail and bus expenses. She said, "Transportation experts say that operating losses will be more debilitating to Northern Virginia and to similar urban areas, that the capital (construction) costs".

On March 14, 1974, Mary Ames of the Journal in an article headlined "Compromise Saves Metro Aid", told of a eleventh-hour agreement that guaranteed Northern Virginia a $15 Million contribution to rapid transit over the next two years - but left taxpayers with no guarantee beyond that time. The money, from the highway fund, represented half the amount area taxpayers had been assessed for Metrorail construction costs.

In an article headlined "Interstate Funds Go To Metro", Arlington Journal staffer Susan Garland on February 5, 1976, described the complex question raised when the Federal government decided to use interstate highway funds for urban mass transit purposes. She wrote there was a question of whether Virginia State government would hand over the highway money to Northern Virginia for Metro construction, and even it did, could the local jurisdictions come up with the required 20 percent in local matching funds. She said Arlington and Fairfax Counties were running out of construction funds

Major Community "Battles" and Controversies

and would have to ask skeptical constituencies to approve more bond proposals with a very uncertain outcome.

Frank Davies of the Arlington Journal, on March 11, 1976, in an article headlined "Battle Due in Senate on Metro Funding", told of the frustration and disagreement in the Virginia legislature over Metro funding. He wrote that controversy swirling around whether highway money expected from a scaled down I-66 should be used for other roads or for Metrorail..

David Brooks of the Northern Virginia Sun, on January 21, 1980, wrote in an article headlined "Metro Subsidy Figure Angers Officials", told of the concern and discontent of Arlington County Manager Vernon Ford and fiscal analysis Chief Tony Gardiner over the money the county was called upon to pay to keep bus and subway servicing going. Brooks wrote, in part that the count had "...jumped by almost a million dollars to a level 20 percent over what the county says it is willing to pay, leading to a potential breakdown between local and transit authority officials. He wrote further that the County Board had reacted angrily to a Metro statement that Arlington's subsidy for the upcoming year had risen from $9.9 million to $10.8 million and that the County was considering the possibility of establishing substitute service to replace some of the more costly Metro bus lines.

Sandra Hemingway of the Alexandria Gazette wrote on December 12, 1980, in an article headlined "Rough Time Seen for Future Metro Funding", that "Northern Virginia officials (at a conference in Arlie House) found themselves staring into the uncertain future of Metro funding once again". She wrote that the officials felt the recently enacted higher gas tax would "be nothing more than a pittance", and that "somewhere down the line we may have to find another source of revenue".

All of these media accounts, and many others not recited here, highlight the continuing funding difficulties over the Metro construction and operational years. From this history, it is clear that Arlington County, and its sister jurisdictions, have toiled hard to persevere and "maintain the momentum of the assault" in their efforts to find ways around the fiscal obstacle and challenges of building and operating a modern, popular, and efficient mass transit system. Nor is the war yet won. There are battles ahead that may be even more frustrating than those of the past.

PUBLIC ATTITUDES

Over the years, public attitudes on the emergence of a rail rapid transit system have varied greatly, and are difficult to assess accurately. The best indication of support probably lies in the votes on bond issues in the various local jurisdictions. Letters to the editors in newspapers also provides some clues of citizen opinions. Robert Moore of Tacoma Park in a letter in the September 17, 1972 issue of the Post wrote that he "Did

ARLINGTON COUNTY VIRGINIA - A Modern History

*Metrorail.
An improvement?*

not dig Metro". He wrote "...it becomes clear that this much heralded and hugely expensive 'public transportation' system may in reality be no more than a windfall for those who would profit from making every street a superhighway and every front yard a passing zone...it now appears we are to have a 1,100 parking garage for us...the insanity of this..."

Robert Smith of Falls Church, in a letter to the Arlington Journal on December 11, 1975, urged a Metro cutback. He claimed the Journal had not conveyed the whole picture about Metro operations and that WMATA proposed budgets "contemplated large increases in current costs and deficits...which will be passed on to taxpayers". He wrote the increases in taxes were not inevitable, essential or mandatory. He urged the elimination of marginal bus service, a stretch out of construction, and a postponement of some metrorail operations.

Another writer in the Washington Star on October 10, 1976, complained that the Arlington County Board action in opposing the construction of I-66 was imperiling funds for Metrorail, and that "Many taxpayers are shocked with the adverse impact Metro is having on local governments' ability to provide other necessary public services and adequate education. He suggested that Board action in opposing I-66 contributed to the defeat of the $25 million bond issue on the Arlington ballot the year before.

CURRENT STATUS OF SYSTEM

In its 1994 "Fiscal Budget" report, the Metro Authority reports that it has 74 rail stations in operation with 89.5 miles of subway. There has been a steady, but not dramatic, increase in revenue from $164 million in 1988 to $242 million (projected) in 1995. It reports a modest, considering the growth and expansion of the system, increase in rail ridership from 97 million trips in 1988 to 112 million trips (projected) in 1995, and bus-rail ridership from 39 million in 1988 to 45 million (projected) in 1995.

Of particular concern in coming years could be the Authority's report on the aging of its rail rolling stock and station facilities and the expense this will likely impose on its already pressing operational deficits. Of its 764 rail cars, the Authority reports that 298 are nearing 20 years of age and will be, or are, up for mid-life rehabilitation. Another 200 or so are nearing ten years of age and use. The Authority reported that it had spent $128.4 million in fiscal 1992 and 1993 on capital rehabilitation projects to include stations, tracks, cars, escalators, elevators, service facilities and other equipment and planned to spend another $425 million over the next four years. The system reports that it recognizes that the "new and gleaming original system will not stand up to the demand of new ridership (and financial viability) unless rehabilitation and improvements continue to be made".

The bottom line of all this seems to be that the heavy demands on local jurisdictions to underwrite Metro deficits are not likely to ease but, rather, if anything will increase. Thus, the battle to establish and retain an efficient mass transit rail and bus system in the Washington, and Arlington areas is far from over and seems sure to continue. The Washington Post reported on December 16, 1995 in an article by staff writers Alice Reid and Stephen Fehr that Metro officials were proposing fewer and shorter trains and buses with longer waits by passengers to slow service and limit ever rising area subsidies. They reported that the system needed $13.8 million more in subsidies for the next year that were already running at $320 million. Arlington's share amounts to $26.8 million. It remains to be seen how much support for Metro there will be as the system places ever heavier burdens on area taxpayers to underwrite the operational deficits of the system..

On a more upbeat note, in spite of the ever rising deficits and need for subsidies, it seems that overall public confidence in the rapid rail transit system has not ruinously diminished although many people seem to be rather ambivalent in their opinions. On December 9, 1995, the Washington Post reported in an article by writer Fehr headlined "Poll Finds 74% Favor Extending Mass Transit", that a poll of area residents indicated a broad willingness to pay more taxes for transportation projects. Fehr wrote that respondents indicated a need for more trains and buses, and also more highways. He reported that the results of the survey were released in connection with a Council of Governments (COG) conference to develop long-range transportation and land-use plans for the area.

Writer Fehr quoted Robert Krebs of the Greater Washington Board of Trade as saying, "...people in surveys say they support mass transit more than highways (but) those same people would not actually use mass transit once it is built". He also quoted Mahln Anderson of the AAA as saying, "Transit ranks right up there with motherhood and apple pie...but when you ask people if it is practical for them, then it's not such a great idea." Fehr wrote, "About 74 percent of those surveyed said they favored mass transit, such as extensions of the Metro system as a solution to traffic congestion, whereas 58 percent said they favored more roads. He also wrote that support for mass transit was higher in Maryland and the District than in Virginia.

SOME IMPORTANT METRO DEVELOPMENTS

Jul 10, 1952	Congress passes National Capital Planning Act mandating preparation of plans for movement of people and goods in the region
March, 1954	Maryland, Virginia and DC form commission to implement
July 1, 1959	Resulting survey presented to Pres. Eisenhower. Calls for $500 million rapid transit rail system by 1980
Sept 8, 1965	Pres. Johnson signs into law bill authorizing $431 million 25 mile rapid transit system capable of future expansion
Feb 4, 1966	Gov Mills Godwin signs bill authorizing Virginia participation in interstate compact authority (WMATA)
Oct 20, 1967	WMATA submits proposal for 95.6 mile system - 34.6 in D.C., 27.8 in Maryland, and 33.2 in Virginia
Aug 10, 1968	Congress withholds Metro funds from D.C. budget. Rep Natcher states will release as soon as freeway system gets underway beyond recall

Nov 5, 1968	Voters endorse Metro funds in 5 jurisdictions
Sep 24, 1969	Rep Natcher approves $18.7 million for Metro previously deleted.
Dec 9,	First construction contracts awarded - includes Gallery Place and Judiciary Square stations. Ground breaking ceremony with officials and 1,500 persons
Jun 17, 1971	Ground breaking in Rosslyn, Virginia
Jul 13, 1972	Nixon signs bill to provide Federal guarantee of $1.2 billion Metro revenue bonds to expedite their sale
Sep 1, 1974	The last 151 AM General buses of 620 ordered are placed in service
Nov 14,	Costs of Metro recalculated at $4.5 billion due to inflation
Nov 26,	Pres Ford signs act providing first subsidies for mass transit from Highway Trust Fund
Oct 1, 1975	New ordnance takes effect making smoking, eating, or playing radios without earphones on Metro illegal
Mar 27, 1976	Metro opening day on 4.2 miles on five stations of system. Free rides for 51,000 persons
Mar 29,	First revenue service. 19,913 persons, 188 train trips
Aug 26,	WMATA revises estimated cost of system at $5.5 billion
Feb 19, 1978	125 Metro bus routes changed to terminate at newly opened stations instead of downtown
May 18,	One day wildcat strike following rape of woman bus driver
Jul 19-25,	Week long wildcat strike over cost of living clause in contract
Feb 19, 1979	Three day shut down due to blizzard and deep snow on tracks
Jul 16,	Congress authorized $1.7 billion to complete 101 mile system
Dec 1,	Four stations on Orange line in Virginia go into service
Nov 22, 1981	Blue Line Addison Road segment begins operation. Metro system totals 41 stations and 37 miles of line
Jan 13, 1982	First Metro passenger fatalities when car derails at switch south of Federal Triangle. 3 dead, 25 injured. Crash is preceded by major snow storm, early release of federal employees and crash of airliner into the 14th street bridge and Potomac River.
June, 1982	Metro launches two prong attack to control spread of graffiti
Apr 30, 1985	Metro announces new high of 400,000 daily trips in ridership.
Jul 31,	Metro claims system safety record is best in the transit industry
Jun 7, 1986	Vienna station opens completing Orange line in Virginia. Average weekday ridership jumps to 30,000
Mar 16, 1989	Re-authorization legislation introduced
May, 1991	Metro manager proposes $775 million capital improvement program
Jun 7-8,	Desert Storm Victory celebration on Mall generates record 786,000 riders
Nov 1994	Metro claims it has created 87,000 new jobs and that Virginia has realized a 12.4% return on its investment in Metrorail.

* * * *

Major Community "Battles" and Controversies

Round V
THE PROSPECT HILL REZONING

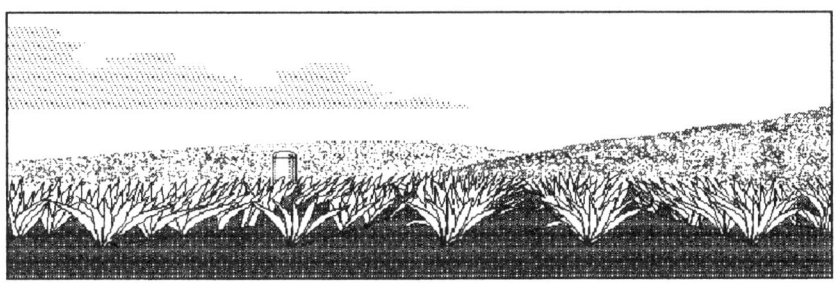

In the late 1830s, Phillip Roach, with his wife and two daughters and son James arrived in Alexandria from his former home in Ireland. He immediately set about to find land upon which to establish a new world home for himself and his family. In due course, he focused in on one of the most desirable and attractive pieces of real estate in Northern Virginia. The site was well elevated, located about a mile from the Potomac River and afforded a spectacular panoramic view of the National Capital area. It was identified on land records as "Hoe Hill" as recorded by historian Templeman in her _Arlington Heritage_, cited below in FN 29. The land had been a part of the estate of 18th Century settler John Alexander after whom the City of Alexandria was, and is, named.

From Hoe Hill, an observer could perhaps have seen through the trees, also about a mile to the North, the majestic Arlington House completed by about 1818 by George Washington Park Custis. To the right and southeast, could probably have been seen Abington, the home of the Alexander family, the ruins of which are now preserved near the modern day main terminal at National Airport. After passing from the Alexander family to a member of the Washington family in 1811, the Hoe Hill land was taken over by the Bank of the United States in 1836, and bought by Roach on March 30, 1838.

Roach and his son James promptly set about to build a plant on the clay lowlands below Hoe Hill to make bricks for a new home. The senior Roach, however, died in June at the age of 50, before construction could get underway, and the lands passed to his son James, who then proceeded to build the family residence. He completed it in 1841, and named the mansion "Prospect Hill". [29]

Templeman, in 1959 about eight years before the house was demolished, in the article footnoted below, described the Roach home as follows:

---

[29]_Templeman, Eleornor Lee, Arlington Heritage, Avenel Books, New York, 1959, p. 58._

> "The house is beautifully proportioned and detailed, with a two-story center section and one-storied wings on each side. Brick-walled pathways lead to servants quarters which are also of brick. The original huge brass locks remain on the doors. One of the most interesting rooms is the kitchen with the oven built into the wall beside the massive fireplace."

Several years later, Arlington County Planning Director Richard E. Arms, would write about Prospect Hill the following: [30]

> "...the (Prospect Hill) tract has an excellent panoramic view overlooking the National Airport, the Pentagon and Arlington Cemetery with the District of Columbia in the background...the residence is an excellent example of colonial architecture, (and) has been kept in good repair by the owners except during and immediately after the War years of 1860-65. The House sits majestically atop this ridge (Arlington Ridge) among a setting of beautiful old trees overlooking the valley below...there are few other historical landmarks in Arlington with the architectural character of Prospect House which are situated in so prominent a location."

During the Civil War and afterwards, the Prospect Hill house and the Roach family fell on hard times. Both were subjected to abuse and misuse in numerous ways. In a letter obtained by Templeman from a great grand daughter of the builder of the house, it is related (FN 29, page 221) that Union soldiers came to Prospect Hill at 2 a.m. on May 24, 1861 and took possession of the house. The builder and his son James Carson Roach were taken prisoners and the elder was not released until almost six months after the fighting ended. "The soldiers burned the two story farm house and a large barn, killed ducks, turkeys and chickens, rooted up the vegetable garden, and turned government cattle in to graze in the front yard to destroy shrubs and everything. Many a night the family members were awakened by the soldiers tramping through the house under the pretext of finding fire arms."

The Templeman letter writer relates that trees were cut down to built Forts Albany and Runyan located on the property and that they gathered all grain into the grist mill and burned it. The Roaches moved into Alexandria after the war and the property was later sold under court order in 1869 to settle claims against the estate.

In 1913, the Prospect Hill estate was purchased by Mrs Phillip Campbell, who died in the early 1960s, leaving four children as heirs to the property. All four were located in places far from Arlington and apparently had no interest in returning to the property to live, or even to retain it. It appeared to local residents that the property, in essence, constituted a "white elephant" for the heirs, and that they, therefore, entered into a contract to develop the property if it could be profitably rezoned for higher density uses such as a high rise apartment building.

---

[30] *Memorandum, March 10, 1965, to the Arlington County Board, from Bert Johnson, County Manager; Subject: Application for rezoning, Z-1794-65-2.*

Major Community "Battles" and Controversies

The James Roach mansion on Prospect Hill on South Arlington Ridge Road before its destruction in November 1965.

In 1964 an application for rezoning of the property designated 1230 South Arlington Ridge Road, and 164,000 square feet (3.8 acres) in size, was filed by Arlington Attorney William B. Lawson on behalf of Charles Rose and associates as "contract owners". The application requested a change from "R-10" (single family detached housing on not less than 10,000 square feet of land), to "RA-H", Hotel District. The RA-H classification would permit a condominium type apartmental building larger and higher, and with greater density than other adjacent apartment buildings on three sides that were built under RA 6-15 and RA 7-16 zoning.

The rezoning application came before the County Planning Commission and County Board in January and February 1965, respectively but was deferred several times over the following months at the request of the applicant, or the County Manager's staff, for additional time to prepare, study, or modify the site plan. [31]

A "site plan" is an architectural drawing of a proposed building that would be constructed on a given piece of land. Such a plan is expected to reflect the general

---

[31] *The Arlington County Board has required that "site plans" accompany rezoning applications for higher density and the plans are taking into account by the Board in deciding whether to grant a requested rezoning.*

appearance of the building as well as its size, style, number of floors, total square feet and relationship to the square feet of the land on which it would be located, and other similar design or engineering characteristics or features.

During the months that the rezoning application remain on file and pending Board action, numerous groups filed responses opposing the requested rezoning and urging that the site be maintained in its existing state with its mansion intact, by public purchase if necessary. These groups included, the Arlington County Civic Federation, Patricia Barker on behalf of the Aurora Hills Women's Club, Shannon Trumbo on behalf of the Jefferson Civic League on South 23rd Street, The Arlington Ridge Civic Association, and Helen Bullock on behalf of the National Trust for Historic Preservation. No documents in support of the rezoning, other than those for the applicant, were filed with the County Office of Zoning. The Roscoe-Ajax Construction Company, Washington D.C., wrote "...we do not recommend construction of an apartment house on the proposed site, since excessive aircraft noise can be expected...(but) should you nonetheless proceed, generous sound proofing should be used..."

In numerous communications to the County Board, the County Planning Commission and Manager, opposed the rezoning and urged that the property be purchased and retained for its historical significance. On March 10, 1965, in a Memorandum signed by Planning Director Richard Arms and Manager Bert Johnson, the County Board was advised, in part, as follows:

> *"It is recommended that the County acquire this prominent overlook for open space purposes ...the site has historical significant since the earliest days of development in this area...*
>
> *"Arlington Ridge Road, known in the early 1800s as the Alexandria-Georgetown Road connected Alexandria with Georgetown, climbing the ridge of "Hoes Hill" (later called Prospect Hill" and subject of this zoning), and crossing the plain near Arlington Cemetery to reach the ferry as Rosslyn.*
>
> *"In 1841, James Roach, a leading citizen and contractor of that day credited with masonry work for the Chesapeake & Ohio Canal and early railroad construction, built his home on the crest of Prospect Hill. This residence, an excellent example of colonial architecture, has been kept in good repair by the owners except during and immediately after the War years of 1860-65. The House sits majestically atop the ridge...suggesting a role in the preservation of Arlington's and that Nation's Heritage...*
>
> *"It is the Office of Planning opinion that this property with its heritage, its size, condition and setting offers much to justify public ownership. There are few other historic landmarks in Arlington with the architectural character of Prospect House which are situated in so prominent a location. The foreground of Shirley Highway right-of-way and the low silhouette of the Pentagon and Arlington Cemetery (below) assure a continued prominence of this site as a landmark."*

Major Community "Battles" and Controversies

At its meeting on March 20, 1965, the Board made no decision on the matter, deferred a further hearing until May 8, and requested additional information on the feasibility of public acquisition of the site. On April 27 the Manager advised the Board that acquisition could "be quite costly", and difficult to justify "although the staff feels that the combination of historical, architectural value and prominence of location is unique in Arlington County." The Manager also reported that the applicant had been requested to study, and had studied, the feasibility of moving the main residence to the north end of the property and onto adjacent land owned by the Virginia Highway Department, but that such a movement was concluded not to be feasible because of steep topography and other reasons.

In following months, numerous work sessions were held with the applicants representatives, the county staff, and interested citizen activists. During this period the staff explored the feasibility of public acquisition, and the applicant indicated a willingness to create, dedicate, and maintain a small open space on the north and east end of the property as an overlook for public uses.

The County Board scheduled the matter for final hearing and decision for November 20, 1965. On November 18th, the Manager furnished the Board a "Statement concerning Prospect Hill", indicating a reversal of its earlier position that the site should be acquired for public preservation and open space. The statement follows, in pertinent part:

"In the past six months it has been our pursuit to see if opportunity for public acquisition could be implemented. The most promising course was to get this property registered as a National Historic Site by the U. S. Department of Interior. If this could be achieved, federal financing could be expedited.

"After a call to Secretary of the Interior Udall's office, (we learned) that the Advisory Board agreed it could not recommend Prospect Hill as a National Historic Landmark, that the historians, architects and archeologists agreed that any interest in the property must be local not national...

"Accordingly, we recommend that this property be rezoned, and that the County Board accept the contract owner's proposal to preserve for the public that portion of the tract which is by far the most important to the public - the overlook. The developers are offering...to obtain an easement over approximately 100 feet of the northerly portion of the property. We believe this goes a long way toward the goal of preserving for the general public the most important factor of the tract - the vista of Arlington and the nation's capital...we find it most difficult to justify the amount of money required to purchase the entire tract to obtain the additional southerly portion of the tract...

"Accordingly, it is recommended that the zoning be granted and the site plan be approved preserving the northerly portion of the tract with an easement for public purposes..."

The consideration of the Prospect Hill rezoning request by the County Board at its November 20th meeting was extensive and, at times, heated. No public witnesses testified in favor of the rezoning other than the applicant, or its representatives including attorney William Lawson. Numerous individuals appeared in opposition, but perhaps the most articulate and outspoken were the members of the Arlington Ridge Civic Association within whose boundaries the site was located.

Association member William Frederick told the Board that it was not obligated to act on the application at all - that there was no law or rule requiring the Board to approve the application in any form or to any extent; that the Board could simply deny the request as a matter of discretionary judgment.

Member Francis Hewitt urged public acquisition to preserve the mansion and property and pointed out that the assessed value as shown by the County tax assessor was only a little over $300,000, which was not prohibitive.

Association member Sherman Pratt, this author, showed the Board home movie amateur film clips of the site to demonstrate the unique panoramic view of the National Capital as seen from the site's promontory north end. Included in the clips were tourist shots Pratt had taken on trips to the Holy Land in the Mid-east and to the cultural city of Florence in Italy. Pratt showed the Board views of Jerusalem as seen from the high ground on the Mount of Olives above the Garden of Gethsemane, and of the famed Ponte Veccio over the Arno River, and the medieval Churches and other buildings of Florence as seen from the public overlook in Garibaldi Park on the south side of the Arno River. Pratt told the Board, in part:

> *"None of these spectacular panoramic views of these historic and cultural places would be available to visitors and the public today if someone in history long ago had not had the foresight and courage to set aside the overlooks to the benefit of posterity. That preservation did not just happened. Someone made it happen.*
>
> *"You gentlemen in Arlington County on this zoning Board stand at the same cross roads this evening at this point in time. You have a similar opportunity to preserve the only remaining significant overlook in the National Capital area, and the only remaining oldest structure in the county in its original condition, other than Arlington House in Arlington Cemetery. We beg you not to forfeit this opportunity. If you do, the possibility of preservation will be lost forever. Once an immense and costly structure is built, there will be no turning back. You will never ever be able to undo what has been done."*

Following the testimony by public witnesses, the Board discussed at length its course of action. Some members expressed doubt that funds could be allocated for public acquisition of the property at its marketable value. One member said he felt that if the Board did not grant the rezoning, the Board would be reversed in the Courts; that adjacent properties on three sides were already zoned and occupied by high rise apartments and that it could be found to be unreasonable and arbitrary for the Board not to also classify the subject property also as high rise. Whereupon, one public witness rose to point out that the existence of so many high rise apartments in the area constituted

Major Community "Battles" and Controversies

the strongest reason possible for not creating more if control of congested development was to be achieved.

Finally, near midnight, the Board voted 3-2 to grant the rezoning with Board members Thomas Richard, Harold Casto and Leo Urbanske voting for and Joseph Fisher and Roye Lowry voting against. Early the following morning, bull dozers and other razing equipment were at the site, knocking down the mansion and surrounding structures. By night fall, destruction was completed and the site devoid of any indications that it once contained a stately and historic structure. Local civic activists were convinced that the developers had moved with all deliberate speed to accomplish their goals before any legal or other challenges could be taken to reverse or otherwise interfere with the County Board's approval of the rezoning application.

Reaction among Arlington Ridge Civic Association members, and perhaps many others, was bitter disappointment, acrimonious, resentful and openly critical. There was a general conviction that the Board, consisting of four members who resided in the far northern areas of the County, had acted with great insensitivity to the interests and views of the South Arlington residents in whose area the subject property was located. There was the strong feeling that had the property been located in North Arlington, the Board members who voted for approval, would have taken a different course of action. The weakness of that attitude, however, was that one of the Board members, Urbanske, himself lived in South Arlington, on South 18th Street, only a few blocks from the Prospect Hill site.

The Representative condominium apartments on South Arlington Ridge Road overlooking the Pentagon and Crystal City.

In the years following the Board approval of the rezoning, after several additional chances in the site plan, construction began on the massive condominium Representative Apartments, that now stands as one of Arlington County's most luxurious and prestigious residential structures. It stands high on the Arlington Ridge and can be seen easily from numerous view points in North Virginia and from across the Potomac River in

Washington, D.C. Listed among the more famous and well known personalities that have resided in the Representative was the late Admiral Hyman Rickover, often called the father of the atomic submarine.

True to their promise, the applicants did in fact create the 100 foot overlook public access area complete with concrete patio, benches and lighting that is a clear asset to the Arlington Ridge community and the County. Sadly, however, the unique, historical, and stately Prospect Hill mansion of James Roach of long ago, is but a memory. It will forever, however, be an indelible, historically fascinating and lasting part of Arlington's past.

* * * *

"Great bird's eye view, fellows, from here at the Prospect Hill RidgeRoad overlook?"

"That's for sure! Thoughtful and cagey of ole James Roach to build his home on this property so long ago. Saved much space for wildlife".

"Where is his mansion now? Wasn't it used in the American Civil War by those two legged earthling humankinds for a hospital?"

"Sure was, and was very prestigious in design much like the bird sanctuary down the Potomac called Mt Vernon. Became quite an historical treasure. But locals tore it down in 1967 to make way for a high rise apartment building."

"How did that happen? Didn't anyone object?"

"Almost everybody, including our cousins. But all lost in a bitter rezoning struggle."

"Pity!!"

Major Community "Battles" and Controversies

Round VI
THE SICKELS TRACT REZONING

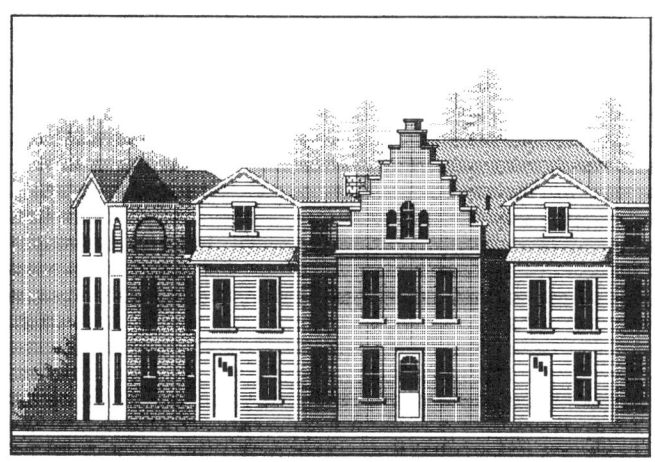

THE FOREST HILLS TOWNHOUSES

By the mid 1960s most of the scarce available land in Arlington County zoned for single family, or low density, residential use was rapidly being developed. Other open or under-used tracts zoned for higher density uses, commercial and/or residential, were on the threshold of being developed and would be fully developed by the late 1970s and 1980s. Those areas would become known as the Rosslyn, Crystal City, Pentagon City and the Ballston Corridor developments.

A sizeable piece of undeveloped land, and probably the largest such tract anywhere in the County, zoned R-10, was situated just east of Shirley Highway (later I-95 and then I-395) near Glebe Road. The land was known among local citizens as the Sickels tract, or, as sometimes labeled in the media or elsewhere, the Sickles tract. It was just under 16 acres in size and bounded on the west by Army-Navy Drive, on the north by South 23rd Street, on the south by the existing Shirley Park garden apartments, and on the east by single family detached homes along South Pierce Street and the Oak Ridge Elementary School. Open space R-10 land just to the north of the Sickels tract between South 20th and 23rd Streets and about two thirds up the slopes of Arlington Ridge from Army-Navy Drive had been developed into single family detached homes in the early 1960s.

The Sickels tract was so known because it was owned, at the time of her death in 1956, by Frances Lee Sickels who was born in 1878. She was the daughter of Presha Antonia Fraser Sickels and Jackson Sickels, a Civil War engineer who had built Federal fortifications around the City of Washington, and later became a county engineer who worked with Frank Hume a school supervisor. Presha Sickels had inherited the lands from her father Anthony Fraser.[32] Fraser owned not only the Sickels tract, but also considerable adjacent lands to include those on which is now located the Army-Navy Country Club and golf courses, and the Gunston County School. Fraser died in 1881 and was buried on his property. [33] All those lands were earlier known, generally, as Green Valley. Fraser's granddaughter Francis Lee Sickels died in England in 1956. Her daughter, Mrs David dePackh and her daughter lived in later years in Washington, D.C.

*"Green Valley Manor", home of the Frazier family.
Built 1821. Burned 1924.*

In 1821, Anthony Fraser built his handsome residence on that part of the Sickels property that remained undeveloped in the 1960s, and named it the "Green Valley Manor". The estate was among the first lands in Northern Virginia to be occupied by Federal troops when they crossed the Potomac in May, 1861 and its grounds were used for a hospital and convalescent camp in the Civil War. It is recorded that the camp was one of the worst in the war with a higher death rate than most others. Historian Eleanor Lee Templeman wrote that nearby Rapid Run ran "red with blood from the amputations performed there." Fraser was a leader and active in local affairs. On June 26, 1849 was elected "Overseer of the Poor" as recorded in the Minute Book of Alexandria County (Arlington Historical Society Magazine, October 1963, page 42.)

---

[32] *For a more detailed account of the Fraser family see "The Frasers of Green Valley", Eleanor Lee Templeman, Arlington Heritage, p.60, Avenel Books, a division of Crown Books, New York, NY, 1959.*

[33] *The Frazer family grave site remains within the Army Navy Golf Course enclosed within an iron fence near the 26th green and just off Interstate highway I-395.*

Major Community "Battles" and Controversies

In 1924 Green Valley Manor was destroyed by fire, but foundations and parts of the fireplace and walls remained until modern times almost completely concealed and hidden in the midst of heavy over growth. One of the few items of furniture retrieved from the fire is a desk known as the "Desk of Infamy". Legend has it that the desk was once owned by Jefferson Davis who so called it because of its use when he penned his fatal refusal to consider a carte blanche request from President Lincoln to write his terms for ending the war at a time when losses on both sides had become overwhelming. Davis later presented the desk to his good friend Frederick Sickels a noted New York marine engineer and brother of Jackson Sickels mentioned above.[34]

* * *

On a wintry evening in early 1967 the executive committee and some others in the Arlington Ridge Civic Association met in the home of Frances Hewitt on South Hayes Street. Those in attendance included civic activists and local residents Alice Campbell, William Frederick, Sherman Pratt, Phil Arends, and Hewitt. Prominent on the agenda for discussion was a report floating around that an application was about to be filed for development of the Sickels tract. It was understood that the heirs of Francis Sickels were not interested in retaining the property and were negotiating with the Chaiken development firm to buy and develop the tract.

The Arlington Ridge neighborhood group was in agreement that the matter was of major concern to them and the community for fear that an effort would be made to develop the land in any way, and especially if into high rise and high density uses in conflict with the single family residential character of the neighborhood. Only months earlier, the community had experienced periods of near panic with respect to dense development of the property. Residents were appalled at the prosects of crippling increases in traffic and parking congestion and related problems. On October 3, 1967 the County Board considered, but rejected, a petition to rezone the property to RA7-16, that would have allowed high rise buildings. Additionally it learned about the same time that the owners of the adjacent Shirley Park garden apartments were considering redevelopment of those units, a section at a time, into high rise apartment buildings. That plan was abandoned when the owners were confronted with intense community opposition.

The Arlington Ridge Association had long been on record since earlier consideration and adoption of a General Land Use Plan by the County Board, as favoring the retention of single family residential areas to the maximum extent possible and maintaining the lowest density possible throughout the county in all types of land uses. There was general agreement that such a policy would minimize congestion and pollution, not strain utility, school or other community facilities, and would help to avoid other adverse consequences that were perceived to detract from enjoyable living or otherwise be detrimental to the citizenry. The prevailing view in the Association, as generally

---

[34] *The desk is a permanent acquisition of the Arlington Historical Society, donated by Mrs Davis de Packh, the daughter of Francis Lee Sickels, and is located in the Society's museum in the former Hume School at 1805 Arlington Ridge Road.*

elsewhere throughout the county, was also to resist the intrusion of commercial and high density areas into existing low density neighborhoods. Soon after the subject 1967 meeting of the Ridge Association members, notice was received from the County Zoning administrator that an application had been filed for rezoning of the Sickels tract. The matter was promptly taken up by the Executive Committee of the Association. Before the group was the question of what position to take on the application to rezone the Sickels tract from R-10 to R-10T, or, in short from single family detached residences on lots of at least 10,000 square feet to townhouse use that could allow as many as 5 or more houses per acre depending on configuration and layout.

There was general agreement among the Ridge Association members over the following months at numerous meetings that the Association should urge the County Board, as a first choice, through a bond issue if necessary, to acquire the land for park or other public use and retained the land as open space. In its desires to retain the Sickels tract as open space, the Association had solid support from numerous other civic activists or groups to include the County Planning Commission. In a later report to the Commission its Site Plan Review Committee recommended that the "Commission reaffirm its previous position that this site be purchase for public open space"[35] The Committee reported, in pertinent part:

> "...the Commission has already recommended the subject site as its number one priority for purchase for public open space...however County Board action has not been taken...
>
> "The...staff report on open space clearly indicates the critical need for open space in the Gunston Junior High School District. The Chaiken or Sickles Tract, (valued at about a million dollars) ...represents the *cheapest* site of significant size in the Gunston District. The Committee identified many advantages for maintaining this site undeveloped:
>
> Historical significance: The old dirt road existing through a portion of the site is part of the original Rosslyn Ferry to Alexandria road dating back to the 18th Century. Ruins of an original manor house are on the site.
>
> Accessibility: The site is located on 23rd street, easily reached by foot, bicycle or auto from the surrounding area.
>
> Wild life abounds on the site. A Staff member recently visiting the site reported observing wild ducks in Long Branch stream."

Although the Ridge Association and other local activists were firmly on record as favoring the public purchase of the Sickels tract, it was recognized that the County Board might never agree to do so. There was recognition of the need for deciding what position should be taken on the townhouse rezoning application if the Board refused to

---

[35] *Planning Commission Site Plan Committee Report, Forest Hills Town Houses*, July 26, 1973. Actions or reports such as this by County government offices are on file in either the County Manager's Office or the Virginia Room archives of the Central Library, or both.

buy the land. The clear preference, absent a public purchase, was that the R-10 zoning be retained, but some expressed doubt that even that position was realistic.

Hewitt pointed out that the prospects of public purchase were bleak since it would involve a bond issue with much uncertainty of voter approval, and even doubt that the Board would put the matter before the voters.

"All the Board members live in the far north end of the county." pointed out Alice Campbell. "They are not about to approve the purchase of the Sickels tract with a price of almost a million dollars."

"I think we should take a hard stand and oppose any rezoning even if the Board doesn't buy the land," argued Phil Arenson.

"But if the application is denied, and the land not bought, then where are we?" asked Bill Frederick. "We will live in fear that another application will be submitted sooner or later, and perhaps for a much more undesirable use, as before, such as garden type apartments or even high rises. We can't go through life with that prospect hanging over our heads."

"I don't think we can rely on this County Board listening to us very much," responded Hewitt. "They all live up north. Not a single member is in the Southern half of the county and they have increasingly demonstrated great insensitivity to our interests. I have the feeling that they don't even listen to us when we appear before them with our position on problems here."

"Are you saying we should cave in and concur in the townhouse rezoning?" asked Sherman Pratt.

"Of course it's not the citizens first choice," Frederick answered, "but it might be the most practical approach. I'm led to believe the developers are eager to work with us with a view of making concessions if they can get our agreement not to fight them, at least for the townhouses if not too thick and dense".

Arenson didn't agree. "I think you're giving in too soon and easily. No Board in this county would dare to rezone that land for high rise uses. It would conflict with the land use plan they just got through adopting. I think we should hold out for purchase, or keeping the existing R-10 zoning."

"But Board membership changes from election to election", Frederick countered. "This Board might not rezone for high rise, but how can we depend on what the next might do?"

In the months that followed, the Association met repeatedly and anguished over the matter. Representatives met with the developers to learn precisely what was proposed. Finally, when the applicants consented to amend their plan in several critical respects as desired, the Association agreed, with reluctance and little enthusiasm, "not to oppose" the town house application.

In their amendments to the site plan, the developers agreed that the total number of units would be reduced from 141 to 129; a buffer strip should be left between the development and the existing single family residences on South Pierce Street; the streets should be widened to 36 feet in accordance with County requirements; off street parking would be increased; and only detached houses should be constructed on 23rd Street to conform to other houses on that street.

With these changes in the site plan the developers appeared before the County Board on February 6, 1968 in support of their application for rezoning. Numerous recreational, environmental, historical and other groups were on record as opposing the rezoning and urging that the land be acquired for park or other public uses. Also on file was the County Planning Commission's position advocating public acquisition of the site. Spokes persons for the Arlington Ridge Association testified that while they did not expressly favor the rezoning, the Association had voted not to oppose it after specified modifications and concessions had been made by the developers. After prolonged discussion, the Board approved the application and rezoned the property from "R-10" to "R-10-T", One-family Town House Dwelling District.[36]

On January 25, 1969, almost a year later, the County Board approved the tentative site plan that had been used by the applicant and shown to the Board at the time of the rezoning hearing.[37] The final site plan included the modifications recommended by the Ridge Association and was not therefore opposed by the group. In fact, since public purchase had been declined, the Association was now eager to have townhouse development move ahead and it urged the County Board "to approved the revised Town House Site Plan".[38] The site plan approval was subsequently extended for one year on January 21, 1970 and for six months on January 9, and July 10, 1971, and finally on

"We're breaking ground for the new Forest Hills townhouses on Army-Navy Drive at South 23rd Street?"

"Yes! On some very historical Arlington County lands."

"Why historical?"

"Because the early settler Anthony Fraser built his "Green Valley Manor" here which stood until burned in 1924. It was used as a hospital during the Civil War and accounts say so many amputations took place that nearby Roach's Run turned red with blood! General Lee and others were known to have stayed here."

"Wasn't Fraser in charge of the first election district that met at the Thompson House at Balls Cross Roads following the 1846 retrocession?"

"He was indeed! Or at least it is so recorded in the Alexandria County Court Minute book entry of March 9, 1848."

---

[36] *Minutes Arlington County Board, Book 22, Page 82.*

[37] *Under a procedure adopted in the early 1960s pertaining to applications for rezoning, applicants must present draft "site plans" for a site at the time of a rezoning hearing that were subject to later resubmission for Board final consideration and approval.*

[38] *Letter, January 13, 1969, Francis S. Hewitt, President, Arlington Ridge Civic Association to Dr Kenneth Haggarty, Chairman, Arlington County Board.*

January 26, 1972.[39] At each of these actions, Civic Association representatives appeared and did not object to the extensions but increasingly expressed apprehension that the developer was going to break faith and not proceed with construction. Fear prevailed among Association members that with his foot in the door with a townhouse rezoning, the developer would abandon plans for townhouses and submit a new proposal for higher density uses in sharp conflict with the desires of the Ridge Association community, and the General Land Use Plan. The Association became increasingly suspicious of the good intentions of the developers. The new Association president wrote to the County Board as follows:

> *"Although our Association Agreed to the rezoning ...several years ago, we remain apprehensive over the continued delay in the consummation of this project...we have agreed to previous extensions...based on the understanding that the delay ...was due mainly to the tight money market...*
>
> *Until construction is well under way, our residents will not rest at ease for fear that the developers may abandon their town house plans and seek authority for more dense development...*
>
> *We do not plan to oppose the application for renewal of the site plan...but in view of the history of repeated delays...we request that the Board question the applicant, publicly, and in detail, on his specific plans and schedule...with respect to the dates on which construction and completion of this project can be expected."* [40]

On February 6, 1973 the Zoning Administrator for the County ruled that the 1969 site plan approved and extended had expired on July 26, 1972. Thereafter the applicants resubmitted their site plan and it came before the County Board on May 12, 1973 and was heard in a late night session that continued until well after midnight.

Arlington Ridge spokesmen appeared in opposition and protested vigorously that the new site plan differed significantly from the one initially approved by the Board at the time of the rezoning action on January 16, 1969. Association President Pratt, and past Zoning Committee Chairman, pointed out that the new site plan constituted, essentially, a return to the original proposal that was objected to by the Association. He said townhouses once eliminated had been again included, townhouses were proposed for 23rd street instead of the agreed to single family detached residences, and off street parking had been reduced. Pratt added;

> *"I am at an utter loss to understand how you could ignore the virtual mandate to buy this land. Almost every responsible organization*

---

[39] *Letter, March 12, 1974, from Tom Parker, Planning and Zoning Chief, to Charles Flynn, County Attorney's Office, Subject: Forest Hills Town House Plan.*

[40] *Letter, January 7, 1971 from William K. Skaer, President, Arlington Ridge Civic Association to the Arlington County Board.*

and individual, including a unanimous Planning Commission wants the tract for open space." [41]

Member Bill Frederick proclaimed that Board approval of the new site plan would constitute a breach of faith with the citizenry and a violation of earlier agreements made in order to obtain Association approval of the townhouse plan.

Notwithstanding these protests by Ridge Association representatives, the County Board voted to approved the new site plan before them.[42] One member, however, Ellen Bozman, an "Independent" candidate for the County Board, disassociated herself from her other colleagues on the Board and asked the Board to buy the tract.[43]

The Arlington Ridge Civic Association, and particularly its members who resided in the areas immediately adjacent to the Chaiken-Sickels tract took the strongest umbrage at the action of the County Board in approving the site plan they opposed and decided to file suit in an effort to overturn the Board's action.

A suit later filed in the Arlington County Circuit Court was dismissed but the filing of the suit resulted in voluntary changes in the site plan more in keeping with the desires of the citizen plaintiffs.[44] The developers proceded with their plans and built townhouses on 23rd Street, contrary to the wishes of the plaintiffs who had insisted on single family residences as proposed in the first site plan submitted and approved by the County Board. The developer did agree, however, to more off street parking and more townhouses with garages, and also to a wider buffer strip of open space between the development and the residences adjacent on South Pierce Street.

Although not completely acceptable to the residents, the project as finally completed mostly conformed to the original proposals not objected to by the community and the Forest Hills townhouses stand today as one of the County's most distinguished, reputable and impressive housing projects. Citizens involved in the struggle are convinced that it would be detrimentally less so but for their efforts and struggles.

* * * *

---

[41] *Arlington Journal* May 17, 1973, p. 1 & 7

[42] Letter, March 12, 1974, Tom Parker, ibid.

[43] *Arlington Journal,* May 17, 1973, p.7. Several members of the Board ran for election as "independents" but they were supported by, and included on the campaign literature of, the County Democrat Party, and the dominant political organization known as Arlingtonians for a Better County.

[44] Details of the suit are unavailable due to a fire in the Court Clerk's office that destroyed many records including the file on this law case.

Major Community "Battles" and Controversies

The Forest Hills townhouses at South 23rd Street and Army-Navy Drive near the I-395 and Glebe Road intersection.

ARLINGTON COUNTY VIRGINIA - A Modern History

Round VII
THE I-66 CONTROVERSY

Interstate Highway I-66 in Arlington at Glebe Road

BACKGROUND AND HISTORY

By the closing years of the Eisenhower administration in the late 1950s, the design and planning for his new national highway system of freeways was in full swing. Construction was, in fact, underway in many parts of the country. It was to be known as the "Interstate" highway system and was to criss-cross the country from north to south and coast to coast for tens of thousands of miles.

One leg of the Interstate system, to be identified as Interstate 81, or I-81, was to run the entire length of Virginia from Bristol in the Southwest on the Tennessee border, to the West Virginia State line in the north about 12 miles beyond Winchester.

A shorter 75 mile link in the Virginia system to connect I-81 to the National Capital area was planned to run east from the Front Royal area to and through Fairfax and Arlington Counties and then cross the Potomac at Washington. That segment was identified as I-66 and in 1959 was placed on the National Interstate Map by the Federal Bureau of Public Roads, later Federal Highway Works Administration (later FHWA). Its proposed general location and route inside the Washington beltway (I-495 then about to be constructed), was also approved in June, 1959.

Major Community "Battles" and Controversies

ARLINGTON BECOMES INVOLVED

Arlington quickly became involved in that planning process. On October 28, 1958, Wilbur S. Smith of the consulting firm Wilbur Smith and Associates wrote to Mrs Leone Bucholz, Chairperson of the Arlington County Board concerning "the location of Interstate Route 66 through Arlington County".

Smith advised the Board that after consulting with engineers and officials in the Virginia Department of Highways, he had made reconnaissance and surveys of the Arlington area concerning possible routes for the highway from the standpoint of costs, feasibility, benefits for the County, and other pertinent considerations. He said, in part, "...it will be necessary to carefully work out interchange needs, traffic assignments, approach roads...to integrate the designs not only with the roadway network of the County and adjacent counties, but also to integrate it with over-all planning factors of the County." He expressed hope that the forthcoming results of his studies would assist the County "...in arriving at a sound recommendation to present to the State and Federal authorities relative to the location of Interstate Route 66".

The route through Arlington County for I-66, based on the studies of Smith, the Department of Highways, and others, was to be through "East" Falls Church, along portions of the W&OD railroad right of way, Fairfax Drive, northeastward to Spout Run and other nearby parks, through Rosslyn, and to cross the Potomac River into Washington via a new bridge at the southern tip of Roosevelt Island. The route became known as the Fairfax-Bluemont corridor. There was to be a spur road, identified as I-266, partly in the Spout Run Park, for an additional crossing of the Potomac in the area of the Three Sisters Islands, a mile or so north of the Key Bridge over the Potomac between Rosslyn and Georgetown.

That early planned I-66 route remained fixed and uncontested, for the most part, through following years of controversy, except for some uncertainty at the beginning with respect to its precise route through Falls Church. Later there would be objection to the additional crossing at the Three Sisters Island, as well as the road itself, as we shall see. With respect to the route in the Falls Church area, Jay Waldron, the Northern Virginia Sun business editor, reported on September 17, 1958, that the Chamber of Commerce was urging a more easterly alternate route at the north western tip of Arlington County through a mile or so of the City of Falls Church.

In an effort to resolve differences in the route through the Falls Church area, and some other questions, the State Highway Commission in October held a public hearing on the matter. It was attended by over 800 Arlington, Fairfax and Falls Church residents to determine which of four possible routes in the Falls Church area should be adopted. The aim of those in attendance, generally, was to keep the new thoroughfare out of, or away from, their properties. The Washington Evening Star on February 19, 1959, reported that the Commission had chosen, of the four proposed routes, the so called Fairfax-Bluemont corridor as roughly described above. That route had also been recommended by the Arlington County Board.

On August 14, 1958, the Virginia Department of Highways accepted the first bids for construction of I-66 beyond the Falls Church area under consideration. The bids were for a 3.3 mile section near Marshall in Fauquier County with construction to begin before winter.

Through the 1960s, work, or planning, on the Northern Virginia portions of the Interstate system continued. In 1961, the first sections of I-66 were opened and on November 18, 1964, the first segment in the Washington metropolitan area, 12.9 miles from the Beltway west to Centreville in Fairfax County was opened. By 1968 "...93.9 percent of all dwellings and 84.4 percent of all necessary right-of-way had been acquired...". [45]

PROBLEMS EMERGE

In this time frame several events occurred that complicated matters and delayed final planning and initiation of construction along those portions of the route closest to the terminus at the Potomac River. They included a public controversy and litigation concerning the Three Sisters Island Bridge, the desire of some commuters to keep the Washington and Old Dominion Railroad in operation where I-66 right of way was needed, a need to coordinate the I-66 plans with those for the coming Metro rail system for the Washington Metropolitan area, and growing public discontent and opposition to the construction of the road.

While these events were perculating, in 1966, the Department of Transportation Act was passed with a requirement that no park land could be used for road projects unless there is no "feasible and prudent alternative" to the use of the park land. And in 1970 the National Environmental Policy Act (NEPA) became law. Section 102 of that legislation required hearings and studies and an environmental impact statement (EIS) for Federal action "significantly affecting the quality of the human environment"

CITIZEN OPPOSITION DEVELOPS

In the late 1960s, as stated, criticism and disenchantment with I-66 within the beltway, especially within Arlington County, intensified and became more organized and assertive. By 1970 a group known as the Arlington Coalition on Transportation (ACT) was formed (later incorporated) and began meeting and planning steps to prevent the construction of the road. They adopted what some considered to be delaying tactics. The group was led by an energetic couple, James and Emilia Govan, who lived next to the proposed route for the road.

The Govans were relatively recent residents of Arlington County. James grew up in Indiana in an area southwest of Harrisburg and attended Wabash College where he met Emilia. Emilia was raised in Brooklyn, New York and attended St Joseph College. Upon arriving in Arlington they took up residence in the Barcroft neighborhood near Washington Boulevard and No. Glebe Road. Both became active in the Woodlawn-Barcroft Civic Association and Emilia worked in the County Board campaign of ABC-

---

[45] *Dept of Transportation, Secretary's Decision on I-66, January 5, 1977, p. 2.*

Major Community "Battles" and Controversies

Democrat Joseph Wholey. They both taught political science and international relations.[46]

ACT was joined by other groups and individuals to include the Arlingtonians for the Preservation of the Potomac Palisades, a community civic association led by Leslie Logan. Logan was a retired employee of the Voice of America, a self proclaimed environmentalist, and an established opponent of developments perceived by him to adversely effect the natural state of the lands along the Potomac River in Arlington.

Some of the individuals involved in this effort to stop I-66 were home owners who were in the I-66 pathway, or close along side. They complained of the loss of their homes or adverse environmental impacts on them such as noise, congestion, air pollution and destruction of desirable natural features. They were joined by others who also considered themselves "environmentalists" and stated they were opposed to the trend to "pave over the whole landscape from the Potomac to Dulles airport". Most of the opponents objected to the local and national trend to rely on the individual automobile rather than mass rail or bus transit, car pools and other means, for commuting and for other transportation needs. Without doubt, as with many crusading causes of this nature, there probably were others more interested in the matter as an issue on which they could assert themselves and seek publicity, attention, praise and self gratification as supporters of a "just cause".

All those making public statements, or taking positions, on the roadway were not just opponents of the road. Many were supporters from highway officials charged with building the road, and the governor and Senator Harry Byrd, to ordinary citizens. They saw the road as relieving congestion on local roads, as synonymous with progress, a time saver for commuters, a vital link between the Shenandoah Valley and Washington, and other reasons. Norman Worthington, of the Arlington Chamber of Commerce, in a letter published January 17, 1972, took the Washington Post to task for "inadequate reporting" in its coverage by dwellng on the positions of opponents but not mentioning that there was support for the road "..by a large segment of the community". Worthington said that the Chamber "has been a party to the suit since its inception.." and had filed briefs in support of the road.

Some Arlington citizens in the middle or southern half of the County viewed a failure to build the road as resulting in further adding to strangulating traffic and trucks already saturating Route 50, Columbia Pike, the Jeff-Davis, Route 1 highway, and Interstate 95 (later 395). One South Arlington citizen and long serving civic activist, John Dabinett, said, in a remark overheard by this author, "As if we don't already have enough traffic down here, those North Arlingtonians are now eager to send down to us the traffic from the west that should be traveling through their neighborhoods."

ACT and other opponents met regularly with members of the Arlington County Manager's staff and with County Board members, and appeared at County and VDHW and other public hearings in 1970 to make known their views. They were articulate, outspoken, contentious, and persistent. They particularly seemed to have a sympathetic forum when before the Arlington County Board whose members frequently praised the

---

[46] *Oral Histories, James and Emilia Govan*, Archives, the Virginia Room, Arlington County Main Library.

opponents and commented at board meetings on the value of the public service they were rendering the community in opposing the road.

The Govans remember their early experiences in opposition to I-66 as follows, in part: [47]

> "...we went to the early design hearing of September 29, 1970...at that time we weren't opposed to the highway...didn't know enough about it and whether to oppose or support it...it was quite an experience at W&L High...about 600 people attended...we were quite taken back that there were only engineers there...no elected officials from any level of government...we later consulted with the highway people in Richmond and asked about noise from the highway...they said there would be a chain link fence - with ivy...we thought this was not a decision to be made behind closed doors by officials without serious public input.
>
> "...early on we organized an 'educational' walk along the right of way...stopping at parks and schools...this got the media and elected officials' attention...2 or 3 weeks later 20-25 of us met in the offices of Audrey and Patty Wyatt on Wilson Blvd...it was decided that we would organize and call ourselves the Arlington Coalition on Transportation and there was a consensus that the group would be chaired by James and Emilia Govan...
>
> "We attended a reopened hearing in December...Bright Springman, a map maker with the USGS made a sketch of a 14 lane highway with the battleship Missouri sailing down the median...it got wide attention and was published in the Northern Virginia Sun...Laura and Harold McCoy rallied to defend their widely famed azalea gardens that would be threatened by the highway...our committee had experts on various aspects of the road...Betty Jo Berland on noise, Rudy Wendelin with his sketch of Smokey Bear on design alternatives, and others on landscape and architecture...we even had a delegation of farmers fly in from Wisconsin for advice on their efforts in fighting a road there...our efforts attracted much attention from the media...not at first. Ben Bradley of the Post showed scant interest at first...said there wasn't significant community interest...but later we had reporters from the National press including the NY Times, LA Times, and even the Wall Street Journal in our living room for interviews..."

A LAW SUIT IS FILED

Following repeated meetings and hearings, and widespread public discussion, and probably as a consequence of or preliminary thereto, the Board, through its specially

---

[47] *Oral Histories, Govans, Ibid.*

retained attorney and long time County resident and practitioner Edmund D. Campbell [48] filed suit in the U. S. District Court for the District of Columbia. It sought to enjoin the construction of the I-266 spur through the George Washington Parkway in Virginia, and the construction of the Three Sisters Bridge across the Potomac River. [49]

The County Board suit named as defendants GEORGE B. HARTZOG, JR.,, Director of the National Park Service; STEWART L. UDALL, Secretary of the Interior; ALAN S. BOYD, Secretary of Transportation; The DISTRICT OF COLUMBIA, a Municipal corporation; WALTER E. WASHINGTON, Commissioner of the District of Columbia; and the twelve members of the National Capital Planning Commission. [50]

In its suit the Board challenged the right of defendants to locate the Interstate Highway through the George Washington Parkway, and the Spout Run section thereof, and thus the bridge, without the express consent of The Congress and the governing body of Arlington County. The Board, as Plaintiff cited various laws and agreements entered into with the National Government in earlier years in connection with the acquisition of land from Virginia for the construction of the George Washington Parkway providing, among other things, that "...the United States will never use the land so acquired for any other purpose except with the consent of the County of Arlington and of the Commonwealth of Virginia".

The Plaintiff asked the Court to render a judgment concerning the authority of the Defendants to authorize the construction of the highway and bridge pending litigation of the matter and to permanently enjoin them from any further action for the purpose of "planning, designing, constructing, maintaining or operating the highway and bridge". The cause went to the Appellate Court in October, 1971. The court ordered Transportation Secretary John A. Volpe to make a new determination as to whether the bridge was necessary.

The issues in the Arlington County Board suit were eventually rendered moot and the case was closed when the Federal and State highway departments canceled and abandoned their plans for I-266 and the Three Sisters Bridge in view of the opposition and modification of plans for I-66.

ANOTHER LAW SUIT

1971 and 1972 were to see dramatic developments over whether or not the I-66 highway would be built. Armed with the new Federal law requirements for environmental impact studies, and the provision that park lands could not be used for

---

[48] *Campbell had earned, among other reasons, wide recognition in the 1950s as council in school desegregation litigation during the Virginia's "massive resistance" stand.*

[49] *Civil Action No. 2838-66.*

[50] *Phillip G. Hammer, C. Franklin Edwards, James O. Gibson, Paul Thiry, Conrad L. Wirth, Walter E. Washington, George B. Hartzog, JR., Wwilliam A. Schmidt, William F. Cassidy, Francis C. Turner, Alan Bible, and John L. McMillan.*

environmental impact studies, and the provision that park lands could not be used for highways unless there were no other "feasible and prudent alternatives", ACT and other highway opponents also undertook to halt construction of the highway by means of litigation. On February 19, 1971, the group filed suit in the U. S. District Court for the Eastern District of Virginia in Alexandria [51] to block construction of I-66 through Arlington County. They contended the road could not legally be built without the required EIS and a determination that there were no other alternatives. They claimed there were in fact other alternatives such as use of other existing roads, use of METRO rapid rail, car pools, and other recourses. They also argued that the road could not run through five acres of Spout Run Park and 9.6 acres of Bon Air Park until the government decided that was no feasible and prudent alternative.

On October 9th, Judge Oren R. Lewis dismissed plaintiffs cause. He held, among other things, that the location of I-66 had been approved by the Bureau of Public Roads in June of 1959 long before the enactment of the legislation requiring EISs and findings that there were no other alternatives. He held that those requirements were not retroactive in effect and thus did not apply to this project.

The plaintiffs promptly appealed Judge Lewis's dismissal and ruling to the Fourth Circuit Court in Richmond. In a January 6, 1972 article, Washington Post reporter Jay Mathews wrote that the Federal government, through its lawyer Robert S. Lynch, in arguments before the Circuit Court appeared to retreat somewhat from its earlier position. Lynch told the Court that even though the highway was approved before the law requiring consideration of alternatives, the government decided to comply with the law "because it was a matter of public concern and we thought we ought to do it."

Judge John D. Butzner on November 24, had already ordered condemnation of land stopped until the appeal was processed and until the government completed the final draft of the EIS. The Arlingtonians for the Preservation of the Potomac Palisades, through its lawyer Larry Latto also argued that a restudy was needed to see if, after 13 years of delay, the highway was still needed.

THE CIRCUIT COURT REVERSES

On April 4, 1972, a Fourth Circuit Court panel of three judges reversed Judge Lewis, and enjoined any further action toward constructing I-66 until the EIS and available alternatives requirements studies and hearings were completed. In its reversal decision, the Appellate Court did not address directly, or dispose of, the substantive question of whether the road could or should be built. Rather, it limited its consideration to the procedural issue of whether work could move ahead in the absence of an EIS and other administrative determinations and on this the Court said it could not.

On the same day of the Circuit Court action, to the surprise and delight of opponent plaintiffs, the U. S. Environmental Protection Agency announced its conclusion that the construction of I-66 through Arlington County "could have a significant adverse effect on the environment." It was never clear what impact this announcement and

---

[51] *The action, upon later refiling, was designated Civil Action No 77-559-A.*

statement had, if any, on the eventual outcome of the court suit, or the later decision of the Transportation Secretary on the road project.

On April 19th the Virginia Attorney General asked the Court to reconsider its decision. He pointing out that applying new laws retroactively to projects already underway could cause widespread harm and cause "terrific expense and delay". The Court, however, was not receptive to those arguments and refused to reconsider its decision of April 4th.

On August 7th, Virginia asked the U. S. Supreme Court to review the matter and on October 7th the Court declined to do so. The Arlington County Board in May had voted 3 to 2 to ask the State not to proceed with its appeal to the Supreme Court.

An interesting twist at this point in the litigation was a change in position by the U. S. Justice Department. In the lower courts, the Department had supported the Virginia highway planners and proponents of the road. In a brief to the high court, the Department attorneys departed from their support of the appeal of the Virginia authorities and opposed a further review. They said construction on I-66 could begin sooner if the state devoted full attention to organizing the hearings and stopped spending time on further court appeals. There is no way of knowing the extent, if any, that the Department's position influenced the High court in refusing the review the matter. The Court does not make public its internal thinking in such instances. For certain, however, the Departments change of position did not harm the cause of the road opponents who did not want the Supreme Court to review the matter and possibly reverse the circuit court's order for new hearings and an EIS.

REACTION TO COURT ACTION

Opponents of the road were overjoyed and elated at the Circuit Court's order to stop construction and conduct new hearings and the refusal of the high court to interfer. Post writer Jay Mathews in an April 6th article quoted James Govin as saying, "We won on all counts. This is going to require a fresh look (at the project) and I don't see how they can continue to justify the decision to build the road." Opponents termed the decision a "major victory". A side issue at the time was the effect the cancellation of the road might have on the construction of the METRO rail rapid transit system then being built and whether there would be added land acquisition costs for Metro that was to use a part of the I-66 right of way for its own tracks.

The Washington Post too, joined in applauding the Circuit Court for putting a hold on I-66. On April 15th its editors wrote, in part:

"...the passage of time has raised numerous questions about I-66...by our new awareness of the ecology and the decision to built Metro...these will not repeal the automobile, obviate the need to find creative solutions to the problem of traffic or put the Highway Department out of business. But it does...justify the ruling of the Court that further work on the freeway be stopped until these questions have been duly considered and answered..."

"We think the new hearings on location ... must not only seek information about social effects..its impact on the environment, and community urban planning goals, but also must seek information about economic effects in the light of the proposed rapid rail service..."

Post writer Mathews, in an article headed "Road Ban to Delay Metro in Virginia", wrote on April 7th that a decision not to build I-66 at all would force Metro to spend much more money on the project, as alluded to above. Mathews quoted Metro general manager Jackson Graham as saying, "..Metro would have to pay the state for the right of way that runs from Glebe Road in Arlington to the Beltway in Fairfax, and pay for drainage facilities it had expected the state to build (if I-66 were built)."

CONTENTION CONTINUES AND GROWS

By May, on the close heels of the Circuit Court decision halting I-66 work, contention between proponents and opponents of the road steadily increased and grew more heated. In a May 11th article, Mathews, again in the Post, told of a "sharp, wide-ranging attack on environmentalists" by Highway Commissioner Douglas B. Fugate, Virginia's top highway official. He quoted Fugate, in part, saying that further delays in I-66 would create "chaotic congestion and...an unnecessary toll in tragedies resulting from traffic accidents". He said Fugate added he wanted to get "a few things off my chest" charging environmentalist groups with forcing delays to the detriment of the overwhelming majority of residents.

Mathews further quoted Fugate as saying in a talk before the Virginia State Chamber of Commerce, "In my judgment, many of the worthwhile environmental gains in recent years...are being jeopardized by those whose principal interest is to delay, denounce and delude, who appear bent on obstruction for the sake of obstruction alone." The article said Fugate quoted from a letter received from a taxpayer who complained that "the costs have risen with so many delaying tactics...as a road user my frustration grows each time I must drive into Arlington ...by bottlenecks of traffic and congestion on the existing roads." Mathews also pointed out the enormous increase in cost of the road by inflation by almost a decade of delay.

I-66 HOV Lane ?

In August, the Highway Department selected the consulting firm of Howard, Needles, Tammen and Berendoff of New York City to undertake the studies directed by

Major Community "Battles" and Controversies

In August, the Highway Department selected the consulting firm of Howard, Needles, Tammen and Berendoff of New York City to undertake the studies directed by the Court at a cost of half a million dollars. Also in August, the Department voluntarily delayed building a two mile stretch of I-66 inside the beltway outside the boundry of Arlington County. Residents opposing the highway had complained that building that segment would violate the spirit of the court order blocking work in Arlington County.

Commissioner Fugate said the consulting firm had been picked because of its familiarity with the area and a past record near the Florida Everglades in ironing out environmental problems for a new airport. He announced that five members of a regional transportation group would monitor the consultant's study. They were: Martha Pennino, Chairperson of the Metropolitan Council of Governments (COG), Joseph Alexander, of the Northern Virginia Transportation Commission, Joseph L. Fisher, Chairman of the Metro Board; A. Leslie Phillips, vice chair of the area transportation planning board, and Jimmie Singleton, chair of the Northern Virginia Planning District Commission.

The selection of the consultants, and the monitoring panel, came under the immediate criticism of Emilia Govan of ACT. She was reported in the press as saying, "this means the same firm will re-evaluate its own study." She charged that the five monitors, as far as she knew, favored construction of I-66 and none had ever publicly opposed the highway. Fugate dismissed those concerns saying that opponents would have several opportunities to express their views while the year long study was in progress.

On November 15th, a meeting termed a "public participation workshop" on the proposed I-66 road was held in the Kenmore Junior High School on Carlin Springs Road in Arlington (Washington Post, November 15, 1972, p. A-10). The results must have brought great joy and encouragement to opponents of the road, and particularly their leaders to include the Govans. As Emilia Govan spoke to the crowd and castigated highway officials as "nonelected bureaucrats" that could veto decisions made by citizens she was frequently interrupted by loud applause. An estimated 250 people attended the meeting, and when Govin spoke to them, it was a clear case of the preacher preaching to the choir. She was saying what a crowd, already persuaded to her point of view, wanted to hear. Govan urged the audience to adopt three criteria to form the basis for the ongoing study, to wit: maximize the use of mass transit for commuting and other travel; prevent the degradation of natural and human environment; and to move the greatest number of people in the most efficient, economical and convenient manner. Although one audience member, a Fairfax County supervisor who was one of the monitors selected by highway Commissioner Fugate, urged the group to go slow and not "have a plebiscite tonight", the group adopted the criteria by enthusiastic acclamation.

UNCERTAINTY OF PUBLIC ATTITUDES

During the remainder of 1972 and on into 1973, community dialogue on I-66 continued. There were constant letters to the editor in the press for and against the road. Bumper stickers for and against the road proliferated. Ellen Bozman, an ABC Democrat candidate for the Count Board, stressed her opposition to the road in her campaign. Opponents, especially the Govans, continued to receive wide attention to include human interest feature articles on their personalities and involvement in the dispute. An Arlington Journal article by writer Beth Price described the Govans' background in Brooklyn before coming to Arlington and how dedicated, committed and involved they were in the I-66 struggle. Price wrote, "the Govans are a young dynamic couple, intelligent and articulate. How they became involved in this fight against I-66 is a story basically of two people doing what they felt needed doing." She also wrote that by taking up the I-66 fight, the Govans had "virtually sacrificed their private lives since November 1970. In their regular appearances before the Arlington County Board, the Govans were invariably well received and listened to with sympathy. They were undoubtedly highly influential with the Board when it formally adopted its position opposing the construction of the highway.

Another interesting aspect of the I-66 controversy, for reasons not easily explained, was the extent to which the issue seemed to drift into a liberal versus a conservative issue - at least insofar as the participants, if not the substance, was concerned. ABC-Democrats, known in Arlington for their liberalism, on the County Board or elsewhere, tended to be almost entirely opposed to the road and supportive of the Govans and other opponents. The Govans were thanked at Board meetings by the Chairman for the great public service they were performing in fighting the road.

It's not likely that it will ever be possible to determine, with any degree of certainty, whether the opponents of the road spoke for a majority of the population. In one poll conducted by Republican Congressman Joel Broyhill, it appeared they did not. In his poll, roughly two out of three constituents surveyed indicated they were for the construction of the road. It may be that those favoring the road were not living alongside the I-66 corridor and thereby would not be directly harmed by any adverse impacts of the road. From the raucus and noisy testimony provided at hearings and meetings, and words of approval and praise from those to whom they spoke, one could conclude that the road opponents were correctly conveying the prevailing attitude in their community. On the other hand, Emilia Govan in her Oral History in the Arlington Library alluded to the Rosslyn Ramada Inn hearing in 1973 attended by hundreds of people and lasting several days, and said that speakers supporting the road out numbered those against - but by a margin of only two. She is recorded also as saying, "As a matter of fact, the surveys were showing that many people, particularly in the outer suburbs, really wanted the highway very badly".

(AN AUTHOR OBSERVATION)

It can be noted also that most proponents of the road seemed to be from sources usually considered quieter and more conservative in their actions as well as their philosophy. Such groups generally include Republicans, business interests, retired people and the like. They often were not so outspoken, dedicated to their cause, and persevering in their support for the road as were the opponents in their protests against the road. It is not likely that it will ever be known with precision just how many people favored or opposed the road. There was no plebicite on the matter. Unlike Metro rail and some other local projects, funds for I-66 did not come in part from local bond issues that called upon the voters for approval at the polls. Thus voter reacton in the voting booths provided no clue of community support for the I-66 road.

Major Community "Battles" and Controversies

THE ENVIRONMENTAL STUDY

In December of 1973, the VDHT announced that its environmental study was complete and it held a public hearing on the study in the Ramada Inn in Rosslyn over a four day period. 239 citizens had indicated a desire to speak at the hearing. They represented civic organizations, churches, chambers of commerce and others. The Arlington Journal reported that Barry Hyman, a spokesman for ACT said the hearings would be filled "with a tremendous outpouring of anti-highway sentiment", but that Dorese Bell, a spokesperson for pro-highway forces predicted the opposite. "We will have our own large contingent..we expect the hearing to come out in our favor." No decisions were announced at the conclusion of the hearing. Observers and participants were compelled to await future announcements of the Departments decision.

As 1974 rolled in, the community waited for the results of the December hearings in Rosslyn and the release of the VDHT decision on I-66. In the opening weeks of the year, there was a flurry of publicity concerning the extent of additional costs for Metro in event I-66 was not built. On April 11th, the Journal reported that the costs for just the EIS for I-66 had jumped to more than $1 million, "making it one of the most expensive studies of its kind in the nation," according to federal highway officials. On January 24th, the Journal editorialized on the I-66 controversy. It said, in part:

> *"Another 'final decision' in the seemingly endless battle over I-66 is expected shortly...should the decision be made to proceed...you can bet your last gallon of gas that the anti-freeway forces will go back to court again. What can be done to terminate the bitter battle which has cost us millions of dollars in lengthy court fights and expensive studies? The anti-freeway groups must recognize that there is strong support and demonstrable need for a more adequate northern highway corridor...opponents of I-66 (see) this conflict as a struggle between the 'people' and the big bad highway department. This is ridiculous. There are thousands of decent Northern Virginians who want I-66 built...we believe a scaled down version would take care of traffic needs with minimal adverse environmental effects"*

The Journal suggested the time had come for more realism and compromise and outlined numerous approaches that could result in a settlement of the issue.

Predictably, on February 14th, ACT co-founder James Govan responded and took the Journal to task in vigorous opposition. In a letter to the editor he said the Journal editorial "reflected considerable lack of realism" and that the Journal "exhibited the same kind of auto-oriented bias that continues to wreak havoc in our urban communities across the country".

On July 9th, the State Highway Commission released the results of its EIS and modified road proposal and submitted them to FHWA, and then, at the request of FHWA, further modified the proposal and resubmitted it to FHWA in November, 1974 for approval. The modified road plan proposed, among other things, to: (1) reduce the number of lanes from eight to six; (2) prohibit heavy duty trucks from using the facility; (3) provide for four passenger only vehicles during rush commuter hours; and (4) redesign the segment through the Spout Run Parkway area to provide a ground level road rather than a two-level structure as opposed by both proponents and opponents.[52]

On the following June 21, 1975, the Federal Transportation Secretary held a public hearing to learn the positions of elected officials and civic organizations on the road as proposed at that point by the State. The Secretary then took an action that surprised many of the participants in the I-66 controversy. He disapproved the proposal of the VDHT and FHWA for the road segment inside the beltway calling for six lanes and some other aspects of transportation in the I-66 corridor. A revised proposal for a road with only four lanes, except for short exit and access or other incidental lanes, was then resubmitted and approved by the Secretary on January 5, 1977.

Only a week earlier, on the near eve of the Secretary's final decision on the road, the Arlington County Board at its own hearing again considered the I-66 question. The Board had gone on record a year earlier as opposing any kind of road in the I-66 corridor, but now seemed pressed to consider their position further in view of the impact that not building the road may have on the availability of funds for Metro which the Board was on record as strongly favoring.

Journal writer Chris Jensen reported that the citizen advisory Transportation Commission members, and Senator Edward Holland and Delegate Mary Marshall, who were also members of the Northern Virginia Transportation Commission were known to be opposed to a highway in the corridor. Jensen wrote that they told the board, however, that Metrorail must be built and if there was no other way to obtain federal funds, then the highway should be approved. The Board heard over 30 speakers, but postponed any decision on the issue. Before again considering the matter, the Secretary releaed his decision of January 5th.

Four days after the Secretary released his decision, the FHTA made the determination as required by the Transportation Act and the District Court order of August 18, 1972 that there was no feasible or prudent alternative to the use of the land from Bon Air Park and that the proposed four lane multi-model concept included all possible planning to minimize harm to the park.[53] Virginia Governor Mills Godwin accepted the version approved by the Transportation Secretary and the Virginia and Federal highway departments moved the District Court to dissolve its injunction of August 18, 1972 so that the completion of I-66 as approved could be resumed.

EVENTS IN THE COURTS

Meanwhile, back in the courts another scenario was unfolding. Far from giving up, and even as their cases had been heard extensively in and out of the courts and at every level of government, the perseverance of ACT and other opponents and their supporters never diminished. Apparently sensing that they were about to lose in the District Court in Alexandria that had in 1972 enjoined further work on the road, the

---

[52] *DOT Secretary's Decision, Ibid, P.4*

[53] *Memorandum Opinion and Order, U.S. District Court, Eastern District of Virginia, 4 August 1977, Civil Action No. 77-559-A, p.2.*

plaintiffs suddenly jumped the Potomac River and filed suit in the District Court for the District of Columbia. The Federal Courts in the District had long been known to be more liberal than those in Northern Virginia and it is probable that ACT and its friends thought they would have a more sympathetic ear there.

In their new filing, ACT and the others attacked the legality and sufficiency of the Transportation Secretary's decision of January 5th, six months earlier, that approved the construction of I-66 as modified. But they did not get far with that ploy. The case was promptly, on April 14th, transferred from the District Court to the Alexandria Court for hearing. Back in the Alexandria court, the plaintiffs on July 15th renewed their motion for a preliminary injunction on numerous enumerated grounds, and requested time to take discovery and inspect the defendant's files. The Virginia Department of Highways moved to dismiss the plaintiffs motion on the grounds of res judicata., i.e. that the complaints filed had already been heard and disposed of. Judge Oren Lewis, however, apparently desired to give plaintiffs the benefit of every doubt. He declined to rule on whether the matter was res judicata so he could take a careful look at the plaintiffs' contentions. He granted additional time for discovery, with the understanding that defendants would cut no trees in the meantime, while he considered each of the plaintiffs claimed grounds.

THE COURT'S FINAL DECISION AND ORDER

When Judge Lewis released his final order in this matter on August 5, 1977, for the most part he gave the complaintants short shrift.

Judge Lewis reminded the plaintiffs that he had heard and determined their invalidity claims when he dismissed and disolved the August 18, 1972 injunction in Civil Action No 59-71-A (the original suit). He also held, in pertinent part:

1. That the latest proposal was not a new project requiring a new hearing, as plaintiffs would have one to believe; that it was nothing more than a modification in design necessitated by the abandonment of the Three Sister Bridge and the Old Dominion Railroad, and the Transit Authority's plans for using the medium of I-66 west of Glebe Roar for Metro Purposes;

2. That the Secretary had held the required hearings and made the necessary findings and there was no requirement or need for more hearings as claimed by plaintiffs;

3. That plaintiffs' contention the Secretary's decision was based on unsupported assumptions and unreliable car pool and traffic projections lacked evidentiary support;

4. That plaintiffs' charge of unlawful political pressure was too nebulous to warrant discussion;

5. That there was no need for a new corridor hearing as claimed by plaintiffs since the location of I-66 had been established since 1959 and there had been no change in location between the December 1973 hearing and now;

6. That the Secretary was clearly correct in determining that the completion of I-66, as approved, will have no adverse effect on the District of Columbia or any historical sites located therein; and

7. That plaintiffs' claim that there are feasible and prudent alternatives to the use of Bon Air Park lands was not supported by the record, and was in accordance with the Transportation Act.

Judge Lewis then found that the Secretary of Transportation had acted within the scope of his authority and in good faith judgment after considering all relevant factors including possible alternative or mitigative measures in approving the construction of I-66, and he ordered that the Virginia Department of Highways could proceed with the construction of I-66 from I-495 to Rosslyn Virginia. [54]

A LAST DITCH STAND

Following their failure administratively and in the courts to stop the construction of the I-66 highway, the Govans and their supporters in January 1977, took to the streets in a last ditch, all out effort to rally support from the "court of last appeal". In Lafayette Park, on Pennsylvania Avenue in Washington, across from and in full view of the White House, with banners and placards waving, they marshalled their troops and closed ranks in an effort to lay their cause on the door steps of no less than the President of the United States. Emilia Govan in her Oral History above referred to relates that her I-66 forces did get the attention of the Jimmie Carter staff, but that the staff had advised the President that "this is such a contentious issue - very hard between the highway and Metro activists - the best advice was to leave it alone." And the President did.

CONSTRUCTION AND COMPLETION

In due course, following Transportation Secretary Coleman's approval of January 5th, and Judge Lewis's Order of August 5, 1977, construction began on the disputed leg of I-66. The road was completed, dedicated and the last 10 mile segment between the beltway and the Potomac River at Rosslyn was opened to traffic on December 22, 1982 amidst extensive broadcast and printed media coverage . The Washington Post devoted more than half a dozen pages to the event, including biographical features on the principals involved in the dispute, many photographs, detail maps and descriptions of the road's route and a history background of its creation.

ASSET OR LIABILITY?

Whether the completion of I-66 to include the last link from the beltway inward is an asset and credit to the communities through which it passes, or not, is a matter on which reasonable and sincere people can and do widely differ in their opinions.

Those favoring the road will complain that the delay of almost a decade of time in completing the road deprived for years countless thousands of travelers and commuters of the necessary means of moving more cheaply, quickly, and conveniently by means of a freeway rather than slowly in gridlocks through congested neighborhood streets with engines idling at redlights and in heavy traffic, or over greater distances around the beltway to the George Washington Parkway, or via I-395 in South Arlington to get into, or out of, the National Capital.

---

[54] *Memorandum Opinion and Order, ibid, p. 10*

Major Community "Battles" and Controversies

engines idling at redlights and in heavy traffic, or over greater distances around the beltway to the George Washington Parkway, or via I-395 in South Arlington to get into, or out of, the National Capital.

I-66 supporters will also be quick to point out the significant additional final costs of the over $275 million roadway that at the beginning was expected to cost less than $25 [55] million if built promptly before inflationary developments. Proponents of the road will ask whether the public interests were really much served by the expense of these additional millions of dollars resulting from the efforts of opponents to prevent construction of the road.

On the other hand, opponents can argue with not a little justification, that even if they were not successful in stopping the road in its entirety, they did succeed in getting a road that has become an enviable and model interstate highway for the Nation. I-66 has no trucks, and fewer lanes than as originally proposed. It also has unique and precedent setting beautification through creative architectural design and vegetational plantings, a $3 million bike trail, and more sophisticated sound control features than probably any other comparable interstate road in the country. It should, therefore, have minimal adverse impact on the environment.

Those who fought the road as originally proposed and thereby caused extensive modifications and improvements are due much credit for this. Of more complexity is whether, in a cost versus benefit scenario, these pluses outweigh the price paid in spent effort, time of delay, and added costs. That question is hardly likely to ever be fully resolved to the satisfaction of everyone concerned.

Whether it was wise for opponents to insist on fewer lanes, and highway officials to approve them, stands as yet another perplexing question. Will this be only a temporary and inadequate feature that will result in enormous amounts of money sooner or later to correct? That remains to be seen. At this writing with the highway only a bit over a decade old, there is already pressure underway to increase the number of lanes to handle a greatly increased number of vehicles or to allow for dedicated High Occupancy Vehicles (HOV) traffic. The entire highway was initially restricted to such traffic during morning and afternoon rush hours for vehicles with four or more passengers. Each year has seen a significantly heavier use of the road. Even in most non rush commuter hours the road remains saturated with endless columns of vehicles at almost any hour of the day or night, although a little lighter in rush hours when only HOV traffic is permitted. Because of lighter HOV traffic on I-66 inside the beltway, that number was in time reduced to three passengers due to the efforts of Northern Virginia Congressman Frank Wolfe, and others. At this writing additional efforts are emerging to further reduce the HOV passengers to only two.

Equally difficult to resolve is the question of whether the new road will add to or subtract from overall atmospheric pollution. Freeway adversaries seldom see eye to eye on this factor. Road opponents here and elsewhere have argued that the more roads society builds, the more it encourages greater use of the polluting and environmentally wasteful automobile. They urge that the public not drive, or drive less, or rely on other means of transportation to include mass transit. They often view road proponents as irresponsible and as bent on destroying the environment just to allow the luxury of greater and unnecessary use of the automobile.

---

[55] *The Washington Post, December 22, 1982, page 5, Virginia Section.*

ARLINGTON COUNTY VIRGINIA - A Modern History

Road proponents, conversely, are likely to say "Hogwash and Bull feathers." They will say that mass transit will never fill all needs for all people - that you cannot run a rail or bus line to everyone's place of residence or work, nor can you expect mom or pop to take a rapid rail train to the kids' school, the supermarket or shopping center, or the weekend picnic. Most of those favoring better roads will concede the need for Metro, but insist that at least some highways are also essential. In this instance, they will contend that this highway has been built with little or no harmful impact on existing parks or the environment, the opponents to the contrary notwithstanding. Proponents will also likely view those who oppose any kind of freeway as extremists and obstructionists, and as being unreasonable and unrealistic.

All of these sentiments have been expressly repeatedly at public forums, before governing bodies, and in letters to the editor in the media during the running of the I-66 confrontation over past years. There is, of course, no shortage of merit to both sides of the question. Fortunately in our society reasonable men and women can still disagree without detracting from the credibility of either. The outcome with the most benefit to the public and the participants in this, as well as most disagreements, is a compromising consensus, and one can hope that this is what has emerged from this long. burdensome, costly, and frustrating dispute.

Perhaps the Govans who fought so long and hard on this issue are entitled to the last word. In their Oral History they philosophized in pertinent part, as follows:

> *"We never had any qualms about being totally opposed to the road...we always took a no compromise position...(and) were criticized by many as being extremists...but others were articulating alternatives or other courses, so we didn't have to...I think our efforts contributed to the kind of highway (the least offensive) finally developed and helped in developing Dulles. The minuses are that it stimulated further development in the country side and I believe the pressure will be there to build it eventually into a bigger highway...there are some downs - graffiti is already appearing...but worse of all, the highway further locks us into an (undesireable) dependance on the automobile for our transportation needs..."*

* * *

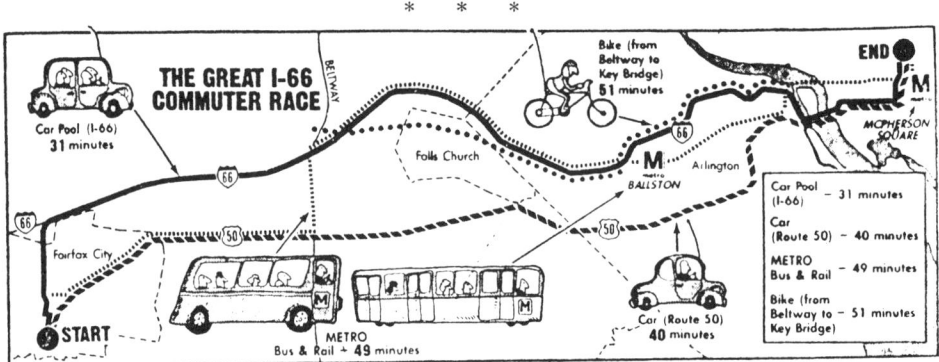

Major Community "Battles" and Controversies

Round VIII
THE FIGHT FOR SINGLE MEMBER ELECTORAL DISTRICTS

A fundamental concept of the framers of the American constitution was that law makers should come from the lowest possible political subdivisions so as to be as near as possible and responsive to, and in closest contact with, the citizens represented. Provision was made for each State to have two Senators in the National government, each elected by all the voters of the State thereby running "at-large". There was no requirement concerning place of residence of a candidate in a State. Thus, a State such as Virginia could have both its senators residing in a remote corner such as Bristol, far removed from the centers of population and all other activity. While this could result in an undesired consequence to that degree, at least the people of a State were guaranteed they would have senatorial representation from their state in the Federal Congress.

Delegates to the House of Representatives, on the other hand, were not to be elected at-large, but rather from several designated geographical districts each of which were to be represented by a single member to the House. Thus the delegates could be said to be elected from "single member" districts since no two delegates could represent the same Congressional district, nor do they today.

The single member electoral system has prevailed, generally, at all levels of American government until recent years. In the wake of the civil rights movements following World War II, single member districts at the municipal level were replaced in many cities and towns with single district, multi member, voting arrangements. The usual objective, or at least effect, was to water down minority voting strengths and thereby prevent the election of minorities. The courts, in response to Supreme Court landmark decisions outlawing "at-large" voting arrangements have been busy ordering a return to single member districts throughout the country.

DETAILED TREATMENT HEREIN

The controversy over at-large versus single member electoral districts in Arlington is being treated in somewhat greater detail than most other "battles" herein because of what the author perceives as exceptionally high feelings on the matter by many residents, and because it continues at this writing to be an on-going and far from settled challenge facing the citizens, and especially voters, in the County even as the century ends.

ARLINGTON COUNTY VIRGINIA - A Modern History

BACKGROUND AND HISTORY

Following the 1930-32 Arlington County adoption of the county manager form of government, and the multi-member single electoral district, with "at-large" voting for the County, repeated efforts have been made in recent years to return to the multi-district, single member electoral arrangement. These efforts were based on the belief and contention that the "at-large" system had not been operating fairly and evenly, serving all sections of the County effectively, or affording all political groups and individuals equal opportunity and access to the democratic process.

As alluded to or mentioned in various places herein, Arlington County Virginia, at the Commonwealth's Northern extremes across the Potomac River from the Nation's Capital, is governed by a five member elected County Board of supervisors, and a County Manager appointed by the Board members. The Manager serves as the chief executive officer and exercises direct supervision and operational control, generally, of the executive branches of the County local government.

The County Board thus, is, ostensibly, free of day to day operational duties and performs only policy making or legislative functions within the scope of its statutory and constitutional authority. Positions in government, except for the judiciary, several "Constitutional" elected officials,[56] and the clerk and staff to the County Board, generally are filled or vacated by the Manager.

The board members are elected for terms of four years each with all the registered voters of the entire county eligible to vote for each candidate. There is no requirement that a candidate for the office, or, if elected, the office holder, must reside in any particular part of the county. The terms of office are for four years with elections staggered so that each year one, and on a fourth year two, positions are filled.

The Arlington County Manager form of government with elected governing body members and an appointed manager appointed by the board, was adopted by voters by a public referendum in the November, 1930 election. It was the first community in the United States to adopt the county manager form of government that provides for the election of governing body members who then appoint the manager, or "mayor". This concept of local government differed from the three member Magisterial districts then in existence in Arlington and from the mayor and ward alderman systems generally in use throughout the rest of the country. The manager system was hailed by its proponents more efficient, innovative and progressive.

THE 1930 REFERENDUM

Arlington voters, pursuant to new Constitutional amendments and resultant enabling legislation were asked in the 1930 election whether they desired the County Manager form of government, and if so, did they want their governing body members elected "at-large" or by single member districts. The voters indicated they did desire to change to the County Manager form of government by a rather close vote. They also

---

[56] *The Commonwealth Attorney, Commissioner of Revenue, Sheriff and Treasurer.*

Major Community "Battles" and Controversies

voted by a margin of about 2 to 1 to elect the board members "at-large" in County wide elections.

THE 1932 AT-LARGE ELECTION

New board members, therefore, were elected for four year terms in the election of November 1931 and they took office seven weeks later on January 1, 1932. It was the first county manager form of government to be adopted in the United States and the forerunner of many more in later years. The arrangement has continued to date with no significant change, except that just before World War II, voters chose by referendum to stagger the board member four year terms with annual, instead of quadrennial, county board elections. [57]

STATUTORY AUTHORITY

The Virginia Statutory authorization for the adoption and operation of the County's manager form of government is contained in Chapter 14 of Title 15 of the Code. That Chapter per Section 15.1-669 is applicable only to Virginia counties with more than 500 inhabitants per square mile and with less than "sixty square miles of highland". Since Arlington is the only county in the State with these characteristics, the section applies only to Arlington.

Section 15.1-694 of the Chapter, in essence, provides that whenever 200 or more voters so petition, the circuit court will order an election in which voters will be asked (l) do they desire a change in the form of government, and (2) if so do they desire the specified Modified Commission Plan[58] or the County manager plan, and (3) and if changed do they want the governing board elected at-large or by districts. As stated above, Arlington voters in the l930 election chose to change, to adopt the manager form, and to elect board members at large.

DIVISIONS OF OPINION

Overall, it seems the adoption of the County Manager form of government for Arlington was greeted at the time with enthusiasm by most citizens. There was, however, some discontent in minority neighborhoods at the election of board members at-large rather than by single member districts as will hereinafter be discussed.

The late Arlington historian C.B.(Cornelia) Rose, Jr., describes the adoption, and especially the at-large voting, in laudable and complimentary terms. On page 197 of her

---

[57] *For a more comprehensive account of the County's adoption of the Manager form of government, and the at-large elections, see article this subject by Robert Nelson Anderson, page 58, AHS Magazine, October, 1958.*

[58] *The provision in Article 2 of Chapter 14 describing this option was repealed and editorially dropped from the Statutes in 1976 after a Court decision subsequently in Vollin v. Arlington County Electoral Board, 216 Va. 674.*

book <u>Arlington County Virginia - a History</u>[59] she wrote in part, "...the County Board elected at-large meant a governing body more responsive to the needs of the whole County rather than pitting once section against another."

RACIAL DISCRIMINATORY OVERTONES

While it is difficult at this late date to dispositively document all the circumstances surrounding the adoption of the manager and at-large voting arrangement there is evidence to indicate that certain elements of the community did not view at-large voting in the same light as did Rose later, and others who supported that approach or voted for it. There is reason to believe that the change in the form of government and voting method, or at least the tactics and speed with which it was achieved, may have been racially motivated to discriminate against Arlington's black population, deny them equal access to the democratic process and to prevent the election of Black candidates to local public office.

One senior Arlington citizen from the black community who was born in the county almost 90 years ago and was alive and residing in Arlington during the time the manager form and at-large voting were adopted is the late (died 1997) Mr George Vollin who lived in the Arlington View neighborhood next to the "mixing bowl" of I-395 at Washington Boulevard. His past neighborhood is near the extinct Freedman's Village where freed slaves were temporarily located after the Civil War and that is now partly the southeastern tip of Arlington Cemetery.

Mr Vollin testified in 1974 in Federal Court under oath in a civil rights suit[60] brought by him and several other citizens almost 50 years after the adoption of the at large voting system. The Vollin suit was filed for the purpose of having the at-large system declared unconstitutional in line with recent U.S. Supreme Court decisions on the subject that had outlawed at-large voting in numerous other Northern as well as Southern cities.

Vollin testified that he was born in the county before the turn of the Century, had lived in the black Queen City section of the Jefferson Magisterial District. That section of the county was razed in World War II for the Pentagon South parking lot and Vollin has since resided in the Arlington View community of Arlington on South 13th Street.

Vollin, related that he remembered the circumstances that surrounded the referendum voting in 1930 and the election of board members in the at-large election of 1931. He contended the that movement to secure enabling legislation, the solicitation of petitions to place the item on the 1930 election, and the subsequent voting on the matter all occurred immediately after, and as a consequence of, heightened black political activity for the first time since the days of reconstruction after the Civil War.

---

[59] *Port City Press, Baltimore, Md., 1976, copyright Arlington Historical Society, Inc..*

[60] *U. S. District Court, Eastern Division of Virginia, Alexandria Division, Civil Action No. 173-74-A, George Vollin., et al., v. Mills E. Godwin, et al.*

Major Community "Battles" and Controversies

Vollin further testified, and has related to this writer with recordings on tapes, that there were meetings in the black community early in 1930 where it was decided that there would be black candidates fielded in the coming November elections. He related that when that knowledge became known publicly, there were demonstrations in the County and especially through the black neighborhoods.

Vollin asserted that hooded Klu Klux Klan men paraded in motor convoys through the black neighborhoods in the old Jefferson Magisterial District where he lived, rattling noise making instruments and shouting threateningly to intimidate black residents. Vollin stated that it was only after it became known that blacks intended to run for elective office, that delegations from the white community traveled to Richmond and appeared before the legislature urging the new law described above to permit a vote on changing the government form to include the election of governing body members at-large instead of by several single member districts.

Vollin also contended that the movement on Richmond to press for the new legislation and its implementation, or at least the speed at which it was undertaken, and especially the timing just after word that black people planned to file for elective offices, was racially motivated and a consequence of Black election plans. Vollin's testimony and version of events and political environment in Arlington at the time was reinforced with similar corroborative testimony by his co-plaintiff Harrison Douglas, another very elderly black Arlingtonian and life long resident of the County.

IMPACT OF AT-LARGE VOTING ON BLACKS

There may, of course, be no shortage of Arlingtonians who then, or today, will disagree with Vollin's version of events at the time of the change in the County government. It can certainly be rationally argued that the changes were appropriate, needed, and bound to come sooner or later regardless of whether there were to be politically active black citizens at the time of the changes, or an adverse voting impact on them.

In any event, following the adoption of the Manager and at-large voting arrangement in the election of 1930, none of the four black candidates on the November, 1931 ballot, three for a county board position, and one, Mr Vollin, for sheriff, were elected.

Whether or not the adoption of the at-large voting system in itself resulted in the defeat of the black candidates, in the 1931 election, or to what extent, may never be conclusively known. It is clear, however, that by adopting the at-large arrangement, the black voting clout, for whatever it may have amounted to, was substantially reduced in a county wide election as compared to one for a smaller area comprised mainly of their own segregated neighborhood.

Following the defeat of the four black candidates in the 1931 election, no black person was elected to public office from Arlington for almost a half century until the late

1980s when a black attorney[61] ran for and was elected to the county board. During that period only one other black candidate[62] ever bothered to file for office. Mr Vollin, and the other elderly black witness, testified that the cause of this black disinclination to run for office stemmed from the adoption of the at-large system and the defeat of the candidates in 1931. They stated that black people in Arlington were discouraged from running for election and that they considered it an exercise in futility since there was no chance of their prevailing in county wide elections in a community where they were greatly outnumbered by whites.

EFFECTIVENESS OF THE AT-LARGE SYSTEM

Aside from the possibility, as described, that the Arlington form of government and electoral system may have been adopted, to some degree, for racial discriminatory reasons, the arrangements seems, as stated, to have been generally acceptable to the citizenry. There is little or no evidence of any significant community disenchantment or dissatisfaction with the system in principle or in operation in those early years of its existence.

Notwithstanding the absence of any geographical residence requirements for board members, the at-large board at its beginning, in varying degrees from time to time, was composed of members from all the principle sections of the county. For a brief period after World War II the board was comprised of a majority, three members, from South Arlington. Additionally, for most of the years, there was reasonable representation of both, or all, the main partisan political parties or movements in the County. Board members were elected that ran as Democrats, Republicans, AIMs (Arlingtonian Independent Movement), or Independents either with or without endorsement by these groups.

CHANGES IN BOARD COMPOSITION

By the early 1960s, however, the situation began to change significantly with respect to the political composition of the board and the geographic residential location in the county of its members. The highly effective and energetic group, the Arlingtonians for a Better County, steadily gained dominance in controlling county government as is covered in more detail in Chapter Four herein under political movements.

---

[61]*Arlington Attorney William Newman, an ABC-Democrat backed candidate, won election to the County Board in the November, 1987 election, and took office on January 1, 1988.*

[62]*In the November, 1969 general election, a South Arlington Black minister, Rev. Arthur W. Walls was defeated, not for a local office, but for a position as one of four Arlington delegates in the Virginia legislature.*

Major Community "Battles" and Controversies

POLITICAL IMBALANCE

By 1960 the ABC organization had gained all five of the county board seats and for most of the next 32 years they would occupy most, and again in many years all, of the five positions. Only in the years 1967, 1969, 1970, and 1979 to 1982, would Republicans gain a majority and control of the board with three of the five positions.

One Republican elected to the board in 1983[63] did not run for reelection in 1987 at the end of his term. After his departure the board was again composed of only ABC or ABC supported members, until 1993 when Republican Benjamin H. Winslow, Jr., was elected, but then defeated in 1995. At this writing, the Democrats (ABC) not only have their members in all five of the County Board positions but also in every other elective office in the County. Additionally, all Arlington delegates to the General Assembly are also Democrats.

Until the recent legislation providing for the election again of school board members, the County Board also appointed the five members of the School Board, the ABC-Democrat organization has seldom been known to appoint a Republican, or a political opponent, to that body in excess of the number on the County Board, and rarely anyone from the southern half of the county. Thus the Board, and the county government, under ABC domination has become badly unbalanced with respect to participation by the County's Republican or independent minority which, as indicated in election results through the years, amounts to just under half the county population.

GEOGRAPHICAL BOARD IMBALANCE

Arlington seems to be generally, at least by street designations, divided into Northern and Southern halves as delineated by Arlington Boulevard (U.S. Rte 50) running roughly from the Potomac River and the Ft Myer Army Post on the east, to the county line near Seven Corners in the west. In 1962, Mr Leo Urbanske, Jr., who resided on South 19th Street near what is now Crystal City, was elected to the County Board with the support and endorsement of the ABC organization. He was the last citizen from South Arlington to be elected to the Board for almost 30 years until the election of Board member William T. Newman, Jr., in 1988, as mentioned above.

During the many years in between the elections of Urbanske and Newman, the Board was comprised not only of members from North Arlington but also mostly from the Northernmost tip of North Arlington. The members mostly resided in a tiny area immediately around the Washington Golf and Country Club in the extreme northern and most affluent tip of the County just inside the boundary from Fairfax County and farthest from the Southern half of the County.

---

[63] *Mr Michael E. Brunner, a resident of North Arlington.*

ARLINGTON COUNTY VIRGINIA - A Modern History

The residential location of the governing body members far from the Southern edge of the County where most of the urban problems were perceived to exist was a source of growing discontent by citizens in that end of the county. Those urban problems stemmed from, or were related to, the location of many undesirable, even if necessary, community facilities in the southern sections of the county. They included the National Airport, the railroad yards, the trash collecting and compacting facility, the sewage treatment plant, massive traffic, and pollution on and near I-395. Also, the southern areas were where most of the lower income neighborhoods and concentrations of new immigrants from Asia, Latin America, the Caribbean and other World areas were located. It was in such communities that most of the poverty, drug traffic, crime, and other social problems thrived. Yet there was no one on the county governing body that lived in or near those areas that had first hand knowledge of conditions there.

BOARD INSENSITIVITY TO SOUTH ARLINGTON

Over a period of years South Arlington neighborhood leaders were repeatedly rebuffed in their representations before the county board on matters they considered to be of utmost importance to their section of the county, as will be detailed below. The "Southerners" increasingly concluded that the county elected officials were insensitive to them and they attributed it to the fact that there was no one from their area, aware of and sympathetic to their problems, on the governing body. The relationship of South Arlingtonians with their elected governing body officials steadily became confrontational, contentious, and adversarial.

Iluminating the severity of the geographical imbalance on the Arlington County Board was an article in the Washington Post by staff writer Jay Mathews on Nov 11, 1973, headlined, "Many South Arlington Residents Unhappy at Dominance of the North". The article explained the nature of the problems faced by South Arlingtonians that were not resolved by their elected supervisors.

The Post article was accompanied with a map that pin pointed the residences of senior county officials to include the Board, the County Manager, the School Board members (all appointed by the County Board), the Constitutional elected officials, and the County's representative in the State Legislature. All of the officials, except for State Delegate Warren Stambough and School Board member Eleanor Monroe, were shown to reside in the Northern half of the county, and mostly in the extreme Northern neighborhoods as stated.

The Post article, and map, appeared one week after the November election in which one candidate ran against the Republican and ABC-Democrat candidates for a County Board position. In the campaign the candidate mainly stressed the need for representation on the Board by someone from the Southern end of the County. The Post had, during the campaign, announced its support for the ABC candidate who lived also in the northern tip of the County off Glebe Road near the Chain Bridge Road. It can only be speculated as to the effect the article would have had on the election had it appeared before, instead of after, election day.

Major Community "Battles" and Controversies

BASIS FOR SOUTH ARLINGTON DISCONTENT

Beginning in the late 1960s a number of major community actions involving land use or provision of public facilities were considered by the County Board under its zoning, spending, or policy making authorities. A disproportionate of these actions seemed to effect properties in the southern half of the county. The Board actions greatly displeased the nearby citizens and they are listed and described in some detail elsewhere herein, either in this or other chapters. They are briefly listed below for convenient reference. In each of the instances, the County Board, comprised only of members who resided in the northernmost sections of the county, took action contrary to the expressed views and recommendations of South Arlington civic leaders or associations and caused them to question whether their section of the county was received equitable attention and treatment from a board with only members from the northern half of the county and functioning under the at-large electoral arrangement. The subject actions include, but are not limited to, the following. We mention them only briefly here since they are discussed in detail elsewhere herein.

a. THE ROACH HOUSE REZONING ON RIDGE ROAD:

The property, with a 140 year old historical mansion and panoramic view of the Nation's capital, was rezoned from single family to high rise apartment use over the vigorous and unanimous objections of citizens and other groups.

b. THE AURORA HILLS BRANCH LIBRARY:

In 1973, County officials announced plans to build a new replacement branch library on the front of the existing Nellie Custis Elementary School on South 23rd Street. Citizens vigorously objected on grounds of poor design, and violations of zoning law concerning set backs from streets and off street parking requirements. The county yielded and dropped the plan only when citizens filed suit to stop the project.

c. THE SICKLES TRACT - FOREST HILLS TOWNHOUSES:

When the developer of a large tract of open space on South 23rd Street at Army Navy Drive departed in 1974 from his agreement made with local citizens in order to obtain rezoning, the County Board ignored the citizens protests and objections to Board approval of a site plan for townhouses. The citizens then filed suit to obtain relief judicially when they did not obtain it politically through the governing body. The matter was settled when the developer agreed to substantially comply with commitments to the citizens with respect to density in the project, street widths, and off street parking, and some other related matters.

d. THE WIDENING OF JEFF-DAVIS HIGHWAY (Rte 1/I-595):

In the early 1970s, plans were published for the widening of U.S. Route 1 through Crystal City in South Arlington and to convert it into Interstate 595. Citizens protested the project on grounds of appearance, perceived adverse environmental impacts, and other reasons. The County Board, however, strongly favored the proposal, notwithstanding the citizens disapproval, and urged its completion. Whereupon, citizens filed suit that resulted in changes of design more in keeping with the recommendations of the protesters. Only after suit was filed did the County Board cease to urge the completion of the project as proposed.

e. THE COUNTY SEWAGE TREATMENT PLANT:

Through the years, the County sewage plant on South Glebe Road at U.S. Route 1 (Jeff-Davis Highway) has undergone repeated enlargement and expansion over the objections of nearby residents who questioned the need and the procedures followed. They claimed the county officials were insensitive to their concerns and to the adverse, or unknown environmental impacts on them of the operations at the plant. In 1974, the citizens filed suit to halt work on the plant, at least until an environmental impact study was conducted and satisfactory results were obtained. The suit resulted in some changes in approach, but did not stop the project. Plant operations again created intense citizen concern in the mid-1990s when plans were made to substantially increase sludge burning.

f. THE PENTAGON CITY DEVELOPMENT:

When developers began moving forward in the early 1970s to build a massive complex to become know as "Pentagon City" in open space just off I-395 opposite the Pentagon Building, citizens began consulting and meeting with them. Over the months the developers adopted many citizen recommendations concerning density, parking, types of uses, and other matters. When the matter came before the county board, however, there remained major reservations on the part of the citizens. They urged unsuccessfully that the Board not approve the rezoning. The citizens then filed suit against the Board in an effort to seek redress through the courts since they felt they were not satisfactorily heard by their at-large elected officials, all of whom lived in the northern parts of the county.

EFFORTS TO CHANGE THE AT-LARGE VOTING SYSTEM

Repeated efforts, both judicial and political, have been made over the recent years to discard the at-large electoral system in favor of several single member districts, or at least, to provide direct representation on the governing body for South Arlington by someone living in the area.

JUDICIAL EFFORTS

In 1974, a suit was filed in the U. S.District Court in Alexandria[64] on behalf of citizens and residents of Arlington County[65]. The complaint stated that the plaintiffs

---

[64] *George Vollin, Jr., et al v. Mills Godwin, et al., Civil Action No. 173-74-A.*

[65] *George Vollin, Jr., Deloris Lurito, Harrison Douglas, Ethel Tucker, Frank Walsh, Kay Lou Papanicolas, Philip J. Kaczmarek and Dora Curtis.*

Major Community "Battles" and Controversies

were all from minority (Black and Hispanic) or lower income neighborhoods. Plaintiffs asked that the at-large voting arrangement of the County be declared unconstitutional and that it be ordered discontinued. They asked too that single member districts be adopted on the bases that the at-large system racially and otherwise discriminated against them, diluted their voting strengths, and denied them equal access to the democratic process. The suit cited as authority several recent U. S. Supreme Court landmark cases where at-large voting systems had been found thus defective and ordered discontinued.[66]

When the matter was heard on October 2, 1974 by District Court Judge Albert V. Bryan, Jr, the suit was dismissed after several plaintiffs testified as to the history and conditions of the matter in Arlington County.

Judge Bryan said, in part, "Even assuming that there was racial motivation behind the passage of the referendum in 1930, that happened so long ago that it can't be considered as a background of racial discrimination which shifts any burden to the defendants" and "..there is no showing here of any actual impact on individual voting power as a result of the multi-member (single) district." (emphasis supplied).

The plaintiffs did not agree with Judge Bryan's reasoning, which they considered tortured and wrong and appealed his decision. The 4th Circuit Court of Appeals in Richmond, however, did agreed with the District Court and affirmed his action. The U. S. Supreme Court later refused to hear the case. Thus, the effort to end at-large voting in Arlington Country by recourse to the Federal courts had failed.

During the course of the suit above in the Federal Courts, a development occurred to the surprise and temporary delight of the plaintiffs. In response to an interrogatory from plaintiffs, the Assistant Attorney General for Virginia, Anthony F. Troy, stated that "...an argument exists that State law would allow a procedure to take the sense of the people on the question of whether Arlington should change its form of government. See e.g. Sec 15.1-694 of the Code of Virginia".

The section quoted is the same cited hereinabove and used as the bases for the 1930 referendum in which the form of government was changed and the at-large system adopted. As stated, it provided that "whenever 200 or more" voters so petitioned the Circuit Court an election would be held to take the sense of the voters on specified questions. The statute did not expressly provide that its provisions could be used only one time. In earlier consultations on this subject, the County Attorney, and some other attorneys in the County, had taken the position that the Statute section, having been used in 1930, could not again be so used.

Armed with the suggestion from no less a legal authority than the Governor's own senior attorney's office that the subject Virginia Code section could indeed be used again, contrary to the views of local Arlington attorneys, plaintiffs set about promptly to implement and take advantage of its provisions as interpreted by the State Attorney General's office. Petitions were quickly circulated, well over 200 signatures were

---

[66] *e.g., Chavis v. Whitcomb, 305 F Supp. 1364 (S.D. Ind. 1969), Connor v. Johnson, 402 U.S. 690 (Miss.1971), and their progeny.*

ARLINGTON COUNTY VIRGINIA - A Modern History

obtained, and the Arlington Circuit Court was requested to order an election to take the sense of the voters on the questions in the statute to include whether they desired single member or at-large voting districts.

When the petition for an election came before the Arlington Circuit Court, Judge William Winston heard the case and after arguments he agreed with the County Attorney and with local attorney Larry Latto who appeared at the hearing to the surprise of the petitioners and their attorney. Latto was well known in the community as a long time supporter of the controlling political group and had appeared, presumably on behalf of the County government or the ABC-Democrat Board members in opposition to the petitioner citizens and voters.

Judge Winston ruled, to the petitioners great disappointment, that the subject statute section could not be used a second time, notwithstanding any suggestion by the State Attorney General's Office that it could be so used.

The Circuit Court ruling that dismissed the plaintiffs petition for a special election on the statute questions was appealed. After arguments in Richmond before a State Supreme Court panel, the State Supreme Court upheld Judge Winston and affirmed his decision.[67] Thereafter, no additional efforts were made by Arlingtonians to have the at-large electoral system declared unconstitutional, or otherwise unlawful, through either the Federal or the State Courts.

POLITICAL EFFORTS

In an effort to achieve South Arlington representation on the governing body through the political process, a South Arlington citizen, this writer, ran in 1973 as an independent for a seat on the County Board against two opponents, one an ABC-Democrat and the other a Republican. He lost with only about 10% of the votes cast. He ran again as an Independent with Republican backing in 1977 against the ABC-Democrat incumbent Board member Bozman, and again lost, but this time narrowly.

In both campaigns the candidate stressed throughout what he considered to be the urgent need for representation on the board from the Southern end of the County, as well as issues of board insensitivity, excessive borrowing and ineffective school administration. The political effort to achieve South Arlington representation on the County Board had twice failed.

The candidate attributed his inability to prevail to the handicaps of running at-large in a county wide, "winner take all", election where he could not effectively

---

[67] *Vollin v. Arlington County Electoral Bd.*, 216 Va.674, 222 S.E. 793 (1976).

communicate his message, and when running as a "David" against a "Goliath" opponent supported by a political organization far better organized, orchestrated and financed.

An additional effort was made in 1977 to open the door to a return to the single member district electoral system when the County Board adopted an item in its legislative proposal agenda for new legislation to allow a referendum vote by Arlingtonians on the matter. The County Board at the time was comprised of three ABC-Democrat members and two Republican party members. The legislative proposal concerning a referemdum on returning to single member districts was adopted on a 3 to 2 vote when ABC-Democrat Board member, John Purdy, to the surprise of proponents of the measure, voting with the two Republican members in favor of the proposal.

The proposal to allow a referendum was not acted on in the legislature. At the time, all Arlington Delegates, and its Senator, were from the same political organization as the one that controlled the County Board and who were widely known to strongly oppose a return to a single member district voting system. Such a proposal has not been included in any County Board legislative proposal package for any other year in recent history.

ATTITUDES ON AT-LARGE VOTING

The defenders of the status quo at-large electoral system do not appear to be apprehensive over their prospects of retaining the at-large arrangement. They have many philosophical arguments to make for its retention. They usually contend that the at-large system is more efficient and effective. They claim that with it, each voter has not one, but five representatives on the board since all voters vote for all five members of the board. They are also quick to point out, in agreement with historian Rose's opinion, that the at-large voting avoids "parochialism" that would exist if Board members were elected from smaller, neighborhood areas, and that they can be more objective, and honest, in county wide problems when elected by county wide voting.

One long time, loyal and dedicated ABC-Democrat, and perhaps the most vocal spokesman, publicly, in defense of the at-large system, is Arlingtonian Maurice "Maury" Flagg. Flagg writes periodically in the Letters to the Editor columns of the local media, often in response to critics of the existing electoral arrangement. Flagg has contended that the at-large system results in Board members who are "representatives of the entire citizenry, not just one piece of it"... "Its why we get first class county government management...and why we are spared the evils of logrolling and dealing common ... with single member districts ... and (it) saves us from single-issue, narrow minded hacks."[68]

Flagg, on another occasion, wrote, in pertinent part, concerning the opponents of the at-large system and the ABC-Democrat candidates, "Their candidates don't win elections because they are noncredible, have no ideas that add value to the community...

---

[68] *Arlington Journal, Letters to the Editor, June 30, 1989.*

are ...ineffective and will continue to be no matter whatever gimmicks (they) may pursue."[69]

Critics of the at-large electoral system, on the other hand, usually claim that it is unfair, undemocratic and inefficient, does not serve well all sections of the county, and is used by the controlling political faction mainly as a tool to remain in power.

One Arlingtonian, Jim Charleton, wrote, in part, "It is ironical that the county's dominant political machine, virtually alone in Virginia, clings to this legacy of segregation, while communities like Norfolk have been forced to give it up because it discriminates against minorities.. the unrepresentative at-large system will continue to limit, if not exclude, ethnic and racial, as well as political, minorities from equal participation in public life... If the shoe were on the other foot and Mr Flagg in the opposition, I am sure we would now be hearing how unfair this at-large system is..."[70]

Another critic, Jack Marks, asserted that the at-large Board's treatment of South Arlington was a "history of neglect". He wrote further that "...Board members are mediocre people and most of them serve on to board to feed their egos... The Board is not responsive to the people...So long as we have people who have been there many years and suffer from 'executive arrogance' the board will not provide superior leadership."[71]

Finally, another Arlingtonian, Harry Almond in Crystal City wrote, "...voting by districts...is the best alternative available to move toward a democratic process of accountability and responsibility...in the authorization and spending of taxpayer funds...and opportunity for introducing badly needed new talent, new thinking and new and innovative ideas" as a basis "...for shaping the County into a truly desirable residential community." [72]

The author with Plaintiff George Vollin.

No matter what may be the merits of the philosophical arguments for, or against, the at-large electoral system, it is clear that the system, in operation in Arlington County, (1) denies to a large percentage of the County residents, any meaningful and actual participation in County government, (2) operates to the distinct disadvantage of political factions or movements or individuals who are not highly organized and well funded, and (3) does not insure that all geographical sections of the county will be represented on the governing body by a person residing in

---

[69] *Arlington Journal, Letters to the Editor, March 2, 1992.*

[70] *Arlington Journal, Letters to the Editor, April 22, 1992.*

[71] *Arlington Courier, Letters to the Editor, June 15, 1992.*

[72] *Arlington Courier, Letters to the Editor, June 26, 1991.*

the section or neighborhood that is more likely to be directly familiar with local conditions and problems.

Critics of the at-large voting system are quick to point out that Arlington's political situation exists almost nowhere else in the American legislative process at the Federal, State, or most municipal levels. They argue that the system and its consequences also contrasts sharply with the historical American governmental concept dating from the days of the Founding Fathers that there should be maximum and equitable representation in government from the lowest possible levels of society and political subdivisions.

In accordance with that philosophy, the American people have historically had single member districts in State and Federal legislatures and, except only for U.S. Senators, have not elected law makers at-large. Critics of the at-large system contend that the principle is equally applicable at the municipal level in any sizeable community. In numerous communities where at-large systems were adopted in recent years with the advent of the civil rights movements the Federal Courts have ordered the systems disestablished on the grounds they were unconstitutional. The Courts said, in cases involving Indianapolis, Dallas, Birmingham, Milwaukee, and a long list of other communities, that the at-large systems were discriminatory in that they diluted the voting strengths of minorities and denied them equal access to the democratic processes.

Control of an American legislative body anywhere and at any level may shift from time to time, but its political minority composition nearly always democratically reflects rather closely the percentage of the minority in the overall constituency. Arlington's governing body does not. Through most of the recent years the minority party has been under represented, or not represented at all as at present although it usually has received as much as just under half the votes cast in most elections since the early 1960's.

While the individual qualifications of Arlington candidates for public office may certainly be a factor from time to time in the success of their electoral efforts, as contended by the systems supporters, there are strong reasons for concluding that this is not the primary reason for the continued success of ABC-Democrat candidates. By and large, with only the rarest of exceptions, Mr Flagg and some others to the contrary notwithstanding, Arlington candidates for public office over the recent years have been of high calibre, no matter what their partisan political positions or connections. The candidates almost totally have been dedicated, committed, honest, ethical, above any reasonable reproach, and fully qualified to hold public office. The County has been remarkably free of any incidents of dishonesty, graft, corruption, or other misconduct by those in public office.

PROSPECTS FOR CHANGE

Although it is clear there is considerable dissatisfaction by a large percentage of Arlington citizens with the at-large voting system which leaves the sizable political

ARLINGTON COUNTY VIRGINIA - A Modern History

minority, and many neighborhoods, unrepresented on the governing body, the prospects for any change from the system appears to be quite remote.

As stated, since recourse to the courts for remedies have proven fruitless, and since there is currently no statutory authority for a referendum on the matter, it seems the only avenue open for the citizenry to express their choice on changing from the at-large electoral system, would be new legislation authorizing a referendum on the matter.

New enabling legislation, however, would ordinarily have to be initiated and introduced in the State Assembly and Arlington's representatives there are hardly likely to take any action to bring that about. Those representatives continue to be from the same political organization that now dominates local government. This was not changed in 1995 with the election of Democrat (ABC) Mary Margaret Whipple to the Senate and the reelection of Democrat Karen Darner to the House of Delegates. The group collectively has firmly and long opposed any change in the at-large system under which they have retained tight control on local government.

The situation could change if Republican, or other non-ABC-Democrat candidates were elected to the State Assembly and would introduce and fight for new laws to allow Arlington citizens to have a referendum voice in choosing their form of local government.

If could well be, in the end, to the delight of at-large proponents and the disappointment of critics, that the citizens, by free democratic choice, might vote to retain the at-large system on its merits or as a matter of preference. That uncertainty will never be resolved however, so long as the matter is kept off the ballot as those in political control have thus far succeeded in doing.

* * * *

"We're moving from South Arlington to North Arlington?"
"That's right! and as fast as possible!"
"Why?"
"We're tired of all the unpleasant conditions all around us!"
"Like what?"
"For starters, sewage treatment plants, railroad yards, airports, massive highways, drug dealing neighborhoods, noise pollution and the unsafest streets."
"Aren't we over-reacting?"
"Perhaps. We shall see and return if we are wrong."

Major Community "Battles" and Controversies

Round IX
THE AURORA HILLS BRANCH LIBRARY
Where to Build

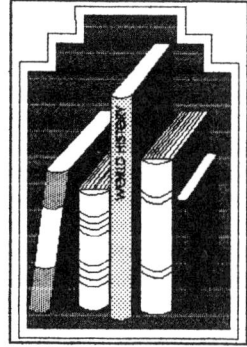

By the middle of the 1960s, residents in the South Arlington neighborhoods adjacent to the Jeff-Davis Highway corridor (U.S. Route #1) began to think in terms of improving the local County Branch library that was intended to serve their needs. The corridor with mostly low density, industrial and commercial activities to include a brick, junk, wrecked cars, sand and gravel and similar yards, and some open undeveloped areas, was on the threshold of massive redevelopment. Under a new and somewhat more relaxed zoning policy adopted by the County Board, with less stringent requirements concerning height and off street parking, applications for rezoning to permit high rise office and residential buildings were beginning to pour into the county government offices. Over the next decades the area would be fully developed with dozens of structures and become know as Crystal City.

The County library, serving that southernmost part of the county generally east of Shirley Highway, later to become I-95 and then I-395, was the Aurora Hills Branch, located on South 23rd and Eads Streets. The library was located in an old three room, one story, store front without any off street parking. It had long been considered to be inadequate in size, facilities and book stocks to even serve the existing neighborhoods even without the spectacular growth then being commenced.

Citizen agitation for a new library reached a point by 1965 that could no longer be ignored by the county government officials, and, steps were taken to replace the existing library. Following vigorous study by county and citizen groups, provision for a new library at a cost of $550,000 was included in a $5,000,000 bond authorization proposal on the ballot in the general election in November, 1969, and was approved by the voters.

In the months following, a coalition committee composed mainly of members of the nearby Arlington Ridge and Virginia Highlands Civic Associations met to explore possible sites for the library, and to formulate recommendations as to style, size, and other characteristics and features.[73] The committee was assisted by Jane Nida, the County Director of Libraries.

In due course the committee appeared before the local civic associations with the results of their deliberations. The committee, assisted by consultants, reported that the most, and perhaps only, feasible location for a new library was at the intersections of South 23rd and Grant Streets, and they provided a sketch and plan for the library. The plan proposed to construct the library in the yard and on the front and side of the existing Nellie Custis Elementary School on that site. The library would in effect be a "wrap

---

[73] *The group of civic activists was headed by Linda Lillinger and included Donna Jensen, Mary Nicholson, Phillip Robbins, Isolde Weinberger.*

The former Aurora Hills Library at South 23rd and Eads Streets.

around" attachment to the school building extending to within inches of the street side walks of the two streets. Further, the plan envisioned extensive alteration and modification of the school building in order to accommodate and incorporate the new library and school into a single building.

The committee, and the county planning staff, recognized that the lack of sufficient off street parking was a matter of major significance. They proposed that this be overcome by using a part of the school playground for parking, together with some spaces made available by Our Lady of Lourdes Catholic Church one block away under an arrangement that could be terminated at any time at the option of the Church. A similar proposal to the Calvary Methodist Church across Grant Street from the proposed library site to use its church parking lot spaces to meet the library off street parking space requirements, was rejected by the church.

As the details of the study became more widely known in the community and among the citizens, opposition and dissention steadily developed which at times became tense and acrimonious. In the Spring of 1972 the Arlington Ridge Association considered the matter at a regular monthly business meeting and received a briefing on the status of the library project. Several members expressed opposition and voiced concern about the location of the library on a highly impacted site with

The Nellie Custis Elementary School. (Sheltered Occupational Center)

a structure extending to within inches of sidewalks at a busy intersection in an area already beset with traffic and congestion problems of serious magnitude caused by the enormous developments only a block away in the Jefferson Davis corridor of the county. Other members expressed opposition because of the absence, at that time, of adequate off street parking facilities. Following the discussion, the Association adopted a resolution urging speed in completing the library, but "...not attached to the school building as proposed".

About a year later, when it appeared that plans to construct the library as proposed were proceeding despite known opposition and its earlier stated position, the

Association, adopted a resolution in outright opposition to the library attached to the school building.

In November 1972, the Executive Board of the Calvary Methodist Church, directly across the street from the proposed location of the library, took a position in opposition and appointed an ad hoc committee to explore means of conveying church opposition. The committee rejected resorting to legal recourse and decided that representations to and before the County Board would be successful in achieving the desired results of blocking construction of the library as proposed.

On March 6, 1973, the Arlington County Civic Federation, an organization with about 40 neighborhood civic groups, described elsewhere herein, adopted a resolution opposing the library as proposed, at least until the matter could be further studied and reviewed by the County Board at an advertised public hearing. The position was communicated to the Chairman of the County Board, but no response was received. Additionally, during this period, the Executive Committee of the Oakridge Elementary School, located in the area to be served by the library, considered the matter and recorded its opposition to the project as proposed. One of its members, Emmy Lou Runyan, a resident on South 23rd Street, circulated an opposition petition, obtained over 300 signatures, and forwarded it to the Chairman of the County Board.

The question of where to built a replacement for the Aurora Hills library was clouded during this period by a concurrent issue involving the expected closing of the Nellie Custis School in a period of downsizing the county school system because of a steady drop in school population. Many local residents and parents with children in the Custis school did not want their neighborhood school closed, and their children bused elsewhere and they hoped that by building the library onto the school, it would result in keeping the school open. One such parent, John K. Mallery, a member of the Virginia Highlands Civic Association in whose area the school was located, wrote to the Editor of the Arlington Journal newspaper, (clipping on hand but date missing) in part:

> *"...what might be more important than a local library (and) our local neighborhood school...a report made to the school board recommended the closing of Nellie Custis. However, the school board pursued their plans to remodel the school in conjunction with the library...this present hope to those of us who have children in Custis because it seemed unlikely the school board would spend up to $200,000 of their money on a building only to turn it over to someone else...(if) there are no plans to remodel the school we can probably look forward to it's (sic) closing in the near future..."*

Another Virginia Highlands resident with children in the Nellie Custis school voiced similar sentiments to the editor of the Northern Virginia Sun newspaper, and bitterly attacked opponents of the proposed library. George W. Downes wrote (date missing) "If you kill the library, you kill Nellie Custis school because of its small size..." He alluded to certain opponents as "those rich people up on the hill" and said their statements "help me understand why a library issue is used as a cover-up (shades of Watergates) for a school issue...if this sounds like a neighborhood squabble, Well, it is."

On April 25, 1973, the matter came before the County Board for a decision as to whether to continue with the project by advertising for construction bids. Numerous citizens appeared and spoke on the subject for over two and a half hours. Most expressed opposition to the proposal, including four individuals who spoke for organizations or for organized groups.

Among the reasons advanced by the speakers for not constructing a public library as part of an elementary school, were the following:

==the library detracts from the usability and functionability of the school building as designed, constructed and used;

==the concept of a joint public school and library used simultaneously by the public and school children is contrary to accepted and generally recognized practices as recommended by professional librarians and school administrators;

==the availability and merits of other, more desirable sites was not adequately considered;

==the proposed library building, extending almost to the corner of the busy intersection on a main thoroughfare would obstruct vision of drivers entering or leaving Grant and 23rd Streets and thus create an unnecessary traffic and safety hazard;

==the library, extending to the intersection corner without required setback, compromises and encroaches on the visability and exposure of the Calvary Methodist church to its detriment, and;

==the proposal violates County policy with respect to off street parking requirements and structure setbacks from streets requirements.

In the Board members' discussion that followed the citizens comments, the Chairman stated that he was not inclined to hold up on the project. One Board member suggested that perhaps a review of the matter was needed, but no motion was made to do so, and thus the Board moved on to the next item on its agenda without taking any action to cancel or hold up on the planned library on the school front.

Soon after that Board meeting of April, citizens frustrated and displeased with the Board's failure to hold up on the library proposal filed suit, through their attorney Sherman Pratt, also a local resident in the area and active in the matter, in the Arlington County Circuit Court (Equity # 23394, John T. Dabinett[74] et al v. The Arlington County Board, the County Manager, and Staff). The plaintiffs asked that defendants be enjoined from proceeding with, or advertising, the library project until such time as a hearing on the merits would be held. They alleged that the County authorities had acted illegally, arbitrarily, unreasonably and capriciously in that there had been no required environmental impact study, and that the County's own ordinances concerning street set

---

[74] *Other plaintiffs were: H. Anderton, a member of the Calvary Methodist Church, Daniel Ragalie, a local businessman, Emmy Lou Runyan, a member of the Oakridge PTA, Frances Shraison, a local businesswoman, Joyce Velde, a member of Our Lady of Lourdes Catholic Church, and Patrick Monohan.*

Major Community "Battles" and Controversies

backs and parking spaces were being ignored and violated. They charged that County imposed requirements on these matters for private sector were equally applicable to the county for its public buildings and activities.

On the day before the case was scheduled for hearing, County Attorney Jerry Emrich contacted the plaintiffs' attorney and reported that the County Board had met and decided to cancel the proposed plans for the library, thus making the court dispute moot. He asked if the plaintiffs would object if he moved for dismissal. Plaintiffs' attorney said he would not. Whereupon the complaint was dismissed and the litigation ended.

The Arlington Journal reported in an article by Judy Gillis:

> *LIBRARY PLANS SHELVED: Controversial plans for a community library at the Nellie Custis School in South Arlington have been shelved this week by the Arlington County Board. The County Board also directed County Manger Bert Johnson to "formulate a new plan for the providing of essential library facilities to serve the citizens of the area."*

"This will be a good time to get together and make a fresh start," said Dick Staley, Chairman of the coalition. "Maybe we can get the ball rolling again."

In the months and years that followed, the County purchased open space land at 18th and South Hayes Street over the underground right of way of the Metro rail system and built a combined fire station, recreation center, and library. That facility now serves the area without any known discontent or criticism from citizens who use its services. There is wide open space area on all sides of the joint facility, there is adequate on-site parking space, and in its unconjested surroundings on a wide divided lane street, there is clear passage for departing and returning fire fighting equipment.

"We think this arrangement is far superior to the earlier proposal from many standpoints," said Joyce Velde, one nearby citizen served by the library, "and especially because it has the library and rec-center in the same building with the firemen. That provides peace of mind and a considerable measure of safety and security for visitors, especially during the evening hours of darkness", she added.

ARLINGTON COUNTY VIRGINIA - A Modern History

The Aurora Hills joint Library, Recreational Center and Fire station at South 18th and Hayes Streets in Crystal City.

The Citizen
Fall 1995

The masthead of the Arlington County monthly newsletter.

Major Community "Battles" and Controversies

THE PENTAGON CITY REZONING

The Pentagon City complex in South Arlington between I-395 and Crystal City on Jeff-Davis highway (U. S. Route 1). On the right from foreground to background are; the Macy Department Store, the MCI Office Building (and main entrance to the Fashion Center Shopping Mall), the Ritz Carlton Hotel, the Nordstrom Department Store and the Park Vista Apartments. To the left and out of the photo is the Pentagon Center with additional shops and services to include the Costco/Price Club warehouse type discount outlet. A view of the area from the opposite direction can be seen in Chapter Six on developments.

By the early 1970s, most open, or "under-developed" land in Arlington County that was designated on the land use map for high rise uses, mainly in the Rosslyn, Ballston and Crystal City areas, was rapidly being developed. One notable exception was a tract of about 116 acres of open space adjacent to Shirley Highway (I-395), directly opposite the Pentagon between the River House apartment complex and the Western Electric warehouse on South Fern street at 15th Street. The tract was owned by a group known as Cafritz-Thompkins that also owned the adjacent River House apartments. The area was soon to become known as Pentagon City.

In early 1973 word and rumors circulated and spread rapidly in the South Arlington neighborhoods that the Pentagon City tract was about to be developed. Community reaction varied greatly. At the September Planning Commission meeting the Dewberry, Lealon and Davis Company, a land development company retained by the owner/developer as consultants, outlined its proposal for developing the tract as a shopping center, hotel, apartment and nursing home, and other community facilities. Although never developed, the tract had long been zoned for high rise use.

In a September 27 article headlined "Pentagon City? What's That?", the Arlington Journal reported that few of the nearby residents had ever heard of Pentagon City and only 5% knew of any plans to develop it. The article also described the results of a survey of citizen attitudes conducted by Hollander Associates of Baltimore and presented to the Arlington Planning Commission. The Journal article quoted consultant Sidney Hollander as saying that the survey consisted of a sampling of 500 adults living near the Pentagon City tract and proportionately divided between single-home and apartment residents. Hollander explained before the Planning Commission, "We're convinced Pentagon City is not yet a burning issue in the community because so few people have even heard of it." That indifference, or lack of awareness, was soon to change as we shall see.

Hollander also asserted that of the 40% of the people interviewed, only a few of those who knew of the development plans felt the shopping center would be of value, while another 25% favored park uses for the site. Of those with any interest, most suggested that the development include a library, movie theater, a good restaurant, a concert hall and an arts and crafts center. Hollander said 25% of those interviewed could not see the development "as a use to them". Sidney Dewberry of the land development company said their plans "hopes to minimize automotive trips and pedestrian automotive conflicts and encourage the use of mass transit".

THE REZONING APPLICATION

In the following months, the Cafritz-Tompkins group, through their attorney Barnes Lawson, filed its application for site plan rezoning that began to wind its way through the County Managers staff to the Planning Commission and the County Board. In this period, community interest and involvement steadily grew with extensive meetings and consultations with the developers and the county government. There was extensive "give and take" and concessions between and among the citizens, county staff and developers in efforts to minimize differences when the matter reached the county Board for public hearings. Citizen representation and leadership in this period was mainly through a group known as the Pentagon City Coordination Committee (PCCC), later to become incorporated and renamed the Center for Urban Education (CUE). The PCCC group consisted mainly of members of the local civic associations. The precise composition and detailed activities of the group is described at length in Chapter IV herein.

The developers proposal, generally, envisioned a complex with about 7,000 dwelling units, 2 million square feet of office space, over 800,000 square feet of commercial space, and a hotel/motel with 1,200 units. In the period leading to consideration of the proposal and rezoning application by the Planning Commission and County Board, differences arose between the developers, the citizens and the county planning staff as alluded to above. Most of these concerned density, height, off street parking, and the amount of open space to be provided in and around buildings. Many, but not all, of the differences were resolved at the many meetings leading to Board consideration. A major concern of citizens not resolved was their continued concern over the feared adverse environmental impact of the development by noise, air and other pollution and by vehicular traffic congestion.

PLANNING COMMISSION POSITION AND ACTION

The Pentagon City development proposal was considered by the Planning Commission and its ad hoc committee for the study of the matter chaired by John McCracken, in numerous meetings in the closing weeks of 1975. By a narrow vote, the Commission recommended that the County Board approve the applicant's proposed zoning and site plan. In its report, the Commission said it had "studied the proposal within the frame work of accomplishing the following objectives :

1. Encourage development of densities lower than Rosslyn and Crystal City.
2. Minimize adverse impacts on adjacent single-family areas.
3. Minimize secondary impacts on other parts of the County.
4. Encourage a mixed residential, commercial, motel and office usage.
5. Design pedestrian and vehicle traffic patterns that will encourage Metrorail and Metrobus usage.
6. Encourage highest possible use of public transportation systems and multi-passenger vehicles.
7. Provide sufficient open space and green space within the high density development.

In its report the Commission addressed numerous aspects of the development to include building heights, measures to control congestion, traffic circulation, noise and air pollution, crime, parks, open space, transportation, parking, street configuration, housing, lighting, and other similar considerations that might affect the enjoyability of life in the area for all concerned.

COUNTY MANAGER POSITION

On November 19, County Manager Bert Johnson reported to the County Board that his staff had recommended approval of the Pentagon City site plan subject to 57 conditions, 43 of which had been agreed to by the applicant. He listed the remaining not agreed to conditions to be:

No. 5 - A new 15th Street, South, sanitary sewer to be constructed by the applicant.
No. 7 - A disagreement between the applicant and utility companies on the location of electric and telephone utilities and whether on street right of way.
No. 19 - Whether applicant should pay full cost or pro-rata share of cost of required off site 320 feet of storm sewer.

No. 21 - Disagreement concerning the extent to which street construction should proceed concurrently with actual development.

No. 26 - Whether applicant should pay full or half the cost of construction of 15th street, and medium, considering that applicant agreed to deed the county a 12-acre park on the south side of the street.

No. 28 - Whether applicant must be responsible for construction of a medium and street widening on South Joyce where developer owns property on both sides of street.

No. 34 - The extent to which the applicant is responsible for pedestrian grade separation facilities to avoid conflict between pedestrians and automobiles at street level.

No. 38 - Disagreement as to whether applicant must provide 12 feet major, instead of 10 feet minor, sidewalks in four block faces.

Nos. 46 and 47 - Disagreement as to whether applicant should be responsible for landscaping all street mediums within the project.

No. 48 - Disagreement as to whether street trees should be spaced at staff desired 40 foot intervals, or at 50 foot as desired by applicant.

Nos. 53, 54, and 55 - Disagreement as to the location of the 650 unit nursing home on one site, or several as desired by the applicant.

PRESS COVERAGE AND CITIZEN REACTION

On December 7, the Washington Star reported that the application of Cafritz-Thompson group had come before the County Board for consideration but that the Board had deferred the matter until January 24, 1976. The Star article reported; "About 50 people attended the meeting to speak...and most were expected to seek either deferral or denial of the rezoning", or downsizing of the project. Board Chairman John Purdy was quoted as saying that if the matter was deferred [to the 24th] there would be "no sense listening" to those desiring to speak on December 7. By deferring the matter to the following month, and year, action on the Cafritz-Thompkins application would be heard by a new Board that would include newly elected members Walter L. Frankland and Dorothy Grotos who would replace departing members Richards and Munsey.

Star writer Lynn Dunson wrote that South Arlington opponents of the Pentagon City development were "not arguing so much for a no growth policy as they were questioning how much more growth the area can withstand." She alluded to the owners gift of 12 acres for the expansion of a park and acreage for construction of a fire station, library and nursing home. She added;

> *"But the prospect of a mini-town with an estimated 10,000 residents attracting 9,000 office workers, plus shoppers and other commuters and generating some 25,000 additional cars making an estimated nearly 50,000 trips a day and inevitably overflowing into nearby neighborhood streets is giving some South Arlington citizens the shudders."*

Dunson quoted South Arlington resident Dirk Swain as predicting the proposal would produce "a complete breakdown in transportation because of the number of cars

Major Community "Battles" and Controversies

jockeying for ramp access positions, taking short cuts through residential areas and copping local parking spots". She wrote that even Richard Barton, chairman of the planning commission, admits he doesn't feel comfortable about making a decision on the proposal now, and asking the board to defer its decision and 'chew over' the possibility of down zoning.

On the eve of the County Board's January 24 meeting to consider the Pentagon City proposal, community dialogue continued and intensified. On January 8, Chris Jensen in the Journal reminded his readers of the Planning Commission's admonishment that before approving the higher density zoning for the Pentagon City tract, the County Board should make a "strong commitment to protect single family homes from adverse traffic and noise impacts." He wrote that the rezoning if approved "would allow the construction of 12 story office buildings and a 16 story hotel and apartment buildings with an estimated 8,700 additional office workers and 10,700 residents.

Civic activist Louise Chesnut took issue with public statements made by Planning Commission member Joel Eigen and wrote in the Arlington News on January 15th, in part, "We must stop turning farm land into sprawling developments and stringing out our urban areas so that a car is necessary every time we leave the house. We need to relearn the habit of mixing our land uses. There is a METRO station in the center of the Pentagon City tract. The plans call for a mixture of land uses. We should be happy. But (there is) a fault. As it is presently conceived it will generate over 46,000 additional auto trips a day in the already overcrowded Pentagon-National Airport-Crystal City area...it will increase air pollution. This does not seem like a profitable trade off."

In response to Chesnut, Eigen wrote, also in the News, "I (am) in wholehearted agreement with Mrs Chesnut in her concern with the deteriorating environment...the automobile is indeed our greatest polluter...we should give those citizens who wish to live in a less extravagant and more resource conserving manner the opportunity to do so...the Pentagon City development would be quite consistent with official policies in the recently adopted Long Range County Improvement Program...(and it would) encourage development of housing and employment within walking distance of Metro transit stations, to minimize auto travel."

On January 20, four days before the scheduled Board action on the Cafritz-Thompkins application, the Washington Post editorialized, in part:

> "In many respects the developers have taken the right approach in planning Pentagon City...what worries us-and what seems to have been somewhat blurred over in the presentations to the citizens-is what this high density development will do to traffic and air quality. The density the developers will request on January 24 will nearly double that permitted under present zoning adopted in the late 1930s. At that time no one could anticipate the extent of traffic, noise and pollution generated by National Airport, Shirley Highway (I-95) and other commuter roads, the Pentagon, Crystal City and Arlington's new incinerator...Zoning, as the Virginia law puts it, is 'to protect and enhance the quality of life and protect health and welfare'. The County Board should therefore reject the request for higher densities and send the Pentagon City developers back to the drawing boards."

ARLINGTON COUNTY VIRGINIA - A Modern History

On January 22, two days before Board consideration of the rezoning, Derk Swain (mentioned above) and his wife Nancy, both active in the PCCC, wrote letters to the editor of the Arlington News. They too took issue to some extent with the views of Joel Eigen and further elaborated on the anticipated adverse impact of the developers' proposal, particularly with the County's failure to keep its vows "to maintain existing neighborhoods". They asserted, for reasons voiced by others as detailed above, that "the proposed zoning should and must be denied".

Also on the 22nd, the Arlington Journal in a page one banner headline item characterized the upcoming Saturday rezoning hearing as a "Mini-City Showdown", by "geared up" South Arlington residents. Staff Writer Chris Jensen wrote that the hearing was expected to bring about marathon public testimony and that litigation would probably occur if the application for rezoning was approved. He quoted South Arlington resident and PCCC member John Quinn as saying, "...if the Board persists in flying in the face of the facts (on air pollution and other adverse impacts) we have no choice but to litigate the matter." Peggy Horton, president of the Aurora Hills Civic Association added, "People are so much up in arms and so disturbed by the [expected] traffic they would be very willing to consider a suit."

MORE PRESS REACTION

The Washington Post too, gave the Pentagon City rezoning conspicuous attention. In an article by Patricia Camp on the day of the hearing, it quoted Francis Hewitt, a 29 year South Arlington Resident and past president of the Arlington Ridge Civic Association as observing, "We find ourselves a little island in the sea of concrete. Crystal City brought (many) problems and Pentagon City will enlarge on them. It makes life as we have known it a little difficult. They call it progress". Her article continued, "'There has never been anything like it before and there will never by anything like this again,'" said Sherman Pratt, a South Arlington resident and unsuccessful 1974 County Board Candidate". She also quoted Sidney Dewberry, the consultant in the rezoning matter, with a converse position saying, "The citizens are comparing no development to my proposal and that's not fair. They should compare it to the existing zoning. I think my plan is better than what's there now."

"More concrete?"

In letters to the Editors of the Washington Post and Arlington News on February 7 and 19 respectively, John T. McCracken, the Chairman of the Arlington Planning Commission, and Ad Hoc Committee on Pentagon City, defended the Commission's earlier vote of 9-1 to grant the requested rezoning, took issue with many of the positions of the opponents concerning numerous adverse environmental impacts, and wrote that "Approval of our recommendation would be a responsible act and would help protect the quality of life of Arlington residents and workers alike." Commission member Chris Oynes, however, in a letter to the editor of the Arlington News, not published until February 26th, after the Board's action on the 25th as described below, took issue with the views of his chairman, faulted the Board because it "refused to mention, let alone discuss the merits of the 2 inch thick analysis document prepared by the citizens'

Major Community "Battles" and Controversies

Pentagon City Coordination Committee" and charged that the Board "so far, is not doing its duty.",

Thus on the eve of the Board hearing, opposition forces were aligned on the field of contest and ready to do battle with rhetorical or other weapons at the ready.

THE COUNTY BOARD HEARING

On February 25, 1975, after giving tentative approval a few days earlier, the Arlington County Board met in an all day session attended by an over-flowing crowd, and after hearing many speakers, approved the Cafritz-Thompkins application for site plan rezoning of the Pentagon City tract in a 4 to 1 vote. Board Chairman Ellen Bozman, and members Joseph Wholey, John Purdy and Walter Frankland, Jr., voted for rezoning, with Dorothy Grotos voting against. Washington Post staffer Deborah Sue Yeager wrote the following morning, in part:

> "The Arlington County Board rezoned the 116-acre Pentagon City site last night to permit development of a long planned office, apartment and commercial complex there...(it) will enable the owners to build 1.25 million square feet of office space,[75] 800,000 square feet of shopping center, 2,000 hotel units, a nursing home and about 6,200 apartment units, along with 13.5 acres of park land...the Board insisted there be no on street parking...requested that office building developers encourage mass transit ridership by constructing fewer (off street) parking spaces and allocating them on a preferential basis to car pools...William B. Lawson, the attorney representing Cafritz-Thompkins agreed to these conditions..."

REACTION - THE COURT SUIT

Critical reaction by opponents of the Board's approval of the Pentagon City application was intense and immediate. South Arlington citizens and members of the PCCC moved promptly to continue their opposition in the courts. They retained the legal firms of Covington, Covington and Burling and Siciliano, Ellis, Sheridan and Dyer to represent them, and the PCCC became incorporated. On June 3, a suit was filed in the Circuit Court of Arlington (Chancery No. 26523), asking for a declaratory judgement to overrule the county Board's decision.

The Plaintiffs in the suit were the Pentagon City Coordinating Committee, Inc., John H. and Joan C. Quinn, D. Derk Swain, Richard J. and Deborah Herbst, and Robert F. and Calista L. Steadman. The County Board and its members Bozman, Wholey, Purdy, Grotos and Frankland as individuals were named as defendants.

The Plaintiffs asserted that the defendants had proceeded upon the erroneous legal premise that they were legally foreclosed from maintaining the existing zoning and that

---

[75] *This was a developer concession from its original proposal calling for 2,000,000 square feet.*

they had an affirmative legal obligation to change the zoning in such a way as to permit higher density. In their complaining petition, the plaintiffs listed all, or many, of the above enumerate claimed adverse community and environmental impacts. These included pollution, noise, congestion and other consequences they had long voiced in the press, in meetings with county officials and elsewhere. They claimed the Board's action in granting the rezoning was arbitrary, capricious and therefore unlawful. They also cited provisions in the Virginia Constitution and Statutes requiring that rezoning must insure that a tract would provide "healthy surroundings for family life", reasonably free of environmental pollution and thus promote the health, safety and welfare of those who would eventually live in and around the tract. Plaintiffs claimed the Board had failed to consider these questions. The Plaintiffs, therefore, prayed that the Court enter a declaratory judgment that the Board's decision was null and void.

In the weeks immediately following filing of Plaintiffs petition, the Court disposed of interlocutory procedural issues concerning parties to the suit and other matters and on November 15th began hearing testimony in the matter in sessions that lasted for several days and some evenings.

On December 23rd Judge Paul D. Brown released his decision that, in effect, denied Plaintiffs' requested action to reverse the County Board decision to grant the requested rezoning, and dismissed the case. Judge Brown held, in pertinent part:

> *"The issue is not whether the Court favors or does not favor the building of the proposed 'Pentagon City' The issue is whether the County Board in enacting the zoning legislation acted in a manner which was clearly unreasonable, arbitrary and capricious and without reasonable or substantial relation to the public health, morals or general welfare. A further legal principle involved is that: The Court will not substitute its judgment for that of a legislative body, and if the reasonableness of a zoning ordinance is fairly debatable, it must be sustained...the Court finds that the reasonableness of the zoning site is clearly debatable. Accordingly...the prayers of the Petitioners are denied."*

The Court also held that the petitioners had a right to complain and it examined the question of the impact of pollution on the area and petitioners. Concerning the possible pollution, the Court held that insufficient evidence had been presented on this point to justify granting petitioners' request. It said, "...reasonable men may differ as to whether this pollutant (auto exhausts) will violate standards for the horizon year...plaintiffs have been unable to show that man's knowledge of this kind of pollutant as of the zoning date was such that a zoning of a thirty two million dollar property should be delayed...the complaint of the air pollution must fail...Overall the zoning action has not been proved to be arbitrary and capricious. The result is to sustain the action of the County Board."

In January of 1977, PCCC appealed Judge Brown's decision to the Virginia Supreme Court. On July 28th, the Supreme Court held there was "no reversible error" and denied the appeal. On September 8, the Court denied a petition for rehearing as related elsewhere herein. On December 1, the PCCC petitioned the U. S. Supreme

Court to review the decision of the Arlington County Board (via a writ of certiorari). The Court, on January 28, 1978, issued its order declining to review the matter and thus bringing the Pentagon City litigation and rezoning challenge to final end.

PENTAGON CITY AND "CENTRE" TODAY

In the ensuing months and years, the development of the Pentagon City tract proceeded and at this writing has been long completed. The South Arlington citizens involved in the struggle pursued their opposition with an intensity, vigor, skill, determination, and full commitment rarely matched elsewhere or at other times by any civic group locally or in other American communities. While some may view them as unsuccessful and undertaking a futile task having not achieved all their desires before the zoning Board or in the courts, it can probably also be correctly argued that while they lost the battle, they won the war overall. Because of their persistent and unyielding demands on the developers, numerous concessions were made that has resulted in the development being a less dense and congested asset to the community. The "mini city" is remarkably popular and well accepted as demonstrated by the crowds of shoppers and others who are continuously and increasingly attracted to the hotel, office, apartments, department stores, "Fashion Center" shopping facilities, and other amenities offered.

In a March 23, 1995 update on the Pentagon City and its across the street more recently opened partner the Pentagon Centre, the Arlington Journal details the success of the numerous operations in and around Pentagon City. Writer Michael Scully points out that the converted former AT&T/Western Electric warehouses across Hayes Street from Pentagon City now sports numerous new shopping and commercial activities. In addition to a branch of the Price Club there are tenants such as Best Buy, Linens and Things, Marshalls Department Store, Fresh Choice, Borders Books, California Pizza Kitchen, Starbucks Coffee and Chevys Mexican Restaurant, each of which are stores usually bustling with customers.

Scully reported that in interviews shoppers agreed they were pleased with the newer Pentagon Centre complex as well as the Fashion Center at the main Pentagon City shopping complex. He quoted Kristin Davidson of Alexandria as feeling that the area had many factors working for it and saying, "...it is right off the George Washington Parkway, the Metro and I-395. For me it's halfway between work and home."

Undoubtedly the "battle" over the Pentagon City development, and its commercial colleagues later opened around it, notwithstanding early criticisms, will stand for long times to come as one of the more successful Arlington urban struggles involving land use and development. Credit for this must rest to a large extent with those South Arlington civic activists who fought without yielding at their own inconvenience, without pay or other financial compensation, and today largely without any recognition. For sure, the community owes them a debt that will never be adequately paid.

ARLINGTON COUNTY VIRGINIA - A Modern History

The Crystal City Nursing Center on South Hayes, a part of the Pentagon City rezoning proposal.

Pentagon Center across South Hayes Street and to the east of the Pentagon City Fashion Center with retail outlets to include the COSTCO/Price Club, Best Buy, Borders Books, Marshalls and other shops.

Major Community "Battles" and Controversies

Round XI
THE BATTLE FOR SOUND WALLS

WALLS DOWN AND UP

In the closing years of the 20th Century and the ending of the Communist Cold War, the world witnessed walls tumbling down in Berlin, Germany to the great satisfaction of residents nearby and around the world.

In Arlington County, Virginia, many residents were vastly more interested in seeing walls go up. Sound barrier walls that is - that would provide some relief from the distressing and blaring noise pollution from modern high speed highways through urban residential neighborhoods. With the ever increasing number of interstate highways and freeways, and constantly expanding numbers of lanes on them, and nearly 24 hour daily traffic of noisy trucks, motorcycles, and other vehicles, life for many city dwellers had become nerve wracking and in some locations all but totally intolerable. People found that they could not sleep peacefully, go onto their patios, or into their yards without shouting at each other to be heard above the roar of traffic noise.

SOUND WALLS IN NORTH ARLINGTON

Arlingtonians living in the northern half of the county had met with considerable, or some, success. Interstate Highway I-66, discussed elsewhere herein, had been designed and completed with extensive sound walls, bermes, vegetation, and other measures to reasonably insure that the road would have minimum or no adverse impact on residents along its borders. Moreover, trucks were prohibited from being operated on the road. The road has been widely viewed as a model for the nation in dealing with noise problems. It is safe to say, allowing for some isolated disagreement, that most Arlingtonians living in its general area, do not even know, from sound levels, that the highway is even there.

Other Arlintonians living in mid-county, but literally just barely in the northern half of the county in their neighborhood along the north side of U. S. Route 50

(Arlington Boulevard) had obtained some sound walls and relief through litigation. Route 50 marks the dividing line between the north and south halves of the county and winds its way around Ft Myer and thence westward to the county line in the Seven Corners area.

In a law suit filed on December 23, 1988 [76] by Attorney Cary P. Sklar, who also lives in the subject area, the plaintiffs outlined the nature of the harmful noise effects of U. S. Route 50 on them, and asked for declaratory and injunctive relief and a mandamus. The Plaintiffs contended that the defendants had failed to comply with their statutory requirements concerning noise abatement in road construction in plaintiffs' area to their harm. They asked that defendants be required to implement noise abatement measures by constructing an appropriate barrier on the north side of Route 50 between Carlin Springs Road and Manchester Street.

In a Memorandum Opinion (and Order) released May 16, 1990, following extensive filings and testimony, Judge Norma Holoway Johnson essentially agreed with the plaintiffs and granted them the relief requested. She stated, in part, that the defendants' "decision not to incorporate a noise barrier at ... the Route 50 project must be set aside, because it was based on a policy that was contrary to federal law". In her discussion of the defendants' obligations in addressing the reasonableness of noise abatement measures she quoted from a Federal Highway Administration Guideline of the factors that should be considered, which she concluded had not been met. They were:

(1) noise abatement benefits,
(2) cost of abatement,
(3) views of the impacted residents,
(4) absolute noise levels,
(5) change in noise levels,
(6) development along the existing highway, and
(7) environmental impacts of abatement construction.

* * *

SOUND WALL EFFORTS IN SOUTH ARLINGTON

Residents of Arlington County living in the southern half of the county had not been as successful as their neighbors in North Arlington in obtaining sound barriers along the two major roadways, one of which could be expected to generate oppressive traffic noise.

The transformation of U. S. Route 1 (Jeff-Davis highway) into Interstate I-595 in the 1970s did not include the construction of any significant sound barriers, nor were any particularly needed. The roadway is not a high speed throughway, is only a little over a mile in length, and is not usually a route chosen by truck drivers or motorists for use for other than local deliveries or destinations.

---

76 *Civil Action No. 88-3645, Boulevard Manor Civic Accosiation, et al, v. U.S. Secretary of Transportation, Administrator, Federal Highway Administration, Virginia Secretary of Transportation, et al.*

Major Community "Battles" and Controversies

The situation on Interstate I-395 (formerly Shirley Highway and then I-95) with respect to traffic noise was and is quite another matter. That roadway constitutes, in effect, a part of the principal east coast north-south "main street" of America from Florida to Maine. While much of the through traffic may by-pass Arlington and flow around the inner metropolitan area by way of the I-495 "beltway", a sizeable amount of it with inner city destinations or departures points will not. The road is also the primary Northern Virginia north-south commuter road and, except during congested rush hour periods of slowly moving bumper to bumper traffic, is a high speed route that generates the most shrilling and penetrating traffic noises.

There are also no restrictions for I-395 on the size or number of trucks not only from the north or south, but also from the west. Since trucks from or to the west are not permitted to travel on the portions of I-66 inside the beltway that includes the Arlington portions of the road, they must find other routes. Nor are heavy trucks permitted on Route 50 in Arlington also running, generally, east-west. Thus east-west traffic must exit from, or approach, I-66 outside the beltway by way of the beltway and most likely use I-395 through Arlington in the process.

In the 1970's the Virginia Department of Highways (VDH) with mostly Federal financing was in full swing on its massive project to greatly widen and "upgrade" to interstate standards the World War II four lane Shirley Highway that ran southward through Arlington and Fairfax Counties from the Potomac River and the 14th Bridge. Upon the completion of the project, first labeled as Interstate I-95 and later I-395, residents along the sides of the road began to understand in full measure the profoundly adverse impact the new road was having on them.

Interstate Highway 395 at South 20th Street in Arlington showing no open space buffer zone between the highway and adjacent homes on Army Navy Drive.

Unlike interstate and many other principal highways in rural areas, and even some urban areas, I-395 in the Arlington location was not bordered by a 150 feet or more open space between its shoulders and the nearby residents. Most of the residents lived along Army-Navy Drive that parallels I-395 with no open buffer space whatever between them and the high speed multi-lanes of I-395. Residents in the Fairlington housing complex between Glebe Road and Route 7 were and are a little better off. There was, and is, some open space between them and I-395, but their location on a hill side over looking the highway insures that they too are subjected to a substantial amount of traffic noise. The highway traffic noise quickly became oppressive and overbearing. Peaceful and enjoyable living ceased to be the norm for homeowners and others in the area. The citizens became restless and aggressively sought relief from public officials. Their annoyance, impatience and demand for assistance steadily increased with each passing month and year.

THE START OF CITIZEN PROTEST

In the period of the late 1970s, citizen activists from the Arlington Ridge Civic Association, or individuals on their own to include this author, made repeated visits and appeals to County officials for relief. They asked for sound barriers and for replacement of ineffective reed vegetation that had been planted in their areas along the chain link fence of the highway at the time of the Shirley highway upgrading project of the 1970s.

The lack of protection from traffic noise received wider public attention on October 29, 1980, when Arlington Journal writer Jim Wolfe in an article headlined "Residents Rap I-395 Shrubbery" described the irritation of the situation on residents. He described the topography of the area and the fact that the neighborhoods were mostly on a sloping hill side running from Arlington Ridge above, downward to the edge of the highway. Wolfe quoted one resident as saying, "its like being in the first row balcony of the Eisenhower Theater in Kennedy Center. The acoustics are magnificent and the over powering sound comes right at us. Not a decibel of sound goes unnoticed ".

In due course, with the help and cooperation of the County Director of Public Works, H. S. Hulme, Jr., the matter of vegetation screening was resolved to some satisfaction of the residents. The original buckthorn and reed plantings of the Virginia Highway Department were replaced with evergreen Leland Cypress and Red Cedar plants that do not shed leaves or growth in winter and also are taller than the former bushes. The vegetation provided some relief from the visual pollution of glaring vehicle lights and air pollution from engines. Still remaining, however, was the far more odious and  obnoxious impacts of traffic noise. Wolfe wrote that Hulme had said, "The only way to make a big dent in the noise level, would be to build sound barriers, but I don't think anyone is proposing that."

As if to disillusion Hulme of any misimpressions that no one was proposing sound barriers, Joseph Pisciotta, a resident on Army Navy Drive, and this author appeared before the County Board on October 15, 1981 and advised the members that a poll had been taken of the affected residents on the question of their positions on the matter of sound barriers along I-395. The results of the poll in a signed petition form was submitted to the Board. It contained the names of residents in the 20 acre Forest Hills Townhouse development at 23rd and Army Navy Drive, all residents on Army-Navy Drive and on intersecting side streets in houses close enough to be within reasonable hearing of traffic noise. All of the several dozen signatories of the petition, except two who were indifferent, indicated they desired that an effective sound wall be constructed.

YEARS LATER

Over the next several years, the proponents of sound walls along I-395 continued to prod the County and State officials for forward movement on the matter. On July 1, 1987 this author wrote to Public Works Director Hulme again and referred to the petition of citizens submitted to the County Board more than five years earlier. The letter read, in part:

> "While countless bucks are being spent elsewhere in the (Washington metro) area for magnificent (noise) screening in areas where there is a wide buffer right-of-way between major interstates and abutting neighborhoods, we here have 395 practically in our living rooms and there is not a shred of protection of any type".

On July 23rd Director Hulme answered the above letter. He said he had contacted the Virginia Department of Transportation (VDOT) to see if their policies on sound walls had changed in the past 6 years. Hulme reported that the policies had not been changed and were still not to "retrofit" walls along a highway "unless some other major work is being done at the same time."

MEDIA ATTENTION

By summer's end help from the media for sound wall proponents began to emerge. On August 31st, the Arlington Journal in an editorial headed "Wall of Silence", the editor wrote, "There is plenty of reason to sympathize with people who live within a stones throw of Interstate 95 (later 395)...they want sound walls to keep the noise of the highway from intruding on their lives. It's a reasonable request." Then, on October 7th, the Journal published a feature article with a banner headline on page one, referring to this author, "Lawyer wants State to wall out noise." The article effectively and in convincing detail outlined the severity of the noise problem for citizens along I-395. The Journal article included a staff photograph of the author with neighbors Frank Delatour and Admiral Gustave Johansen standing alongside the highway and demonstrating the close proximity of homes to the road shoulders.

On October 5th, this author again wrote to Director Hulme and stated that his letter of July 23rd was not considered "satisfactory or very responsive to our problem and needs", nor indicate that, "you are in fact very much concerned about our situation", and whether Hulme had made any effort to persuade the VDOT to change its policy on sound walls for completed projects. The letter stressed that not providing sound walls for I-395 in South Arlington, while extensively doing so in other less critical areas was unfairly discriminatory, and that the Director should carry the matter back to the State where his voice as a public official would carry more weight than that of private citizens. On October 9th, Hulme responded in writing and said he would again "raise the issue of noise abatement along Shirley Highway" with the State, but he pointed out that "VDOT's six year construction and funding plan contains no funds for any project within Arlington County that is not already under construction."

On November 23rd, Hulme again wrote and said he had heard from VDOT Commissioner Ray Pethtel who stated the State did not have a retrofit noise abatement program nor did they anticipate developing one in the foreseeable future," that "there is no fiscally feasible way" to maintain such a program, and that "an exception for Shirley highway would neither be legally nor morally an acceptable option" for VDOT (emphasis supplied). Hulme did not explain Pethtel's basis or rationale for concluding that providing sound walls for besieged residents along I-395 would not be legal or moral.

"Noise relief immoral?"

In November of 1987, the Journal, in a graphic and explicit article by writer Mark Grossman added further light on the adverse impacts of interstate highways on residents living along an interstate highway. He alluded to the situation of Fairfax County residents living along I-66 but who were farther from that road than were the Arlington residents from I-395. Grossman wrote in part,

> "...residents equate the constant highway noise they hear to a roaring ocean...windows stay shut and conversations can't be held in back yards facing the busy highway...the noise also has taken the joy out of playing Little League baseball (in a nearby park)."

Following the 1987 developments outlined above, highway noise, tempers and frustrations continued to rise in the South Arlington I-395 corridor. Citizens searched for any additional avenues in which to seek relief. Responses from State Officials had contended that the Virginia policy on not retrofitting completed highways with sound barriers was not of their making but, rather, a requirement of the Federal highway Department.

Finally, on November 15, 1990, U.S. Air Force Retired General C. M. Talbott, President of the Forest Hills Community Association, and Mary Dabinett, President of the Arlington Ridge Civic Association, wrote letters on the matter to the Members of the Arlington County Board, U. S. Senators John Warner and Charles Robb, and Representative Frank Wolfe, VDOT Secretary John Milliken, and Virginia State Senator Edward Holland and Delegate Warren Stambough. [77]

In their letters, Talbott and Dabinett pleaded for "meaningful and serious assistance on a matter of critical importance to our citizens who live along I-395...and are painfully impacted to their great detriment by constant and deafening noise from that highway". They alluded to the extensive sound barriers being constructed throughout the

---

[77] *Stambough died before receiving the letter addressed to him.*

Major Community "Battles" and Controversies

Washington metro area, asserted "our need is clearly greater", and described the topographical and other features existing in their residential area that added to the noise impact. They asked the addressees to let them know promptly what they planned to do to help and offered to meet with and conduct them through the subject area.

The elected officials in January and February 1991 responded to the letters of the civic association presidents and reported that they had forwarded the letters to the appropriate highway officials for response. Some included responses that simply reflected the previous positions of the VDOT. Senator Warner, however, provided a copy of a letter to him from T. D. Larson, the Administrator of the U. S. Department of Transportation, that clearly and directly contradicted the earlier contentions of the VDOT that the State policy of no retrofitting was required to meet Federal standards. Larson wrote, in part;

> *"The Federal noise regulations...apply to construction projects for which a State highway agency has Federal funding. Each State agency administers the Federal-aid program in its own respective state. Federal law and regulations do not require the State to implement noise abatement along existing highways (retrofit noise abatement). States may voluntarily initiate this type of abatement. They are solely responsible for making this decision." (emphasis supplied).*

Virginia State Transportation Secretary Milliken [78] in his reply to the Civic Association Presidents mostly reiterated the existing State policy of no retrofittings. He offered to meet with all parties concerned to explore local cooperation and funding for noise abatement but cautioned that all levels of government "are painfully financially strapped" at this time.

The Arlington Journal reported on these developments with a November 28th article by staff writer Peter Kaplan headlined "Residents raise ruckus for barriers". Kaplan reported that South Arlingtonians "have renewed demands that the state erect sound barriers to protect homes from noisy traffic on Interstate 395." He wrote they were prompted by the VDOT decision to build noise walls along a stretch of I-66 in Fairfax County and that "residents in Arlington Ridge and Forest Hills...want the same treatment". He wrote further that "Arlington County has planted trees and bushes to put the highway out of sight, but VDOT has steadfastly refused to consider more expensive measures, such as barriers."

"Why no barriers?"

Shortly after the Journal article, on December 14th, County Board Chairman Albert Eisenberg wrote the Civic Association presidents and advised them that the VDOT policy had changed somewhat, and would now allow the funding of sound walls along existing highways up to 50% of costs. Eisenberg added that the County Staff would

---

[78] *Milliken was a past Arlington County Board member and resided on Arlington Ridge Road above and about a city block away from the subject stretch of I-395.*

contact the VDOT "to express our support, to request its evaluation, and to estimate the costs of the I-395 highway project." He said "once we have this information, we can decide on its inclusion in our CIP". (Capital Improvement Program).

1993 FOLLOW UP

On March 31, 1993, new Arlington Ridge and Forest Hills Civic Association Presidents Army General(Ret) Donald M. Babers and Paul Haire wrote new Board Chairman James B. Hunter concerning the matter of sound barriers along I-395. They again referred to the earlier 1990 correspondence, and to Board Chairman Eisenberg's December 1990 letter and his commitment to staff action and possible inclusion of a project in the county's CIP. The Presidents wrote that two years had passed and they had not heard further from the Board or Staff on the matter and asked for a report of any progress to date.

Shortly after the above letters, a news item appeared in the Washington Post, on April 17th, by writer Stephen C. Fehr. With a headline "Va Breaks its rule, Offers to help pay for Noise Walls Near I-66". Fehr wrote that the state transportation board had made an exception to its policy and would pay about two-thirds of the $1.1 million cost of walls on Route 28 in the Centreville area. He wrote further, in part,

> "The decision puts pressure on county officials, who say building barriers on interstate highways is the state's responsibility and the county does not have the money. They worry the state has set a precedent that could lead more neighborhoods along the Capital Beltway, I-66 and Shirley Highway to ask the county for money for barriers, which reduces the noise that can be heard from traffic."

In the aftermath of the Post news item, Presidents Babers and Haire again wrote Board Chairman Hunter. Alluding to the news item, they wrote that "...it appears we too could benefit by such a policy reversal. We again urge you, and the Board as our elected officials to get actively and meaningfully involved in this matter and throw your weight behind our efforts to obtain relief...May we hear from you promptly...?"

Shortly afterwards, Fehr wrote another article for the Washington Post headlined "Along Noisy Interstates, a Hue and Cry for a Wall". In that article he discussed in depth the traffic noise conditions along area interstate and other heavily traveled roads. He included an inset box headed "Understanding Highway Noise" in which he outlined methods for measuring sound, factors in traffic noise including volume, trucks and speed, and guidelines in the various metropolitan jurisdictions. Journal writer Amy Resnick on April 9, 1993 published a similar article headed "Tempers rise along I-395". She quoted VDOT spokeswoman Stacy Pruitt who again outlined the policy against retrofitting highways with sound barriers, and said "...we simply do not have funds to put up sound walls on any road."

On July 24, 1995, Post writer Fehr again addressed the highway noise problem in an item headed "Highway Noise Studied". He wrote that "Under increasing pressure from people who live near noisy highways, officials in Maryland and Virginia are considering ways to make it easier to have sound barriers erected in suburban

Major Community "Battles" and Controversies

neighborhoods of Washington and Baltimore". He said Virginia DOT officials said they were evaluating the state's wall policy with "a report by the policy setting Commonwealth Transportation Board due before the end of the year".

On that more optimistic note, it appeared more hopeful than ever that the besieged residents of South Arlington may yet realize relief from the oppressive noises of traffic on one of the largest and heaviest traveled highways in the country running through their neighborhood. At this writing, however, it remains to be seen whether that result will materialize or the form that it will take. The promised policy report by the end of the year had not been released "by the end of the year" (1995) as promised. Nor was the report forthcoming in 1996.

* * *

A HISTORY VIGNETTE - A Break in the Text

Dawson Terrace Recreation Center on North Taft Street in Arlington. A part of the structure is the remains of the original Dawson family home.

The Dawson home, Abingdon at the National Airport, and the John Ball house on South Third Street, all dating from the early 18th Century, are the oldest extant homesites in the County. As indicated on the above marker, and some later reports in the Virginia Room of the Central Arlington Library, there is some uncertainty concerning the precise age of the Dawson structure.

Round XII
THE US RT 1-JEFF DAVIS UPGRADE TO I-595

BACKGROUND

With massive high rise and dense development in and around the Crystal City most southeastern parts of Arlington County beginning in the late 1960's, it was generally known that major redesign of the area's Route 1 "main street" was about to take place. It also was recognized that any major work could only be carried out by obtaining Federal funds for construction.

In the period 1966 to 1969 the Virginia Department of Highways and Transportation (VDH&T) completed their proposed plans for a new highway on the Route 1 location. In March 1970 the Department held "location and design" hearings in the local community and in September the Department approved the features as presented at the March hearings. Federal Highway Administration (FHWA) approval followed in October. In the following months, the FHWA also removed the road from the Federal-Aid Urban program and added it to the Interstate system which increased the Federal contribution from 50% to 90% of the costs.

At the March 1970 public meeting, Virginia State highway officials unveiled their plans for the new road. It was to be about 3/4 mile in length, of 6 or 8 lanes, and be designated I-595. It would run from I-95 (now I-395) on the north, to the National Airport overpass on the south. The road was to have elevated overpasses at three intersections. The roadway would peak at about 30 feet on south 15th street, return to street level near 20th street, and rise again to 18 feet at south 23rd street. The projected cost was expected to be around $20 million, but perhaps more if construction was delayed for any reason. The purpose of the road was represented to be "to provide a better link between the airport and I-95 and to reduce traffic congestion and safety hazards" along the then four lane, no median strip, Route 1.

CITIZEN REACTION

Citizen reaction to the VDH&T proposal was overwhelmingly in opposition. Washington Post Staff writer Nancy Scannell in an article headlined "Citizens Decry Crystal City Freeway" quoted speakers from the nearby Aurora Highlands and Arlington Ridge Civic Associations as testifying that while they wanted "the area's chronic traffic problems solved" they "opposed the solution offered by the state highway department".

Shortly after the public meeting a local civic activist, Steve Krum, later to become Chairman of the County Planning Commission, formed the Jefferson Davis Corridor Transportation Coalition [79] to oppose the road as planned and met with the

---

[79] *Not to be confused with the later Board appointed Jefferson Davis Corridor Ad Hoc Committee. Members included civic activists and nearby residents Robert*

Major Community "Battles" and Controversies

Virginia Governor. Barry Bretschneider, a coalition member said that the proposed highway would constitute a "Great Wall of China" separating the office and residential complexes on the two sides of the road, and would be visually objectional by looking "like a roller coaster" with its up and down elevations. Herman Jensen of the Aurora Highlands Association said he opposed any zoning that would mean more development and suggested having as much green open space as possible. Another Association member, George W. Downes said the whole area "should be designated as polluted and if anyone wants to build there, they should consider its pollution aspects".

Citizens also claimed, among other things, that there would be unacceptable noise and pollution from the new road, gridlock traffic congestion, and that there had been no environmental impact assessment as required by Federal Law.

Following the intensity of citizen complaints, and probably as a result of them, VHD&T decided not to proceed with the construction of I-595 until an environmental impact statement had been prepared. In January 1973 VHD&T announced plans to prepare such a statement and on April 1973 it held another location and design public hearing.

COUNTY BOARD REACTION

Notwithstanding the avalanche of opposition from residents near the highway, and from elsewhere in the county, the County Board on December 13, 1973 by resolution unanimously urged immediate construction of I-595. Board member Joseph Fisher, however warned that the action might throw the county into a long legal dispute that would block construction since there had not yet been an environmental statement, and he said he was backing the resolution "reluctantly". Board member Everard Munsey urged the Board to notify the State authorities of the Board action and called for immediate improvements along South Glebe Road between Route 1 and Shirley Highway (I-95). Nancy Scannell wrote in the Post under the headline "Arlington Board Backs Link From I-95 to National" that there was disagreement as to whether an environmental statement was required. While Board members and county transportation director Henry S. Hulme claimed they did not know if a statement was required, opposition activists strongly insisted a statement was required, Scannell wrote.

In the following months, and years, dialogue on the road by opponents continued, and County Board enthusiasm for the projected widening of Route 1 seemed to wane. Opponents continued to feel that the widening would add to traffic congestion and pollution. Proponents insisted that I-595 would eliminate bottlenecks and relieve traffic problems on nearby residential streets. VDH&T completed its environmental study and statement and opponents immediately criticized it as inadequate. Citizen opposition continued to build and in February, 1976 the Arlington Board appointed a special task force to be known at the Jefferson Davis Corridor Ad Hoc Committee. The group was to be comprised of two representatives each from the County Planning Commission, Transportation Commission and Environmental Improvement Commission, and one

---

Merchant, Emmy Lou Runyan, Herman Jensen, Richard Staley (later to become chairman), and Barry Bretschneider.

representative each from the Arlington Ridge, Aurora Highlands, River House Tenants, and Crystal City Civic Associations. Later, a representative from the Pentagon City Coordinating Committee (PCCC) joined the committee. The PCCC at the time was active in fighting the Pentagon City rezoning matter.

In a March 4, 1976 Arlington Journal article, headlined "Interstate: Pedestrian Roadblock", staff writer Marilyn Chase quoted Board Chairman Ellen M. Bozman as feeling that the proposed road was "totally unsatisfactory from the pedestrian point of view." She wondered if the road could not be reduced from 6 or 8 lanes to four lanes and said "...pedestrian crossing is most acutely needed between the south side of 23rd street and the north side of 18th Street, particularly around 20th Street. Chase wrote that Transportation Planning Division Chief John Hummel shared that view. She wrote further that Bozman felt there was not much the Board could do at that point and "our only recourse would be to file our objections" with the State authorities. Board member John W. Purdy noted other shortcomings in the proposed road. He said, "With regard to air quality the environmental impact statement appears to rely on data of questionable applicability". He alluded to meteorological data from 1950 that, he said, did not take into account "the mass of high rise buildings to the west of Crystal City and (as far as) Arlington Ridge.

Former President of the Aurora Highlands Association Herman Jensen found little he liked in the road proposal or the environmental statement. In a letter to the Editor of the Arlington Journal published March 11, he wrote in part:

> *"It is almost unbelievable that VDH&T would continue to consider building I-595...and even more incredible that the Federal Highway Administration would approve it...the I-595 will not work without the Potomac Expressway which has been removed from all Arlington County Planning maps...the pedestrian has not been considered at all...free right turns will be allowed on and off the ramps...if autos have free right turns how is the pedestrian going to get across...the highway will cut off the east side of Route 1 which contains shopping offices and apartments primarily from the west...it will be very difficult to get to the Metro station...there are no provisions for express buses...the impact statement (does not) contain any statistics or explanation to explain their claim that vehicles miles will be reduced by constructing this highway...these are only a few (of the drawbacks)...others are air quality, noise, aesthetics and loss of green space."*

The County Board considered the matter of I-595 further at its meeting on March 22, disapproved any I-595 construction until certain conditions were met concerning design and environmental impacts as reported by Keith Girard in the Northern Virginia Sun. As a result of that meeting, Girard wrote, "the Board informed federal and state highway officials as well as the U. S. Council on Environmental Quality that the highway was unacceptable" and it requested another plan for the corridor. He wrote further that the Board considered key issues to be "increased consideration of bus and car pool lanes, improvements of South Glebe Road near Shirley Highway (I-95) and (construction of) pedestrian bridges, especially in the Clark Street area at State expense".

Major Community "Battles" and Controversies

A view of the Jeff-Davis corridor looking east from the National Airport overpass.

Arlington Journal writer Chris Jensen wrote, concerning the Board's disapproval of the road's design, that county officials were not certain that such action could stop the highway since Federal and State officials had already approved the plans and the environmental statement. He quoted County Transportation Director Henry Hulme as saying, "The process is a bit cloudy at this point". Jensen wrote that Planning Commission Chairman Stephen Krum had suggested that Arlington might try to have the Council of Government remove the highway from the regional transportation plan which could prevent use of Federal funds for the project. Jensen wrote, however, that some transportation officials had quietly expressed doubt that such action could be taken retroactively since the project had already been approved.

On August 2nd, Girard of the Sun wrote that the Board had again met (on July 31st) and discussed the I-595 situation. The Board, no doubt aware by now of increasing citizen discontent, seemed to further retreat from its earlier strong insistence that the highway be built immediately and the Board agonized over what to do next. Girard wrote that "The County Board is looking for a way to express its displeasure with I-595 in South Arlington - but doesn't know how to say it". He reported that "a contractor had been selected to begin construction on the project (and) citizen alarm arose over the unaddressed conditions set by the Board".

Board member John Purdy advocated that the Board take a strong stand in opposition and "stand fast". He moved that the Board go on record as favoring the abandonment of the current design in favor of a new proposal. He said "what we are finding is a state bureaucratic dictatorship which snowballs once it is set in motion and there is no turning back." Board member Ellen Bozman commented, "what this calls for is to stop the project and conduct a complete examination (but) I don't believe, more pragmatically, that it will happen". Member Joseph Wholey said he feared the highway would be constructed without the changes sought by Arlington that are in the process of being met. The intent is to insure a coordinated design." In the end, Purdy's motion was tabled by a vote of 3 to 2 with Wholey and Bozman voting in favor. Wholey argued that the road was needed to avoid strangulation in the densely developed area and that concessions in the design were more likely if "we don't upset the apple cart".

On August 10th the County Board again considered the I-595 matter and specifically the resolution of member Purdy that had been tabled at the July 31st meeting. The resolution, among other things, asked the State to defer final awarding of contracts on I-595 until certain specified alterations were made and to submit a new plan for the highway. Purdy moved that his resolution be removed from the table (and now considered), but his motion died for lack of a second. This left the Board's position on I-595 the same as it was in March. Purdy told the Arlington Journal reporter Katie Elberfeld, "I don't think that tabling a motion is a complete act; it's burying it...I would have hoped that the motion could have been brought up and voted up or down".

The action by the Board in not voting on the strong resolution of member Purdy was perceived by opponents of the highway as being less of a strong stand in opposition than they desired. It clearly moved them ever closer to resorting to litigation in an effort to obtain relief from what they considered the adverse effects on them of the I-595 construction.

Reporter Girard wrote that Purdy's position that the project should be abandoned in favor of a new proposal similar to one from the Pentagon City Coordinating Committee (PCCC), the recently formed ad-hoc citizen group from South Arlington. That group had filed suit opposing the rezoning of land for Pentagon City and was threatening to do the same to stop construction of I-595.

LAW SUIT CONTEMPLATED

On August 4, attorney Geoffrey Judd Vitt, of the Alexandria Law firm of Cogen, Vitt and Annand, wrote to the members of the Arlington County Board and advised that it was representing citizens' groups who were opposed to the construction of I-595 as planned, to wit: The Hospitality House Motor Inn; Stouffer's National Center Hotel; the PCCC; and the Arlington Ridge and Aurora Highlands Civic Associations.

Attorney Vitt stated that his clients supported the Resolution passed by the Board on March 23 and urged that the Board again go on record in opposition to I-595 as presently contemplated. He enumerated the extent to which his clients considered the plans deficient with respect to:

(1) improvements beyond the Airport Viaduct to the county line;
(2) the failure of Stae officials to satisfactorily address the matter of pedestrian bridges;
(3) inadequate improvements for Eads Street;
(4) failure to make the Ball Street connection a part of the project;
(5) insufficient attention to aesthetic consideration that will result in I-595 becoming an austere, monolithic structure with a "Great Wall of China" effect on South Arlington;
(6) no noise abatement measures are planned;
(7) uncertainty of VDH&T position in solving obvious safety hazards between 20th and 23rd Streets;

Major Community "Battles" and Controversies

(8) no VDH&T commitments regarding the mass transit oriented request of the Board; and

(9) insufficient attention to likely heavy airport traffic problems and traffic flow into Crystal City from 15th and 18th Streets.

# # #

In its August newsletter, the Aurora Highlands Civic Association reported that its President, Peggy Horton, had recently joined a delegation that met for three hours with John Harwood, the State Highway Commissioner. Delegation members included John Quinn, President of PCCC, Derk and Nancy Swain of the Arlington Ridge Civic Association, Ellen Bozman, Chairman(person) of the County Board, Henry Hulme, Arlington Transportation Director, and civic activist Louise Chesnut. The delegation urged the Department to abandon the present design and consider alternative designs of smaller scale. Harwood told the delegation, however, that the project was already too far along to consider abandoning it, but that he was open to suggestions for modification.

As the August days rolled past, events surrounding the I-595 project moved steadily and ominously closer to litigation for a resolution of opposing positions. On August 5th, Journal writer Suzi Shuman reported that the State highway commission had awarded a contract to Slattery Associates, Inc., of New York to begin construction on the highway, which would only be three-quarters of a mile long in length, or only to the airport overpass and far short of the county line at Four Mile Run. She wrote that a suit by three civic associations and two prominent hotel owners was expected to be filed within two weeks.

Writer Shuman quoted attorney Stephen D. Annand, council for the plaintiffs, as saying that his clients were reluctant to file suit, but that "the department has not adequately answered the questions the plaintiffs ask, which mainly concern noise and pollution levels", but also included the items enumerated by the law firm in its letter of August 2nd to the Board. The Shuman article explained that John Reiss, of the Stouffer Hotel opposed the highway because of a 20 foot concrete ramp that would obstruct the public's view of the hotel and complicate access for guests arriving from the airport.

The probable cause of the Hospitality Inn's opposition to the road as planned, was revealed in a Journal article by reporter Chris Jensen. He told of a dispute, and law suit, between the State highway department and the Motor Inn over the price of a parcel of land needed for the construction of the road, resulting in the filing of a condemnation suit against the American Realty Trust Company that owned the property. The land in question bordered on the Hospitality Inn along the highway and on the south side of 20th Street. The state offered the Trust company about $100,000 for the property which was rejected. The company contended that its loss of its full use of the land came closer to $750,000. It claimed the highway would "bring a ramp right across the fourth floor" and "cars would be driving through right by the swimming pool". The suit was not aimed at stopping construction of the highway but only to determine how much the owner should receive for the property. This writer has been unable to learn the outcome of the suit which was probably settled by out of court compromise and such settlements are usually confidential and thus not made public.

ARLINGTON COUNTY VIRGINIA - A Modern History

LAW SUIT FILED

True to predictions, on August 24, 1976, suit was filed in the U. S. District Court for the Eastern District of Virginia in Alexandria, by the Vitt, Annand and Cohen law firm to enjoin the construction of the I-595 highway in Crystal City. The plaintiffs in the suit were The Pentagon City Coordinating Committee, Inc.; the Arlington Ridge Civic Association; the Aurora Highlands Civic Association; The Stouffer Corporation; and the Hospitality Management Company, Inc. The defendants were shown as William T. Coleman, U. S. Department of Transportation, Norbert T. Tiemann, Administrator, Federal Highway Administration, and John E. Harwood, Commissioner, Virginia Department of Highways and Transportation.

The complaint for injunctive relief outlined the history of the proposal to build the I-595 road, and listed eight claims for relief, to wit: (paraphrased)

(1) Defendants have violated the National Environmental Policy Act of 1969 (NEPA) by not providing the required environmental impact study and statement;

(2) Defendants did not hold the proper type of public hearings as required by NEPA that should have considered design and corridor factors and economic and social impacts on the environment;

(3) Defendant Coleman failed, with respect to a related public park, to consider feasible and prudent alternatives to the use of the park;

(4) Defendant Coleman failed to promulgate guidelines to assure full and appropriate consideration as required by NEPA of "possible adverse economic, social and environmental effects", such as air, noise and water pollution, disruption of man-made and natural resources, adverse employment effects, injurious displacement of people, and disruption of desirable community and regional growth;

(5) Defendant Coleman failed to follow required NEPA requirements concerning noise levels, and acted illegally and was arbitrary, capricious and abused his discretion when he granted the State exemptions from applicable noise standards;

(6) Defendants Coleman and Tiemann were arbitrary, capricious and acted with an abuse of discretion in violation of law when they improperly approved a plan for implementation of air quality standards and regional quality control for the I-595 highway;

(7) Defendants Coleman and Tiemann violated law when they approved the plan for I-595 that did not adequately consider whether the road would be a "safe" highway; and

(8) Defendants Coleman and Tiemann violated NEPA when they failed to consider the merits of I-595 as a part of a continuing comprehensive planning process that included considering the views of responsible local officials, i.e., the Arlington County Board and the Alexandria City Council.

In the months following the filing of the I-595 suit, numerous meetings took place between the Plaintiffs and Defendants and their legal councils. Out of court concessions were made by the Defendants that narrowed the differences in their positions with respect to the character of the proposed road and thus helped to avoid a full dress trial in the case. These developments did not result in the reduction in lanes to four as desired by most of the plaintiffs, but they did achieve certain objectives favored by plaintiffs. Chief among these were (1) the modification of designs by eliminating elevated crossings at 18th, 23rd, or other intersections, (2) the inclusion of a pedestrian underground crossing at 23rd Street, and (3) the extension of the improvements beyond the airport overpass and farther to the county line at Four Mile Run.

Additionally, concerning concessions in design by Defendants, on December 6th State Assistant Attorney General John J. Beall, Jr., wrote that VDH&T had directed its contractor to do the following as had been requested by plaintiffs:

1. Remove cement barricades.
2. Patch test holes made by utilities.
3. Replace most gutters and curbs that had been removed.
4. Remove shoring and sheet piling on wall, west side of Route 1, between 12th and 15th streets.
5. Finish swimming pool at the Americana Motor Inn.
6. Resurface 23rd Street between Route 1 and Eads Street.
7. Replace the old entrance to the Americana.
8. Replace soil and reseed demolition sites at 15th and 20th streets.
9. Remove detour preparations at the Airport connector.
10. Relocate traffic signal pole at 15th Street.
11. Eradicate and repaint pavement markings.

In his letter, the Assistant Attorney General did not indicate whether or not some of these measures were "concessions" or whether they merely constituted routine construction steps that would have been taken even if a law suit was not pending. He did state that it was the Department's overall intention to "restore the Route 1 corridor to its condition ante as best it can given the demolition work".

In due course the trial judge issued his final decree that took into account the above agreed to provisions and work on the roadway continued and was completed.

CONCLUSION OF CONTROVERSY

On May 2, 1977, Chris C. Oynes, Chairman of the Jefferson Davis Corridor Ad Hoc Committee, submitted the Committee's report on land use in the Corridor to Planning Commission Chairman Fred Berghoefer. The report contained the Committee's findings and recommendations for best land use in the corridor if that part of the county was to remain, or become, a "more desirable place to work and live in the 1970's, 1980's, and beyond".

In general, the Oynes report called for maximum retention of existing single family residential areas, and more rigid control on high rise development, particularly offices buildings that generate more workers, traffic, air pollution, and parking problems. The committee recommendations seemed to closely coincide with the positions taken by plaintiffs in their suit over the construction of I-595. Whether the report would have been helpful to the plaintiffs in the law suit in their resistance to I-595 construction will

ARLINGTON COUNTY VIRGINIA - A Modern History

never be known with certainty and can only remain as a matter of conjecture since the report was released just as the court suit was in its final stages.

The matter of the construction of I-595 has constituted one of Arlington County's major controversies in recent history. In a way if can be said to have been a classic example of democracy at its best. Before it was ended the community saw its governing body completely reverse itself when confronted with intense citizen opposition and indignation. At one point early on, the Board official took a firm stand, contrary to citizens expressed preferences, in favor of construction of the road and officially urged that the road be "promptly" built. Before the matter ended, the Board reversed itself and objected to any further work until questions raised by energetic citizens and citizen group were satisfactorily resolved.

Most of those citizens so heavily involved at the time seemed later to feel that their efforts were clearly worthwhile and productive in persuading their governing body to alter its position. While they may not have had their way in every respect, they can surely take credit for a far better designed roadway emerging from their efforts. Many of their predictions of dire consequences concerning traffic gridlocks and adverse impacts on their neighborhoods, however, do not seem to have developed. Conditions in their neighborhoods have not significantly changed or worsened.

Concerning air pollution, and the extent of its harmful effects, one can only say the jury is still out. The Northern Virginia area, including Arlington County remains at this writing one of the most highly air polluted parts of the State. Automobile emissions are generally blamed for this and the Northern counties are some of the few required by the State to have vehicles inspected for emmision control purposes.

Freeway proponents argue that with ease of movement and less need to stop and idle engines less air pollution results. Freeway opponents, on the other hand contend that better and more roads simply attract wider use of the automobile instead of mass transit facilities, and therefore cause more pollution. The day may come when additional measure will be required to better control pollution in the regional area, and especially close in neighborhoods such as the Jefferson Davis corridor. Time will tell.

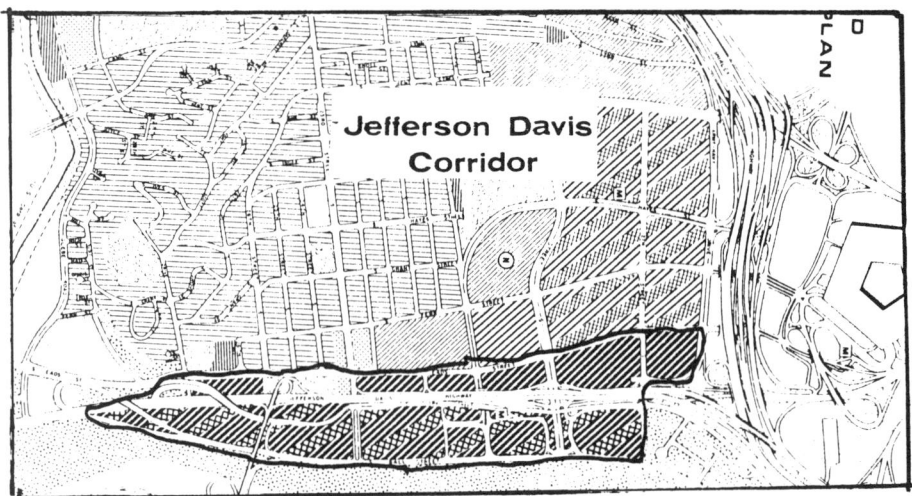

Major Community "Battles" and Controversies

Round XIII
THE SEWAGE TREATMENT PLANT EXPANSION

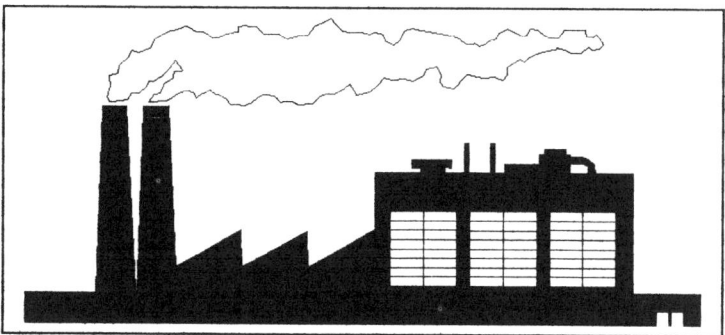

THE LOCATION

The higher elevated residential neighborhoods in the extreme southeastern tip of Arlington County are relatively remote and somewhat isolated. There are no main through roads for commuters to exploit and congest with traffic or fringe parking. The streets are mostly quiet, clean and well kept with comfortable middle to higher middle income families. There are no mansions or "estates", or castles or chateaus, but neither are there any slums, or depressed or run down sections, or "economically depressed" groups of houses. The area is usually referred to, or known, as the Arlington Ridge, Aurora Hills, Fort Scott Drive, or Oakcrest neighborhoods. It is bounded loosely by Interstate highway I-395 to the west, Glebe Road and Four Mile Run to the south, the mostly developed high rises of Pentagon City to the north. Many homes here overlook the Virginia Highland neighborhoods and the Jeff-Davis, U.S. Route 1 and I-595 corridor high rises and parts of the City of Alexandria to the southeast.

During the Civil War period, this part of the County was the center of intense military activity when the Union Army crossed the Potomac and occupied the Northern Virginia high ground to establish a series of fortifications, known by historians as "Mr Lincoln's Forts" for the defense of Washington. One such installation was Fort Scott now preserved as a County Park and from whence the main artery Ft Scott Drive gets its name. Except for some stately residences along Ridge Road that were built around the turn of the century and World War I during the days of scattered open spaces and dirt and muddy roads, most of today's homes date from the period following World War II. Some rather distinguished, or well known, figures have resided in the area over the years

ARLINGTON COUNTY VIRGINIA - A Modern History

to include most recently former President Reagan's press aid James Bradey who was shot and disabled in the Connecticut Avenue assassination attempt, Security Advisory Bill Allen, Star War proponent retired General Daniel Graham, Virginia Secretary of Transportation John Milliken, and Senator and later Vice President Albert Gore.

Its probably quite safe to say that most residents of the area consider it as one of the most affluent and desirable places to live in Arlington County. It is not, however, without its distractions or disadvantages. It overlooks some modern urban facilities that many residents would probably just as soon do without if it were feasible. There is, first off, just out front of the eastern slope in the lowlands on the banks of the Potomac River, the National Airport with its almost continuous and unmuffled , and sometimes near deafening whine and scream of countless numbers of jet aircraft taking off and landing, or warming up idling during times of maintenance or waiting in long backup lines for takeoffs. There are also, a short distance away and in full view, the unsightly, and at times very noisy, railroads yards on the main east coast tracks of freight and AMTRAK passenger trains. And then there is nearby truck and other traffic on Glebe Road and the Jeff Davis corridor with its noise and visual pollution to detract from the enjoyment of life on the patio or in the home yards. Until recently there was also the noise, odors, smoke, fumes and unsightliness of the trash collecting and compacting point on Eads Street that could easily also be seen and heard and smelled from most locations on the eastern slope of the residential neighborhoods above.

MOST UNDESIRABLE RESIDENT

Without a doubt, in the view of the local residents, the neighborhood characteristic most detested, obnoxious, odious, offensive, revolting, undesired, plus any number of other adjectives that could be thrown in, has been, and still is, the sewage treatment plant at the intersections of South Glebe Road and U.S. Route 1, or Jeff-Davis Highway. Necessary as such a facility may be for any community, if local residents had their way, the plant would be located elsewhere, away from dense and built up communities. For years the citizens complained that they suffered greatly from the plant's oppressive stenches, especially when the winds were from the east and south as they often were.

The sewage plant, at an elevation of ten feet above sea level, the lowest spot in the county, has served as the collecting point for sewage from most of the county, and some areas outside the county, at elevations of as much as 400 feet above sea level at Minor Hill, and generally in the Four Mile Run watershed. The facility has been located on land where once existed the 40 acre amusement center known as Luna Park with its Gothic, Moorish, Japanese style structures that housed exhibits. The park also had a carrousel, an aerial ride, a chute-the-chutes, a lagoon for boat rides and some animals to include elephants that sometimes escaped and generated area wide animal hunts.[80]

By the 1960s, with the country and Arlington compelled by new Federal legislation to take measures to minimize water and other pollution, attention was focused

---

[80] Baker, Gail, <u>The Great Northern Virginia Elephant Hunt</u>, The Arlington Historical Magazine, Arlington, Virginia, October, 1994, p.41.

Major Community "Battles" and Controversies

on the need to improve the efficiency of Arlington's sewage treatment to dramatically minimize the discharge of effluent into the Four Mile Run and then the Potomac River, and eventually the Chesapeake Bay and Atlantic Ocean.

The Arlington County sewage, or "wastewater" system is described in an April 30, 1973 report by the Alexander Potter Associates, Alexandria, Virginia,[80] as one that was first placed in primitive service in 1933, increased in capacity in 1953, and again with secondary treatment facilities in 1968 capable of removing 90% of the BOD (biochemical oxygen demand)from an average daily flow of 24 million gallons.

POLLUTION CORRECTIVE MEASURES

The Potter Associates reported that under a joint agreement with neighboring jurisdictions, Arlington handles some Alexandria, Falls Church and Fairfax County sewage within the Four Mile Run watershed, and that sewage from about one third of the county areas outside the shed are handled by those jurisdictions.

By 1970, the Virginia State Water Control Board had directed Arlington County to proceed with the preparation of plans for tertiary treatment facilities in its water pollution control plant, as was being done in other nearby jurisdictions. Potter described tertiary treatment as a method of "increasing sophistication to render the secondary effluent almost completely free of solids and free of bacteria by the addition of chlorine...to remove up to 99% of the organic matter". The Associates explained that phosphorus and nitrogen had to be removed to prevent the growth of algae in lakes and estuaries that caused secondary pollution. They reported that "this involves the use of physical-chemical processes, using lime or alum for precipitation of phosphorus, followed by filtration, using mixed media filters, carbon columns for absorption, ion exchange units for nitrogen removal, reaeration to restore dissolved oxygen and finally chlorination and disinfection."

An estimated $30 million was required to upgrade the Arlington County treatment facilities to meet new Federal standards and to be financed 55% by a Federal grant, 25% by a State grant, and 20% ($6 million) by local funds. Bond issues to finance the Arlington share of this cost were placed on the ballots in the 1971, 1972, and 1973 elections, and approved by the voters by comfortable margins.[81].

CITIZEN REACTION

As plans for the expansion and upgrading of the sewage treatment plant crystallized and were made public by the County Office of Public works, citizen interest and concern intensified. Residents and members of nearby civic groups, and especially the Arlington Ridge Civic Association, appeared in sizeable numbers before the County

---

[80] *On file in the office of County Public Works.*

[81] *The vote in the 1973 bond ballot for sanitary sewage was 13,613 for and 5,744 against.*

ARLINGTON COUNTY VIRGINIA - A Modern History

Manager Staff, the Planning Commission, the County Board, and other involved offices, seeking maximum information.

The worried and distressed citizens pressed county officials for specifics as to plant capacity in millions of gallons flowing daily, numbers and scheduled hours of chemical or hazardous material vehicles entering and leaving the area daily, plus routes of ingress and egress, and other characteristics of operations they perceived would adversely impact them and their enjoyment of life and movement in the community.

The citizens also expressed deep concern over a proposed design that would accommodate more sewage by far than would be produced in the County, and whether Arlington would not in effect become the sewage plant for the whole region, to the detriment of nearby residents who would bear the brunt of the unpleasantness of the operation.

Francis Hewitt, as spokesman for the Civic Association and clearly reflecting the views of his neighbors, wanted to know why all the effluent for the entire county and beyond had to be treated only in his "backyard", and whether any thought had been given to multiple treatment stations spread along the Four Mile Run at various elevations so as to more equalize the disadvantages of the problem and spread its undesirable consequences more evenly through the county. The citizens also expressed alarm at the prospects of another of the severe "100 year" floods in the area that could cause overflows of the collecting basins and disperse raw sewage far up and down the Four Mile Run valley and into adjacent residential communities.

The answers and responses to these citizen concerns were, in short, that the plant "improvements" were mandated and had to go forward; that it was not economically, or practicably feasible to perform the operations elsewhere in the county; and that the adverse consequences to the public and nearby residents of the future plant operations were not precisely known. County officials conceded that no meaningful environmental impact study for the project had been undertaken, and insisted that fears of sewage tank overflows caused by flooding in the plain would soon become moot because of a $42 million flood control project for the area about to be undertaken by the Federal Government through the Army Corps of Engineers.

"Sewage tank overflow?
No Problem! I'll handle"

Major Community "Battles" and Controversies

On June 12, 1973, Robert Machen, President of the Arlington Ridge Civic Association, in a letter to Everard Munsey, Chairman of the County Board, reported that the Association in its June 6th meeting had adopted a unanimous resolution concerning the sewage plant, that encompassed the above described concerns.

The letter asked for a study and environmental impact evaluation statement; that the county immediately cease the incineration of sewage sludge, or at least insure that incineration was controlled to prevent harmful emissions; that a more pleasing aesthetical design with less height for the tallest structures be drawn; that a limit be placed on the quantity of sewage handled daily with time limits and adequate charges for non-county users; and that a limit of 30 million gallons per day be established for the plant. Machen stressed that these measures were considered necessary to "minimize the immediate and long range adverse environmental impact of the plant on this area", and that additional costs should not be an acceptable justification for rejection.

Civic Associations leaders also expressed their flooding concerns to their U. S. Congressman Joel Broyhill who, in due course received some assurances on December 26, 1973 from Col. Robert McGarry, Baltimore District Army Engineer, at least for the long term. The Colonel wrote, in part:

"In the development of the plan for flood protection along Four Mile Run, the Baltimore District coordinated closely with the plans being prepared for the sewage treatment plant in Arlington...(our) project would be completed in June 1977...this leaves a 3 1/2 year period in which the existing plant and the proposed station will be subject to flooding...additional facilities at the proposed location prior to completion of the Corps' project could worsen environmental health problems associated with flooding of a sewage treatment facility...flooding...is expected at average intervals of about 3 years..."

On January 2, 1974, Association President Machen again wrote the Board Chairman, now Joseph Wholey, about the communities concern "that we have an example of State, Local, and Federal government processes going awry". He charged that in the past six months there had been no progress toward a more rational review of the project, or outlining what steps the County would take to assure against hazards to public health caused by flooding, or air pollution in the Crystal City-National Airport-Jefferson Davis Corridor. He reminded the Chairman that County Planning Commission members regarded the site to be suitable for a park ground. He said the Association continued to believe that an environmental impact study was essential for the plant expansion.

On January 21st, Machen sent a similar letter to Russell Train, Administrator for the Environmental Protection Association (sic). He charged that the National Environmental Policy Act of 1969 was being violated by the absence of a required impact study, and that if assistance was not forthcoming, the Association would exercise its right to file suit to litigate the matter if no satisfactory response was received within the 60 days the statute allowed the EPA to answer.

ARLINGTON COUNTY VIRGINIA - A Modern History

* * * *

CITIZEN LITIGATION

On February 29, County Manager Bert Johnson advised the Board that "Construction plans are essentially complete", and on March 6th, Arlington Attorney L. Lee Bean filed suit in chancery in the Arlington Circuit Court for a declaratory judgment and injunction concerning the sewage treatment expansion project. The suit, # 24141, named Alvah L. and Carole M. Rogers as complainants [82] and as defendants, Commonwealth Attorney Claude M. Hilton and County Attorney Jerry K. Emrich, and Board members Everard Munsey, John Purdy, Joseph Wholey, Ellen Bozman and Joseph Fisher.

The Bill of Complaint outlined the history of the complainants efforts to achieve relief from local and Federal officials on the matter of expanding the sewage plant, and alleged zoning irregularities and violations with respect to permitted industrial uses, public notices and hearings, required set backs and height limitations, and other requirements for buildings in a flood plain.

COURT ACTION ON CITIZEN SUIT

With respect to the complainants' allegation of zoning and administrative violations and requesting an order to enjoin further construction, Judge Charles Russell for the Circuit Court issued an interim decision refusing to stop construction. In an April 18th article on page B5 by writer Doug Brown, the Washington Post reported:

> "...Russell said yesterday that he agreed with neighbors suing to stop construction that the county had violated its zoning ordinance numerous times...but that...the county had changed its zoning ordinance to make its previous acts legal...the former deficiencies created by the county in not obtaining a permit to build on a flood plain, failing to obtain construction permit and building the plant on land that probably was not zoned for that purpose were corrected when the County Board changed the law after the suit was filed."

On April 20, Judge Russell heard the complainants' witnesses, received their exhibits on the remaining issues, and considered the Defendants motion to strike their evidence and grant a motion to dismiss their cause. The Court then held that the evidence was insufficient to maintain the issue, and granted defendants' motion and dismissed the cause. On July 18th, Attorney Bean appealed Judge Russell's decision, but

---

[82] *Additional complainants were; John and Diane Pickett, Louis and Dorothy Mendosa, Walter and Phyllis Tudor, Jack and Patricia Gates, J. Hunt Brassfield, John and Mary Dabinett, Harrison and Patricia Lobdell, Alfred L. Stoessell, Robert and Dorothy Machen, and Paul J. Hyman.*

Major Community "Battles" and Controversies

on February 24, 1976, the Virginia Supreme Court held (Record No. 751235) that there was no reversible error, and affirmed (upheld) the lower courts action, thus ending the litigation, absent further appeal which was not undertaken.

* * *

In the years following the failure of the South Arlington citizens and civic groups to halt the enlargement of the sewage treatment facility, construction continued and was completed by the late 1970s. With the completion of that enlargement project, and the earlier dismissal of their law suit, most nearby South Arlington residents resigned themselves to the inevitability of an expanded sewage plant in their midsts and the futility of further resistance. They held their noses and turned their attention to other civic matters. While they did not like the outcome, they considered the matter laid to rest and that it would command their attention and haunt them no more. But that was not to be. On the contrary, the sewage plant controversy, like the ancient Egyptian Phoenix would rise again from the ashes seemingly like a symbol of immortality and resurrection. On a new 1995 go-around, there arose the matter of increased capacity for sludge burning.

On July 3, 1995, the County Manger, through the Division of Public Affairs released an announcement advising that there would be a hearing on July 27th at the Aurora Hills Community Center on the County's application to expand the sewage sludge treatment (i.e., burning) capabilities at the plant. The announcement hit the community like an explosion. It explained that the expansion proposal called for increasing the capacity of two existing sewage sludge incinerators from 45 to 60 tons of sludge a day to meet state and federal clean air regulations and as an alternative to the more costly approach of hauling the unburned sludge to distant land fills or by other disposition.

The alarmed reaction of neighboring citizens was almost instantaneous. Many quickly asserted that they not only did not want the burning capacity not increased, but rather wanted it discontinued altogether. On July 28th the Arlington Journal reported on citizen reaction with banner headlines proclaiming "Neighbors protest proposed sludge increase" and "Residents fear more incineration". Retired Colonel and engineer Bruce Jones was reported in that Journal article as stating, "The residents want incineration to cease. They do not wish to be subjected to any further emissions." The Northern Virginia Sun on August 3rd, quoted Rebecca Gray, chair of the Arlington Ridge Civic Association's Incinerator Effects Assessment Committee, and later President, as saying, "the county has been less than honest about the effects of burning sludge." She said further that when the Association discovered that among the "non-toxic" substances emitted were nitrous oxide and lead, members were "mortified" by the lack of better knowledge about the effects of pollutants. "This stuff is blanketing the community and staying in our neighborhoods and local surroundings", Gray said.

On August 15, the area's State Senator Robert L. Calhoun wrote to Albert Eisenberg, Chairman of the County Board on the matter. He said, in part:

> "...Based on my review of the application and the testimony at the July 27 public hearing, I am persuaded that the project should not go forward...

"...the Northern Virginia area has a difficult and challenging air quality problem...such being the case I find it hard to understand why the County would be promoting an air pollution source that will have to be 'traded off' elsewhere. Although there seems to be some dispute as to whether the new facility will be more polluting that the present one, I do not find that to be a relevant consideration to this central issue...I think it strongly argues that more serious consideration needs to be given to alternatives, in particular the alternative of transporting the sludge for recycling at a land application site.

"The principal objection to this approach (transporting) are ones of site availability and cost...the city of Alexandria and other jurisdictions seem to have worked out the siting issue...Government imposes the costs of compliance with the Clean Air Act on the private sector as a matter of course. I submit that it is not unreasonable for the County...to bear these costs in the case of its own programs."

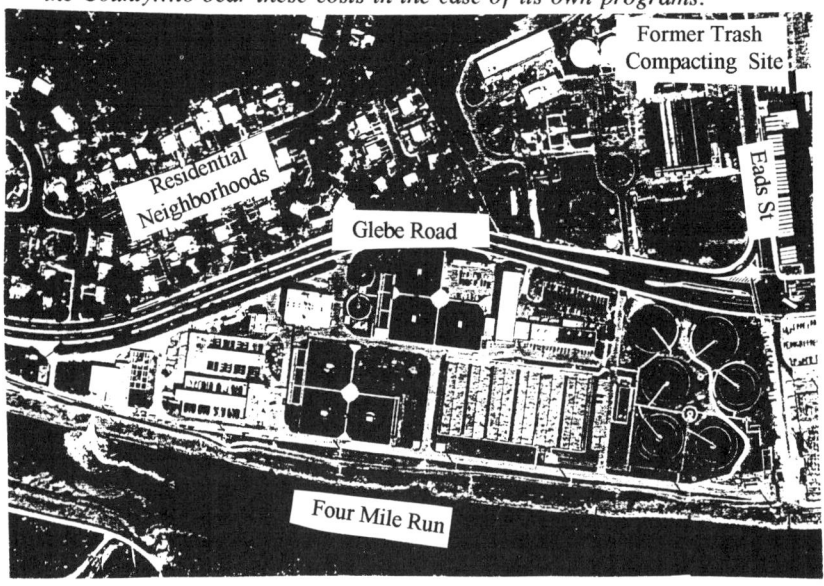

Waste Treatment Plant at So. Glebe Rd and U.S. Rte #1

In its regular newsletter released just before the July 27th public hearing on the sewage plant expansion, editor David Jones listed a detailed discussion of the adverse health effects of the toxic substances to include Mercury, Lead, Carbon monoxide, sulfur dioxide. He urged Association members to attend the hearing "to let the State know we are against this expansion and are requesting their denial of the permit". He added, "You will hear from Arlington County that the emissions are within EPA restrictions. HOWEVER, we cannot believe these limits were set to include a site which dispenses toxic materials such that people are actually LIVING in the plume cloud."

Major Community "Battles" and Controversies

The issue of the sewage plant expansion also became an issue in the 1995 County Board race when the proposal came under attack by Republican county board candidates. The Journal headlined on August 29th, "GOP blasts sludge fires - Democrats: 'its politics'". Republican Board member Ben Winslow, running for reelection, proclaimed, "We are concerned that county staff and the County Board are not giving enough attention to this problem. We really ought to look at other means of removing sludge."

Closely following this political campaign exchange, and perhaps as a consequence of it, County Manager Anton Gardner on September 8th, in a memorandum to the County Board, reported that the "County recently requested that the Virginia Department of Environment Quality defer action on a permit application for an upgrade and expansion of the biosludge incinerator, pending the outcome of a sludge management alternative study." He wrote that the preliminary scope of work for the proposed study was before the County Board for consideration. In an article headlined, "Gardner to Review Sludge Options", Northern Virginia Sun writer Nita Rao on September 29th alluded to the county board political campaign and wrote that the sewage incineration had become a divisive issue. She wrote further in part:

> "In the latest development in the sludge incineration controversy, Arlington County Manager Anton S. Gardner presented a memorandum to the county board, outlining preliminary plans for a study considering alternative means of waste disposal in Arlington.
> "It is a victory for the Republican team of Benjamin Winslow, the county board's lone GOP member, and Henriette Warfield, both of whom advocate recycling...to haul away sludge until other viable options to sewage burning could be arranged."

Rao quoted Winslow as saying "It looks like Gardner has finally heard (the) complaints and is now, seven years after citizens started complaining, acting in their best interest." She quoted Warfield as saying that Gardner "was not initially aware of alternatives to sewage incineration and did not have a plan, he was just barreling down the road."

The Washington Post on July 22, 1995, in an article headlined "Arlington Ridge Residents Rally to Protect Community", staff writer Linda Wheeler described the Ridge community. She called attention to some of its problems and concerns of its citizens that included the sewage treatment plant as well as the trash collecting, compacting and burning facility that was once there until protests by citizens resulted in its removal. Concerning the trash facility, writer Wheeler quoted retired engineer, and past Association President Bruce Jones as saying, "They wanted to put the plant at the bottom of our hill. We got concerned. We rallied around this thing." Following complaints by the Association, Arlington joined Alexandria to build a plant several miles away. She explained that now the community is similarly concerned about plans to expand the capacity of sludge incineration. Quoting current Association president Rebecca Gray, Wheeler pointed out that residents have done their own research on the harm caused by the smoke from the plant at current capacity that is believed to have killed several 200-year old oaks by pollution from the plant.

ARLINGTON COUNTY VIRGINIA - A Modern History

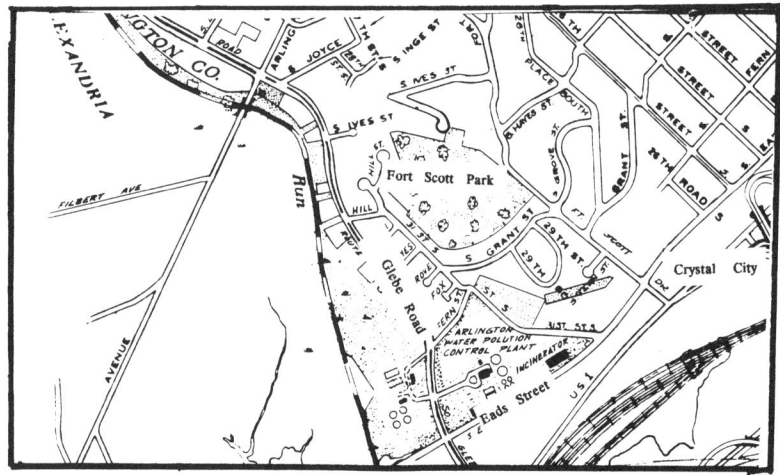

The Sewage Treatment Plant Location

The Post article outlined how Doris Bangs, a longtime resident of the Ridge, in the 1920s and well before the modern day air pollution from the trash and sludge burning by the sewage plant, used to walk as a child in fresh air to the Hume School on Ridge Road that now houses the museum of the Arlington Historical Society.

At this writing, no one knows with any certainty what will be the eventual outcome of this sewage plant's overall operations or whether, or to what extent, if any, it, or other future developments, will result in further environmental adverse impacts and thus continue the controversy on or with the surrounding neighborhoods.

The sewage facility and its grounds are now almost surrounded by dense urban development. As stated, on one side on the slopes of a hill is a mostly single family dense residential neighborhood. To the North, the massive high rise office and residential units of the Crystal City-Jeff Davis corridor-Route 1/I-595 complex has reached the boundary of the sewage plant.

In the years to come pressure for similar developments must be expected to the South across the Four Mile Run in Alexandria along the mostly undeveloped and, in places, run down commercial stretch on the Jeff-Davis corridor and the railroad marshalling and switching yards on the opposite side of U. S. Route 1. Most railroad activities in the area have been discontinued except for the Metro lines and the main north/south through lines of the railroad company.

The railroad area across Route #1 east of the sewage facility and locally referred to as the "Potomac Yards", is the subject of much speculation in the early and mid 1990s as to its eventual use. Development of some kind is expected and seems at this writing to be only a question of time. When that time arrives, the sewage plant will be entirely surrounded by urban developments. Some citizens have pointed out that it will not be much unlike locating such an essentially industrial and odorously obnoxious facility in downtown New York on Grand Central Park, or in Washington in Lafayette or Farragut

Major Community "Battles" and Controversies

Parks. How long the citizens or community will tolerate such a condition will remain to be seen.

With respect to sludge burning it appeared to distraught citizens in the closing weeks of 1995 that relief was at long last in sight even if still a bit far away on the horizon. As citizen opposition to incineration mounted, the County Board scheduled the matter for hearing on December 9th to determine, essentially, whether to push forward with plans to enlarge the plant sludge burning capacity. In the Spring the County government had applied to the State for a permit to expand the capacity from 45 to 60 tons daily. The question of sewage treatment plant operations had been a hot issue in the County Board political campaign only days earlier with Republican Ben Winslow accusing the ABC-Democrat board majority of indifference to the concerns of citizens living near the plant.

At issue at the board hearing, essentially, was whether the sewage, or sludge, would be burned or hauled away; i.e., "incineration, or land application". Northern Virginia Sun write Nita Rao, on November 21st, had written that other options that had been considered and ruled out were "...composting the sludge; drying it by heat (the capital and operating costs were too steep); hauling it to a landfill (the closest one is 85 miles from Arlington); and co-incineration, a process in which sludge is burned with solid waste". County Director of Public Health Susan Allan had stated that "the current operation of the biosludge incinerator is safe and poses no safety or health threats to the community". Citizens living nearby, however, strongly disagreed. They insisted that there was no reliable and conclusive proof available that emission were harmless to residence living nearby and within the plume of exhausts from the furnace smoke stacks. They pointed out that the top of the stack was roughly the same height of numerous houses on the slopes or top of the Arlington Ridge land mass, and was therefore dumping emissions practically into the bedroom windows of nearby residents. They contended that while increasing the height of the stack might be helpful by elevating the contaminated plume higher above the homes of residents, it was not an available recourse because it would constitute a hazard for aircraft arriving or departing from nearby National Airport and thus be opposed by the FAA. The Arlington Journal editorialized on November 11th:

> "...the smoke stack emissions include sulphur dioxide, carbon monoxide, nitrogen oxides and volatile organic compounds that combine to form smog and even some lead...The amount of sludge already is straining the capacity of the plant, and the county would be better off investing in equipment to make recycling -- not burning-- possible...(these) are solid reasons for moving ahead with a proposal to truck the sludge out to farm country..."

The hearing room when the County Board next considered the sewage plant matter, was filled to seating capacity with citizens standing around the walls and over flowing into the halls outside. The hearing began with a briefing by the County Manager's staff, led by County environmental planner Jeff Harn and other staff members. They declined to recommend to the Board whether sludge should be hauled

ARLINGTON COUNTY VIRGINIA - A Modern History

or burned, but explained that hauling at about $40-45 per ton was slightly more expensive than burning at $35-40 a ton. They stated that hauling would result in a plant operational cost of about $48.65 per household per year, or about $6.68 more than burning sewage sludge.

Following the staff presentation, citizens began to speak against burning the sludge; no one spoke in favor. Speakers included Arlington Ridge Civic Association President Rebecca Gray, residents Arlene Cam, Mary Dabinett Woolnough, Bruce Jones, Nancy Swain, Ernest Ragland, and many others, some of whom were not living near the sewage plant.

When some dozen or so citizens had spoken, Board Chairman Al Eisenberg announced that the Board was leaning in the direction the speakers desired and that perhaps the proceedings could be shorten if those on the long list of speakers could abbreviate their comments by simply indicating they concurred with the views of previous speakers. Some later speakers did so and by around five o'clock the Board went into executive session. It then unanimously adopted a resolution presented by Board member Mary Margaret Whipple to switch by 1998 from burning sewage sludge to recycling it for farm use, as practiced by a growing number of cities and counties across the country. By its action, the board capped months of debate on the issue.

"Burn sludge? Phewee!"

Ridge Association president Gray said, "We are very, very pleased. Recycling is absolutely the right thing to do. The County Board made the right decision." Gray indicated afterward that the concerned citizens would next concentrate their efforts on the question of whether the sludge burning could be discontinued sooner than 1998. The achievement of that goal, however, did not appear to be very likely. That county staff had informed the board that about that much time would be required to remodel the plant to handle recycling. They said a dewatering building would be needed, plus a second truck bay, storage hoppers for sludge, a silo for lime used to treat the sludge, and a scrubber system to remove foul odors.

Local citizens are sure to continue to fear that even if sludge burning ceases and the current controversy is resolved, they will continue to be confronted years down the road with a sewage plant Phoenix that will periodically resurrect itself from the ashes and return to haunt them and detract from the enjoyment of living in their community.

* * *

Major Community "Battles" and Controversies

Round XIV
THE FOOTBALL AND BASEBALL STADIUM BATTLES

"Not in my Backyard"

For many Arlingtonians, and especially those in the southernmost parts of the County, it must have seemed in the 1990's that they were destined to spend the rest of their community times in resisting efforts to establish sports stadiums, contrary to their desires, on their figurative door steps - or "backyards" as the media most often phrased it. Some times these efforts appeared headed by outsiders, but also, on occasion, by their own elected officials.

THE POTOMAC YARDS FOOTBALL STADIUM

The first of these efforts emerged when the decade was barely underway. In 1992 it became known that football owner and magnate Jack Kent Cooke was looking for a place to put his Redskins football team other than in the District of Columbia at the RFK stadium. Locals knew also that he had his covetous eye on the mostly abandoned railroad former marshaling and switching yards between U.S. Route 1 (Jeff-Davis highway/I-595) and the national airport, a site known as the Potomac Yards. Most of the area was and is located within the boundaries and political jurisdiction of the City of Alexandria, but a small portion extended into Arlington County and the extremities of the Crystal City high rise office, hotel and apartment building areas.

The development of the railroad yards had for some years been on the front burner of municipal planners in Alexandria, developers, and others. The Arlington Journal on April 3, 1992 reported that the Alexandria City Council on the following day would hold the first of a series of workshops and public hearings to discuss Potomac Yards and an adjacent stretch along the George Washington Parkway known as Potomac Greens.

There had been repeated proposals for the area presented and discarded for various reasons mostly because of unresolved problems with traffic flow, access into and

ARLINGTON COUNTY VIRGINIA - A Modern History

out of the area from nearby road nets, uncertainty as to how much density to permit and some other ramifications. Journal staff writer Jay Sherman reported on April 3, that a proposal was under consideration by the Planning Commission at the time for a project with 2.75 million square feet of office space, 300,000 square feet of retail space, a 625 room hotel, and 4,000 residential units that would include 15 percent affordable (low income) housing. Sherman added that the proposal was on hold for the moment while a substituted plan of Planning Director Sheldon Lynn was studied. Lynn's plan called for more office, retail, hotel and residential space. Sherman quoted Lynn as feeling that his plan "isn't as great as the tract's developers want, but could be more economically viable" and "legally defensible".

While these developments were unfolding on the city stage, there suddenly entered from the wings one Jack Kent Cooke, who felt that the best use of the Potomac Yards would be for a new stadium home for his Washington Redskins ball team. He was aided and supported by Virginia Governor L. Douglas Wilder, but not by many others. Citizens in the Auburn Village, Del Ray, Brenton and adjacent residential neighborhoods, and in South Arlington's Aurora Hills, Virginia Highland and Arlington Ridge communities rose in clamorous and rebellious opposition. It became the main matter for business at civic association and other community meetings and letter writing to newspaper editors. Plans were made for campaigns to oppose a stadium in the Potomac Yards.

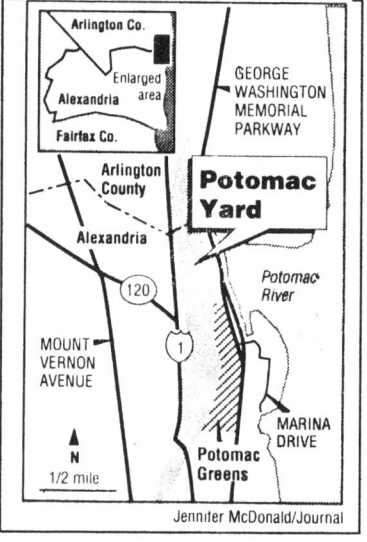

Jennifer McDonald/Journal

One letter writer to the Journal on September 16, protested that most media articles had concentrated primarily on the claimed economic benefits of a stadium and claimed that too little consideration had been given to adverse impacts on nearby communities. He wrote, in part, "Many of us are more fearful of the inevitable increase in congestion, traffic, crime, insecurity, pollution, trash and other undesirable consequences of being next to such an activity, and the resultant costs to our community of coping with it."

The Arlington County Board remained mostly aloof from the swirling controversy, but the County Manager reported that the County could lose up to $40 million in tax revenues over the coming years because of stadium land removed from the tax rolls, and that Arlington could be stuck with $100,000 a year or more in costs for police, fire and traffic-control services for a facility that wouldn't even be mainly in the County. With respect to the Arlington Board's relatively quiet position on the stadium, the Journal editor opined that even if the matter "was out of its (the Board's) hands...when an ostrich buries its head in the sand, other parts of its anatomy are vulnerable." The Journal editor scolded the Board and wrote that it should stand up and shout loud and clear, "We don't want the stadium at Potomac Yard."

Major Community "Battles" and Controversies

In due course, and in the face of withering fire from opponents, the Cooke baseball stadium proposal for the Potomac Yards eventually died on the vine. The matter passed into history, at least for the time. Discretion became the better part of valor for its proponents. Owner Cooke had apparently concluded that the effort was not worth the candle to mix a metaphor. The launch was aborted and alarmed and indignant citizens breath a sigh of relief and relaxed - but not entirely or for long.

THE TWIN BRIDGES BASEBALL STADIUM

The comfortable relaxation of Arlingtonians over the cancellation of plans for an unwanted sport stadium in their midst was to be short lived. As early as 1994, soon after taking office, Virginia's new governor George Allen, himself from a sports family with a father who was the past coach of the Washington Redskins football team, let it be known that a high priority project for him would be to bring baseball to Virginia. He wanted a team located in the State, which for all practical purposes meant Northern Virginia since that is where the heavy population necessary to support a team is located. The prospect of returning baseball to the District of Columbia was not given serious thought since it was known that major league baseball authorities considered the District to be within the Baltimore Orioles geographic territory and for other reasons.

The Governor recommended, and the State Assembly passed, a measure to create a commission to attract and locate a team. The Commission, to be known as the Virginia Baseball Stadium Authority (VBSA) was to have a total of nine members, four each from Fairfax and Loudoun Counties, and one from the City of Alexandria. It was charged with selecting a site, negotiating a lease with a baseball team, and the building of a stadium. Arlington County was not included initially because of an understood lack of interest and more outlying counties were not included because their distances from the Metropolitan Washington urban center was considered to be too great and that fans would not travel great distances for games.

The Authority was vested with a mandate to locate a site for and build a major league baseball stadium in Northern Virginia. They promptly invited stadium bids from Fairfax and Loudoun with a filing fee of $150,000. A filed deadline of June 15, 1996 was set since the goal was to begin construction of a stadium by the fall of 1996 with playing to begin by the 1997 or 1998 season.

By January 1996, the newly establish Virginia Baseball Stadium Authority, headed by George L. Barton IV, former chairman of the Loudoun County Board of Supervisors, had held meetings on the matter and several suggestions for location of a stadium were being circulated and discussed in the community with mixed reactions. On January 11, Washington Post writer Eric Lipton reported that Arlington and Prince William Counties were considering putting forward their own sites for a baseball stadium, and thereby causing friction within the other two counties vying for the complex. Days

ARLINGTON COUNTY VIRGINIA - A Modern History

later Arlington County officials formally filed their request that Arlington County also be considered as a possible site location.

RUMBLINGS OF PUBLIC REACTION

Voices from the public were also being heard in Arlington for the location of the stadium in the County. Citizen Gene Van Arsdale a resident in Crystal City in a letter to the Arlington Journal published January 23, thought a stadium in Arlington "would be perfect", and "good business for the community". He dismissed the usual "not in my backyard" objections to a stadium. County Board members Albert Eisenberg and James Hunter let it be known publicly that they favored a stadium in, or near, the County and listed as "practical locations" the Potomac Yards at the southern end of Jeff-Davis corridor, and a site at the northern end of the corridor known as the Twin Bridges area.

Increasingly, voices were also being heard in opposition to a baseball stadium at either of the suggested locations. In a January 16 Journal article headlined "Another Stadium fight looms", writer Gigi Whitley, reported that Arlingtonians who geared up to keep the Redskins stadium out were saying they would do the same to the baseball project. Whitley quoted Rebecca Gray, president of the Arlington Ridge Civic Association as saying the county "shouldn't even waste the money (to respond) to a request". Sue Super, President of the Aurora Highlands Civic Association said she was surprised to learn that the Board members were even considering a site in Arlington. "We are concerned that any decision made are on firm factual grounds...not emotional appeals of whether people like baseball or not", Super said.

Whitley wrote, however, that Pro-Sports Arlington member Matthew Cary, a management control consultant said, "Our proposed site (Twin Bridges) would be away from residents in terms of noise or lights." Whitley wrote that the Virginia Baseball Club Corporation, a group formed to fight for a stadium, estimated the state's economic benefits as $113 million annual and $183.4 million during construction. Lipton pointed out that a group led by telecommunications executive William L. Collins III, was working to attract the Houston Astros team but was prepared to buy any other team that is for sale.

Also high on the stadium agenda in this early period were the questions of how the stadium, estimated to cost $250-300 million, would be paid for and whether by private or public funds during the construction and later the operational periods. On January 11, Post writer Lipton reported that on January 10, the VBSA panel met and voted

Please!! No stinky, noisy, messy stadium in my front yard!!

unanimously to ask the legislature to authorize special lottery games estimated to raise $11 million a year to pay off stadium debts. Lipton also wrote that there was a "growing

Major Community "Battles" and Controversies

consensus among advocates that the stadium cannot be built without a major infusion of public funds".

STADIUM MOMENTUM GROWS

On January 19, Post Writers Lipton and Tod Robberson wrote that the proposals to build the stadium in Arlington "was gaining momentum after baseball officials indicated they have reservations about sites under consideration in Fairfax and Loudoun counties. He also described the mounting disagreements among supporters and opponents over traffic, parking, safety and other considerations for the Arlington sites which were steadily being narrowed down to the Twin Bridges location.

Apparently to allay fears by citizens of premature Board movement Chairman James Hunter, was reported by Northern Virginia Sun writer Henry T. Dunbar on January 25 as saying that no major league baseball stadium would be built in the country without a thorough public process. "Let me repeat that the county board is fully committed to a widespread and comprehensive public process prior to any submission of a proposal", Dunbar quoted Humter as saying. One South Arlingtonian promptly responded to Hunter with a letter to the Journal editor saying, "Of course there will be public participation...but after such input will the Board, composed mostly of North Arlingtonians simply dismiss the opposition and do as they jolly well please as they have so often done over the past." The writer added, "...it is safe to say that our community is overwhelmingly opposed to any such activity on our doorsteps...a stadium means traffic, noise, lights, congestion, raucous misconduct, massive litter, even muggings and other crimes, and an obnoxious nuisance not needed or wanted on the edge of our residential community".

Dunbar also wrote that Mark Jinks, the County Director of Management and Finance had reported to the Board at its January 20 meeting that the only step taken by the County toward building a stadium was to request the Authority to allow Arlington to also be considered. Shortly thereafter, the Authority granted Arlington's request. Additionally, Arlington was authorized to have a member on the panel to be appointed by the Governor.

On February 1 the Arlington Ridge and Aurora Highlands civic associations held a joint meeting at the Aurora Highlands Library with an overflowing attendance. Every speaker or participant voiced opposition to the stadium some in exceptionally strong and emotional terms. No one spoke in favor of it.

A COUNTY BASEBALL COMMITTEE

On February 3, the County Board voted to establish an Ad Hoc Baseball Stadium Advisory Committee consisting of 18 members and to authorize funds for a study. On February 5 the Board appointed members to the Committee and named as Chairman local attorney and stadium supporter George D. Varoutsos. Some committee members represented the community at large. Others represented specific organizations to include the Arlington Ridge and Aurora Highlands Civic Associations, the County Civic Federation, the Planning Commission, the Environmental and Energy Conservation

ARLINGTON COUNTY VIRGINIA - A Modern History

Association, the Transportation and Sports Commissions, the National Parks Service and the Metropolitan Airports Authority. The Commission were to hold 12 meetings and two public forums attended by hundreds of citizens. Traffic and economic studies were prepared for the Committee by outside consultants.

During much of the months of February and March, 1996, dialogue on the stadium centering on both location and financing. Opposition among county residents, particularly in the southern portion crystallized and intensified. The stadium Authority set a deadline of June 17 for Northern Virginia communities to propose locations, saying it wanted to select a site by August so that ground breaking could take place in March, 1997, with stadium opening by 1999. Post writer Lipton reported that investors eager to bring major league baseball to Northern Virginia had offered to pay about a third of the $300 million building cost.

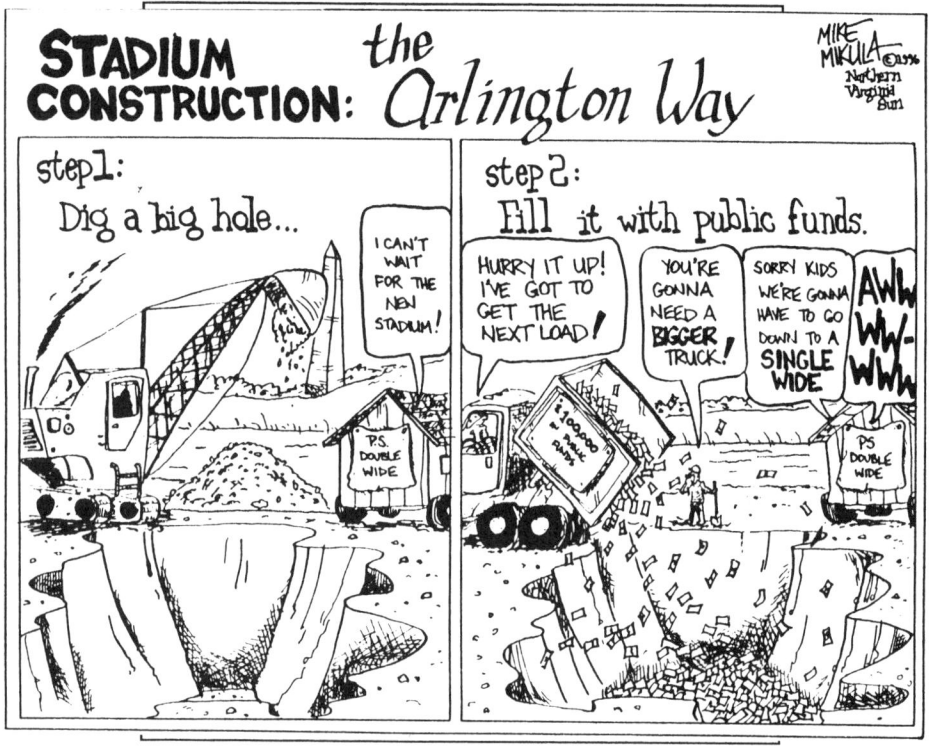

In the face of mounting public opposition to the stadium, Board members favoring the project did not seem to waver. An article by Stephen C. Fehr in the Post in this period shed some light on why some Board members appeared so strongly to support the stadium, but not why they did so almost in defiance of increasing community opposition. Fehr focused on the economic considerations and shifting employer composition in the County. He called attention to the loss of thousands of jobs expected from the movement of major Navy operations from Crystal City, the planned move of Gannett Company in

Major Community "Battles" and Controversies

Rosslyn to Tysons Corner, the American Management Systems move from Rosslyn to Fairfax County and the Patent and Trademark Offices announced plan to move 5,000 employees from Crystal City. He suggested that these losses would not offset some gains in jobs the Electronic Industries Association, the National Rural Electric Cooperative Association and the Manufacturers Association. Fehr quoted Board member Eisenberg as saying "...he stadium would send the clearest message to the region that Arlington intends to be a major player in economic development", and member Whipple as saying, "..we increasingly are having to complete with cheaper (office) space further out."

On March 24, the two local civic association Presidents Gray and Super requested that Scott McGeary, President of the County-wide Civic Federation, include the matter of the stadium on the agenda for the federation May 2 and 7 meetings. In a jointly signed letter, they wrote, in part, "...our communities would be directly and negatively impacted if the stadium were to be built...problems would be greater (than the football stadium earlier rejected at Potomac Yards) because there would be so many more games (and) on weekday rush hours...impacts include traffic congestion, parking on neighborhood streets, extremely expensive 'fixes', increased crime, environmental problems since the site borders on the waterfowl sanctuary, and disappearance of open spaces..."

BASEBALL HEADLINES

By April and May, stadium discussion and attention by the public and involved officials, and coverage by the media, soared to lofty peaks. Hardly a day passed without some story in the Washington Post and Times, the Arlington Journal and Courier, and the Northern Virginia Sun, as well as non local publications, on some aspect of the stadium. Headline writers had a field day with captions. They seemed to delight in tieing in a news item, an editorial, or a new development with baseball rhetoric. Common headlines or phrases included; "...made a pitch for stadium", "Arlington plays economic hardball", "More swings at a ball park", "Ballpark may hit a homer", "Agency says baseball near National won't fly", "Don't bat us around", "Fairfax Citizen Federation cries Foul", "Arlington baseball strikes out", "Baseball plan strikes out in Fairfax", "FAA throws curve", "DC officials ready to make pitch for ball team", "Poll: play ball, not pickpocket", "Late in the game, ballpark site draws new offers", "Bottom of ninth for N.Va. baseball", "Foul play: stealing signs", and "Covering the bases for a stadium".

NEWS COVERAGE ABOUNDS

News coverage during this period revolved around such questions as to whether the stadium would create a safety hazard for aircraft operating to and from National Airport; whether the FAA would sanction the stadium so close to the National runways; whether sufficient parking could be arranged either at the stadium or from nearby lots at the Pentagon or in Crystal City or Pentagon City; whether or to what extent stadium traffic would be "manageable" or clog arterial major roads or local neighborhood streets; the Department of Interior attitude concerning possible adverse impacts on GW Parkway; whether aircraft noise would be unbearable for stadium patrons; and perhaps most fundamental of all, how the stadium would be financed and whether the stadium would be located at the Twin Bridges or at several possible places other than in Arlington.

On April 4, the Arlington Journal, and on the 11th, the Northern Virginia Sun reported that traffic consultants Wells & Associates had submitted the results of the study they were commissioned to do by the Ad Hoc Committee. Journal writer Whitley wrote that the consultants said, somewhat hedgingly, "...it appears (emphasis supplied)...traffic is manageable at this site", but conceded that motorists at several Jeff-Davis intersections, and especially at South 20th and 23rd Streets "would experience delays after weekend games. The Sun's Nita Rao wrote that the Wells study challenged local civic association claims that gridlock would result, and that the report indicated major changes in I-395 and Boundary Drive would be needed at a cost of about $6.6 million. Whitley quoted Arlington County planner Richard Viola as saying that Arlington "would need to encourage baseball fans to use public transportation, car pools, or walk to the stadium". Viola did not elaborate on what public transportation he alluded to, or, if it was Metro rail, how fans would, especially in bad weather, get to and from the stadium via the nearest three stations, none of which were less than a mile or so away.

LEGISLATURE COOL ON PUBLIC FINANCING

On Tuesday April 9, the South Arlington civic associations held a heavily attended evening forum in the South Lang Street Gunston Center on the subject of the stadium. The Journal's Whitley wrote that speakers "ballyhooed and bemoaned putting a Major League Baseball stadium near Crystal City and he quoted Sherwin Landfield, a member of the Citizens for the Abatement of Airport Noise as saying, "Should we speculate on the unthinkable worst-case scenarios like a huge fireball, when glaring lights 100 feet high snag a passing plane and bounce it into a crowded stadium?" Landfield continued, "Yes, it's a convenient location for a stadium, just as National is a convenient airport site. But don't forget that the ultimate convenience for a passenger is to leave and return safely. And the ultimate convenience for a baseball fan is to watch yet another game." Whitley quoted several speakers, however, who were in favor of the stadium at the Twin Bridges to include Donald Redmond who maintained that the stadium "is far enough away from the residential neighborhood to have little impact." Whitley wrote that Redmond lived "a few miles from the proposed site."

Rebbeca Gray of the Arlington Ridge Association asked, "What happens if the stadium is not successful - if it turns out to be another white elephant like RFK and there sits a monumental core?" Dick Smith, chairman of the Arlington Independent Party said the County was ripe for a stadium, but not at the Twin Bridges. He did not indicate where else in Arlington there was space for a stadium.

Another speaker at the forum, John Russo, a member of the County Fiscal Affairs Advisory Commission and former President of Arlington County Taxpayers Association expressed concern about funding and the County right of eminent domain. He asked "Since Arlington County has requested the State to grant them authority to do the eminent domain condemnation, rather than the original concept of the Authority, will the Authority be able to repay the County its costs ... and will the County utilize

Major Community "Battles" and Controversies

Enterprise Bonds to finance the acquisition, thus leaving Arlington taxpayers 'morally' responsible for repayment?"

Post writers Lipton and Steve Bates on April 10, reported on Virginia legislature developments with respect to funding in an article headed "Most Support Funding for N. Va. Ballpark". Speakers at a committee hearing on whether taxpayer dollars should be invested in the enterprise asserted that the stadium was "an opportunity of a lifetime", and that legislators should disregard "naysayers" and commit to using general taxpayer funds or lottery revenue. Lipton and Bates wrote that key members of the panel indicated that taxpayer financing of the $250 million stadium remained unlikely and that the complex would be built "only if it can largely support itself."

On April 23, Journal writer Whitley reported again on the financial aspects of building a stadium and quoted Fairfax Delegate Vincent Callahan as saying that the legislative panel studying the matter probably would not ask taxpayers outside Northern Virginia to "foot the bill"; that there was little support for a statewide tax to lure the Houston Astros or another team to the state.

The following day on the 24th, the Ballston-Virginia Square Civic Association held yet another community forum on the subject of the stadium in the Renaissance Hotel on North Stafford Street. The results were much the same as for the earlier forum in South Arlington. Most speakers voiced reservations, or out right opposition to a stadium anywhere in the county and especially at the Twin Bridges site. With respect to financing the stadium, William Collins, president of Virginia Baseball Club, Inc., as reported by Whitley in the Journal, said he didn't care whether taxpayer came from the entire state or only from a group of localities. "A team and a new stadium would be a boon to all of Virginia and put the State on the economic map." The Virginia Baseball Club had been formed in August 1994, expressly for the purpose of securing a Major League team in Virginia. [83]

Kierstan Gordon reported in the Journal two days later, in what could well be a master piece of understatement, that "residents are at odds over where to put (the stadium)", which seemed to be boiling down to either Springfield in Fairfax County or the Twin Bridges in Arlington. Gordon also wrote that the Metropolitan Airports Authority, that operates National and Dulles, had stated publicly at the above forum that it had many concerns about the Twin Bridges proposal, but that the authority had not yet taken an official position.

FINANCIAL IMPACT STUDY REPORT

The next day, on April 26, Journal writer Whitley reported, in what was becoming almost a day to day running account of stadium developments, on the rosy economic picture that a stadium presented according to George Varoutsos, chairman of the Ad Hoc Advisory Committee. Varoutsos indicated that he was relying on the results of an economic and fiscal impact study for the Ad Hoc Committee just released by

---

[83] *Included among the Club's members was Mark Warner, President of Columbia Capital, former Virginia Democratic Party Chairman, and a 1996 candidate for U. S. Senator.*

Arthur Anderson, a real estate advisor in Washington. Varoutsos said the study "indicates the economics would be favorable to Arlington". He said it would generate $22.3 million for the County and gross $7.1 million in tax revenues, with 4,800 additional hotel rooms being rented a year but that the restaurant industry would appear to be also a large beneficiary. The Anderson study also predicted $11.0 million impact in salaries and wages from annual operations, and a $38.5 million total economic activity, $4.7 million from salaries and wages, and $1.4 million in tax revenues during the stadium construction period. Anderson predicted more than three times these benefits for the Commonwealth of Virginia as a whole.

On May 2, Governor George Allen added two Northern Virginia men to the Virginia Baseball Stadium Authority; William G. Buck of Arlington, of the firm Bucks and Associates and former member of the County Planning Commission and Chairman of the County Site Plan Committee, and David G. McWatters of Loudoun County, a retired Marine Corps master gunnery sergeant and member of the Loudoun County Board of Supervisors. McWatters expressed the opinion that his county would be chosen as the site for the stadium.

On the same day, the Airports Authority announced that it had "strong" objections to a stadium near the National Airport. Journal writer Robert White wrote that the move came one day after the FAA said it had questions about the safety of having a stadium at the Twin Bridges, less than half a mile from the end of a runway. White cited an Authority tersely worded statement from General Manager James A. Wilding that placing the stadium next to the airport "would not be good public policy because it would endanger spectators and add to traffic congestion." Also on May 2, Governor Allen announced that he opposed a sale tax increase to pay for the stadium, and that user fees would be a better way to finance the project..

These events apparently prompted another wry editorial from the Arlington Journal. The editor said the Twin Bridge proposal had been "beaned" three times. First, he wrote, when the FAA voiced doubts, Second when the Regional Authority voted unanimously to fight the plan, and Third when the Defense Department would not allow fans to use the Pentagon parking lots. The Journal editor concluded that the best available site was the General Services Administration Warehouse complex across the County Parkway from springfield Mall. He also suggested that user fees or taxes on tickets, concessions, parking, etc., and not general taxpayer money, would be the best approach for a stadium. In the meantime, newspaper dialogue by way of news items and letters to the editor continued unabated.

THE COUNTY BOARD HEARING

On May 9, the County Board conducted a hearing on the question of a stadium in Arlington County. The Board room was filled with overflow spectators standing in the halls and listening to the proceedings from exterior mounted speakers. After opening comments, some lasting 15 or more minutes, by Board members, the Chairman directed the clerk to call public speakers based on slips submitted. The Board heard only 3 minute speakers until the meeting was recessed shortly before midnight at which time it

Major Community "Battles" and Controversies

was recessed with an announcement by the Chairman that 5 minute speakers would be heard when the meeting was resumed on Saturday morning.

Reporter Steve Bates wrote in the Post the following morning that "more than 120 people signed up to speak...". Civic Federation President Scott McGeary informed the Board that the Federation two nights earlier had voted 51-1 against the stadium. Civic Association Presidents Rebbeca Gray and Sue Suter reported that their associations with record turnouts had voted unanimously to oppose the stadium.

Most of the speakers for and against a stadium, and the arguments they advanced, were the same that had appeared, or been made, at the forums in April in the Gunston Center and the Renaissance Hotel. At the conclusion of the public testimony, and/or comments, the Board members discussed the matter at some length over a period of about two hours. The discussion included comments with emphasis on considerations such as transportation to and from the stadium by vehicle, buses from Metro stations, or otherwise; methods of financing, traffic and routes into and out of stadium parking lots; whether the $150,000 application filing fee should be paid, or waiver requested; and the economic viability of a stadium with respect to expected attendance.

Board members Hunter, Eisenberg and Bozman conveyed the impression, in varying degrees, that they were in favor of a stadium in principle, provided that known reservations of airport and other Federal agencies could be overcome. They did not address the matter of widespread citizen opposition as established by speakers at the hearing. Board Member Ferguson, one of the Board's two newest members, did not participate extensively in the discussion. All of the members expressed either outright opposition, or at least deep reservations about having to pay a $150,000 application fee up front as required by the Stadium authority. They talked of either filing an application without the fee as a test, or of requesting a waiver of the fee. Member Zimmerman was the only member who clearly indicated that he was concerned about citizen opposition to a stadium and that he might be against it even if known reservation by the Federal agencies did not exist. He commented, in part, as follows. [84]

> "I want to talk about the economic benefits...while there might be some..it is also clear if you look at the studies that have been done...not advocacy research done by people seeking public funds to subsidize this activity, but the more balanced...the impact is minor, measurable, but minor...a baseball team should not be set up as a test of our commitment to economic development...the major economic players in the area in which this would be located, and presumably benefit the most, have not embraced the idea...it is not clear that Major League Baseball or anyone associated with it really thinks this site is so good...(there's uncertainty) about where the community is...it seems clear to me that the community is very much divided on this...the problems are just as significant now and seem no more likely to be resolved...so I can't see expending more resources on this...I think that

---

[84] *County Board minutes, 9 May 1996, Newsletter, Ballston Virginia Square Civic Association, May/June 1996, p.25.*

ARLINGTON COUNTY VIRGINIA - A Modern History

in this case they (the proponents) are pursuing a dead end...so I don't think I'm prepared to support going further on this at this time"

Post writer Bates in his article of the following morning reporting on the Board meeting wrote that Chairman Hunter and member Ferguson had said they "... planned to vote against (the stadium)." That account appears to be an incorrect overstatement, however, in view of Member Zimmerman's comment quoted above that he was not prepared "to go forward" with the matter "at this time"(emphasis supplied). Available records do not support Bates version of the reported statements. At the follow-up session of the hearing on Saturday May 11, 28 five-minute speakers testified with 3 in support of a stadium and 25 opposed. This, of course, conflicted with the testimony at the May 9 session of the hearing of Chamber of Commerce President Richard Doud, on record as strongly favoring the stadium, that in a straw poll conducted by John Hudson, the community was shown to be heavily in favor of a stadium by a margin of 4-1.

Two days later, Post letter writer Harold E. Foster injected what he might have thought to be a new element into the equation. He asked "Why not RFK?" He wrote why not leave the team in the DC stadium where investors plan to have their team play while the new stadium is under construction. He elaborated on the economic and other benefits of doing so. The short answer of course to Foster's query is that the investors were known to have no sympathy for putting a team in the District of Columbia with its fiscal, social, management and other current problems where attendance would likely be low and thus not a viable solution as had been the case in the past with other sport events in the RFK stadium. And also, as stated, because the District was considered to be within the geographical territory of the Baltimore Orioles.

Perhaps the most comprehensive press coverage of the entire period of stadium controversy occurred on May 13, with a Washington Post page 1 and 3 Metro Section feature article by writer Eric Lipton. Lipton's constant coverage of the matter over many weeks must have made him an in-depth authority of sorts on all aspects of a stadium at the Twin Bridge site. His article was headlined:

"At Ballpark Site, a Not-so-Joyful Noise
Roar of Jets could dampen Roar of Crowd near National Airport

Lipton included in his article a dramatic and frightening photo of a jet in a landing approach barely above tree top at the edge of the proposed stadium site He also included a chart showing decibel levels for various day-to-day sounds (lawn mowers, motorcycles, trucks, etc) showing the levels for a jet at take off was the highest of all. Another chart showed the height and location from the proposed stadium of several dozen passenger planes approaching National Airport, and indicating that most would be within 1000 feet of the stadium. Lipton compared the expected decibel levels at a Twin Bridge stadium with those for other major airports such as LaGuardia in New York, but he drew no dispositive conclusions from his comparisons. He quoted Michael Scanlon, executive vice president of the Virginia Baseball Club as conceding that noise "is one of the many things we need to examine."

Major Community "Battles" and Controversies

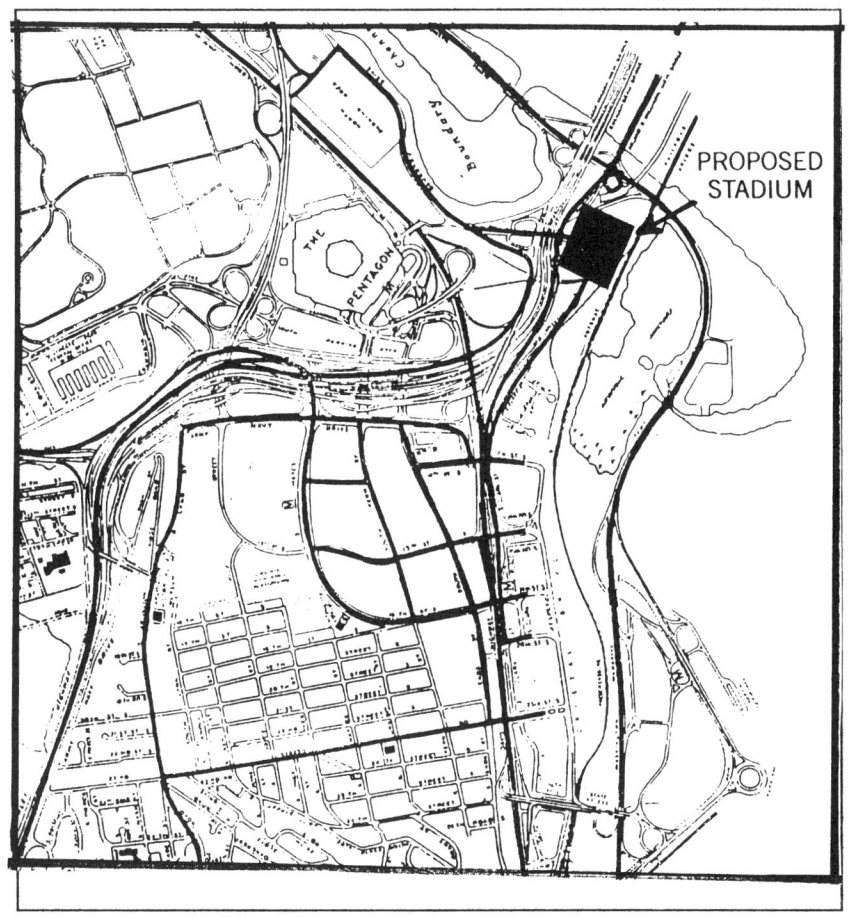

As the deadline of May 15 for filing applications for a site approached and none of the local jurisdictions had filed any applications, the question of extending that deadline became critical. Post writer Tod Robberson reported on May 11 that Fairfax was joining Arlington in requesting an extension of the deadline until June 15. After first indicating to Arlington officials that the dead line would not be extended, Stadium Authority chairman George L. Barton on May 13 sent letters to officials in Arlington, Fairfax, Loudoun and Stafford counties notifying them that the deadline had been extended to June 17.

Whether the extension of the application filing deadline would have any meaning for Fairfax County was thrown into much doubt only days later when the County-wide Civic Federation comprised of 165 local associations and 160,000 residents of the county advised that it would oppose a stadium at either of the two sites under consideration. Post writer Robberson reported on May 18 that the Association voted on oppose the two stadiums near the Springfield Mall. Robberson wrote that Fairfax Supervisor Dana Kauffman had harshly criticized stadium advocates and that most county Board members had said they would defer to him since the proposed site were in his district. Robberson also quoted Kauffman as saying, concerning financial problems for a stadium, "There's no way they're going to get financial support from Fairfax County."

The matter of a stadium in Fairfax County appeared to become moot several days later when the supervisors voted to abandon their efforts to nominate a site for a major league stadium. Post writers Lipton and Spencer Hsu said the action resulted from "...a sudden backlash from residents near the proposed sites (Springfield)", and that only two other sites were being considered, one at National Airport (Twin Bridges), the other 40 miles away in Stafford County. The writers added that Virginia Baseball Club President Collins "vowed to press on", that investors would "pare their list of wanted Fairfax sites to one or two and then propose them", and that Collins expected to step up talks with competitors in Arlington and Loudoun counties. Lipton and Spencer wrote, however, that Stadium Commission Chairman Barton said that if the panel "ends up with only Stafford County applying as of June 17, he will move to call off the site selection process...that it would mean the end of the effort to buy the Houston Astros."

On the 22nd, the Journal editor opined

"...Fairfax County struck out Monday...Loudoun two weeks ago. Arlington is in danger of striking out (as it should) and Stafford County should strike out...The real shocker is how Fairfax rolled over and voted not to endorse the most promising site, the GSA warehouse in Springfield...that's not leadership...We can understand why Loudoun supervisors withdrew from the site west of Dulles...too far from the center of the region and has no transit nearby...the Arlington site is smack in the core of the region but has one screaming drawback: it is a half mile from the National runway...too close for comfort. As for the Stafford county site, 28 miles south of the beltway, get real...maybe the team can find a site on their own...on the World Wide Web and post results on a bulletin board...that's something the Center for Innovative Technology can work on..."

The closing days of May saw baseball stadium proponents licking their wounds from the several setbacks and wondering what next to do to keep the issue alive. Post writer Lipton summarized developments on the 23rd in an article headlined "Backers of N. Virginia Baseball Strive to Revive Stadium effort". He wrote that the Fairfax Chamber of Commerce issued a plea to supervisors to reconsider, and quoted Baseball Club President Scanlon as suggesting a new possibility for a stadium site was at the Shirley Industrial Park complex just inside the beltway on the west side of I-395. Cold water was thrown on that possibility, however, by Supervisor Penelope Gross who called attention to the fact that there was no Metro station nearby and "without a subway stop (this location) is probably not viable.

Major Community "Battles" and Controversies

South Arlington resident George Strauss wrote to his Congressional delegation protesting the location of a stadium in Arlington and especially at the Twin Bridges site. Sen. Charles Robb replied that state and local officials would decide where the stadium would be located and that he couldn't control the decision but that he shared the desire that it be where it would have no negative effect of the surrounding community. Senator John Warner simply wrote Strauss that he was paying close attention to the selection process and if a decision required assistance from Congress he would keep Strauss's comments in mind. Congressman James P. Moran wrote Strauss in a reassuring tone implying that there was a non-problem with respect to the stadium. He wrote that it appeared neither Arlington nor Fairfax County "are prepared to do anything more to support construction of a stadium" and this "may be the most prudent course of action".

At month's end it appeared the final crushing blow for a Twin Bridge stadium fell when the FAA repeated its concerns about safety and asked Arlington to pick up the tab for a study estimated to cost $75,000 which Board members had indicated they would not do. The agency told the Board again that glare from stadium lights could hamper the vision of pilots and air traffic controllers and that electromagnetic radiation from the stadium would interfere with electronic flight-guidance equipment.

The prospect that there would be no stadium in Northern Virginia apparently prompted District officials to move aggressively into the competition. D.C. Sports Commission officials argued that the stadium belonged in the city anyway, and not in the suburbs and, as Post writer Lipton wrote on May 31, the Commission schedule a meeting for June 10 to make a case for locating the stadium in the District.

Although it began to look as though the Virginia opponents of the stadium were prevailing, leaders in the battle were not yet ready to relax and let down their guards. There was suspicion that their adversaries would roll with the punch, recoup their strength, and come lashing back when opponents were not vigilant or willing to continue the fight. They had still not heard their local governing body members state as a panel or individually that they were against a stadium in Arlington at the Twin Bridges. On the contrary, the perception was that most of the Board members were very much in favor of a stadium if opposition or reservations mainly by Federal agencies could be overcome.

AN OPPOSITION COALITION IS FORMED

Accordingly, South Arlington and some other stadium opponents resolved to continue the fight and solidify their defenses. On May 31, a group of activists and concerned residents, at the invitation of Scott Sterling, an executive in the Charles E. Smith construction company, met in the 11th Floor conference room of the Smith Building at the foot of South 23rd Street. In attendance were Sue Super, David Jones,

ARLINGTON COUNTY VIRGINIA - A Modern History

Rebecca Gray, Bruce Jones and Sal Cangialosi who had been particularly active in leading the fight against the stadium. [85]

The aim of the group was to form a coalition for stronger and more collective action and to launch a better organized and orchestrated campaign to prevent the location of the stadium in Arlington and especially at the Twin Bridges site. The agenda for the initial meeting of the group included issues of Logo and name, structure, a store front headquarters, materials (bumper stickers, front yard signs, lapel stickers, T-shirts, volunteer cards), a mailing program, telephone trees, and "backgrounders" and press releases for the local media. The group decided that Gray and Super would serve as co-chairpersons, and that they would meet weekly until further notice.

At the first and succeeding meetings, it was decided that the coalition would be named CO$T (Coalition Opposing Stadium Site, Taxes and Traffic); that they would prepare and distribute as widely as possible flyers setting forth the statistics and arguments against the stadium and organize a "telephone tree" to better inform the citizens locally and regionally on the anticipated adverse impacts of a stadium on the community.

In the early days of the coalition several flyers were prepared and distributed door to door, to the media, and posted on recreation center, library, and other bulletins boards to the maximum extent possible. One flyer titled "Get the Facts Straight (on stadium costs) detailed the construction and annual operation costs to Arlington. Another titled "Impact on National Airport: Safety, Noise and Access" explained what the coalition felt would be the adverse consequences of a stadium on these matters. Still other flyers dealt with the matters of "traffic chaos" on principle highways and neighborhood streets, and "Stadium Parking" described as grossly inadequate and that would result in strangulating overflow into nearby neighborhoods.

On June 3, nationally syndicated business columnist Rudolph A. Pyatt, Jr., indirectly jumped into the Northern Virginia baseball stadium fracas with an article Published in the Washington Post, entitled "Stadium Opponents Aren't just NIMBYs. They're Not-From-My-Wallet Types too." Pyatt referred to the Virginia controversy and wrote that the debate was not just a "Not in my backyard" issue. He said, "The stadium proposal is a pocketbook issue - pure and simple. What it really comes down to is that taxpayer financing of nonessential services and projects is not a popular choice when local budgets are tight and the economy isn't growing as fast as it did six or seven years ago." Local stadium opponents, as indicated in their flyers, were clearly in agreement with Pyatt on the economic considerations of the stadium, but they were also on firm accord as opposing it on grounds of adverse impacts on their neighborhoods and the overall enjoyment of life in the community.

Throughout June there continued to be almost daily news items on the baseball stadium issue. On the 12th Nito Rao wrote in the Sun that Arlington would likely submit an offer by the June 17 deadline. The deadline came and went, however, with no offer by Arlington. On June 20, the Journal's Robert Gehl told in an article "Foul Play:

---

[85] *Also in attendance were Ted Saks, Richard Pfordte, Judy King, Martin King, Elaine Woods, Arlene Camm, Janet Doukelberger, Brent Spence, Allan Schell, William Wallace, R. F. Sanders, Ruth Sanders, and Sherman Pratt.*

Major Community "Battles" and Controversies

Stealing Signs", of the stealing of over 100 "No Arlington Stadium" front yard signs around the Aurora Highlands neighborhood. The signs had been distributed at a neighborhood picnic on June 8th and otherwise. The supposition generally was that the stealing was mischievous or vandalization by stadium supporters, but Gehl quoted Richard Runkle, chairman of the pro-baseball group "Play Ball Arlington" as responding in outrage "I was shocked to hear about it...this is not the way we want things to happen", and he guaranteed it was not anybody in his organization.

As June arrived, the matter of the application filing fee continued to be a matter of concern and discussion. On the 4th, The Arlington Chamber of Commerce, a supporter of the stadium, advised the County Board that unnamed members had agreed to pay the $150,000 fee but only if used to meet the June 17 deadline. Board Chairman Hunter advised the Chamber, however, that while "the Board appreciates the efforts of the private business community to help...we just can't submit a site without having a public hearing. There are major unanswered questions that remain". [86]

Type yard sign posted and stolen in South Arlington neighborhoods.

Also on June 4, the County Board again deliberated on the stadium issue and discussed the process for deciding whether to formally nominate a site near the Twin Bridges. While citizens near the bridge that felt they would be harmed by a stadium there might have been piqued at the County Board for not considering more closely their views, they surely could not fault the Board members in not putting efforts, although perhaps unproductive, into trying to find a solution consistent with the best interests of community.

Post writers Nakashima and Peter Baker on June 13 described the Board members' frustration at the June 4 meeting. She described member Eisenberg's sarcastic faulting of Loudoun officials for spending money, allegedly, on baseball trips to Chicago of questionable justification, and suggesting that the Authority Chairman condescendingly agreed to an Arlington meeting only if the County nominated a site. "He's coming over here (just) to get the check!" Eisenberg charged. The Post writers, even after Chairman Hunter complained at 10 p.m. that it was past his bedtime and he had a meeting the following morning, reported that the meeting did not adjourn until 3:15 a.m. the following morning "setting a record".

---

[86] *Washington Post, Metro Section, June 4, 1996, page 4.*

ARLINGTON COUNTY VIRGINIA - A Modern History

On June 11, the Stadium Authority, made a tactical switch that did not cause rejoicing in the ranks of stadium opponents. After announcing that it was ending the previous site selection approach (offers by local governments) the Authority voted to encourage private developers and landowners to submit sites by July 22nd. The Authority said "the new process, which bypasses local jurisdictions, at least for the time being, is better." No opponent voices in agreement were heard.

As June melted into July, the fate of the stadium for Northern Virginia remained most unclear to put it mildly. Conflicting and contradictory events recurred almost daily. On June 17, as the filing deadline passed without any Arlington application with the required filing fee, the Journal's Gehl wrote "Arlington out of the Ball Game", but then on the 26th he wrote "It ain't over yet on ball sites."

At that time, Gehl reported that Stadium Authority member Michael Frey, also a member of the Fairfax Board of Supervisors, had said concerning the absence of application; "This is absolutely not the end of it...just a minor glitch...I am not (sure) that the Arlington site has not been taken out of consideration. We're going to be dealing with this issue for a long time." A new and late site in Prince William County west of Bull Run and Manassas was suggested but no follow up occurred.

Then on July 4th, in what could hardly be termed helpful publicity, Post writer Hsu revealed that $256,000 had been spent on lobbying for a stadium by the Virginia agency (the Stadium Authority) created to oversee the construction of a professional baseball stadium. Hsu wrote "Virtually all the money was spend by the Richmond based law firm of McGuire Woods Battle and Boothe, which, according to lobbying disclosure reports, assigned four lawyers and other workers to serve as the Stadium Authority's staff". Fairfax Delegate Vincent Callahan was quoted as saying, "I wish they'd told us about this ahead of time...it does raise some questions...perhaps there ought to be some modification of the law."

Sun writer Rao wrapped up the stadium situation as of mid-summer in a July 18 article "Stadium Panel takes a new Approach". She reported that the Authority had pushed back to September 11 the deadline for stadium site applications from the private sector and that Arlington's representative Buck said, "I feel real positive about it...if I'd had any suggestions or any say in the matter before, this is the way I'd have wanted to go." She wrote that Buck estimated that the Authority would receive 10-12 or more proposed site submissions from private sources. She did not say where Buck thought these sites might be located but it would seem that Arlington citizens

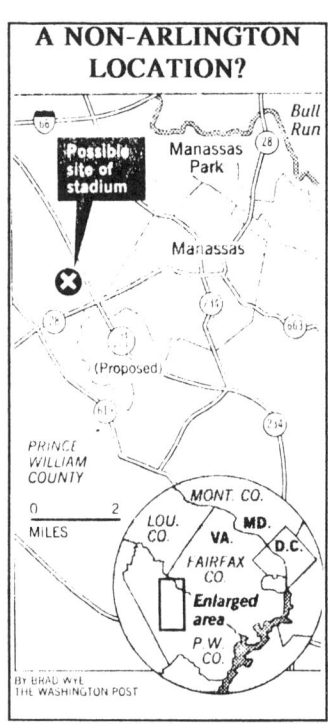

A new site suggestion.

Major Community "Battles" and Controversies

opposed to the stadium in their county need not be unduly upset. No one knew of any available open and unused space in Arlington County sizeable enough to accommodate a baseball stadium. On July 18, 1996, writer Spencer Hsu in the Washington Post on page 3 of its Virginia Weekly section reported that the Virginia Baseball Stadium Authority had, at $256,895, had spent more on lobbying expenses for 12 months ending April 30 than any other single organization.

By summers end there were no other or new startling developments in the drive to establish a major league baseball stadium in Northern Virginia. By mid-autumn, however, in an October 15 article by staff writer Eric Lipton, the Washington Post reported that consideration was being given to locating a stadium on the grounds of the 3,200-acre Lorton Correctional Complex in southern Fairfax County slated to be closed by the year 2001. The reaction of Virginians outside the beltway to locating a stadium at that site remained to be seen as this narrative goes to press. For Arlingtonians opposed to a stadium in their county the development appeared to provide better hope that the prospect of a stadium in their midst might not rise again like the mythical phoenix from the ashes to haunt, taunt and intimidate them.

* * *

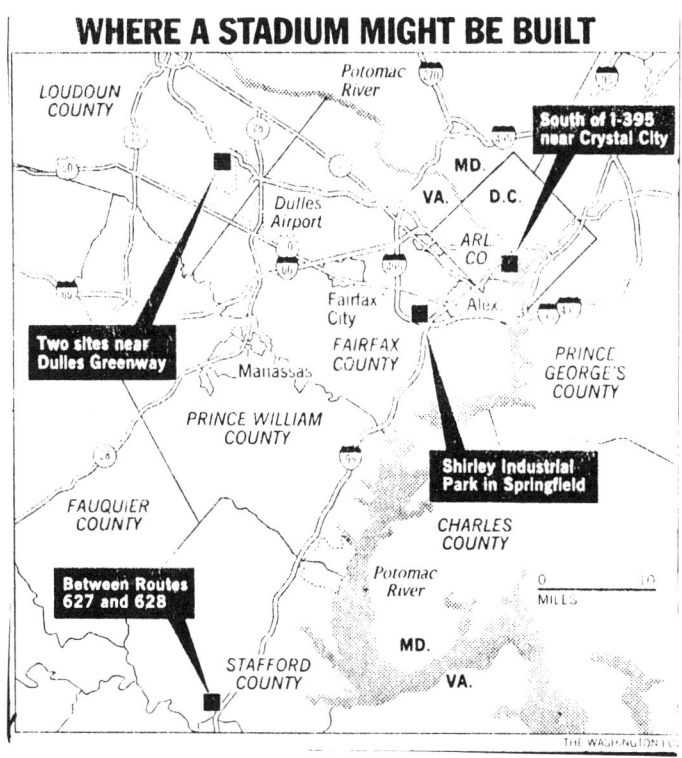

Round XV
THE EFFORT TO SAVE THE ABINGDON RUINS

Abingdon Plantation Manor about 1929. A movement to restore the manor was abandoned when the structure was destroyed by fire in March, 1930.

As 1991 drew to an end, area media reports indicated that the Washington Metropolitan Airports Authority planned to demolish the ruins of the Abingdon plantation manor [87] house and site at National Airport to make way for new multi-level garages. The Authority was well along on its major project to enlarge and modernize the National Airport. The news hit Arlington historical preservationists, as well as many others, like a nuclear explosion. They had been long fighting to preserve the site and its ruins in place and had thought they were making meaningful headway.

The battle to save the Abingdon site and what was left of its manor ruins had been going on for several years before 1991 with periods of optimism and pessimism by preservationists who wanted no airport parking lot on the site. As recently as mid-1990, to the delight of those fighting to save the site and ruins, the airport authority indicated that they would be spared.

---

[87] *By modern standards the Abingdon house would hardly qualify as a manor, or mansion, but in its primitive day of log cabins it was probably looked upon as such and has been so called by writers in the media and elsewhere. Herein we will resolved any doubts in its favor and refer to it as a manor.*

Major Community "Battles" and Controversies

The Abingdon Manor ruins as seen in 1995 on the eve of the Airport Authority Preservation project.

On July 23, 1990, in a page one article by staff writer Peter Kaplan, with the banner headline "Airport won't dig up old digs", the Arlington Journal reported, in part; "The Metropolitan Washington Airports Authority last week backed away from plans to dig up the ruins of Abingdon House, part of the Colonial estate with connections to George Washington. Faced with growing opposition, the authority's 11-member board set aside a recommendation that it excavate (the site of) Arlington's oldest structure to make room for a 7,000 space garage at Washington National Airport...Critics of the excavation plans greeted the airport authority's move as good news." The article quoted Arlington County Board Chairman Albert C. Eisenberg as saying, "I always had great faith that common sense would prevail."

Eisenberg's euphoria, and that of others of like mind, would soon be dampened, however, by the later announcement of a reversal and change of position by the Authority to the effect that the site would be excavated instead, and the area used after all as part of a concrete parking garage.

Abingdon and its ruins were not a run of the mill historical artifact. The present city of Alexandria nearby is named after Abingdon's early Alexander owners. Abingdon was also, as explained in more detail below, the birthplace or childhood home of some exceptionally noted people in early National and Arlington County history to include Nelly Custis, the granddaughter of Martha Washington.

The Abingdon manor had burned in 1930 and all that remained within a wrought iron fenced enclosure, about a quarter of an acre in size, was the lower portion of the brick walls and some of two fireplaces. Its location was and is on a grassy knoll, about 100 yards in front of the airport main terminal relatively inaccessible to pedestrians or air travelers and not very visible to motorists passing by on the George Washington Parkway or other nearby airport roads.

ARLINGTON COUNTY VIRGINIA - A Modern History

HISTORY OF ABINGDON

The Abingdon manor was revered and famed locally as the first structure in what is now Arlington County that was lived in by a known owner. There were other land owners in its day, such as George Washington, George Mason and others, but they lived not on their Arlington lands, but outside the County at their mansions such as Mt Vernon. Abingdon was also, before it burned, the oldest structure in the County, even predating Arlington House in Arlington Cemetery built in the period 1804 to 1814, and the Ball-Sellers House on South 3rd Street built about 1840 but with a log cabin interior believe to date from 1750.

The Abingdon manor probably was built sometime before 1746 by Gerrard Alexander, who had inherited the land from his father. The land was part of a purchase in 1669 by his great grandfather John Alexander from the ship captain Robert Howson. The elder Alexander had bought a strip of land about two miles wide on the West bank of the Potomac extending northward from Hunting Creek to a point up the river about a mile above the confluence of the Potomac and Anacostia rivers.

In 1778, John Parke Custis, son of Martha Washington by her first marriage, purchased a part of the tract generally north of Four Mile Run that was to become known as the Abingdon plantation. He and his wife Eleanor Calvert Custis promptly moved into the manor house. A year later a daughter, Eleanor "Nelly"[88] Custis, and two years later in April 1781, a son, George Washington Parke Custis, were born to the couple. Nelly was born at Abingdon and George nearby across the Potomac at Mount Airy, Maryland.[89]

Later that year, the father of the two children died of a fever during the battle of Yorktown and young Nelly and George Custis were adopted by their grandmother, Martha Washington and her husband George Washington. In 1799 George Washington died and three years later, upon coming of age in 1802, Custis took possession of "land inherited in Alexandria County from his father John Park Custis...(and)...in addition George Washington left him lands on Four Miles Run...on what must have been the finest location overlooking the Potomac and the new national capital."[90] He then looked around for a place on the tract to build his own manor to be known initially as Mount Washington and eventually as "Arlington House". It was so named after the

---

[88] *The nickname Nelly has sometimes been spelled by writers with an "ie" ending instead of a "y". The "y" was used by her mother and thus seems the preferred spelling. Her adoptive father George Washington is known to have used either ending.*

[89] *Mount Airy survives as a preserved historic manor and plantation outside Andrews AF Base at 8714 Rosaryville Road, in Upper Marlboro, Prince George County, Maryland.*

[90] Netherton, Nan and Ross, <u>Arlington County Virginia, A pictorial History</u>, The Donning Company/Publishers, Virginia Beach, VA, 1992, p.47.

Major Community "Battles" and Controversies

family manor built around 1657 near Cheriton on the eastern shore of Virginia near the mouth of Chesapeake Bay.

George Washington Custis selected the spot for his manor on high ground with the most spectacular panoramic view of the Capitol Building, possibly the Presidential Mansion, and other Washington and Georgetown sights. In 1831 his daughter Mary was married in an elaborate Arlington house ceremony to a young Army officer and fourth cousin, Robert Edward Lee from Stratford on Virginia's Northern Neck east of Fredericksburg. In later years, the George Custis manor on the Potomac was also to be known by some as the "Custis-Lee Mansion".

A FAVORITE TOPIC FOR WRITERS

Abingdon, before and after it burned, has been the subject of many articles in magazines, newspapers, and elsewhere. George Washington frequently stayed at Abingdon when traveling through the area and especially when visiting his timber lands along the Four Mile Run (now roughly the Shirlington area west to about Columbia Pike) to prevent timber poaching. [91] In a book by Alexander Hunter,[92] a Confederate soldier who once owned Abingdon, and was on the lands during the Civil War, the author tells that he was

> "determined to run the blockade to Washington City...we donned citizen's dress and went to a certain farm (Abingdon) three or four miles above Alexandria (of which I was the prospective owner) where a row boat was kept, and bribed the gardener, Old Uncle Sandy, to row us to Washington, reaching there about noon. Then commenced our tour. How thick the blue-coats were! How many officers in the city! How elegant their uniforms...We wended our way to Willard's Hotel; the lobby was filled with an excited crowd, in the bar-room the discussions were fiery. One officer said to a group around him 'I'll tell you, gentlemen, in two months from the word go we will march from the Potomac to the Rio Grande and drown the last d--n Rebel in the Gulf' So the talk drifted on and proved they had no higher opinion of their foes than said foe had of them".

A footnote on page 40 of the Hunter book describes the Abingdon estate and manor thus:

> "Between Washington and Alexandria, on the banks of the Potomac, is one of the oldest and finest estates in Virginia. It was the family seat

---

[91] Wise, Donald A., *George Washington's Four Mile Run Tract*, Arlington Historical Society Magazine, Vol. 5, No. 3, (October 1975), p. 19,20.

[92] Hunter, Alexander, *Johnny Reb and Billy Yank*, The Neal Company, New York and Washington, 1905, p. 34 et seq.

ARLINGTON COUNTY VIRGINIA - A Modern History

of the Alexanders and Hunters, and has been in the family for nearly three centuries. The family is descended from the powerful clan of MacDonald of Scotland, from Alexander, son of John, Lord of the Isles, by Lady Margaret his wife, who is the daughter of Robert the second King of Scotland. John IV, son of the Earl of Sterling, emigrated to Virginia in 1659 and had all the land from Georgetown to Hunting Creek, by letters patent. When he died in 1677 his will bequeathed to his son John all the land from Four Mile Run to Hunti ng Creek, (sic) so that the historic home referred to became the home of the Alexanders. The mansion is still standing and is most solidly constructed. The beams and rafters are of solid oak, two feet in diameter, and strong enough, as was proven, to bear weight of two centuries.

In an Outlook Section article of the Washington Post on April 22, 1990, writer Sherwin Landfield provided additional background on the history of Abingdon. Landfield pointed out that during the Civil War Abingdon had been occupied by the troops of the Federal Government and that the owner had to sue in court after the war to get the plantation back. In that successful suit, the owner was assisted before the Supreme Court by the lawyer James Abram Garfield. When Garfield later became president he was shot at the Mall railroad station in Washington on July 2, 1881 and died of blood poisoning from the wound.

EARLY EFFORTS TO SAVE ABINGDON

On February 20, 1928, a feature article appeared in the Washington Evening Star newspaper, telling of the efforts of prominent Alexandria citizens to save the historic mansion of Abingdon "which in the past few years has become almost a total wreck". The article related that the Richmond, Fredericksburg and Potomac Railroad, owners of Abingdon, had been approached by the Alexandria Washington Society with a plea to defer the razing of the building until financial arrangements could be made to restore it.

Major Community "Battles" and Controversies

The article included some colorful history surrounding Abingdon. It reported that Dr David Stuart, who with the help of George Washington, had married the widowed mother of Nelly Custis in 1873, had lived at Abingdon, was one of the first Commissioners to the new federal city of Washington and "with Daniel Carroll, established the boundary lines for the District in 1791".[93]

In the June 1929 edition of the Daughters of the American Revolution Magazine the article Sketch For the Restoration of Abingdon by writer Delos Smith appeared on page 325. The article consisted of an in-depth history of the Abingdon estate with sketches of the floor plans and external appearances. It also included a drawing of nearby "Mount Airy" manor in Prince George's County Maryland where the above mentioned John Parke Custis (father of George Washington Park Custis who built Arlington House in Arlington cemetery) met and later married Eleanor Calvert, and where the Arlington House builder was born as stated herein. The DAR article told of the visit of three men in 1928 to Abingdon with almost chillingly prophetic observations concerning the coming fate of the manor house:

> *"A year ago, three men went down from Washington to see Abingdon with a view to discovering what remnants of the old original house might yet remain in spite of decay, vandalism, and alterations. They were familiar with many other old houses of the Tidewater country where the serene old mansions stand in dignity, hallowed and trim, amid ancient trees and box-bordered gardens...(in) dismay they approached the building for it was empty and dilapidated, the gardens gone, the fences rotten, and the grounds littered with rubbish...(but) there was something clean and honest in the old framework. The basis of a true colonial character was here which, if restored, would show itself to be worthy of the admiration we reserve for the best work of our pioneer forbears...the goodly steep roof...gables walls, sloping rafters...were enough to show the graceful outline of the time of John Parke Custis...an Abingdon restored today (could) stand as a memorial on the new Mount Vernon Boulevard which is soon to pass its doors!*
>
> *"Within the month a party was found tenting nearby while they enjoyed the splendid view of the river and basked in the warmth of a <u>large campfire</u> The premises are untenanted and uncared for. If Abingdon is to go out like <u>a candle flame</u>, the memory of it must still live to those who have visited here."* (emphasis supplied).

---

[93] *This is an overstatement of the role of Stuart in the boundary survey. The project was under the overall control of Major Andrew Ellicott, who was assisted by Stuart, Benjamin Banneker, and others. Stuart did, however, participate in the placing of the first (South) corner stone at Jones Point near Alexandria on April 21, 1791. Stuart also, with two other Commissioners, named the capital the "City of Washington in the Territory of Columbia", a designation later changed.*

ARLINGTON COUNTY VIRGINIA - A Modern History

THE BURNING

Little did writer Smith know in June 1929, or the three visitors in 1928, just how soon their predictions of the demise of the Abingdon manor "like a candle flame" perhaps from brush fires from a "large campfire" of intruders would take place. In March of 1930, only months after the DAR article, Abingdon was to be utterly consumed by flames in circumstances almost precisely as conjectured by the three visitors. The Washington Post on March 6, 1930, reported it thus:

OLD NELLIE CUSTIS HOUSE DESTROYED BY BRUSH FIRE FLAMES LEVEL ABINGDON MANSION ONCE PROPERTY OF GEORGE WASHINGTON

"Abingdon, one of the oldest houses in the Nation, the birthplace of Nellie Custis, and once the property of George Washington,[94] burned to the ground late yesterday afternoon at its isolated site on the Four Mile Run in Arlington County, a short distance south of Virginia Highlands along the route of the Mount Vernon Boulevard.

"Fanned by high winds, (sparks) from one of the numerous brush fires which have menaced other parts of the country during the last few days, swept through bushes and dead weeds over the gracious front lawn and quickly enveloped the large two-story frame structure with flames...

"In recent years many pilgrimages have been made to Abingdon by hundreds of school children and tourists, many of whom chipped off wood as souvenirs...private individuals in Richmond have salvaged the beautiful marble mantels which long graced the open hearths...

"Several attempts have been made in recent years to seek restoration...At a convention of the DAR of Virginia last year, the Arlington County Chapter presented a resolution to commit the State organization to the proposal (to restore the manor) but the resolution was defeated".

Although records are scarce of latter day residents in Abingdon there is evidence that it was occupied shortly before it burned. In an "Informal Memorandum" [95] of the Arlington County Manager's office dated August 13, 1987, the "Beckworth" family

---

[94] *This is an error by the Washington Post writer. Washington never owned the land on which the Abingdon manor was located. He did, however, as stated herein, own land nearby along Four Mile Run. The writer may have meant to allude to the fact that Washington often visited Abingdon when entering or passing through the area.*

[95] *The Abingdon files, Virginia Room, Arlington County Main Library, Arlington, Virginia.*

Major Community "Battles" and Controversies

members are reported as the last residents in the Abingdon property. The Memorandum reflects that the family lived there from 1923-1927, and farmed the plantation for four years. It lists an "Aunt & Uncle were E. W. Beckworth (Edward Payne) and Hollis A. Phillips who, after renting Abingdon, lived at 621 S. 21st Street in Virginia Highlands."

ABINGDON PUBLICITY

Over the years since the burning of the Abingdon manor, there have been regular articles to keep alive the memory of the historical and meaningful structure and its grounds. Noted historian Eleanor Lee Templeman wrote of the history of Abingdon in a March 28, 1957 issue of the Northern Virginia Sun. In her article headlined "Abingdon Oldest House in County", Templeman recapped the history of Abingdon and wrote that the "remains of the Alexander family (in the) burying ground were in recent years moved to Pohick churchyard, along with those of "Long Tom", legendary treacherous Indian who had been killed while ambushing a member of the family".

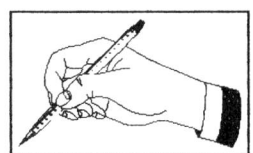

Writer and photographer James Barron also wrote of the history of Abingdon in a February 5, 1974 Northern Virginia Sun article and a July 12, 1974 Alexandria Gazette article. He related the site to the radar station towers and other operations at National Airport. His articles included photographs of Abingdon as it appeared before and after the 1930 fire. Barron wrote in the Gazette article that, "...Tourists who descend from jets at Washington National Airport probably never realize that the runways are on historic ground once owned by the Custis family and seen by George Washington..." [96]

Other recent articles of particular note on Abingdon include; Abingdon: a place of historical beginnings, by Lloyd R. Decker in the July 15, 1976 issue of the Arlington News; Lost Heritage: Early Homes that have disappeared from Northern Virginia, by Ruth Lincoln Kaye in Northern Virginia Heritage, February, 1987; Abingdon Plantation, in the Summer 1990 edition of the Crystal City Magazine; and Abingdon Plantation: A National Airport Dilemma? by Charles Baptie, in the Summer 1990 issue of the Metropolitan Washington Airport Magazine. Writer Kaye in her article, mentioned that some of the foundation bricks from the Abingdon manor were recovered and used to restore the garden wall in Gadsby's Tavern in Old Town Alexandria on South Royal Street.

* * * *

---

[96] Writer Barron was probably only partly correct. The runways are mostly on "fill" ground. The main terminal building more likely is about where the Abingdon wharf, alluded to by Hunter, would have been located.

ARLINGTON COUNTY VIRGINIA - A Modern History

EARLY CONCERN FOR PRESERVATION

As stated at the outset above, the concern of local preservationists and historians over the fate of Abingdon did not begin in 1991. The site and what was left of its ruins had been under the watchful eyes of many observers for some years.

As a means perhaps of keeping some focus on Abingdon, the Alexandria Gazette in a feature entitled "News of Long Ago", ran the following item on April 27, 1977 that had apparently been originally published after the Civil War:

> *"THE ABINGDON STOCK YARD. - It has always been a subject of surprise to many that the Virginia shore opposite Washington has not been utilized for many purposes outside of mere agriculture...One of the great needs for this section is a stockyard...the present stockyard is above Georgetown and in a very unapproachable situation. There is no railroad near...cattle have to be driven several miles on hoof to reach it...Mr Alexander Hunter is now building a stock yard on his Abingdon estate...This location will be of great convenience both to the cattle drovers and butchers."*

THE 1980s - THE BATTLE TO SAVE IS LAUNCHED

On August 1, 1985, H. Gray Gillem, Chairman of the Arlington County Historical Affairs and Landmark Review Board (HALRB) wrote to John Milliken, Chairman of the Arlington County Board urging him to write to the U. S. Department of Transportation to carry out an evaluation of Federally owned National Airport buildings and grounds to determine eligibility for listing on the National Register of Historic Places. Gillem referred to recent legislation introduced in Congress to allow the transfer of the airport, and also Dulles airport, to local control. He pointed out certain historical preservation needs at National for such action , particularly with respect to the Abingdon plantation site.

A letter to the Hon. Elizabeth Dole, Secretary of Transportation, was prepared for the Board Chairman, dated August 7, 1985, as requested by Gillem, but a penciled notation "Not sent" is on the copy in the Virginia Room files in the Arlington Main Library. A letter some weeks later on December 6th from Milliken to Gillem seems to shed some light on why the August 7th letter was not sent. In that letter, Milliken advised Gillem that he had referred the matter to the County Attorney to "consider the question of whether or not Arlington might reasonably request Secretary Dole to consider buildings on site at National Airport for inclusion in the National Register". Milliken wrote he had been told "the airport does not fall under one of the expressly defined categories for inclusion..."

On January 16, 1986, Russell V. Keune, AIA, the new chairman of HALRB, wrote the new County Board Chair Mary Margaret Whipple. He said the HALRB had requested him to "reopen the issue of a formal request to the Secretary of Transportation for a survey", and that "I believe the County Attorney is in error in his belief that nothing at National Airports falls under one of the expressly defined categories for

Major Community "Battles" and Controversies

inclusion ..." He urged that the Board reconsider the HALRB original August 1, 1985 request.

The entrance to the Abingdon ruins.

Over the following months, developments must have occurred that persuaded the Arlington County Board to alter its position of apparent uncertainty over whether or not it was reasonable for the County to request the Department of Transportation for its position on the matter. At any rate, on August 11th Whipple wrote Keune that, "I would be willing to send the request to the Secretary of Transportation", a position just the opposite of the one taken by her predecessor Milliken less than a year earlier. It can, perhaps, be assumed that persons favoring the preservation of the Abingdon site, were able in the intervening months to persuade Whipple to reverse the County Board's position on the matter.

Keune then advised Whipple on September 18th that HALRB had voted unanimously "to accept your willingness to pursue the matter with the Secretary." He also wrote, "We are interested in insuring that the Federal government discharges its required responsibilities for historic preservation before transferring the property to another authority."

The following year, in May and June, a "Programmatic Memorandum of Agreement" (MOA) was executed by the Chairman of the Advisory Council on Historic Preservation, the Virginia State Historic Preservation Officer (SHPO), and the Director of the Metropolitan Washington Airports, Federal Aviation Administration. The Memorandum alluded to Public Law 99-591 (Acts of 1986) concerning capital improvements at National and Dulles airports, and to Section 106 of the National Historic Preservation Act (16 USC 470f), under which the transfer of properties at the airports would have "an adverse effect" on properties eligible for the National Register of Historic Places. In the memorandum the parties to it agreed in essence, among other things, to develop and implement plans to survey and identify portions of the airports that contain properties that meet the National Register criteria. It was further agreed that such portions would be protected, preserved, rehabilitated, stabilized and maintained where appropriate, and to "consider reasonable alternatives to undertakings that would have an adverse effect on resources" The Memorandum provided for guidelines and standards for (1) archeological survey, (2) preservation planning, and (3) historic preservation and set dates for the completion of these actions.

ARLINGTON COUNTY VIRGINIA - A Modern History

THE ISSUES ARE NARROWED

In the months and years to follow, the efforts to save the Abingdon site and its ruins would narrow, essentially, to the questions of;

(1) whether preservation of the entire site with its ruins would be saved in place, or,

(2) whether the site would be excavated and paved over with its ruins removed to another location for display,

(3) if the latter, could this be done without first an affirmative determination, as required by law, that continuing with garage construction would have "no adverse impact" on the historical Abingdon site and ruins, and

(4) whether it would be feasible and possible to save Abingdon and its ruins.

On July 19, 1988, the new HALRB chairman, Jim H. Charleton wrote to Milliken, who had resumed chairmanship of the County Board, and reported that citizens had inquired about the "apparent failure of the Airports Authority to consider appropriate archeological and interpretive measures regarding the remains of the historic Abingdon estate on the grounds of Washington National Airport. Charleton stressed the historical importance of the Abingdon remains. He pointed out that Federal agencies were obligated by Executive order to determine "whether historic resources are being impacted by their undertakings." He also wrote that a "Determination of Eligibility" must be requested from the National Park Service and that HALRB was of the opinion that the process was not functioning for both Abingdon and the Main Terminal at National. Charleton urged the Board to bring the matter to the attention of the appropriate authorities.

On August 9th, Milliken replied to Charleton. He referred to the 1987 Programmatic MOA among the parties responsible to comply with the Section 106 of Federal Law concerning historic preservation. Milliken said an agreement had been reached regarding "the scope of work for a consultant to develop the historic property plans" for the airports. Milliken also wrote that the "Master Plan for National Airport does not propose any new construction in the area of the Abingdon ruins currently enclosed by a fence." Milliken pointed out, however, that the approved Master Plan was a planning document and not a specific design document. Soon after, however, just the opposite appeared to be in prospect for the ruins.

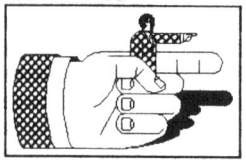

A little over a year later on November 21, 1989, Hugh C. Miller, the Virginia SHPO, and Director of the Department of Historic Resources, wrote to Francis J. Conlan the Airports Authority Engineering Division Manager. Miller referred to the copy he was provided of the Phase II of the Archaeological Investigations of the National Airport and specifically to the Study of the Abingdon Plantation Site. He wrote, among other things, that his office "concurs with the assessment that Abingdon is potentially eligible for inclusion to the National Register of Historic Places under Criteria D" (as an "archaeological resource"). Miller also included a statement that was

Major Community "Battles" and Controversies

to later shock and infuriate citizens who were fighting to prevent the destruction of the Abingdon manor and site by airport expansion. He wrote:

> *"It is the understanding of this office that Abingdon Plantation cannot be retained in site without jeopardizing a portion of the proposed project. Therefore, this office is willing to accept a determination of <u>No Adverse Effect</u>, provided the site is one hundred percent cleared archaeologically and all relevant pre-1940 archeological features undergo data recovery."(emphasis supplied).*

The position that the Abingdon plantation could not be retained without jeopardizing the airport project and that the project would have "no adverse effect" on the plantation ruins or site was one to which Abingdon preservationists could hardly have more strongly objected to as we shall see below. It would be precisely on these points that preservationists would make their strongest stand in the coming months.

* * * *

The closing weeks of 1989 and most of 1990 were to be some of the most active and contentious for the participants in the struggle to save the Abingdon site and ruins. There were to be times when it appeared the battle was both lost and/or won, with uncertainty as to which side had emerged victorious. The tide of battle would ebb and flow.

An opening shot to signal a resumption of hostilities was fired on December 5th at a meeting of the Arlington County Civic Federation, as reported in the January, 1990 issue of the Historical Society newsletter. The newsletter reported that "The news leaked out" by Representatives of the Airports Authority in a Federation appearance that "the Virginia Department of Historic Resources had approved a 100 percent excavation of the Abingdon site". On the heels of that disappointing development, the Society met in special session two days later on December 7th to consider action to take. At its next regular meeting in January, the Society adopted resolutions aimed at preserving the Abingdon site in place.[97]

On December 12, 1989, a time of particular dismay for preservationists, Arlington Journal writer Martin Finucane in a page one article headlined "Colonial Home Site Threatened" reported that the Authority planned to build a new parking garage on the Abingdon site. He described the worries of historical activists that the National Airport rebuilding "would wipe out traces of history that go back to Colonial times."

Finucane wrote further, that the Arlington Historical Society had voted to work for the preservation of the ruins of Abingdon and quoted the President June Robinson as saying, "We voted to do whatever we can to see that the remains of it, if possible, are saved." Finucane wrote that the authority's plan, as announced by its spokesman David Hess, was not to preserve the site intact, but to "excavate and remove any historic artifacts before building on the site", a position fiercely opposed by most of the

---

[97] *Arlington Historical Society Magazine, Vol. 9, No. 2 (October 1990), p. 64.*

ARLINGTON COUNTY VIRGINIA - A Modern History

preservationists. "The airport authority has worked with state historic preservation authorities in deciding how to handle the site", Finucane wrote. That course of action and position seemed to be consistent with the views and position contained in the November 21st letter of the SHPO alluded to above.

The Arlington Courier, only two days later in an article by John Riley, announced the formation of a new historical group in Arlington, the Arlington Heritage Alliance (AHA), headed by historians Bruce McCoy and Sara Amy Leach. Riley wrote that the group had thrown itself into the battle in support of efforts to save the Abingdon ruins, as well as some other historically important buildings such as "Lawyers Row" to include the Jesse Building on North Court House Road across from the court house. [98]

On December 13th, Hilary Adams wrote in the Alexandria Gazette, in part, that the historic site "will be removed from National Airport to an undetermined location to make room for a parking facility." She said that David Hess, spokesman for the Airports Authority, indicated the removal would be completed in "late summer or early fall" to a new location not yet known. Adams quoted Sara Collins, a member of the Arlington Historical Society, "So much of our visible history has already disappeared. It's important that we can be reminded of where the original plantation sat. If it's moved, you'd never have the same sense of where it really was."

In still another Abingdon site preservation article Northern Virginia Sun writer Yvonne French reported on December 20th of the efforts to historian Eleanor Lee Templeman to save the ruins. French wrote that Templeman had written letters to numerous local politicians and had obtained the intervention of State Senator Edward Holland of Arlington. As a result of negotiations with Holland and others, French wrote that the project manager for historic preservation had under consideration several alternatives to accommodate the site.

On the 26th of December, Journal writer Finucane revealed what seemed to some as a ray of hope and an indication that the pendulum might be swinging in the direction of the ruins preservationists. He reported Authority spokesman David Hess as saying "We're not going to touch the site until we look at it further". Hess conceded that the plan was to remove the ruins "to an appropriate place" until preservationists launched their all out offensive to save the ruins in place. Finucane quoted County Board member Milliken as saying he didn't know if he would try to save Abingdon but wanted to learn more about the site's historical significance.

In the closing days of 1989 some shots "for good measure" were fired on behalf of preservationists efforts. On December 28th, Gail Baker, new Chair of HALRB wrote to Ellen Bozman, current Chair of the County Board and urged the Board, in effect to

---

[98] *The efforts of the group to save "Lawyers Row" was unsuccessful. The buildings were razed to make room for the new jail and court house completed in 1993-95.*

Major Community "Battles" and Controversies

cease being an idle "standby" in the Abingdon dispute, and become an active and "consulting party" under section 106 of the Federal historical preservation Act. Baker wrote, in part; "HALRB discussed this matter (Abingdon) and unanimously passed the following resolution: HALRB encourages the Arlington County Board to become a consulting party in the federal Section 106 process...Consulting parties are the primary participants in the Section 106 process...as a consulting party the County can play an active role in the decision making and convey to the Airports Authority the considerable public interest in Abingdon's future...Individuals too may become consulting parties, and several Arlington citizens have expressed their interest in doing so".

Then, on December 29th, Bozman wrote Don Klima, Director, Eastern Office of Project Review of the Federal Advisory Council on Historic Preservation and expressed the Board's interest and concern over the fate of Abingdon. She wrote, in part, concerning a new proposal; "..we understand it calls for archaeological excavation of the Abingdon site rather than its preservation intact as previously proposed...We would appreciate receiving any materials and documents relevant to this issue."

1990 - A YEAR OF INTENSE ACTIVITY

As 1990 arrived an ever increasing number of players arrived on the field of combat to throw their weight into the fray. Arlington residents mentioned herein, and some others to include Barcroft resident Randy Swart, were among those known in the community to be especially interested and active in the drive to save the Abingdon ruins. Swart had written to the Board and reminded it of the Arlington County ties with the plantation and that a street and elementary school bore the names of Abingdon.

On January 3rd, Alexander Keyes, President of the Civic Federation, wrote County Board Chairman Eisenberg requesting that the Board become a consulting party in the development of the Master Plan for National Airport and that the design options for retaining the ruins should consist of "enhancement and embellishments at the site". Keyes wrote further, "While some (Federation) delegates pointed out that the deteriorated conditions of the ruins did not display enough historical merit to warrant preservation, the large majority...considered the sense of history embodied within this site to be worth strong preservation efforts and recommended further improvements to explain and enhance its historical significance."

In a January 4th memorandum to the County Board Chairman, County manager Anton S. Gardner outlined the status of the Abingdon matter to date and described the HALRB involvement. He also wrote; "Because of the existing Memorandum of Agreement to comply with Section 106, it was assumed that any proposed changes ...would be subject to public process to which the County would be invited...this has not occurred and staff has recommended that Arlington formally request participation as a consulting party..."

A MAJOR DEVELOPMENT

In a January Briefing Paper on Abingdon ruins, the Virginia Department of Historical Resources, to the particular interest of preservationists, stated; "Preservation is always preferred...(but) if it can be demonstrated that preservation is neither prudent or feasible, then other options must be explored." This position was greatly encouraging to Abingdon preservationists. They were contending that it had not been demonstrated that preservation was neither prudent or feasible and, therefore, no other option should be explored.

On January 8th, Congressman Frank Wolf and State Senator Clive DuVal, wrote to preservationist Bernard Berne. Neither took a particularly strong stand in favor of reserving the Abingdon ruins and site in place. Nor did State Delegate Mary Marshall in a January 24th letter to Berne. Wolf wrote that he had written to the Airports Authority General Manager "encouraging steps that best preserve the <u>historical significance</u> of the ruins (emphasis provided), and DuVal wrote merely that he hoped the Authority "will find some way to build the garage without destroying Abingdon". Berne considered "preserving the significance", which could be done in a display at another location, as far short of insuring the preservation of the ruins and site in place.

June Robinson as president of the Historical Society had on February 5th distributed materials on the dispute to all Society members to bring them "up to date on matters concerning Abingdon".

Of special irritation to preservationists at this time was the release of a National Airport sketch in a January consultant report for an Airport System Revenue Bond Prospectus. The prospectus showed a continuous parking garage that included the Abingdon site and stated that the plan would provide "an opportunity for the Authority to charge premium parking rates in the new facilities." To the Abingdon preservationists it appeared that the site and ruins were to be sacrificed so that additional parking revenues could be realized.

* * *

In what was to be a next step in these dramatic developments to save Abingdon, on March 9, 1990, James Wilding, General Manager of the Airports Authority, released a notice of a 7 p.m., March 29th "public hearing on the Abingdon Plantation Historic Site" at the Crystal Gateway Marriott Hotel, 1700 Jefferson Davis Highway in Arlington. The notice included an explanation of the background and said "It is presently considering alternative means of handling the site, including archeological excavation with full data recovery, and <u>retention of the site</u>" (emphasis supplied). The notice invited public comments in person or in writing concerning" 1) whether the plantation site should be preserved undisturbed; and 2) if the site must be disturbed, what should the Authority do with the historical artifacts and materials that are excavated. It said the hearing would be strictly an information gathering session for the staff or members of the Authority's Board of Directors present and that the public should not expect responses from the Authority for any comments or proposals during the hearing.

Also on March 9th, the Northern Virginia Sun writer Peter Mullaney reported that the Arlington County Board would hear a staff report on the Abingdon site and he said that Board Chairman Albert Eisenberg had indicated "the board will fight for the site's preservation". He said Eisenberg "was convinced of the site's historic value by the

Major Community "Battles" and Controversies

well-researched appeals of county residents". The staff report urged support for the effort to save the ruins in place, and the Board's Task Force on Arlington Open Space would shortly thereafter recommend "Preserve and discourage adverse construction" in the area of the Abingdon ruins..

On March 10th, the County Board, as an agenda item, requested the Airports Authority, among other things to "demonstrate that options to achieve construction goals which will not adversely impact the Abingdon site have been considered" and (if they) are not feasible and evacuation cannot be avoided that total recovery, public display and placement of historic markers be assured." Some preservationists were not highly pleased with that Board action which seemed to them to present the Authority with an undesired alternative to preservation on site.

On March 19th, Arlington's State legislative delegation threw its weight behind the efforts to preserve Abingdon in a somewhat ambivalent letter to Daniel Feil, the Authority's staff architect. In the letter signed by State Senators DuVal and Holland, and Delegates Almand, Marshall and Stambaugh they wrote, "..we approve of a study that would disturb the site minimally if at all". The language was considerably short of outright opposition to excavation, but there was the addition, "In sum, let us keep the ruins where they are"'. Some days later U. S. Senator Charles Robb in a stronger position advised Feil of his "full support for the preservation of Abingdon", but he did not indicate whether that went as far as favoring preservation on site with no excavation.

The March 29th hearing was held as scheduled and attended by several dozen citizens most of whom spoke strongly in favor of not excavating the ruins but retaining them in place. Speakers included County Board Chairman Eisenberg who called attention, according to Arlington Journal writer Martin Finucane on March 30th, to a long list of celebrated figures in American history who had been associated with Abingdon to include Captain John Smith, George and Martha Washington, Robert E. Lee, President James Garfield, and Arlington's Custis family. He quoted Eisenberg as saying in part, "Abingdon is one of our treasures, and we ask you to preserve it." The meeting was presided over by the Chairman of the Airports Authority Planning Commission, Carrington Williams, who was the only member of Authority's Board of Directors present.

Richmond Times-Dispatch writer William Rubarry indicated in an article several days later on June 4th that the issue at that time was still in much doubt despite the Authority's hearing and the County Board favorable positions. He reported that the Authority had not yet reached a final decision on the matter, that its initial proposal "envisioned a parking lot around the ruins, but not to disturb them" but that "last year the officials began to have second thoughts".

Rubarry also reported that Klima of the Federal Council on Historic Preservation, had complained that the Council's position had been misrepresented by the Authority at the March public hearing and asked why the Council had not been invited to the hearing. Rubarry further reported that the council had approved the 1988 airport renovation plans, but that plan "portrayed Abingdon Plantation as being avoided, unlike the current plans". In other words, Klima was objecting to the Authority's misrepresentation that the Council had approved the plans on the table and under consideration at the March 29th public hearing.

THE HEIGHT OF BATTLE

As Spring drifted into Summer in 1990, opponents of paving over the Abingdon ruins rolled out their heaviest artillery and most vocal combatants. Withering fire was directed at any and all officials in a position to influence an outcome on the matter, but the barrage did not appearing to have much impact on the designated, well entrenched targets.

SOME OF THE DARKEST HOURS

At an Airports Authority planning committee meeting of June 21st, airport architect Daniel Feil distributed a memorandum outlining the background of developments as of that date. Feil reported that the SHPO had made a "no adverse effect" determination of the parking system on the Abingdon site, "provided a 100% archaeological data recovery program is implemented". His memorandum alluded to the earlier March 29th public hearing and reported that the consensus of the 43 respondents was to leave the site "as it is", but that some agencies and groups had taken the position that if it were not possible to do so, then they favored an "archaeological excavation with full data recovery and an interpretive exhibit open to the public". The memorandum also stated that to preserve the site would result in a loss of 740 parking spaces, unless those spaces were provided at other airport locations, or by adding an additional parking level. The architect apparently considered that neither of those options were feasible. He recommended that "there be excavation and full data recovery" and that a "museum quality" interpretive exhibit be developed. The Planning Committee concurred in this recommendation to destroy the Abingdon site, a development that could hardly have been more disappointing to the Abingdon preservationists. Preservationists were beginning to wonder if they would ever prevail.

In the Washington Post coverage of the June 21st Authority meeting writer David Lindsey quoted Carrington Williams, chairman of the Planning Committee of the Authority as saying, "We think the excavation plan is the best way to go". To the contrary and in unequivocal disagreement, Lindsey quoted Judy Muniec, chair of the AHA as saying, "We would much prefer to have it preserved. It's a part of our history, one of the riverfront plantations that were between Arlington and Mount Vernon."

* * *

INTERDICTORY FIRE

The last shot, however, had not yet been fired. The battle raged on. On June 25th, historical preservationist and civic activist Bernard Berne wrote to the Chairman of the County Board. Berne outlined arguments for preserving the Abingdon site. The more salient were:

Major Community "Battles" and Controversies

o) Abingdon foundations date from at least 1746, longer than any other historical structures in Arlington, Alexandria, and Washington including Georgetown;

o) All the above received their names from people who lived at Abingdon;

o) George and Martha Washington lived near Abingdon, and often visited it. It was one of four famous plantations, including Mount Vernon, associated with the Washington family. All are national shrines except Abingdon;

o) Abingdon is near a METRO station, ideal for tourist visits;

o) The Virginia State Historic Preservation Officer has stated that Abingdon can only be destroyed if there is no <u>feasible and prudent alternative</u>, and the airport architect, Dan Feil, misrepresented the State's position when he failed to inform the Authority on this point.

o) Abingdon is one of the County's most treasured historical resources ranking with Arlington House and the National Cemetery.

o) Virtually every local historical group and elected officials supports preservation in place, and the airport staff did not tell the Planning Committee about this wide support; and

o) Only one member of the Airport Authority's Board attended the public hearing, and thus it cannot be assumed that absentees are aware of these points.

On the heels of Berne's letter with the above points, support fire continued from other sources. On July 3rd, County Board Chairman Eisenberg wrote to Klima at the and to Hugh Miller the Virginia SHPO. He referred to the recommendation of the Authority's Planning Commission to demolish the Abingdon Site that would be presented to the Authority at its upcoming July 19th meeting. He wrote that the recommendation was presented to the Planning Commission by Project Manager Feil who had quoted the SHPO as having made a "no adverse impact" determination concerning the impact on Abingdon of the proposed parking facilities, and had also said that the Authority had complied with the terms of the MOA. Eisenberg added, "Mr Feil's report is a disturbing development following assurances from your office and Mr Don Klima...that the Section 106 Review had not been initiated." Eisenberg expressed concern that "demolition and excavation of the site could ensue without our knowledge", and he asked what steps would next be taken on the matter and what action was available for Arlington County.

On July 5th, H. Bryan Mitchell, the Deputy Director of the Virginia Department of Historic Resources reiterated in a letter to Berne that the Department's position "has been, and still is, that of preservation in place at the Abingdon site". He wrote, however, that, "...due to the controversy involved with the Abingdon site, it would be our recommendation that a MOA be developed specifically for Abingdon."

On July 9th, a detailed letter to the editor from Berne was published in the Washington Post relating the issues involved in the Abingdon preservation efforts and faulting airport officials for thinking of replacing the site with a garage.

ARLINGTON COUNTY VIRGINIA - A Modern History

On July 16th, Betty Clements, President of the Arlington Historical Society wrote to the Airports Authority Board Chairman Governor Linwood Holton, and advised him that the Society had adopted a resolution favoring preservation of the site, and said it was disturbed at the "apparent misrepresentation" of the State position before the Authority Planning Committee. Clements urged the authority to halt any plans for demolition of the site and to initiate a Section 106 review. On July 17th, Arlington citizen Sara Collins, a professional historical librarian, also wrote Chairman Holton and presented a petition by concerned citizens who supported "preservation of the Abingdon Plantation House site as a visible, tangible symbol of our historic heritage". 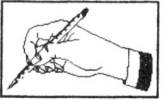 *Clements writes*

On July 16th, U. S. Senator John Warner joined the others in pleading for the preservation of the Abingdon site. He outlined historical reasons for doing do and wrote that it was his hope that the Authority would decide "to preserve the Abingdon site in place (emphasis provided).

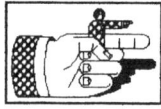 Perhaps the real and most telling "coupe de grace" in the exchange of fire of this period came from the guns of the State Department of Historical Resources. On July 13th, Deputy Director Mitchell wrote County Board Chairman Eisenberg and advised him that no determination of "no adverse effect" had ever been made concerning the Abingdon ruins. He wrote that the Authority staff report to the Authority Planning Commission to the contrary "was in error" and that Chairman Governor Holton had been so advised. Mitchell added:

> "We believe that the Abingdon ruins are eligible for the National Register as an archaeological site. Destruction...would constitute an adverse effect. It is our preference that the expansion of the airport be designed in such a manner as to allow the retention of the site. We recognize...that may not be feasible, but at this point it is the burden of the Authority staff to present us with documentation to that effect."

Finally, Mitchell wrote that the site might not be eligible for the Register "as a site associated with historic events or persons" since such a resource "must have significant association and it must retain its (structural) integrity" (which Abingdon did not have since there was no extant "structure" - only ruins). He wrote further, however, that "This finding in no way alters our previous determination that the site is eligible for the Register because of archaeological significance.

A WELCOME TURN IN THE BATTLE?

Finally, at a point when preservationists were confronted, seemingly, with only the most despairing of news and events, a bright ray of sunshine and hope burst full upon them. It appeared that the Authority was reversing itself and would move after all toward preserving the Abingdon ruins in place. In an article headlined "Airport won't dig up old digs", Peter Kaplan wrote in the July 23rd Arlington Journal that the Authority "last week backed away from plans to dig up the ruins of Abingdon house", and "Faced with growing opposition, the authority's 11-member board set aside a recommendation

Major Community "Battles" and Controversies

that it excavate Arlington's oldest structure to make room for a 7,000 space garage at National Airport". He quoted Authority Board member Bette Anderson as saying, "All of us have been deluged with letters...we need to take another good close look at it." However, he also quoted Board Chairman Carrington Williams as saying, "I've done a lot of agonizing on the subject (but) We've got what we consider our marching orders from Congress."

Some clouds of doom seemed here to reappear just when all seemed sunny and rosy. On August 24th, Williams wrote to Senator Robb and explained the lengthy history of the Authority's involvement with the Abingdon ruins. He pointed out that if the ruins remained in place, they would be surrounded by garages on three sides, and thus have a view of only Crystal City to the west. He said "few people know of or visit the ruins". He also wrote, "...to make Abingdon a public attraction as it now exists would, I believe, require access and parking space which, with existing constraints, would not be feasible...we incline to the view that preservation...in place is less than consistent with(our) mandate from Congress...to rebuild National Airport and make it more functional and convenient for air travelers, including maximum use of available (parking) space for passengers...(but) we are reviewing the matter further..." Sometime later, on November 2nd, Williams wrote to Berne along similar lines and said, in part, "I believe the overwhelming sentiment...is in favor of transportation improvements...and historic preservation must give way to that."

Some good news arrived soon afterwards from Authority Chairman Holton. On September 5th, he wrote to Eisenberg and referred to a misunderstanding by the Authority architect that led to the earlier misrepresentation of the State's position before the Authority Planning Commission. He said that "it is now clear that the State Historic Officer believes that preservation in place is preferable", provided it is a "reasonable and prudent" alternative. At this point, it seemed that preservationists might have some basis for cautious optimism.

1991 ARRIVES - AND LEGISLATIVE ASSISTANCE

As 1990 rolled into 1991, the Abingdon site controversy did not see a resolution satisfactory to the proponents of preservation on site. Big guns arrived on the battlefield, however, in the form of meaningful, but not quite dispositive, legislative assistance for the Abingdon preservation efforts. In early 1991 on February 21st the Virginia Senate agreed to House Joint Resolution No. 475, sponsored by Delegate Karen Darner and others, calling for appropriate elected officials and others to take all steps necessary to preserve and interpret to the public the Abingdon ruins. The resolution was welcomed by preservationists, although it was non-binding in effect.

Considerable indecision and uncertainty dominated events for the next several months until September 18th when State Director Miller wrote to Virginia Delegate Bernard Cohen with some discouraging language. Miller wrote, in part, "...The General Assembly urged the Authority and us to explore all feasible possibilities for saving the ruins," (emphasis provided) and "We agree with the Authority that preservation of the ruins in place cannot be feasibly accommodated within the expansion of the airport". Miller's representation of the legislative action was misstated. The language used in the

Miller letter was not precisely that which was contained in the Joint Resolution of February 21st, which read not to "explore possibilities", but, rather, the much stronger language "to take all steps necessary to preserve".

On the same day, Miller's Deputy H. Bryan Michell wrote to Authority managing engineer Conlon in a similar vein to Miller's letter to Cohen. He alluded to the matter of determining "no adverse effect", and wrote "the site and its resources continues to be adversely affected by its present context" and "we understand the severe limits (of site preservation) to MWAA's ability to locate parking in the vicinity of the Main Terminal...we find the mitigation measures are clearly described and realistically considered in light of what is prudent and feasible..." Michell seemed to be saying, inferentially, if not expressly, that his office concurred in excavation and removal of the Abingdon ruins.

A few days later, on the 25th, Peter Kaplan in the Arlington Journal delivered what seemed to be the final blow. He confirmed that the SHPO had approved the Authority plans to "remove the Abingdon ruins...despite protests by Virginia preservationists and lawmakers. He referred to the SHPO letters of the week before and wrote that the SHPO concluded the Authority had no "prudent and feasible" alternative to removing the ruins to make way for parking spaces. Kaplan wrote that approval by the state agency "removes the largest obstacle to the Authority's plan for Abingdon."

By years end, the Arlington County Board included in its 1992 Legislative package the position statement, in part; "Arlington County supports legislation which would ensure the preservation in place (emphasis provided) of the Abingdon...ruins". That statement met with strong approval from preservationists.

1992 - A DECISIVE YEAR

Steve Bates in the Washington Post reported on January 30, 1992 that a decision from the Authority as to whether or not to excavate the Abingdon site was expected in the Spring and that measures aimed at forcing the agency to preserve the ruins had been introduced in the Virginia General Assembly. [99] The Authority's staff discussed the measures, a bill and a resolution, in its February "Briefing Paper" to the Authority's Planning Commission..

On March 4th, Washington Times reporter Frank Wolfe wrote that the Virginia General Assembly had passed the measure requiring the Authority to leave the Abingdon site untouched until April 1, 1993 by a House vote of 78-20 and a Senate vote of 21-19. Wolfe quoted Authority spokeswoman Tara Hamilton as saying, "We're disappointed". He wrote that the measure would need to be passed by the D.C. Council and Abingdon

---

[99] *House Bill 726 requiring the Airports Authority to "take all steps necessary to insure the preservation in place, the study, and the interpretation to the public" of the Abingdon ruins was offered on January 21, 1992 by Delegate Karen L. Darner and others. On March 20, Virginia Governor L. Douglas Wilder signed it into law as Chapter 402 of the 1992 Acts of the Assembly. The law expired on April 1, 1993 and was not reenacted.*

Major Community "Battles" and Controversies

supporters expected the Authority "to lobby the council against the bill as strongly as it lobbied the Virginia Assembly to reject a proposed study of its preservation".

As word of the Airports Authority announcement of intent to destroy the Abingdon site spread, so did community interest and alarm at the prospects of losing forever the historical and treasured plantation manor site.

Another Abingdon supporter wrote to the Washington Times in a letter published February 6, 1992, in part:

> *"...The Abingdon ruins at National Airport are in danger of disappearing forever from this planet. Now is the time for concerned citizens to rally to this historical preservation cause. What's left of the Abingdon plantation -- in the path of the new National Airport parking garage -- must be saved. Posterity will thank us if the site is spared. We will be faulted if it is not. It can be done if there is enough public outcry. Few today may understand the importance of Abingdon. Its ruins, scant as they may be, are about the only pre-Revolutionary War artifacts in Arlington County other than the Ball-Sellers house on South 3rd Street. Even the prestigious Arlington House in the National Cemetery (Custis Lee Mansion) dates from well after the war. Both George Washington Parke Custis, who later built Arlington House, and Nellie Custis (grandchildren of Martha Washington) were born at Abingdon. Also, the City of Alexandria is named after Gerrard Alexander who built Abingdon in about 1741..."*

As the days passed following the revelation that the Abingdon ruins were in danger of elimination, numerous individual citizens rose in defense of the ruins and urged the Airport Authority to reconsider its plans to do away with the Abingdon site. One of the most energetic and persistent critics was Arlingtonian and Historical Society member Bernard H. Berne, mentioned repeatedly herein. He was in time to become known around the community as "Abingdon Ruins Bernie". He became heavily committed to the "crusade" to save the ruins and must be given a major share of credit for alerting the community of the threat to the Abingdon site and in encouraging the General Assembly to become effectively involved. Additionally, various organizations joined in the drive to save Abingdon. The 1992 legislation had only granted Abingdon one additional year of life. With that in mind, on Chairman Michael Glick of the Arlington HALRB in a September 30th letter to County Board Chair Ellen Bozman, urged the County Board to include in its legislative package for the Virginia General Assembly a proposal "to insure the continuing (emphasis supplied) preservation in place, the study, and the interpretation to the public of the Abingdon Plantation House ruins and Historic Site at Washington National Airport". Similar recommendations were made to the Board on October 8th by Arlington Historical Society President Bruce Gregory McCoy, and on October 28th by the AHA by its President Terri Brown. By the end of the year, the governing bodies of the City of Alexandria, and the Counties of Arlington and Fairfax recommended that permanent legislation, as desired by the HALRB, AHA, the Arlington Historical Society and others, be transmitted to their respective legislative delegates and senators.

THE EXISTENCE OF OPPOSITION

Not all reaction in this and other periods was necessarily in opposition to the Authority's plan to eliminate the Abingdon ruins. Some, perhaps most, citizens were clearly indifferent or at least expressed little or no interest in the matter. Some even seemed to approve the loss on the ruins and site. In an editorial headed "All this to save a few stones?", the Arlington Journal on November 30th suggested that the there was not enough of the manor remaining to make it worthwhile to try to save.

The Journal editorial resulted in a stream of letters to the editor taking the newspaper to task for what was felt by some readers to be a cavalier position concerning a historical site of major significance. This writer in a "Counterpoint" article in the December 9, 1992 issue, pointed out that certain sites are historically of value and worth saving even if little

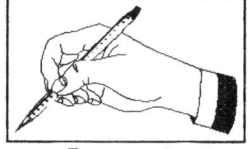

Pratt writes!

remains of what was once there, or even if there was never any structure of any kind but was just a place where a major historical event took place. The article cited the area in Montana where the Battle of the Little Big Horn took place, or where the 300 Spartans held off the Persians at Thermopile in the 5th Century B.C. that are preserved for all posterity to visit and marvel. It was stressed that those and innumerable other historical sites are preserved not for any structures intact or in part, but because of great historical events that occurred on the land. The article included a contention that no one would even think of erecting any structure, or otherwise consider any other non-historical and unrelated development, on such historically important sites, and that it should not be done on the Abingdon site.

ANOTHER TURN OF THE TIDE

As 1992 neared an end, the Authority appeared to be wavering and regrouping in their insistence that the Abingdon site was essential for their expansion plans for the airport. On November 19, to the excitement of preservationists, an article headlined "Plan may spare Abingdon from airport lot", Arlington Journal writer Norman Gomlak seemed to signal an about face and possible capitulation of the Airport authority concerning the survival of the Abingdon ruins in place. Gomlak wrote, in part, that the Authority "appears to have found a way to save the historic plantation ruins at Washington National Airport from being destroyed when a parking lot is built."

Gomlak also quoted James Wilding, general manager of the Airports Authority as saying "...the Authority will probably not need to build as much new parking as originally planned..." A similar article headlined "Manor's Ruins May Be Saved, Airport Says", by writer Steve Bates appeared in the November 20th issue of he Washington

Major Community "Battles" and Controversies

Post. Preservationists felt that the tide of the struggle was changing, that they were regaining the initiative and were effectively advancing on the field of battle.

Gomlak also wrote in his article that Daniel Alcorn, a member of the Authority board was pleased with the news, that he'd like to see the Authority set aside money to restore the site, and "if we do it, we need to do it well...to retain its historical integrity, and be done to a quality standard". Gomlak also reported that Jean Federico, director of the Office of Historic Alexandria noted that Wilding's statement "was almost a 100 percent change from previous Board policy".

A December "Status Report" by Wilding to the Authority's Planning Commission, presented at its January 5, 1993 meeting, listed as actions presently being implemented concerning the Abingdon matter included (1) "designing into the Middle and North Parking Structures the capability for future construction of a sixth level", and (2) proceeding the MOA negotiations relating to the effects of the parking structures on the Abingdon site. Wilding concluded that multiple options were identified to provide adequate parking without having to excavate the Abingdon site. In so concluding it appeared the Airports Authority had found it was indeed feasible and prudent to preserve the Abingdon site.

1993 - SECURING THE OBJECTIVE

On January 7, 1993, Gomlak of the Journal wrote in an article headlined "They won't pave ruins or put up a parking lot", "After years of debate, the regional airports authority has agreed to preserve the ruins..." of Abingdon. He quoted Jean Federico, director of the Office of Historic Alexandria as saying she was pleased to see that the plantation ruins will stay where they are...There is a difference between not building on it and making it look attractive. The next step is to preserve it properly. Gomlak wrote that Wilding, general manager of the Airports Authority said, "It was a relatively slow build up of use...(one garage had opened during the previous year) that had the light bulb go off in my mind..."

Only days later on January 15th and 20th, 1993, Virginia Delegates Vincent F. Callahan, Jr., and Karen Darner wrote to Bernard Berne and Bruce McCoy, respectively, that they did not believe any further legislation (to replace the expiring 1992 law) to insure the preservation of the Abingdon ruins was necessary in view of the Airport Authority's change of position and apparent commitment to save Abingdon. Darner wrote that she had become convinced through conversations and written communications with members of the Authority that "good faith" was in operation. She alluded to the Authority's promise to draw up a memorandum of understanding to the satisfaction of all concerned.

A MEMORANDUM OF AGREEMENT

In due course a proposed MOA and a Preservation Program (Plan) for Abingdon was prepared and released in March 1994 by Frank D. Holly, Jr., the Authority's Engineering Division Manager. At a public meeting at the National Airport, Holly distributed copies of the MOA and plan to all interested parties for their information and comment. The Virginia SHPO, the Advisory Council on Historic Preservation, and the Airports Authority were parties to the MOA. The memorandum contained ten stipulations, concerning Authority obligations. In essence they provided the Authority would:

    1. Endeavor to have the Abingdon site nominated to the National Register of Historic Places;
    2. See that resources and the historic setting of the site are protected and disturbance of archaeological deposits avoided;
    3. Continue to provide public access to the site and make provision for disabled visitors;
    4. Develop a site stabilization program;
    5. Remove, as necessary, all vegetation that causes, or could cause, damage to structural remains or archaeological deposits and avoid adverse effects by any new plants introduced;
    6. Make historic and archaeological information related to the Abingdon site available to the public, and develop on-site interpretive exhibits and displays;
    7. Provide an opportunity for SHPO and the council to review and comment on elements of the plans, and take any such comments into account;
    8. Initiate consultation, as needed, if any future airport development is determined to have potentially adverse affects on the site;
    9. Consent to consultation and amendment of this Agreement if changes in the scope or specifications of the project results in additional detrimental or harmful effects on the site; and
    10. Consult to remove any objections by SHPO or the Council to any plans or specifications pursuant to this agreement, and if the Authority determines that the objection cannot be resolved then to request further comments of the Council using the process provided for in the Code of Federal Regulations.

SOME DESIRED MODIFICATIONS IN THE MOA

In response to the above proposed agreement, and at the instance of its member Berne and other concerned members, the Arlington Historical Society President Seymour Stiss wrote the Airport Authority on May 3, 1994. He stated that the Society agreed with most of the planning and design efforts but offered three recommendations. The Arlington County Board and the Civic Federation, by inference, joined in these recommendations. They were;

FIRST, the Society recommended the MOA be amended to require the Authority to preserve the ruins and site "in perpetuity" or for so long as the Authority has control of the site.

Major Community "Battles" and Controversies

SECOND, that the MOA be amended to stipulate that the Authority will maintain the notable yew trees on the site and that no trimming take place except as necessary to protect the trees and the integrity of the historical site.

THIRD, that the Abingdon Plantation Site be nominated to the National Registry of Historic Places and the Virginia Landmarks Register, and that Abingdon be referred to as an historic site rather than a structure.

The Airports Authority agreed only to protect the yew trees. Thus the MOA signed later in October, did not provide for the permanent preservation of the Abingdon site to the keen disappointment of Abingdon preservationists.

On May 18, 1994, David M. Foster, of the Arlington Civic Federation wrote Frank Holly, the Authority's managing engineer and said the Federation had long supported the preservation of Abingdon "in place" and suggested that the final MOA provide that such preservation be permanent. He also said the Federation urged that the Abingdon site be considered for nomination to the National Register of Historical Places and the Virginia Landmark Register.

THE PRESERVATION PROGRAM DETAILS

The March 1994 Preservation Program, or plan, for Abingdon contained a description of the Authority's proposal providing for the stabilization, public access, enhancement, and historic interpretation of the Abingdon Site.

The plan noted the unstable conditions at Abingdon that have caused deterioration and past inadequate efforts to prevent further damage caused by uncontrolled plant growth and weathering. Major elements of the site preservation program for the primary structure ("Main House"), Secondary structure ("Kitchen") and Ancillary structure ("Shed") included:

a. removal of non-historic plants, pruning of others;
b. repair and capping of foundation remains;
c. uncover and repair the North Chimney base;
d. filling the basement to stabilize the foundation, discourage vandalism, and promote the safety of visitors; and
e. replacing existing wooden bracing on standing walls/foundations with appropriate permanent supports.

To make the new Abingdon more accessible to the walking as well as the motoring public, the Authority plan provided for a new "pedestrian bridge" to connect the site to the Metrorail station and the New North Terminal. Additionally, the existing Mount Vernon Trail would be extended with a Site access path. Site parking would be available in either the South or Middle/North nearby parking structures, and there would be a handicap accessible path from the Pedestrian Connector to the plantation site. The plan also called for pedestrian access to the side open to the east that had previously been designated for more parking in the Authority's recommended Master plan. With these features, the Abingdon Site should be easily accessible to visitors in cars or to air travelers when waiting in the terminal for planes, or when transferring between flights.

ARLINGTON COUNTY VIRGINIA - A Modern History

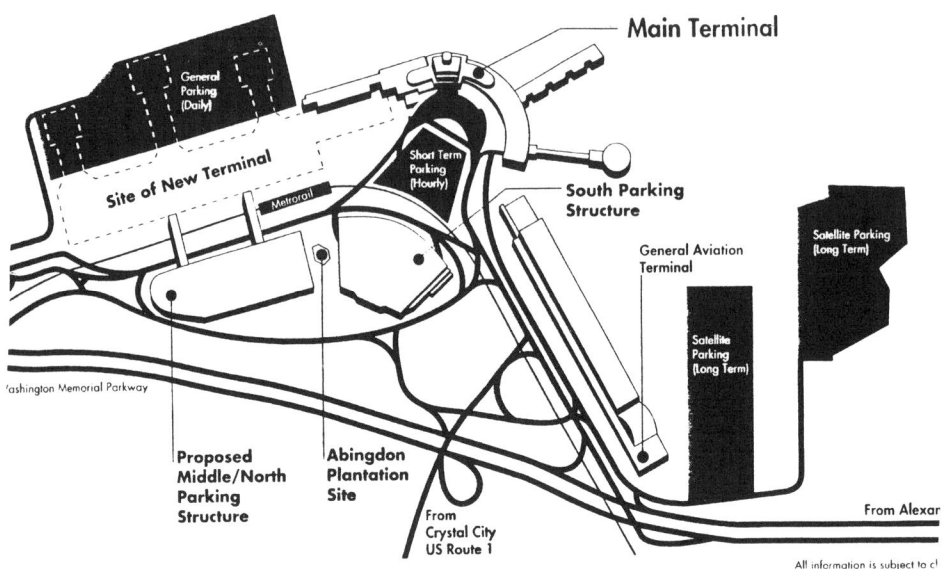

The Airport Authority sketch showing the location of the Abingdon site in relations to the airport roads, terminals and other structures.

To aid visitors in finding the Abingdon site, or better understanding it when on the site, the Authority plan included the erection of directional signs and interpretive displays of weatherproof informative placards as had been earlier suggested.. These were to contain historical and other significant archaeological information concerning the site to stress its importance and the role it played in the development of Arlington and Northern Virginia.

In preparing its preservation plan the Airport Authority related that it had worked closely with the Virginia State Historic Preservation Office and the Federal Advisory Council on Historic Preservation. The Authority did not indicate the extent, if any, to which it had taken the positions of those agencies or the public into account.

THE BATTLE ENDS

Thus ended, at least so hoped many participants, a tedious, exasperating, protracted and often acrimonious and uncertain campaign with many maneuvers, skirmishes and battles on a matter of utmost importance to those involved and their supporters. There were widespread sighs of relief. Although the proponents for saving

Major Community "Battles" and Controversies

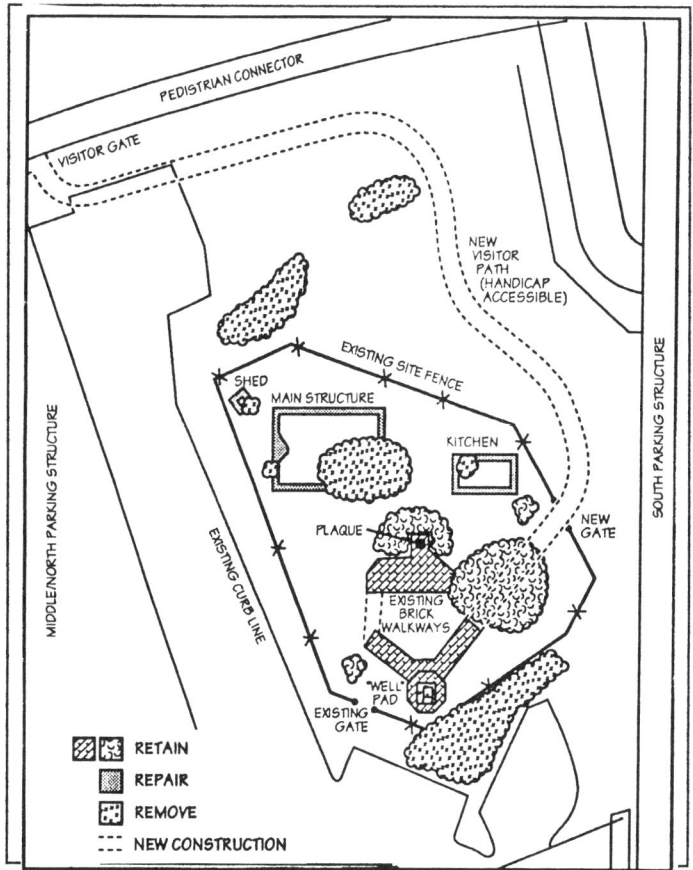

Airport Authority sketch of Abingdon showing work proposed to preserve.

Abingdon were no doubt gratified at the final outcome of the matter, many were also convinced that but for them it would have been otherwise, and Abingdon and its ruins would, in due course, have been only a memory. The perseverance and skill with which they had mounted their campaign, and steadfastness with which they maintained the momentum of the assault throughout, had paid off.

One can only wonder whether future visitors to the Abingdon site would ever know just how much "blood" of community and history lovers had been spilled on the field of battle in the great campaign of the 1980' and '90s to save the site from extinction so that it could be viewed for many years, and hopefully forever, as a vital element in Arlington County, Virginia and National history.

* * * * *

Round XVI
THE ACQUISITION OF FORT SMITH

The Hendry Tract

On July 19, 1994, The Arlington County Board in an Executive session not open to the public voted 5-0 to acquire a 14.7 acre tract of land owned by the Ernest S. Hendry family at a cost of $5,250,000,[100] based on a purchase agreement dated just the day before. There was no advance public notice, or clear indication on the agenda available to the public, that the Board was to consider the purchase of land at that session. The property had been assessed at the time at $4.5 million. The County promptly acquired the property less than two months later on September 9, 1994. The deed, signed by Elizabeth Hendry Vercoe, several other family part owners, and Andrew R. McRobert, the Assistant County Attorney, is recorded in Arlington Circuit Court Deed Book 2695, page 0081, et seq. County Board Chairperson Mary Margaret Whipple stated that the acquisition "was one of the most significant land acquisitions in the County's history", a view clearly shared by many in the community.

The tract, identified as 2411 North 24th Street, mostly open space and woodlands, had been used as the residence and farm of the Hendry family for many years. It contained the sizeable Victorian residence of the family, a cottage, a farm equipment barn, and several out-buildings. It also contained about two thirds of the earthen remains of Civil War Fort C. F. Smith, and the land on which was located the barracks, parades ground, stables, and other amenities of or for the troops that manned

---

[100] *Arlington County Board Minutes, July 9, 1994, page 233.*

Major Community "Battles" and Controversies

the fort. About one third of the western earth remains of the fort had been destroyed by the earlier opening of 24th (formerly Malvern) Street, and the construction of several homes on the street side opposite the Hendry property.

The Hendry property is located on the high ground in the northern half of the county above and about a mile North of Rosslyn. It adjoins the George Washington Memorial Parkway and the Potomac River Palisades to the northeast and northwest, Spout Run Parkway to the east and fronts on North 24th Street to the south. The land was described by Board Chairman Whipple as having "unique historical and ecological potential" and has received a historical designation. There could be no doubt that most Arlingtonians shared her view.

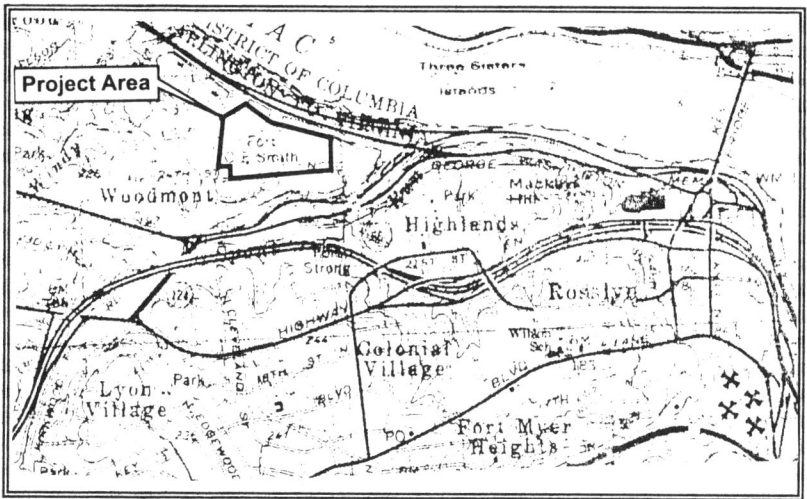

The Ft Smith location relative to Arlington surroundings.

SOME DISSENTS ON THE PURCHASE

The purchase of the Hendry property was looked upon by some South Arlingtonians, however, with considerable disenchantment and irony. The purchase was made in 1994 although only a few years earlier in 1979 a ballot bond proposal to buy the Hendry tract and local parks was defeated 16,577 to 9,465.[101] South Arlingtonians remembered that in the late 1960s their efforts to have the County Board, composed only of North Arlingtonians, purchase an open space tract at Army-Navy Drive and South 23rd Street had met with failure. That 19 acre R-10 zoned tract, discussed elsewhere herein, was known as the Sickels/Chaiken land (now the Forest Hills Townhouse development), and was the largest extant undeveloped tract of open space in the County.

---

[101] *The ballot merely showed $4 million for "local park acquisition" but it was widely understood in the community that the funds would be used to acquire the Hendry tract.*

ARLINGTON COUNTY VIRGINIA - A Modern History

Civic Association leaders pleaded for denial of a rezoning application for R-10T (townhouses) and urged the County Board to buy the land for park or other open space uses. They pointed to recent surveys showing far less park lands per resident in the southern than in the northern half of the county. The Sickels tract was assessed at the time at about $1 million, about a fifth of the value of the Hendry tract.

The County Board, however, refused to buy the Sickels tract and granted the rezoning as requested. Residents around the former Sickels property wondered if the different attitudes and action of the Board in the two instances did not constitute unfair discriminatory treatment that favored North Arlington over the Southern half of the County. Long time civic activist John Marr said, "How strange the county refused to buy the Sickels tract but only a few years later bought the Hendry tract, about the same size, at five times the price, but located nearer where the Board members live."

"But the Hendry tract had great historical importance as the site of one of the main civil war Forts of Abe Lincoln, and the best preserved in the County", said Col. Bruce Jones another local civic activist and member of the Arlington Ridge Civic Association.

"No South Arlington Parkland?"

"Not quite so", said Marr. "The Sickels tract also had its historical claim to fame. Remember, it was the lands of some of the County's earliest settlers and contemporaries of John Ball, James Roach, Samuel Shreve and others. Indeed, it was Anthony Fraser who built Green Valley Manor on the land, who is now buried in the family grave sites on the Army-Navy golf course and whose daughter Presha married the Civil War engineer Jackson Sickels from whence the land got its latter day name."

"I suppose you are right," admitted Jones. "If the Board felt it had justifiable reasons for buying the Hendry tract, then it surely had equal or better reasons for grabbing up the Sickels tract instead of letting it go for more residential development." The County Board, of course, as reflected by the course of events, did not see it that way.

To buy the Hendry tract, the County Board used part of the $9 million of bond money under a general heading for "Land Acquisition and parks development" that had been approved by the voters in the election of 1992, and perhaps some of the land and park bond money approved in the 1990 election.[102] It is pertinent here to again point out, for whatever interest if may be, if any, that only a short time earlier, as related above, Arlington voters had turned down a land acquisition bond proposal specifically designated to buy the Hendry tract.

There is further evidence that approval in the County for the purchase of the Hendry tract was not quite universal. In its newsletter "The ACTA Watchdog" of October 5, 1992, the Arlington County Taxpayers Association (ACTA) had opposed the

---

[102] *According to David Miller in the County Fiscal office, the sale of bonds at times of best available interest rates, and when they are most needed, is a complex and delicate challenge and it is not always possible to determine with precision from what voter authorization bonds are being sold.*

Major Community "Battles" and Controversies

$9 million bond proposal for land acquisition (and some other bonds for playgrounds, ball courts, bike trails, lighting, etc) on the question of need and propriety. It said, in part, "...except for the land acquisition, none of these belong on a bond issue..they are all operating maintenance and should be accommodated with the annual operating budget". Concerning the $9 million for land acquisition, the association asked, "...is it appropriate to buy and develop more park land? Northern Virginia...abounds with parks. The County already owns many properties utilized as parks, and also owns 162 acres for parks that has never been developed as such."

Later, in its 1995 newsletters, ACTA continued to question the propriety of Board action with respect to the Hendry tract. In its September 8th newsletter the Association alluded to the Board session of April 29, 1995, when, in another executive session with a 5-0 vote, a decision was made to purchase from Robert E. Hemphill, Jr., adjacent property known as Parcel B of the Hendry tract for $2,850,000, or $660,181 an acre. ACTA claimed that Hemphill, Executive Vice President of Arlington's Applied Energy Service Corp., had purchased the 4.317 acre property in March, 1993 from the Hendry family for $2.4 million and thus in only a few months had earned a "hefty profit" of $450,000. ACTA noted from election records that Hemphill had contributed "at least a total of $1,250" to the campaigns of board members Eisenberg and Newman, and at "least $1,190" for the campaigns of Hunter, Bozman and Whipple. ACTA wanted to know "if there had been a violation of Virginia law since members of the Board received over $2,400 in campaign contributions from the seller of the property". ACTA observed, "If there wasn't an actual violation of Virginia statute, there is certainly the appearance of one."

In its next newsletter in October, ACTA reported that it had queried the Commonwealth Attorney and asked that the purchase of Parcel B be reviewed for a possible violation of law, or the appearance of a violation. Deputy Attorney Barbara L. Walker [103] replying to ACTA on August 30th answered that Board members did not violate the Virginia statue and that her office had no "jurisdiction to opine on the 'appearance' of a violation". She wrote that Sec. 2.1-639.4.5 of the pertinent Virginia Act, that prohibits gifts, money or acts that tend to influence public officials in the performance of duties, did not apply to any political contribution and that Hemphill's campaign contributions had been reported as such. This writer has been unable to determine that ACTA pursued the matter further.

Notwithstanding any disenchantment, or disapproval, of the County Board's purchase of the Hendry tracts, and the earlier refusal of voters to approve bonds intended for the purchase, the action seems to have been generally well received by the county citizenry. At least this writer has not been able to establish a record to the contrary through examination of letters to the editor or otherwise. It seems likely that the public purchase and setting aside this last remaining large tract for park and historical preservation purposes will in future years be looked back upon as ranking in wisdom and foresight with the purchase years ago of the lands alongside Rock Creek in the District

---

[103] *Ms Walker worked as Deputy to the Commonwealth Attorney who had ran for office on the Democratic Party ticket or support, as had all five members of the County Board.*

ARLINGTON COUNTY VIRGINIA - A Modern History

of Columbia that are now known as Rock Creek Park. That land has long been an oasis of open space in the midst of clusters of high rises, business districts, traffic and congestion. The Hendry tract seems destined to become for Arlington County and Northern Virginia, perhaps on a smaller scale but with more historical aspect, what Rock Creek Park has become for the Nation's Capital.

EARLY HISTORY OF THE LAND

The Hendry tract as located on pre-Civil War map showing Mason property.

    Probably the best easily available recorded evidence of the earliest ownership of the Hendry tract is on a full page supplement in the Northern Virginia Sun published during the 1976 Bicentennial Salute. The map entitled, "Land Ownership Map:1669-1796" was researched by the Arlington Historical Society member Donald Wise, who also served at the time on the County Bicentennial Commission. That map shows the Hendry tract to be well within a much larger tract once owned by Thomas Going.

368

Major Community "Battles" and Controversies

The Beth Mitchell map (previous page)[104], one of the most reliable early maps, identifies Fairfax County land owners in that year (which included what is now Arlington County). The later and somewhat more definitive Wise map identifies owner tracts in Arlington that later became Alexandria County of the District of Columbia. Both maps show the property of George Mason in which the Hendry tract would eventually be located. Mason's lands ran along the Potomac Palisades, inland for about a mile or two from about the present Arlington/Fairfax County line on the north, to Rocky Run about where the present day Iwo Jima Marine Monument is located. The property included Roosevelt (Analostan) Island, shown on the map as Mason's Island.

The Mason shown on the Mitchell map would have been George Mason III, the father of George Mason IV who was the builder of Gunston Hall and the author of the Virginia Bill of Rights. Neither of these early Masons seems to have made any significant improvements on the land according to the John Milner Associates of Alexandria, Virginia (referred to hereinafter) who made a survey of the Fort Smith area and its history for the Arlington County Department of Parks and Recreation.[105] The survey, with detailed and scholarly annotations and references, is available for examination in the Virginia Room of the Arlington Central (Main) Library, and in the County Department of Parks and Recreation. The following background information is mostly from the survey.

THE JOHN MASON & WILLIAM JEWELL PERIOD

Upon the death of Mason IV at the end of the century and around the time of the establishment of the new national capital, his lands were transferred to his son John Mason and the land became subject to several changes in ownership over the years. Early in Gen Mason's stewardship, he built an elegant estate, described elsewhere herein, called Analostan on Mason's Island. The home and estate became gathering places for the new capital's diplomatic, political and social elite. Mason also began developing property on what eventually became the Hendry tract between Spout and Windy Runs. According to the Milner Associates, he built a mill along the north side of Spout Run and constructed a bridge across the Run to provide access to it. He engaged in various commercial enterprises including the ownership of the Henry Foxhall Columbia foundry, Washington's largest business.

Mason founded the Bank of Columbia in 1793 and served as president of the Potowmack Company, the predecessor of the Chesapeake and Ohio Canal Company. When the bank collapsed in 1833 he became bankrupt and was forced to sell his home and much of his land. In the years following, the lands went through a period of sub divisions and changes in ownership with various efforts to develop. Farming was also attempted at times. In 1848 Lots 20, 21 and 16 (essentially the Hendry tract) were

---

[104] *Published by the Office of Planning, Fairfax County Government, Fairfax, Va., 1987.*

[105] *John Milner Associates, Architects, Archaeologists, Planners,* Historical and Archeological Survey of Fort C. F. Smith, Vols. 1-5 *Alexandria, VA., 22312, 1995.*

ARLINGTON COUNTY VIRGINIA - A Modern History

purchased by William Jewell who held the property until 1887 except for the Civil War years when it was occupied by the Federal Army for Fort Smith and other purposes as described below.

In the period 1888 to 1927, the Hendry property was owned in whole or in part by such people as Robert Lamborn, Charles Bradley, A. C. Yates, George Deming and a syndicate known as the Ivanwold Corporation. In 1898 10 acres of the property south of the present day Hendry tract was purchased by the Col.Charles Doubleday family with a building they expanded with wings to create an elegant mansion they called, The Cedars. The configuration and size of the property seems to have varied during this period of complex exchanges but by about 1907 the 22.29 acres containing Fort Smith had taken, for the most part, its present form. In 1924 Charles R. Lindsey of the Lindsey Light Company in Chicago purchased the 22.29 acres but there is little evidence that his family ever lived on the property. He did, however, make extensive alterations to the main residence "Idlewild" and built a cottage to the west. The Hendrys claimed that Herbert Hoover, President Woodrow Wilson's Secretary of Commerce during the first World War, and later also President, was a frequent visitor at Idlewild.

THE CIVIL WAR PERIOD

Within a month of the inauguration of President Lincoln in 1861, the opening shot of the Civil War was fired in the Charleston, South Carolina harbor and on April 15th, Fort Sumter surrendered. The fat was in the fire and the war had begun. An apprehensive and concerned President was told by his senior military advisors, including  the aging General-in-Chief Winfield Scott, that the capital city was not "defensible". It was considered accessible to an enemy from any side, but especially from the South where Confederate armies were forming. Most of the capital city and its federal buildings could be shelled from the heights of Arlington (then the "county" part of Alexandria County) only a couple of miles away, or less, at most points. The president and his advisors quickly realized that the Arlington high ground had to be occupied either for defense from an attacking force, or to keep it out of the hands of the enemy.

During the night of May 23-24, 1861 the occupation of Arlington heights and other related grounds was launched. Regiments crossed the Aqueduct Bridge at Rosslyn, the Long Bridge near the present "twin bridge" area and arrived in Alexandria by boat. They quickly set about to erect earthwork Forts Corcoran, Haggerty and Bennett to guard the Georgetown Aqueduct, and Forts Runyon and Albany to cover the Long Bridge. Fort Ellsworth was established as a point of strength for the city of Alexandria. The pace of work was intensified when two months later in July the Federal troops were routed in the first Battle of Bull Run (Manassas).

By the time construction of the Virginia forts was complete the system consisted of several main or base forts, such as Forts Whipple, Scott, Corcoran and Richardson with smaller, supporting, or "lunette" fortifications (satellite moons?) such as Forts McPherson, Morton, Cass or Tillinghast nearby. Somewhat unlike the larger forts, lunettes consisted of two faces and two parallel flanks. The larger forts were usually

Major Community "Battles" and Controversies

more star shaped in design. Eventually there would be a total of 48 works surrounding the Capital in Virginia and Maryland. The work was under the charge of 46 year old Major General John G. Barnard, a slightly deaf 1833 graduate of West Point who finished second in his class. He became known as the "Father of the Defenses of Washington".

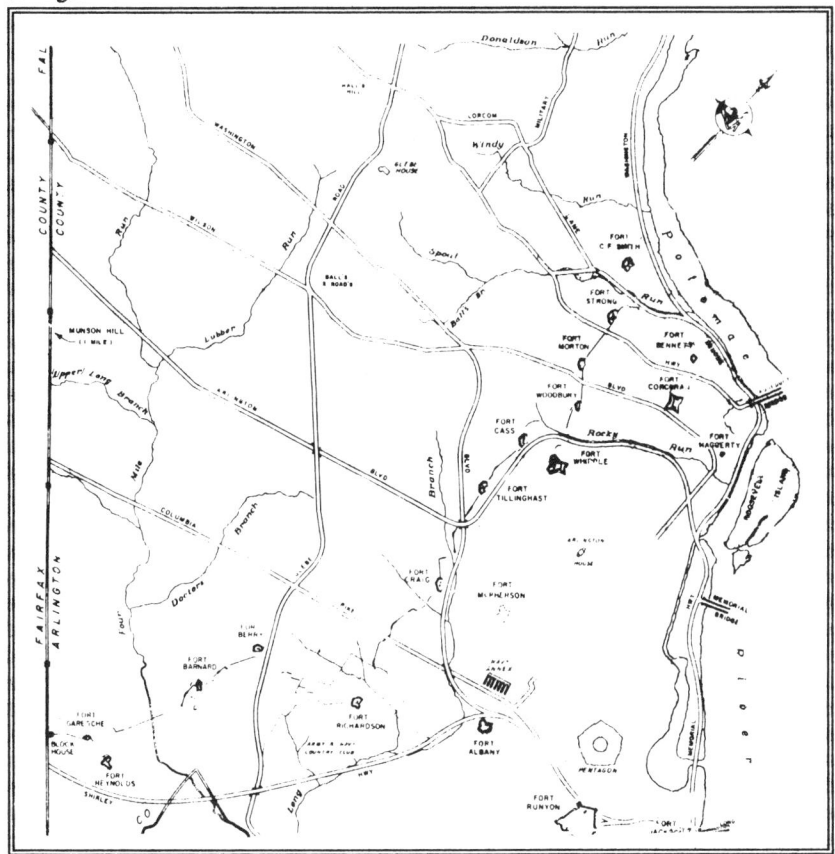

President Lincoln's Northern Virginia Civil War Forts.

Following and in the light of ill fated Federal campaigns near Fredericksburg and Chancellorsville and at Antietam there was renewed concern for the safety of the Capital. A commission was appointed by Secretary of War Stanton. As a result it was decided to establish two new fortifications in the line of forts; one a couple of hundred yards northwest of Arlington House used as a military headquarters that would eventually become named Fort Whipple, the other on the William Jewell palisades property above the Georgetown Aqueduct.

ARLINGTON COUNTY VIRGINIA - A Modern History

The design of the fort on the Jewell property shared many of the same physical characteristics of the other "lunette" forts being constructed at the time. They were described, as set forth below, in some detail in a preservation plan for Fort Smith that was prepared and circulated in 1986 during public discussion and consideration of rezoning to allow a retirement home that is discussed below.

> *"...The forts had a slanting parapet (wall) seven to nine feet high that was eight to twelve feet thick (fronts were twelve to eighteen feet). A six-foot-deep ditch was dug at the bottom outside edge of the parapet. Usually the outside walls were sodded. On the interior of the parapet a banquette or wooden platform was built for the infantry to stand on. Vertical posts were rivetted to the inside of the parapet where possible. The magazines and bombproofs were constructed of timber covered with a composition of tar, resin, sand and clay. The bombproofs were centrally located and had an opening to the rear with overhanging roofs. The entrances to the forts were at ground level and faced Washington. Wells were present at all the important works. (but perhaps not at Fort Smith: AUTHOR). They were hand-dug and lined with brick and stone, and were eight to ten feet in diameter."* [106]

Construction of the Jewell tract fort began in early 1863. It was first called the "fort at Red House", then Fort McDowell. In June of 1863, however, it was named Fort C. F. Smith in honor of Major General Charles Furgeson Smith, in accordance with the practice at the time of naming the Northern Virginia forts after Union generals killed in the war. Smith had died on April 25, 1862 of a leg infection, aggravated by dysentery, while serving in the Tennessee campaign with General Grant. When Smith jumped from a small boat he slipped and badly scraped his shin. The wound became infected and he died bedridden about a month later in Atlanta.

General Charles F. Smith

Smith was born in Philadelphia on April 24, 1807, the son of an army surgeon. He graduated from the Military Academy 19th in a class of 37. He soon returned and served 13 years as an instructor and commandant of cadets. He was looked upon as an ideal example of a career soldier by then cadets Ulysses S. Grant and William T. Sherman.

Smith experienced a colorful and active military career in the years leading to the Civil War. He served in the Mexican War with Zachary Taylor and Winfield Scott and achieved an outstanding reputation for bravery and meritorious conduct. In 1856 he led a peaceful mapping expedition to the Red River in Idaho to establish a site for a suitable post. In 1857,

---

[106] Witthans, Wynn E., *A Preservation Plan - Fort C. F. Smith and the Hendry Estate,* December 10, 1985, revised January 6, 1986, Plan 830, (on file in the Virginia Room, Arlington Main Library).

Major Community "Battles" and Controversies

Smith participated in Federal policing action against the Mormons in Utah territory. President Buchanan had sent 2,500 troops to back a new non-Mormon governor who was being harassed by Mormon militia who captured wagon trains, stampeded livestock and burned grass before the issues were settled by mediation.

> REVISED REGULATIONS
> ARMY OF THE UNITED STATES
> 1861
> ARTICLE IX
> Care of Fortifications
> * * *
> 40. No person shall be permitted to walk upon any of the slopes of a fortification, excepting the ramps and glacis. If, in any case, it be necessary to provide for crossing them, it shall be done by placing wooden steps or stairs against the slopes. The occasional walking of persons on a parapet will do no harm, provided it be not allowed to cut the surface into paths.....
> 41. All grassed surfaces, excepting glacis, will be carefully and frequently mowed (except in dry weather), and the oftener the better, while growing rapidly--the grass never being allowed to be more than a few inches high. In order to cut the grass even and close, upon small slopes a light one-handed scythe should be used; and in mowing the steep slopes, the mower should stand on a light ladder resting against the slope, and not upon the grass. Crops of hay may be cut on the glacis; or, if fenced, it may be used as pasture; otherwise it should be treated as other slopes for fortification. On all slopes, spots of dead grass will be cut out and replaced with fresh sods. All weeds will be eradicated. A very little labor, applied steadily and judiciously will maintain the grassed surfaces, even of the largest of our forts, in good condition.
> (as republished by the Pennsylvania Historic Society)

An example of Civil War Army Regulations

Early in the Civil War, Smith led a charge at Fort Donelson at the head of his 3rd Division. He breached the Confederate defenses and was given major credit for the ensuing Confederate surrender. It was shortly after this success that he slipped and injured his leg with resultant infection and death.

ARLINGTON COUNTY VIRGINIA - A Modern History

William Jewell died in 1856 and his lands, the Hendry tract, passed to the control of his son Thomas. The Jewell family did not fare well with the take over of their lands and property for the establishment of a Federal fort, according to claims filed after the war. Thomas said he lived on his property with his family until "soldiers robbed my house and ordered me off". [107] His two and a half story frame house was first used as a headquarters until the structure was demolished because it was located within the forts ditch boundaries. In his 1877 claim #20709 for damages, [108] that was mostly denied, (he claimed $17,123.05 and was allowed $4,887.34) Jewell charged that his out buildings were destroyed, his farm tools taken, and his barn taken down and removed. His testimony in support of his claim included the following, in part:

> "...they took our land for guard and mess houses...the barn was pulled down and moved to Fort Albany...it was of wood with a stone basement...the dwelling house stood on ground now occupied by the fort; it was torn down before 1864...I live in Georgetown, employed by W. W. Corcoran; my brother Henry Clay is loyal; another brother was in the Navy (he is crazy and lives now with my brother Henry); my third brother...and other (siblings) live in California; another is wife of Thomas Dawson [109] they live on their farm adjoining...I am 65 years old; the farm is 1 1/4 miles from the Aqc.(sic) Bridge...after the war I bought the Fort and 5 or 6 houses for which I paid...our house was destroyed...it was 2 1/2 stories high...the house was built two years before the war and was completely finished...other buildings were also destroyed...the soldiers ordered me off...I lost a child trying to stay there."

Fort Smith had a perimeter of 368 yards and gun emplacements for twenty-two cannons. Quartermaster property on the fort at the end of the war included three barracks, two mess houses, cook houses, a guard house and officers quarters. It is known that there was also a parade ground for training horses and men among other things. Most of the trees and vegetation was removed for some distances from the fort to clear fields of fire for weapons. The fort's guns and armament varied during the war but at war's end in 1865, it is shown as:

> One 8-inch Sea Coast Howitzer
> Three 12-pound Howitzers
> Four 24-pounders on Siege Guns
> Two 10 pound parrott Rifles
> Six 4 1/2 inch Rodman Guns

---

[107] *Milner survey, Vol 1, p.2-12.*

[108] *Jewell family files, Virginia Room, Arlington Central Library.*

[109] *Apparently the early family from whence the nearby historical Dawson home and Dawson Terrace Recreation Center on North Taft street gets their names.*

Major Community "Battles" and Controversies

Three 8-inch siege Mortars
Six vacant platforms. [110]

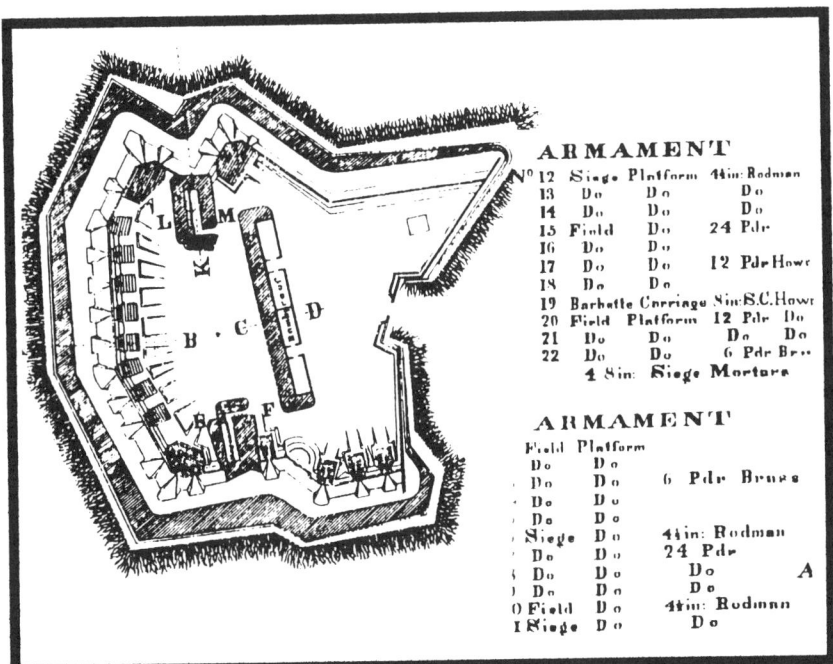

The layout of Fort C. F. Smith showing shape and other features.

A 1994 brochure prepared and distributed by the Arlington Department of Parks and Recreation, contained the following description of Fort Smith, and the practices employed in building the Washington area forts, based mainly on materials available from the Virginia Room of the Central Library.

> *"In fortifying Washington, Union troops altered forever the agricultural base of what is today's Arlington County. Since this was a livelihood of most people at that time, many area residents relocated to the cities of Alexandria or Washington. A great deal of the County's*

---

[110] *Milner Survey, Ibid, Vol 1, p. 2-12.*

forestation was decimated during this phase, as the need for lumber was nearly endless. Local folklore is full of stories of how the troops cleared hills of trees from top to bottom freeing the way for weapons fire and creating barriers to approaching Confederate soldiers.

"Fort Smith was built to fortify the Union's position along the Palisades and to extend the line of forts to the Potomac...the center (was) fronted by Halls Farm at the distance of about 3,000 yards. At the right is the Telegraph road crossed by ravines to Fort Ethan Allen at the distance of about three miles. On the left is a ravine 600 yards wide.

"The road to Fort Smith is outside the rifle pits ...there is no well water within the fort, all the water being brought in...the only water supply is a small spring, unequal to the wants of the garrison...the fort gave a perfect view of the Potomac River...only a few Confederate soldiers were ever sighted at the fort...Daily life was similar to that of many of the other forts...at dawn, enlisted men filled their time with drills, parades and inspections. At night they had plenty of time for mischief, including forays to the local taverns...officers were often invited into the homes of Washington's 'society'. Several even met and married their wives during their tours (at Fort Smith)."

In mid 1863, as Confederate General Lee's army passed west of Washington on its way to Pennsylvania and eventually the Battle of Gettysburg, there was again concern for the defenses of the Capital. General Barnard's engineer wrote to him, "Sir: The frequently recurring alarms on the south side of the river have created a nervous apprehension of danger in the minds of our hired laborers (i.e., working on Fort Smith) and many of them have left work. I understand that large numbers have determined to leave today..." When news of the Union victory at Gettysburg reached Washington the fear of an attack on the Capital diminished and work on the forts continued. By October, General Bernard was able to report to the Secretary of War: "Fort C. F. Smith, commenced last winter, was in readiness early this spring. It is a powerful work, and is essentially complete...with few exceptions, (it has) undergone important improvements." [111]

As is well recorded by numerous historians and alluded to above, the Forts around Washington saw little actual fighting during the Civil War. Operations consisted mostly of reactions to rumors of, or actual minor penetrations by, Mosby's raiders who were sometimes in the area. Troops in the forts spent much of their time incapacitated by malaria or typhoid and other camp diseases. A civil war soldier, Stephen Blanding in his unpublished In the Defense of Washington, or Sunshine in a Soldier's life wrote,

"With the exception of drilling, guard mounting, and inspection of knapsacks, we had but little to do, and the time passed pleasantly enough as each day shortening our term of service"

---

[111] *Milner Survey, Vol 1, p. 2-13.*

Major Community "Battles" and Controversies

August 1865 view of Company L, 2nd NY Heavy Artillery in Fort Smith looking west. Photo courtesy US Army Military History Institute.

At the end of the war, the War Department listed 25 forts around Washington to be retained and Fort Smith was included in the list. Guarding Fort Smith in peace time proved to be a challenge for some soldiers. One wrote;

> *"If there had been a thousand years of life before us and we had no definite plans in living, the stay in these forts might have been enjoyed. As it was there was a dull succession of inspections, parades of all sorts and make-believe guard duty that was hardly creditable to any one concerned. The constant query with us was, 'What are we here for?'".*

ARLINGTON COUNTY VIRGINIA - A Modern History

Disposal work on the remaining forts of the Washington defenses began in the fall of 1865. In November the order for dismantling the last of them was issued - on it was the name of Fort C. F. Smith.

THE HENDRY PERIOD - 1927 to 1993

The last owner of the Hendry tract before purchase of the land in 1927 by Dr. Ernest D. Hendry was Robert F. Watson, who had purchased it only about a year earlier from Charles R. Lindsay. The area where the land lay was known on land plats as the Woodmont community. It was not incorporated and relied on the post office in Cherrydale for postal service.

Hendry was a graduate of John Hopkins Medical College in Baltimore and decided to begin his medical practice in the Washington area. He was warmly attracted to the rural-like, uncluttered settings of the Potomac Palisades across the river from Georgetown and tried to buy land there with some others he tried to interest in subdividing. For whatever reasons, his efforts failed and he decided to buy all the property now known as the Hendry tract. In 1939 he married Anne Pearce of Norfolk who had studied in Washington and was teaching at St. Agnes, an Alexandria parochial school.

The Hendrys concentrated in developing the gardens and landscape of their property, but apparently made few changes in the buildings. They engaged in farming of sorts over the years. The extant 1960 Sanborn map available in the Arlington Library and at the Historical Society Hume School Museum on Arlington Ridge Road shows about the same number and configuration of buildings in 1936 as exists today. The map, as mentioned elsewhere, shows North 24th Street to still be named Malvern Street. Anne remained in the house and on the property after she was widowed by the death of Dr Hendry in 1976. In 1988, the Hendrys, Anne and her son Ernest, Jr., began renovating the main house with the aim of establishing a "bed and breakfast" type inn. The project, however, never reached fruition.

EARLY EFFORTS TO REZONE FOR DENSER USES

From available information, it appears that Dr Hendry always considered the 20 plus acres of his land to be a bit more than he could handle. As recorded, he originally bought the entire tract in 1927 only after he was unable to interest some others in joining him in buying smaller, subdivided portions of the land. As the years passed and he aged, he no doubt found it increasingly difficult to maintain and handle such a large piece of land. At any rate, by the mid 1950's, almost three decades later, he tried twice unsuccessfully to have the property rezoned from its R-20 classification, i.e. single family residential use with lots at least 20,000 square feet in size. On May 13, 1952 and

Major Community "Battles" and Controversies

November 13, 1953, the County Board denied his applications for rezoning to "RA6-15" and "RAR", respectively.[112] a classification for high rise or more dense residential units.

1985-86
THE RETIREMENT HOME REZONING EFFORT

The efforts to break up the tract and obtain permission for more intensive uses was continued by his widow Anne. On January 23, 1985, Anne Hendry, and her son Ernest S., Jr with his wife and children as sellers, entered into an agreement with George I. Bonaface, a real estate broker, to sell and buy the Hendry tract, subject to successful efforts to rezone. It was widely known locally that Anne Hendry strongly desired that the remains of Fort Smith be preserved and that if the land were to be developed for residential use as much open space as possible should be retained.

The agreement provided that the property was to be developed by Bonaface's partner John G. Georgelas and Sons, Inc., Builders and Developers, McLean, Virginia. A flyer dated September 20, 1985, with the Georgelas firm heading and signed by George Georgelas was circulated throughout the neighborhood addressed "Dear Neighbor". In it, it was explained that the Hendrys were paying over $25,000 a year in property taxes, "a rather handsome sum" and that Georgelas with the Hendrys were studying and evaluating development alternatives. He invited suggestions or criticisms from the community. He said the easiest and most obvious plan would be to divide the property into 38 half acre lots as permitted by current zoning. He said other plans would consist of "an elegant and refined" retirement community, or for a cluster residential development. The flyer invited the public to visit the Hendry tract "and visit with us" on Sunday, September 29, 1985 between 10:00 A.M. and 4:00 P.M.

Later that year an application was filed for rezoning from "R-10" to "S-D" to allow the establishment of a 295-unit retirement home on the tract for people over 65 years of age. Under the proposal the Hendry family home, the remains of Fort Smith, and most old trees would be preserved. There would be 358 parking spaces provided and shuttle bus service to the nearest Metro would be furnished.

On May 17, 1986, the application, was denied by the County Board, together with an accompanying proposed site plan. The proposal turned out to be highly

---

[112] *Memorandum, Larry J. Brown, County Manager, February 23, 1987, to The County Board, Subject: Site Plan Request for approval of cluster development (on Hendry Tract).*

controversial in the neighborhood and the county overall in the months before the formal filing of the rezoning application and consideration by the County Board.

If the Hendrys and their contract buyer/developers were running their proposal up the flag pole to see who might salute, they were getting their answer. Almost no one was saluting. On the contrary, as reported by Washington Post staff writer Marcia McAllister in the Virginia Real Estate section of October 5, 1985, the proposal angered numerous homeowners along quiet residential streets of North Arlington who were to appear before the County Board and voice their opposition when an application was filed and a hearing held. They asserted that the retirement home would "destroy the single-family residential character of their neighborhood".

McAllister reported that some neighbors, however, were "eyeing it as a future residence when they no longer are able to maintain their large houses". She also wrote that developer Georgelas and its partner Boniface had paid (or were to pay?) more than $4 million for the land, according to a source familiar with the deal.

CONCERNED RESIDENTS MEET

McAllister wrote also that more than 400 residents showed up on September 29th in response to the invitation to visit and that many had expressed concerns about service truck traffic on the narrow 24th Street, disturbances from ambulances and other undesired impacts on the neighborhood. A local resident, Tom Richards was quoted as saying, "this is a particularly sensitive tract..." and that the development would affect not only Arlington, "...but all of the national capital area."

McAllister added that Tom Georgelas, an architect and brother of the developer, said the home would leave most of the Hendry tract undisturbed and would be three stories high on the uphill side on 24th Street, and seven stories high on the back side done the hill toward the Potomac River.

Additional evidence of tough going for the applicants on their proposed retirement home, and an indication of probable forthcoming County Board action was contained in a March 27, 1986 letter from Board Chair Mary Margaret Whipple to Mrs. Joseph L. Fisher, widow of the late Board member and U. S. Congressman. Mrs Fisher, who lived nearby, had written to the Chair and voiced her opposition to the rezoning of the Hendry tract for a retirement home. Whipple replied and said, in part, "I have several concerns...We have already received complaints from residents ...about an additional traffic burden on the limited street network...the tract also seems a little isolated from shopping and public transportation for a retirement home..."

On May 1, 1986, County Manager Larry J. Brown recommended to the County Board that the Use Permit and Site Plan for the retirement home be denied. He said his staff considered the density proposed was "out of scale with the low density of the neighborhood surrounding the site", that there would be adverse traffic on local streets, and that it would be inconsistent with the County Board policy of protecting the Potomac palisades. At the next Board meeting on May 17, as stated, the application was denied.

Major Community "Battles" and Controversies

THE 1986-87 EFFORT TO REZONE TO "R-10" CLUSTER

Following the refusal of the County Board to grant the application for a retirement home on the Hendry tract, the owner/developers submitted a new application for rezoning from the existing "R-20" to "R-10" with a site plan for a residential cluster of forty-eight units. The application was set for hearing by the County Board on January 10, 1987.

On December 11, 1986, County Manager Larry J. Brown in a Memorandum to the County Board recommended that the application be denied because there was no justification for the increased density that would result from the rezoning. In addition, he said other goals of the county such as preserving the Fort Smith site and retaining maximum open space would not be met and that such a change would exert pressure to similarly rezone other nearby sites zoned "R-20" along the Potomac River.

Brown explained that under existing zoning the applicant could create 43 lots and 86 under the requested "R-10" zoning. He said the applicant's plan called for 48 units, more than existing zoning but less than maximum under requested "R-10" zoning, and that open space would be provided in the form of preservation of a portion of Fort Smith and a portion of the river palisades adjacent to the George Washington (GW) Parkway. Brown discussed some of the advantages and disadvantages of the options available to the County under each zoning arrangement, but pointed out that "the preservation of Fort Smith is not a requirement of any by-right development."

In other words, Brown stressed, if the some mutually agreeable arrangement with the owner/developers was not reached, and the tract was developed under existing zoning as the applicants had every legal right to do, then there could be no assurance that Fort Smith would not be wiped out entirely and lost forever by the establishment of homes.

On the following day, December 12, the manager fired off another Memorandum to the County Board, this time recommending that a Historic District Designation be approved for the Fort Smith portion of the Hendry tract, and that $6,000 be appropriate to carry out an archeological study of the Hendry tract to delineate just where are the boundaries of the Fort. In his memorandum, Brown reported that neither Mrs Hendry nor the developers supported historic designation "at this time". He added that the Historical Affairs and Landmark Review Board (HALRB) had found the property contained significant historical, cultural and architectural resources and that his staff concurs in the findings as pertained to the Fort, but not the entire 20 acres of the tract. Brown included in his memorandum a discussion of trees on the tract that might be rare or unique, a matter over which there would be some disagreement in the coming months, until finally resolved in the affirmative. He also called attention to the absence of a "clear and defined County policy to preserve the Palisades."

On December 30, Andrew McElwaine, a member of the Arlington Republican Committee wrote to Michael Brunner, the Republican member of the County Board and "in no uncertain terms" and urged him to "support a historic designation for the Hendry

ARLINGTON COUNTY VIRGINIA - A Modern History

Tract". To do otherwise, he added, "could well cost Arlington the last vestige of a critical part in her history".

On January 7, 1987, on the eve of Board consideration of the Hendry tract application, Arlington Historical Society member John D. Sinks, Chairman of the Society's Committee for Arlington Civil War Heritage, wrote to County Board Chairman Albert Eisenberg. He reminded the Chairman that the Hendry tract "contains the remnants of a Civil War Fort, (Smith) which not only are the best preserved in Arlington, but are preserved in their original context of commanding the terrain from a Confederate attack from the west." He said the Society urges the County Board to (1) immediately appropriate funds for an archaeological study, (2) protect the site, and its field of fire, and (3) acquire the fort and land to its west (the field of fire) for an historical park. Sink included in his letter a recapitulation of the fort's history, contributions, and importance, and why the creation of a historical park would be in the community's best interest.

The same day of Sink's letter, Board Member Brunner wrote to the County Manager and referred to the Hendry tract. He said he was interested in discussing the development of a policy for the Palisades and asked the staff position on designating the entire 20 Hendry acres historic as favored by the HALRB.

Manager Brown swung into high gear. Apparently as a matter of top priority, he responded to Brunner the following day with an explanation in some depth of the county policy on developments along the Palisades. He wrote that the policy was one of single family development with density from one to ten units per acres. He said the staff also supports single family cluster development "as a means of preserving even more open space." He  listed three alternative approaches that might also preserve the palisades, i.e., (1) an ordinance that would provide for greater tree/landscape preservation in all developments, (2) some modifications in the ordinance governing Historical Designation Districts, and/or (3) imposition of scenic easements.

Brown added that these approaches might help to insure the preservation of the palisades, but that such a policy would have to be crafted carefully to avoid legal challenges by property owners and that the County might be faced with decisions to purchase easements or even titles to properties.

With respect to the Hendry property, Brown wrote that no recommendation as yet had been made to designate the entire property historic for several reasons. He said there was clearly no historic significance to the main house, the property in general, or the landscaping on the site; that while the property was once a part of a larger Mason property, it was difficult to justify only a 20 acre remnant of the larger 2,000 acres as constituting a significant historic feature; that the Hendry house was similar to many others of like age in Arlington, none of which have been designated historic; and while the Palisades may be a unique feature of the Washington area, none of it has been designated historic. Finally, Brown pointed out the consequences for property owners of historic designation such as increased restrictions and required approvals on alterations, remodeling, or other changes in historic features.

Major Community "Battles" and Controversies

ACTION ON THE "R-10" CLUSTER APPLICATION

On January 10, 1987, the County Board held its hearing on the application for re-zoning of the Hendry tract. It denied the request for rezoning from "R-20" to "R-10", and for a residential cluster development for 48 single family detached homes. The Board then advertised, instead, for a public hearing for a cluster development of 43 such homes, and deferred action on all other aspects of the matter to February 28.

The Board, after holding its public hearing, decided to ask several citizen groups, the developer, and the staff to review the matter and report back to the Board with recommendations on the Land Use Plan, the Historical District Designation and a use permit for possible cluster development. The Planning Commission, HALRB, Park and Recreation Commission, Parkway Citizens Association, and the Historical Society were specifically asked to participate in the review. Additionally a special ad hoc committee chaired by former County Board member, civic activist and nationally known environmentalist Thomas Richards was appointed to also review the matter and report its recommendations to the Board.

There followed a period of intense activity with respect to the Hendry tract with the future of prized Fort Smith hanging precariously in the balance. At times the County became so deeply involved in the Hendry tract affair that an outsider happening upon the scene might well imagine that the county was confronted with no other community problems of any great significance. Hardly a day passed when one of the groups, or their numerous sub-committees, were not meeting and deliberating on the Hendry tract. The Richards Task Force met on five occasions during January and February, and repeatedly visited the Hendry tract for on-site examination and familiarization. The planning Commission held hearings and heard testimony from the applicant, Task Force Chairman Richards, and numerous citizens to include Antoinette Lee, John Jessup, Alice Nicolson, William Nolden, John Sinks, Richard Bacas and Bernard Berne.

Citizens agonize over Hendry tract?

On February 20, 23, and 25, the Special ad hoc Committee, HALRB, and the Planning Commission submitted their reports on the Hendry tract to the County Board. Additionally, on February 23, the County Manager forwarded his report of the staff position on the matter. Motivated primarily by a desire to save the Fort Smith site from elimination, which could happen if the tract was developed to the maximum under existing "R-20" zoning, none of the parties favored development under existing zoning.

With the understanding that the Fort Smith site would be dedicated by the developer to the County and thus preserved, there was general agreement among all parties that the Land Use Plan should be changed from "Public" to "Low" residential use;

the entire tract should be designated a Historic District;[113] the applied for "R-20" Cluster Site Plan for 41 single family detached homes be approved; and that lots and open spaces north, west and east of the Fort be acquired, by County purchase or developer dedication, to preserve the "fields of fire" of the Fort.

There were some minor differences among the parties with respect to:

(1) whether all or only a part of the tract should be designated "historic",

(2) as to whether curbs and a sidewalk should be installed on 24th Street along the Fort boundaries,

(3) as to precisely how much land around the Fort should remain open in order to protect its historical integrity,

(4) the disposition of the Hendry house and whether or not it should be designated historic,

(5) as a separate but closely related matter, the appropriate Board action with respect to establish a Potomac Palisades policy,

(6) whether the County or the developer should financially assist in the archeological research and renovation of the fort and if so to what extent, and

(7) the exact number of houses the developer should be permitted to build after the purchase or dedication of some lots to the County.[114]

In due course all of these differences were either resolved by the Board at its hearing or otherwise ameliorated. The special Task Force in its report also commented on the fate of the Hendry House, views into the Hendry tract, fort, tree and palisades protection, and the financing of a recommended archeology study.

There was also news coverage of the developing events. In an article in the February 25 issue of the Washington Post headlined "Va. Riverfront Houses Backed", staff writer Sandra Evans described the Planning Commission approval of the 41 lot cluster proposal at its meeting of the night before. She wrote that Commission members had proposed that the county buy three of the building lots to create more open space but noted that the cost, "..perhaps $600,000 could be prohibitive." She wrote also of the switch in the Commission's position when it had on only the evening previously of the 23rd, supported a "commercial project, including office building and an apartment hotel, in exchange for the setting aside of about seven acres of the 11.6 acre tract as park land. The Commission had apparently abandoned that position since no such proposal was under consideration." She added that a nearby resident Bill Nolden, representing the Parkway Citizens Association, stated that 41 houses on the site would be "an unwarranted burden on the community".

---

[113] *This represented a change of position by the County Manager. In his December 12, 1986 Memo to the Board, and his January 8, 1987 letter to Michael Brunner, on the matter of Historical Designation of the Hendry tract, he wrote, that the Staff concurred in designating the fort historic but not the entire 20 acres.*

[114] *On February 21 citizens Ruth and Andrew Poggenpohl on nearby Lorcom Lane wrote to the Planning Commission that they were "opposing more than 36 units on the Hendry Tract".*

Major Community "Battles" and Controversies

At its scheduled meeting on February 28, the County Board, heard numerous speakers, public and otherwise, who commented on various aspects of the proposed cluster rezoning. None of the speakers outright opposed the proposal. Whereupon, the Board approved, 5-0, the General Land Use Plan amendment for the Hendry tract to show "Low" residential use from "Public", gave the entire tract a Historic District Designation, and approved a site plan for a residential cluster development for up to 43 single family detached dwellings with the expectation that only 37 houses would be built, with the county acquiring some of the lots.

The Board's approval of the Historic District designation contained the following specifics:

    a. It included 92,000 square feet of dedicated open space encompassing the Fort C. F. Smith earthworks;

    b. there would be an additional 19,000 square feet of open space designated for the Fort's "fields of fire" based on drawings submitted,by the applicant;

    c. there would be dedicated to the county 30,000 square feet shown by applicant as Lots 1,2 and 41 and the back 25 feet of lots 37, 38 and 40 as shown by applicant's drawing.

The Board also indicated its intention to purchase two lots by the end of 1987 and others later. In the months following the February 28, 1987 County Board action, several applications for amendments to the approved site plan were submitted but as the months stretched into years, leading to the decision to buy the land in 1994, no construction or implementation of the site plan took place and Mrs Hendry retained the property unchanged. Although extensive time and effort by large numbers of people had gone into the complex studies and reviews leading to the rezoning action, no one seemed to particularly mind that development was side tracked.

In response to an inquiry by citizen Charles T. Householder, zoning administrator Susan A. Ingraham wrote on April 28, 1989, in part, "The owner's decision to generally retain the property in its present form is an asset to the community. There is a considerable amount of unique history on the site which is not found elsewhere in the County." Householder was a neighbor and known close friend of the Hendrys and was working with them to restore portions of the estate aimed at establishing a "bed and breakfast" facility.

THE HENDRY - GEORGELAS LAW SUITS

All of the reasons for Mrs Hendry's changed position on developing her property are not necessarily a matter of public record, but it would appear that the primary cause was a deterioration of relations between Ms Hendry and the contract buyer/developers that resulted in some protracted and complicated litigation. There were claims and counter claims, and finally suits by each party against the other.

The first suit arose in 1987 when it became apparent that Mrs Hendry was not going to concur in developing the property. Georgelas apparently felt as contract owner it had the right to do so over Mrs Hendry's objections and it filed suit in the Arlington County Circuit Court (Chancery #87000-671) asking for "specific performance" (i.e. that the Hendrys be forced to sell their property as contracted). Georgelas also asked for

ARLINGTON COUNTY VIRGINIA - A Modern History

$18.547 million in damages, the amount he claimed he lad lost in income because of the failure of Hendry to go forward with development. Aside from various issues not very relevant to our narrative, Judge Thomas Monroe after exhaustive filings and pleadings, held that the Hendrys had been enriched by the rezoning of February 28, 1987 whether development was pursued or not, and he urged they settle in the amount of $1.5 million damages to Georgelas. On the advice of their counsel Francis J. Pelland of a Washington law firm Hendry reluctantly agreed to pay Georgelas $150,000 and to execute a note for $1.2 million due May 31, 1997.

A little over a year later, the second suit was filed, this time by Mrs Hendry, on October 20, 1989, in the Arlington County Circuit Court (Chancery # 89000-969) against the Georgelas firm. She sought to have the first suit, in effect, reversed. Again, all of the details of the suit are not within the scope of this narrative but in general it seems there was continued disagreement between the parties centered around the legal rights and obligations or contractual standing of Georgelas and exactly what both parties had agreed to in the contract to sell and buy the Hendry tract. Hendry claimed the contract had expired when the County rejected the application for the residential home. Georgelas disagreed, contending that contractual wording providing for renegotiation within two years if the rezoning were denied kept the contract alive, and it had remained a contract owner.

A copy of the January 23, 1985 contract between the parties was attached to the complaint as Exhibit A. In it, a purchase price of $4.5 million was agreed to, subject to the County accepting changes in the land classification to allow construction of a 400 unit residential home and that if the county rejected the request, the contract could be renegotiated in 24 months. The contract stipulated that the assessed value of the land was $1.75 million, and the improvements $2.4 million.

Mrs Hendry asked for damages and again contended that the contract expired when the County Board rejected the proposal for a residential home on May 17, 1986. She claimed that the grant of cluster rezoning on February 28, 1987 was null and void anyway because the application was signed by Georgelas who was not an owner by contract or otherwise of the property. She asserted further that the earlier settlement agreement stemming from the 1987 suit, was the result of a mutual misunderstanding of fact and should be set aside. She asked the Circuit Court (Judge Benjamin Kenrick) to vacate its order of June 1, 1988 by Judge Thomas Monroe.

On December 22, 1989 Judge Kendrick dismissed the complaint of Mrs Hendry on grounds it "...fails to state a cause upon which relief can be granted." Following Kendrick's order of dismissal, a series of legal maneuvers took place that clearly were not the norm for judicial proceedings. Upon release of Judge Kendrick's dismissal order, Hendry through her attorney immediately filed a motion for recusal, [115] requesting that

---

[115] *A plea objecting to the jurisdiction of a particular judge on grounds he is disqualified from hearing the matter by reason of interest or prejudice; Black's Law Dictionary, West Publishing Company, 1968, St Paul MN.*

Major Community "Battles" and Controversies

the matter be heard by another judge. On December 29, Judge Kendrick denied the motion, sustaining his December 22 Order.

In filings on January 5 and February 7, 1990, to Chief Circuit Judge William Winston, Hendry through her attorney Joseph Hyman asked that Winston hear the matter "as the only judge who has taken no position...", and that the December 22 order of Judge Kendrick be vacated. Instead of hearing the matter as requested by Hendry, Judge Winston referred it back to Kendrick who on April 18, 1990, again denied the motion. On May 11, Hyman filed a notice to appeal to the Virginia Supreme Court, and later a petition to appeal, that was denied by the Supreme Court on October 3. The public record in the Circuit Court Clerk's office does not indicate what judicial developments, if any, thereafter occurred.

The following year, in 1991, Mrs Hendry filed suit against her former attorney Frank Pelland in the Federal Court in Washington, alleging malpractice and claiming damages. As reported by Arlington Journal staff writer Joe Farruggia on September 22, 1993, the court found Pelland "not guilty of malpractice and ordered the Hendrys to pay more than $37,000 in unpaid legal fees to Pelland's law firm, Sadur Pelland and Rubinstein."

As if the above legal hardships were not enough, the Hendrys were involved in yet another legal tussle during the period when a required "certificate of appropriateness" was obtained from the County for some work on their land for a building addition and utilities needed to open their bed and breakfast establishment. The Arlington Heritage Alliance, a preservation group, filed an appeal against the county for issuing a permit for construction work near the historic earthworks of Fort Smith. The Alliance contended the permit was invalid since it had not been signed by the Hendrys as owners and because there had been no hearing as required by the HALRB.

Northern Virginia Sun writer Yvonne French on February 1, 1991 wrote that the Hendrys did not obtain a certificate because they refused to recognize that their land had properly been designated historic. She wrote that the Hendrys contended the designation" was enacted when they sought to build a retirement home which never went up." French wrote that Sara Leach of the Alliance said the county acted improperly when it filed for a certificate not as owners but on behalf of the Hendrys. French indicated that the Hendrys had prevailed in the appeal and she quoted Board Chairman Eisenberg as saying, "If the County takes out (a certificate) and the owners agree to abide by it, then it's enforceable.". The matter apparently became moot in time when negotiations were undertaken for sale of the land to the county and the Hendrys abandoned plans to establish a bed and breakfast facility.

For the next several weeks the community lived through a period of wait and see wondering just what the next step would be and whether the County Board would bite the bullet and purchase the Hendry tract. Park enthusiasts and preservationists hoped they would do so. Fiscally conservative citizens and taxpayers for sure hope the Board would not do so.

ARLINGTON COUNTY VIRGINIA - A Modern History

!!! - THE HISTORIC PARK IS ESTABLISHED - !!!

Soon after the July 19, 1994 the uncertainty was resolved. The Board voted to approve the purchase of the Hendry tract, and the purchase was consumated. On September 1, a ceremony was conducted on the site to honor the event.

On October 22, a "Commemoration of Acquisition of Fort C. F. Smith" was held. A welcome was extended by Parks and Recreation Department Director Alice E. Foster, and "reflections" on the Fort were given by Dr Benjamin Cooling, Historian and Co-Author of the book Mr Lincoln's Forts. He told how the fort came to be located where it was, and how it got its name. About the fort, he said, "Hopefully there will be some restoration, but not too much..." Patriotic Civil War songs were sung by the Choir of the Mt Olive Baptist Church, and remarks were made by Board Chairman Mary Margaret Whipple. About the site, ArlingtonCourier writer Joe Farruggia in the October 26th issue wrote, in part,

> "It has a rambling Victorian home, an old barn dating back to the 1850s, a well kept garden of exotic plants and is lined with rare species of hybrid trees."

In the closing weeks of 1994, the County Department of Parks, Recreation and Community Resources (DPRCR) began preliminary actions to convert the Hendry tract into a meaningful historical park with maximum usefulness and value to the public. On January 16, 1995, it issued the first of a series of "Fort C. F. Smith Park News" bulletins. In that issue it was announced that Stan Ernst, Assistant to the Director for Planning and Design of DPRCR would head the planning effort for the park and that Landscape Architect Chris Munson would lead the Park Master Plan Core Team. It was also announced that the staff was visiting other historical parks in the regional area, that clean up of the park to remove dangerous debris and junk would begin in January 1995, and that a search would be made for an engineering/architectural consultant to survey and evaluate the existing site utilities and buildings and their historical significance. On March 9, the DPRCR staff led by Chris Munson appeared before the Historical Society and reported on park developments and plans to date, and answered questions from the membership.

In news bulletin #2 of April 18, it was announced that John Milner Associates, Inc., of Alexandria, Virginia had been selected to conduct the historical and archeological survey of the tract, and that upon receipt of the survey draft it would be distributed to interested parties for comment.

On May 15, DPRCR distributed a "Dear Neighbor" bulletin in which it related that it had acquired the Hendry tract, that it had been officially designated a Historic District, and that work was underway to convert it into a park. DPRCR advised that the park would remain closed until preparations for opening were completed and urged the public to report to the police, but not approach, any persons or vehicles not properly escorted by County staff, or using metal detectors or mountain bikes, or tampering with plants, trees or buildings. The bulletin also advised that "someone chain-sawed and removed a valuable specimen tree over the weekend of May 6".

Major Community "Battles" and Controversies

In June the County Board, with the concurrence of the HALRB, the Parkway Citizens Association adjacent to and surrounding the park, and the staff, officially named the park the "Fort C. F. Smith Park", and changed the zoning from the R-20 category to S-3A for public land classified as Natural Resource Open Space as defined in the County's Open Space Master Plan.

In news bulletin #3 of September 22, DPCRC announced that the draft of the "Historical and Archeological Survey of Fort C. F. Smith" had been completed and circulated to the staff and the Technical Advisory Council for review and comment. The Council included members from the Arlington Historical Society, the Potomac Overlook Regional Park, the U. S. Department of Interior, Mark Gionet from the Vienna Virginia Landscape and Architect firm of Lewis, Scully and Gionet, W. Dale Waters, the staff Historic Preservation Coordinator, Kim Hohen, Ft Myer Historian, Bruce McCoy, Arlington Historian and past president of the Historical Society, and various members of the county staff involved in the project.

The Milner survey was described as a "massive study" consisting of five bound volumes, with over 450 pages and 90 maps and figures in addition to numerous historical and current photographs. The volumes were titled, "Volume 1, Management Summary", "Volumes 2 and 3, Archeological Resources", "Volume 4, Landscape Resources", and "Volume 5, Planning Study".

The newsletter indicated that opening of the park was scheduled for Spring 1996 that would see the completion of phase 1 of the Master Plan. Phase 1 included:

      a. existing trail drainage improvements,
      b. dead and hazardous tree removal as required for safety,
      c. utility installation,
      d. protective measures for the fort's earthworks,
      e. a park sign and interpretive brochure,
      f. temporary rest rooms,
      g. telephone and security systems installation, and
      h. establishing a temporary manager's office in the Tractor Barn.

It was also announced in the newsletter that two land acquisitions were approved by the County Board which raised the total Park acreage to 19.0. The first was 4.5 acres of the Hemphill property to the east of the site that will add protection, prevent encroachment and ease pressure on the more natural and historical parts of the Park. The second property was a 20,000 square foot lot in the center of the property that was exchanged for an equivalent corner of the Hemphill property.

On November 14, Project Coordinator Munson wrote to Dr. Charles D. Cheek, of Milner Associates and advised him that the staff review of the Milner report, after circulation among the members of the Council, had been completed. With the understanding that all parties interested and involved agreed that in general the fort should be stabilized and preserved essentially as it is, fields of fire cleared, and existing buildings retained, Munson conveyed the staff and council comments concerning the various structures on the site, essentially, to wit:

    a. The Main House (formerly the Hendry residence),

To remain in its present configuration, except some wall removals to enlarge rooms, a first floor conference and meeting room, 2nd floor to be finished as offices, two bathrooms to be finished, kitchen completed and equipped to permit catering, laundry room in basement to be converted to bathrooms with exterior access to serve visitors.

    b. The Cottage.

To be restored to function as a park office and visitor center, with a one room museum, sleeping porch will be an office, upstairs for storage, needs new electric, water and heating facilities, upstairs bathroom for staff.

    c. The Bank Barn.

To be stabilized and restored to late 1800 appearance and used as a storage barn open to visitors.

    d. Tractor Barn and Shed.

No work or estimate required at this time.

Munson also pointed out that the staff did not agree with a recommendation in the Milner survey that contemplated allowing visitors access onto the earthworks.

In 1996, work by the staff and others to establish the Fort Smith park moved ahead apace and with vigor. On January 31, Project Coordinator Munson released DPRCR newsletter #4, containing progress reports on various aspects of the project, and he notified Technical Advisory Council members that a Cultural Resources Management Plan (CRMP) was in preparation and would be presented to the public and County Board in the Fall of 1996. He also held a public forum on March 14 in the Central Library Auditorium to solicit comments and suggestions to be incorporated into the CRMP.

On March 28, the Advisory Council met at the Long Branch Nature Center off Carlin Springs Road to achieve a consensus on such matters as the park open schedule, park capacity, on-site parking, use of Main House, the trail network, fencing and earthwork protection, citizen requests for horse riding on-site, access from GW Parkway, and foot paths on Earthworks. Many suggestions were offered by members to be taken under consideration in the coming months.

At the Long Branch Center meeting, Munson also distributed an outline for the forthcoming Resources Management Plan that included the following items.

    a. Goals concerning community involvement, compliance with the County Open Space Master Plan, natural and historic resources preservation, interpretation of resources, and land and existing structure uses;

    b. Relationship to county policies concerning zoning, open space, the palisades and citizen associations;

    c. Site history, archeological surveys, topography, habitats, overall plan for Fort Smith, and interpretation and development;

    d. Management of park carrying capacity, Main House, interpretive programs and maintenance;

Major Community "Battles" and Controversies

e. Architectural plans for the Main House and other buildings; and
f. Developmental standards for parking, roads, trails, signs and landscaping.

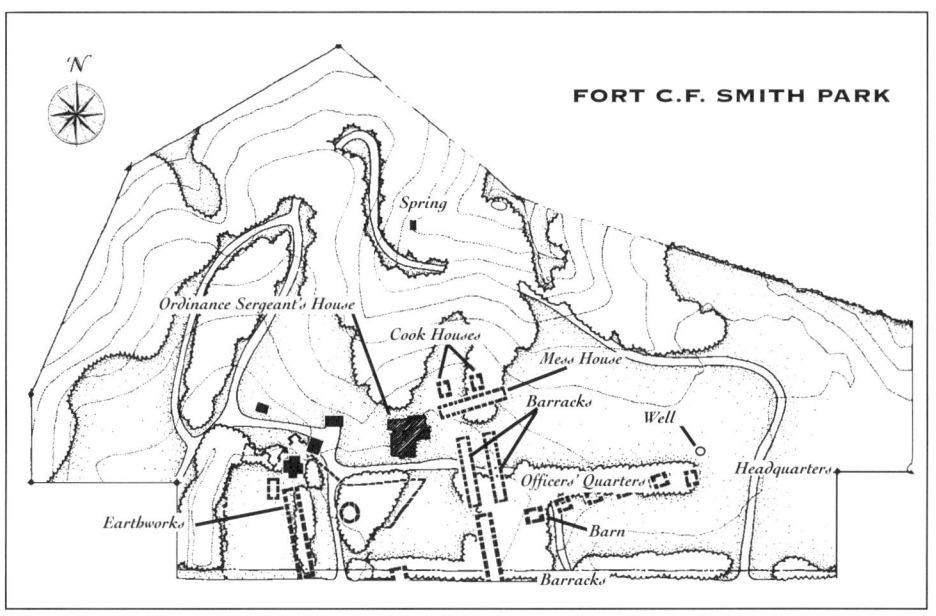

Fort C. F. Smith showing trails, description stations, buildings, the Fort site, and other features.

During the Spring, special pre-opening walking tours and orientation visits were conducted for individuals and groups especially interested in the park, and a brochure was prepared as a handout for park visitors. The brochure included a history of the property from 1707 to 1996, a map with a tour trail outlined, and numbered stations along the trail with a brief narrative for each station. The brochure is designed for folding to fit neatly and conveniently into a shirt or other pocket.

* * * *

ARLINGTON COUNTY VIRGINIA - A Modern History

SUMMARY

Thus the long and painful struggle over the open and spacious acres of the Hendry tract drew to a close. At this writing there remains mainly the completion of the transformation of the Hendry farm and open spaces into an organized, delineated, and operating historical park. It seems clear that future generations will not doubt that the result was more than worth the effort. A priceless and treasured historical fort site and area was spared the degradation and indignity of the developer's bull dozer. Another island of meaningful and useable open cultural space in the midst of urban congestion will remain to serve as a much needed breath of fresh air for future generations to enjoy.

* * *

Visitors at the Main House in Fort Smith Park on opening day in October 1996.

Major Community "Battles" and Controversies

ROUND XVII
SAVING ARLINGTON HOUSE WOODLANDS

Members of the Arlington Historical Society at the Custis-Lee Plantation woodlands (to their rear and left) in May 1996 for a TV Channel 8 newscast.

As pointed out repeatedly herein, Arlington County over the decades has witnessed dramatic and explosive growth and development and a consequent disappearance of woodlands, farms, and other open space. With the constant march of population growth and the accompanying advent of housing, malls, schools, hospitals, roads, and other amenities to accommodate people, the wherewithal to preserve rapidly disappearing open spaces, especially those of historical, or archeological importance, has grown ever more difficult or even impossible. Once such lands are lost to development the opportunity to reclaim them seldom ever returns for practical as well as economic and political reasons.

A case in point within the State of Virginia and County of Arlington but on Federally owned lands not subject to local control is a small 24 acres tract of woodland that is a part of the Custis-Lee mansion grounds in Arlington Cemetery. It is administered by the National Park Service. Although most of the rest of the plantation's 1100 or so acres have long since been taken for approximately 245,000 grave sites in the cemetery managed by the Army, or for use by the Army's adjacent Ft Myer military reservation, cemetery officials have long pressed for more land for burials. Eligibility for burial in Arlington National Cemetery is more restrictive than in most or all other national cemeteries. It is limited generally to active duty personnel; those retired for length of service or disability; those awarded the purple heart or the Silver Star or higher; recently died former POWs, certain dependents, widows or spouses of persons buried or about to be buried in the cemetery; and cabinet members or other high level government officials or chiefs of missions. [116]

In the mid-1960's Cemetery Superintendent John Metzler, father of the current Superintendent John "Jack" Metzler, Jr., launched a major plan to cut trees and begin using the woodlands around the Custis Lee mansion for burials. When Arlington House Curator Agnes Mullins learned of the tree cutting by the elder Metzler she with some others moved quickly and succeeded in halting the cutting. Soon afterward the Department of the Interior signed an agreement with the Army to stop all tree cutting and to protect the historic woods with a scenic easement. A few years later, in 1975, the 24.4 acres were transferred to the National Park Service for protection thereafter.

The Custis-Lee Mansion Woodlands

Thus the National Park Service has been responsible for protecting and preserving the historic landscape for more than 20 years.

The present Superintendent Metzler is an energetic and industrious official. He was born in Brooklyn New York, and was a helicopter crew chief in Vietnam during his army service from 1966-69. He was selected for his Arlington Cemetery assignment in 1991 from two applicants based on his service and training in the field of cemetery management in the National Cemetery System.[117] In recent years, with the filling of the Cemetery, Superintendent Metzler, like his father before, has been known to also be energetically searching for more land for graves either from within the cemetery or from the surrounding areas in Arlington County.

As early as 1993 there were even suggestions in the press that the huge "temporary" Navy Annex building on Columbia Pike next to the cemetery be razed and the cemetery expanded there to provide additional burial grounds. Another area that caught the fancy of the Superintendent was land at the Netherlands Carillon and Marine Iwo Jima Monument, also administered by the Park Service. He was rebuffed on that

---

[116] *32 Code of Federal Regulations (CFR) 553.15.*

[117] *Interview with author, June 28, 1996, in office of the Superintendent, Arlington National Cemetery.*

Major Community "Battles" and Controversies

request and the site was recently approved for the new U. S. Air Force Memorial. In a later interview with this author [118] the Superintendent stated that both these areas were still on the top of his list of possible lands for expansion of the cemetery, but he conceded that he had little hopes of securing land at either of these two locations. He indicated, however, that he held out hopes for land next door at Fort Myer for future burial grounds. When asked where on that crowded, small post he thought there might be unused land available, he answered, "The picnic area in that part of the post alongside the Cemetery wall." He did not indicate how he thought the troops and their families would react to the taking of their picnic grounds and the post's only such recreational area.

In the interview, the Superintendent was asked whether the campaign by him for additional burial grounds was self generated, or whether he was under orders or pressure to do so by higher authority or others.

"Only by me," Superintendent Metzler answered. "No one else is exerting any pressure on me. There is no one else I must answer to".

"Isn't the cemetery under the control of the Department of the Army? What is the chain of command above you?", I asked.

"There is none," he said. "We are an independent agency. We go directly to the Hill to testify for our budget or other matters."

"So you are acting independently and on your own in seeking more burial grounds for the cemetery?"

"Absolutely."

"Then may I ask, what motivates you to do so?", I next asked. "If no one is pushing you on the matter, why persist?"

"Because I feel it is my responsibility and duty to accommodate as many requests for burial here as is possible. Arlington is unique among all the National Cemeteries. It has more prestige and fame. Many individuals desire to buried here more than anywhere else. The Tomb of the Unknowns is here. President Kennedy is buried here, and by far more national heros and famous figures than anywhere else. Arlington is a symbol of freedom and peace. We should fill as many requests from our veterans and service people for burial here as possible."

"But the Cemetery's space and capacity is not infinite. Sooner or later it will be filled, and as surrounded as it is by the Arlington County community and other installations there will be the day when no further expansion is possible."

"True, but we have not reached that day yet, and I intend to expand the cemetery as much as possible until that final day is reached."

"Even to taking the woodlands next to the Arlington House?"

"Yes - or at least the Internment Zone that is farthest from the House, on level ground, out of sight of the house, and of no historical or archeological character or value. The Lee Memorial Preservation Zone may not be the same. Much of it is on a steep slope and therefore not very suitable for burial grounds. As reflected in the interagency agreement, it may also have a high potential for archeological resources pertaining to the significance of the Arlington House. The forest dates from the Lee

---

[118] *June 28, 1996, Ibid.*

occupancy in the mid-1800's and may contribute greatly to the setting of the Arlington House. We shall have to await the results of forthcoming studies mentioned in the agreement and the pending transfer legislation in Congress."

"You are aware that many history and preservation buffs, and some national environmental groups, are strongly opposed to your aims of taking the woodlands for burial sites. Does this not deter you?"

"No, but some of the things they are saying as reported in the press does annoy me."

"Such as?"

"Some say we are going to cut down all the trees and that we are going to menace the Arlington House. We are going to do neither. We have over 14,000 trees in the cemetery. We like trees and will always protect them."

I told the Superintendent that I had not heard or read such statements, but there were many who felt he was going to cut down many of the older trees, and for sure destroy most of the native woodlands that was habitat for wild animals and countless forest plants. The Superintendent did not further respond.

With respect to the independence of the Arlington Cemetery operations and lack of higher echelon control, it appears the Superintendent may have over spoken or be in error. Statutorily and by Federal Regulations, the Secretary of the Army for Civil Works, through the Military District of Washington, is expressly and "directly responsible" for the "administration, operations and maintenance" of Arlington Cemetery.[119] The Federal Regulations further provide, in pertinent part, "new burial sections will be opened and prepared for burials only with the approval of the (Army) Adjutant General, and after types and sizes of monuments on permanent sites have been established". [120] Concerning his operational relations with the Secretary of the Army and the MDW, the Superintendent may have meant, based on his day to day experience, that he had been given such wide leeway in discharging his duties that it appeared he was indeed independent as a matter of practice.

When possible expansion of Arlington Cemetery was first discussed in the early 1990's the Washington Post published a letter in opposition on July 23, 1993 from this writer, a veteran of two wars with extensive combat service. The letter pointed out that veterans do not have a constitutional right to be buried in Arlington Cemetery; that there are countless other national cemeteries for their use. I wrote that while I was fully eligible under current criteria to be buried in Arlington, and preferred to be, I would willingly forego that option if it could avoid the taking of more land for the cemetery. I wrote further, "I prefer my children and their progeny to have any unused land for their use as the living, rather than for my use in death". Other lands around the cemetery are also known to have been considered by the superintendent for taking for burial grounds.

The transfer of the 24 acres of woodlands next to the Arlington House in the cemetery took a surprising and major leap toward consummation at 8:30 a.m. on February 22, 1995 at Arlington Cemetery when representatives of the Army, Interior and

---

[119] *38 U.S. Code 2400 et seq., and 32 Code of FederalRegulation,553.4.*

[120] *32 CFR 553.7 (b)*

Major Community "Battles" and Controversies

the Cemetery superintendent met to execute an inter-agency agreement. The agreement was signed by Dr John H. Zirschky, Acting Assistant Secretary of the Army for Civil Works, George T. Frampton, Jr., Interior Assistant Secretary for Fish and Wildlife and Parks, and Arlington Cemetery Superintendent Metzler.

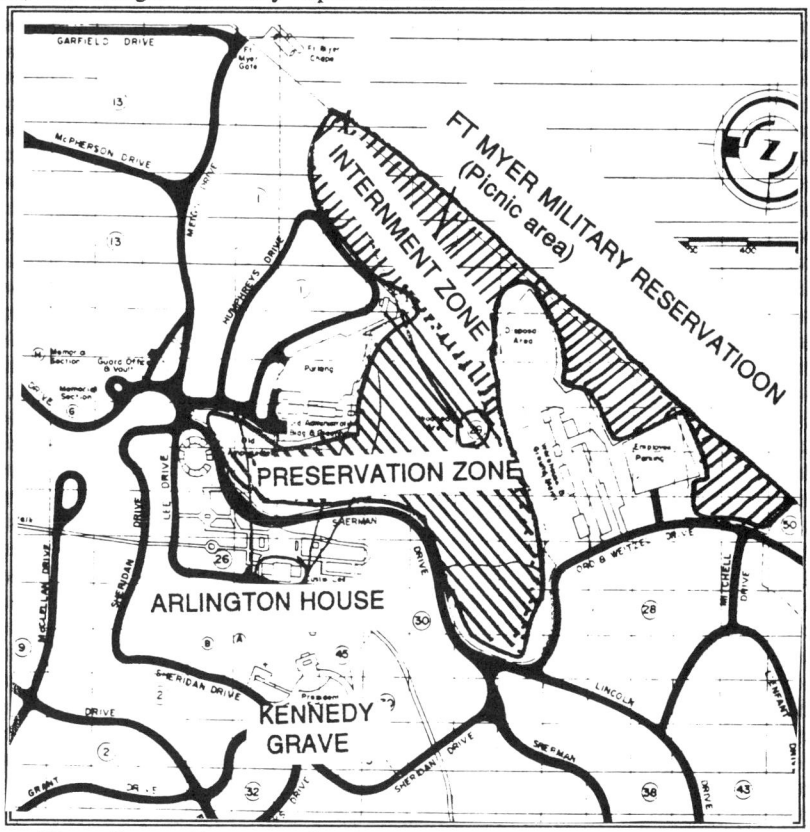

The Arlington House woodlands Internment and Preservation Zones as drawn by Cemetery Superintendent Metzler.

The agreement, as announced one day in advance by the Public Affairs office of the Military District of Washington, provided that 12 of the 24 acres to be transferred known as Section 29, would be earmarked for use as "an internment area". The area ran generally along the Fort Myer northwest wall of the Cemetery, wrapping somewhat around the Cemetery's warehouse and ground maintenance facilities. The remaining 12 acres, comprising the Lee Memorial Preservation Zone, began directly behind the Arlington House between Sherman Drive and the Old Amphitheater Building and its parking lot, and extended to the limits of the internment area. The agreement specified that the Memorial Preservation acres would be "preserved in a park-like setting of Arlington House" but further studies were to be made "to determine its possible suitability as additional burial areas".

The agreement acknowledged that the Memorial Preservation Zone, encompassing approximately 12.5 acres with steep slopes, has "a high potential for archeological resources pertaining to the significance of Arlington House, and forest cover dating to the Lee occupancy of the mid-1800's which contributes significantly to the setting of the Arlington House."

Local Historians and environmentalists strongly opposed to the transfer of the land were and caught off guard. They reacted with alarm, resentment and indignation. They pointed out that there had been inadequate advance public notice of the signing ceremony, and that they were denied the opportunity for the filing of opposing comments or otherwise to participate in the matter. Opponents of the transfer began to dig in deep in preparation for all out assault on the agreement and to defend the woodlands. They were aware that Congressional approval of the agreement was required and the opponents determined to make known their objections before committees or otherwise when the matter came before The Congress.

On June 5, the Executive Board of the Arlington Historical Society adopted a resolution opposing the transfer stressing that the land should remain in its "present pre-civil war condition." It issued a press release on its resolution and provided copies to the Interior and Defense Departments. Society members pointed out that the tract is the only remaining native or primitive woodlands on the plantation grounds and that it should remain wild, overgrown and undisturbed to show visitors how the estate looked when it was taken over by the Federal army during the Civil War. Society President Sherman Pratt stated that "the site abounds with native plant life and has oak trees and other timber known to be over two hundred years old, and numerous animals to include turkeys, fox, and deer".

On June 25, The Washington Post printed a letter from Maurietta M. Schoolfield who wrote that she had been a docent at Arlington House for 14 years with the belief that the Park Service "was committed to protecting the house and the few surviving acres of pre-civil war woodland in its historical setting."..."as a part of our national heritage".

On June 29, the Arlington Journal editorialized that the cutting of trees (for graves) would be "a serious mistake" and that "if we save the trees, we will have a shrine that will prove much more valuable for living Americans in the centuries to come". On the same day, the newspaper's lead story on page one by reporter Vincent Morris with banner headlines reported on the cemetery land transfer plans and featured an interview with Schoolfield, with color photos and maps. Several days later, on July 6, the Washington Post joined in the coverage with an article by staff writer Ellen Nakashima headlined "Environmentalists Fear effects of Expanded Arlington Cemetery." She quoted James F. Wright from the Virginia Chapter of the Sierra Club in opposition to the transfer as saying "...we need to protect natural areas..." and not harm "the historical value of Arlington House." She also pointed out that the transfer would require Congressional approval.

In the following months, opponents of the land transfer met and considered their options. Their plans included the submission of materials and appearances before Congressional committees that they expected to hold hearings before any final action was taken.

Several months went by without any further information as to the status of the matter when suddenly, in mid June 1996 information was received that the House of

Major Community "Battles" and Controversies

Representatives had quietly approved the transfer with little or no notice, fanfare or publicity and that it was about to be voted to the floor by the Senate.

A tiny and innocent sounding provision mandating the transfer of the land was included in the massive $240 billion Defense Authorization measure for the Fiscal Year 1997. The provision simply read, in pertinent part, "Interior shall transfer lands" known as the Internment Zone and...the "Robert E. Lee Memorial Preservation Zone...". No mention was made of the number of acres involved, nor was there a description of the land, or any indication that it was adjacent to the mansion and a part of the original Custis Lee plantation grounds, or that it was the only remaining part of the antebellum Civil War estate that had not been taken for use or development of the cemetery, the abutting Fort Myer Army reservation, or otherwise.

"Lose woodlands forever?"

Preservationists, scholars and history buffs were appalled at this development and the prospect of losing the only remaining acres of the pre-Civil War plantation. Arlingtonian Catharine T. "Teddy" Saulmon, a docent and guide at Arlington House for 28 years, pointed out that the "woods appear today much as they did before 1861. Over the years winds and lightning strikes have taken most of the historical oaks but some of the surviving trees are more than 200 years old. The majority of the trees here today are naturalized, mainly oak, and are the direct descendants of the trees that grew here in General Lee's day." Saulmon added, echoing the sentiments of Schoolfield and others, "The floor of the woods is thickly covered with native Virginia wild flowers and plants...proving an invaluable habitat for a population of red and gray fox, wild turkey, and a wide variety of birds. Deer have also been seen here. With almost all of the original Arlington estate now covered with graves, this small section of woods alone provides today's visitor with a vivid glimpse of the historical landscape as it was before the Civil War."

* * * *

Arlington House, also referred to as the Custis-Lee mansion, is treated at several places herein. A brief recap here, however, of the House and its contemporary setting may be helpful to the reader. The structure dates from the beginning of the 19th Century, and enjoys a most remarkable and, at times, painful history. It is the oldest extant major structure in Arlington County. An older residence, Abingdon at National Airport, also discussed in detail herein, built by Jerrard Alexander around 1741, from whence the City of Alexandria gets its name, was destroyed by fire in 1930. Its ruins are being preserved and not paved over for parking lots by the airport authorities as a result of vigorous protests by local historical preservationists.

When George Washington died in 1799, and his wife Martha in 1802, at Mt Vernon, some of his lands along the Potomac River across from the Capital passed to his adopted son George Washington Parke Custis. Custis, the grandson of Martha Washington, was born at Mt Airy, the Calvert homestead across the Potomac in Maryland, while the family lived at Abingdon. Upon taking possession of the lands,

ARLINGTON COUNTY VIRGINIA - A Modern History

Arlington House during the Civil War

young Custis looked around for the most desirable place to construct his home. He chose the existing site with its magnificent panoramic view of Washington directly across the river.

Custis began building his home in 1802 and two years later took for his bride 16 year old Molly Fitzhugh of Alexandria. In 1831, in an elaborate ceremony at Arlington House, their only surviving daughter, Mary Ann Randolph Custis married a young Army lieutenant from Stratford east of Fredericksburg and just out of West Point, Robert Edward Lee. In the following years Lee departed for the Mexican War, and for various duty assignments to include ones at St Louis and the Military Academy.

In 1853, Molly Custis died and four years later her husband (and Lee's father in law) also died. The two are buried on the grounds of their estate about midway between their mansion and the Ft Myer Chapel gate in a wrought iron enclosure amidst a group of trees near the junction of McPherson and Meigs Drives. Lee then took leave from the Army to manage the run down and financially ailing estate. Friends advised him to sell some of the slaves to raise funds for repairs and upkeep but, as related by the late Arlington historian Eleanor Lee Templeman in her book Arlington Heritage,[121] General Lee declined to do so because he had plans to free the slaves instead. Custis also was

---

[121] *Avenel Books, a division of Crown Publishers, In., New York, 1959.*

Major Community "Battles" and Controversies

opposed to slavery and provided in his will that the slaves were to be freed but after they had been taught a trade.[122]

At the beginning of the Civil War in 1861, after the Virginia legislature voted to secede on April 17, 1861, Lee declined the new President's request to take command of the Union Armies. The Lees promptly fled southward, and on May 24th Union Armies spilled across the Potomac and occupied high grounds along the river including the Custis Lee plantation and Arlington House. In a bazaar set of circumstances that smacked of invidiousness and lack of candor on the part of the Federal authorities, the Custis Lee estate was bought by the Federal Government at a 1864 delinquent taxes auction for $26,800. The Lees had failed to pay a real estate tax of only $92.07 because of a special law applying to conquered territories that required payment only by the land owner in person which Mrs Lee could not do when in Richmond as a semi-invalid. General Lee, of course, was otherwise preoccupied in the Battle of the Wilderness and other engagements.

After the war, the Lee's eldest son and heir to the property sued to recover the land claiming illegal seizure. The Supreme Court agreed and affirmed title in the Lees in 1883. Lee, however, did not want the property that had been by then extensively filled with the graves of union soldiers. Instead, he accepted $150,000 in compensation, thus clearing the Government's title.

With the occupation of Northern Virginia highlands across from the Capital in 1861, a vigorous construction program was launched to build forts to defend Washington. A line of primary and secondary, or "lunette" forts stretched through Arlington (then Alexandria) County from Ft Marcy in Fairfax County to the town of Alexandria. One of the primary forts, later named Fort Whipple, was located on the Custis Lee grounds about where the present day flag pole of Ft Myer is situated. Smaller forts on the plantation grounds included Fort McPherson located inside present day Arlington Cemetery roughly opposite the Radar Clinic in Ft Myer and Forts Tillinghast and Cass near the Ft Myer Main Gate on or about opposite U. S. Route 50/Arlington Boulevard.

The Custis-Lee plantation grounds also became the location, during and after the Civil War, of housing for freed slaves moved from grimy and sordid slums in the District of Columbia. The housing, known as Freedman's Village, demolished in the 1880's, was constructed on the portion of the plantation where the southern edge of the Cemetery is now located just short of Columbia Pike and the Henderson Hall Marine Barracks.

Thus, all of the Custis Lee plantation grounds have been converted to Federal or other uses, mostly burial grounds, over the years, except for the relatively tiny 24 acres of pristine woodlands that now awaits its fate.

* * *

As stated, the Arlington House woodlands transfer provision had been included in the legislation with little fanfare or public knowledge and thus escaped the attention of local persons interested in, and monitoring, the matter. With word that the transfer provision had passed the House, indignant local historians and preservationists swung into

---

[122] *A copy on file in the Virginia Room, Arlington Central Library.*

action in an effort to have the provision deleted from the Senate bill. They knew their chances of success were not great. They knew that most Senators, as with the Representatives, or anyone else concerned about such preservation, would not even know of the provision. Equally damaging, they knew that even if any senator or aide chanced to spot the provision, it was highly unlikely anyone would know that it applied to a critical, last remaining piece of Arlington Cemetery woodlands next to the Custis Lee mansion.

Nevertheless, a handful of Arlingtonians in whose county the land rested, determined to make a try at attracting Congressional and other attention and support to kill the transfer provision. The authorization bill was expected to arrive on the Senate floor for debate on Wednesday, June 19. On Tuesday the preceding day, a hastily assembled team from the Arlington Historical Society prepared a packet of materials for distribution on Capital Hill and the media. The packet included a copy of the land transfer provision of the bill with the seemingly innocuous and misleading language highlighted, an earlier background press release by the Public Affairs office of the Military District of Washington, and copies of media articles that included maps or drawings of the Custis-Lee grounds and the location of the 24 acres. Telephone "trees" also were launched to spread the word as widely as possible to persons or organizations that could be expected to be interested and supportive. Progress was slow and tedious, however, because each call to a completely uninformed source required lengthy and complex explanations. Workers often wondered if they had any chances of prevailing in their efforts.

Additionally, on the day the Senate began considering the matter, a delegation of past Presidents of the Society visited the offices of Virginia Senators John Warner and Charles Robb to brief them or their staffs, to deliver letters pleading for support, and to convey the Society's opposition to the transfer or development of the land. The Society delegation included past presidents Catharine "Teddy" Saulmon, Sherman Pratt and Evelyn Syphax, an African-American long prominent in Arlington and Metropolitan Washington affairs. The Syphax family ancestors had lived on the Custis Lee plantation either as slaves or freed persons.

On June 21, the Arlington Journal again opposed the transfer in an editorial titled "Keep the Trees", and pointed out that "the land in question is historic in its own right". The Journal also featured the event with banner page one "Trees or graves? Annex in tug of war" headline and a color photo of the Arlington House. The article by writer Robert Gehl described in detail the developments in the matter since House passage of the Defense bill, and he quoted Superintendent Meztler, concerning Arlington House as saying, in part, "We would never use that (Arlington House), in fact we would never even think of that. It's a historic landmark." The Superintendent did not say that he also considered the plantation grounds next to the Arlington House historic, nor why he did not so consider them to be as equally historic as the mansion.

The following day on the 22nd, Washington Post writer Ellen Nakashima again wrote in detail on the transfer developments in an article "Plan to Expand Cemetery Angers Preservationists". Her article was accompanied with an explanatory map of the Arlington Cemetery and subject section. She wrote that "Congress is on the verge of passing legislation..." (to transfer the land), but that an environmental assessment also had to first be completed. She added that while Senator Warner's aides had said the

Major Community "Battles" and Controversies

Senate is likely to approve the legislation that such a prospect had not daunted the expansion foes. Her article reflected the concern of both senators of the possible reaction of veterans if a stand was taken in opposition to a project aimed at providing more burial grounds for veterans. She quoted Warner's communications director Eric Ruff as indicating there was a need to balance veterans interests with those of "environmental and historical aspects of this proposal".

In the hours and days following, other Arlingtonians joined the Society's protest group including James Wright of the Virginia Chapter of the Sierra Club, author and architect Russell Kuene, and Arlington County Board member and past Chairman Albert Eisenberg now with an association primarily concerned with preserving open and undeveloped spaces. The opponents also solicited the help of other national organizations including the Nature Conservatory in Rosslyn in Arlington and Julia Coombs in the Regional Office of the National Trust for Historic Preservation in Philadelphia.

A background paper prepared and released by the delegation from the Arlington Historical Society (AHS) read in part:

> *"The irreversible loss of this historic woods and landscape is too high a price to pay for burial land. Such destruction amounts to outright stealing from future generations. The Secretary of Interior and the Director, National Park Service must be held accountable for preserving and protecting these woods - it is not theirs to give away for destruction."*

On June 22nd letters were written to both Senators Robb and Warner to formally document for the record the AHS's opposition to the land transfer. In the letter to Senator Warner, the Society spokesman referred to the senator's reported concern about balancing preservation and veterans needs and advised the senator that on this point there was no disagreement, but that a question could be as to just where that balance may be. The Society's letter writer, himself a veteran, argued that almost all the Custis Lee plantation grounds had already been taken for the 245,000 burials in the cemetery, and asked:

> *"Does a 'balance' require that we veterans have every last square foot of land around the plantation manor? We contend not. As advanced by us, the relatively small 24 acres in the pending legislation should not be gobbled up for burial sites but should be preserved in its natural state to prevent further imbalance in favor of us veterans. These small remaining grounds of the Custis Lee plantation are no less historical and irreplaceable as the manor itself."*

On June 26th a sudden development occurred that seemed to be cause for some encouragement for the opponents of the woodlands transfer. Their efforts, at least to some extent, seemed to be paying off. From Senator Robb's office came notice that the Senator's aids had drafted substitute language in the legislation that the Senator, along with Senator Warner, were planning to jointly introduce from the floor. The language in the bill providing that the Secretary of the Interior "shall transfer jurisdiction to the

Secretary of the Army" (that manages Arlington Cemetery) "administrative jurisdiction over the following lands...All lands in the Robert E. Lee Memorial Preservation Zone, other than lands in the ...Zone that the Secretary..determine must be retained <u>because of historical significance of such lands, or for the maintenance of nearby lands or facilities"</u> (emphasis supplied) was retained; but the following new language was proposed:

> *The Secretary...may not make the transfer...until 60 days after the date on which the Secretary submits to the (Congressional committees) --*
> *(i) a summary of the document entitled 'Cultural Landscape and Archaeological Study, Section 29, Arlington House, the Robert E Lee Memorial',*
> *(ii) a summary of any environmental analysis required with respect to the transfer under the National Environmental Policy Act (NEPA) of 1969, and*
> *(iii) the proposal of the Secretaries setting forth the lands to be transferred and the general manner in which the Secretary will develop such lands after transfer."*

The opponents of the land transfer greeted this development with mixed reactions. On the down side, the three conditions specified seemed to be little more than rhetoric and not very substantive. The requirement for a NEPA study was already a requirement of existing law and further was included in the February 22, 1995 agreement of the Secretaries. With respect to the requirement in paragraph (iii) that the Secretaries "set forth the lands to be transferred" and the general manner they "will develop such lands after transfer" that requirement also was included in the inter-agency agreement. Paragraph II of the agreement reads in pertinent part, "The Exact acreage and legal description of the property in the Interment Zone...shall be determined by a survey..." and paragraph VI reads, in pertinent part, "The exact acreage and legal descriptions of the property in the Preservation Zone to be transferred shall be determined by a survey satisfactory to the respective secretaries...". With respect to "development" of the lands, paragraph V of the agreement reads in part, "...the NPS (National Park Service) will issue a permit to the Army, which will allow the Army to study and survey the property and to plan for its use..." Thus there appeared to be little if any gain for the transfer opponents in the substituted Senate language.

On the plus side, however, the new language seemed to insure that at least the transfer would not immediately be a "done matter" as it would have been by Senate approval of the House version of the bill. In short, they pointed out, while a short term battle may have been won if the Senate adopts the amended language, the longer range war was still to be fought.

In the midst of the 1996 summer struggle, some of the opponents recognized that the arena of conflict could now be changed to the Departmental and not the Congressional level. Plans were made to file letters with the Secretary, and to encourage as many other organizations or persons as possible to do likewise, expressing and documenting their interest in the matter and demanding an opportunity to participate in and be kept informed of any hearings or studies undertaken. Some opponents also

Major Community "Battles" and Controversies

grudgingly recognized, as a practical matter of reality, that all 24 acres of land may never be saved, but they were determined to make a vigorous effort to at least save the 12 acres that the agreement of 1995 indicated would be "preserved in a park-like setting" pending further studies "to determine its possible suitability as additional burial areas". (emphasis supplied).

By early September, 1996, the Congressional measure, known as the Defense Authorization Bill for Fiscal 1997, with the provision authorizing transfer of the Arlington House woodlands to the Army, had cleared Congress and on September 24, the Washington Post announced it had been signed into law by the President.

Following the signing of the measure by the President, Historical Society President Robert Watson and Sierra Club Virginia Chapter Chair James Wright sent letters to the Army and Interior Secretaries and the Park Service Director. The letters reminded the addressees of the writers' (1) continued strong opposition to the transfer, (2) that there was a loss to understand how Interior, as the Federal agency primarily charged with protecting open space and historical treasures, would have agreed to such a transfer, (3) that the transfer would constitute a breach of the 1975 Congressionally expressed commitment that the land should be "set aside in perpetuity to preserve an appropriate setting for the mansion, and (4) that the writers' organizations were determined to do whatever they could to ensure that the woodlands remain undisturbed and an appropriate setting for the mansion.

On October 18, Martin Lancaster, the Assistant Secretary of the Army for Civil Works responded to Watson and Wright and wrote, in part, "...some of the land found in Section 29 will be transferred to the Army...none of the land...found to be historically significant, however, will be used for burials. Any of the land deemed to have sensitive and historical resources will be retained by the Department of Interior".

A few days later on October 31, Terry Carlson, National Capital Area Field Director for the National Park Service also responded to Watson and Wright on behalf of Interior and the Park Service and wrote, in part, "Prior studies and experience in our management of Section 29 indicate resources exist within the Preservation Zone (half the 24 acres) that make it likely that all those lands must be retained by the National Park Service because of historical significance."

The statements from Interior and the Army were received with some pleasure and surprise by preservationist opponents of the woodlands transfer, but also with some apprehension because of uncertainty as to possible interpretations by Interior of what might be concluded to be "cultural and historical significance."

On November 18, Watson and Wright wrote to Carlson and said, in part, "We have received with considerable relief your letter...which sounds like a near guarantee that at least 12 acres next to the mansion will be retained in its present undeveloped and wooded condition...we confess, however, a degree of apprehension on your possible interpretation as to what constitutes 'historical significance'...we hold there is clearly historical significance by the mere location of the grounds that were once a part of the ...plantation and next to the mansion whether or not any specific artifacts are ever found on those grounds...". Several days later Watson and Wright formally asked Interior to record the Society and Club as "consulting parties" as provided for in Section 106 of the EPA in order to insure them an opportunity to be heard on the matter before any final

ARLINGTON COUNTY VIRGINIA - A Modern History

decisions were made. Additionally, they sent letters to other interested parties, to include the County Board, urging that they too request recordation as consulting parties.

In the closing days of June, 1996, the groups opposed to the Custis Lee plantation lands transfer awaited further word from Interior and they vowed to continue the fight to retain at least some of the acres next to the Custis Lee Mansion in a natural woodlands condition. The inference from the legislation wording, from the correspondence with Interior and the Army, and from public statements of Cemetery Superintendent John C. Metzler, Jr., seemed to provide some hope that at least the Preservation Zone 12 acres of the 24 acres may be saved from use as burial grounds.

As 1996 drifted into 1997, the Society members, and others supporting them, knew well that they still had an uphill fight before them but they proclaimed their determination to pursue the matter so long as there is any recourse available that might save any part of the last plantation woodland acres at Arlington House.

At the year neared its end, there appeared to be some basis for encouragement for those seeking to save the mansion woodlands. On August 26, Audrey Calhoun, National Park GW Memorial Parkway Superintendent, forwarded her draft Environmental Assessment to her higher authorities for review. The draft listed three alternatives concerning the 24 acres in Section 29, i.e: (A) to retain all significant resource areas (all of the memorial zone and most of the internment zone); (B) to retain only the preservation zone and transfer the interment zone for the cemetery; and (C) to retain the entire Section 29. The draft assessment included a recommendation, essentially, that alternative (A) be adopted. While preservationists would obviously favor adoption of alternative (C), no land transfer at all, the adoption of alternative (A) would yet save most of the subject woodlands and all of the areas closest to the mansion.

At this writing, however, the outcome is far from settled.

The Mount Airy plantation, home of the Calvert family, descendants of Lord Baltimore, in Prince George County Maryland just outside the U. S. Air Force base Andrews Field where the President's Air Force One is based. Eleanor Calvert from Mount Airy was the mother of George Washington Parke Custis who built Arlington House. Custis was born at Mount Airy in 1781 where his mother was visiting and away from the Custis family home at Abingdon Virginia.

Major Community "Battles" and Controversies

ROUND XVIII
Arlington-Falls Church Boundary Park lands

At the recommendation of the Falls Church Historical Commission on September 17, 1993, and following an invitation of the Northern Virginia Planning District Commission, nominees from four jurisdictions and other concerned organizations participated in the Northern Virginia Boundary Stones Committee (NOVABOSTCO) which held fifteen meetings and two field surveys between March 17, 1994 and August 28, 1995.[123] The Committee's area of interest involved boundary stones that once marked the Northern Virginia boundary of the National Capital as laid out and surveyed in 1791 by Major Andrew Ellicott, with celestial sightings and other assistance from the free black scientist Benjamin Banneker.

After the 1846 retrocession to Virginia of that part of the National Capital that had been ceded to the Federal Government in 1791 for the Capital, the boundary stones in Northern Virginia no longer marked the division line between the Capital and Virginia. That boundary line was changed and became the southern shore of the Potomac River at high tide. The previously installed boundary stones in Virginia then became markers to delineate the boundaries between the County of Alexandria (Arlington later) and the City of Alexandria, the County of Fairfax, and the City of Falls Church.

The South corner stone (# 1) that constituted the initial point for the survey was, and is, at Jones Point alongside present I-495 (the "beltway"). It is now under an abandoned U. S. Coast Guard lighthouse that is preserved as an historical artifact in a small municipal park. Boundary stones from there lay northwestward at one mile intervals to the West cornerstone (boundary stone # 10), near the intersection of Williamsburg Blvd and North Arizona Streets (Merridian in Falls Church) in North Arlington. The West cornerstone is located on a small tract 24x12.5x13 parts of which lie within Arlington and Fairfax Counties, and part in the City of Falls Church. The land on which the stone is located is known as the West Cornerstone Park.

Boundary stone #9, (SW9) one mile to the southeast, is located in publicly owned open space of the Four Mile Run flood plain that once was the right of way for a line of the Old Dominion railroad. The stone is on the Arlington-City of Falls Church boundary line and is a few feet from the Van Buren and North 18th Street intersection.

---

[123] *NOVABOSTCO Findings and Recommendations, September, 1995, ps.1 and 2 (on file in the County Dept. of Parks, Recreation and Community Resources).*

In the late 1970s, SW stone #9 was designated a National Historic Landmark after nomination by the Afro-American Bicentennial Corporation. On the surrounding fence there is a marker identifying the stone as the Benjamin Banneker SW 9 stone and a statement that the site possesses national significance in the History of the United States. The land on which stone #9 is located has been known as the Four Mile Run Park on the Falls Church side of the boundary, and as the East Falls Church and Isaac Crossman parks on the Arlington side of the boundary. All of the lands and surrounding areas for some distance was once owned by the early settler Isaac Crossman, some of whose progeny still live in nearby historic houses in Falls Church.

ANDREW ELLICOTT

Major Andrew Ellicott, commissioned by the new American President George Washington to survey the capital boundaries in 1791, came from a Pennsylvania Quaker family that moved to Maryland in 1771 and established extensive mills in an area that eventually became Ellicott City. Ellicott was a talented mathematician and with his first cousin George Ellicott became skilled in astronomy. He surveyed, or was involved in surveying, much of the boundaries of Pennsylvania on the west to Lake Erie and on the south next to Virginia (now West Virginia). He finished the work started by Mason and Dixon on the Pennsylvania-Virginia boundary. He was surveying the western boundary of State of New York when he was summoned to survey the new District of Columbia, at which time he requested the assistance of Benjamin Banneker. [124]

BENJAMIN BANNEKER

Benjamin Banneker was born in 1731 as a free black man. His father, Robert Banneker, bought 100 acres of land in Maryland which was later inherited by Benjamin. Banneker was exceptionally talented and mostly self educated in mathematics and other subjects. He was one of the first students to take advantage of free lessons in astronomy offered by Andrew Ellicott's brother George. By extensive practice and persistent application he became extraordinarily proficient at astronomical observations and sightings. Legend is that he designed and carved a wooden clock, the first in America, that worked for over 50 years. [125]

In the Washington Post Sunday features sections in 1995 in a series of segments also available in booklet form from Red Rose Studio in Willow Street, PA, 17584, cartoonist Patrick M. Reynolds depicts highlights of Banneker's life and career. He relates that Banneker worked at Jones Point lying on his back to find the exact starting point on the ground by plotting about six stars as they crossed his spot at a particular time of the night. From that plotted spot the surveyors started at Hunting Creek in Alexandria and crossed the Potomac into Maryland, and then northwest into Virginia. The field

---

[124] Study, *Proposal to Renam[e] ...Parks,* by Pamela Fisher, East Falls Church Civic Association, January 25, 1996, p. 4, NOVABOSTCO Findings, Ibid.

[125] Ibid, p.5.

Major Community "Battles" and Controversies

team armed themselves with axes, choppers and earth tools since much of the routes were through dense woods, swamps and undergrowth to clear four 40 foot wide swaths each of ten mile lengths. The strenuous pace soon proved too much for Banneker in his 60s and in April 1791 he left the team and went home to Howard County in Maryland while Ellicott and the others completed the survey. At home Banneker wrote a compendium of mathematics, astronomy, essays, proverbs and jokes and, with the help of Thomas Jefferson, succeeded in having it published. He wrote an almanac published in 1795 that accurately predicted an eclipse. He died in October 1806 at the age of 75.

A 1996 CONTEST FOR BANNEKER ARTIFACTS

Considerable attention and some controversy arose in August, 1996, when an inheritor of Banneker's few possessions, Elizabeth Wilde, an Ellicott descendant in Indianapolis, Indiana, made them available for auction in Bethesda, Maryland. As reported by staff writer Jon Jeter in the Washington Post on September 9, "...supporters of a planned museum for the legendary black scientist had hoped to buy the few remaining possessions from money they had raised when learning that the Colonial-era treasures would be for sale." They were thwarted, however, when a stranger later identified as Emanuel Friedman, quietly appeared and launched an energetic bidding contest that drove prices for items beyond the reach of the museum organizers. When the auction was over, Jeter wrote, Friedman, had paid over $85,000 for Banneker artifacts including one drop-leaf table for $32,500 that would normally sell for about $10,000. In the end the museum supporters had managed to buy only a handwritten ledger. They could have taken some comfort, perhaps, from the fact that it was an especially treasured item, since it was personally used by Banneker in his work on the District of Columbia Boundaries.

With respect to the auction of Banneker's artifacts, the Washington Post editorialized on August 22, several weeks before the auction, as follows, in part:

> "...The Ellicott family to whom (Banneker) bequeathed his possessions have the right to dispose of them any way they see fit...[and] to auction off the 20 or so artifacts for whatever they may bring...Still if the objects are dispersed and the memory of Mr Banneker stripped from them, the sale will be a sad one...it would be a significant investment in this area's own historical awareness if someone could be found---or come forward--to keep the collection together."

To the dismay of historians and museum proponents, and contrary to the hopes of the Post, no one did step forward and, as stated, the possessions passed to Friedman. Time only can tell whether they will someday be returned to "keep the collection together".

* * *

Ellicott began his boundary survey as stated above, at Jones Point in Alexandria, Virginia a place that is now a park and almost beneath the approaches to the I-495 "beltway" highway Woodrow Wilson Bridge. The operation was not without its perils. The region was still heavily wooded and several men assisting Ellicott lost their lives during the survey's course. One was killed by a falling tree. Accounts differ on the extent of personal commitment and involvement by both Ellicott and Banneker. Some writers have said that Ellicott spent most of his time in the observatory tent and left the field work to younger and more energetic helpers. Others have written to the contrary and claim that he repeatedly visited every one of the 40 mile and corner marker stones that stretch through Virginia and Maryland and back to the South stone at Jones Point. Probably, without in any way detracting from his magnificent and meritorious achievement, the truth lies somewhere in between.

PROPOSED CHANGES IN PARK NAMES

In early February 1996, the Arlington Historical Society (AHS) learned that the Falls Church Historical Commission and the Advisory Board for Recreation and Parks in October 1995 had proposed that the name of the Arlington Isaac Crossman park area at the Falls Church/Arlington boundary adjacent to Van Buren Street at SW boundary stone #9, and certain other nearby park lands, be renamed the "Benjamin Banneker Park at Four Mile Run". The Society also learned that nearby civic associations and affected park and historical authorities had also been advised of the proposal.

On February 12, the President of the AHS wrote to the Chairman of the County Board on the matter and reported that the AHS Board of Directors had considered the matter. The President pointed out that the Board did not understand the need for any change in name, but that if the park was to be renamed a better designation would be the "Ellicott-Banneker Park".

The President in explaining the rationale of the Society position pointed out that Banneker had already been recognized for his significant role in the sightings for the boundary survey with a marker plaque at SW stone #9, but that Ellicott who was in overall charge and worked mostly in the field for the entire forty mile operation had not been commemorated anywhere along the boundary, or perhaps elsewhere. The President added, "We think our suggested alternative would be a reasonable compromise that will afford Banneker additional recognition while not diminishing or overlooking the far more extensive role of Ellicott."

When responses to the proposed name changes were received from all parties concerned it was determined that there was no support for the name changes as proposed. Whereupon an ad hoc inter-jurisdictional work group was formed for the purpose of reaching a mutually acceptable solution for the naming of parks that straddled jurisdictional boundaries. The ad hoc group met on March 29, 1996 in Conference Room 2, Falls Church City Hall. The meeting was chaired by Maurice J. "Rick" Terman of the Falls Church Historical Commission and attended by:
> from Arlington County;
>> Paul Zingg, East Falls Church Civic Association,
>> Sherman Pratt, AHS,
>> Lawrence Goldschmidt, Historic Affairs & Landmark Review Board,

Major Community "Battles" and Controversies

and
Donald Mozingo, Parks and Recreation Commission,
from Fairfax County;
Jack Hiller, History Commission,
Jeanne Niccolls, Park Authority, and
from Falls Church City;
Barry Buschow, Advisory Board for Parks and Recreation, and
Mark Gross, Chair, Planning Commission.

After several additional meetings, and some exchange of correspondence, the ad hoc group succeeded in resolving differences in preferred park names and at its final meeting on May 30th reach a consensus that the parks should be named as follows:

1. The name "Isaac Crossman Park at Four Mile Run" should apply for all of the Arlington and Falls Church parkland west of Van Buren Street.

2. The Arlington and Falls Church parkland between Van Buren and Sycamore Streets should be named the "Benjamin Banneker Park".

3. The name "East Falls Church Park" should be retained for the Arlington Parkland east of Sycamore Street.

4. The land at the at the West Cornerstone west of Arizona Street in Arlington should be renamed "Andrew Ellicott Park at the West Cornerstone".

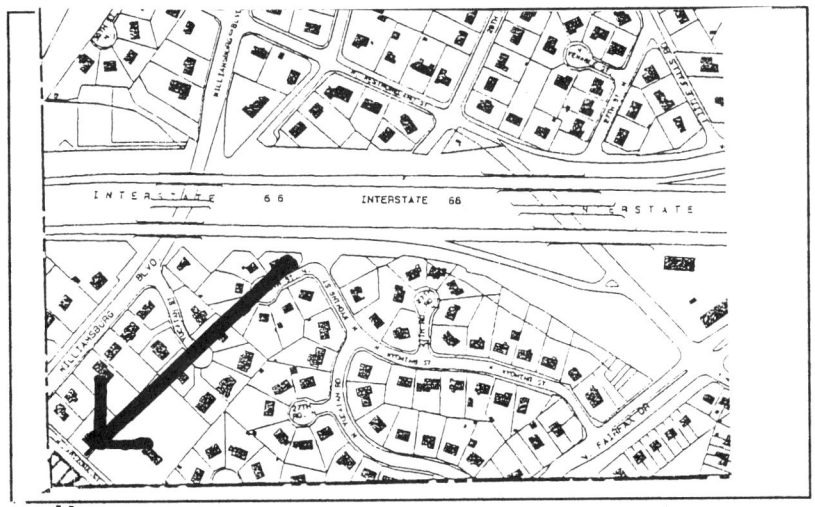

Andrew Ellicott Park At The West Cornerstone

On July 16, Arlington County Manager Anton S. Gardner prepared an agenda item for the County Board recommending approval of the ad hoc committee proposal for change of names of the parklands in Arlington County. The manager advised the Board that the name changes would be in accordance with the Board policy for naming County facilities adopted on November 26, 1988. The manager recommended that the renamings be contingent upon approvals from the authorities in Fairfax County and Falls Church.

ARLINGTON COUNTY VIRGINIA - A Modern History

On August 3, 1996 the County Board on a motion by Chairman James Hunter and seconded by member Ellen Bozman, approved the parkland renaming as recommended by the County Manager. [126]

Thus, with the County Board approval the curtain was brought down successfully and peacefully on what might otherwise could have become a cantankerous, contentious and bitter fought controversy. Citizens of all jurisdictions concerned could be relieved and pleased with the outcome. Even Crossman, Banneker and Ellicott may well have cheered with satisfaction were they still around to do so.

> A JUNE 26, 1791 ELLICOTT QUOTE: Surveyors Camp, State of Virginia "The country through which we are now cutting one of the ten mile lines is very poor...there is not one house that has floor except earth...we find little fruit, except huckleberries,..laboring hands in this country can scarcely be had ...I have had to wade slowly thro' with [only] six...this scarcity of hands will lenthen out the time much beyond what I intended..this country intended for the permanent residence of Congress bears no more proportion (to Philadelphia) than a crane does to a stall fed ox.." (From Papers in VA Rm, Arl. Central Library)

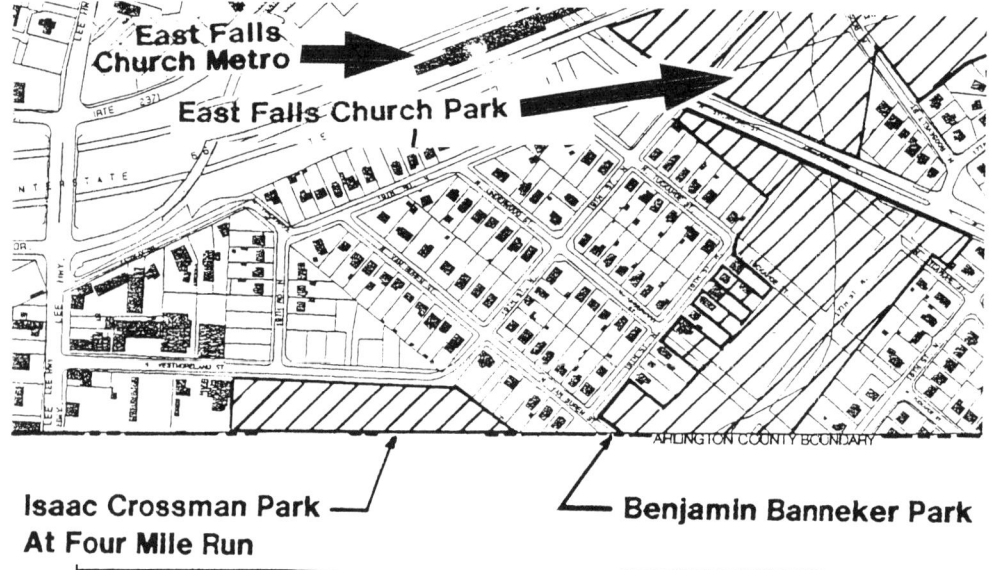

New names for Arlington Boundary Parklands at Falls Church

* * *

[126] *Arlington County Board Minutes, August 3, 1996, page 283, item #9.*

Major Community "Battles" and Controversies

PART XIX
THE HOME DEPOT PROPOSAL

For many years in modern times one of Arlington's better known features and landmarks has been the Sears Roebuck store between Wilson and Clarendon Boulevards and Daniel and Filmore Streets with its auto service store and parking lots behind to the south.

Early in the 1990s media accounts reported that the Arlington store would be closed as a consequence of the Sears Company's nationwide cost cutting down sizing. The other nearest northern Virginia Sears store in the Landmark shopping Mall at Route 236 and I-395 (Shirley Highway) was to remain. In due course the Arlington store was closed and the grounds and buildings became idle and unoccupied. There was much community speculation on what would become of the area. Some members of the Courtlands Civic Association, within whose boundaries and area the site was located, were known to favor redevelopment of the Sears site as park lands or low density residential uses.

By early 1994, it became generally known in the Arlington community that the Atlanta based nationally operating Home Depot company was interested in the site for one of its warehouse-style hardware and home needs stores. Staff writer John Lavey in the Northern Virginia Sun quoted Tom Miller, a planner in the county's Department of Community Planning as saying, "Home Depot has not filed for any rezoning, but they're out there and we know they're out there." It was understood that Home Depot planned a 102,000 square foot store with a 28,000 square foot garden center, approximately 60 feet high, with a three level garage for 864 vehicles, and bounded Clarendon Boulevard on the north, 11th Street to the south, Filmore Street to the west and Danville Street to the east.

SOME FIRST COMMUNITY FORUMS

On February 24, the first of a series of community forums on what to do with the Sears site, and certain surrounding areas, was held in the County Board Room. The meeting signaled the start of a public process to determine the future of a 13-acre special zoning district comprised largely of the Sears site. Sun writer Lavey reported that Joe Rahner, President of the Courtland Civic Association had said, "The overriding issue is regardless of what goes in there of a commercial nature, it must be compatible with the surrounding neighborhood" and that "the Sears site juts into the Courtland [area] like a giant fist."

In a later article on April 4, following the second meeting of the community forum on the Sears site, Lavey wrote that nearby neighbors were working on their own plan that envisioned a park and open space with a mix of commercial and residential uses for the tract. He also wrote that planner Miller was processing data from a questionnaire that was distributed and indications were that "most residents are in favor of mixed uses...[but] some who are not directly affected are in favor of the Home Depot [store]."

On June 27, the County Planning Commission held a hearing on the matter of a Home Depot store on the Sears site. Sun writer Andrew Cain reported on June 29 that all but one of the 254 speakers at the meeting opposed the Home Depot proposal. He wrote that residents of the Clarendon and Courtland neighborhoods said the store would "ruin the surrounding community by creating noise, air pollution and 20,000 car trips per week". Cain quoted Planning Commission member James Charleton as saying, "I do not believe Clarendon is an appropriate (site) for an industrial park". Cain wrote that Home Depot officials did not make a presentation at the hearing but that they were known to expect to win approval because of the economic advantages involving the employment of about 200 people, 85 percent of which would be full time employees.

On July 22, Sun writer Cain reported that Home Depot, faced with a likely County rejection of their sprawling single-story store, were considering stacking their store into a two story structure. He quoted Board Chairwoman Mary Margaret Whipple as saying that while such a change would not insure approval, it "would at least give Board members something to think about". Cain wrote further that while stacking would provide more buffer area between the store and nearby residents, it still would not satisfy residents who believed a Home Depot store would be inconsistent with a community planned for pedestrian walkways and subway use.

As Summer waned into Fall of 1994 the Home Depot matter continued to slowly percolate without resolution. Arlington Courier writer Joe Farruggia wrote on September 28, that the County Board had approved a revision of its General Land Use Plan (GLUP) that would expedite consideration of an upscale grocery store on a part of the Sears site. He also reported that the Home Depot officials had appeared before the Planning Commission and asked for a 60-day deferral of its site plan amendment request (for stacking), a request that was scheduled for Board consideration in October. The Commission rescheduled the matter for a special meeting on February 13, 1995.

A TRAFFIC STUDY

As the date for the special hearing approached, a traffic study by a Home Depot consultant was released and it generated additional controversy and dissention. The study, done by the Washington based Barton Aschman Associates, Inc., claimed that store traffic would not disrupt the neighborhood [because] "there would be no through traffic from the Home Depot on neighborhood streets".

Clarendon residents, however, viewed the study with skepticism and disenchantment. Journal writer Michelle Meyers wrote on January 12, that the Courtland Association President Jon Eklund described the study's numbers as "suspicious" and "pretty low". Meyers also quoted another Courtland resident, Ronni Freeman, as believing the study numbers were low and unsubstantiated, and quoted her, "They seem unbelievable. I'm not happy with the study. I was hoping for something less slippery and more honest. We hope the study is met with the same skepticism at other levels." Meyers reported that Planning Commissioner Vice Chairman Thomas Korns and others were concerned that "there is no pedestrian entrance on Clarendon or Fillmore. We won't want a warehouse on the corner of the street".

* * *

THE PLANNING COMMISSION PONDERS

The February 14 Commission meeting took place with a packed audience in attendance. Home Depot attorney Nan Terpak presented an elegant scale model of the site, with several dozen drawings, traffic studies and made articulate and lengthy arguments on behalf of the proposal. She noted improvements in the designs and architecture, "far from what you would see in a traditional Home Depot", to cope with the "urban village" concept suggested by county officials. These changes and steps apparently failed to satisfy a majority of the Commission, whereupon the Commission deferred the matter to April 1. Notwithstanding that deferral, however, the Commission considered the Home Depot proposal again in late March at a six hour "work session" meeting lasting until 2 a.m. Numerous speakers and staff and commission members had reservations with the Home Depot latest proposals and in its deferral the Commission listed major conditions it wanted met, to include:

= Adding more space for retailers on North Fillmore and a store entrance on Fillmore.
= Limiting store hours to 8 a.m. to 9 p.m. Monday through Saturday and 11 a.m. to 5 p.m. on Sunday.
= Creating a traffic management plan acceptable to neighbors.
= Designing a pedestrian link to neighborhoods.
= Linking construction to adjacent townhouses.
= Sharing parking spaces with nearby business such as the planned Bread and Circus grocery.

ENCOURAGING DEVELOPMENTS

By the end of March, things seemed to be looking up somewhat for Home Depot. Journal Writer Whitley wrote on March 27, in an article headed, "Board Wants to OK Home Deport" that most Board members preferred to approve the development of a Home Depot store "but not at the risk of altering long established plans for developing that area". Whitley wrote that the decision of the Board was hinged on the company's revised plans that were due before its carry-over session scheduled for April 4. She quoted Board member James Hunter, "We need to have economic development in the county...but development that makes sense." A few days later on March 30, Whitley wrote that seven Planning Commission members, in a four page letter, had written to the County Board and cautioned it on the possible adverse precedent setting consequences of the Home Depot rezoning request. The Commissioners pointed out that retail lumber yards and construction materials were not on the specified list of uses for special exceptions in the subject zoning district.

* * * *

COUNTY BOARD HEARS ARGUMENTS

On April 4, the County Board considered the Home Depot proposal that included requests for rezonings for some of the properties involved. There were about 60 speakers and over four hours of public testimony. The Board, however, did not approve the proposal. Instead, it instructed the applicant and opposing citizens to return to the negotiating table and work out a compromise on the company's store. The Board gave the parties until the Board's June 24 meeting to reach a consensus on plans for the store and adjacent townhouses and said that regardless of the outcome it would make a binding decision on that date rather than defer the matter again. Journal writer Whitley reported that the County planned to hire an independent mediator skilled in handling public disputes of this type.

Most of the speakers at the April 4 meeting of the Board were opposed to the Home Depot project. Of the few speakers in favor one said that he believed Home Depot would benefit the county if the Board imposed "appropriate conditions on the store to protect the neighborhoods." Whitley wrote that citizen Peter Fallon, president of the Donaldson Run Civic Association, that favored the project, testified, "I would offer that the silent majority of Arlingtonians are staying at home and waiting for opening day. People fear the big box but it is clearly what the consumers want as evidenced by the success of Pentagon Centre with stores such as Best Buy." Whitley added, "One of the opponents who cornered Fallon after the meeting, suggesting(ed-sic) that Home Depot put their store in Cherrydale, which borders Donaldson Run. Fallon responded he would gladly trade Cherrydale's strip of auto body shops and service stations for Home Depot".

During the months that the Home Depot proposal was pending before the community and its government officials, numerous letters from interested citizens appeared in the local letters to the editor columns of the press. Although the letters for and against the proposal were about evenly divided, it appears unlikely that this would reflect the positions of the public at large. As with most community projects or proposals concerning land uses, those who perceived themselves to be most directly and adversely affected, as did residents next to the Sears site in this instance, are more likely to be active and articulate in their opposition, than would be the public generally that is only indirectly affected. Thus, it is clearly hazardous to draw dispositive inferences as to public support or opposition based on the number and position of letters to the editor writers.

As late as early May, it appeared that the Home Depot proposal could be headed for approval. The Board was on record as telling all parties to work out their differences before its June 24 meeting to decide on the matter and Chairman Eisenberg, as reported by Journal writer Whitley, stated "We think the process can work...but only if there's goodwill and good sense on the part of participants".

A THUNDER CLAP - A LIGHTENING BOLT
HOME DEPOT WITHDRAWS

Then, like a clap of thunder and a blinding flash of lightening, to the surprise of all and no doubt the dismay of many and the delight of others, Home Depot suddenly announced on May 11 that it was abandoning its plans to put a store in Arlington at the Sears site. In a letter to Board Chairman Eisenberg, Home Depot Senior Vice President William E. Harris explained why the corporation was withdrawing its request. Harris wrote, in part:

> "Despite innumerable compromises and a substantial expenditure of funds by Home Depot over the last two years the delays, expense and conditions associated with the site plan process in Arlington County have made the Clarendon project commercially infeasible...it is no longer prudent to pursue approval for a Home Depot store in Clarendon.
>
> "It was a situation where the stipulations that Arlington County was going to put on our approval would make it impossible for us to operate our store profitably. We are looking at additional sites...that would not be in Arlington"

On page one the following day the Journal headlined "Home Depot bows out - Retailer gives up on Clarendon site". In its next edition on the 16th, the Sun proclaimed also on page one, "Home Depot Gives Up on Clarendon Site; Mixed Reaction from Officials, Residents." Journal writer Whitley wrote that the Atlanta-based company submitted at least four designs for a Clarendon store and attended a plethora of meetings to include day-long public hearings. He said Home Depot had been knocking at Arlington's door for two years, although the company did not actually submit its plans until October.

COMMUNITY REACTION

Community reaction to the startling Home Depot announcement varied greatly as reported by Sun writers Valerie Franchi and Mark Garris, and Journal writer Whitley. Board member Whipple said, "I'm disappointed that they decided to pull out...I thought we had set up a good community process..." Board Chair Eisenberg said, "I think part of the problem was that Home Depot showed up on the scene very, very early, before we had planned a future for this site...I think the process might have been instructive for us for the future, but that's history now...I would have preferred to see the process through to the June 24th decision date".

Journal writer Whitley reported on the community reactions to the Home Depot withdrawal in a May 12, 1995 article headed, "Home Depot Bows Out". He wrote that Courtland and Lyon Village residents Bill Gearhart, John Ekland, and some others who had opposed the Home Depot project and were "mostly stunned to hear Home Depot had pulled out" (Whitley), were generally pleased with the announcement. Gearhart said, "...its a great victory for planning in the county for the Clarendon sector plan". Alisa Cowen, President of the Lyon Village Association said, "We're delighted we will not have a chance to work with the Jones family [owners of the Sears tract] to ensure the property is developed to maximize Metro ridership..."

Whitley wrote that Courtland Association past President Joe Rahner, however, who had also strongly opposed Home Depot, seemed, as reported in the press, to have some second thoughts following the withdrawal of the proposal, at least insofar as where the blame rested. He said, "It cost me a ton of money personally and it does irritate the hell out of me that our County Board caused us to waste our money on this...I don't blame Home Depot for this mess. The whole fault belongs squarely with our county government...I would love to know if they [Home Depot?] are fed up with Arlington because the county has treated these people terribly..."

Pamella Gillen, who had testified in favor of Home Depot said the store, "could have been an asset..." Richard Doud, president of the Chamber of Commerce seemed to join in the sentiments expressed by Rahner. He said,. "I think it speaks poorly of the process that it takes this county over a year to make up its mind whether it wants somebody or not...as far as its effect, I don't know the message that Arlington is open for business...rang true in this case.. The process is clearly flawed and obviously skewed against the applicant."

Writer Garris in the Sun on May 19, quoted Republican Board member Benjamin Winslow, at the time running unsuccessfully for reelection as saying, "If we are going to be a business friendly community, we have to explain our position...we've been running around saying all this time if they want to come to our house they've got to live by our rules...but they (Home Depot) didn't have any idea what the rules were because we never made them explicit." Barbara Favola, another candidate for the County Board voiced similar sentiments. She said, "Improvements need to be made in the application process. No developer or neighborhood should have to go through a 14-month process. And Jill Rathbun, active in local politics, agreed. She stated that, "We have no pro-active marketing strategy for the entire county - we don't go out and recruit businesses into Arlington...we get into a process that is unfriendly." She somewhat cynically added that the issue would be forgotten by election day and would not have much impact on those chosen for the County Board in November.

SOME AUTHOR OBSERVATIONS

As can be seen herein, and reasonably inferred from undocumented sources, opinions within the community did and will vary greatly as to the need for and value of a Home Depot at the Sears site and therefore whether the collapse of the Home Depot proposal is welcomed or not. It seems likely that the great majority of people who must travel for home maintenance or improvement and must go to the more distant Hechingers at Baileys Crossroads or to the Home Depot stores near Landmark in Alexandria County, or at Seven Corners in Falls Church would welcome an outlet of this type much closer to them even if they did not expressly say so during the Home Depot consideration. Arlington has no stores or this type nor does it seem likely, from the stand point of land availability or economic feasibility that such a facility could be located anywhere else in Arlington. The Home Depot store, as pointed out by the company and supporters, would have created jobs and business and tax income for the county, but also might have forced into bankruptcy smaller businesses in the area that market products handled by the large home improvement stores such as Home Depot.

Whether Home Depot operations would have had the adverse residential neighborhood impacts perceived by the opponents of the Sears site proposal, or whether any such disadvantages would have been far outweighed by the overall advantages to the county generally, will never be known with certainty. Adverse impacts of proposed developments or business activities are often exaggerated and do not materialize to the extent feared. Some residents in South Arlington painted grim pictures of the

Major Community "Battles" and Controversies

consequences of allowing a Price Club to operate in the Pentagon City area. They cited air and visual pollution, traffic and parking congestion and gridlocks but at this writing, after some three years of operations, these conditions have not arisen, at least to the extent feared.

Although seeming to display a degree of guilt complex in some of their statements over the decision of Home Depot to abandon their efforts to locate a store in Arlington at the Sears site, county officials nevertheless were optimistic about the future for the area. Both Eisenberg and Whipple expressed confidence that the Sears site area would yet be developed in a manner that would be beneficial to the county. Later Board member Paul Ferguson said, "Home Depot's decision ...is a victory for the citizens of Arlington." Eisenberg said he was confident that the site would attract other businesses, and "We fully expect that attractive and appropriate retail uses will succeed on this site". Whipple too said that Arlington remains a very desirable business location and, "...in other places we have been successful and I don't think that one episode counteracts all those years of success." The citizenry of Arlington County, even if disappointed that there is no Home Depot for them, seem to agree. They have continued to elect governing body members from the political party that, at least to some extent by omission or commission, are responsible for the Home Depot withdrawal.

* * *

THE ROSSLYN BOATHOUSE

Perhaps one of the strangest controversies to arise in the county in modern times centered around the efforts of governmental authorities to establish a boat house in the Rosslyn area just south of the Key Bridge since it involved an area over which the county had no jurisdiction or control and a project that was opposed by those who did. The Arlington County line ends at waters edge on the South shore of the Potomac River, and the river is within the District of Columbia. Further, the County shore line along the

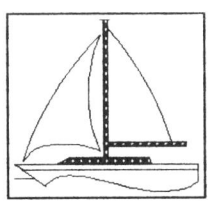

River at that point and mostly elsewhere in Arlington County where the George Washington Parkway is located is under the jurisdiction of the National Park Service. Neither the Park Service nor the District of Columbia have expressed any approval for placing a boat house in that area. In fact, both have indicated they disapproved the idea.

For many years, rowing enthusiasts in Arlington high schools had dreamed of having a boat house on the Virginia side of the Potomac river rather than using the facilities of the more distant and inconvenient Potomac Boat Club and Thompson Boat Center, private facilities on the Washington side of the river. Students participating in rowing programs at Arlington's Washington-Lee, Yorktown and Wakefield High Schools, and at JEB Stuart in Falls Church have numbered around 200.

Late in 1991, rowing enthusiasts, led by Charles S. Butt who had retired after coaching at Washington-Lee for 42 years, submitted a plan to county authorities and the

National Park Service for a 15,000 square foot boathouse on the Potomac River in Rosslyn. In a Journal article dated December 11, staff writer Peter Kaplan said the rowing group would soon meet with skeptical National Park Service officials about its plans for a two story boathouse just south of the Key Bridge.

Kaplan quoted Butt as saying, "We feel that Arlington has the right to have access to the river." He also explained that the Park Service had opposed a boathouse on the Virginia side of the river saying it would worsen traffic and parking problems as stated by Arlington parks and recreation spokeswoman Lisa Daniels.

The boathouse matter percolated along over the following months with letters to the editor for and against appearing intermittently in the press. On June 17, 1992, Kevin Curnyn and Maurice Spraggins, Co-Presidents of the Washington-Lee Crew Boosters wrote in the Arlington Courier in Letters to the Editor that the boathouse deserves support. A few days later John S. Gottschalk wrote against the "folly" of a boat house and said "Don't spoil the Potomac".

Some encouragement developed in 1993, however, when the County Board seemed to give a favorable nod to the idea of a boathouse. In a Northern Virginia Sun article on July 12, headlined "County Board Throws Weight Behind Arlington Boathouse", staff writer Roberta Holland reported on a Board work session at which speakers had pleaded for favorable consideration of the idea. Robert Gazzola, Chairman of the County Sports Commission told the Board, "It may be an impossible task, but it needs the full support of the county to see if it's feasible." Holland said Board members had agreed to work with the National Park Service on the matter but he quoted Board member Eisenberg as saying the project would cost between $3 and $5 million which must be paid by private groups or individuals. He also quoted Park Service spokesman Earle Kittlman who said that while the agency has been historically against adding anything to the Arlington shore, the policy was not "set in stone".

The boathouse matter continued to percolate into 1996 and with increased interest and support from the County Board. On May 13 Journal writer Whitley, and on May 30, Washington Post writer Lan Nguyen reported that the Board, despite objections from the Park Service, had voted to spend $1-million for the boathouse on condition that the remainder of the $5-million needed be raised by private supporters. Both writers reported continued opposition by the Park Service but that the attitude of the Board members was that they would "call the bluff" of the Park Service.

By the end of 1996, boathouse supporters seemed to be well organized and unrelenting in their campaign. In a flyer widely mailed within the county by the Arlington Boathouse Foundation, PO Box 4610, Arlington, 22204, signed by Carole Robinson, President, addressed to "Dear Friends" recipients were jubilantly advised of the action by the County Board on May 11 and the $1-million contribution in park bonds toward construction of the boating facility. The flyer further announced "this is a big step in the right direction" and "More Good News!. We have received our tax exempt designation".

At this writing in early 1997 it remains most unclear how the boathouse project can possibly succeed in the face of continued opposition by the Federal agency who has jurisdiction and control over the proposed location, or how supporters hope to raise the $4-million needed for their share of the costs.

Major Community "Battles" and Controversies

* * * *

MISCELLANEOUS CONTROVERSIES LESS THAN MAJOR OR STILL INCUBATING

There have been, of course, no shortage of other less than "major" controversies from time to time in Arlington County that are not treated in detail herein. They could include the establishment of the detoxification center on Columbia Pike, the efforts to create low cost "affordable" housing in the Buckingham Village apartment units or the Cafritz-Truland corporation proposal for town houses on the Potomac Palisades.

Worthy too, of at least brief mention in passing, was the County action in 1969 involving the use 17.9 acres of undeveloped land between Arlington Blvd. and South 2nd Street, known at the Van Every and Lassiter tracts. Bond money was available to purchase the land for public use but recreational and educational advocates were in sharp disagreement over whether the site should be used for a proposed Thomas Jefferson Junior High School or for a Central Arlington Recreational Center, or both. The matter was laid to rest and a possible bitter controversy avoided when a compromise and decision was reached to buy and use the land for both uses as reported by the Northern Virginia Sun on November 20, 1969 in an article headed, "Arlington Buys Van Every Tract for $789.000." A combined facility was built and has been used for over two decades for many community purposes to include a site for the annual County fair.

Also unresolved at this writing is the question of where to put a 14,500 or 24,000 square-foot complex so that sports and other non-school programs can be removed from the Gunston Middle School at South 28th and Lang Streets. Nearby residents strongly oppose placing the complex in the Gunston school yard because of perceived adverse impacts of noise, littering, congestion, traffic, and inadequate space for parking. Some supporters, as an alternative, favored locating the center in the Barcroft area on Columbia Pike at Four Mile Run. As we near publishing time for this narrative, it appears that the facility will be located in the Barcroft area where adverse impacts will be minimal and where there is no known significant opposition.

Word on these matters, however, must await the attention of a future chronicler or they must rest in peace until or unless further addressed.

CHAPTER SIX

POST WORLD WAR II DEVELOPMENT

The spectacular and dramatic transformation of Arlington County in only a few recent years from a semi-rural or suburban county without a single high rise residential or office building at the end of World War II into a highly urbanized community saturated with masses of towering buildings concentrated in Rosslyn, Pentagon City, and the Jeff-Davis and Ballston corridors is truly unique on the National Capital landscape and probably not duplicated in scope in any other American community.

Insofar as this writer can establish, there was not a single elevator anywhere in the County at the end of the War, except perhaps in the Defense Department Pentagon building. As described elsewhere herein, the county consisted in the years just prior to the war of the several neighborhoods established around the turn of the century such as Glyncarlyn, Clarendon, Cherrydale, Lyon Village, Virginia Highlands and some others. Open or underdeveloped spaces in between or elsewhere had gradually filled with mostly single family detached residences largely erasing any lingering bucolic or rural appearances from past years.

Two and three story "garden" type apartments, and townhouses, or rowhouses as they had long been classified, had made their appearances in the years just prior to and

Post World War II Development

during the war.[1] Garden apartments usually had a common entrance and stairway with individual apartment entrances on each of the two or three landings, or levels. In some instances, however, as with the Fairlington and Shirlington complexes mentioned elsewhere, some multi-level apartments were designed with individual exterior entrances. Among the first of these larger garden-type apartment developments were the Community apartments on North Pershing Drive in 1927, Langhorne Courts on North Lincoln Street in 1930, the several Colonial Villages on Key Boulevard in the period 1934 to 1940, Duff Manor on North 21st Street in 1938, the Lee Terrace apartments on North Lee Street in 1938, and the Buckingham apartments on North Glebe Road in 1939.

During the war, the massive 3438 unit mix of garden apartments and townhouses was built at the intersection of King Street and Shirley Highway, now I-395. The complex became known as Fairlington, a title drawn from the names of the counties whose boundaries the complex straddled; i.e., Fairfax and Arlington). Other major complexes of garden apartments construction during the war years included the 595 unit Arlington Village (formerly Claremont Apartments) on South Walter Reed Drive in 1939, the Rudd apartments on North Washington Boulevard, Kenmore Apartments on North Kenmore Street and Gates of Arlington on North Pershing Drive in 1940, Queens Court on North Quinn Street in 1941, Cambridge Courts on Arlington Boulevard in 1943, Pierce Green apartments on North 16th Street and Arna Valley apartments on South Glebe Road in 1942, and the Westover Courts on North Lancaster in 1943.

In the early years following the War, garden type apartment constructions of significant sizes included the Barcroft Apartments on South George Mason Drive and the Fillmore Gardens on South Walter Reed Drive in 1946, the Stafford Apartments on North Stafford Street, Westmoreland Terrace on North Fort Myer Drive and Walter Reed Gardens (now Commons of Arlington) on South Walter Reed Drive in 1947, the Buchanan Gardens on South Buchanan and Greenbrier on South Greenbrier in 1949, the Arlington (formerly Claremont) Apartments on South Walter Reed Drive in 1950, the Lee Albemarle apartments on North 20th Street, and the Colonial Terrace apartments on North Colonial Terrace in 1954. Numerous other garden apartments as well as townhouses were also built in this period, and increasingly in the following years.

---

[1] *Computer readout from Housing Division, Department of Community Planning, Housing and Development, Arlington County Government.*

ARLINGTON'S FIRST HIGH RISE

The first buildings that could be considered as "high rise", that is, higher than 2-3 floor garden types apartment or office buildings requiring elevators, were the Arlington Towers, now known as River Place, in Rosslyn at 1011 Arlington Boulevard across from the Iwo Jima Monument. There are a total of four separately standing buildings in the complex. They were built in 1954-5 and converted from rental to condominiums in 1981-83. There are a total of 1,650 units in the four buildings.

For several years, the Arlington Towers stood as the only high rises in the County, but in the next decade or so, additional high rise residential buildings requiring elevators were constructed at various locations generally outside the soon to be redeveloped areas that would become known as the Rosslyn-Ballston and Pentagon City-Jeff Davis Metro corridors. Some of the more conspicuous and well known of these included the Roberts Towers (now Cavendish) on South Ridge Road (1958), Cardinal House on Spout Run Parkway (1959), Cleveland House on North Cleveland Street (1960) Carlyn Towers on Lorcom Lane (1961), the Columbia (formerly Diplomat) and the Lancaster on Columbia Pike (1963), the Horizon House on Army Navy Drive and Ridge House and Prospect House on South Arlington Ridge Road and Palazzo Apartments on Columbia Pike (1964).

RiverPlace
(Formerly Arlington Towers)

Aside from this scattered and spotty high rise construction in the 1950 to early 1960 years, development elsewhere in the Rosslyn, Jeff-Davis and Ballston corridor areas was at a virtual standstill notwithstanding a widely recognized realization in the community that the areas were ripe for development, "upgrading" and redevelopment. The Rosslyn and Jeff-Davis areas were for the most part not attractive community assets and were largely non-productive as sources of taxable revenue. Both were generally regarded as eye sores, filled mostly with junk yards, a little used drive in movie, brick factories, lumber yards, pawn shops, car body shops, and various other types of unappealing commercial activities.

DEVELOPMENT AT A STANDSTILL

Community leaders were receptive to applications for rezoning to permit more viable, desirable and tax revenue producing uses of the areas, but such requests were not forthcoming from developers. From comments heard by this writer at civic, county board, planning commission and other meetings there was a general feeling among business and financial interests that development was not economically feasible or sufficiently financially attractive under the existing zoning code. Developers and investors were known to object to zoning requirements concerning building heights, floor-

Post World War II Development

land area ratios, off street parking, and other factors that were considered to be excessively restrictive and costly to implement.

In view of this stalemate and stagnant development activity in the county, it was clear to many observers and activists that some changes must be made in zoning and planned land uses if further developments, and a broadening of the tax and revenue base to pay for needed growth, were to be achieved. Speakers pointed to the steady population increase and stressed the need for additional revenue to finance schools, roads, fire and police forces and other public services, and also to meet the coming Arlington staggering obligation to help finance the anticipated metropolitan area rapid rail transportation system. Some voices maintained that only by vibrant county growth and development could these needs be met and paid for. Others were not so sure and asked if it would be beneficial in the long run to transform Arlington into what could simply be an extension of downtown Washington D.C. with all of its pollution, congestion, parking, crime and other social problems by permitting massive and dense high rise developments immediately across from the District on the Virginia side of the Potomac River. Dialogue continued and increased as community leaders pondered these questions and sought solutions and a workable direction in which to proceed.

A CHALLENGE IS FACED

As early as the mid-1950s, and even before, some Arlingtonians were convinced that thought should be given to establishing a more effective plan that would govern the manner in which the County used, or desired to use, its land in both the public and private sectors and then to establish zoning rules to implement such a plan and see that it is adhered to.

Some early thinking about community planning had occurred years earlier in the County after World War I. In 1927, the County government adopted an ordinance providing for limited control of land use upon approval of plats by the Directing Engineer. This was followed in 1930 with a Zoning Ordinance to be implemented by a Zoning Administrator. In 1937, the County Board established a five member Planning Commission with an assignment to prepare and recommend a Master Plan for the physical development of the County.[2] The following year a Planning Division within the Engineering Department was established and for the first time land planning in Virginia was set up as an official function of local government. Detailed information on the accomplishments, if any, of that Commission and Division is lacking, but in 1953 an Office of Planning was created as a function in the County Manager office.

One of the first moves of record following World War II to meaningfully move ahead in adopting a land use plan, and zoning to implement, was a paper, "Study on

---

[2] Kirkbride, Gary W. and Wheeler, Robert C., *A Guide to Arlington Planning*, July 1983, on file in the Virginia Room, Arlington Main Library.

425

ARLINGTON COUNTY VIRGINIA - A Modern History

Planning and Zoning for Arlington County", dated May 1948 and prepared by the Board of Directors of the Arlington Chamber of Commerce.[3] The paper is signed by W. Morrell Stone, Chairman of the Committee on City Planning and Zoning, and W. E. Hoge, Jr., Chairman of the Zoning Advisory Council. The paper indicates that it was prepared with the legal counsel of Thomas W. Phillips of the law firm of Jesse-Phillips-Klinge and Kendrick.

The Chamber study states that its purpose was to analyze proposed amendments to the Zoning Ordinance of the County, point out differences in the existing zoning ordinance and evaluate the effects on county business interests. The hope was expressed that the effort would be of assistance in formulating "a sound and practicable Zoning Ordinance...which will protect and advance interests in the proper development of our community".

The Chamber study included a discussion of the history, judicial interpretation, and Virginia legislative action pursuant to the Constitution adopted in 1927, and an explanation of the purpose and scope of authority of the County in acting on zoning matters. The study pointed out that existing legislation permitted the county "to regulate and restrict the height, number of stories and size of buildings and other structures erected in the county, the percentage of a lot that may be occupied by buildings and structures, the size of yards, courts and other open spaces, the density of population, the location and use of buildings and land for trade, industry, residence and other purposes, and the types of materials to be used..." But, the paper stressed, the regulations "must be made in accordance with a comprehensive plan designed to lessen congestion in the streets, roads and highways" and "designed to secure safety from fire, panic and other dangers and to promote health and general welfare" among other things. The Chamber paper included comments on the functioning of the Zoning Commission.[4]

A NEXT SMALL STEP IN PLANNING

The next, even if small, step in movement toward the development of a comprehensive land use plan for Arlington seems to have occurred on 21 December 1955, at which time the Arlington Development Committee, Chaired by Wilfred Owen, transmitted its prospectus for future action to the County Board.[5] In its prospectus the

---

[3] *Documents on file in The Virginia Room, Arlington Central Library.*

[4] *Zoning authority was later transferred by the General Assembly from a commission to the governing authority, or County Board.*

[5] *On file under "Arlington County Growth and Development" in the Virginia Room, Arlington Central Library.*

Post World War II Development

Committee pointed out that the county is "maturing rapidly" and that in 15 years its population has nearly tripled and in the same period "more than 32,000 dwelling units have been added, leaving approximately 2,100 acres vacant and available for development." Chairman Owen pointed out that "how the County's land is to be used will determine the character of future development" and that all governmental actions "must be guided by a comprehensive land use plan if the goals of a better community are to be achieved." He wrote that any comprehensive plan must incorporate the following objectives or provisions;

+++ plans to provide satisfactory living and working environment for the next 25 years,

+++ a County determination of desirable population limits and service that must be provided and the economic base necessary to provide financial support for future growth,

+++ a County determination of the functions, dimensions, characteristics and design of the central business district and neighborhood commercial developments,

+++ a determination of transportation facilities needed for intra-county and through traffic and transit needs,

+++ the government building requirements and capital improvement programs related to general plans for the county so that a progressive financial program will be realized, and

+++ a program designed to enhance and preserve the remaining natural beauty and to promote and assist in neighborhood improvement programs aimed at the eradication and prevention of deterioration and blight.[6]

The Owen Committee report asserted that land use will be the basic guide for future development in the County and pointed out that "two thirds of Arlington's development has taken place in the last fifteen years". Owen asserted that Arlington development "must be related to the economy elsewhere in the Washington Metropolitan region". His report outlined recommended courses of action as (1) the preparation of a pilot [land use] plan in collaboration with County government officials and citizens committees, and (2) close examination of priority problems that will become elements of a comprehensive County plan.

Two years after the Owen report the County Office of Planning in May, 1957 released its own early report on land use and plans for same entitled "Fiscal Aspects of Land Use in Arlington County, Virginia".[7] Report Number 3, Master Plan Study, in Part II of the report centers on a Master [land use] Plan and contains a report from James

---

[6] *It would appear that this recommendation was the forerunner of the County neighborhood conservation programs alluded to elsewhere herein and especially in the next chapter concerning fiscal affairs and bond programs.*

[7] *In the file "Arlington County Planning", Virginia Room, Arlington Main Library.*

ARLINGTON COUNTY VIRGINIA - A Modern History

Berkey, Chairman of the County Planning Commission to the County Board, then chaired by Mrs Leone Buchholz.[8] The Berkey report examined numerous aspects of residential, commercial, industrial, private and government uses of land in the County and ended with the following summary and somewhat startling, at least to some, conclusions (in part).

> *"In terms of the Arlington County Government's income and outgo, land used for multi-family dwellings and especially land in commercial and industrial uses produces a surplus of land for single and double family homes, [and] requires a greater expenditure of County funds to provide services and facilities than it yields in real property taxes or other revenue...because considerably less land is devoted to multi-family dwellings than other categories, residential land as a class results in a deficit...on the expenditure side, the dominant factor is...the cost of public education...by far the costliest of Government functions and there are relatively more children in single family than in multi-family dwellings...this study deals with 7,687 acres of land in the County...47% of the total area of 16,350...the balance is vacant, or in public and other non-revenue producing uses.[9]*

The Berkey report also concluded that multi-family housing land occupied 12% of the area with 38% of the population, contributed 25% of the revenue and required 21% of the expenditures. Land used predominantly as single family homes in 78% of the area and with 62% of the population provided only 48% of the revenue while requiring 68% of the expenditures. In other words, while multi-family residential land more than sustained itself by a ratio of 25 to 21 percent, single family residents constituted a loss to the County by providing only 48% of the revenue needed to operate local government while consuming 68% of the costs. Berkey concluded that commercially used land constituted no drain on the county fiscally since, while occupying only 4% of the land it contributed 18% of the revenue and required only 7% of the expenditures.

The clear inference of the Berkey conclusions seemed to be that either more revenue producing uses must be found for land in the county, occupied and used or not, or substantially more revenue must be raised through tax increases to cover the fiscal deficit caused by the relatively high percentage of land devoted to single family land uses.

---

[8] *The Planning Commission stationery heading indicated its Executive Secretary was then Lyle C. Bryant, described elsewhere herein as exceptionally active in Arlington civic affairs and a leader in founding the Committee of 100.*

[9] *These figures would be drastically altered in later years with the intense high rise and other developments in the Metro corridors*

Post World War II Development

LAND USE PLANS MOVE AHEAD

In the months following the Berkey report, and other studies, on land use and plans for the County, interest in the matters continued and news coverage increased. In a July 15, 1958 article headlined "Higgins to Head Planners", Northern Virginia Sun writer Jerry Doolittle reported that furniture store owner Kingsley Higgins had been selected, by unanimous vote, to head the Arlington Planning Commission. Doolittle wrote also of a contentious confrontation in the competition for a new chairman. He reported that the Commission had split in a 3-3 vote between Higgins and J. Fuller Groom, another local business man, to replace Commission Chairman James Berkey, mentioned above. Doolittle wrote, that Berkey was considered by ABC County Board members as "too political for the job". The appointment of Higgins to head the Planning Commission was viewed by some as a forward step to accelerate land use planning.

By the end of 1958, news items indicated additional forward movement in the direction of adopting a County land use plan. In an article headed "Top Arlington Planner Lays Out 6-Point Master Plan Crash Program" in the December 1, 1958 Northern Virginia Sun, staff writer Dana Bullen reported that County Planning Director Tom Moore would on that date unveil to the Planning Commission a crash program on Arlington's master plan efforts. Moore's plan specified dates during the coming year of 1959 for completion of various phases on open space, thorofares (sic), public buildings, and a review, revision and re-evaluation of the plan's provisions to include a revision of the County's zoning ordinance. Bullen reported that Moore had set December 1959 as the time for presenting the master plan to the planning staff.

A PARTIAL MASTER PLAN IS UNVEILED

On December 1, 1959, the Northern Virginia Sun with the page one banner headline "Centralized Arlington Master Plan Unveiled", announced that planner Moore had, at least in part, met his December schedule for presenting his master land use plan. Sun writer Bullen wrote that the plan presented applied only to public buildings and mainly to the "court house" area around Wilson Boulevard and North Court House Road. The plan was accompanied by a map showing the northwest corner of the county and a large west central area that lacked sufficient fire fighting equipment and stations.

Bullen wrote that the plan called for:

(1) a 23 acre, 7-building community facilities center on North Quincy Street for a library, recreational center, art gallery, convention hall, health clinic, welfare building, and a sports area and plaza;

(2) an expanded County government center around the existing Court House for a new post office, and a 7-story tower for state and federal offices;

(3) a public safety center at the intersections of George Mason Drive and Arlington Boulevard for police, fire and civil defense offices;

(4) an enlarged hospital and health center with wings for Crippled and Retarded Children Clinics;

ARLINGTON COUNTY VIRGINIA - A Modern History

(5) Four or five neighborhood service centers with library, recreation and health facilities; and

(6) increased fire fighting power and new stations at Glebe and Little Falls Roads, and Carlyn Springs Road at Arlington Boulevard.

Although many of these proposed projects never reached fruition, Moore's proposed plan was imaginative and proved to be clearly an advancement in the community's desire and need for a more organized and practical program of land management and uses.

A PROPOSED GENERAL LAND USE PLAN EMERGES

In the weeks following the release of the public buildings portion of planner Moore's proposed master plan, additional portions of his overall plan were unveiled. On June 4, 1960 he formally submitted his proposed General Land Use Plan to the County Planning Commission.[10] The document was over 50 pages in length and contained detailed discussions of related regional considerations and the use of Arlington land for residential, commercial, industrial and open space. Moore also discussed the relevance of Federal Government installations in the County, which included the Pentagon building, Fort Myer, and Arlington Hall Station.

Moore asserted that the objectives of the land use plan was to provide a policy that would preserve the County as "a relatively low density residential community with a high level of public service", and to develop the physical, social and economic potential of Arlington so that "it remains a safe, stable, convenient and attractive place in which to live and work".

Moore asserted that his plan was based on certain assumptions, the dominant of which were "that the majority of Arlington's citizens chooses to resist these forces acting for intense urbanization and desires rather to retain the predominantly single-family residential character of the County" and with "such commercial activity as it can support and such industrial and multi-family housing as available space and the requirements of a high quality residential community permit".

CURRENT ADOPTED GENERAL LAND USE PLAN

Planner Moore stressed the importance of retaining and acquiring more open space and he outlined the requirements for additional water, sanitary and storm sewers, and other public services that would be required to sustain expected future growth. In his summary, Moore wrote that there was virtually no large undeveloped areas in the county suitable for subdivision so the planning for residential areas must more accurately be termed "replanning", and the techniques employed in such replanning would be "population density, the design of planning districts or neighborhoods, and conservation and rehabilitation".

---

[10] *File 711.4/A724p, Virginia Room, Arlington Central Library.*

Post World War II Development

Part Two of Moore's proposed plan consisted of a County map showing land use or zoning changes that would be needed to implement his proposed general land use plan. Areas of the county where such changes to different classes of residential, or to new commercial, industrial, or open space uses, were shown by color shading as explained in a "Legend" on the map border.

After extensive public hearings, and numerous revisions based on Planning Commission, staff, citizen and other recommendations, the County Board on August 27, 1960, adopted a General Land Use Plan which became known locally as the GLUP. In this period, the Board also created the Neighborhood Conservation Advisory Committee to handle citizen generated recommendations and programs concerning land use, public facilities and environmental issues. Since these projects were primarily involved not in development, but in conservation, upgrading and preservation of existing neighborhoods the subject will not be treated here but will be addressed in more depth in the following chapter on fiscal and bond matters.

The action of the Board in adopting the Land Use Plan was in accordance with the requirements of the Code of Virginia that requires all governing bodies in the Commonwealth to adopt Comprehensive Plans. The Plan consisted of five elements; a General Land Use Plan, a Water Distribution System Master Plan, a Sanitary Sewer System Master Plan, the Storm System Plan, and a Major Thoroughfare (Master Transportation) Plan. The Transportation Plan included a Master Transit Plan, a Paratransit Plan and a Bicycle Transportation Plan. In later years, a Recycling Program Implementation Plan, a Chesapeake Bay Preservation Ordinance, and an Open Space Master Plan were added. [11]

The General Land Use Plan, or GLUP, has been amended numerous times over the following years usually to bring it into conformity with rezoning actions undertaken by the County Board. One of the first questions asked by Planning Commission and County Board members upon consideration of a rezoning application has been "Does the rezoning conform to, or conflict with, the Land Use Plan?" Ordinarily, only for the most compelling public interest reasons has the Board granted rezoning and Land Use Plan changes that have been departures from the use shown in the General Use Plan adopted in 1960 and subsequently amended.

A notable example of such action was the change in the classification and zoning of the 20 plus acre Hendry family tract on North 24th Street from R-20 (single family detached housing on 20,000 square feet lots) to open space upon the July 1994 County Board action to acquire  the land for park uses and to preserve the remains of the Civil War Ft Smith. This action is discussed in more detail in Chapter Five herein.

---

[11] Page 4, *Five-Year Review of Arlington County's Comprehensive Plan*, June 21, 1995, Planning Division, Department of Planning, Housing and Development, Arlington County government.

ARLINGTON COUNTY VIRGINIA - A Modern History

THE DEVELOPMENT LOG JAM IS BROKEN

As stated herein, development of high rise buildings, or "urbanization" in Arlington stood at a virtual standstill through much of the County's history and after World War II until the early summer of 1962. At that time an event occurred that was to open the doors on a building boom unprecedented in the National Capital area, or probably anywhere else in the Country. The County Board, consisting of members Ernest Wilt, Ralph Kaul, Roye Lowrey, Thomas Richards and Leo Urbanske, on June 13, 1962, unanimously enacted sweeping changes in the zoning ordinance. It relaxed many provisions applying to the construction of high rise office and residential buildings. Especially significant and pertinent, as mentioned above, were provisions disliked by development interests concerning the number of off-street parking spaces required, the permissible height and number of floors of buildings, the acceptable ratio of floor-area space, building set backs from the street, and certain other features considered to be prohibitively costly, and a barrier to profitable design and construction of a building.

Included in the zoning changes were sections providing for optional "site-plan" rezoning in addition to "by-right" development in accordance with the existing zoning classification. Most of the dozens of new buildings to be erected in the following decades would be under the site-plan rezoning. Under the site-plan arrangement, applicants for rezoning could, in exchange for concessions from the County concerning heights, densities, or other matters, submit with the applications a plan and sketch of their proposed building for County Board consideration. This arrangement provided the Board with a degree of control over the style, appearance, service features and configuration of a proposed building. For example, permission for additional floors could be granted in return for desired commitments from a developer concerning streetscapes and setbacks, street level shops, locating utilities lines underground, or the provision of public service features to include additional open space for public parks.

The zoning changes resulted in a near avalanche of construction applications and launched an intense building program over the next three decades that has changed Arlington County from a near rural community to a pulsating, energetic, and greatly more congested urban community.

By the mid-1990s almost every available tract of land designated for high rise building construction has been so used. Massive "downtown" areas of clusters of office and apartment buildings and hotels sprang up in Rosslyn, Pentagon City and the Ballston and Jeff-Davis Corridors. As documented by the County government's Planning Division in a 1990 booklet "Development in the Metro Corridors", in the thirty year period from 1960 to 1990, 264 residential, hotel, office, commercial and mixed-use buildings were erected in the Metro rail corridors in the County. In terms of office/commercial space this translated into 62 million square feet of floor area, with an additional 12.3 million square feet of space under construction or

Post World War II Development

site plan approved. In terms of residential units, it translates into 55,000 units completed at the end of 1990, with another 25,000 under construction or approved.[12]

Remaining space available for further development in Pentagon City and the two corridors was estimated in the county staff's Planning Information Report No. 16, October, 1991, as follows:

	Square feet office space	Residential units
R-B Corridor	3,400,000(13%)	4,084(14%)
J-D Corridor & Pent. City	4,076,176(23%)	1,615(10%)

The staff did not include in PIR No. 16, the space in a number of sites outside the Metro station areas such as Shirlington and a section of North Glebe Road from Arlington Boulevard to 5th Street North.

Through special dispensations to developers under the site-plan re-zoning procedure, almost all of the buildings were built under the site-plan zoning arrangement and of those all exceeded the 75 feet, or about 8 stories allowed by the by-right zoning classifications. The height of most of the site-plan buildings, according to the Planning Division booklet, ranged between one and two hundred feet, but four in Ballston ranged from 221 to 246 feet. In Rosslyn, the booklet shows, there were in 1990 three buildings in the 200 feet range, but the highest structures in the County were the East and West Towers in the Arland USA Today Towers complex on Wilson Boulevard at 312 feet each.[13]

As stated, a guiding concept for growth and development in the county has been to preserve the single family neighborhoods adjacent or surrounding high rise areas and to attempt a balanced and medium or low density mix in high rise areas between single family residences and office/commercial buildings.

In the Rosslyn-Ballston corridor mixed high density concentrations were to be located near the five Metro stations in "bulls eyes" approximately 1/4 mile in radius and within easy walking distance of the stations.[14] The bulls eyes in that corridor were identified as Rosslyn, Court House, Clarendon, Virginia Square and Ballston. In its May 1989 "Mid-Course Review" of the Ballston corridor, the staff described Rosslyn as the

---

[12] *Pages 4 and 6, Planning Information Report No. 16, October 1991, Planning Division, Department of Planning, Housing and Development, Arlington County Government.*

[13] *Much lower future heights ranging from as little as 30 feet to a maximum of 110 feet with additional setbacks are envisioned in the Clarendon zoning "bulls eye" where an "urban village" environment is planned. (staff report Clarendon, Sector Plan, May 19,1990.)*

[14] *The Rosslyn-Ballston Corridor, Page 3, Mark R. Parris, County Planning Staff, February 25, 1989*

"dense office center", Court House as the "government complex", Clarendon as an "urban village", Virginia Square as a "blend of residential and cultural/educational facilities", and Ballston as the "new downtown". Particularly noteworthy new structures in the government complex bulls eye has been the Courthouse Place and Plaza around 14th Street and Clarendon Boulevard to house the county offices, and the new Criminal Justice Center (jail and court buildings) on North Court House Road. The former county offices and tower building across the street to the west was demolished in late 1996 and early 1997 with a spectacular "big loud bang" explosion in February to make way for an underground garage and a street level open space park.

As urban high rise development goes, Arlington's efforts stand unique. On the plus side, most buildings are mostly attractive, functional, and innovative in style, appearance and design. Only a few are not. Of the dozens of buildings now standing, no two touch each other so that there are all-around windows to the benefit of occupants. Light and air can circulate around and among the buildings with ease. People can look out and see other than an alley, or the side of another abutting building. Thus, Arlington has no dark and gloomy streets as does many American cities and especially the District of Columbia on its L and M Streets NW that are lined for blocks with high rise buildings almost to the curbs that literally constitute downtown "canyons". Those District streets are shaded most of the day, the sun can only be seen when directly overhead on the few days in a year when it is so located and building occupants can only look out from front windows or perhaps into the alley if in the rear of the building.

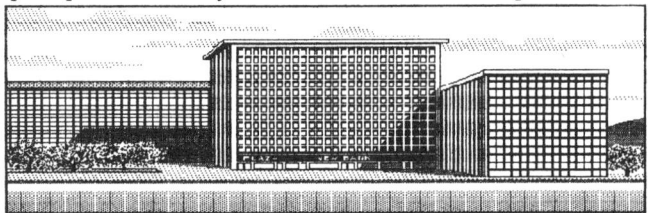

In Arlington, to the extent that a balance has been achieved between residential and office, or "work" buildings, parking, traffic and travel has been at least to some extent reduced by providing living space for people within walking distance of their work places.

BUT IS GROWTH DESIRABLE?

Many citizens will question whether Arlington's growth has been beneficial from the standpoint of providing additional tax revenue so as to lighten the burdens on the individual home owners. The disposition of this complex question is beyond the scope of this narrative and can perhaps never be settled to the complete satisfaction of all sides. A cursory examination of the county tax income will surely show impressive amounts flowing from the real estate and business taxes generated by all the new growth. On the other hand, critics have complained that demographically, the growth has imposed painful new demands for water, sewers, schools, police, fire and other public services the costs of which have more than off set any new revenues realized by the high rise developments.

Post World War II Development

The consequent question, therefore, is whether the price paid, even if tax relief for the individual home owner was realized, and many argue that it was not, is too great. In terms of a deterioration of the quality of life caused by increased and strangulating traffic, air pollution, noise, congestion and other distractions of dense urban environments and constantly rising real estate taxes many Arlingtonians may well wonder about the professed advantages of mushrooming growth.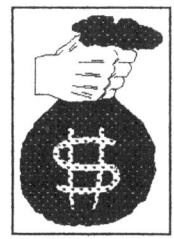

In an editorial titled "Sprawl and the Grass Roots" on June 27, 1996, the Arlington Journal alluded to developers encouraging urban dwellers to new ground and asked if the rules were being changed to discourage any would-be followers. The Journal said "the answers should not lie in exhausting the remaining spaces as well as public funds with open invitations to clear and build at will".

County staffer Mark Parris in his "Early Visions" cited in the footnote above, put the question of tax benefits by development this way, in part:

> *"[there are] public questions in Arlington County and elsewhere of the desirability of new growth. In response to traditional arguments that redevelopment would broaden local tax bases, expand commercial opportunities and provide jobs, no-growth advocates raised quality of life objections in terms of the effect of development on established neighborhoods and existing commercial establishments. By the early seventies, it could no longer be assumed that County residents agreed that growth was a desirable end in itself..."*

Nor, apparently, has all the new growth met the desired expectations of its advocates in and out of local government. In the case of Rosslyn, one of the first areas to be re-developed from "a tawdry collection of warehouses and service establishments", as contended by Planner Parris and others, mistakes were made that proved to confound County leaders. In the draft study "Rosslyn Station Area Plan" dated September 18, 1991, the staff pointed to "drawbacks" in the Rosslyn experience. On page 5 the study drew attention to "...the lack of integration between Rosslyn's various elements and other problems [that] prevent it from being the premiere office and residential area it can and should be". Page 6, contains the following comments:

> *"The full impact of adjacent residential development upon the livability of Rosslyn and the economic vitality of area merchants is decreased because the residential areas are not well connected physically or socially to the office core. Many of Rosslyn's original buildings are undistinguished architecturally and are nearing the end of their economic lives. There is little continuity in the streetscape with large expanses of blank walls and office towers isolated one from another. Retail establishments are scattered through the area and have little or no visibility from the street. The system of parks and open spaces is disjoined and provides few recreational or cultural activities. Finally, the duality of pedestrian systems, one of the hallmarks of the original*

plan, create confusion for the pedestrian and disperses necessary activity over too large an area."

The study also points out on page 17 that there is a "severe shortage of publicly owned recreational open space or facilities within Rosslyn" and that community facilities "are limited to a post office and the Wilson Center" but that "getting to these facilities is often either inconvenient or difficult..." It adds that the one nearby recreational center, Dawson Terrace, "is very small and is located in a residential area which does not have a street system that could accommodate a large influx of recreational users. Nor does the center have the capacity to support additional activities."

Planner Parris in his referred to "Early Visions" alluded to a specially organized Rosslyn-Ballston Corridor Committee and wrote that the group was adamant that the Rosslyn experience should not be repeated elsewhere in the corridor. He quoted the committee, in part,

> *"While Arlington can live with a Rosslyn...on the periphery, to have a development that size in an interior locations, such as one of the Metro stations in RB corridor, would have a devastating impact on...adjacent residential communities. The committee is deeply concerned about the nighttime 'ghost town' atmosphere in Rosslyn, which seems to result from the concentration of office space and the virtual exclusion of dwelling units and commercial retail space..."*

Further evidence of the shortcomings of the Rosslyn growth, and an indication of staff and community awareness of the need to not repeat those mistakes, is contained in a study prepared for the County by an evaluation team of four self described "community design experts", chaired by Charles Rucker.[15] Under "Station Area Opportunities" on page 11 of the study, the team expresses rather harsh assessment of the design, architectural, circulation and other errors made in the re-development of the Rosslyn area. They wrote, in part, :

> *"The area has a chaotic image...the architecture is mediocre...the pedestrian circulation is incomprehensible. There are lots of short blocks and narrow, unorganized skyways but no sense of a system. There is no focus or central place...there is an over emphasis on accommodating vehicles. There are too many roads and the street level is full of parking entrances, bus stops, garages and vast blank walls..."*

Under a section headed "Opportunities", the Rucker team inferentially adds to its criticism by pointing to the lack of a dramatic gateway into Rosslyn as a main entrance

---

[15] *Threshold of Opportunity: Rosslyn-Ballston Corridor Mid-Course Review*, Prepared for the Arlington County Board and Citizens, Organized by Partners for Livable Places, May, 1989.

Post World War II Development

into the County, [from the Key Bridge or I-66] and that with a day-time population of approximately 100,000, and served by two Metro rail lines, there could be a profitable increase in retail space. They further wrote that with the street facades dominated by garages, redesigning the second level walkways with "a more easily understood and grandiose gesture" might be both an economical and attractive way to accommodate pedestrians. The team suggested that potential options for improvement could be "extending the walkway system to overlook the Potomac River, widening and focusing retail activity on the walkway systems and making the system legible by highlighting its location and path through special lighting, painting and art".

In "A Few Last Words" on page 21 of the study, the team states that the study "raises more questions than answers" and there is an admission of skepticism that the opportunities for improvement will be lost. The team wrote not very convincingly that, "There is the distinct, sometimes daunting, possibility that things might actually change." Alluding to the fact that there is much growth yet on the horizon [as of 1989], the team volunteered the thought that such growth could be guided "with wise leadership -- to become an even more wonderful environment". The team did not undertake to assess fault for the many mistakes they listed in Rosslyn development but one inference that could surely be drawn from the above statement would be that they felt that past leadership [by the staff, Planning Commission and County Board] had not been very "wise". The team may have desired to be charitable in not more directly expressing their conclusion with respect to past blame for what they considered the "chaotic", "mediocre", and "incomprehensible" past adverse experience in Rosslyn re-development.

Not everyone, of course, takes such a dismal view of the development in Rosslyn. In an April 1, 1995 article headed "Arlington's Rosslyn Rises High Above Its Tawdry Past", Washington Post writer Heather Salerno painted a much warmer assessment of Rosslyn. She wrote that the enclave was once "a tawdry enclave of pawnshops, lumberyards and warehouses, ...but now, aside from offices, it is also the home to more than 10,000 residents." She quoted Mike Critz, operator of the Pawnshop Restaurant on North Fort Myer Drive as saying, "...the building we're in used to be an actual pawnshop...everyone sees Rosslyn as just high-rises, but there is a lot more history here than people realize...look at the pictures on the wall of what Rosslyn used to look like and compare it to now...the difference is amazing." Salerno quoted other residents as saying that in Rosslyn one gets more money for less since it is right near Georgetown in the District without paying Georgetown prices. Salerno also quoted Rosslyn resident and worker John Muschette, "I'm so happy about the Newseum [a planned museum dedicated to journalism] and Freedom Park [created from a failed

"Rosslyn? It's a planning disaster!"
"Oh yeah? You could do better?"
"No. But my ten year old at Swanson could."

loop road]. They've taken some of the eyesores of Rosslyn away, and really improved its appearance...and now it seems like things in Rosslyn are just getting better".

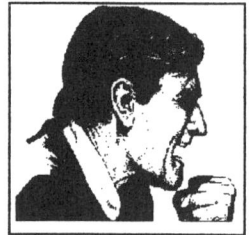

Development over the recent decades in Arlington has not been without periodic controversy. Many of the proposed structures were opposed by civic organizations and activists who appeared before the Planning Commission, the County Board, and other community groups, or wrote letters to the editors of area newspapers. Some rezoning actions resulted in court suits such as the Pentagon City rezoning of 1976 as described elsewhere in detail in Chapter Five herein. Perhaps the rezoning that commanded by far the most attention and publicity over the years consisted of the County Board grant of rezoning for the USA Today towers of the Gannett publishing Company in Rosslyn. The 29 story twin towers that soar over 300 feet almost on the banks of the Potomac River are almost twice the height of most nearby buildings.

In a March 15, 1978 article headed "Interior Lays New Challenge to Rosslyn", Washington Post writer Sandra Boodman reported that U. S. Interior Secretary Cecil Andrus had filed a 12 page memorandum, personally signed, with the Arlington Board of Zoning Appeals to block the construction of the USA Today towers.

Although Interior objected to the towers in substance, the memorandum sought to procedurally block Zoning Administrator Van Caffo from issuing a certificate. Interior asserted that the developer was required to begin construction before the expiration of its building permit and that the moving of some earth on the day before expiration did not suffice to meet that requirement. When Interior lost before the Zoning Board, it later filed suit in the Federal Court in Alexandria arguing that the "monster" buildings would despoil Washington's skyline.

District Court Judge Oren R. Lewis ruled against the Interior Department and dismissed the suit. On December 22, 1989, Washington Post writer Stephen Lynton reported that, upon appeal, the 4th U. S. Circuit Court of Appeals in Richmond upheld Lewis. Lynton wrote that the Circuit Court agreed with Lewis that Arlington officials had "properly complied with the zoning ordinance and could not be accused of acting unreasonably or arbitrarily". Lynton reported that Appellate Court Judge  Donald S. Russell wrote for the Court that the "single issue" was whether Arlington officials properly interpreted zoning procedures in granting the height-limit waiver and the court concluded they did.

In a "Viewpoint" article in the Arlington Journal on October 15, 1980, this writer sided, in substance, with the Interior Department in its opposition to the height of the USA Today towers. I wrote, in part, "Here for years, as a national and local policy, the height of buildings in the District have been rigidly controlled and limited so as not to adversely impact on our national monuments. To what end, one must ask, if adjacent jurisdictions do not do likewise?" I added, "It is my hope that the ...Board will ensure voluntarily that there are no more 'sky-scrapers' and unnecessary higher-density rezoning...if it does not, however, I for one will welcome federal intervention in efforts to compel my local government to do what it should to protect the national capital

Post World War II Development

interests". I did not fault the Court decisions, however, believing that Interior had waited too long to voice their opposition to the rezoning action by not appearing before the County Board when the matter was under consideration. Also pertinent and widely discussed in media letters, cartoons and articles at the time, was the hazardous impact that many felt the buildings could have on commercial air traffic using National Airport a short distance down the Potomac river, which are required to adhere to flight paths over the river and alongside the USA Towers.

In another high profile zoning case, contrary to its action in the USA Today towers rezoning, the County Board rejected proposals for exceptionally high hotel and office buildings in the Jeff-Davis corridor. In a May 13, 1978 article Post writer Boodman reported that the Board in a 3-2 decision had denied applications by New York developers to build a 692-room, 18-story hotel and a 15 story office building at 2765 Jeff-Davis Highway. Board Chair Dorothy Grotos, and members John Purdy and Ellen Bozman had voted against and members Stephen Detwiler and Walter Frankland had voted for the proposal.

Boodman quoted Grotos as saying, "Usually they toss us a crumb...but in this case they wanted additional height and really offered us nothing in return...the developers are completing roads...they said they didn't know who would build the hotel and while I'm sure the office building would be built, I'm not so sure they wouldn't come back in a few months and ask that the hotel be substituted for another office building". Boodman added, no doubt with the Rosslyn USA Today towers in mind, that "Arlington County officials have come under attack from several federal agencies for approving high rise projects along the Potomac which critics claim have harmed the beauty of the Washington skyline, which County officials have denied".

There are a great many pluses and minuses in Arlington County growth in the volatile and explosive decades at the end of the 20th Century. Perhaps future generations will be able to determine to what extent, if any, the pluses outweigh the minuses.

*Blight in Arlington about 1920
near the modern day Arlington Hospital.*

ARLINGTON COUNTY VIRGINIA - A Modern History

Rosslyn in 1960 as seen from the Potomac River.

Rosslyn in the 1990s following extensive re-development.

Post World War II Development

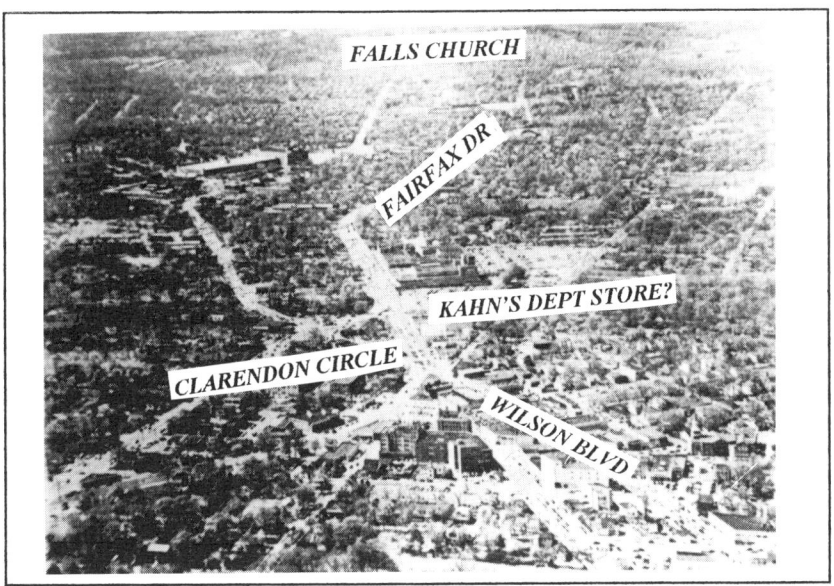

An early view of the Ballston corridor looking west before development.

The Rosslyn-Ballston corridor in the mid-1990s nearing full development.

ARLINGTON COUNTY VIRGINIA - A Modern History

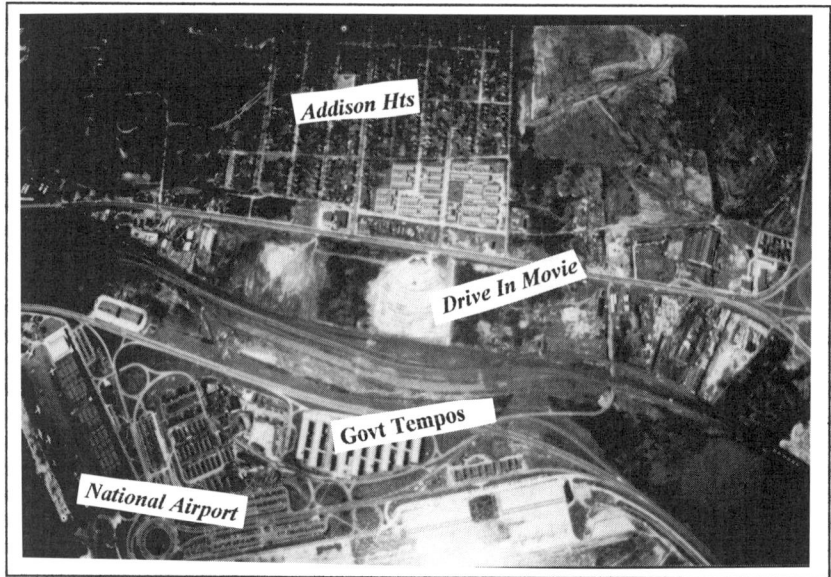

The Jeff-Davis corridor around World War II before development.

View of Jeff-Davis corridor in mid 1990s following development.

Post World War II Development

Early view of Court House hill before re-development showing the 1898 original court house with WWII wings and before addition of the tower of the 1950's. Note absence of hi-rises to the rear and around. The entire area was cleared by demolition in early 1997 to make way for an underground garage and a surface park.

1990s View of Court House "bulls eye" in Rosslyn-Ballston corridor.

ARLINGTON COUNTY VIRGINIA - A Modern History

The Pentagon City complex on Hayes Street in South Arlington between I-395 and Crystal City. From the foreground are the Park Vista Apartments, the Nordstrom Department Store, the Ritz Carlton Hotel, the MCI Office Building (and main entrance to the Fashion Center Shopping Mall), and the Macy Department Store at the far end on Army-Navy Drive. To the right and out of the photo is the Pentagon Center with additional shops including a restaurant, book, clothing, and appliance and electronic stores, and the Price Club/Costco warehouse type discount outlet.

The combined Aurora Hills Library, Fire Station, and Recreational Hall in the Pentagon City-Crystal City area of South Arlington.

CHAPTER SEVEN

FUNDING AND FINANCING OF THE COUNTY

"Joy, joy! Arlington has a triple A bond rating. We can borrow, borrow!"

This narrative on Arlington County Virginia and its recent experiences would not be complete without at least some brief comments on the engine that has kept the entire machine running and functioning. That engine is money! - funding, financing, loans, bonds, revenue, expenditures, appropriations, borrowing, taxation and other costs and outlays.

The treatment of this matter in depth is well beyond the scope of this treatise, and certainly even more beyond the capability of this writer who holds no claim to any great scholarly grounding in economics. But some discussion in passing may be needed in order to provide a framework into which some of the other matters herein covered can meaningfully be fitted.

Arlington's approach to financing its operations is, in most respects, not much unlike the techniques used by its nearest sister jurisdictions in the Washington Metropolitan area; Fairfax, Loudoun, and Prince William Counties, and the Cities of Alexandria and Falls Church in Virginia, and Montgomery and Prince George's Counties in Maryland. All have governmental operations, programs, tax rates and expenditures that bear a remarkable degree of similarity and equality. All can be distinguished from the District of Columbia that has serious financial and other complex social and operational problems of every kind at this writing. These have resulted in a partial return of the Capital City to Federal control with more extensive and perhaps even complete Federal control being discussed.

There are, however, some fundamental and controversial differences in the Arlington approach to paying for its operations and it is to these that we will briefly turn our attention herein.

Arlington's recent elected, and some senior appointed, leaders, all of one political faction, are not hesitant to tout what they consider to be the progressive qualify of life of the County and the highly efficient manner in which the county government is operated. They regularly contend that this has resulted from the practices they have followed in what they identify as "The Arlington Way". The undeniable truth of the matter, however, as we shall see below, has been that Arlington county has operated its government not by "pay as you go" financing but by heavily borrowing to underwrite what would otherwise be significant operational deficits. The question of whether this deficit operation and heavy borrowing through bond sales is necessary or wise is a matter on which critics and supporters of the County leadership have sharply disagreed.

EXPENDITURES

Arlington's budgeted expenditures have, as elsewhere generally, steadily increased through recent years from only $15-million in 1957 to $24-million in 1967, $118-million in 1977, $254-million in 1987 and $478-million in 1996 (totals rounded).[1] The pie slice graph below from the Comprehensive Annual Finance Report of 1996 shows the breakdown of county spending for that year which to a degree can be considered typical of recent years, except the figures are all higher.

In its 1968 Financial Report, the Department of Management and Finance listed the expenditures under headings of General Government, Public Safety, Sanitation, Transportation, Health Social Services, Libraries, Environment Affairs, Non-Departmental, Debt Service, Contributions to Regional Agencies, and Education. In its 1974 Report, the Department began listing Regional Transportation consisting, essentially, of County contributions to underwrite its share of the losses of Metro bus and rail operations as distinguished from the County's share of construction costs which were funded by bond sales. . Those contributions grew from $.4-million in that year to $8.5-million in 1996. In its 1977 Report, the Department dropped the headings of Sanitation, Transportation, Social Service and Environmental Affairs and added the categories of Public Works, Welfare, Culture and Recreation. Presumably funds allocated for the

---

[1] Arlington County *Comprehensive Annual Financial Reports* for the years cited on file in the County Manager's office, or the Virginia Room, Arlington Central Library.

Funding and Financing of the County

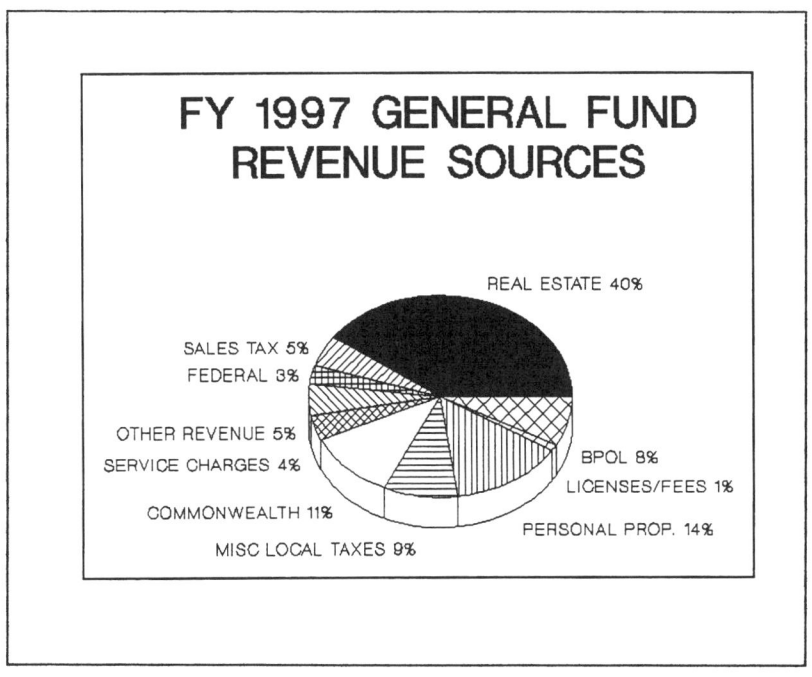

categories dropped were included in the newly listed categories.

While much, but by no means all, of the above increases in County spending can be attributed to inflation locally and nationally, considerable increases must be traced to a County Board that responded sympathetically and favorably, with no apparent adverse political consequences for elected County Board members, to public demands for more services and new or improved facilities. Annual budget hearings witnessed by this writer were almost without exception attended by large numbers of citizens who pleaded for their special or favorite programs or projects. The hearings were often held in school auditoriums, rather than the County Board hearing room, to accommodate the unusually large number of people attending the budget meetings and testifying. Speakers favoring more, rather than less, spending usually were in an overwhelming majority by ratios of ten or more to one. Thus, it can with much justification be said that by steadily increasing County spending the elected officials were merely responding to the wishes, wise or not, of the electorate and taxpayers.

Of much significance and concern to fiscal conservatives has been, is, and will be the debt service costs (interest and principle payments on outstanding bonds) that also rose steadily from $4.4-million in 1968 to $33.3-million in 1996. In the 33-year period from 1968 to 1996, the total costs of debt services is shown in the annual reports as approximately $420-million. When the additional interest costs of $127-million in future years, as reflected on page 356 of the 1997 adopted budget for General, School and Metro bonds already sold at this writing are factored in, the total debt service costs for about three decades will easily exceed a half billion dollars.

ARLINGTON COUNTY VIRGINIA - A Modern History

This, then, can be said to be the cost over four decades to Arlington citizens and taxpayers of the governing body not following, attainable or not, a pay-as-you-go policy with respect to county spending.

REVENUES

Over recent years, tax rates and revenues have been set and controlled by the County Board so as to insure that revenues were adequate to provide a balanced budget with no deficits, except to the extent that borrowing through the sale of public bonds was undertaken as mentioned and as will be discussed in greater detail below. In the 1996 Annual report general revenues were shown to be $478-million with $302-million of this derived from taxes (real estate and personal property) and $99-million from "Inter-Governmental", e.g., State and Federal aid.

The overall amount of revenue raised by the County is determined mainly by the tax rate on real estate and personal property set by the County Board. Those rates have fluctuated up and down over time. In years of steadily rising inflation no, or little, rate increases in the tax rates were made by the Board. Increased values resulted in increased assessments and ever increasing taxes collected. During those years the Board was able to continue spending at former, or higher, amounts and yet claim correctly that it had not taken any specific action that resulted in raised taxes.

About the time of the arrival of the 1990s, however, real estate values leveled off and in some neighborhoods even dropped. Revenues therefore, also dropped, or did not keep pace with rising operational costs. The Board was then faced with the unpleasant task of either raising the tax rate or substantially reducing expenditures. It chose several times to significantly raise the rate while making modest cuts in some expenditures assumed to be not widely or strongly supported by the public.

In a March 22, 1992 Washington Post article headed "Arlington Tax Rate Increased - Bills Will Go Up An Average of 4.5%", staff writer Charles W. Hall reported that the Arlington Board lifted the real estate tax to 82 cents per $100 of property value, up from 76.5 cents. Hall added that Arlington was the first of the area jurisdictions to take such action. Hall quoted Board member Eisenberg as saying, "I have never voted for an increase in the tax rate...and I had hoped, as things merrily rolled along, that I would never have to". Hall also wrote that the revenue shortfall occurred because average property assessments, had fallen 4.5 percent which, consequently, as stated above, reduced revenues.

Again, in 1995, the Board raised the tax rate. In a March 23, article headlined "County Board Votes to Increase The Real Estate Tax Rate Again" Northern Virginia Sun writer Leslie Maria reported that the Board in a 4-1 vote, with the lone Republican member Benjamin Winslow dissenting, approved a 4.3 cent increase in the real estate tax rate. That action brought the then existing rate to 94 cents per $100 of assessed value.

Arlington Courier writer Joe Farruggia covered the tax rate and revenue developments of the County in some detail in an April 4, 1994 article headed, "Trend: Tax revenues increase as rates drop". Farruggia depicted a several year honeymoon period for the County Board when rising home values resulted in ever increasing revenues and they could take the politically popular route of reducing the real estate tax rate without reducing revenues.

Funding and Financing of the County

Farruggia included graphs in his article to show that the value of the average single family home in the county rose steadily from 1977 to 1991, and stayed high through 1994, and in the same period, the tax rate declined steadily until 1991, and then rose only slightly through 1994. The graphs showed that the value of a home in 1986 was about $112,000, yielding a tax of $1,064 and that the value rose until it reached $190,000 in 1991, yielding a tax of $1,453. His graph on the tax rate indicated a tax of $1.53 in 1977 (the year in which assessments began to be based on 100% of fair market value instead of 40%) and dropping steadily to a low of 76 cents in 1991. Farruggia's charts are shown below, courtesy of the Arlington Courier.

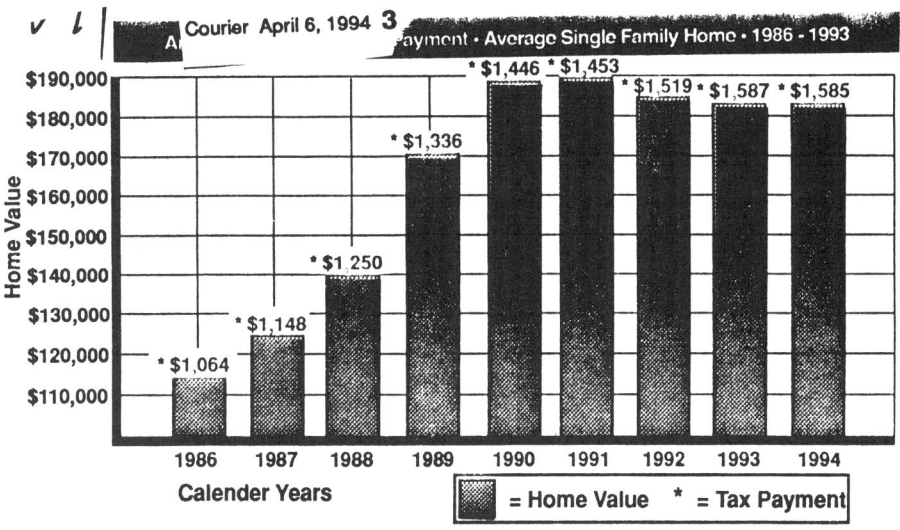

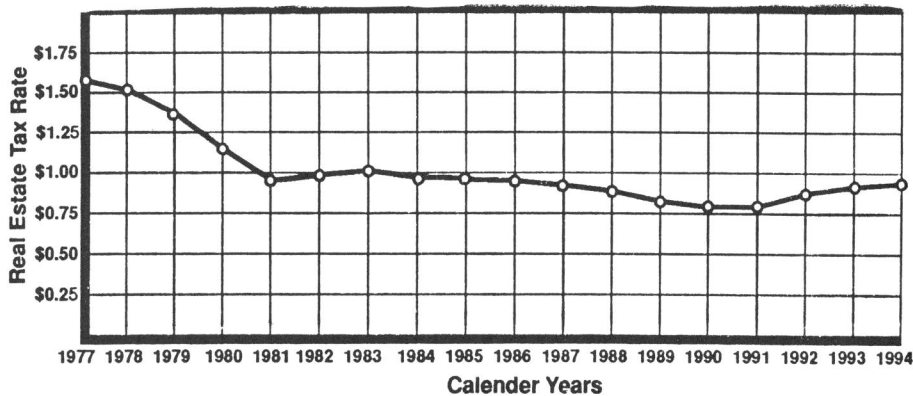

ARLINGTON COUNTY VIRGINIA - A Modern History

Personal property (autos, boats, business machines, etc) and the real estate taxes have been the County's principle source of income amounting to over 50%, as reflected in the pie slice graph below from page 46 of the FY 97 Adopted Budget. The balance of the revenue is shown to come from licenses and permits, charges for services, fines and forfeitures, and miscellaneous.

A MOST UNPOPULAR TAX

The personal property tax has been clearly among the most unpopular taxes imposed on Arlington, and perhaps other, residents. The tax is authorized by the State but local jurisdictions are authorized to set the tax rates. The rate at this writing and since 1987 as appearing on page 51 of the FY 97 Adopted Budget, is $4.40 for each $100 of assessed valuation. For most Arlingonians not having business property, and with no marinas and thus no large boats in the county, this property tax translates essentially into an auto tax. A little more than half of the personal property tax revenue comes from the tax on vehicles, as shown in the budget chart below from page 51 in the FY97 budget report.

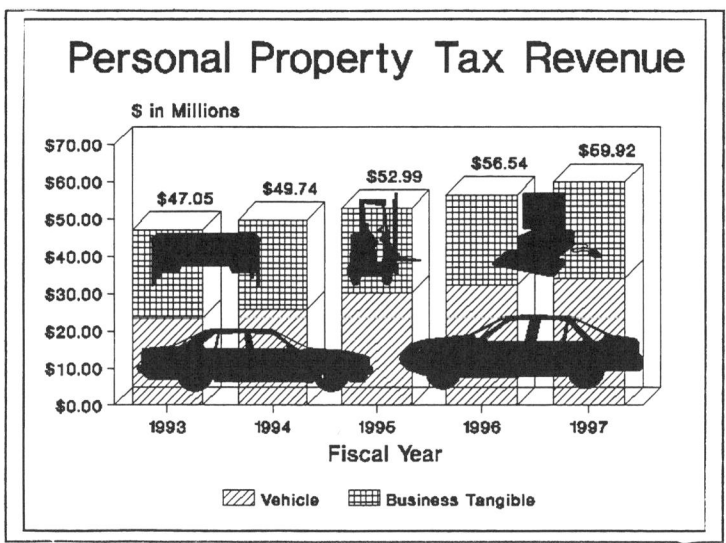

Over the years, numerous efforts or suggestions have been made to end the personal property tax, especially for vehicles. In a January 22, 1997, article headlined "Vehicle-Tax Repeal Plan Hits Va. Senate Roadblock", Washington Post writers Spencer Hsu and Mike Allen reported on a "rambunctious hour-long Virginia Senate hearing" attended by citizens who "oozed disgust for the [auto] tax bills that arrive every fall". Hsu and Allen wrote that the Northern Virginia residents touted a proposal by Senator Charles J. Colgan of Prince William County that would "kill the levy and make up lost revenue to local jurisdictions by increasing the statewide sale tax to 6 percent from 4.5

Funding and Financing of the County

percent". Witnesses were quoted as complaining that the tax discouraged purchase of new cars to replace older and more polluting "clunkers". Powhatan resident Carolyn Finney testified that when she purchased a new Oldsmobile for $33,000, her tax bill rocketed from $151.20 to $976.50. Finney was reported as saying, "It's no longer a nuisance tax. This is an injustice and it is an outrage."

There are of course practical and philosophical considerations for and against repealing the vehicle tax. On page 51 of the FY 97 Budget the vehicle tax revenue is shown to be over $30-million an amount certainly difficult to replace in the tax structure.

Arguments are also made, as alluded to by writers Hsu and Allen, that replacing the tax with an increase in the sales tax would place a harmful and disproportionate burden on the poor. They wrote that a family making $25,000 per year, driving a cheaper car taxed lower, might buy about the same food and other necessities as a family making $100,000 and therefore would pay less taxes under the existing system. They wrote that the distinction could disappear under Senator Colgan's plan. The fate of the personal property tax, at least as it applies to personally owned non-business vehicles, remains to be seen at this writing.

"Stinky taxes!!"

The prospect for much agonizing hand wringing by law makers lies awaiting. Unpopular as the tax is with the average resident, its elimination and replacement will not be an easy hurdle to overcome.

COUNTY DEFICITS

Arlington County has remained fiscally viable and moving progressively ahead in the view of some and operating without deficits because, as stated above, like the Federal government it has borrowed heavily each year. The enormous Federal deficit has been the subject of widespread concern, discussion and even recommendations for a Constitutional amendment to require a balanced budget. What could be a comparable situation with respect to local Arlington fiscal affairs seems to have escaped attention, or has been deliberately ignored by the County leadership.

While the Arlington budget shows an ostensible balance between income and outgo, this is misleading. Millions of dollars paid out each year from money derived from the sale of County Bonds are not shown in the expenditures and revenue pages of the budget, although such information is listed in other pages of the budget report. The Federal borrowing shows up on the Federal budget as a towering deficit that at this writing has approached, or perhaps passed, $5-trillion. The President's budget shows this borrowing as a deficit. Since the County budget does not list bond funded projects in the general expenditures pages or columns, a disingenuous impression is created that the County is operating within, or at a par with, its revenues.

FINANCIAL AFFAIRS - WELL MANAGED?

On occasion, there has been uncertainty and disagreement with respect to the extent to which managers were keeping track of County money. In 1993 at the height

ARLINGTON COUNTY VIRGINIA - A Modern History

"Let's Borrow,"

of a Board member campaign between Republican challenger John Barr and Ellen Bozman an argument erupted over whether there was a spare and unaccounted for $45-million somewhere in the budget. Courier staffer Joe Farruggia on November 3, 1993 in an article headed "Does Arlington have a spare $45 million?", quoted Taxpayer Association President John Rosso as saying, "We believe some of that surplus money should be applied toward next year's budget to offset any increases in taxes". Farruggia reported that County finance director Mark Jinks had responded that there might be a $45 million surplus but if so it was earmarked for unfinished projects and could not be used for other purposes. Jinks was reported as saying "Most of the cash on hand is bond money, and it is illegal for the County to use that money for general operating expenses". Interest in the matter subsided a few days later after the election in which Barr was defeated and Bozman was reelected, but many citizens were left with indecision as to who was more correct in this controversy.

ECONOMIC SURVIVAL THROUGH BORROWING

The Arlington County Board has placed the matter of bonds on the ballots for voter approval more often than not and thus demonstrated its preference for paying for numerous community needs, real or apparent, through borrowing to be paid by future and not necessarily current, taxpayers. Bond items have become the rule rather than the exception. In the 45 years from 1951 through 1996, bond issues have not been on the ballot in only 13 years, or about one third of the years.

A January 15, 1995 compilation titled "Bond Referenda History" by the Department of Management and Finance, shows that a total of over $780-million of bonds were placed on the ballots in the 1951-95 period. The ballot items specified that the bonds were for about every kind of county activity to include schools, public buildings, storm and sanitary sewers, streets and highways, curbs and gutters, local and regional parks and playgrounds, the water treatment plant, Metrorail, jails (1969-81-88), libraries, and swimming pools. $110-million of the bonds were for Metrorail construction. Another major bond item in the years beginning in 1969 has been $78-million for neighborhood (later shown as "Community") conservation.

The voters of Arlington have demonstrated a perhaps surprising willingness to approve bond issues. It could almost, but not quite, be said that they never saw a bond item they did not like. Perhaps like individuals with plastic credit cards, the public attitude may have been that to "charge it", meant an easier way out and one that others down the years may have to pay rather than the voter approving of the bonds at the time on election day. For elected officials the bond approach permitted the financing of many maintenance or upkeep projects such as curbs, gutters, streets, and repairs that would otherwise require handling in the regular annual budgets and probably only by the politically unattractive recourse of raising taxes or by paring other favorite but marginally essential projects.

Other than the election of 1960 and 1975 when voters rejected every bond item on the ballot (except the self liquidating water treatment bonds on the 1975 ballot), voters have rarely defeated a ballot bond item. Voter disapproval has been scattered with rejection of bonds in 1951 for a courts building and parking lot, in 1954 for a county building site and swimming pools, in 1955 for streets and highways and storm drainage, in 1956 for schools, in 1961 for land acquisition, in 1965 and 1968 for schools, in 1969 for a park authority, in 1973 for schools and a county property yard, and in 1979 for local and regional parks. No bond item has been rejected by voters in the 16-year period from 1980 to 1996.

NEIGHBORHOOD (COMMUNITY) CONSERVATION

In 1964, the County Board established by resolution a program identified as the "Neighborhood Conservation Program (NCP)." The Board resolution stated, in part, "the concern for the good health of an entire neighborhood is the focus of the program". The goal of the program as described by the County Manager alluding to the Board Resolution was, and is, "...the improvement and maintenance of the living environment suited to the nature and desires of the people who are a part of it..."[2] The Manager further explained that the initial program was seen primarily as a land use planning and curb, gutter and sidewalk program, but that it has expanded over the years to include traffic, historic preservation, parks, beautification, drainage, crime and public safety, pollution abatement, business conservation, and green space preservation. The Manager referred to similar programs in the metropolitan area, but said that Arlington's NC Program "is unique in its level of citizen participation".

The fundamental concept envisioned for the NCP was neighborhood self-direction with strong citizen involvement. Its operational concept consisted of the preparation of a plan by citizens of a designated portion of the County, usually corresponding in boundaries and identification to the particular neighborhood civic association. The plan would contain the concensus of the neighborhood as to needed work to upgrade and improve public areas with respect to blight, run-down or unkept conditions, needed maintenance or improvements, or other actions on public property to improve and upgrade appearances. Plans adopted by neighborhood groups, usually with county staff assistance, were to be submitted to the Planning Commission and County Board for consideration and, if approved, for funding through the ballot bond and sale process. An NCP Committee was established to consist of one member and one alternate member from each NCP neighborhood. Staff support was and is provided by an NCP Coordinator, a County employee in the Department of Planning, Housing and Development. At this writing the Coordinator is Elizabeth Hagg.

---

[2] *Memorandum, July 10, 1989, from County Manager Anton S. Gardner to Board Chair Ellen M. Bozman, Subject: Neighborhood Conservation Program 25th Anniversary reception.*

The NCP Committee is chaired by an appointee of the County Board. Chairpersons have been the following:

1964-1969	Hall Gibson	1979-1980	John Marr
1969-1970	Anthony T. Lausi	1981-1982	Herman Jensen
1970-1973	Elizabeth Weihe	1983-1984	Edward Knowles
1974-1975	Richard Barton	1985-1986	Helen Hedges
1976-1977	Joan Allen	1987-1988	Marguerite Savard
1/78-5/78	Phil White	1989-1990	Monica Craven
6/78-12/78	Herman Jensen	1990-1991	Nancy Jennings & Gary Bowman
	1992-1993	Christopher Zimmerman	
	1994-1995	Charles Monfort	
	1996-1997	Joan Culver	

Soon after the establishment of the NCP by the County Board in 1964, three neighborhoods, Arlington View, High View Park, and Maywood drew up their programs for neighborhood conservation and submitted them to the County Board for consideration. The Board approved those three plans in July 1964. The plans for Central Arlington and Alcova Heights, as well as the first stage for Nauck were approved later in the 1960s. Since those early years, 39 more neighborhoods have entered the program for a total of 44, of which the Board has formally adopted the plans for 29 of that number. At this writing almost all county neighborhoods are participating in the program either partially by "commitment" or fully by having their plans formally adopted. The most notable exception is the northeast tip of the county around the Washington Golf and Country Club along the Potomac palisades. That area of the county is widely considered to be newer and more affluent, and therefore least needing repairs and upkeep.

In later years, the Board revised and expanded the NCP and in 1984 incorporated NCP plans into the County's Comprehensive Plan, described in Chapter Six herein. It has also, from time to time and with the passage of time, reviewed and updated some of the plans earlier adopted. For example in 1994, the Board updated the Plan of the High View Park neighborhood first committed in 1964, and adopted in February, 1965.

FUNDING FOR NEIGHBORHOOD CONSERVATION

Funding for the NCP has consisted of money borrowed by voter approved bond sales although on one occasion the Board appropriated $800,000 from the General Fund.[3] There were no bond items on the ballots for Neighborhood Conservation in the early years so it would appear that NCP projects were funded from the General Fund or, to some extent, in 1965 and 1967 from bonds shown on the ballots as for "streets and sidewalks" ($7.1-million in 1967), or as "Recreation Facilities" ($2.5-million in 1968). Bonds specifically designated for "Neighborhood Conservation" were on the ballots in 1969, 1971 and 1977 in the amounts of $.8-million, $.8-million and $2.5-million respectively. The designation for NCP bonds was changed to "Community Conservation" for the ballots of 1975, 1981, 1983, 1984, 1986, and 1988 and totaled $26-million. On the 1990, 1992, and 1994 ballots "community conservation" is merged under a line item

---

[3] *County Manager Memorandum, Ibid. page 3.*

Funding and Financing of the County

identified as "Streets, Highways, and Community Conservation" and the bonds authorized by voters in those years was $11-million, $13.4-million and $17.7-million respectively, or a total of $42.1-million. This writer is informed by Coordinator Hagg that bonds sold for "community conservation" were used for purposes other than neighborhood conservation.

Information is lacking as to the distribution of funds from bonds sold under the authority of the "Streets, Highways, and Community Conservation" designation. This may require complex research of numerous items in the budget reports. Thus, while total bond sales in the period from 1969 to 1994 that could have been used for neighborhood conservation total over $72-million, it is not clear just how much of this was used precisely for this purpose. "Streets and highway" bonds on the ballots listed above, or even on any number of other ballots over the years, could supposedly could also be used for neighborhood conservation if such work was included in a NCP plan.

In a document titled "Arlington's Neighborhood Conservation Program" released by the Department of Planning, Housing and Development in May 1994, it is stated that "From 1964 to 1993, Arlington voters have approved bond sales of $13,250,000 for the Neighborhood Conservation Program". That figures seems clearly at odds with the much greater bond approvals listed above. This writer is without the means to reconcile the differences in the amounts and the Coordinator has stated that she is too busy to pursue the matter. Whether the County has and is using for other purposes bond money inferentially or expressly approved by voters for Neighborhood Conservation is clear, but it strongly appears that it may be doing so.

ARLINGTON RELIANCE ON BONDS - SOUND PRACTICE OR NOT?
--Some author observations--

The question of whether Arlington has managed its fiscal affairs properly, and whether too many routine expenses have been improperly and detrimentally paid for by borrowing has been a matter of continuing contention in the County. On the up side, it must be said that many worthwhile and desired benefits have been provided today to citizens that otherwise might have been unavailable if a strict pay-as-you-go policy had been followed by the governing bodies. It must also be conceded by critics, or others, that this approach has been endorsed and approved by a comfortable majority of citizens as reflected by the repeated election, and reelection of the same political faction that has dominated County politics and government for most of the last half of the century and almost exclusively is responsible for the approach used. Additionally, voters have faithfully and consistently approved almost all bonds presented to them on the ballots.

Spokespersons for the entrenched establishment take obvious pride in repeatedly claiming that Arlington has the lowest per capita tax rate of any of the metropolitan suburban jurisdictions. This claim may be true if only the real estate tax is taken into account but is likely subject to challenge as only partly true when other taxes such as personal property, sales tax, utilities and some others are included as claimed below by the Taxpayer Association, or some others. It is also pointed out with regularity by the County leadership that the county enjoys a AAA rating among the Wall Street money moguls that rate the credit of municipalities. The annual budget reports of the County also regularly include charts to show; (1) the favorable position of the County with respect to ratio of general obligation debt to the market value of the County's overall wealth; (2) the general obligation debt per capita; and (3) the ratio of tax-supported debt service to general expenditures.[4] All of these charts purport to show, and certainly to an extent correctly, that compared to other local jurisdictions, or on national average, Arlington is far better off than most other comparable communities. Whether this, to the extent it is true, is the result of superior management by the elected leadership, or simply due to the affluence and relatively high social and economic level of county residents is debateable.

It should also be noted that the County's use of bond money for routine maintenance and upkeep has not been limited to neighborhood conservation bonds. Bonds shown on the ballots for other items such as parks and playgrounds, streets and sidewalks, recreation facilities, and other uses, have often been used not for strictly capital improvement, but for routine maintenance that many financial advisors would argue should be handled from annual expenditures.

An example of the use of bond money for routine maintenance can be the $12.8-million item for school bonds on the November 8, 1988 ballot that was approved by the voters by a ratio of 49 to 12. A breakdown of the proposed uses of some of those bonds was provided by the County staff to the Arlington Ridge Civic Association for the Oakridge Elementary, Thomas Jefferson Intermediate and Wakefield High Schools that serve the Ridge area. The breakdown showed that substantial amounts of the bond money was to be used for replacing windows, boilers and ceilings, landscaping, adapting bathrooms, dumpster screening, modification of air conditioning, redesigning classroom spaces, and certain other uses all clearly within the category of routine maintenance and upkeep. It can only remain a matter of conjecture as to whether voters would have approved bonds supposed to be used for capital improvements if they had known the bonds were not to be so used but, rather, were used for maintenance as outlined above by the county staff.

PUBLIC CRITICISMS OF COUNTY FISCAL PRACTICES

Dialogue and discussion on the manner in which Arlington County finances are handled, and whether bond or other monies are used properly has been lively over the years. Letters to the editors and comments by citizens testifying at annual budget or other meetings have been numerous.

Foremost among critics of County fiscal policy, as some observers might point out, has been the Arlington County Taxpayers Association, or ACTA, described elsewhere herein in Chapter Four. The group has often questioned county expenditures line by line and asserted that many projects or programs could be carried out more cheaply, postponed, or eliminated altogether.

---

[4] *Pages 351, 352 and 353 in the Adopted Budget for FY 1997.*

Funding and Financing of the County

Washington Post writer Charles Hall wrote that "ACTA in recent years has vigorously challenged the county government's cherished self-image as one of the best-run, and most lightly taxed [jurisdictions] in the Washington area". [5] Hall wrote that ACTA claimed credit for "forcing some savings by publicizing three swimming pool jobs that paid $65,000 each annually..." that were later downgraded in a staff reorganization. Hall quoted ACTA President Rosso as saying, "It's a glaring example of how they have ignored the public..." and that the county had "kept the public in the dark about other projects that threatened tax-payers interests".

Most issues of the ACTA newsletter "Watchdog" have contained critical comments on the County management of its fiscal affairs, and especially the marketing of bonds to finance programs and the increase of tax supported debt.

In the August 5, 1992 newsletter, ACTA quoted from the June 15 issue of City and State newspaper reporting Arlington County long-term debt of $1,306 as "the second highest per capita of 50 counties surveyed nationwide." The newsletter said its members have watched the County's general obligation per capita debt "skyrocket from $585 per person in 1990 to $1,255 in 1992" and that the County "should not continue this rapid escalation of debt...and not be trying to outdo the Federal Government". ACTA reported that its members supported bond items in the forthcoming election for Metrorail and the Water Treatment Plant, but not for school projects, higher education, parks, and streets and highways.

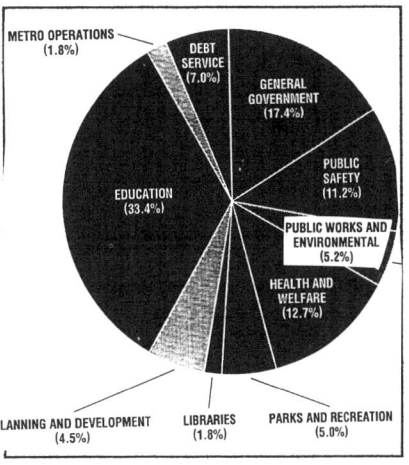

In the February 16, 1993 Watchdog, ACTA member Jeffrey Fogel, with an obvious tongue in cheek offered some "Predictions for the New Year". They were, in part, "tax burdens on residents will increase...highly visible though relatively inexpensive programs will be cut in a brief flurry of symbolic Spring cost-cutting...the County Manager's six-figure salary will be increased...the bureaucrats' fleet of cellular telephone equipped unmarked take-home cars and the exorbitant fleet of other non-law enforcement County passenger cars will not be reduced...the County will buy more land at prices substantially in excess of assessed value...and sell land and easement at prices well below sale prices of adjacent land...the County government will vehemently advocate 'neighborhood conservation'...and it will open two new County government highrise buildings [with] embarrassing interior extravagances, planned and approved without public notices when the public was being told of the need for higher taxes".

In its October 1, 1993 newsletter "The ACTA Watchdog", the editor commented in reference to the Arlington tax rate, "[Board member] Hunter trotted out Arlington's

---

[5] *Merits of Taxpayer Association Questioned*, Washington Post, July 8, 1993, Virginia Section, page 1 and 3.

real estate tax rate which is the lowest in the metropolitan area...[like] any good politician, he tells only a small part of the truth...although the county does have the lowest real estate tax rate, Arlington either collects taxes which others do not or collects taxes at higher rates than do other jurisdictions..."

In its July 12, 1996 newsletter, ACTA complained that tax supported debt per capita would increase 21.5% from $1,633 in 1995 to $1,984 in 2002; that debt service as a percentage of expenditures would increase almost 47% from 6.02% in 1995 to 8.84% in 2002; that tax supported debt as a percentage of market valuation of county real estate would increase and that debt service per capita would increase over 68% during the period from $154 to $260. The news letter editor quoted the words of Thomas Jefferson, "The fore horse is public debt. Taxation follows that, and in its train wretchedness and oppression."

MORE CRITICISM

In an August 1993 letter to the Journal editor, Arlington activist and past Republican candidate for public office, Halvor O. Ekern charged that the county was over-staffed. He wrote that a recent study and survey revealed that the average number of employees in 94 of Virginia's counties was 6.34 per 1,000 employees, in cities it was 16.25, but that Arlington topped the list with 19 employees per 1,000 population. Ekern asserted that Board member Hunter's defense that Arlington was unique because it provided service for a daytime work force of 224,000 should be discounted as so much rhetoric.

In an October 13, 1993 editorial concerning "Arlington's millions in bonds", the Journal alluded to the sale of $105-million of bonds for the sewage treatment plant and the George Mason University law school. It said it had opposed some of the bonds - for street repairs, parks and recreation and higher education - for a variety of reasons, not the least of which was that the bonds will cost the taxpayers nearly $200 million in the long run and increase per capita indebtedness to more than $1,200 a year. The editor added, "[There] is even a more compelling reason to oppose some of the referenda: The County team that trundled to the paper to pitch the sale had nary a clue as to how the County would pay operating expenses for the projects the bonds would pay for...it is an opportune moment to remember why bond referenda are generally a bad idea".

On May 12, 1994 the Washington Post headlined "[Arlington] Bond issue [on the 1994 ballot] may Rise to Near $100 million". On the following day it published a letter from Larry E. Naake, Executive Director for the National Association of Counties headed "Counties are Losing Control of Their Budgets". Alluding to the recent trend of the Federal government to place increased financial burdens on local government through mandated programs, Naake wrote that "...counties relieved their budgetary stress in a

Funding and Financing of the County

number of ways: [by] budget reductions...raised fines, penalties or fees, raised property taxes, postponing capital projects or placing a freeze on hiring". He did not write, as might be applied to the Arlington situation, that some counties meet the problem by considering many routine expenses as capital improvement projects that are paid for with borrowed money through bond sales.

THE EDITOR SPEAKS AGAIN

On March 15, 1995, the Journal editor again spoke out critically on the County Boards sale and use of bonds for various purposes. The editor referred to Board Chairman Al Eisenberg's statement that well educated and affluent Arlington residents "knew what they were doing when they approved bond issues" that sent county debt soaring by 61 percent in three years. The editor admitted that some projects are long term and should get long term financing, but that "putting it on plastic [saves] almost nothing and worrying about it later are virtually American hobbies". The Journal said it had opposed half the bond referendums on the 1993 and 1994 ballots but that "...blaming - or crediting - voters for inevitable tax increases doesn't cut it. The bills will come due and even generous Arlington taxpayers will one day take umbrage at the rising tax bills. The buck should stop with the County Board".

On December 10, 1996, Journal writer Robert Gehl in an article headed "County's debt service jumps 19%" wrote that "Arlington now owes $1,780 for every man, woman and child living within its boundaries". He quoted Tim Wise, the new president of ACTA as saying, "...the highest-possible bond rating which Arlington currently enjoys is in greater jeopardy than County Board members realize. Without the burdensome debt load, the county board would feel significantly less pressure to raise taxes. Instead of paying debt service, taxpayers would enjoy paying less taxes". Gehl alluded to the county debt service burden that was approaching 10% of the general fund and quoted Jodi Hecht, an analyst with Standard & Poors, one of the two credit rating agencies that gave Arlington it high rating. Gehl said Hecht felt the 10% level would concern her, that "10 percent is considered somewhat high - not necessarily a positive or negative", and that she was "more concerned about where the money is coming from to pay the ever-increasing debt". But she added, according to Gehl, that the county is in good shape and has been "well run".

On December 13, 1996, the Journal editor again spoke out to Arlington voters on the "Sky High [bond] Debt" that "has jumped by 19 percent". The editor wrote "You [voters?] approve every bond referendum the Arlington County Board puts in front of you and what do you get? No surprise here: rising amounts of debt for which each county taxpayer is responsible...". The editor reminded readers that bonds don't cost just the amount voters approve and that the $12.9 million park bond approved in November will cost more than $25 million when the interest to bond holders is paid off in 20 years or so. The editor added "How much do residents think about it before they sign off on bond referendums: How much does the County Board ponder that before they put the referendums on the ballot? Not enough". The editor referred to a statement by the Wall Street analyst from the credit rating agency who said, "We'd like to see what departments are being cut to pay for the increase in debt service" to which the editor responded,

"Silly wabbit, why cut spending when the County Board can just take a few dollars from the taxpayers wallets".

BOARD MEMBER RESPONSES TO CRITICS

As might be expected, elected and other Arlington officials have been quick to respond to criticism directed at them concerning their management of the county financial and bond operations.

In a letter to the editor of the Journal published August 10, 1993, the then Board Chairman James B. Hunter III, reacted to criticisms by Arlington civic activist Joe Evans that the County is "over-indebted and over-staffed". With respect to over-indebtedness, Hunter referred to the Moody's Investors Service characterization of the county debt position as "moderate" and wrote that "While the county's per-capita debt level is higher than many surrounding communities, Standard & Poor's ..has stated that...the county's outstanding debt level is 'low' with 'rapid' debt repayment".

"How dare they criticize!"

Concerning Evans charge that there is over-staffing, Hunter asserted that "any discussion of this...should recognize that Arlington County's unique unitary form of government results in a statistical distortion". He wrote that Arlington operates as both a city and a county while most of the counties on the City & State list do not have urban, city functions, nor do they carry a school budget or debt responsibilities. He added that Arlington had undertaken street, park, highway and public health functions not taken on by any other counties in Northern Virginia and that employees are counted in Arlington statistics that are not counted in Fairfax or Prince William Counties. "Arlington is an efficient government [sic] and can justify its employee levels", Hunter wrote.

In a letter to the Courier Editor published June 2, 1994, Board member Albert C. Eisenberg, then Vice Chairman, asserted that the County budget process worked. Eisenberg referred to critical comments by the Northern Virginia Sun editor on May 5 and asserted that the Board had balanced the budget, met surging school enrollment, provided funding for policing, opened a new jail, addressed rising public health needs, cut small business taxes, provided cost of living increases for county employees, and "identified" $94.5 million in savings through budget cuts and efficiencies over five years while maintained the "lowest overall tax burden in the region along with one of only 26 city and county AAA/aaa bond ratings in the nation". In his lengthy reply of three columns, Eisenberg responded point by point to Sun criticisms and insisted that the process followed by the Board "produced an outstanding budget that no other major community in the region can match for low taxes and high quality of services". Eisenberg repeated his arguments on numerous other occasions at Board meetings, on the campaign trails, or otherwise.

* * * *

Funding and Financing of the County

STAFF RESPONSE TO CRITICS

With respect to criticisms that Arlington's debt is not manageable, the County director of Management and Finance Mark Jinks lashed out in a letter to the Journal editor published on December 20, 1996. Jinks asserted that a Journal news article and editorial of December 10 was "misleading" and that "important information was omitted".

Jinks charged that the news story had failed to mention that Wall Street bond rating agencies had affirmed the county's "top notch financial condition", and that Arlington remains in the "select group of 34 cities and counties out of more than 20,000 with respect to its standing in the bond market. Jinks also complained that the Journal had failed to consider the primary debt measure: the value of a community property tax base in comparison with the amount of tax-support debt outstanding and that in that measure Arlington scored well. Jinks referred to bond rating agency information that had been supplied by his office to the Journal that reported that Arlington's "debt position reflects moderate debt level" and that the county had "a growing but yet manageable debt burden".

Public statements defending the policies and practices of the County leadership have also been made from time to time in letters to the editor, or otherwise, by the County Treasurer Francis X. O'Leary, who is an elected official from the same political party comprising total membership of the county Board.

Additional support for the County leadership's point of view with respect to the soundness of Arlington fiscal management was contained in a 1993 Washington Post article by Peter Baker. The article was headlined, "Arlington 8th in Fiscal Survey of 50 Jurisdictions Nationwide".

SOME AUTHOR OBSERVATIONS

It is not the role of this writer to evaluate and dispose of the arguments for or against the path the county leaders have taken in handling Arlington's fiscal affairs. That must remain a challenge for the voters and so far at this writing they have clearly supported the elected officials and their appointees. Nevertheless, some points bear mentioning.

An observer, even if not cynical and skeptical, could surely be entitled to question the wisdom and necessity of borrowing for capital improvements that could be delayed or even eliminated and that will cost a great deal more in the long run when paid for by borrowing with interest. Questions could also be asked about the prudence of borrowing for maintenance items, not capital improvements, that should be paid for from annual and routine operational funds.

Surely no financial advisor worth his or her salt would, absent the most extenuating of circumstances, condone Harry Homeowner borrowing money and going into costly debt for money to mow the grass, rake the leaves, replace a broken step or hand rail, repaint the house or handle other routine maintenance and upkeep needs that do not constitute any increases in the capital investment involved. Sound financial planning would dictate that such expenditures be fitted into the monthly budget even if adjustments of other expenses is required. The new deck, automobile, solarium, driveway, air conditioning or house wing may be clearly capital improvements, as distinguished from routine maintenance, that fully justify borrowing to finance, providing payments on the loan can be handled by normal income. Isn't the homeowner courting disaster if he goes ever deeper into debt to cover day to day expenses?

If these concepts are right for the home owner are they any less applicable to our governmental operations? Is the County leadership proceeding on the right course when it pays for upkeep and repairs and maintenance projects, as it has done consistently and especially regarding neighborhood conservation items, with borrowed money? Has it been fiscally responsible to pay for even a needed capital improvement item with expensive borrowed money rather than more slowly from annual revenues even if an unpopular increase in tax rates is required?

Although it may be politically more palatable and easier for an elected official to resort to borrowing to provide a community with desired projects, does it necessarily follow that the approach is in the best interests of the taxpayer who must eventually foot a much larger, perhaps doubled, bill? Have elected officials given too little attention, as the Journal editor asserts, to their responsibilities to peer long and dubiously at every bond item before placing it on a ballot? Isn't this an area where the voter depends heavily on the elected officials to weigh carefully the need for every bond item and excercise the soundest of judgment as to essential need since the individual voter does not have the expertise or detailed data to do so? Some citizens surely must have felt that board members have not exercized sound judgment in this respect and have cavalierly placed bonds on ballots for expenses that should not be paid for with borrowed money.

Certain Board members have asserted that voters must know what they are doing when approving bond issues placed on the ballots by the County Board. Perhaps so, but also perhaps not. Like the public practice of relying excessively and sometimes unthinkingly on the plastic credit card for their personal needs and thereby floundering in debt, so too in all likelihood does the voter not fully realize the ultimate cost to the public of borrowing to run the local government. Few voters will understand in detail the uses to which bond money will be put and especially whether it will be used only for necessary capital improvements. Nor will they always examine closely, some board members to the contrary notwithstanding, just how urgent is the need for a particular bond item to be on a ballot.

Having said this for the record, it must be conceded, no matter what the degree of public knowledge and understanding, or lack thereof, concerning what they are voting for, Arlington voters have clearly sanctioned the courses sailed by their leadership to date and this, after all, is democracy in action.

Journal writer Robert Gehl has had a late, but surely not the last, word on this subject. In an article featuring Arlington taxes on March 1, 1997, he wrote in part; "Arlingtonians pay more than their counterparts in three of the seven other local jurisdictions and, if the tax rate climbs again this year, will slip even further." That assesment is not likely to please the County political establishment who have long touted Arlington as the lowest taxed jurisdiction in the Metropolitan area.

* * * *

Funding and Financing of the County

SIGNS OF GROWING PUBLIC DISENCHANTMENT

Indications that the public attitude may be changing with respect to support for the County practice of financing much of its operational costs by borrowing began to appear in no less a county wide and prestigious organization than the Civic Federation. At the regular monthly Federation meeting on June 3, 1997, the assembled delegates heard Robert Nester of the Bellevue Forest Civic Association speaking for the Revenues and Expenditures Committee. In a report on the County's Proposed Capital Improvement Plan for 1998-2003, the Committee commented on "cost overruns for the Department of Human Services building", "School Board capital requests that exceeds the County Board guidelines by $21.7 million", "...potential unforeseen costs of providing facilities and staffing...for the educational system...", and "Continued costs of implementing the Courthouse and other sector plans".

In its recommendations, the Committee urged the county "to curb its new capital spending"; "...continue to pursue alternative methods of constructing and financing the DHS building to contain costs..."; "...that (CIP) expenditures for Parks be deferred to allow for re-evaluation..."; and that "funding for leasing of [school] relocatables [sic] (trailers) be deleted from the CIP and included in the operating budget". Finally, the Committee recommended that the budgets should better identify projects earlier funded but not begun, that a unified inventory be prepared of properties requiring capital expenditures for renewal or maintenance, and that projects for the "out years" be eliminated until they can be clearly identified for inclusion in the CIP.

After some minor modification of wordage, the Committee recommendations were adopted overwhelmingly by the Federation.

* * * *

For the distinction of having the very last words on county fiscal affairs and particularly bonding and budget practices, we will defer to Arlingtonian Sophie B. Vogel and Chip Hoagland, the editor of the Arlington Courier.

Both these writers addressed these subjects, Ms Vogel in a letter to the editor of the Northern Virginia Sun on March 6, 1997, and Mr Hoagland in an editorial entitled "Is the County Budget Relevant?" in the Courier's March 20-April 2, 1997, issue. Mrs Vogel is a retired Arlington school librarian, has long been active in county civic affairs and is editor of the Historical Society's newsletter.

The observations of both these writers are thoughtful, scholarly, timely, and incisive. The thoughts are also, while undoubtedly contentious or provocative to some, clearly on point with many of the taxation and related circumstances mentioned in this chapter. There is thus no more constructive and fitting way to end this chapter and this narrative, than with the thoughts of these two gifted writers.

Sophie Vogel

The school system's fiscal 1998 budget contains a wealth of information on the financial status of the debt program, which was proposed and spent by a mixed (appointed/elected) School Board and the school administration over the past decade...the real cost of the five bond referenda that have been passed in Arlington County far exceeds the amount voters checked off on their ballots... Principal and interest payments on all five bond issues will continue to be made until the year 2017, for a total of 29 years, [even] if no additional bonds are floated before then.

When did it become board policy to float a CIP bond every two years? The budget estimate, when the 1996 yet-unsold bonds are sold in 1997, is that the principal and interest in fiscal 1998 alone on the debt incurred since 1979 will be $10.1 million! Arlington residents are still paying on the 1979 Virginia Literary Fund loan which financed the Washington-Lee auditorium, and on the 1983 Virginia Literary fund loan which covered renovation on a science wing at W-L. A mortgage on this proportion, repeated every year, is competing with dollars needed for school programs. The programs will suffer and test scores will tumble further.

We want our children to be housed in safe schools, wired to receive new technology. But will columns, free-standing curved cement walls, fancy fenestration and entrances add to the students' education?

Prior renovation in the 1970s was accomplished at the least possible cost...the then superintendent had been a math instructor...local businessmen sat on the School Board. They did not muddle through, but kept track of every dollar voted for each project."

S.B. Vogel, Arlington

Chip Hoagland

"...Bragging [by county officials] about our triple A rating and our large tax base is a tiresome theme. Such a rating simply means that the rating agencies believe that the tax base has yet to be completely harvested through taxation...Let's not agonize over the details of the budget. Set a cap. The ceiling should be our current revenue base. Set priorities. There are probably a number of services...whose termination would go largely unnoticed...let's spend the money where it makes the most sense. In the school system that would be the classroom - not the

Funding and Financing of the County

white building next to the planetarium. Let's swap middle management administrators for teachers and teachers aids.

"Consider numbers...there is something like 200,000 residents in Arlington...and 10,000 [county] employees...or one for every 20 residents...we have a budget of a half billion dollars...or $2,500 for each household person...that seems a bit steep...if we changed to a fee-based system where the users paid the cost for what they used, would you spend that much for what you are receiving? That would be the true test for true accountability in our budget process. Value for money.

"The county has experienced amazing growth...mostly through development and redevelopment of real estate...prospects for future growth appear to be good, but there is no assurance about the future. Arlington should plan for the future. We should not run our tax rates up every year in order to deal with an uncontrolled county budget. Each time we increase the rates we lose a little bit of flexibility to deal with potentially larger needs in the future. At some point there is a limit...We should make the marginal decisions and choices now, a little bit at a time so we don't have to make bigger and harder ones in the future. Most large institutions in the United States have dealt with downsizing. Municipal governments should not be exempt from this trend. Arlington County has yet to begin the process."

Chip Hoagland

Eureka! Arlington has lowest area tax rates!!

*   *   *   * ʻ *   *

EPILOGUE

This then, is one author's efforts to document some recent events of historical significance in one of America's, if not the world's, most unique communities. Unique in many respects.

Arlington County clearly stands tall and above most other areas in its historical background. The list of important events in the formulation and development of America is lengthy. Arlington was that part of Virginia, until the retrocession of 1846, that formed the 100 square miles of Virginia and Maryland territories for the capital of history's first lasting and workable democracy. Founders and leaders George Washington, George Mason, James Madison, and many other early patriots owned land or worked in, visited, or traversed what is now Arlington County. It was mostly in Arlington that Abraham Lincoln built his forts, the remains of some which remain today, to protect the capital from attack during the dark days of the American Civil war.

It was also in Arlington, then Alexandria County, that Martha Washington's grandson, and adopted son, George Washington Parke Custis built his magnificent mansion Arlington House, eventually occupied by General Robert E. Lee who married Custis' daughter Mary Anne. The mansion remains today as one of the country's most cherished and meaningful symbols of our national heritage. Both our County and America's largest National Cemetery are named after Arlington House, the Custis-Lee mansion.

Arlington is also the locale of the world's first aircraft casualty in 1908, Lieutenant Thomas Selfridge, and in 1909, the first cross country aircraft flight which started at Fort Myer and reached to Shooters Hill in Alexandria where today The George Washington Masonic Memorial is located. The military installation, Fort Myer, within the boundaries of Arlington County, has been the assignment station for renown military figures to include Generals George Marshall, George Patton, Douglas MacArthur, John Pershing, and countless other famous military leaders.

In Arlington National Cemetery, within the boundaries of Arlington County, is the Country's Tomb of the Unknowns, graves of Presidents John F. Kennedy and William Howard Taft, and the greatest collection in the Country of burial sites for national figures to include Supreme Court Justices, cabinets officers, wartime heros, astronauts, literary and musical figures and other personalities who have contributed to America's greatness.

Arlington County is also unique in its geographical location. It is on the door steps of the Capital of the most unique nation ever to appear on the historical stage of this planet. Never has there been a nation, or empire, or kingdom, of such super power as is the United States of America today. Nor has there ever been a country so committed to freedom, rule by its people, and the preservation of human rights and dignity, rather than oppression, cruelty, and domination, as is America today. Arlington County is privileged to be closer to the heart, soul and mind of that great Super Power than any other community in the Country.

ARLINGTON COUNTY VIRGINIA - A Modern History

Arlington County also, simply, is just a splendid place to live, work, raise a family and enjoy the fruits of living. The County is relatively clean, neat and tidy, and the rate of crime and misconduct is among the lowest, not the highest, in the nation. The County's government and leaders, although not universally accepted by all, is still devoid of any record of corruption or misconduct. This author has found only one instance of an elected official in the county ever having been tried and convicted of any serious or ethical offense while in office, or perhaps even out of office (a County treasurer about 1930). Elected officials of the political group in power at this writing, loudly proclaim repeatedly that the County has the lowest tax rate, and the highest quality of services, of any of the Washington Metropolitan jurisdiction. While critics may not wholly agree with this claim, they are hard pressed to disprove it to any significant extent.

All in all, Arlingtonians have many reasons to be proud of their community and highly content to be living in the County. Perhaps typical of the compliments that could be showered on Arlington, and especially its geographical location next to the Nation's Capital, were the comments of Washington Post columnist Steve Twomey in an October 14, 1996 article. Twomey attended a function high in a Rosslyn towering building and recorded his impressions from an Arlington 24th floor terrace. He wrote, in part:

> "...I wasn't prepared for what unfolded as I got off the elevator and walked onto the terrace...Rosslyn, the high rise village ... is one of our area's genuflections to height...spread beneath my feet was a capital that I had never seen...directly below [was] the Potomac hefty and serene dividing to pass on either side of Roosevelt Island [Analostan and Mason Island of past Arlington history days] and then coalescing again to pass beneath the Theodore Roosevelt and Arlington Memorial Bridges... taking a big turn to the right and flowed out of sight on its way to the sea...I was having a religious experience...[perhaps] the warm late afternoon sun had something to do with that because its rays were painting the city gold. It glowed...I eye-cruised for landmarks...the biggies were right there - the Jefferson Memorial, the Lincoln Memorial, the Washington Monument, the Capital - plus the Supreme Court, RFK Stadium, the Washington National Cathedral, the Basilica of the National Shrine, Georgetown, everything...Farther right, downriver, jets were silently lifting into the sunlight from (Arlington's) National Airport...maybe [the view] is a secret Rosslyn [and Arlington] shouldn't keep to itself..."

Twomeys impressions from modern day Arlington County are surely those with which Arlingtonians can fully agree and with no reservations adopt as their own. It is my hope, among others, that the writings herein will better enable my fellow citizens to improve their perspectives and knowledgeability of their community and its position of importance and uniqueness on our local and national scene.

* * * *

APPENDIX

Arlington County Board Members 1870-1931

The following are the members of the Arlington County Board (of Supervisors) in the period following the Civil War until the adoption of the County Manager form of government in the election of 1930, and the running of Board members in the next election of 1931 (the first under the County Manager form with at-large election of board members). The list is the product of the Arlington Historical Society Research and Records Committee and was in the October 1967 issue of the Society annual Magazine.

The election of the new Board of Supervisors was held on May 28, 1870, with the following Judges of Election appointed by the Court:

Jefferson Township	*Arlington Township*	*Washington Township*
James C. Roach	Garrett B. Wibirt	John R. Minor
Thos. Sanborn	Edward [Edwin] Ball	———— Stallcup [sic] [7]
W. E. Carter	S. B. Wibirt	H. A. Lockwood

The new Board of Supervisors held its first meeting on August 29, 1870, when it elected a Chairman and proceeded to "lay the levy." The following data are from the "Minute Books" of the Board of Supervisors, of the County Board, and of the County Court which until 1904 had the power to fill vacancies in many offices and before which officials qualified. There are some gaps in the record, and some mysterious appearances and disappearances of individuals. The Research and Records Committee would welcome any corrections or supplementary information.

BOARD OF SUPERVISORS

July 1, 1870—September 5, 1870
    H. Dwight Smith, Arlington Township, Chairman
    Charles W. Payne, Washington Township
    Supervisor elected for Jefferson Township (Storm V. Boyd) failed to qualify

September 5, 1870—June 30, 1871
    H. Dwight Smith, Arlington Township, Chairman
    Charles W. Payne, Washington Township
    James C. Roach, Jefferson Township (Appointed)

July 1, 1871—June 30, 1872
    H. Dwight Smith, Arlington Township, Chairman
    Edward Deeble, Washington Township
    William A. Rowe*, Jefferson Township
        *Given variously as Wroe, Roe, and Rome. In later years, consistently Rowe.

July 1, 1872—December 5, 1872
    William A. Rowe, Jefferson Township, Chairman
    Henry W. Febrey, Washington Township
    John B. Syphax, Arlington Township (Resigned 12/5/72)

December 5, 1872—March 3, 1873
    William A. Rowe, Jefferson Township, Chairman
    Henry W. Febrey, Washington Township
    H. Dwight Smith, Arlington Township (Appointed 12/5/72; resigned, 3/3/73)

March 3, 1873—April 8, 1873
 William A. Rowe, Jefferson Township, Chairman
 Lott W. Crocker*, Arlington Township
 Henry W. Febrey, Washington Township
  *Appointed 3/3/73; probably did not qualify as see Schutt, below.

April 8, 1873—June 30, 1873
 William A. Rowe, Jefferson Township, Chairman
 Henry W. Febrey, Washington Township
 Francis G. Schutt, Arlington Township, "Associate" (Appointed 7/8/73)

July 1, 1873—July 8, 1873
 William A. Rowe, Jefferson Township, "President"
 Supervisor elected for Arlington Township, ? ? ? , failed to qualify
 Supervisor elected for Washington Township, Edward Deeble, failed to qualify

July 8, 1873—December 1, 1873
 William A. Rowe, Jefferson Township, "President"
 Francis G. Schutt, Arlington Township, "Associate" (Appointed 7/8/73)
 (vacancy), Washington Township

December 1, 1873—June 30, 1874
 William A. Rowe, Jefferson Township, "President"
 Francis G. Schutt, Arlington Township, "Associate"
 Samuel Titus, Washington Township, "Associate" (Appointed 12/1/73)

July 1, 1874—June 30, 1875
 Francis G. Schutt, Arlington District, Chairman
 William A. Rowe, Jefferson District
 Gilbert Vandenburg*, Washington District
  *This name also appears in the records as Vandebergh and Vandenburgh. Properly, it is Vandenberg.

July 1, 1875—June 30, 1876*
 Francis G. Schutt, Arlington District, Chairman
 William A. Rowe, Jefferson District
 Gilbert Vandenberg, Washington District
  *Term changed to two years.

July 1, 1876—June 5, 1877
 Francis G. Schutt*, Arlington District, Chairman
 William A. Rowe, Jefferson District
 Gilbert Vandenberg, Washington District
  *Notation on June 5 that he was no longer on the Board as he had moved from Arlington District, date unspecified.

June 5, 1877—June 25, 1877
 Gilbert Vandenberg, Washington District, Chairman
 William A. Rowe, Jefferson District
 (vacancy), Arlington District

June 25, 1877—June 30, 1877
 Gilbert Vandenberg, Washington District, Chairman
 William H. Robinson*, Arlington District (Appointed 6/25/77)
 William A. Rowe, Jefferson District
  *Also appears as Robertson, as it does on the 1878 map of the County, but more frequently as Robinson.

July 1, 1877—April 2, 1879
 Charles W. Payne, Washington District, Chairman
 William H. Robinson, Arlington District
 William A. Rowe, Jefferson District (Resigned 4/2/79; moved from Jefferson to Arlington District)

Appendix

April 2, 1879—June 30, 1879
    Charles W. Payne, Washington District, Chairman
    William H. Robinson, Arlington District
    (vacancy), Jefferson District

July 1, 1879—June 30, 1881
    William A. Rowe, Arlington District, Chairman
    Travis B. Pinn, Jefferson District
    Francis G. Schutt, Washington District

July 1, 1881—August 15, 1881
    William A. Rowe, Arlington District, Chairman
    Christopher Costello*, Washington District
    Travis B. Pinn, Jefferson District (Resigned 8/15/81)
    *Also given as Costollow or Costolow.

August 15, 1881—June 30, 1883
    William A. Rowe, Arlington District, Chairman
    Christopher Costello, Washington District
    Francis M. Mills, Jefferson District (Appointed 8/15/81)

July 1, 1883—April 1, 1884
    Christopher Costello, Washington District, Chairman
    John W. Pendleton, Jefferson District
    Perkin W. Squier*, Arlington District
    *Postmaster of Alexandria City. Court declared seat vacant under the Virginia law prohibiting Federal employees from holding office in the State, and appointed a successor.

April 1, 1884—November 15, 1884
    Christopher Costello, Washington District, Chairman
    Curtis B. Graham, Jr., Arlington District (Appointed 4/1/84)
    John W. Pendleton, Jefferson District

November 15, 1884—June 30, 1885
    Christopher Costello, Washington District, Chairman
    Curtis B. Graham, Jr., Arlington District
    George W. Saulisbury*, Jefferson District
    *Nothing in the record shows why Saulisbury took Pendleton's place, nor exactly when; the meeting of 11/15/84 is the first in which he is shown as "present."

July 1, 1885—June 30, 1887
    Richard W. Johnston, Jefferson District, Chairman
    John D. Payne, Washington District
    George W. Veitch, Arlington District

July 1, 1887—November 13, 1888
    A. B. Grunwell, Washington District, Chairman
    Tibbett Allen, Jefferson District (Resigned; date ?)
    Horatio Ball*, Arlington District
    *This was Jr. as his father had died in 1873 at the age of 88 of "old age."

November 13, 1888—June 30, 1889
    A. B. Grunwell, Washington District, Chairman
    Horatio Ball, Arlington District
    Frank Hume, Jefferson District (Appointed: date ?)

July 1, 1889—June 30, 1891
    Frank Hume*, Jefferson District, Chairman
    Frederick S. Corbett, Arlington District
    Walter G. Willson, Washington District
    *Hume was also Delegate to the General Assembly in 1890 as he was 1899-1900.

July 1, 1891—June 30, 1892
>   Frank Hume, Jefferson District, Chairman
>   Millard F. Birch, Arlington District
>   Walter G. Willson, Washington District

July 1, 1892—June 30, 1893
>   Frank Hume, Jefferson District, Chairman
>   Millard F. Birch, Arlington District
>   William N. Febrey*, Washington District
>   *The record does not show why Febrey succeeded Willson who presumably had been elected for the two year term in May 1891.

July 30, 1893—June 30, 1895
>   Frank Hume, Jefferson District, Chairman
>   John W. Clark, Arlington District
>   R. Henry Phillips, Washington District

July 1, 1895—June 30, 1897
>   A. B. Grunwell, Washington District, Chairman
>   Frederick S. Corbett, Arlington District
>   William Duncan, Jefferson District

July 1, 1897—October 11, 1897
>   George N. Saegmuller, Washington District, Chairman
>   William Duncan, Jefferson District
>   A. D. Torreyson*, Arlington District
>   *The election in Arlington District was contested with Torreyson and F. S. Corbett each getting 209 votes on the first count. The Court found for Corbett who was declared to have been a member of the Board since July 1 though Torreyson had been sitting.

October 11, 1897—June 30, 1899
>   George N. Saegmuller, Washington District, Chairman
>   William Duncan, Jefferson District
>   Frederick S. Corbett, Arlington District

July 1, 1899—June 30, 1901
>   George N. Saegmuller, Washington District, Chairman
>   Frederick S. Corbett, Arlington District
>   Dr. D. N. Rust, Jefferson District

July 1, 1901—December 31, 1903*
>   Rezin W. Darbey, Arlington District, Chairman
>   C. J. Costolow, Washington District
>   William Duncan, Jefferson District
>   *The Constitution of 1902 changed the term of office to four years on a calendar year basis. The extra six months of this Board covered the transition period.

Calendar Years Unless Otherwise Specified

1904—1907
>   Dr. D. N. Rust, Jefferson District, Chairman
>   W. W. Douglas*, Arlington District
>   W. N. Febrey, Washington District
>   *The election was contested by F. S. Corbett, the Court held for Douglas.

1908—1911
>   W. N. Febrey, Washington District, Chairman
>   Frederick S. Corbett, Arlington District
>   Edward Duncan, Jefferson District

1912—1915
>   Edward Duncan, Jefferson District, Chairman
>   Robert L. Walker, Washington District
>   W. C. Wibirt, Arlington District

Appendix

1916—March 27, 1919
    Robert L. Walker*, Washington District, Chairman
    Edward Duncan, Jefferson District
    W. C. Wibirt, Arlington District
        *Resigned 3/27/19 to take post of Sanitary Inspector for the County.

March ?, 1919—December 31, 1919
    W. C. Wibirt, Arlington District, Chairman
    Clarence R. Ahalt, Washington District (Appointed; date ?)
    Edward Duncan, Jefferson District

January 1, 1920—February 20, 1920
    Thomas J. DeLashmutt, Arlington District, Chairman
    Edward Duncan, Jefferson District
    (vacancy)*, Washington District
        *Clarence R. Ahalt elected but moved from District before term began.

February 20, 1920—April 12, 1920
    Thomas J. DeLashmutt, Arlington District, Chairman
    Edward Duncan, Jefferson District
    Frank Upman, Washington District (Appointed; date ?)

April 12, 1920—December 31, 1923
    Thomas J. DeLashmutt, Arlington District, Chairman
    Edward Duncan, Jefferson District
    W. T. Weaver*, Washington District
        *Appointed. The record does not show why (nor exactly for how long) Upman served such a short time.

1924—1927
    E. C. Turnburke, Washington District, Chairman
    Edward Duncan, Jefferson District
    W. J. Ingram, Arlington District

1928—1931
    Edward Duncan, Jefferson District, Chairman
    B. M. Hedrick, Arlington District
    E. C. Turnburke, Washington District

COUNTY BOARD

County Manager plan of government

January 1, 1932—May 31, 1933
    Harry A. Fellows, Chairman
    John C. Gall (Resigned 5/31/33)
    Fred A. Gosnell, Sr.
    Lyman M. Kelley
    Elizabeth B. Magruder

June 1, 1933—December 11, 1933
    Harry A. Fellows, Chairman
    Fred A. Gosnell, Sr. (Resigned 12/11/33)
    Lyman M. Kelley
    Elizabeth B. Magruder
    B. M. Smith (Appointed 6/1/33)

ARLINGTON COUNTY VIRGINIA - A Modern History

County Board Members 1932-1994

This list prepared by Historical Society member Norman S. Novack appeared in the 1994 annual Society Magazine. The terms of Board members Bozman, Eisenberg and Hunter should be extended to 1996, the time of this writing, and the list should be amended to include members Chris Zimmerman and Paul Ferguson elected for four year terms in 1994 and 1995 respectively.

Name	Term of Service
W. P. Ames	1936-1939
Lucas H. Blevins	1957-1960
Ellen Bozman	1974-
(Served as Chairman in 1976, 1983, 1984, 1989 and 1992)	
(Served as Vice Chairman in 1975, 1978 and 1991)	
Herbert L. Brown, Jr.	1958-1961
(Served as Chairman in 1960)	
Michael E. Brunner	1984-1987
Leone B. Buchholz	1952-1958
(Elected to filled unexpired term on Nov. 10, 1952)	
(Served as Chairman in 1954)	
M. Rex Byrne	1952
(Appointed on Sept. 18, 1952, to fill vacancy until filled by election on Nov. 10, 1952.)	
Edmund D. Campbell	1940-1946
(Served as Chairman in 1942 and 1946)	
Florence Cannon	1948-1951
(Served as Chairman in 1951)	
Harold J. Casto	1964-1967
(Served as Chairman in 1967)	
F. Freeland Chew	1936-1951
(Served as Chairman in 1939, 1941 and 1945)	
Wesley W. Cooper	1954-1957
(Served as Chairman in 1956 and 1957)	
Robert W. Cox	1950-1952
(Served as Chairman in 1952)	
(Removed from office on Sept. 17, 1952, under a ruling of the Virginia Supreme Court of Appeals that the exemption of members of the Arlington County Board from the prohibition against federal employees holding office in Virginia had been granted by an unconstitutional statute.)	

Appendix

Name	Term of Service
Harry W. Cuppett	1947

(Appointed on May 17, 1947)

Alan L. Dean 1952
    (Removed from office on Sept. 17, 1952
under a ruling of the Virginia Supreme Court
of Appeals that the exemption of members of
the Arlington County Board from the prohibition against Federal employees holding office
in Virginia had been granted by an unconstitutional statute.)

Basil M. DeLashmutt 1940-1949
    (Served as Chairman in 1943, March-December 1947, and 1949)

Robert H. Detwiler 1952-1953
    (Elected to fill unexpired term on Nov. 11, 1952)

Stephen Detwiler 1979-1982
    (Served as Chairman in 1981 and 1982)
    (Served as Vice Chairman in 1980)

Daniel A. Dugan 1947-1952
    (Served as Chairman in 1948 and 1950)
    (Removed from office on Sept. 17, 1952
under a ruling of the Virginia Supreme Court
of Appeals that the exemption of members of
the Arlington County Board from the prohibition against Federal employees holding office
in Virginia had been granted by an unconstitutional statute.)

Albert C. Eisenberg 1984-
    (Served as Chairman in 1987 and 1990)
    (Served as Vice Chairman in 1986, 1988-1989 and 1994)

Harry A. Fellows 1932-1935
    (Served as Chairman in 1932-1933)

Joseph L. Fisher 1963-1974
    (Served as Chairman in 1963 and 1971)
    (Served as Vice Chairman in 1968)
    (Resigned following his election to the U.S.
House of Representatives)

Name	Term of Service
Walter Frankland	1976-1983

    (Served as Chairman in 1980)
    (Served as Vice Chairman in 1979)

Alfred E. Frisbie 1947-1952
    (Appointed on Nov. 26, 1947)
    (Served as Chairman in September-December, 1952)

John C. Gall 1932-1933
    (Resigned on May 31, 1933)

Christopher B. Garnett 1933-1935
    (Appointed on Dec. 11, 1933)

Fred A. Gosnell, Sr. 1932-1933
    (Resigned on Dec. 11, 1933)

Dorothy Grotos 1976-1983
    (Served as Chairman in 1979)
    (Served as Vice Chairman in 1981 and 1982)

Dr. Kenneth M. Haggerty 1966-1973
    (Served as Chairman in 1969)
    (Served as Vice Chairman in 1967)

James B. Hunter III .... May 1990-
    (Served as Chairman in 1993)
    (Served as Vice Chairman in 1992)
    (Elected in a special election in May 1990 to
    fill the unexpired term of John G. Milliken,
    who had been appointed as Secretary of
    Transportation of the Commonwealth of
    Virginia.)

Ralph Kaul 1956-1963
    (Served as Chairman in 1958)

Lyman M. Kelley 1932-1934
    (Served as Chairman in 1934)
    (Removed by court order on Nov. 3, 1934)

Alvin F. Kimel 1952-1955
    (Elected to fill unexpired term on Nov. 10,
    1952)

David L. Krupsaw 1956-1960
    (Served as Chairman in 1959)
    (Died in office on Jan. 21, 1960)

Appendix

Name	Term of Service
Leo C. Lloyd	1940-1947

   (Served as Chairman in 1944)
   (Died in office on Nov. 3, 1947)

Roye L. Lowry 1962-1965
   (Served as Chairman in 1964)

W. A. E. McShea 1934-1939
   (Appointed on Nov. 8, 1934)
   (Served as Chairman in 1937)

Elizabeth B. Magruder 1932-1947
   (Served as Chairman in 1938, 1940 and 1947;
   Resigned as Chairman on Feb. 11, 1947)

Howard R. Massey 1952
   (Appointed on Sept. 18, 1952 to fill vacancy
   until filled by election on Nov. 10, 1952.)

John G. Milliken 1981-Feb. 1990
   (Served as Chairman in 1985 and 1988)
   (Served as Vice Chairman in 1983, 1984 and 1987)
   (Resigned in February 1990 following his
   appointment as Secretary of Transportation of
   the Commonwealth of Virginia)

Everard Munsey 1972-1975
   (Served as Chairman in 1973)
   (Served as Vice Chairman in 1972)

William T. Newman, Jr. 1988-March 1993
   (Served as Chairman in 1991)
   (Served as Vice Chairman in 1990)
   (Resigned in March 1993 following his
   appointment as a Circuit Judge)

Robert A. Peck 1952-1955
   (Served as Chairman in 1953)

John Purdy 1973-1980
   (Served as Chairman in 1975 and 1978)
   (Served as Vice Chairman in 1973 and 1977)

A. Leslie Phillips 1969-1972
   (Served as Vice Chairman in 1970)

Name	Term of Service
Thomas W. Richards	1961-1968; 1975

(Served as Chairman in 1963 and 1968)
(Appointed in 1975 to fill the unexpired term of
Joseph L. Fisher, who had been elected to the
U.S. House of Representatives.)
(Only Board member to serve in two non-
continuous time periods)

Jay E. Ricks	1968-1971

(Served as Vice Chairman in 1971)

George M. Rowzee, Jr.	1953-1956

(Served as Chairman in 1955)

B. M. Smith	1933-1935

(Appointed on June 1, 1933)
(Served as Chairman from Nov. 8, 1934 to
Dec. 31, 1935 — Acting Chairman)

Ned R. Thomas	1967-1970

(Served as Chairman in 1970)
(Served as Vice Chairman in 1969)

John A. Tillema	1952

(Appointed on Sept. 18, 1952 to fill vacancy
until filled by election on Nov. 10, 1952.)

Leo Urbanske, Jr.	1959-1966

(Served as Chairman in 1961 and 1966)

Mary Margaret Whipple	1983-

(Served as Chairman in 1986 and 1994)
(Served as Vice Chairman in 1985 and 1993)

Joseph S. Wholey	1971-1978

(Served as Chairman in 1972, 1974 and 1977)
(Served as Vice Chairman in 1976)

Ernest D. Wilt	1960-1963

(Appointed on Jan. 29, 1960)
(Served as Chairman in 1962)

Benjamin H. Winslow, Jr.	April 1993-

(Elected in a special election in April 1993 to
fill the unexpired term of William T. Newman,
Jr., who had been appointed a Circuit Judge.)

George M. Yeatman	1936-1939

(Served as Chairman in 1936)

Appendix

Chairs of Committee of 100

1954 - Lucas H. Blevins
1955 - B. Allen Lillywhite
1956 - Kingsley Higgins
1957 - William Backus
1958 - Stanley Mayer
1959 - Kenneth Ludwig
1960 - William Watt
1961 - George Terborogh
1962 - Jules Guedalia
1963 - Harold Stone
1964 - James McHugh
1965 - John Palmer
1966 - William Bartlett
1967 - Barnard Joy
1968 - Henry Lampe
1969 - Malcolm Miller
1970 - Ellen Bozman
1971 - James McMullin
1972 - Theodore Taylor
1973 - M Patton Echols, Jr
1974 - Clye W. Elliot
1975 - Allen H. Harrison, Jr

1976 - Gustave C. Zader
1977 - Larry T. Suiters
1978 - Ruth C. Cocklin
1979 - Robert E. Skinner
1980 - Elizabeth Weihe
1981 - J. Newman Carter
1982 - W. Grady Malone
1983 - Hilton Peel
1984 - Bette Clements
1985 - James B. Hunter III
1986 - James M. Wright
1987 - Theodore Weihe
1988 - Marjorie S. McCreery
1989 - Scott McGeary
1990 - Margo Horner
1991 - Connie McAdams
1992 - Jinny DeSimone
1993 - John McCracken
1994 - Rex Wackerle
1995 - Robbin Stombler
1996 - James Mayer

CIVIC FEDERATION MEMBERSHIP

American Assn of University Women
Arl. Education Assn.
Arl. Heritage Alliance.
Arl. Historical Society.
Arl. Housing Corp.
Arl. Taxpayers Assn.
Arl. Forest Citizen Assn.
Arl. Heights Citizen Assn.
Arl. Jr Chamber Comm.
Arl. Oaks Community Assn.
Arl. Ridge Civic Assn.
Arl. View Civic Assn.
Ashton Heights Civic Assn.
Astoria Unit Owners Assn.
Aurora Highlands Civic Assn.
Ballston-Virginia Square Civic Assn.
Barcroft School and Civic League.
Bellevue Forest Citizens Assn.
Boulevard Manor Citizens Assn.
Buckingham Tenants Assn.
Center for Urban Education.
Cherrydale Citizens Assn.
Civic Coalition for Minority Affairs.
Claremont Citizens Assn.
Colonial Village Community Services Assn.
Columbia Heights Civic Assn.
Concord Mews Unit Owners Assn.
Courtland Civic Assn.
Delta Kappa Gamma Alpha Omicron
Dominion Hills Civic Assn.
Donaldson Run Civic Assn.
Dover-Crystal Civic Assn.
Fairlington Citizens Assn.
Forest Glen Citizens Assn.
Friends of Arl. Parks.
Glencarlyn Citizens Assn.
Gulf Branch Citizens Assn.
Highland Park-Overlee Knolls Citizens Assn.
Hyde Park Condominium Assn.
Langston Citizens Assn.
League of Women Voters.
Leeway Citizens Assn.
Lyon Park Citizens Assn.
Lyon Village Citizens Assn.
Madison Manor Citizens Assn.
Maywood Community Assn.
Nauck Citizens Assn.
New Arl. Douglas Park Citizens Assn.
North Highlands Citizens Assn.
Old Dominion Citizens Assn.
Organized Women Voters of Arl.
Parkway Citizens Assn.
Rivercrest Civic Assn.
Riverwood Citizens Assn.
Rock Spring Citizens Assn.
Stonewall Jackson Citizens Assn.
Tara-Leeway Citizens Assn.
Waycroft-Woodlawn Civic Assn.
Westover Civic Assn.
Williamsburg Civic Assn.
Yorktown Civic Assn.

DORMANT OR DEAD ASSNS
Buckingham Tenants
John M. Langston
Pro-Bolivian Comm.
Waverly Hills Civic Assn.
Wilde Oaks Homeowners Assn.
Alcova Heights Civic Assn.
Barcroft Apt. Tenants Assn.
Columbia Pike Citizens Assn.
Glebewood Civic Assn.

Appendix

CIVIC FEDERATION PRESIDENTS

1916 - Frederick C. Handy
1919 - Frank G. Campbell
1922 - Clarence R. Ahalt
1925 - Robert E. Plymale
1928 - Leslie C. McNamar
1929 - William C. Hull
1931 - Harry A. Fellows
1932 - Robert N. Anderson
1934 - Arthur Orr
1936 - I. Chance Buchanan
1938 - Dr. Victor Meyers
1940 - Alva D. Adams
1942 - Florence E. Cannon
1944 - Charles A. Cobbins
1945 - William G. Watt
1947 - Ruby G. Simpson
1949 - Charles M. Smith
1950 - T. Oscar Smith
1951 - Ruth O'Dell Cox
1953 - Clyde E. Merriman
1955 - Edward B. Hincks
1956 - Walter Kingsbury
1958 - William C. Backus

1960 - Mary C. Hackman
1962 - Robert W. Cox
1964 - Robert Reynolds
1965 - Clarence Salisbury
1966 - William M. Graham
1968 - Joseph H. Newlin
1970 - Edward J. Kelly
1972 - Sherman W. Pratt
1973 - Robert L. Weinberg
1975 - Charles A. Fun
1975 - Joseph N. Pelton
1977 - James A. McCaskill, II
1979 - Anne M. Noll
1981 - N. Edwin Demoney, Jr.
1983 - Godfrey E. Barber
1984 - Kenneth Ingram
1985 - Kenneth Ingram
1987 - William Gearhart
1989 - Alexander Keyes
1990 - David Foster
1992 - Jean Mostrum
1994 - Scott McGeary
1996 - William F. Nolden

FEDERATION MEMBERS
DISTINGUISHED MERITORIOUS SERVICE

1936 - Frederick E. Mann
1938 - Grover C. Payne
1942 - Robert E. Plymale
1943 - Florence E. Cannon
1949 - Ruby G. Simpson
1950 - Dr. Victor Meyers
1954 - William G. Watt
1960 - Walter Kingsbury

1978 - Lorna Hutchins
1978 - John Lohman
1982 - Anne M. Noll
1985 - Bernard Joy
1987 - Godfrey E. Barber
1995 - Scott McGeary
1995 - Roye Lowry

FEDERATION JOURNAL (Formerly Washington Star) TROPHY AWARDS

1938 - Public Util. Comm.,
   Robert E. Plymale, Chair
1939 - Julian D. Simpson
1940 - Albert A. Carretta
1942 - Hospital Comm., Carlton K.
   Lewis, Chair
1943 - Parks & Playgrounds Comm.,
   Dr. Victor Meyers, Chair
1944 - Welfare Comm., Florence
   Arnheim, Chair
1945 - War Memorial Coordinating
   Comm., Beulah Goss, Chair
1946 - William G. Watt
1947 - Oscar R. Lebeau
1948 - Ruby Simpson
1949 - Rev. & Expend. Comm.,
   Robert W. Cox, Chair
1950 - Malcoln D. Miller
1951 - Local Govt. Comm.,
   Harley M. Williams, Chair
1952 - Shirley P, Wheeler
1953 - Ruth O'Dell Cox
1954 - Alice Campbell
1955 - Walter Kingsbury
1956 - William A. Backus
1957 - Mary Cook Hackman
1958 - Schools comm.,
   Lorna Hutchins, Chair
1959 - Robert Reynolds
1960 - Clarence Salisbury
1961 - Howard William Gammon
1962 - John Lohman
1963 - William M. Graham
1964 - Marie Dresser
1965 - Schools Comm.,
   June Lohman, Chair
1966 - Leslie & Muriel Logan
1967 - John C. McComb
1968 - James M. Warnock
1969 - Edward J. Kelly
1970 - Lawrence D. Moracher, Jr
1971 - Sorine J. Preli & Richard
   Golrick
1972 - Herbert Shaffer
1973 - John Steven Chwat
1974 - Constance M. Allard
1975 - Robert L. Weinberg
1976 - Robert B. Machen
1977 - Anne M. Noll &
   Joseph N. Pelton
1978 - N. Edwin Demoney, Jr
1979 - James H. McCaskill, II
1980 - Godfrey E. Barber
1981 - Jean Harrett
1982 - Susan Zajac
1983 - Shirley Pallansch
1984 - Kenneth J. Ingram
1985 - Catherine DeScisciolo
1986 - Alexander Keyes
1987 - Edward Knowles
1988 - Karen Darner
1989 - William Gearhart
1990 - Jennie Davis
1991 - Helen Hedges
1992 - David Foster
1993 - Monica Craven
1994 - Jean Mostrum
1995 - Evelyn Staples
1996 - Ernest Ragland

Appendix

CIVIC FEDERATION PUBLICITY

The following article was written to publicize the Civic Federation upon its annual banquet and was printed on March 4, 1975 in the Northern Virginia Sun and other regional newspapers.

THE ARLINGTON COUNTY CIVIC FEDERATION
A Public Forum
by Sherman Pratt

The History of the Arlington County Civic Federation prior to 1916 is somewhat sketchy, but since that date there is no shortage of documentation to show the Federation's very real contributions to the civic life of the community.

Down through the years it has served as a public forum and as a source of advice and information to public officials on almost every issue or controversy facing the county. Through its delegates from member neighborhood civic associations and other groups who serve on the Federation committees and make up its leadership, the Federation has studied, aired and made recommendations concerning taxation, education, public services, zoning, utilities, and every other facet of government and county activities.

The Federation has played a particularly active and influential role, going to the very roots of the county governmental structure in 1930 when Arlington residents voted on and adopted, before any other American community, the county manager form of government.

In that same election, the voters opted to discard the old magisterial single member districts in favor of the multi-member single district, or "at-large" electoral system, which is used to this day to elect members to the governing body.

The Federation has also concerned itself with important matters of recreation, legislation, public safety and transportation. Perhaps one of the most time consuming and sensitive areas of Federation activity has been in the area of land use and zoning, and the chairpersons of that committee particularly have repeatedly distinguished themselves and the committee with the results of their prolific hard work and worthwhile recommendations.

Certain meetings during the Federation's annual schedule are set aside to honor and hear from county elected or appointed officials and on these occasions the delegates and public visitors have an opportunity to make comments or ask questions on matters of current interest or importance.

The Federation's social highlight of the year is the annual banquet, normally in late April, which in recent years has been held at Mary Mount College. The banquet normally features a distinguished guest speaker or a program of current interest and it serves as an appropriate occasion to honor citizens with certificates of appreciation for exceptional community services, and to award the annual Washington Star-News Trophy Cup to the delegate or committee that has made the most outstanding contribution during the year. The Federation encourages maximum attendance at its annual banquet by the public generally as well as its own delegates and officials.

During its existence the Federation has served as the principle training ground for community leaders as most elected or senior appointed officials of the county had at one time or another, been a Federation delegate of officer. This includes the present Chairman of the County Board, John Purdy, and four of the five present members of the School Board. Numerous members of the Planning Commission have also been delegates to the Federation.

At times the Federation has been accused of being political. In the broad sense of the term, as pertaining to the body politic in the community, the Federation is probably the most political of all groups in the County since it involves itself in virtually every aspect of Arlington life and is the only activity with such a county wide base of participation and representation.

From the standpoint of partisan politics, however, the Federation by its constitution is forbidden to take sides in elections or political campaigns. The constitution provides that its activities "shall be strictly non-partisan, non-sectarian, non-sectional and non-political."

The Federation has also been accused of indecisiveness by not taking positions on particularly controversial matters. Years ago it was charged with being dominated by conservatives when it favored changing from the single member district electoral system at a time of heightened Black political activity in 1930 and 1931. More recently, the criticism heard is that the Federation is liberally dominated by an unproportionate percentage of delegates who are part of, or sympathetic to, the partisan group who now prevail on the County Board.

The truth in the charges of Federation domination by certain county political groups probably lies somewhat in between the two charges. The short answer may be that the Federation does indeed, and should, reflect to a considerable extent the philosophical or political views of the electorate, generally, as indicated by the voters at the ballot boxes.

In any event, notwithstanding any criticisms aimed at it, the fact remains that the Federation is performing a vital and worthwhile county service and that it alone, among county activities, is best qualified to fill this role - at least in a community without local electoral districts. Most other county organizations exist to represent a particular political, academic, professional, religious or other point of view, and their memberships can be quite localized in a small part of the county.

The Federation's goals, on the other hand, is to promote the county welfare generally and to create maximum interest in civic matters. Its delegates come from all parts of the county and represent the "grass roots" positions of the ordinary citizens, regardless of political or partisan affiliation. Thus on civic matters, it may be truly said that the Federation is the "Civic Voice of Arlington" and it deserves the strongest possible public support and active citizen participation and involvement.

* * *

Appendix

WHY DO WE CALL IT?........

The following information, comprising the best known and available, on the sources for names of some geographical features in Arlington County is based mainly on two thumbnail reports, the first dated 1960, the second undated but believed to date from about 1975, prepared by the Research and Records Committee of the Arlington Historical Society. In the reports, the Committee indicates that some of the information was collected from a series of articles with the above name that appeared in the Northern Virginia Sun over a period of months. The reports were further updated in 1997 by AHS members Sara Collins and Norman Novack. For brevity, some abridgement has been effected.

ABINGDON

The John (and Gerrard) Alexander estate at the National Airport, and recent efforts to preserve its ruins, is discussed in detail herein and needs no repetition here. The source of the name Abingdon does not seem to be known but is understood to have been acquired by Robert Alexander after the property was returned to the Alexander family. The estate had been sold to the John Parke Custis in 1778 as related herein, but was later returned to Robert Alexander upon non-payment of rent following the death in 1781 of Custis. The name Abingdon has persisted since that time.

ARLINGTON COUNTY

In 1920, the General Assembly of Virginia passed an Act decreeing that henceforth the county which had been known as "the country part of" Alexandria County (that excluded the city of Alexandria) should be known as Arlington County. This was to eliminate the confusion resulting from a city and county having the same name.

The name Arlington is taken from the Custis-Lee estate in the County. This had been the name of the home of the Custis family in Arlington County and earlier in Northhampton County on the Eastern Shore of Virginia. It is a matter of some dispute whether the name was taken by the early Custis settlers from an English town of the same name, or to honor Lord Arlington of England who was a friend of the Custis family in England.

ARLINGTON MILL DRIVE

In 1836, George Washington Parke Custis built a water grist mill on Four Mile Run near where it was crossed by Columbia Pike, and called it Arlington Mill from the name of his estate. When later the railroad came up the valley and a station was established there, it too was called Arlington Mill Station.

The modern highway built generally along the railroad line up the valley has been designated Arlington Mill Drive in recognition of the mill which formerly stood in the neighborhood of the right-of-way.

Why Do We Call It....? Continued

ARMY NAVY DRIVE

Army Navy Drive, was and is so named because it gives access to the Army Navy Country Club. It was formerly known as Old Georgetown Road to distinguish it from the "new graveled road" a block away and running roughly parallel which became known as South Arlington Ridge Road. The Old Georgetown Road was one of the oldest highways in the County and was shown on a survey of the area made in 1746, following the line of an earlier "wood's path" (sic). It ran from Alexandria to the ferry across the Potomac from what is now Rosslyn to Georgetown. George Washington and Thomas Jefferson must have traveled this road on their trips to the Federal City.

For a time after the Civil War the road was known as "Convalescent Camp Road" since it led to the large Union hospital encampment situated at Anthony Frazer's "Green Valley Manor" mansion where the Forest Hills townhouse development is now located at Army Navy Drive and South 23rd Street. The road was altered somewhat with the widening and conversion of Shirley Highway into I-395 in the 1970's and Long Branch, the stream running alongside, has been covered over and placed underground.

AURORA HILLS

This subdivision in the eastern part of Arlington County overlooking the Potomac River, and now Crystal City, the National airport and Potomac railroad Yards, derives its name from the Roman personification of dawn. According to old newspaper clippings, "The rising light of morning first dawned on the subdivision of Aurora Hills in 1914". The concept apparently was a favorite with developers since another subdivision to the north of the Court House is known as Aurora Heights.

ARLINGTON NATIONAL CEMETERY

Gerrard Alexander sold an estate of about 1,100 acres to John Parke Custis in 1778 (at the same time Custis was acquiring Abingdon from Gerrard's brother Robert). This was inherited by George Washington Parke Custis in 1802 who built a house on it and went to live there in 1804. He named it Mount Washington initially, but later changed it to Arlington after the Custis family home in Northampton County on the eastern shore.

Custis' daughter married Robert E. Lee, and the property was confiscated during the Civil War when the Federal Army occupied it on May 24, 1861. In 1864 war dead began being buried on the grounds of the estate and it was soon designated Arlington National Cemetery. After the war General Lee's son won a suit to recover the property but not wanting to return to a cemetery to live settled for a $150,000 payment by the Federal government. The Cemetery has acquired the name of the estate on which it is located.

Appendix

Why Do We Call It....? Continued

BAILEY'S CROSS ROADS

This important intersection was formed when Columbia Pike was constructed (1806-1812) and reached the old road from Alexandria to Leesburg (Seminary Road). The opening of the new Leesburg Road (1818-1838), now Route 7 and Leesburg Pike, made five forks at this point.

In 1837, Hachaliah Bailey of Westchester, New York, acquired the surrounding land. He deed it to Mariah Bailey, wife of Lewis Bailey, in 1843. These Baileys built a house there and operated a store and an inn at the cross roads which began to bear their name. In later years the Barnham and Bailey circus went into winter quarters in the area and led some to believe that the Crossroads derived its name from the circus name.

BALLSTON

John and Moses Ball were among the earliest settlers in what is now Arlington County, acquiring property in the Glencarlyn area in the 1740s. Late in the 18th Century a member of this family established an "ordinary", or tavern, where the road to Alexandria to the Falls of the Potomac (now Glebe Road) crossed the road from Georgetown to Falls Church (Wilson Boulevard). This became known as Ball's Crossroads. The area later became known as Ballstown, or Ballston.

BARCROFT

John Wolverton Barcroft of New York bought 62 acres from George Washington Custis Lee (Robert E. Lee's son) in 1880. This was the Custis mill tract part of Washington Forest. Barcroft tore down the Arlington Mill which George W.P. Custis built and put up another nearby where Columbia Pike crosses Four Mile Run. The name of the railroad station there was also changed from Arlington to Barcroft about the same time. The name of Barcroft is perpetuated today in Barcroft Park and the Barcroft apartment developments, and also with a Civic Association bearing the same name.

BLUEMONT DRIVE

When the Southern Railway succeeded to the ownership of Northern Virginia's first railroad, the Alexandria, Loudon and Hampshire (chartered 1853), it extended the trackage, reaching Bluemont, Virginia in 1900. This line was taken over in 1912 by the Washington and Old Dominion Railroad which ran from Rosslyn to Great Falls. The connection of the two branches became known as Bluemont Junction, and the road which led there as Bluemont Drive. Part of the Drive disappeared with the construction of I-66, but a slab of concrete from the station at the junction, partly covered by a tennis court, remains today in Bluemont Park between Arlington and Wilson Boulevards. There have been efforts by local historically minded citizens to better preserve and identify the concrete block.

ARLINGTON COUNTY VIRGINIA - A Modern History

WHY Do We Call It?.....Continued

BOUNDARY CHANNEL

In 1632, after the establishment of the Virginia colony, King Charles I granted land in America (Maryland) to Lord Baltimore, describing the boundary in part as running along the "farther bank" of the Potomac River. [The grant did not specify, however, whether this meant at high or low water tides and the difference in flat marsh lands could be significant]. Thus it is that the boundary between Maryland and Virginia does not run down the middle of the River as one might expect as is common in many other parts of the country where a river constitutes the boundary between two states.

The exact boundary between the two States - and between the District of Columbia and Virginia after the latter was retroceded to Virginia in 1846 - has been a matter of some controversy ever since the 17th Century. Law courts and Federal and interstate commissions have failed to settle the matter. A Federal Act in 1945 followed by an Act in the Virginia General Assembly in 1946 declared the boundary to lie at the high water mark on the Virginia side of the river. Thus the channel separating Columbia Island and Lady Bird Park from the Virginia mainland between the Memorial and the other bridges to the south, is known as the Boundary Channel. It also explains why one does not see "Welcome to Virginia" signs immediately when leaving the Virginia side of the Memorial bridge but rather after traveling some several hundred yards farther.

CARLIN SPRINGS ROAD

In 1772, William Carlin bought land along Four Mile Run from the estate of John Ball, the first settler. After Carlin's death in 1820, it was divided among his heirs who continued to farm it.

The construction of a railroad through Four Mile Run valley suggested the development of the area around two farm springs on the property as a picnic and excursion resort about 1870. The road which gave access to the property came to be known as Carlin Springs Road. Originally, it entered what is now Wilson Boulevard along the line of present Abingdon Street.

When the County Board adopted the new street naming system in 1934, the Carlin names was misspelled "Carlyn" in the Board Minutes. Thus, it is said the road is now officially (although improperly) called Carlyn Springs Road. The common mistake of dropping the "s" from Springs can be avoided if it is recalled that there were two on the Carlin farm. The spelling may also have been changed at the insistence of the Postal authorities to avoid confusion with another Carlin Spring in the State.)

CAMERON STREET

The Lord Fairfax who inherited the proprietorship of the Northern Neck from his mother, Catherine, the daughter of Thomas, the 2nd Baron Culpeper, was the 6th Baron of Cameron. The first Fairfax to be created Baron of Cameron, in 1627, was Thomas Fairfax of Denton. It was rather ironical that a Fairfax should have inherited

Appendix

Why We Call it....? Continued.

the grant of vast lands made by King Charles II to Lord Culpeper since the 3rd and 4th Barons of Cameron had been leaders of Parliamentary troops under Cromwell.

Grants of land made by the proprietors in the Northern Neck form the first step in the chain of title to all property between the Rappahanock and the Potomac to their "first springs" with the exception of patents (land grants) seated before 1669. The name Cameron appears frequently in honor of the Fairfaxes.

CHAIN BRIDGE

The first bridge at this site - a favorite river-crossing point for centuries - was built in 1779 and is known as the "Fall's Bridge" from its proximity to the Little Falls of the Potomac. It was carried away by high water in 1804, and a second bridge, built in 1808 was suspended by iron chains anchored in stone abutments. It was this bridge which became known as "the Chain Bridge" - a name which has persisted although chains have not been used in its construction since 1852. The present bridge, built in 1938, however, still makes use of masonry piers which photographic evidence proves were in place 100 years ago.

CHERRYDALE

The Community known as Cherrydale grew up around Dorsey Donaldson's cherry orchard. The name of Quincy Street was originally Cherry Valley Road. When a branch post office, and a railroad station, was established there a name was needed for both so the locally used name "Cherrydale" was used for both.

COLUMBIA PIKE

The abbreviation "Pike" for Turnpike, perpetuated in the name of this major thoroughfare through Arlington, traces back to its original status as a toll road.

In 1808, the Washington Bridge Company began construction of the Long Bridge, reaching from the foot of Maryland Avenue in Washington to Alexander's Island. This crossing was approximately on the site of the present Railroad Bridge. In the same year, the Columbian Turnpike Company was chartered by Congress to build a toll road from the western end of the causeway leading to Alexander's Island to connect with the Little River Turnpike in Fairfax County. By 1812, construction had been completed to the Fairfax County line (the boundary then with the District of Columbia of which Arlington was then a part), and the Fairfax Turnpike Company received a Virginia charter to build the final link. The name has continued to modern times.

COURT HOUSE ROAD

That portion of this road that runs past the Arlington County Court House (and now the jail next door) appears to have been appropriately named. But what of the

Why do We Call it....? Continued

section from Columbia Pike to South Uhle Street? Before the construction of Arlington Boulevard, which now interrupts it, the entire road was the most direct way from Columbia Pike to Wilson Boulevard and the Court House. Thus when the Street Naming Committee made its recommendations (adopted by the County Board in 1934) it seemed logical to give that name to this road. Portions of it, on the south side, had been known as Arlington Avenue. On the north side, it was Sherman Street. Prior to the renaming, what is now North Custis Drive had been known as Court House Road.

CULPEPER STREET

Thomas, Lord of Culpeper, a favorite of King Charles II, was one of the original recipients of the royal grant of the Northern Neck and the street name derives from that source. Culpeper was commissioned Governor of Virginia in 1677 but did not come to the Colony until May of 1680 when he stayed only a few months. He again visited Virginia a couple of years later. The names is borne by a Virginia County as well as an Arlington street.

CUSTIS-LEE MANSION

The lovely, pillared home which overlooks the Potomac from the height of the Arlington National Cemetery is officially designated Arlington House but is also known to many as the Custis-Lee Mansion, in honor of the two famous families associated with its history. First named "Mount Washington" by its builder George Washington Parke Custis (grandson of Martha Washington), the home was later renamed "Arlington House" after his daughter's marriage to then Lt Robert E. Lee. The home was occupied by Federal troops on May 24, 1861, after the Lee family fled south and never returned to the former owners. General Lee's son successfully sued after the war to recover the property but accepted a settlement instead of returning to an estate that had been converted into a cemetery with graves almost at the edge of the front porch.

DALE STREET

Dale Street runs a short distance in the southern part of Arlington County and was named for Sir Thomas Dale, "High Marshall" and Lt. Gov. of Virginia for periods in 1611, 1614 and 1616. He is best remembered for the severe laws which were introduced in the Colony during his tenure, but can also be credited with having done much in a critical period to assure the stability and permanence of the Jamestown settlement.

DAWSON TERRACE RECREATION CENTER

This Center is located in a part of Arlington County that was once the farm of Thomas Dawson. A portion of the Recreation Center structure is believed to date from

Appendix

Why Do We Call It....? Continued.

the 1700's. Until the renaming of streets that part of 21st Road North was known as Dawson Road. Dawson with his family, wife, slaves, cattle and horses moved from his father's home in Dawsonville, Maryland in 1847 to the hills so beautifully situation above the Potomac River and next to the William Jewell property, (now Fort C. F. Smith Park). In 1859 Dawson bought property adjoining the Jewell home place and added to the stone building standing there. Although the name of Dawson Road disappeared from the County maps in 1935, the name of this pioneer Arlingtonian is perpetuated in the name of the Recreation Center.

DITMAR ROAD

This road is named after "G. Ditmar and others" who in 1907 applied for permission to establish a road described as "beginning at the junction of Little Falls (Chain Bridge) Road and the road leading to Falls Church, said junction being in front of the Truett place, in a northerly direction through the land of Grunwell, Mcauliffe, Hitchcock, Walker, and others to a point on Chain Bridge Road in from of the land of Merritt".

In 1909 the County Supervisors ordered the road opened for its full length. Today it begins and ends on the same road, but the name of the latter has been changed and is now known as Glebe Road.

DINWIDDIE STREET

This street was named after Robert Dinwiddie (1693-1770) Lt Gov of the Colony of Virginia from 1751 to 1758 who was handed the position, as was the custom in those days, as a political plum. It was Dinwiddie that sent George Washington to Ohio in 1753 to demand the withdrawal of the French from English territory, and again in 1754 with an armed force. The skirmish that followed precipitated the French and Indian War.

DOCTOR'S BRANCH

This stream which flows into Four Mile Run between South Walter Reed Drive and Columbia Pike takes it name from a Doctor Michael Danghill (or "Dunghill" as it was sometimes (mis?) spelled) who rented land in this area from a John Todd in the 1720's. He lived there but a short time, according to the old records, "and then absconded" - but his stay was long enough to put his name, or rather his title, on the map and keep it there for over 200 years.

DONALDSON RUN

This stream, known around 1900, as the "Swimming landing Run", now carries the name of a family that once owned much of the land through which it flows. Just when the Donaldsons first came to this area is not certain, but the William and an

Why We Call It....? Continued

Andrew Donaldson were counted here in the Census of 1782. In 1808, Andrew Donaldson was overseer of the Glebe lands. There are still many representatives of the family in Arlington today.

EADS STREET

This street is named for James Buchanan Eads, a prominent engineer in the latter part of the last century. He was born in Indiana in 1820 and died in Nassau in 1887. His best known work was done on the Mississippi which he bridged at St Louis (1867-1874). During the Civil War he constructed iron clad steamers for use on the Mississippi by the Federal Government. In 1884, he was given the Albert Medal of the Society of Arts (Great Britain), the first American citizen to be so honored. [It is not indicated by the Society researchers whether this engineer ever had any association with Arlington that would have warranted naming a street after him. Author).

FAIRFAX DRIVE

This road derives its name, as it might be assumed, from Lord Fairfax who had inherited the area as part of the proprietorship of the Northern Neck which had come to him from his mother, Catherine Culpeper. The road roughly follows the route of the electric railroad built in the early 20th Century to connect Rosslyn with the Town of Fairfax in Fairfax County. In 1946 the main right of way through Ballston and Clarendon was condemned by the County as the railroad had ceased operation, to be merged with the existing road and developed as a major thoroughfare.

FAIRLINGTON

The large apartment development known as Fairlington was built in 1943 by the Defense Homes Corporation to relieve the war-induced shortage of living units in this area. The property acquired for this purpose lay partly in Arlington County and partly in Fairfax County - thus Fairfax - Arlington as an appropriate name. The portion which lies outside Arlington County was included in the 1952 annexation from Fairfax by the City of Alexandria, so that the name Fairlington no longer has its original significance.

FORT BARNARD

This 1961 fort constructed on a height commanding a view of the Four Mile Run valley as part of the defenses of Washington was named for Maj. Gen. J. G. Barnard of the U.S. Corps of Engineers. The General was in charge of most of the work on the forts and other field works built in the County at the time. Traces of the fort remain in the Fort Barnard Playground across Walter Reed Drive from the County Water tower.

Appendix

Why Do We Call It....? Continued

FORT MYER

This Army installation built during the Civil War was first called Fort Whipple in honor of Maj. Gen. Arien Whipple who died in May, 1963 from wounds suffered at Chancellorsville. It was renamed Fort Myer in 1881 in honor of General Albert J. Myer who, among his many other accomplishments, served there during the war and founded the Signal School and Weather Bureau and became the Army's first Chief Signal Officer.

FORT SCOTT

This fort, built in 1861 as part of the defenses of Washington was named for General Winfield Scott (1786-1866) who was in command of the U. S. Army at the start of the Civil War. The County has acquired part of the Fort Scott area for use as a playground and part of the remaining earthworks to preserve the site. The site overlooks Crystal City and the area of Jeff-Davis highway to the south. The road giving access to this area, and passing alongside, is known as Fort Scott Drive.

FOUR MILE RUN

Grants of land in the early Colonial days were located with reference to natural landmarks if possible, particularly rivers and streams. Great Hunting Creek below Alexandria was one of these reference points. The next sizable stream up the Potomac is four miles away, hence "Four Mile Run". The name was recorded in a land grant of 1694.

In the old usage, the term "creek" was applied to the stream where it entered a larger body of water such as a river. Thus on the old maps we find "Four Mile Creek" near the Potomac, and "the run of Four Mile Creek" further inland. Nowadays, the stream for its whole length is known as Four Mile Run.

GLEBE ROAD

It was usual in Colonial days for each parish to provide a farm, the production of which supplied the wants of its minister. Such farms were called "glebes". When Christ Church Parish was established in 1765, it embraced Arlington as well as Alexandria and in 1770 the vestry bought land in the County for a Glebe. The road leading to the Glebe became known as the Glebe Road. This is not precisely the Glebe Road as we know it today but only a portion since there has been repeated realignments.

GLENCARLYN

Glencarlyn, the first planned community in Arlington, was established as a cooperative development from land that had been owned by William Carlin who had bought it from the estate of the original settler, John Ball. The name of the village was

Why Do We Call It....? Continued

changed in 1896 from Carlin Springs to Carlyn Springs at the instance of the Post Office department to avoid confusion with another town of a similar name.

HOFFMAN-BOSTON SCHOOL

This school, named for two Black (African-American) educators is in the Nauck neighborhood of South Arlington. It was dedicated in 1932 and replaced a four room school known as Jefferson. The school got its name party from Edward Clarendon Hoffman, a former principal of Jefferson School, who was born in 1866 in Freedmen's Village. The other part of the name came from Miss Ella Boston who first taught at the Rosslyn School and then moved to the Kemper School in Green Valley first as sole teacher and then as principal for many years.

HUME SCHOOL

This school on South Arlington Ridge Road was built in 1891 on land donated by Frank Hume, a widely known and prominent civic leader. Hume fought in the Confederate Army and was wounded at Gettysburg. He was a member of the House of Delegates and the County Board of Supervisors, and the Commission to choose a site for the County Court House in 1896. The building is now the headquarters for the Historical Society and is a historical museum.

JEFFERSON-DAVIS HIGHWAY

This highway in South Arlington running from the Potomac River to Alexandria is so named by law. In 1922, the Virginia General Assembly adopted an Act which provided: "That primary road number one of the State highway system, as established by an Act approved January 31, 1918, is hereby designated and shall hereafter be known as the Jefferson-Davis highway in honor of the only President of the Confederate States of America.

JENNIE DEAN PLAYGROUND

This playground near Shirlington is named in honor of Jennie Dean, born of slave parents and founder of the Manassas Industrial School. With an almost missionary zeal she worked, saved and inspired her neighbors for a Baptist church and the school. Her influence was widespread, and her leadership in the field of vocational educations was widely recognized.

JOHNSON'S HILL

This was the site in the vicinity of the Marine post Henderson Hall and the area thereabouts of the farm of John R. Johnson at the time of the Civil War. In 1882 he died

Appendix

Why Do We Call It....? Continued.

and left his land to his wife and children. Gradually all the area was sold off as lots, mostly to Negroes who were being forced to leave Freedmen's Village on part of the Arlington Estate. The Civil War Fort Albany occupied a part of the Johnson land.

LANGSTON SCHOOL

This school is named for John Mercer Langston, a black man born in Louisa County, Virginia in 1829. His parents died when he was only five and he was brought up in Ohio where he graduated from Oberlin College. He studied theology and law and gained admission to the bar. When he was elected Town Clerk in 1854 he became the first Negro office holder in America. Later he served on the City Council and the School Board.

He was appointed General Inspector for the Freedmen's Bureau by President Johnson in 1868 and was minister to Haiti. He held many posts and was active as a writer and speaker. His election to the 51st Congress as a Representative from Virginia was contested and he was not seated until 1890. He died in 1897.

LITTLE FALLS ROAD

This road, leading from Falls Church to Chain Bridge, was one of the earliest roads in Arlington. The river crossing where the bridge was erected in 1797 had been a favorite with the Indians. The path leading there was taken over by the colonists as a rolling road when a tobacco inspection warehouse was established on Thomas Lee's land near the mouth of Pimmitt Run after 1830. At that time the road was known as "the road to the falls". A second "road to the falls" was the predecessor of the present Glebe Road. In the renaming of Arlington's streets, the historic and descriptive name of Little Falls Road was retained.

LONG BRANCH

Two streams have been known as the Long Branch of Four Mile Sun since the early 18th Century when they were distinguished as the "upper" and "lower". The Upper Long Branch rises in Fairfax County and crosses the County line near Glencarlyn School. It joins Four Mile Run near Arlington Mill Drive. The Lower Long Branch is the more important, rising in Lyon Park, running along Washington Boulevard at the edge of Fort Myer, then turning to run south along Shirley Highway and finally east again to empty into Four Mile Run at South Troy Street and Glebe Road. The stream is now mostly covered over and underground as a result of I-95 (I-395) and other construction.

LORCOM LANE

In 1907, Dr Joseph Taber Johnson bought land north of what is now Lee Highway. He named his property Lorcum Farm after his two sons, LORen and

Why do We Call It....? Continued

BasCOM, and the road leading to his place became known as Lorcom Lane. The name was retained when the streets were renamed in 1935. The frequent mistake of spelling this name "Lorcum" can be avoided if this origin in known.

LUBBER RUN

The origins of this name are uncertain but since the stream was known to have been a trysting place for lovers in 1815, it has been thought that the name "lubber" may have been a corruption of "lover" and thus Lovers Run in time became Lubber Run.

MARCEY ROAD

James Marcey, Sr., and his wife Mary Bowlen were the first of this numerous and long-lived family in this area. In 1843 they bought land on both sides of what became Military Road. The general area became known as Marcey-town, and the road which still bears the name Marcey was that which led to their home place.

Contrary to the belief of some, Fort Marcy (without the "e") which lies just outside Arlington County, was not named for this family but for Brig. Gen. R. B. Marcy, Chief of Staff for Maj. Gen George B. McClellan of the Union Army.

MEADE STREET

This street is named after General George Gordon Meade who distinguished himself in the Mexican and Civil Wars. He opposed General Robert E. Lee at Gettysburg. He was Park Commissioner in Philadelphia when he died in 1872. In view of his high and decisive role in the fighting against the South, it would appear that the naming of a street in Virginia with his name was not at the insistence of Arlingtonians.

MILITARY ROAD

This road runs between Glebe Road and Lee Highway in Cherrydale and beyond and comes by its name honestly. It was constructed in 1861 to connect Forts Ethan Allen and Marcy, which guarded the Virginia approaches to the Chain Bridge. It was laid out by Captain B. S. Alexander, "mainly through broken and densely wooden country" and built by troops who completed the job in only three days. When streets were renamed in 1935, citizens who lived along Military Road successfully protested the proposed change to North Chain Bridge Road, and it remains Military Road although the lower part has been absorbed by Lee Highway.

MINOR HILL

This height where the County reservoir is located in on the northwest wide of Little Falls Road near North Powhattan Street. Known in 1731 as "Brandymore Castle"

Appendix

Why Do We Call It....?

it came into the hands of George Minor (born 1753) and in time renamed. Some of the slopes are still occupied by Minor family descendants.

MOORE STREET

This street is name for R. Walton Moore, who was prominent in the affairs of Arlington, Fairfax County where he lived, and of Virginia and the Nation. Moore was born in 1859 in Alexandria and represented the area in the General Assembly from 1887 to 1896. He served with the Constitutional Convention of 1901 and as President of the State Bar Association. On the national scene he served in Congress from 1919 to 1931 for the Eighth District that then covered all of Northern Virginia. From 1933 to his death in 1941 Moore was Assistant Secretary and Counselor of the U. S. Department of State.

NAUCK

This neighborhood in South Arlington derives its name from John D. Nauck, Jr., who once owned the land, part of the Abingdon estate, after the Civil War. His origins are obscure. One Deed book described him as "of Washington", and another "of Alexandria County". He is listed among the white voters of Arlington Magisterial District in a poll book for which the year has not been established. There are records of his service as a special policeman in 1878 and a Justice of the Peace in the Arlington District in 1890 and 1891.

OLD DOMINION DRIVE

The road derives its name from its location on the right of way of the Great Falls and Old Dominion Railway that was chartered in 1900 to run from Rosslyn to Great Falls. The line went into receivership in 1935 and the right-of-way was taken over by Fairfax and Arlington Counties for taxes. Part of the roadbed, with tracks removed, became Old Dominion Drive.

PERSHING DRIVE

This road was named for General John J. Perching, one of the most distinguished leaders in American Military History. The road had formerly been known as Cathcart Road since it led to the estate of Mrs Arthur M. Cathcart who dies in 1960 at the age of 93. The Buckingham community was built on a part of the Cathcart land.

PIMMITT RUN

The exact connection between John Pimmitt and the Run which bears his name is shrouded in the mists of time. It is recorded that in 1687 Robert Alexander deeded

Why Do We Call it....? Continued

150 acres to him - but this was on the north bank of Four Mile Run, some distance away. This property was sold by his son and heir George in 1707. An earlier reference to Pimmitt (as "Pimet") occurs in a deposition before the Crown Commissioner sent to investigate the causes of Bacon's Rebellion. In 1692, there is a record of a piece of property referred to as on "Pimmitt's, alias the Upper Spout Run falling into Potomack River below and near the falls thereof". This would be the Pimmitt Run we know today. Over the years the spelling appears to have taken several forms.

POTOMAC RIVER

Potomac was the name of an Indian settlement at the mouth of a creek which empties into the River just below the mouth of the Acquia. The name first appeared on a map in 1612 and was applied only to the lower part of the river as we know it. Later the whole river from its headwaters to its outlet into the Chesapeake was called Potomac.

The word is usually translated as "trading place", although some give it as "the place where the tribute is brought". In the early days it was spelled in many different ways: Potomack, Petomecke, Pawtomake, Patowmack and Patawomack are some of them.

POWHATAN

This street and spring in the County are named after a powerful Indian chieftain who was the father of Pocahontas. His headquarters was on the James River. At one time his rule extended as far north as what is now Arlington. Legend has it that the chief held councils at the spring which bears his name.

QUINTANA STREET

This street was so named at the time of renaming of streets as one of the few "Q" words that could be found. Quintana is a territory southeast of Mexico and east of the Yucatan peninsula. Its capital is Chetumal.

ROACH'S RUN

The name of the run just off Mount Vernon Boulevard is one of the few evidences left on the map of the extensive activities of James Roach who about 1841 completed his home "Prospect Hill" where the Representative apartment complex now sits and near where the Little Tea House once operated.

ROLFE STREET

John Rolfe (1585-1622) is probably best known as the husband of Pocahontas, daughter of Powhaten. Rolfe's 1614 marriage with Pocahontas helped bring about some

Why do We Call It....? Continued.

friendly relations between the Indians and the first settlers in Virginia. Rolfe also discovered a method of curing tobacco at Jamestown which made it possible to ship to England and thus gave the colonists an exportable commodity. Rolfe was born in Heachum, England and sailed with Sir George Somers in 1609 and reached Virginia only after being ship wrecked in Bermuda. He was killed in the 1622 Indian massacre. Many Virginia families today trace their lineage back to Rolfe and his wife Pocahontas.

ROSSLYN

In 1860, William Henry Ross, husband of Caroline Lambden, received a large farm on the Virginia waterfront opposite Georgetown from his father-in-law, and gave it the name "Rosslyn". "Lyn" or "lynn" is a now an obsolete spelling of "linn" meaning, variously, a torrent running over rocks, a pool of water, or ravine with precipitous sides. It is probably the first of these meanings which the Rosses had in mind since the property is (was) traversed by a rock stream. Today, it is probably mostly under ground from the massive developments in Rosslyn and Lee highway. The Rosses were in France in 1869 after being driven from their home in the Civil War and sold the farm to the Rosslyn Development Company. The company acquired additional acreage which was sold off in lots for the "Town of Rosslyn".

SPOUT RUN

This run that empties tamely into the Potomac above Rosslyn is believed to have once been a wilder stream with waterfalls and hence the name "Spout". The stream became peaceful after extensive quarrying of rock along its route and today, like many other Arlington streams, is mostly underground.

HENRY G. SHIRLEY MEMORIAL HIGHWAY

This roadway is named after the Chairman, or Commissioner, of the State Highway Department from 1922 until his death in 1941. It was the State's first limited access highway, planned by Shirley, and named in his honor. Under Shirley long strides were made in the Virginia highway system and he gained fame nationally and internationally as a master road builder, engineer, executive and administrator.

STRATFORD STREET AND SCHOOL

This school and street are named after Stratford Hall in Westmoreland County, the birthplace of Robert E. Lee and of Richard Henry Lee and Francis Lightfoot Lee, two signers of the Declaration of Independence. Since the Lee family, once residing in Arlington House, was so closely associated with Arlington County it was considered appropriate that this connection be recognized through the use of the name Stratford for

Why Do We Call It....? Continued

both a street and school.

TAZEWELL STREET

This street is named after Littleton Waller Tazewell who was Governor of Virginia from 1834 to 1836. He succeeded John Marshall in the U. S. House of Representatives in 1824, and later moved to the Senate from which he resigned "from pure disgust with Federal politics". He died in 1860.

TUCKAHOE

Tuckahoe was an important staple of the Virginia Indian diet. The roots were dried and ground and used for bread. Tuckahoe Villages was once the name of an Arlington subdivision which originally had Indian street names. With the renaming of streets the name, with three syllables, was used for the appropriate alphabet spot. There is a Tuckahoe school of the side of Lee Highway further west than the subdivision Tuckahoe Village.

VACATION LANE

The site of the Stratford Junior (Middle) High School was at one time the summer home of the Washington Young Women's Christian Association. They bought one of the houses built by Dr Taber Johnson for whose sons Loren and Bascom, his farm and the road leading to it, had been named. The road is still known as Lorcom Lane. The other approach, leading to the vacation lodge of the YWCA, was dubbed vacation Lane by the organization, and has remained so.

VEITCH STREET.

This street is named for a family established in Arlington since the 1800's. Descendants of the family are active in public life in Arlington today although they do not bear the name of Veitch since the connection is on the maternal side.

WALKER'S CHAPEL

This chapel is now a Methodist Church as the intersection of Little Falls Road and North Glebe Road. David Walker, the first of this family in the area, died in 1848 and was buried in a family graveyard near his home. This became the cemetery of the Chapel built in 1871 on land given by his sons, Robert and James Walker. The selection of the name was influenced both by their generosity and by the long connection of the family with this locality.

Why Do We Call It....? Continued

WASHINGTON AND LEE

This name primarily brings to mind the County's first "enduring" high school on North Quincy Street named after two famed Virginians, George Washington and Robert E. Lee. The school does not use the word "and", but rather a "-". Although there actually were two earlier high schools in what is now Arlington County. One high school was in the Delray section (along U. S. highway #1 south of modern Crystal City) that has long since been annexed by the City of Alexandria and thus is no longer a part of Arlington County; the other ceased operation when the building in which it was located was purchased from the School Board by the St. Agnes private school on North Randolph Street.

There was also a shopping center of the same name at the junction of Washington Boulevard and what was once called Lee Boulevard. The shopping center opened in 1947 but was closed in 1985 when the area was redeveloped. The name has lost significance with the designation of the latter thoroughfare as Arlington Boulevard by Act of the General Assembly in 1952 (to end the confusion between LEE Boulevard and LEE Highway).

WESTMORELAND STREET

The street derives it name from Westmoreland County that was carved out of Northumberland County in 1653. This area included what is now Arlington which was part of Westmoreland County until Stafford County was establish in 1664. Westmoreland County is now further reduced in size by the creation of other counties and now covers only a portion of the land between the Rappahannock and the Potomac Rivers.

WISE STREET

This short, little known street, runs for one block between South Uhle Street and 2nd Street, alongside Arlington Boulevard and opposite from from Ft Myer. It was named for Henry Alexander Wise who served as governor from 1856 to 1859. The days of his term have been characterized as "the last of peace and prosperity" for Virginia. He died in 1876.

* * * *

INDEX GENERAL
(Places and events)

A

Arlingtonians for a Better County	
(see Political groups ABC)	
Advent from CCSI	196
Crack in dominance	97
Abbott, Dorthea E.	
Author, AHS mag.	66
Abingdon ruins	
Preservation	361
Efforts to save	335
History	338
Some dark hours	352
Success in saving	359
Burning	4, 342
Building	4
Early designation	4
Addison heights	71
Agriculture Ex. farm	72
Alexander,	
Gerrard	4
John	4
Alexandria County	
"Country part"	6
Apartments, Arlington	
First high rise	422, 424
Post WWII	423
Prior to, during war	422
Arlington Cemetery	
Burials, capacity	22
Expansion	394
Rose garden	21
Superintendent	394
Arlington Coalition on Transportation	
(ACT)	172
Arlington County	
Capital City area	6
Eastern shore	3
"County part"	14
Civil War	12-3
History, chrono.	78
Post Civil War	33-84
Pre-Civil War	7
Retrocession, 1846	11
Settlement	5
Arlington Education Association	169
Arlington Historical Society	40
Custis-Lee woodlands	403
Arlington County Taxpayers Association	
Formation & birth	124
Media analysis	127
Membership	125
Position on Metro	128
Arlington House	
Construction 1802	8
Civil War Damage	20-3
Union troops	14-5, 34
Return to Lees	10
Woodlands loss	393-405
Legislation, 1996	402
Arlington Ridge Civic Assn	224
Prospect Hill	227
Sickels tract	231, 236
Aurora Hills Library	271
Arlington, South, discontent	263
Arlington Independent Movement	
(see Political groups)	
"Arlingtonian", The	171
At-large voting	
(see Districts, voting)	
Aurora Hills Library	
Law suit to stop	274
Where to build	271

B

Baker, Gail, author	61
Backus, Florence, author	61
Bacon's rebellion	3
Ball, Frank, witnessed first	
flight, Ft Myer	19, 44
Ball-Sellers house	44
Ballston development	43

Index

Bannecker, Benjamin	6, 228, 408
Artifacts sale	409
Blatt, William, first Arlington combat burial	21
Boaz, Carolyn Author, AHS mag.	69
Barcroft neighborhood	62
Boundary surveys	408
Artifacts, sale	409
Barrett, Kate, map	52
Boathouse, Rosslyn	419
Board members, county	
1953, conservative	94
1956, liberal	90, 95
1967, flexing period	99
1970 developments	100
1980 developments	102
Republican control	101
Term lengths	87
First "at-large"	87
Philosophy of	89
"Broadview", Lacey house	46
Boundary Park, Falls Church Arlington	407
Buckingham Village conversion, Historic Designation	421

C

Capital boundaries survey	6
Cavalry Methodist Church	273
Center for Urban Education (see PCCC)	
Chamber of Commerce	170, 426
Change of government, 1932	85
Cherrydale	57
Christman, William, first burial	22
Citizens Committee for School Improvement (see Schools CCSI)	
Civic Federation	
Author observations	114
Composition	109
Functions	112
History	110
Membership	113
Clarendon	65
Coalition on Transportation	152

Committee of 100	
Birth of	116
Influence	116
Meetings	118
Membership	118
Goals and purposes	120
Confederate monument, Arl. Cem.	24
Constitution, VA., 1870	34
Cosner, Keven, "No Way Out" movie	31
Custis, George Washington Parke	4, 8, 25, 399
Custis, John Park	4
Custis, Mary Anne	8, 9
Custis, Nellie	4
Custis-Lee mansion	393

D

Dawson Terrace (family)	295
DeBevoise, Ruth C., Author, AHS mag.	46
"Desk of Infamy", of Jeff Davis	231
Detoxification center	421
Development, county	
At stand still	425
Effect of zoning on	425
Growth desirable?	434
Jeff-Davis corridor	432
Law suit over	438
Log jam broken	432
Rosslyn	437
Post WWII	422
Rosslyn	437
Rosslyn-Ballston Cor.	433
Shortcomings	436
USA Towers, Rosslyn	438
Districts, voting	
1930 referendum on	256
At-large attitudes	267
Single member	85, 255
Dodge, George, author	21
Downey, Agnes Mullins, author	20

502

E

Ellicott, Andrew, Major	6, 228, 407

F

Fitzhugh, Mary Lee	8
Fort Myer	19, 45
Fort Myer Heights	59
Fort Smith, C. F.	
Citizen concerns	381
Civil War period	370
County actions	381
Early history	368
Hendry law suits	386
Historic designation	385
Jewell stewardship	374
Park established	388
Acquisition of	364
Fort Whipple	18
Forts, Lincoln's, No. Va.	14
Foster, Jack, authorAHS mag.	180
Frampton, George, Sec.Int.	397
Fraser-Sickels lands (Forest Hills Townhouses)	
Green Valley Manor	57, 230
Fraser, Anthony	231, 234
Rezoning efforts	231-236
Fraser gravesite	234
Freedmen's Village	11, 28-9, 35-9
Friis, Herman, author	2
Funding and Financing, County	
Author observations	462
Board members on	461
Deficits	452
Expenditures	446
Management	452
Media attitudes	460
Property tax	449
Public comments on	457
Revenues	448

G

Gilpin, Susan, author	187
Glencarlyn community	60
Gutshall, Harry, author	48-9

H

Hall's Hill	50
Hannabass, Darline	70
Henderson Hall, USMC	401
Hendry tract	378
High rise buildings, first	75
Historic districts	75
Hoffman-Boston school	98, 199
Home Depot	
Author observations	418
County actions on	415
Proposal	413
Public forums	413
Public attitudes	417
Withdrawal from	416
Hoover airport	72
Hopkins map	40

I

I-66 Interstate construction	
Background	238
Citizens opposition to	240
Court action	244-5
EPA study	249
Final court order to build	252
Law suit filed	242
Problems develop	240
Indians	
Villages	2
Nacochtanke tribe	3
Integration, first school	198

J

Jackson City clean-up	178
Jeff-Davis Hwy (I-595)	
Board actions on	297
Citizens attitudes	296
End of controversy	303
Law suit over	300, 302
Program to upgrade	296

Index

Jefferson Civic League	224
Jewell, William, land owner	369-74

K

L

Land use plan, General (GLUP)	
Beginnings	427
Bekely report	428
Plan (Tom Moore) unveiled	429
Plan adopted, 1962	430-9
Lee, Robert E.	
Assignments	10, 19
Left Arlington House	401
Offered command	10, 14, 19
Marriage	9
Death	10
Liberalism, political	90
Liberty, U. S., Israel firing, crew graves	24
Local government, beginning	83
Luna Park	41
Lyon, Frank	69

M

Major County events, chrono.	76-8
Mackey, Crandal	
Author	12, 53, 180
Cleanup campaign	178-80
Mann, Harrison, author AHS Mag., politician	176
Mason, George	4, 368
Mason, John	14, 59, 67, 369
Mason's Island	14-16
Meigs, Montgomery, Gen.	20, 26
Metrorail	
Background	209
Battle for	208
bonds for	209
Chronology	219
Developments, chrono.	220
Funding	213
Funding problems	214
Public attitudes	217
The system	212
Metzler, John, Supt.,	
Arlington Cemetery	394
Interview with author	395
Michelotti, Cecilia, author	183
Mitchell, Beth, map maker	368
Mt Airy, Md	4
Mullins, Agnes, curator	394
Munson Hill, Bailey's X-Roads	51
Murphy, Audie, gravesite	24
Myer, Albert James, Gen.	17
Nauck, John	55
Neighborhoods, growth of	42
Ballston	43-7
Barcroft	62-4
Cherrydale	57-8
Clarendon	65-8
Fort Myer Heights	59
Freedmen's Village	33
Glencarlyn	60-2
Hall's Hill (High View)	50-1
Lyon Village	69-70
Nauck (Green Valley)	54-6
Rosslyn	51
Virginia Highlands	71-75
Walker Chapel	48-9
Neighborhood Conservation	
Concepts	453
Funding	455

O

Organizations	
County general	108
Non-political	108-9

P

Payne, Louise, author	63
Pentagon Building	74
Pentagon City rezoning	
Background	277
Board hearing on	280
Court suit on	283

Current status	285	(Analostan/Mason)	14, 16, 74
Rezoning decision	277	Rose, C.B.,Jr, author	

Pentagon City Coordinating
Committee (PCCC-CUE)
- Bingo games — 140
- Change of name — 138
- Early activity — 132
- Fund raising — 135
- Future
- Incorporation — 133
- Involvement in Pentagon City rezoning — 277
- Leadership — 137
- Litigation — 136

Peters, James E., historian — 11
Planning, land use (see Land use)
Potomac River — 2
Prospect Hill (Roach)
- Rezoning — 221
- Hearings outcome — 227
- Pro and Con arguments — 225
- Rezoning hearing — 226

Political parties and groups
- General — 144-5
- Democrat Party — 146-56
- ABC — 97, 152-56, 196
- Republican Party — 93, 101, 156-65
- Arlington Independent Movement (AIM) — 165
- Volunteers for an Independent Arlington (VIA) — 167

Q

R

Randolph, Mary, grave — 207
Reconstruction, Post Civil War — 33
Retrocession — 11, 174
Ritchie, Mildred, author — 63
Roach, James (and son Phillip- Prospect Hill) — 221
Robinson, June, author — 51
Roosevelt Island

Rose, C.B.,Jr, author — 1, 6, 12, 16, 27-8, 183
Rose, Ruth, author — 69
Rosslyn bars, streets — 51, 77, 177

S

Schildt, Bobbi, historian — 26-7
Schofield, John, Gen. — 33
School Board
- First elected — 195
- Liberals gain control — 91
- Return of elected — 201

Schools
- Additional openings — 190
- Battle for "good" — 182
- Beginnings — 185
- CCSI — 182-207
- Changing attitudes — 199
- Desegregation — 196
- Earliest in County — 185
- First battles over — 188
- First Council of — 191
- First integration — 198
- Latter day problems — 202
- Philosophy — 204
- Post WWII period — 192
- Sources of info on — 183
- Stratford integration — 198

Selfridge, Thomas, Lt., — 19, 45, 105
Sewage treatment plant
- Board hearing on — 315
- Citizen alarm — 311
- Citizen reaction to — 307
- Expansion of — 305
- Litigation over — 310
- Pollution measures — 307

Shreve, Samuel, early settler — 45
Sickels, Jackson, Civil War — 229
Single Member electoral districts, fight for — 255
- Discontent about — 263
- History — 255
- Prospects for — 270
- Racial overtones — 258

Index

    Versus at-large voting   260
Sound walls
    Citizen efforts for   290
    I-395 impacts   287
    Law suit for   288
    Long term efforts for   291
    Media attention   291
    North Arlington walls   287
    South Arlington walls   289
Spelman, Henry, Captain, 1622   3
Stadiums
    Baseball proposal   319
    Board hearings   326
    Coalition, opposition   331
    Football   317
    Media coverage   323
    Public reaction to   319
    Results and prospects   334
Stiss, Seymour, author   183
Syphax, Evelyn   28, 29, 30, 393
Templeman, Eleanor   9, 51
Three Sisters Islands   240
Town Meeting organization   195
Truro Parish, records, 1743   7
Vollin, George,   29, 260-71
Virginia Highlands Civic Assn.,
    Position on library   274
Ward, Ruth, author   49
Washington Metropolitan Area
    Transit Authority   210
Whipple, Amiel, Gen.   17
Wright, Orville, 1908 flight   19, 20, 45

ARLINGTON COUNTY VIRGINIA - A Modern History

INDEX - INDIVIDUALS

Does not include media writers or most elected or government officials, or others included in the Appendix herein.

A

Abbott, Dorthea, 66
Alexander, Gerrard, 4
Alexander, John, 4
Almond, Harry, 268
Anderton, H., 274
Anderson, Robert, 58, 86, 257
Andrus, Cecil, 438
Annon, Mary & Bud, 132
Antonelli, John, 167
Arcada, Susan, 193
Arends, Phil, 231
Arms, Richard, 222-4

B

Babers, Donald, 304
Bailey, Lewis, 1, 88
Baker, Gail, 61, 306, 348
Bakus, Florence, 61, 193
Bakus, Richard, 383
Ball, Frank, 44
Ball, John, 7, 43, 60
Bangs, Doris, 314
Banks, Lem, 193
Banneker, Benjamin, 6, 228, 407-8
Barber, Josephine, 125
Barkey, Patricia, 224
Barr, John, 452
Baylor, Ralph, 125
Bauman, Walter, 135-7
Berne, Barnard, 350-60, 383
Bickford, Charlene, 152
Bigler, Phillip, 24
Blatt, William, 22
Blevens, Lucas, 117

Boaz, Carolyn, 69-70
Booker, Ivan, 193
Briggs, Henry & Marie, 199
Brown, Paul D., 135, 284
Bryan, Albert, 160, 265
Bryant, Lyle, 117, 428
Bullock, Helen, 224
Butt, Charles, 419

C

Cam, Arlene, 332
Campbell, Alice, 231-33
Campbell, Ed and Elizabeth, 91, 122, 146, 194, 197, 243
Campbell, Phillip, 222
Cangialosi, Sal, 332
Carlin, William, 60
Charleton, James, 167, 202, 268, 346
Chestnut, Louise, 132
Christman, William, 22
Clardy, Warren, 8
Clark, Ralph, 193
Cook, Robert & Sunny, 132
Cuban, Larry, 101
Cummings, Lincoln, 167
Curtis, Dora, 264
Custis, George Washington Parke, 4, 8, 13, 25, 175
Custis, John Parke, 3, 338
Custis, Nellie, 4, 8

D

Dabinett, Mary, 292
Darner, Karen, 101

507

Dean, Alan, 93
DeBevoise, Ruth, 46
Deskins, Peggy, 198
Dixen, Wallace, 184
Dodge, George, 22
Doud, Richard, 171, 328
Douglas, Harrison, 264
Downes, George, 273, 297
Downey, Agnes, Mullins, 21

E

Early, W. A. 92
Ecklund, Jon, 414
Edminston, Elizabeth, 125
Ekern, Halvor, 125, 458
Ellicott, Andrew, 6, 228, 407-8
Emrich, Jerry, 275

F

Fallon, Peter, 416
Finney, Carolyn, 451
Fisette, Jay, 102, 156, 162
Fisher, Joseph, 212
Fitshugh, Mary Lee, 9, 25, 400
Flack, Irene, 193
Flagg, Maurice, 157, 268
Frampton, George, 397
Fruitman, Thelma, 125
Franklin, Harry & Polly, 125
Frederick, William, 231-33
Fugate, Douglas, 246

G

Gannon, W. H., 193
Gaffen, Margaret, 137
Gardiner, Anton, 313
Gault, Benjamin, 125
Georgeles, John, 380
Gilpin, Susan, 84, 187

Goldschmidt, Lawrence, 410
Govan, James & Emily, 240-54
Graham, Daniel, 101, 306
Graham, Ruth, 125
Gray, Rebecca, 316, 320-24, 332
Green, Mason, 125
Griffin, Jewel, 184
Groom, Fuller, 429
Grotos, Dorothy, 125
Gulliford, Andrew, 184
Gutshall, Harry, 48

H

Hadfield, George, 8
Hannabass, Darline, 70
Haire, Paul, 294
Hanwaring, Edward, 193
Harrington, Robert, 132
Harrison, Alan, 125
Haynes, Gideon, 125
Hendry, Ernest, 378
Henley, Theda, 197
Higgins, Kingsley, 117, 429
Hincks, Edward, Mrs, 193
Herbst, Richard & Deborah, 32, 139, 140, 283
Hewitt, Francis, 125, 129, 132, 226, 231-4, 208
Holien, Kim, 389
Hoge, W. E. 426
Horton, Peggy, 301
Hughes, Mary, 139
Hyman, Barry, 249

I

Iandolo, Angelo, 125
Ingram, Joseph, 193

J

James,. Felix, 27
Jensen, Donna & Herman, 271, 297-9
Jessup, John, 383
Jinks, Mark, 452-4, 461
Johnson, Andy, 184
Johnson, Bert, 222-4, 279, 310
Johnson, Norma, 288
Jones, Amy, 167
Jones, Bruce, 125, 311, 332, 366
Jones, David, 312, 331-5
Joy, Bernard, 117, 153

K

Kaczmarek, Philip, 264
Kemp, Fletcher, 184
Kendrick, Benjamin, 386
King, Judy & Martin, 332
King, Philip, 125
Kirkbride, Gary, 425
Kleinsfeldt, Catherine, 184, 187

L

Landfield, Sherman, 324
Lane, Manson, 61,
Latto, Larry, 266
Lawson, William, 223
LeBeau, Oscar, 123, 193
Lee, Antoinette, 383
Lee, Robert E., 9, 10, 14, 17, 19
Lewis, Harold, 193
Lewis, Oren, 244-6, 251
Lightsey, William, 197-8
Lillinger, Linda, 271
Lillywhite, Alden, 117, 193
Logan, Leon, 117
Lurito, Deloris, 264

M

Machen, Robert, 309
Mallery, John 273

MacCoy, Bruce, 109, 359, 389
Mackey, Crandal, 52, 175, 172-81
Macqueen, Donald, 125
Mann, Harrison, 125, 174-6, 194
Marr, John & Willa, 132, 138, 140-1, 366
Mason, John, 14, 60
McCarthy, Walter, 122, 194-5
McCreery, Marjorie, 170
McCune, Timothy, 125
McElwaine, Andrew, 381
McGeary, Scott, 125, 323
Meigs, Montgomery, 21
Merchant, Robert, 297
Merriam, Clyde, 117
Metzler, John, 394-5, 406
Michilotti, Cecilia, 183, 197, 199
Miller, Malcolm, 193
Miller, Norman, 125
Mintz, Alice, 193
Moore, Robert, 217
Munson, Chris, 388-91
Myer, Albert, 18, 19, 20

N

Naake, Larry, 458
Netherton, Nan & Ross, 338
Newbold, Roy, 125, 127
Newdorp, John, 117, 193
Nicholson, Alice, 383
Nicholson, Mary, 271
Nolden, William, 383

Index

O

Olmstead, James 125
Owen, Wilfred, 426
Oynes, Chris, 303

P

Packh, Davis de, Mrs, 231
Papanicolas, Kay, 264
Parker, George, 193
Parris, Mark, 433-35
Payne, Louise, 63-5
Peck, Robert, 43, 93
Pelton, Joseph, 101
Peters, James E., 11
Pettee, James Mr & Mrs, 193
Phillips, Lesley, 212
Phillips, Deborah, 163-4
Planek, Charles, Mrs, 193
Pope, Patricia, 101
Poppenpohl, Andrew & Ruth, 384
Pond, Reed, 193
Pratt, Sherman, 226, 231-35, 332
Pryor, Theodore, Mrs, 193

Q

Quinn, John & Joan, 131-7, 283

R

Ragalie, Daniel, 274
Ragland, Ernest, 167
Rahner, Joe, 417
Randolph, Mary, 207
Reed, Cindy, 125
Rideout, Charles, 221
Richie, Mildred, 63
Rickover, Hyman, 228
Roach, James, 84, 221, 228
Roach, Philip, 221

Robert, Shelby, 193
Robbins, Philip, 271
Robinson, June, 347
Rose, C. B. (Cornelia), 1, 12, 40, 54, 62, 69, 183, 190, 257
Ross, William, 185
Rucker, Charles, 436
Rundle, Judy, 184
Runyan, Emmy Lou, 274, 297
Russell, Charles, 310
Russo, John, 125, 129-30, 324, 457

S

Saks, Ted, 332

Scheips, Paul, 18
Schildt, Bobbi, 27, 37
Schofield, John 33
Sebrell, Thomas, 117
Sefridge, Thomas, 19, 20, 45, 105
Sickels, Antonia Fraser, 229
Sickels, Jackson, 229
Sinks, John 382
Smith, Robert, 218
Smith, Wilbur, 239
Snyderman, Lois, 184-6
Staley, Richard, 275, 297
Steadman, Robert & Caliston, 283
Stiss, Seymour, 183, 191
Stone, Harold & Catherine, 193-4
Stone W. Morrell, 426
Stowe, Mary, 120
Strauss, George, 331
Struther, Edmund, 193
Suter, Sue, 327, 331
Swain, Dirk & Nancy, 132-37, 283
Sweig, Donald, 27, 39
Syphax, Evelyn, 28

T

Talbott, C. M. 292
Templeman, Eleanor, 42, 51, 53, 221-2, 230, 348, 400
Tennyson, E. L., 42
Terborgh, Dorothy, 117
Terman, Maurice, 410
Thatcher, Herbert, 193
Torbet, John, 125
Travesky, Marie, 216
Treadway, Anita, 132
Trumbo, Shannon, 224
Tucker, Ethel, 264
Turner, Francis, 125

U

V

Velda, Joyce, 274-5
Vogel, Arthur, 101
Vogel, S. B., 463
Vollin, George. 30, 163, 264, 258

W

Walls, Arthur, 259
Walsh, Frank, 264
Ward, Ruth, 49
Warfield, Henrietta, 163-4, 313
Waters, Dale, 389
Watson, Robert, 405
Watt, William, 194
Weihe, Elizabeth, 197, 208-9
Weinberger, Isolde, 271
Wendelin, Rudolph, 47
Wheeler, Joseph, Mr & Mrs, 193
Wheeler, Robert, 425
Whipple, Amiel, 17
Winslow, Benjamin, 167
Winston, William, 266, 387

Wise, Donald, 339
Wise, Timothy, 125, 167, 459
Withhams, Wynn, 372
Wright, James, 398, 403
Wright, Orville, 19, 20, 45

X

Y

Z

Zingg, Paul, 416
Zirschky, John, 397

PATRON DONORS

The author expresses deepest appreciation to the following individuals, firms, groups or activities that have contributed significantly, financially or otherwise, to the success of this historical effort.
(random listing)

Mr & Mrs Joseph Cockrell
Doris Bangs Sansbury
Col. Bruce Jones (Ret)
Robert & Laura Watson
David & Dorothy Bates
L. Mitchel Dick
Lincoln C. Cummings
Robert McAtee
Arthur & Anna Hughes
Mary D. Woolnough
LCol. Martha Sachs(Ret)
John & Lucile Phelan
Deem Gillmore
Henry C. Mackall, Atty.
Roye Lowry
Martin Ogle
Col.(Ret) & Mrs William Wright
E. Scott & Rita Cohen
Philip & Ellen Barnhart
Betty Thompson, Atty.
Francis O'Brien
Donald Wise
Ann C. Rudd
Allan & Gertrude Ensign
Janet & James Rogers
Sophie (Mrs Arthur) Vogel
Frances Finta
Dorothy Sue Ferrari
Dow & Jane Nida
Barbara Jacobs
Frank & Arlene Camm
John Schoonvel
Richard Stealey, Army Ranger
  (Ret)

David Foster
Ray Donnelly, Korean War Vet.
Dr. & Mrs Roy Klepser
Col. Warren Wiedhahn (Ret)
  Military History Tours
Dr (Col.Ret) & Mrs John DePauw
Dimitri & Elaine Komis
John & Popi Capetanaki
Viki, Billie & Iris Wilken
Emery J. "Bill" Sanford
Rex Wackerle
Ellen Bozman
Elaine Pratt Pils
Joe Farruggia, Arlington Courier
Robert Gehl, Arlington Journal
Chryssie Tsongos Broadbent
Kazunori Takami, Japanese Historian
George & Hilda Strauss
Claude & Talmadge Bandy, Golfers
Mr & Mrs Harvey Kryder & Family
MGen (Ret.) Lloyd & Mrs Ramsey,
Col. & Mrs Spurgeon Messner
Dorothy & Guenter Grotos
Dr. & Mrs David Ibsen & Family
Kim Holien, Ft Myer Historian
Joan Orvis, Cable TV Producer
Peter & Joyce Velde
Bette Clements
LGen Benjamin Davis,(USA-Ret)
Albert Eisenberg
Michael Kauffman, Surratt Society
Henry Gray Gillem, Sr.
Harold Handerson, Museum Director
Hon. Edward & Joan Holland

PATRON DONORS (Cont)

James & Joanne Palmer, Archivist
Mr & Mrs Leslie Phillips
Mrs Evelyn Syphax & Family
Charlene Bickford, author, political activist
James Charleton
Monte Davis, businesswoman
Judy Muniec, Arl. Heritage
Robert Nester
Joseph Newlin, Atty
John Nicholas
William Nolden
Ernest Ragland
John Rosso
Sue Zajac
Chris Zimmerman
Robert Peck
Chris Munson, Park specialist.
Charlotte Cleary, Voting Registrar
Judy Knudson, Librarian
James & Becki Suma
The Arlington Ridge Civic Assn.
The Arlington Chamber of Commerce
The Committee of 100
The Arlington County Civic Federation

Gail Baker
John Antonelli
Richard Arms
Bernard Berne
Carolyn Boaz
George Vollin
Darline Hannabass
Marjorie McCreery
Scott McGeary
Henrietta Warfield, political activist.
Judge Claude Hilton
Judge Frank J. Cerisi
John M. Melnick, Esq.
Judge Benjamin Kendrick
Ken McFarlane Smith Esq.
Betty Waldow, Bar Assn. Dir.
Barbara Head, Bar Assn. Staff
James (&Mary) Plate, War Vet.
Kevin Appel, Bar Assn. Pres.
Leroy Batchelor, Esq.
Emmit Benjamin, War Vet.
Jack Walker, War Vet.
Larry Driscoll, War Vet.
Andy Barr, Philanthropist
Elizabeth (& Ernie) Saulmon

* * *

It is regretted that contributions received after this narrative has gone to the printers will not be reflected in the above list of Patron Donors. Any such persons, or sources, should be aware that their assistance and support is, nevertheless, greatly appreciated even if not shown above.

Author